# Humanitarian Intervention: A History

The dilemma of how best to protect human rights is one of the most persistent problems facing the international community today. This unique and wide-ranging history of humanitarian intervention examines responses to oppression, persecution, and mass atrocities from the emergence of the international state system and international law in the late sixteenth century, to the end of the twentieth century. Leading scholars show how opposition to tyranny and to religious persecution evolved from notions of the common interests of 'Christendom' to ultimately incorporate all people under the concept of 'human rights'. As well as examining specific episodes of intervention, the authors consider how these have been perceived and justified over time, and offer important new insights into ideas of national sovereignty, international relations and law, as well as political thought and the development of current theories of 'international community'.

BRENDAN SIMMS is Professor of the History of European International Relations and Director of the Centre of International Studies, University of Cambridge, where he is a Fellow of Peterhouse. His previous publications include *Unfinest Hour: Britain and the Destruction of Bosnia* (2001), *Three Victories and a Defeat: The Rise and Fall of the First British Empire* (2007), and *Cultures of Power in Europe During the Long Eighteenth Century* (as co-editor, Cambridge 2007).

D. J. B. TRIM is Director of the Archives of the Seventh-day Adventist Church, in Silver Spring, Maryland, USA. His previous publications include *Amphibious Warfare 1000–1700: Commerce, State Formation and European Expansion* (as co-editor, 2006) and *European Warfare 1350–1750* (as co-editor, Cambridge 2010).

# Humanitarian Intervention: A History

Brendan Simms and D. J. B. Trim

CAMBRIDGE
UNIVERSITY PRESS

CAMBRIDGE UNIVERSITY PRESS
Cambridge, New York, Melbourne, Madrid, Cape Town,
Singapore, São Paulo, Delhi, Tokyo, Mexico City

Cambridge University Press
The Edinburgh Building, Cambridge CB2 8RU, UK

Published in the United States of America by
Cambridge University Press, New York

www.cambridge.org
Information on this title: www.cambridge.org/9780521190275

© Cambridge University Press 2011

First published 2011

*A catalogue record for this publication is available from the British Library*

*Library of Congress Cataloguing in Publication data*
Humanitarian intervention : a history / [edited by
Brendan] Simms & [D. J. B.] Trim.
     p. cm.
   ISBN 978-0-521-19027-5 (Hardback)
1. Humanitarian intervention-History.
2. Humanitarian intervention-Case studies.
I. Simms, Brendan.    II. Trim, D. J. B. (David J. B.)    III. Title.
JZ6369.H85 2011
341.5'08409-dc22

                                                    2010034380

ISBN 978-0-521-19027-5 Hardback

# Contents

# Maps

# Notes on contributors

JOHN BEW is Lecturer in War Studies at King's College London and Co-Director of the International Centre for the Study of Radicalisation and Political Violence. His previous publications include *'The Glory of Being Britons': Civic Unionism in Nineteenth-century Belfast* (2008) and (as co-author) *Talking to Terrorists: Making Peace in Northern Ireland and the Basque Country* (2009).

ABIGAIL GREEN is Tutor and Fellow in Modern History at Brasenose College, University of Oxford. She is the author of *Moses Montefiore: Jewish Liberator, Imperial Hero* (2010) and of *Fatherlands: State-building and Nationhood in Nineteenth-century Germany* (2001). She has also published widely on humanitarianism and Jewish internationalism, and on regionalism and nationalism in nineteenth-century Germany.

MATTHEW JAMISON is Research and Operations Director for The Henry Jackson Society, a London-based think tank, for which he has authored many papers on British foreign, defence, and security policy.

GIDEON MAILER is a Title A Fellow at St John's College and an affiliated lecturer in the Faculty of History, University of Cambridge.

WILLIAM MULLIGAN is Lecturer in Modern History at University College Dublin. His previous publications include *The Creation of the Modern German Army* (2005) and *The Origins of the First World War* (2010). He is currently working on British anti-slavery politics in the late nineteenth century.

THOMAS PROBERT is a PhD student at Peterhouse, University of Cambridge, working on the politics of human rights.

SOPHIE QUINN-JUDGE is Associate Professor of History and Associate Director of the Center for Vietnamese Philosophy, Culture, and Society at Temple University in Philadelphia. She is the author of *Ho Chi Minh: The Missing Years* (2002) and co-editor, with Odd Arne

Westad, of *The Third Indochina War: Conflict Between China, Vietnam and Cambodia, 1972–79* (2006).

DAVIDE RODOGNO is Fonds National Suisse Research Professor of International History and Politics at the Institut des Hautes Études Internationales et du Développement, Geneva. He is the author of *Fascism's European Empire* (2006), and co-editor, with Michael Wedekind, of *Forced Displacement of Civilian Population in Europe, 1939–1947*, special issue of *Storia & Regione/Geschichte und Region* (2010).

MAEVE RYAN is a PhD student at Trinity College Dublin. She is currently working on the history of the British West African settlements between 1830 and 1865.

MATTHIAS SCHULZ is Professor of the History of International Relations and Transnational History at the University of Geneva. Recent publications include *Normen und Praxis: Das Europäische Konzert der Großmächte als Sicherheitsrat* (2009); *The Strained Alliance: US–European Relations from Nixon to Carter*, co-edited with Thomas A. Schwartz (2010); and *Das 19. Jahrhundert* (2011).

MIKE SEWELL is University Lecturer in History and International Relations at the University of Cambridge Institute of Continuing Education and is a Fellow and Tutor of Selwyn College. He has published on late nineteenth-century Anglo-American relations as well as on British responses to the Civil Rights movement, and is the author of *The Cold War* (2002).

BRENDAN SIMMS is Professor of the History of European International Relations and Director of the Centre of International Studies, University of Cambridge, where he is a Fellow of Peterhouse. He is author of *The Impact of Napoleon: Prussian High Politics, Foreign Policy and the Crisis of the Executive, 1797–1806* (1997), *The Struggle for Mastery in Germany, 1780–1850* (1998), *Unfinest Hour: Britain and the Destruction of Bosnia* (2001), and *Three Victories and a Defeat: The Rise and Fall of the First British Empire* (2007).

ANDREW C. THOMPSON is College Lecturer in History at Queens' College, University of Cambridge. He is the author of *Britain, Hanover and the Protestant Interest* (2006) and *George II* (forthcoming 2011), as well as a number of articles on eighteenth-century political and religious history.

D. J. B. TRIM is Director of the Archives of the Seventh-day Adventist Church, in Silver Spring, Maryland, USA, and a Fellow of the Royal Historical Society. Recent books include, as co-editor, *European Warfare 1350–1750* (2010), *The Development of Pluralism in Modern Britain and France* (2007), and *Amphibious Warfare 1000–1700: Commerce, State Formation and European Expansion* (2006).

# Acknowledgements

The original concept for this book emerged from the editors' conviction that humanitarian intervention – normally considered only as a very recent phenomenon – has a long-term history that has remained largely unwritten. Encouraged by a group of scholars based at the University of Cambridge, we felt that an important first step towards recovering that history would be a volume that tackles important episodes and themes in the historical development of what today has emerged as 'humanitarian intervention'. We identified a range of topics, and to write on them we enlisted a group of scholars, some prominent, some relatively junior, but each of them an expert. We are very grateful to all our contributors for providing us, by the agreed deadlines, with stimulating essays which have been a pleasure to edit.

Having worked out the concept of the book, its table of contents, and the contributing authors, we wanted to hold a conference: both as a way to make the scholarly community aware of our concept of a long-term history of humanitarian intervention, and to enhance the quality of the chapters in the book, by presenting drafts to an audience of experts whose comments and criticism would be integrated into the final texts. The conference (entitled 'Towards a history of humanitarian intervention') was held at Peterhouse, Cambridge, in September 2008; it has been an integral and important part of the process of producing this book. Discussion at the conference – between scholars of different academic disciplines, working on different periods, areas, and subjects – was of a high quality; all of the following chapters have been improved by the comments and criticisms raised during formal discussion sessions (and by informal comments over tea, coffee, and dinner). We are indebted to all the scholars who attended the conference, and who thereby helped to improve this book.

We gratefully acknowledge conference funding generously provided by the Trevelyan Fund. We are grateful to: the Master, Fellows, Kitchen Manager and Conference Organiser of Peterhouse, for their support and practical assistance in making the conference happen; to Charlie

Laderman, who worked tirelessly as conference administrative assistant to Brendan Simms; to Frank Tallett, the conference *rapporteur*, for his valuable external overview of all the papers; and to Christopher Hill at the Cambridge Centre of International Studies for his support of the conference and book.

The process of editing was completed while David Trim was Walter Utt Professor at Pacific Union College, Angwin, California. He thanks the College and the Utt Endowment for appointment to the Utt Chair in History, which, with its light teaching and administrative load, greatly facilitated completion of the editing. Finally, we record our thanks to Tarak Barkawi, John Bew, Paul Cornish, Richard Immerman, Matthew Jamison, Davide Rodogno, Andrew Thompson, and Winifred Trim, each of whom helpfully critiqued the overall concept while encouraging us to bring it to completion.

Brendan Simms
D. J. B. Trim
Cambridge and Reading
March 2010

# Abbreviations

| | |
|---|---|
| A. & P. | *Parliamentary Papers* (UK): Accounts & Papers |
| Add. MSS | Additional Manuscripts |
| *AHR* | *American Historical Review* |
| *AJIL* | *American Journal of International Law* |
| AMAE | Archives du Ministère des Affaires Étrangères, Quai d'Orsay, Paris |
| *AZ* | *Allgemeine Zeitung des Judentums* |
| *BDFA*, I, B | *British Documents on Foreign Affairs*, Part I, *From the Mid-Nineteenth Century to the First World War*, Series B, *The Near and Middle East, 1856–1914* |
| BDMB | Board of Deputies of British Jews, Minute Books |
| *BFSP* | *British and Foreign State Papers 1807–1862*, 170 vols. (London: HMSO, 1841–1977) |
| BL | The British Library |
| Bodl. | Bodleian Library, Oxford |
| Broadlands MSS | Hartley Library, University of Southampton: Broadlands Archives |
| CCO | Conservative Party Archive (Bodleian Library): Conservative Central Office |
| CP | HH, Marquess of Salisbury's Manuscripts, Cecil Papers |
| CPC | AMAE, Correspondance Politique des Consuls |
| CP Tr. | AMAE, Correspondance Politique de la Turquie jusqu'à 1896 |
| *CSPFE* | *Calendar of State Papers, Foreign Series, of the Reign of Elizabeth I, preserved in the Public Record Office*, ed. Joseph Stevenson *et al.*, 26 vols. in 23 (London: HMSO, 1871–1950) |
| doc. | document |
| *EHR* | *English Historical Review* |
| encl. | enclosure |
| fo(s). | folio(s) |

xiv List of abbreviations

| | |
|---|---|
| FO | Foreign Office |
| FRUS | *Papers relating to the Foreign Relations of the United States* |
| FSL | Folger Shakespeare Library, Washington DC |
| HH | Hatfield House |
| H HStA | Hannover, Hauptstaatsarchiv |
| HMC | Historical Manuscripts Commission |
| ICISS | International Commission on Intervention and State Sovereignty |
| JC | *The Jewish Chronicle and the Hebrew Observer* |
| KR | Khmer Rouge |
| Lans. | BL, Lansdowne MSS |
| LMA | London Metropolitan Archives |
| MAE | Ministère des Affaires Étrangères, France |
| MS(S) | Manuscript(s) |
| NA | The National Archives, Kew, United Kingdom |
| n.d. | Undated (no date) |
| NGO | Non-governmental organisation |
| NLS | National Library of Scotland |
| NMM | National Maritime Museum, Greenwich |
| n.p. | No place of publication |
| OED | *Oxford English Dictionary* (2nd edn) |
| PP | *Parliamentary Papers* |
| R2P | Responsibility to Protect |
| res. | Resolution(s) |
| SP | State Papers |
| SP Thurloe | Thomas Birch (ed.), *A Collection of the State Papers of John Thurloe*, 7 vols. (London, 1742) |
| TRHS | *Transactions of the Royal Historical Society* |
| UN | United Nations |
| UNSC | UN Security Council |
| VCT (1579) | Stephano Iunio Bruto Celta, *Vindiciae, contra tyrannos: Sive, de principis in Populum, Populique in Principem, legitima potestate* ('Edimburgi' [Basel], 1579) |
| VCT (1581) | Estienne Junius Brutus, *De la puissance legitime du prince sur le peuple et du peuple sur le prince*, trans. [François Estienne] (n.p. [Geneva], 1581). Facsimile edn: *Vindiciae contra tyrannos. Traduction française de 1581*, ed. A. Jouanna, J. Perrin, M. Soulié, A. Tournon, and H. Weber, Les classiques de la pensée politique 11 (Geneva: Librairie Droz, 1979) |

| | |
|---|---|
| *VCT–Apologie* (1588) | Anon., *A short Apologie for Christian Souldiours* (London, 1588) (first (incomplete) English edn of *Vindiciae, contra tyrannos*) |
| *VCT* (1648) | *Vindiciæ contra tyrannos: a defence*, trans. anon. (London, 1648) (second (and first complete) English edn) |
| *VCT* (1689) | *Vindiciae contra Tyrannos: a defence*, trans. [William Walker] (London, 1689) |
| *VCT* (Garnett, 1994) | Stephanus Junius Brutus the Celt, *Vindiciae, contra tyranos: or, concerning the legitimate power of a prince over the people, and of the people over a prince*, ed. and trans. George Garnett (Cambridge: Cambridge University Press, 1994) |

# 1    Towards a history of humanitarian intervention

## D. J. B. Trim and Brendan Simms

> If it bee objected ... that God hath appointed limits and boundes to everie nation, and that we may not as it were thrust in our sickle into their harvest, neither is my counsell to the contrarie, that under pretence of ayde we should invade ... an other nation, or chalenge their jurisdiction ... but rather that we should cut short ... any tyrant afflicting his own people, any king throwing downe the props and stayes of his common wealth.
>
> *Vindiciae, contra tyrannos*, first English edition (1588)[1]

> It is too late in the day ... to tell us that nations may not forcibly interfere with one another for the sole purpose of stopping mischief and benefitting humanity.
>
> John Stuart Mill, 1849[2]

> Is it permissible to let gross and systematic violations of human rights, with grave humanitarian consequences, continue unchecked?

> If humanitarian intervention is, indeed, an unacceptable assault on sovereignty, how should we respond ... to gross and systematic violations of human rights that offend every precept of our common humanity?
>
> Kofi Annan, UN Secretary-General, September 2000[3]

The essays in this book sketch out the long-term history of what, since the nineteenth century, has been termed 'humanitarian intervention' – that is, action by governments (or, more rarely, by organisations) to prevent or to stop governments, organisations, or factions in a foreign state from violently oppressing, persecuting, or otherwise abusing the human rights of people within that state. The problem of how to protect human rights and safeguard human security is one of the most persistent problems facing the international community; although the

---

[1] *VCT–Apologie* (1588), sig. B6; see Chapter 2, by D. J. B. Trim, below.

[2] J. S. Mill, 'Vindication of the French Revolution of February 1848' (1849); see Chapter 5, by John Bew, below.

[3] Kofi Annan, 'Two Concepts of Sovereignty', *The Economist*, 18 Sept. 1999, 49; *'We the Peoples': The Role of the United Nations in the 21st Century*, report to the Millennium Assembly of world leaders, Sept. 2000 (UN, 2000), ch. IV, pt. C, para. 217 (available at www.un.org/millennium/sg/report/full.htm).

'dilemma of what to do about strangers who are subjected to appalling cruelty by their governments' has been particularly pressing in the last hundred years, it is of a truly ancient vintage.[4] Attempts to find answers to this dilemma are also not new. However, until recently humanitarian intervention was treated as though it were a subject without a history.

The chapters that follow examine not only the first episodes that were called 'humanitarian interventions' by contemporaries, but also the concepts and practices from which intervention emerged and which, sometimes after considerable evolution, eventually fused to make the modern concept. They also consider concepts that stood in the way of concern for oppressed people groups, including the concept of sovereignty usually associated with the Peace of Westphalia in 1648 (often identified as the starting point for modern international relations), which almost 400 years later was (apparently) to be endorsed uncritically by the Charter of the United Nations. Because this book is a history, fifteen of the sixteen chapters that follow deal with events *before* 1980; one chapter considers the celebrated (or notorious) interventions of the 1990s in historical perspective. Most of the literature on humanitarian intervention, whether by academics, lawyers, activists, or policy-makers, has been focused on recent interventions. It is precisely for this reason that this book turns the spotlight away from recent events, to history.

*

The term 'humanitarian intervention' lacks clarity, for both conceptual and practical reasons. The literature on intervention reflects a wide range of perspectives, written by scholars of ethics, philosophy, politics, international relations, international law, strategic studies, war studies and peace studies, and by policy practitioners and media commentators. The different presumptions and disciplinary perspectives they bring to the subject are often valuable, but inevitably lead to some conceptual confusion. But the lack of clarity is partly also because, in practice, it can be difficult to distinguish clearly between, for example, coercive diplomacy and 'gunboat diplomacy'; armed participation in foreign civil wars, revolts, revolutions, and insurgencies; and peace-keeping, peace-enforcement, and armed distribution of humanitarian aid. The different types of involvement in another state's affairs can blur into each other. As Rosenau observes: 'So many diverse activities, motives, and consequences are considered

---

[4] Nicholas J. Wheeler, *Saving Strangers: Humanitarian Intervention in International Society* (Oxford: Oxford University Press, 2000), 1.

to constitute intervention that the key terms of most definitions are ambiguous and fail to discriminate empirical phenomena'.[5]

Another common problem is that most definitions of humanitarian intervention, even ones proposed by scholars who take historical examples into account, seem to be primarily concerned with accurately describing interventions since the Second World War. As a result, there can be difficulties in trying to apply their definitions historically. This difficulty is compounded because the meaning of the word 'humanitarian' has changed.

While it has a relatively clear meaning today, it is a rather recent neologism. In the eighteenth century it was used purely theologically, in reference to questions about the humanity or divinity of Christ. In the senses in which it is most often used today, 'concerned with human welfare as a primary or pre-eminent good', or 'with humanity as a whole', and 'action on the basis of [these] concern[s] rather than for pragmatic or strategic reasons', both it and the cognate 'humanitarianism' date only to the mid-nineteenth century.[6] Thus, if by 'humanitarian' one intends to imply a reference to human rights and international human right law, then it self-defines humanitarian intervention as something only carried out since the mid- to late nineteenth century, when the concept of 'human rights' emerged. Yet this cuts it off from the concepts and praxis that gave rise to it – acceptable for a political scientist, perhaps, but not for an historian. In this book, several chapters examine interventions arising from concerns that *today* would be called humanitarian, or relate to what *now* would be called 'human rights' or 'crimes against humanity', but which were not called that in the past. This approach is essential if we are to have a truly historicised understanding of the origins of the modern concept and practice of what, since the nineteenth century, has been termed 'humanitarian intervention'.

In practice, moreover, actions termed (whether formally or informally) 'humanitarian interventions' have usually been undertaken in response to only certain kinds of humanitarian tragedy. When combined with 'intervention', 'humanitarian' typically refers to a response to mortality and brutality inflicted by humans on others, rather than accidentally arising from bacterial, viral, meteorological, or climatic caprice (though it is increasingly being argued that, where human failings in responding to so-called 'acts of God' result in considerably increased mortality, then a humanitarian intervention could be justified). However, if humanitarian, in the context of intervention, generally refers to concern about atrocities,

---

[5] James N. Rosenau, 'Intervention as a Scientific Concept', *Journal of Conflict Resolution* 13 (1969), 154–5.

[6] *OED*, *s.v.* 'humanitarian', A.3, B.2.a, 'humanitarianism', 2: the earliest usages it notes are from the 1840s or 1850s.

the aims of humanitarian interventions can also relate to wider humanitarian concerns: ending tyranny, stopping slavery, or ensuring efficient and equitable delivery of disaster relief or general humanitarian aid.

The term 'intervention' has been much examined, especially by social scientists and lawyers, and for the purposes of this history there is no need to go into detail. We have taken a considerable number of definitions into account in defining, or describing, 'humanitarian intervention' as considered in this book. Despite their different academic disciplinary origins, most definitions have in common three key definitional aspects.[7] These are, as it were, the site, the subject, and the object of the action in question.[8] A humanitarian intervention is:

1. Carried out in, or intended to affect events within, a foreign state or states – it is an intervention;
2. Aimed at the government of the target state(s), or imposed on and only accepted reluctantly by it/them – it is thus coercive, albeit not necessarily involving use of force;
3. Intended, at least nominally (and at least to some extent actually), to avert, halt, and/or prevent recurrence of large-scale mortality, mass atrocities, egregious human rights abuses or other widespread suffering caused by the action or deliberate inaction of the *de facto* authorities in the target state(s).

Because humanitarian intervention involves at least a degree of compulsion of a state with regards to events within its sovereign territory, it can (at least in theory) be distinguished from wider 'humanitarian action' or

---

[7] Rosenau, 'Intervention as a Scientific Concept', 152–6; R. J. Vincent, *Nonintervention and International Order* (Princeton NJ: Princeton University Press, 1974), 3–13; Adam Roberts, *Humanitarian Action in War*, Adelphi Paper 305 (Oxford: Oxford University Press, 1996), 19; S. Neil MacFarlane, *Intervention in Contemporary World Politics*, Adelphi Paper 350 (Oxford and New York: Oxford University Press, 2002), 8–10, 13–16; J. L. Holzgrefe, 'The Humanitarian Intervention Debate', in J. L. Holzgrefe and Robert O. Keohane (eds.), *Humanitarian Intervention: Ethical, Legal and Political Dilemmas* (Cambridge: Cambridge University Press, 2003), 18; Thomas G. Weiss, *Humanitarian Intervention* (Cambridge and Malden, MA: Polity, 2007), 5–8; Eric A. Heinze, *Waging Humanitarian War: The Ethics, Law, and Politics of Humanitarian Intervention* (Albany: State University of New York Press, 2009), 2–9 (with explicit definitional statement at p. 7). Cf. Wheeler, *Saving Strangers*, 42–3, citing proposed criteria for *legitimate* interventions; Gareth Evans, *The Responsibility to Protect: Ending Mass Atrocity Crimes Once and For All* (Washington, DC: Brookings Institution Press, 2008), 11–13, defining 'mass atrocity crimes'; and the introductory comments of Davide Rodogno, in Chapter 7, below.
[8] Vincent identifies six defining features, and MacFarlane four: Vincent, *Nonintervention and International Order*, 4–12 (who intervenes, and the target, activity, types, purpose, and context of intervention); MacFarlane, *Intervention in Contemporary World Politics*, 9 (who intervenes, and where, how, and why they intervene).

assistance, such as that carried out regularly by a range of religious groups and other non-state actors, as well as by state agencies.[9]

The key element is that one state, or a non-state actor, attempts to impose its will on another state or group within it. When a state acts in another state at the request of its government and with its cooperation, it is rarely controversial (at least internationally, rather than internally). When action in another state's affairs is imposed on its government, or occurs in its despite, then intervention is controversial (and, some argue, illegitimate). In consequence, just as humanitarian *action* can take place in a foreign state without *intervention*, so military action in a foreign state does not necessarily constitute intervention either. Where the government of a state, or a party claiming *de jure* or *de facto* authority in that state, invites a foreign power to provide military assistance to deal with a domestic situation, the response is not an intervention, unless there is a clear, credible rival authority, as in a civil war situation. Thus, the despatch, for example, of US Marines to Lebanon and British paratroopers to Jordan in 1958, of French troops to Gabon in 1964, and of French and Belgian troops to Zaire in 1978, were not interventions, as in each case the deployment of troops was approved and/or requested by the governments of the three states in question and no credible alternative authority existed or emerged.[10] In contrast, the United Nations action in Bosnia was an intervention, for though the Sarajevo government invited the UN in, and was widely recognised as the *de jure* authority, it governed less of Bosnia-Herzegovina than Croatian and Serbian separatists and especially the *de facto* government of the Serbian 'state' of Krajina, which objected to the UN presence. The UN thus effectively intervened in a civil war, rather than helping a state to quell internal dissent.[11]

Humanitarian intervention has almost always been perceived as breaking the 'conventional pattern of international relations'.[12] This has been true even when, as has often been the case, intervention has been regarded as perfectly licit within international law; it was still regarded as a last, rather than first, resort. From the authors of late

---

[9] Howard Adelman, 'The Ethics of Humanitarian Intervention: The Case of the Kurdish Refugees', *Public Affairs Quarterly* 6 (Jan. 1992), 62.

[10] Vincent, *Nonintervention and International Order*, 6; MacFarlane, *Intervention in Contemporary World Politics*, 13–14; and ICISS, *The Responsibility to Protect*, 2 vols. (Ottawa: International Development Research Centre, 2001), vol. II: *Research, Bibliography, Background: Supplementary Volume to the Report of the International Commission on Intervention and State Sovereignty*, 56–7.

[11] See Matthew Jamison, Chapter 16, below.

[12] Vincent, *Nonintervention and International Order*, 13.

sixteenth-century treatises on the 'Law of Nations', described in
Chapter 2, to the European statesman planning the nineteenth-century
humanitarian interventions examined in Chapters 7–9, to the Vietnamese
contemplating their Cambodian intervention in 1978–9, described
in Chapter 15, intervention has been seen as an extreme step, to be taken
only in an emergency. Indeed, as R. J. Vincent observes, it is typically
carried out in response to 'extraordinary oppression' – ordinary oppression, persecution, and state violence have been sufficiently common that it
takes the perception of extreme violence to motivate action! By its nature,
then, humanitarian intervention is likely to be controversial.

There is a final point. While it is true that generally the literature of
'intervention focuses on military action', even scholars who define intervention in military terms concede that it may well involve political and
economic, as well as military, action.[13] Economic power can be used to
compel, instead of (or as well as) military power (and economic assistance can be supplied by non-state actors). Diplomatic initiatives can be
effective. At times the threat *not* to use force on behalf of a state with
which an intervening state might otherwise ally can also be an effective
instrument to prescribe action. Yet if the Westphalian principles of
sovereignty are truly normative, as many political scientists and international lawyers aver, then even diplomatic interference in a nation-
state's affairs could be considered illegitimate. Diplomacy and the threat
or use of force are properly conceived not as dichotomous alternatives,
but as points on a spectrum.

This view is reinforced by what the chapters in this book indicate
about the interrelationship of force and diplomacy.

1. The use of military force has usually been preceded by diplomatic
   intercession.
2. When a violent, or human rights-abusive, state has halted repressive
   actions with no coercive force used against it, it has often been partly
   or wholly because use of force had been threatened.
3. On some occasions military or naval forces have been deployed
   without hostilities breaking out, though this eventuality was far from
   certain at the time.

Moreover, even when armed force is used, different types of action are
involved; and again, the boundaries between them and diplomatic or
economic action may be blurred. These include:

---

[13] For example, MacFarlane, *Intervention in Contemporary World Politics*, 13; Holzgrefe,
'The Humanitarian Intervention Debate', 18.

(a) Overt 'humanitarian war' between states, as arguably took place between India and Pakistan in 1971, Tanzania and Uganda in 1978–9, and Vietnam and Cambodia in the same years (the latter the subject of Chapter 15).

(b) The despatch of expeditionary forces whose objectives include using force to compel cessation of atrocities and oppression, as happened in Greece in the 1820s and Cuba in 1898–9 (see Chapters 5 and 13).

(c) Deployment of military and/or naval forces *after* atrocities or violence in order to prevent recurrence and maintain peace, as happened for example in Lebanon and Syria in 1860–1 (Chapter 7), in Haiti in 1994, and in Kosovo in 1999 (Chapter 16).

(d) Employment of military forces to protect and manage distribution of humanitarian aid, as for example in Lebanon and Syria in 1861 (Chapter 7) and Somalia in 1991–2.

(e) Targeted use of naval or military force against specific actors or types of activity, as in British action against the slave trade in West Africa in the early nineteenth century and in East Africa and the Middle East in the late nineteenth and early twentieth centuries (Chapters 10–11).

(f) Limited demonstrations of force, as threats to persuade an unwilling government to accept terms, as happened in the Ottoman Empire in 1905 (Chapter 9).

(g) The provision of military training, supplies and sometimes troops to oppressed and victimised people groups, as by the English government in the Netherlands and France in the sixteenth century (Chapter 2) and some Anglo-American missionary groups in the Sudan in the twentieth century (Chapter 12).

In sum, to confine 'debates about humanitarian intervention to its military dimensions' will be too often to separate 'arbitrarily ... issues that in practice overlap'.[14]

For all these reasons, the chapters that follow consider sustained actions to end oppression, tyranny, persecution, or human rights abuses in another state, where the action was against the will of the government, its ruling elites, or a predominant faction or party, regardless of whether that action was diplomatic, logistical, economic, or military-naval.

★

Having set out what is being considered here, it is important to note the way in which it is treated: historically. This is not the definitive

---

[14] Paul Williams, review of Jennifer Welsh (ed.), *Humanitarian Intervention and International Relations* (Oxford: Oxford University Press, 2004), in *International Affairs* 80 (2004), 541.

history of humanitarian intervention. But one of its goals is to stimulate more treatment of intervention by historians, in the hopes that soon a definitive synthesis will become possible. For to a great extent, humanitarian intervention has been treated as though it did not have a history.

For a decade after the end of the Cold War, even while humanitarian interventions proliferated, analysts tended to argue that they represented a fundamental breach with the rules that had hitherto governed relations between states, and yet did so largely in the absence of 'systematic historical' analysis.[15] From prominent proponents of intervention, such as Michael Ignatieff, to celebrated opponents, such as Noam Chomsky, to more ambivalent commentators, such as Samantha Power (the distinguished writer on genocide), it was taken for granted that both the term and the very concept of 'humanitarian intervention' were recent inventions without any real history.[16] However, assertions that 'humanitarian intervention' originated after the end of the Cold War, and that interventions on behalf of endangered foreign populations to prevent human rights abuses are a creation of the 1990s, betray an almost astonishing lack of historical awareness.

However, in the last decade there has been an increasing awareness that the history of humanitarian intervention did not begin in the 1990s. The Independent Commission on Intervention and State Sovereignty (ICISS), whose 2001 report originated the influential concept that nation-states individually and collectively have a 'Responsibility to Protect' citizens from a range of crimes against humanity, included in that report explicit recognition of the importance of the 'historical, political and legal context' of 'the long history [of] "humanitarian intervention"'.[17] The Global Centre for the Responsibility to Protect (based at

---

[15] Herbert K. Tillema, review of Stephen A. Garrett, *Doing Good and Doing Well: An Examination of Humanitarian Intervention* (Westport, CT: Praeger, 1999), in *American Political Science Review* 94 (2000), 990–1.

[16] Ignatieff is explicit that it originated in 1991, then was shaped by events in Bosnia in the next three years: *Empire Lite: Nation-building in Bosnia, Kosovo and Afghanistan* (London: Vintage, 2003), 57–9; cf. *Virtual War: Kosovo and Beyond* (New York: Picador, 2000), 163. In her article, 'Is Humanitarian Intervention Dead? History Offers some Sobering Lessons', *Slate Magazine*, 29 Sept. 2008 (www.slate.com/id/2200971), Power concurs with Ignatieff. As for Chomsky, while he rejects the ethicality, much less legality, of intervention, he consistently conducts debate in the same limited chronological terms, occasionally briefly considering the 1960s and 1980s, but remaining focused on the interventions of the 1990s: see his 'Humanitarian Intervention', *Boston Review*, Dec. 1993–Jan. 1994 (copy available at www.chomsky.info/articles/199401–02.htm); and 'Humanitarian Imperialism: New Doctrine of Imperial Right', *Monthly Review*, Sept. 2008 (www.monthlyreview.org/080908chomsky.php).

[17] ICISS, *The Responsibility to Protect*, vol. I: *Report of the International Commission on Intervention and State Sovereignty*, 6, 9 (paras. 1.25, 1.39), cf. 84 (App. B).

the Ralph Bunche Institute for International Studies, City University of New York) replies to the question 'Is R2P really new?' with the statement 'No. The core underlying idea that states have an obligation to protect men and women from the worst atrocities is well established.' It then goes on to cite the UN Convention on Genocide of 1948, and the body of international human law governing the treatment of civilians during armed conflict. What R2P added, the Centre continues, was simply the acceptance of a 'collective responsibility' to act against genocide, ethnic cleansing, war crimes, or crimes against humanity. It was thus a development of a longstanding concept of 'humanitarian intervention'.[18]

Scholars and practitioners of international law, especially legal historians, have long been aware that the term 'humanitarian intervention' dated to the nineteenth century, and they had integrated debates over the nineteenth-century precedents into analysis of the legal status of intervention. Unfortunately, most of their studies are not widely known; they have limited applicability, being largely focused on questions of legal interpretation; and they are part of an essentially internal disciplinary debate. As Sir Adam Roberts neatly summarises, even though 'substantial discussion among international lawyers' continued in the last three decades of the twentieth century over 'the question of whether humanitarian intervention could ever be compatible with the [UN] Charter', in particular, or international law more generally, 'this was mainly a debate among schoolmen, especially American schoolmen, and until recent times had relatively little impact on national or international practice'.[19] In the twenty-first century, Simon Chesterman's superb study of humanitarian intervention and international law broadened the context of legal history, taking a comprehensive approach, albeit one still anchored in legal texts, rather than in state practice.[20]

In addition, more and more social scientists writing on humanitarian intervention now take the history of the concept into account. Thus, Nicholas J. Wheeler, in his path-breaking *Saving Strangers: Humanitarian Intervention in International Society*, briefly highlights the fact that legal historians trace the notion back to Hugo Grotius in the seventeenth century and lists some nineteenth- and twentieth-century precedents

[18] See the Centre's website: www.GlobalCentreR2P.org.
[19] Adam Roberts, 'Humanitarian War: Military Intervention and Human Rights', *International Affairs* 69 (1993), 434. Cf. Wheeler, *Saving Strangers*, 2: 'there has been little interchange between the disciplines of international relations and international law'.
[20] Simon Chesterman, *Just War or Just Peace? Humanitarian Intervention and International Law* (Oxford: Oxford University Press, 2001).

ranging from the Greek Revolt of the 1810s–1820s, to Bangladesh, Cambodia, and Uganda in the 1970s.[21] J. L. Holzgrefe has a similar listing in an important chapter in *Humanitarian Intervention: Ethical, Legal and Political Dilemmas*.[22] Likewise, Jennifer Welsh is an expert on Edmund Burke and thus familiar with some of the historical roots of the phenomenon, even if this knowledge is not much to the fore in her edited collection on *Humanitarian Intervention and International Relations*.[23] Historical sociologists are increasingly applying their disciplinary perspective to International Relations, including to issues related to intervention, such as sovereignty; their emphasis that 'history matters' holds out considerable promise of 'a more nuanced, complex' understanding 'of the principal causal flows that lie at the heart of world historical development'.[24] One history of nineteenth-century humanitarian intervention, based on detailed archival research, has recently been published by Gary Bass and another, by Davide Rodogno, has recently been completed.[25]

\*

We believe, however, that these works, welcome as they are, do not yet permit a synthesis of the history of humanitarian intervention. Any claims to have established its history are premature and incomplete.

Gary Bass's recent *Freedom's Battle* unquestionably is a valuable first step towards a more comprehensive history. The tradition of humanitarian intervention, he points out, 'once ran deep in world politics [and] . . . is anything but new'.[26] The author begins with the Greek revolt, and moves via the intervention in Syria of the 1860s and the Bulgarian agitation of the 1870s to the beginning of the Armenian question; he thus ends where Samantha Power's *Problem from Hell* starts.[27] Bass anticipates some of the points made here: the importance of the press (pp. 31–8); the 'flexible' view of sovereignty which made interventions possible in the past (p. 352); the occasionally 'paralysing' effect of

[21] Wheeler, *Saving Strangers*, 45 *et passim*.
[22] Holzgrefe, 'The Humanitarian Intervention Debate', 45–7.
[23] Welsh (ed.), *Humanitarian Intervention and International Relations*.
[24] George Lawson, 'The Promise of Historical Sociology in International Relations', *International Studies Review* 8 (2006), 397–423, at 415; cf. George Lawson and Robbie Shilliam, 'Beyond Hypocrisy? Debating the "Fact" and "Value" of Sovereignty in Contemporary World Politics', *International Politics* 46 (2009), 657–70.
[25] Gary Bass, *Freedom's Battle: Origins of Humanitarian Interventionism* (New York: Alfred Knopf, 2008); Davide Rodogno, *Humanitarian Interventions during the Nineteenth Century: British and French Forcible Interventions in the Ottoman Empire (1820–1909)* (Rome: Laterza, forthcoming).
[26] Bass, *Freedom's Battle*, 3.
[27] Samantha Power, *'A Problem from Hell': America and the Age of Genocide*, 3rd edn (New York: Harper Perennial, 2003).

multilateralism (p. 363); the way in which humanitarian concerns were often linked to confessional solidarity, but also often transcended them (pp. 6, 19, 357–61 *et passim*). He has conducted extensive research in French and British archives as well as having consulted an impressive range of primary printed sources.

A significant part of this book overlaps with *Freedom's Battle*, but Chapters 2–4 and parts of Chapters 5 and 10 cover an earlier period, and Chapters 12–16 cover the century after his terminus. Moreover, while Chapters 10 and 11 examine the same period as Bass, they examine West and East Africa and the Middle East, which he does not, while the intervention in the Ottoman Empire examined in Chapter 9 is one not considered in *Freedom's Battle*.

Furthermore, Bass's approach is very different from that adopted in this volume. He is self-consciously concerned to defend the concept of humanitarian intervention from the charge that it has 'no real historical standing'; this accusation, he rightly notes, 'has been used powerfully to oppose US and European missions abroad' (p. 4). His purpose is to undermine this opposition, not least by refuting claims that cynicism, national aggrandisement, or abusive practical implementation, inevitably characterised historical interventions – hence, by implication, he vindicates present-day interventions (for example, pp. 40–1, 371, 378–82).[28] In contrast, while the contributors to this volume have their own views on intervention in the present day, both positive and negative, our collective purpose here is primarily historical rather than political. In consequence, we take a longer-term perspective than Bass and show that the concept of humanitarian intervention goes back much further than the Greek Revolt against the Ottoman Empire in the 1820s, which produced the first nineteenth-century European intervention to be justified in terms of the emerging discourse of humanitarianism. Despite occasional references to Grotius (p. 4), for example, Bass is essentially unaware of eighteenth-century, much less earlier, precedents and antecedents. Moreover, even in the 'long nineteenth century' (1815–1914) on which Bass focuses, there were many more actions on behalf of suffering foreigners than he chronicles, including unexamined interventions in Crete and Macedonia (the former summarily, the latter comprehensively treated in this book). It is not that Bass is wrong, therefore, but rather that he is even more right than he claims.

This is indicative of a wider problem: even where there is an awareness of the historical dimension, there is still confusion about how far

---

[28] Cf. David Armitage, review in *Times Literary Supplement*, 22 May 2009, 8.

back this history stretches. Even where a history is acknowledged, it is almost invariably one of less than 200 years.

Now, as already noted, legal historians or other scholars of international law have considered pre-1990 precedents for intervention, but most still pay only summary attention to events before the twentieth century.[29] The few studies that do consider a longer chronological span generally begin substantive analysis with, at earliest, the Western interventions in the Ottoman Empire on behalf of the Greek Revolt in the 1820s and pay no more than a kind of lip service, if that, to precedents of the seventeenth and eighteenth centuries.[30] Chesterman's *Just War or Just Peace?* is a partial exception: he considers not only these but also medieval concepts, and while his treatment of the period before *c.* 1800 is still relatively brief, and focused on legal texts, rather than state practice, (pp. 8–21), it is not much shorter than his treatment of the nineteenth and early twentieth centuries (pp. 22–41); however, all this is dwarfed by his analysis of the second half of the twentieth century (pp. 45–217). Martti Koskenniemi's history of the development of international law in the nineteenth century is impressively researched, but while it includes some treatment of developments in attitudes towards intervention, its subject is broader than that, and of course it does not examine the centuries before *c.* 1800.[31] Now, all this is partly natural, since lawyers have as their concern what the law *is* and so are bound to consider recent precedents at length. It is not a criticism of their method, then, but rather an observation of the state of scholarship, to observe that legal scholars, though considering history, actually largely do so superficially – they do not provide a history of humanitarian intervention.

---

[29] For example, Holzgrefe and Keohane (eds.), *Humanitarian Intervention*; and Fernando R. Tesón, *Humanitarian Intervention: An Inquiry into Law and Morality*, 3rd edn (Ardsley, NY: Transnational Publishers, 2005), who despite summary coverage of earlier precedents effectively begins his subject not even in 1900, but in 1945.

[30] For example, Thomas Franck and Nigel S. Rodley, 'After Bangladesh: The Law of Humanitarian Intervention by Military Force', *AJIL* 67 (1973), 275–305; Francis Kofi Abiew, *The Evolution of the Doctrine and Practice of Humanitarian Intervention* (The Hague, London, and Boston: Kluwer Law International, 1999), 44–59 (he briefly covers the writings of seventeenth- and eighteenth-century theorists of the Law of Nations, 33–6); Sean D. Murphy, *Humanitarian Intervention: The United Nations in an Evolving World Order* (Philadelphia: University of Pennsylvania Press, 1996), 49–56 ('The era of the Concert of Europe'); François Rigaux, '"Humanitarian" Intervention: The Near East from Gladstone to Rambouillet', unpubl. paper presented at the International School on Disarmament and Research on Conflicts, 15th Winter Course, Andalo, 2002 (available at www.isodarco.it/courses/andalo02/paper/andalo02-rigaux1.html).

[31] Martti Koskenniemi, *The Gentle Civilizer of Nations: The Rise and Fall of International Law 1870–1960* (Cambridge: Cambridge University Press, 2002) – there is a brief reference to Grotius at 87.

The French Revolution was the starting point for a work that bridged the gap between international law and international relations: R. J. Vincent's classic study of *Nonintervention and International Order*. Although he definitely identifies a long history of debate over intervention and non-intervention, and though he examines early theorists of the Law of Nations, he goes back no earlier than Grotius, in the 1620s, and briefly surveys only three seventeenth-century commentators, Grotius, Hobbes, and Pufendorf (pp. 21–6). His analysis of early and mid-eighteenth-century theorists of the 'law of nations is not much longer' (pp. 27–30). In contrast are his detailed studies of late eighteenth-, nineteenth-, and early twentieth-century theory and practice (pp. 45–141). For practical purposes, then, Vincent identifies the history of intervention as starting around the time of the French Revolution.

This is, finally, also effectively the starting point for the only major studies that consciously attempt to historicise intervention. We have already treated the strengths and weaknesses of Bass's *Freedom's Battle*, which really starts with the 1820s. Mar Swatek-Evenstein's avowed 'history of "humanitarian intervention"' likewise begins in 1822. While it is comprehensive, it is a synthesis, unlike Bass's archivally grounded study.[32] Wheeler's *Saving Strangers*, which like Vincent bridges international law and international relations,[33] actually dehistoricises intervention to a significant degree with his avowal that, with the creation of the United Nations '[f]or *the first time* in the history of modern international society, the domestic conduct of governments was now exposed to scrutiny by other governments, human rights non-governmental organisations (NGOs), and international organisations' (p. 2, emphasis supplied). He has the usual nod to Grotius – but only at second hand (utilising a slightly inaccurate translation that makes Grotius seem even more favourable to intervention than he was);[34] and Wheeler recognises the significance of the interventions in the Ottoman Empire (p. 46); however, having done so in passing, he then overwhelmingly focuses on interventions since 1945.[35] Stephen Garrett and Neil MacFarlane seek to provide historical context for

---

[32] Mar Swatek-Evenstein, *Geschichte der 'Humanitären Intervention'* (Baden-Baden: Nomos, 2008).

[33] Wheeler, *Saving Strangers*, 2.

[34] The quotation from Grotius is from Abiew, *Evolution*, 35; see Tesón, *Humanitarian Intervention*, 59n., on the inaccuracy, in the quoted passage from *De jure belli ac pacis*, of the nineteenth-century abridged English edition that was used (for some quotations from Grotius, including this one, though curiously not some others) by Abiew.

[35] Wheeler, *Saving Strangers*, 55–310.

their studies of intervention, which are largely focused on the present: Garrett begins in 1827, though he surveys some nineteenth-century episodes others miss; MacFarlane notably includes some pre-French revolutionary, as well as nineteenth- and twentieth-century, examples. However, in both cases, analysis of all pre-Cold War instances is brief and not based on original historical research.[36]

Even scholars of international relations who recognise the broad historical context to modern security and human rights challenges, and deal (if only in passing) with the early modern era, treat humanitarian intervention as a late twentieth-century phenomenon.[37] The *Responsibility to Protect* report is symptomatic, in that even though it acknowledged an historical lineage and claimed to have incorporated it into its analysis (as noted above), its work seems to have been based on a very narrow chronological evidential basis. The actual *Report* makes virtually no reference to actual historical episodes – a literally passing reference to the Peace of Westphalia (1648) as the starting-point of the modern concept of sovereignty is the exception (p. 12, para. 2.7). Research commissioned by the ICISS and published as a supplementary volume includes some treatment of history, but only two of nine essays in volume II are on the history of humanitarian intervention, and they examine interventions only 'from the birth of the UN Charter regime' (p. 47). Furthermore, whereas twenty-nine pages cover interventions in the forty-five years from 1945 up to the end of the Cold War (pp. 49–77), forty-eight pages cover the interventions of the 1990s (pp. 79–126). The history of intervention before World War II is dismissed in less than a page in all (pp. 16–17).

In sum, although historical approaches are now more common, the new historical scholarship on intervention assumes, either explicitly or implicitly, that intervention is really a creation of the nineteenth-century world at the earliest.

In any case, historical studies remain few. Most major studies of intervention produced in the last decade remain focused on the 1990s: they betray superficial knowledge of historical precedents; simply lack interest in them; or restrict historical analysis to some events from the

---

[36] Garland, *Doing Good and Doing Well*, 8–13; MacFarlane, *Intervention in Contemporary World Politics*, 19–32 ('Intervention in pre-Westphalian Europe' at 21–3).

[37] For example, Kalevi J. Holsti, 'Reversing Rousseau: The Medieval and Modern in Contemporary Wars', in *The Empire of Security and the Safety of the People*, ed. William Bain, Routledge Advances in International Relations and Global Politics 45 (London and New York: Routledge, 2006), 37–59, esp. 39–40, 42–3, 56–7, 59 n.48.

Cold War, before concentrating on the 1990s.[38] The attitude of a leading authority, one of the co-chairs of the body that produced the *Responsibility to Protect* report, is indicative; in a monograph on R2P and atrocity crimes published in 2008 he dismisses the entire history of 'mass atrocities' before World War II in less than four pages, part of them under the heading 'Centuries of Indifference'.[39]

This reflects the fact that scholarship on humanitarian intervention, *as a whole*, is at present overwhelmingly the preserve of scholars of politics, international law, international relations, strategic studies, sociology, and ethics and philosophy. Academics working in these disciplines, together with analysts from think tanks, NGOs, and the media, often produce well-researched, richly textured studies of recent and current events. Yet their focus on the present and the recent past is a major weakness.[40]

We certainly do not suggest that studies of intervention lacking a historical dimension are therefore poor; nor that works which do have that dimension, but do not take into account pre-nineteenth-century history, are in consequence fatally flawed; nor that only academic historians can conduct effective archival research or write capably on the past. Nevertheless, historical training and perspective has something to offer. Furthermore, much of the history of humanitarian intervention is largely or wholly unwritten.

★

This volume is the first overview of the history of humanitarian intervention from its origins to the present day. Unlike many contemporary analysts, we are not so much concerned with making normative judgments about what *ought* to have happened in the past, but rather with

[38] For example, C. A. J. Coady, *The Ethics of Armed Humanitarian Intervention*, Peaceworks 45 (Washington, DC: United States Institute of Peace, 2002); Anne Orford, *Reading Humanitarian Intervention: Human Rights and the Use of Force in International Law* (Cambridge: Cambridge University Press, 2003); Welsh (ed.), *Humanitarian Intervention and International Relations*; Michael C. Davis, Wolfgang Dietrich, Bettina Scholdan, and Dieter Sepp (eds.), *International Intervention in the Post-Cold War World: Moral Responsibility and Power Politics* (New York: M. E. Sharpe, 2004); David Rieff, *At the Point of a Gun: Democratic Dreams and Armed Intervention* (New York: Simon and Schuster, 2006); Patricia Marchak, *No Easy Fix: Global Responses to Internal Wars and Crimes against Humanity* (Montreal and Kingston: McGill-Queen's University Press, 2008); Heinze, *Waging Humanitarian War*; James Pattison, *Humanitarian Intervention and the Responsibility to Protect: Who Should Intervene?* (Oxford: Oxford University Press, 2010).

[39] Evans, *Responsibility to Protect*, 13–16, at 13.

[40] Cf. Mathias Risse, review of Terry Nardin and Melissa S. Williams (eds.), *Humanitarian Intervention* (New York: New York University Press, 2006), in *Ethics and International Affairs* 20 (2006), 387 col. 2.

exploring what did happen and why. But where the language of the time echoes that of our own, we note and investigate this.

It is important to note that this is not a comprehensive history, which would require a multi-volume work. This necessarily is a select-ive history, although it is intended to be complete in the sense that it ranges across the entire history of humanitarian intervention, from origins to recent examples. We have deliberately sought to draw atten-tion to the earlier history of the subject – to its roots and antecedents, in the sixteenth, seventeenth, and eighteenth centuries. As a result, space does not permit examination of some episodes of the nineteenth and twentieth centuries. In order that the reader will have a complete overview of the history of humanitarian intervention, we briefly high-light here several significant interventions most of which are not examined or referred to in the following chapters; and we point the reader to relevant scholarship.

In 1830, at the Conference of London, the five Great Powers (Great Britain, France, Russia, Prussia, and Austria) recognised the inde-pendence of Belgium, separating it from the Kingdom of the Netherlands. In 1831, the Dutch attempted to reassert their authority in Belgium by force; but French military intervention and a British naval blockade of Antwerp (1831) eventually obliged them to end their campaign. Eventually, the Netherlands formally acknowledged Belgian independence.[41]

In 1866–8, Austria, France, Italy, and Prussia proposed an Inter-national Commission of enquiry into Turkish misrule of Cyprus. The Turks initially rejected it as an unjustified meddling in domestic jurisdiction, leading to Great Power threats of military intervention. This was avoided after Britain and France pressured the Ottoman gov-ernment into making human rights concessions and reorganising local government: the *Règlement organique* of 1868. This in turn was partly along lines inspired by the settlement in Lebanon in 1861 (discussed in Chapter 6). A conference of the five Great Powers (plus Italy) compelled Greece to accept this settlement, despite Greek attempts to mobilise

---

[41] This is an episode that deserves further research. See C. B. Wels, 'The Foreign Relations of the Netherlands between 1813 and 1945', in H. F. van Panhuys *et al.* (eds.), *International Law in the Netherlands* (Alphen aan den Rijn: Sijthoff and Noordhoff, for T. M. C. Asser Institute, 1978), 51–8; see also Barry Howard Steiner, *Collective Preventive Diplomacy: A Study in International Conflict Management* (Albany: State University of New York Press, 2004), 116–17. The episode is referred to in passing as an early possible example of humanitarian intervention by Franck and Rodley, 'After Bangladesh', 284, and Garland, *Doing Good and Doing Well*, 11.

public support in the West for European military intervention in Crete, in the hope it might result in reunion with Greece.[42]

The deployment of US and Belgian troops in the Congo in 1964, to rescue endangered Westerners without the Congolese government's approval, was justified by the American representative to the United Nations Security Council on the basis that the troops had conducted a 'humanitarian mission'.[43] A prominent international jurist, Richard Lillich, was not alone in considering the deployment as 'a valid exercise, at least in the classical sense, of humanitarian intervention'.[44]

India intervened in the Pakistan civil war of 1971, which ended what is generally accepted to have been genocide in what was then East Pakistan and is now the independent nation of Bangladesh. Pakistani troops killed at least one million people in East Pakistan and raped an estimated 200,000 females, including young girls; many more died of hunger and disease in the resulting chaos, and some ten million Bengalis fled as refugees into India.[45] In late 1978, in an episode examined below, Vietnam sent troops into Kampuchea (today's Cambodia), completing in 1979 the overthrow of the inhumane dictator Pol Pot and ending the appalling genocide of the 'killing fields', in which more than one million Cambodians – perhaps as many as 1.8 million – died.[46] In 1978, Tanzania repelled an invasion launched from Uganda, launched by the latter's vicious dictator Idi Amin; in early 1979, Tanzania launched its own invasion, which toppled Amin's brutal regime, which had been responsible for mass atrocities in which some 300,000 Ugandans died.[47] The Indian and Vietnamese interventions rival each other as probably the most effective interventions in history, in terms of the death-tolls in the genocides they terminated, and which might otherwise have increased to unknowable heights.

---

[42] Bass does not examine this episode. See *Cambridge History of the Ottoman Empire and Modern Turkey*, vol. II: *Reform, Revolution and Republic: The Rise of Modern Turkey, 1808–1975*, ed. S. J. Shaw and E. K. Shaw (Cambridge: Cambridge University Press, 1977), 151–2; Maureen M. Robson, 'Lord Clarendon and the Cretan Question, 1868–9', *Historical Journal* 3 (1960), 38–55; cf. Davide Rodogno, Chapter 7, below; and ICISS, *Responsibility to Protect*, II, 24 n.6.

[43] Quoted in Franck and Rodley, 'After Bangladesh', 288.

[44] Richard B. Lillich, 'Forcible Self-help under International Law', *Naval War College Review* 22 (1970), 62; note the title of G. Weisberg 'The Congo Crisis 1964: A Case Study in Humanitarian Intervention', *Virginia Journal of International Law* 12 (1972), 261ff.

[45] Power, *Problem from Hell*, 83; see Wheeler, *Saving Strangers*, ch. 2; Murphy, *Humanitarian Intervention*, 97–100.

[46] See Wheeler, *Saving Strangers*, ch. 3; Power, *Problem from Hell*, ch. 6; see also Murphy, *Humanitarian Intervention*, 102–5; and Sophie Quinn-Judge, Chapter 15, below.

[47] Wheeler, *Saving Strangers*, ch. 4; Murphy, *Humanitarian Intervention*, 105–7; cf. James Mayall, 'Humanitarian Intervention and International Society: Lessons from Africa', in Walsh, *Humanitarian Intervention and International Relations*, 120–41.

In *Saving Strangers*, Wheeler presents meticulously researched and nuanced accounts of the three humanitarian crises of the 1970s and the resultant interventions, breaking a path other scholars are following.[48] The Indian government only ever informally justified its action as a humanitarian intervention to protect ethnic Bengalis, but the revivification of an ancient, but apparently moribund, international-legal principle, along with the fact that there undeniably had been appalling loss of life in East Pakistan, led to a renaissance of legal scholarship on humanitarian intervention in international law, igniting a vigorous debate among lawyers over intervention's legality and legitimacy, a debate that mostly died down, smouldering until the end of the Cold War, when of course it exploded again.[49] Strikingly, however, even though the Vietnamese and Tanzanian interventions could have been credibly presented as humanitarian interventions, they were not; instead they were justified by the respective governments as acts of self-defence and thus in accord with the UN Charter.[50] This attitude was mirrored by US officials who, as Power observes, never 'thought to ask the State Department legal adviser's office' if events in Cambodia constituted genocide, as defined by the International Convention against Genocide.[51] We include in this book (Chapter 15) an analysis of the Vietnamese 'intervention' by Sophie Quinn-Judge, whose expertise on (and first-hand knowledge of) Vietnam enables her to provide a fresh perspective.

*

What follows are empirical studies of the history of humanitarian intervention from its origins to the recent past. The examples are mostly drawn, in one form or another, from the experience of the Western world. This reflects the historical record, at least until the important interventions by African and Asian states in the 1970s. However, the attitudes of the Indian, Tanzanian, and Vietnamese governments were shaped largely by Western concepts of international relations. Indeed, as already hinted, Vietnam's government in 1979 did not draw on long-standing indigenous concepts of the immorality of tyranny to justify its

---

[48] See the preceding footnotes.

[49] For example, Franck and Rodley, 'After Bangladesh'; Richard B. Lillich (ed.), *Humanitarian Intervention and the United Nations* (Charlottesville: University Press of Virginia, 1973), proceedings of a conference organised by the Procedural Aspects of International Law Institute and the Carnegie Endowment for International Peace; Jean-Pierre L. Fonteyne, 'The Customary International Law Doctrine of Humanitarian Intervention: Its Current Validity Under the U.N. Charter', *California Western International Law Journal* 4 (1973–4), 203–70. It probably also influenced Vincent, *Intervention and Nonintervention*.

[50] Mayall, 'Humanitarian Intervention', 125; Quinn-Judge, p. 348, below.

[51] Power, *Problem from Hell*, 124.

intervention in Cambodia; rather, as Quinn-Judge shows, they argued that it was 'in harmony with the principles of . . . the United Nations Charter'.[52] Thus, the Asian and African experiences of intervention in the 1970s to a great extent reflected the experience of the Western world and the 'Law of Nations', which began to emerge in early modern Europe, drawing partly on concepts in late medieval European philosophy and theology.

The seventeen chapters are divided into five Parts, arranged partly chronologically and partly thematically. After an introductory chapter, the three chapters in Part I examine intervention in early modern Europe. The next eleven chapters, in Parts II, III, and IV, deal with nineteenth- and twentieth-century history and are divided by the geography of intervening states or target states. The two chapters in Part V are concerned with recent interventions and what long-term historical perspective suggests about intervention across history and in the present day.

The three chapters in Part I cover two-and-a-half centuries and inevitably more could have been said. While Chapter 2, which covers up to the mid-seventeenth century, examines some military interventions, it also considers the theoretical position advanced in the nascent 'Law of Nations' legitimating intervention against 'tyranny'. Chapters 3 (on the late seventeenth and early eighteenth centuries) and 4 (the eighteenth century) examine humanitarian diplomacy but also pay sustained attention to the developing discourses that delegitimated oppression and argued for the legitimacy of action against it.

The five chapters in Part II are all concerned with interventions by the Great Powers of the 'Concert of Europe' in the Ottoman Empire – this is Bass's territory, but Chapters 5–9 cover a longer period than *Freedom's Battle*, and consider geographical areas and types of intervention that Bass does not. Some of these interventions involved military force, some were purely diplomatic (Chapter 6) or economic, and some involved a mix of methods. Indeed, it is notable that the Great Powers adopted a comprehensive approach to humanitarian trouble spots in the Ottoman Empire, recognising the necessity of reconstruction and preventative measures as well as remedial military action, though in practice comprehensive programmes were not without their problems on the ground.

The three chapters of Part III examine interventions in Africa, though Chapter 11, on late nineteenth- and early twentieth-century action to suppress the East African slave trade, also necessarily deals with the Ottoman Empire, which was then a major market for African slaves.

---

[52] Quoted below p. 343.

Chapter 12, the final chapter of Part III, extends the examination of Africa into the twentieth century, and also expands the coverage from governments to non-state actors – in this case, missionary groups operating in the Sudan. Chapter 12 is extremely important because it shows that intervention need not necessarily by undertaken by a state – it can be undertaken by NGOs. One of the phenomena of the late twentieth century has been the effective transfer of power from states to non-state actors; NGOs (many of them religious in affiliation) are some of the most important and influential of the latter, especially in the developing world, where they have taken on state functions. The missionaries' activity in the Sudan is illustrative of this trend.

The three chapters in Part IV examine interventions by non-European states: Chapters 13 and 14 consider interventions by the United States (one from the 1890s, the other from the 1970s), and Chapter 15 considers Vietnam's intervention in Cambodia, also from the 1970s. The first and last of these were military interventions, the second purely diplomatic. Chapters 13 and 14 consider the debates preceding intervention, the discourses arguing for intervention and the use of the press to promote an interventionist agenda. Chapter 15 is focused on the nature of the Vietnamese intervention and the international debate surrounding it.

Last, in Part V, Chapter 16 is on the post-Cold War years of 'liberal interventionism'; it examines several recent famous (or infamous) interventions and debates surrounding their legitimacy and puts them in historical perspective. Chapter 17 treats the period as a whole and examines key issues in humanitarian intervention in historical perspective; it outlines the chief conclusions that can be drawn collectively from the chapters in this book.

Some chapters of this book naturally examine episodes and debates that have been treated by other scholars (notably Bass and Wheeler). However, this is the first book to trace the history of humanitarian intervention even across the whole of the nineteenth and twentieth centuries, and is certainly the first to treat the subject from the origin of the concept and practice in the early modern world up to today. Even though, as we have seen, it examines neither every intervention nor even every major intervention – which would require several volumes – it examines a significant and indicative sample of interventionist theory and practice. It thus provides an overview of the whole history of humanitarian intervention, from its roots and antecedents in the sixteenth century, up to *c.* 2000.

★

Although conclusions will be drawn in Chapter 17, the remainder of this chapter sets out some of the important themes that subsequent chapters address.

Part I demonstrates that in early modern Europe states threatened or used force, and/or applied strong diplomatic pressure, against foreign regimes which ill-treated minority people groups. It also shows that influential contemporary theorists specifically located the basis for such actions in the nascent Law of Nations. In early modern Christendom, the right to protect foreign populations was widely accepted, perhaps even normative, as Chapter 2 posits; and certainly, as Chapters 3 and 4 emphasise, it was a right provided for by international instruments, for around a hundred years after 1648. In consequence, Part I also collectively shows that the Treaties of Westphalia, which brought the Thirty Years' War to an end in 1648 (and are widely described as creating the modern paradigm of national sovereignty and non-intervention in other states' internal affairs), were much less of a watershed than usually is assumed (a point addressed in Chapter 17).

The early modern period emerges as a time of 'incubation'. Notions of the common interest of 'Christendom' provided a starting point for doctrines that were to evolve and mutate, first in the Enlightenment (Chapter 4) and then in the nineteenth century (Chapters 5–8, 10–11, and 13), via concepts such as 'liberty', 'civilisation', and 'humanity', into the ideas current today. The conceptual and terminological evolutions involved are sketched out later in this introduction, but Chapters 4 and 5, which bridge Parts I and II, and the late eighteenth and early nineteenth centuries, are important; they investigate developments in political thought that helped to make the nineteenth century the high noon of intervention. Subsequent chapters mostly are case studies or surveys of intervention in practice, but these essays in intellectual history and the attitudes of statesmen demonstrate the roots of nineteenth-century state praxis.

It is widely accepted that the emergence of the 'humanitarian' impulse goes back to the universalism of the Enlightenment(s). So far, however, scholarly literature on the subject has tended to concentrate on reduction in the savagery of warfare itself. In fact, the Enlightenment also drove a debate on the use of force to defend and even enforce universal values against transgressing states. Enlightenment values were perpetuated in the liberal constitutional consensus that emerged in some nineteenth-century Western European states; they are very evident in concepts of 'civilisation' and civilised behaviour that motivated opposition to the slave trade and generated much Western concern for imperilled minorities ruled by the 'Sublime Porte' (as the sultan's court was known). The slave trade was largely destroyed, Christian and Jewish minorities in the Ottoman Empire were (sometimes) protected, and tyrannical rule (at some times and in some places) was ended, by the threat or actual use of force. Precisely because of the frequency of such interventions, 'human rights' emerged as a term and legal concept in the mid-nineteenth century and the term 'humanitarian intervention' emerged in the late nineteenth century.

The five chapters in Part II (5–9) and the first two chapters of Part III (10–11) chart the evolution of the concept of intervention, and the way intervention was practised, in the century after the end of the Napoleonic Wars. Chapter 6 includes the role played by non-state actors, in this case religious voluntary groups in European nations, both in helping minorities abroad and in publicising oppression and atrocity, thereby creating a political climate in which diplomatic or military intervention became possible; it is based on their records and publications. Chapters 7–11 are all based largely on evidence from state papers and diplomatic correspondence, and all emphasise governmental, 'top-down' perspectives – an important part of the story of how interventions were conducted.

However, these chapters additionally examine public debates that helped to make intervention possible. Chapters 7, 9, and 11, in particular, bring out the vital importance of the emergence, in the mid- to late nineteenth century, of transnational pressure groups: what Bass terms 'atrocitarians'.[53] Their significance is considered further in the Conclusion (Chapter 17, below), where we suggest that a vitally important factor in the history of humanitarian intervention is the emergence of a 'humanitarian public', which is both consumer and generator of stories about mass atrocities and humanitarian crises, both a source of pressure on politicians and manipulable by them.

A humanitarian lobby also emerged in the United States. Chapter 13 examines the Spanish–American War of 1898, and stresses that the same rhetoric that led some Americans to advocate to humanitarian war was also used to justify acquiring an empire. This tension between intervention and imperialism (which, as already noted also, characterised humanitarian lobbying in Europe) was markedly present in debates before, during, and after the Spanish–American War. But Chapter 13 also brings out that, while the rhetoric and logic of humanitarianism overlapped to some extent with that of imperialism, humanitarians were not necessarily imperialists. Some of the strongest proponents of war with Spain, to save people from an abusive regime, became the strongest critics of the subjugation of former Spanish subjects by the United

[53] Bass, *Freedom's Battle*, 6, 42, 236, 273–81, 288–90, 294, 296, 298, 300, 342, 346, 372, 374, 379, 382.

States, and of arguments that, because American rule would be more benign, the creation of an American empire was justified.

It is clear from the chapters in Parts II, III and IV that Western states did not act against the ailing Ottoman Empire, the equally ailing Spanish Empire, or minor African or Arab princes, simply to save individuals and communities from abuse. Geopolitical aims were always significant. Nevertheless, it is also clear that, in the interventions considered, the rights of individuals were always *an* issue, and that humanitarian motives were present even when not the most important factor in them.[54] These chapters show that there is a long-standing and genuine danger of humanitarian rhetoric becoming 'simply a cloak of legality for the use of force'.[55] But they also show that it actually eventuates less often than is frequently assumed in recent studies.

Chapters 6 and 12 (along with Chapters 7 and 9) show that, even before the twentieth century, 'transnational political movements' were beginning to 'engage in intervention'; although the height of action by the missionaries examined in Chapter 12 was the later twentieth century, non-state actors have taken a 'significant role' in intervention for longer than perhaps most political scientists are aware.[56] John Brown's 1859 raid on Harper's Ferry, intended to spark an uprising that would end slavery in the South of the United States, could be regarded as a failed humanitarian intervention by a non-state actor.

Chapter 14 is a final illustration of the role of pressure groups with transnational concerns. Populist lobbying helped to overcome the opposition of foreign-policy 'realists' in the United States in the early 1970s, allowing a formal linking of trade concessions to the Soviet Union to the latter's human rights record; this established a precedent of diplomatic intervention in the domestic policies of another nation-state. In contrast, Chapter 15 examines the Vietnamese intervention in Cambodia in 1978–9 against the genocidal government of Pol Pot and shows that humanitarian influences could be marginalised in the United States by the rhetoric of *realpolitik* and the geopolitics of the Cold War.

By the late twentieth century, the concept of humanitarian intervention was no longer a solely 'Western' one. Indeed, as we have seen, in the 1970s intervention was the prerogative of former colonies, rather than colonial powers. This was not something highlighted at the time, yet nor

---

[54] This is conceded by modern critics of humanitarian intervention: for example, Franck and Rodley, 'After Bangladesh', 280–3; James Avery Joyce, *The New Politics of Human Rights* (London and Basingstoke: Macmillan, 1978), 21–3.

[55] Adelman, 'Ethics of Humanitarian Intervention', 85.

[56] *Pace* MacFarlane, *Intervention in Contemporary World Politics*, 16, 17.

was it welcomed in the former heartlands of humanitarian intervention. The US government opposed Indian intervention in the Pakistan civil war and genocide; then in 1978, while rejecting calls by US senators for an intervention in Cambodia on humanitarian grounds,[57] it also opposed Vietnam's intervention; indeed, as Chapter 15 stresses, for the next eleven years, it denied 'any positive or humanitarian aspects linked to Vietnam's removal of Pol Pot. Thus, one of the few successful humanitarian interventions in the decades of the Cold War passed without recognition ... by international bodies.'[58] Geopolitical considerations, in sum, can not only generate, and/or taint, humanitarian interventions, they also effect the way they are viewed by other states. *Realpolitik* and its role in decision-making during episodes of mass atrocities is thus a recurrent theme of the chapters that follow. Whether its repeated influence makes truly 'humanitarian' intervention impossible is a point we consider in Chapter 17.

*

Perhaps the most important point to emerge from the following chapters is that the modern phenomenon known as 'humanitarian intervention' is like a river formed from the combination of several different tributaries: these include confessional solidarity, opposition to 'tyranny', abolitionism that transcended race, and belief in a variety of values, including liberty, civilisation, democracy, and (eventually) human rights. A complete analysis of intervention must incorporate the long-term history and must begin, not in 1990, nor in 1945, nor even the 1820s, but in the late sixteenth century.

Our collection is not the first word on this subject, and it will certainly not be the last, for further work is needed from a range of experts: further research, discussion, and debate. Historians need to be part of that process and that dialogue, because 'humanitarian intervention' has a long-term history, developing from a variety of sources, over several centuries, in ways that were complex and historically contingent. Far from being a subject without a history, humanitarian intervention is a subject with a rich and varied history; it demands to be studied in historical perspective.

---

[57] Power, *Problem from Hell*, 133.     [58] Quinn-Judge, below, p. 344.

*Part I*

# Early modern precedents

Map 1 Interventions in early modern Europe.

*Baltic Sea*

Danzig

EAST
PRUSSIA

WEST
PRUSSIA

B R A N D E N B U R G - P R U S S I A

MECKLENBURG-
STRELITZ

Thorn

Vistula

Berlin
Potsdam

BRUNSWICK-
WOLFENBÜTTEL

SAXONY

S I L E S I A

Oder

P O L A N D

Dresden

BOHEMIA

(Seat of
Imperial Diet)
Regensburg

H A B S B U R G
(Austria)

M O N A R C H Y

Danube

Vienna

HUNGARY

Salzburg

| 0 | | 100 | | 200 | | 300 | | 400 km |
|---|---|---|---|---|---|---|---|---|
| 0 | 50 | | 100 | | 150 | | 200 miles | |

## 2 'If a prince use tyrannie towards his people': interventions on behalf of foreign populations in early modern Europe

*D. J. B. Trim*

> If a prince doe violently breake the bonds of pietie and justice, an other prince may justly and lawfully exceede his owne limittes, not to invade the other's, but to force him to be content with his owne. If a prince use tyrannie towards his people, we ought to ayde no lesse, than if his subjectes shoulde raise sedition against him.
>
> *A short Apologie for Christian Souldiours* (1588)[1]

This chapter examines attitudes towards tyranny and extreme atrocities against foreign civilian populations in early modern Europe, and the measures that were both proposed and taken to end them. The period *c.* 1500–1700 was a vitally important one in the formulation of international law, concepts of sovereignty, and the emergence of the modern international system; and governments took what today would be termed humanitarian considerations into account in making foreign policy.

This chapter shows that, in the sixteenth century, a discourse against egregiously abusive government ('tyranny') emerged in influential treatises on political thought and the nascent 'Law of Nations'. This *theoretical* consensus against extremes in government action was matched, to some extent, by state *practice*. Lawyers and statesmen, as well as philosophers and theologians, argued that tyranny and atrocity were illegitimate and that action to end them was legitimate in terms of the Law of Nations. Partly on the basis of such arguments, princes threatened or used force against regimes that egregiously ill-treated foreign civilian populations. Theory and praxis were alike based in the reality of princely

*The concept of this chapter occurred while I enjoyed a fellowship at the Folger Shakespeare Library in 2006; it was completed during a second fellowship in 2009: I am grateful to the Folger for the award of these two fellowships. I am also indebted to a number of scholars. For perceptive comments on earlier versions of the text, I gratefully acknowledge (in chronological order) Brendan Simms, John Reeve, Andrew Thompson, Frank Tallett, Malcolm Smuts, Megan Hickerson, Tarak Barkawi and Winifred Trim. In addition, I thank Hugues Daussy, Megan Hickerson, Gerard Kilroy, Joel Lutes, and Philippe Rosenberg, for practical help with and advice about early modern texts.*

[1] *VCT–Apologie* (1588), sig. B6v.

governing practice, rather than being naively idealistic; there was a widespread recognition that not *all* oppressive or even tyrannical governmental actions could or should evoke an interventionist response by foreign princes. The issue was what a prince could do or ought to do if a foreign prince acted, or allowed some of his subjects to act, in a way that 'excessively exceeds the boundaries of piety and justice' (as one sixteenth-century French text puts it), or that 'shocked the conscience of mankind' (in the language of a study of modern humanitarian interventions).[2] Sixteenth- and seventeenth-century commentators and statesmen directly engaged with, and suggested a solution to, this problem of how the 'commonwealth of Christendom' (in early modern terms) or the international community (in modern terms) ought to respond to excessively tyrannical and abusive misgovernment.

This chapter first examines the intellectual and legal underpinnings of action against tyranny. It particularly focuses on texts produced in the late sixteenth century, by Protestant participants in the French Wars of Religion and the Revolt of the Netherlands against Spain, but it also briefly considers both precursor texts, by Catholic writers, and the views of subsequent seventeenth-century legal theorists, such as Grotius. These texts were important because they were not simply theoretical – though the earliest examples were written by literally cloistered scholars, others were written by statesmen and lawyers, and their arguments can be seen reflected in state action.

The practice of state action is considered next. First, examples of intervention from the sixteenth and early seventeenth centuries, including in the French and Dutch civil wars, mentioned above; then the Cromwellian intervention in Savoy on behalf of the persecuted Vaudois in 1655 which is taken as a case-study of a seventeenth-century 'humanitarian intervention'. This latter episode demonstrates how theoretical concerns that were truly humane were beginning to shape state action.

There is always a need for care when looking for precedents for current events. There are some broad similarities between events of today and, say, those of classical antiquity, or the Middle Ages, but there are so many fundamental differences that comparative historical analysis is of limited value. That said, however, when one looks at early modern Europe, in the sixteenth century and after, despite some major

---

[2] *VCT* (1581), 262: 'outrepasse outrageusement les bornes de pieté & de justice'; Richard B. Lillich, 'Forcible Self-help under International Law', *Naval War College Review* 22:6 (1970), 61.

differences, there are enough similarities to make comparative historical analysis legitimate and potentially valuable.

*

In the thirteenth century, St Thomas Aquinas wrote a series of important and influential treatises on just war, government, and tyranny. Implicit in these was that tyranny was the worst of crimes and could legitimately be opposed, including by military action. Aquinas's theories were significant, but it was only in the sixteenth century that his views that there was a right, or obligation, to oppose tyranny became part of princely practice and were developed in the early treatises of what eventually was to become 'international law'.

The Protestant Reformation (starting in the 1520s) is a large part of the reason why there was a new interest in the status of tyrants, whether in their own domains or in the 'commonwealth of Christendom'. Before the Reformation, persecuted people groups were usually heretics, and accordingly were generally hated. Princes retained, 'even in the bitterest ... quarrels, a sense of solidarity in one Catholic faith'; they usually were unwilling to aid heretics, whose presence in a society invited, it was believed, God's judgment on those who allowed them to flourish. By fracturing 'the unity of Christendom', the Reformation created confessionally opposed polities; the elites of one might regard themselves as the spiritual brethren of oppressed minorities in another. For the first time, then, princes or republics might be strongly disposed to take the side of foreign religious dissidents, whose persecutors naturally were regarded as tyrannical.[3] In addition to a sea change in the religious situation, however, the late fifteenth and early sixteenth centuries had also seen the emergence of relatively powerful and increasingly centralised states, and the discovery of unknown lands and the concomitant question of whether Christian rulers might legitimately acquire and rule them.

New problems thus faced statesmen and scholars considering the principles that regulated relations between princes (or, increasingly, between states), and these new problems prompted the creation of a new concept of law, 'reshap[ing] the familiar concept of a law of nations ... governing the relations of individuals and public authorities within the commonwealth of Christendom, into the notion of a law for sovereign states'.[4] As lawyers and political theorists grappled with issues of sovereignty and interstate relations, some drew on the writings of Aquinas and

---

[3] Garrett Mattingly, *Renaissance Diplomacy* (London: Jonathan Cape, 1955), 18–19; Richard Tuck, *The Rights of War and Peace: Political Thought and the International Order from Grotius to Kant* (Oxford: Oxford University Press, 1999), 28–30.

[4] Mattingly, *Renaissance Diplomacy*, 284–5.

argued that princes had an obligation to protect not only their own, but also other princes', subjects.

The developing discourse that there was a right, indeed a duty, to defend or protect the subjects of a tyrannical and abusive prince from his excesses, is found in the writings of both Catholic and Protestant commentators. In the first six decades of the sixteenth century, Spanish theologian-lawyers (especially the celebrated and influential Francisco de Vitoria ) avowed that it was legitimate to 'defend' neighbouring peoples from 'tyrannical and oppressive laws against the innocent'; war could rightfully be 'declared upon' rulers guilty of 'tyranny and oppression'.[5] The Spanish commentators restricted the application of this right to 'barbarians', i.e., the indigenous inhabitants of the New World; yet their purpose was not to create a general defence of Spanish imperialism, for, having argued for this right, they narrowed it. They argued that it could only apply to those Native American rulers who had actually inflicted harm on 'other men', rather than simply being guilty of offences against Christian morality. There thus was no right to 'eject [them] from their dominions ... at whim' (although, to be sure, if 'there [was] no other method of ensuring safety' than by forcibly deposing the pagan princes and replacing them with Christians, then that would be 'lawful, as far as necessary' to secure safety for the subjects).[6]

In the second half of the sixteenth century, however, the right to act against tyranny and oppression was extended to Christian princes, and was characterised as a duty. This is particularly true of the *Vindiciae contra tyrannos (VCT)*, a treatise first published in the Calvinist Swiss city of Basel in 1579.[7] Its authorship was much debated at the time and remains both uncertain and controversial, but the men most often identified as its author(s) are two Calvinist statesmen and scholars: the French Philippe Duplessis-Mornay and the German Hubert Languet. *VCT* is one of the best-known examples of the so-called 'monarchomach' treatises: works

---

[5] Francisco de Vitoria, 'On the American Indians' [*De Indis* (1539)], 3.5, in *Political Writings*, ed. Anthony Pagden and Jeremy Lawrence (Cambridge: Cambridge University Press, 1991), 287–8.

[6] De Vitoria, *ibid.*, 'On Dietary Laws' [*De usu ciborum* (1538)], 1.4–6, and 'On the Law of War' [*De Indis Relectio Posterior, sive du jure belli* (1539)], 1.3 (*Political Writings*, 224–6, 303); Domingo de Soto, lecture at Salamanca, 1552, quoted in Tuck, *The Rights of War and Peace*, 75; cf. also the slightly later views of Francisco Suarez, *De triplici virtute theologica* (1621), quoted at length in Francis Kofi Abiew, *The Evolution of the Doctrine and Practice of Humanitarian Intervention* (The Hague, London, and Boston: Kluwer Law International, 1999), 34 n.44.

[7] See *VCT* (Garnett, 1994) for a modern translation with excellent scholarly apparatus. I also use a range of early modern editions (including the Latin original and various translations into French and English), because these were what many contemporaries encountered; the translations vary, sometimes slightly, sometimes significantly.

by Calvinists in France (the Huguenots) and the Netherlands to justify their wars against the Catholic Valois monarchs of France and the Spanish Habsburg rulers of the Low Countries. These works 'expound [an] ideology of resistance' to monarchs and come close to asserting a doctrine of 'popular sovereignty'.[8] Many monarchomach works were published anonymously (like VCT), but their authors included, in addition to Duplessis-Mornay and Languet, two more Huguenots: Theodore Beza (or de Bèze) and François Hotman; and two Dutch statesmen and lawyers: Filip Marnix van St Aldegonde and Johan Junius de Jonge. They 'were men of affairs as well as jurists and publicists'. The monarchomach texts were based not only on biblical, classical and scholastic texts, but also on history, law, and personal experience of high politics and diplomacy; they were exercises not merely in abstract theory or academic jurisprudence, but in applied politics and statecraft.[9]

This is important to note, because the Vindiciae's view of (to use a modern term) international relations is innovative. Most scholarly analysis of VCT considers it overwhelmingly as an exemplar of 'resistance theory' and republicanism,[10] which is indeed the focus of the first three (of four) parts, which are, to be sure, the longest and most substantive; but 'the 'fourth and last "Quaestio"' is quite different. The scholarly emphasis on what the Vindiciae says about relations within polities obscures the fact that it has a remarkable view of relations between polities and princes. Indeed, in the words of one of the few scholars to engage at all with Part 4, 'one of the most salient

---

[8] Martin van Gelderen, The Political Thought of the Dutch Revolt 1555–1590 (Cambridge: Cambridge University Press, 1992), 269–71, at 270; Myriam Yardeni, 'French Calvinist Political Thought, 1534–1715', in International Calvinism 1541–1715, ed. Menna Prestwich (Oxford: Clarendon Press, 1985), 317–24, at 317.

[9] J. H. M. Salmon, The French Religious Wars in English Political Thought (Oxford: Clarendon Press, 1959), 17; cf. Mattingly, Renaissance Diplomacy, 287; Yardeni, 'French Calvinist Political Thought', 335. See, for example, Julian H. Franklin (ed.), 'Introduction' to Constitutionalism and Resistance in the Sixteenth Century: Three Treatises by Hotman, Beza, & Mornay (New York: Pegasus, 1969); Ralph E. Giesy, 'The Monarchomach Triumvirs: Hotman, Bèze, and Mornay', Bibliothèque d'humanisme et Renaissance 32 (1970), 41–56; Van Gelderen, Political Thought, 269–76; Hugues Daussy, 'Les huguenots entre l'obéissance au roi et l'obéissance à dieu', Nouvelle Revue du Seizième Siècle 22 (2004), 49–69; Béatrice Nicollier-De Weck, Hubert Languet (1518–1581): un réseau politique international, de Melanchthon à Guillaume d'Orange (Geneva: Droz, 1995); Hugues Daussy, Les Huguenots et le roi: Le combat politique de Philippe Duplessis-Mornay (1572–1600) (Geneva: Droz, 2002); Derek Visser, 'Junius: The Author of the Vindiciae contra tyrannos?', Tijdschrift voor Geschiedenis 84 (1971), 510–25; Donald R. Kelley, François Hotman: A Revolutionary's Ordeal (Princeton: Princeton University Press, 1973).

[10] References to this voluminous scholarly literature are omitted.

qualities of the *Vindiciae* ... is its international aspect'. The fourth and final part 'argues for foreign intervention in a country oppressed by tyranny'.[11]

The grounds for such interventions are set out in both Parts 3 and 4 of the *Vindiciae* and in Beza's *The Right of Magistrates*. Intervention ought only to take place after 'all other remedies have been tried'. A tyrant was not 'a less than good prince, but the worst', guilty not just of extravagance, greed or 'some other vice', but of 'wickedness involving general subversion of the political order and of the fundamental law of a realm'. If a prince had, by consistent and 'thoroughly obvious' actions, proved himself a tyrant; and if, having been 'frequently admonished', he nevertheless 'persist[ed] in his violent courses'; then ultimately 'just force' could legitimately be used against him by other princes. This was because 'tyranny is not simply a crime; but the chief, and as it were, a sort of summation of all crimes'; and so a 'prince which standeth idly by, and beholdeth the wickednes of a tyrant, and the slaughter of the innocent ... is worse then the tyrant him selfe'.[12] The purpose of such a war was not to conquer but 'to defende ... an oppressed people against him, which is neverthelesse a common enemy and a common plague'.[13] Thus, the author of *VCT* follows Vitoria in characterising intervention as defensive, for the people would be defended from a tyrannical ruler's oppression, wickedness, and 'the massacring of innocents' would be prevented.[14]

In addition, the author is much concerned with ensuring that interventions are seen to be legitimate, and deals explicitly with issues of sovereignty.

If it bee objected ... that God hath appointed limits and boundes to everie nation, and that we may not as it were thrust in our sickle into their harvest, neither is my counsell to the contrarie, that under pretence of ayde we should invade the countrey of an other nation, or chalenge their jurisdiction unto us, or convey their harvest into our floures.[15]

As part of his attempt to relieve concerns that tyranny might become merely an excuse for wars of conquest, he repeatedly stresses that

---

[11] Martin N. Raitiere, *Faire Bitts: Sir Philip Sidney and Renaissance Political Theory* (Pittsburgh: Duquesne University Press, 1984), 115–16.

[12] *VCT* (Garnett, 1994), 155; *VCT* (1689), 134; Beza, *Du droit des magistrats* (1574) [*The Right of Magistrates*], in Franklin, *Constitutionalism and Resistance in the Sixteenth Century*, 130–2; *VCT–Apologie* (1588), sig. B5v.

[13] *VCT–Apologie* (1588), sig. B5r.

[14] *VCT* (1648), 146; cf. *VCT* (Garnett, 1994), 183; *VCT* (1579), 262; *VCT–Apologie* (1588), sig. B5v.

[15] *VCT–Apologie* (1588), sig. B6r.

intervention was only to take place against the very worst of tyrants, one who 'violently' or 'outrageously over-pass[ed] the bounds of piety & justice'.[16] But he also argues that intervention against such transgressive rulers was both a *right* and a *duty*.

We should cut short any ... tyrant afflicting his own people, any king throwing downe the props and stayes of his common wealth. And this wee must performe in such sort, having respect not to private commoditie, but to publike societie.[17]

The emphasis on duty is important. Those with the power to 'cut short' a tyrant '*must* performe in such sort'.

What follows reinforces this view. In the passage that provides the title of this chapter and is quoted at its start, *VCT* asserts that, if a prince were to govern with violence and disregard for divine and human law, and thus tyrannically, another prince could, with perfect justice and legality, take military action. This would not constitute an invasion, for the prince's intent was not to conquer his neighbour, but rather to restrain him.[18] This in fact was not an option but an obligation.

If a Prince tyrannize over the people, a neighbour Prince ought to yield succours as freely and willingly to the People, as he would doe to the Prince his Brother if the people mutinied against him: yea, he should so much the more readily succour the people, by how much there is more just cause of pity to see many afflicted than one alone.[19]

'If a prince use tyrannie towards his people, we *ought to ayde*', as the first English translation put it in 1588; or, as the 1648 translation put it: 'a neighbour Prince *ought* to yield succours ... to the People'.[20] In early modern English, 'ought' was used to express 'duty or obligation', especially 'moral obligation'.[21] Moreover, this is not just an addition of English translators; 'ought' in both editions translates *debebit* in the original, which implies a duty; this is reflected in the first French translation, which declares that 'the neighbouring prince must [or has a duty to] give succour to the people'.[22]

---

[16] *VCT* (1648), 147; cf. *VCT* (1579), 234 ('princeps fixos pietatis & iustitie limites violenter transilit').

[17] *VCT–Apologie* (1588), sigs. B6r–v.     [18] *Ibid.*, sig. B6v.

[19] *VCT* (1648), 147: the translation of the final part of the last sentence is given accurately here, having been inaccurately compressed in the 1588 edition; cf. *VCT* (1579), 234.

[20] *VCT–Apologie* (1588), sig. B6v; *VCT* (1648), 147.

[21] *OED, s.v.* 'ought', *v.*, II, 6, 7a.

[22] *VCT* (1579), 234; *VCT* (1581), 262 ('le Prince voisin doit donner secours au peuple'). I am greatly obliged to Gerard Kilroy for his help in translating the original Latin edition.

The author ends on an emphatic note:

> To conclude, as there have beene tyrants some in all places, so there are examples in all historiographers of princes which have resisted the tyrants, and defended the people. The which examples princes in these dayes ought to imitate ... against those which deale tyrannously with their people ... To conclude all in one worde: pietie commaundeth us to defende the lawe of God and the Church: justice commaundeth us to restraine tyrans, and those which overthrowe the common wealth; charitie commaundeth us to helpe the oppressed & such as stande in neede.[23]

Here, too, there is an emphasis on duty: according to the first English edition, 'princes in these dayes *ought* to imitate' the 'examples ... of princes which have resisted the tyrants'; the original Latin provides that 'princes *must* imitate' those examples, using force where necessary; and the first French translation also declares that 'the princes of today *must* follow those examples'.[24] There is also, again, an emphasis on intervention as *defensive* – 'the people' and 'the Church' are alike to be 'defended' from abusive misgovernment.[25]

The *Vindiciae* thus argues that *all* princes had a duty to defend the subjects of other princes against egregiously abusive tyranny and oppression. Part and parcel of sovereignty was what could be termed an 'obligation to aid' or 'duty to defend'. In sum, then, the discourse that tyranny was illegitimate and that, if egregious enough, it constituted a legitimate *casus belli* for foreign rulers, because they thereby were defending the people and ensuring their safety – this discourse, which originated with Aquinas, was developed by Vitoria and others in Spain, and then developed further in the late sixteenth century by Calvinist authors whose works remained popular into the late seventeenth century.

*

However, it is essential, in dealing with the period of the Reformation and the European wars of religion, to stress that the monarchomach authors conceived of 'tyranny' in narrow confessional terms. Roman Catholic regimes were *assumed* to be tyrannical, because of the way they 'oppressed' Protestants.

John Foxe, the English Protestant church historian and martyrologist whose work was immensely influential across Europe, regarded the

---

[23] *VCT–Apologie* (1588), sigs. B7v–B8r.
[24] *VCT* (1579), 236 ('coërcendis, imitari debent'); *VCT* (1581), 264 ('Les Princes d'aujourd'huy ensuivant tels exemples doyvent') – emphasis supplied in all. I am again indebted to Gerard Kilroy for his advice on the Latin text.
[25] Cf. *VCT–Apologie* (1588), sig. A4v (as well as the long quotation above from B7v–B8r); and *VCT* (1579), 236.

'persecutions raysed ... [and] tormentes devised' by the papacy and by Catholic princes 'against the poore flocke and Church of Christ', as proofs 'of 'crueltie & tyranny'. He condemned 'the tyranny of Romain Byshops' and equated 'threates of tyrants' and the 'violence of tormentours'.[26] Other martyrologists followed Foxe in identifying the papal policy of persecuting Protestants as a mark of 'Tyrannie'.[27] Political writers did likewise. The monarchomach François Hotman likewise characterised Rome as innately, permanently tyrannical.[28] During the Dutch Revolt, Habsburg rule of the Netherlands was portrayed as tyrannical on several grounds (see below), but Dutch pamphleteers specifically included Habsburg desires to end 'diversité de Religion' as a mark of 'tyrannie'.[29] As late as 1648, Paul Knell, a Church of England priest, fulminated against the Roman 'Babylon', declaring, in a reference to Revelation 17.3–6, which Protestants uniformly identified with the papacy, that:

the whore must have blood, till she hath made her selfe starke drunk with it; no blood of Beasts, it must be the blood of Men; no blood of sinners, it must be the blood of Saints; not blood of Malefactors, it must be the blood of ... Martyrs of Jesus ... Sad experience of this tyrannie we had in Queen Maries dayes [nearly a century earlier!] ... it is a question whether she would ever have been satisfied, had we not been ... delivered from her tyranny by ... the King of Kings.[30]

But not all persecution equated to 'tyranny'; Knell's language limits it to the persecution of Protestants by Roman Catholics. The category of 'Men' is narrowed down to 'Saints' and martyrs for 'true' religion ('Martyrs of Jesus'); they are pictured in terms of confessional identity, rather than humanity. Foxe, too, saw persecution as tyrannical not because of its brutality *per se*, but because its victims were practitioners of true worship of God ('the poore flocke and Church of Christ'). Indeed, for Jean-Paul Perrin, a Huguenot polemicist, the significance of martyrs was not the horror of their 'being massacred and cast into the fire', but rather that, despite their deaths, the church continued: 'we may

---

[26] John Foxe, *Actes and monuments*, 2nd edn (London, 1570), prefaces, unpag. [pp. 6, 12, 13]; accessed online, *Foxe's Book of Martyrs Variorum Edition Online* (www.hrionline.ac. uk/johnfoxe/edition.html). I am grateful to Megan Hickerson for her guidance on Foxe's writing on tyranny.

[27] For example, the author's preface in Jean Crespin, *Actiones et Monimenta Martyrum, eorum qui à Wicleffo et Husso ad nostram hanc ætatem in Germania, Gallia, Britannia, Flandria, Italia, & ipsa demùm Hispania* (Geneva, 1560), sigs. aii–aiii; the title (and substance) of Thomas Mason, *Christs Victorie over Sathans Tyrannie* (London, 1615).

[28] Kelley, *François Hotman*, 242, 304.

[29] Anon., *Request presentee a son alteze et messeigneurs du conseil d'estat par les habitans des Païs Bas* (N.p., n.d. [1578]), 10.

[30] Paul Knell, *Israel and England Paralelled* (London, 1648), 14–15.

find in their bloud and ashes the seed of the Church'. This continuity in spite of dungeon, fire and sword, and the proof it supplied that Protestantism was the true church, mattered more than the martyrs' experience of human pain and suffering.[31]

However, while it is clear that most Protestant writers regarded persecution as immoral and tyrannical only when practised on fellow Protestants, very often that remains implicit. In their texts, the *suffering* consequent upon persecution, especially that of women and children, is repeatedly stressed, and the victims are often represented simply as people rather than primarily as Protestants. Thus, whatever the propagandists and apologists intended, what many readers would surely have taken away from their reading was that extreme violence was intrinsically wrong because of the human suffering involved, and that this was true for all (or at any rate most) human beings.[32]

Indeed, by the middle to later decades of the seventeenth century, scholars discern a shift in Protestant polemic, from 'martyrology to humanitarianism'.[33] This is particularly evident in responses to the atrocities perpetrated against the Protestant Vaudois (or Waldenses) in Savoy in 1655 (discussed below). As we shall see, some members of the government of the British republic conceived its intervention in literally humanitarian language; and much Protestant propaganda and polemic did likewise, condemning, for example, the 'barbarous & *inhumane* proceedings against the professors of the reformed religion within the Dominion of the Duke of Savoy'.[34] Although it is only 'professors of the reformed religion' the author is concerned for, he nevertheless conceptualises them as victims of cruel, inhuman behaviour – and thus as suffering human beings, rather than only as suffering co-religionists.

Thus, the association of (as it were) state atrocity against minorities with tyranny, constituted an important precedent. Justifying action against tyranny in 'human' terms facilitated widening the conceptual terms of reference for what was 'tyrannical'; the arguments of sixteenth-century Protestant aristocrats were adopted and adapted in ways the authors could not have anticipated. The *VCT*'s arguments

---

[31] [Jean-Paul Perrin], *Histoire des Vaudois* (Lyons, 1618), trans. Samson Lennard as *Luthers forerunners: or, a cloud of witnesses* (London, 1624), 2.

[32] I am grateful to Megan Hickerson and Philippe Rosenberg for sharing their thoughts on this subject.

[33] Philippe Rosenberg, 'From Martyrology to Humanitarianism: Conscience and the Anti-Casuistical Bent in Britain and Beyond, 1683 to 1758', unpubl. paper, read at the American Society for Eighteenth-Century Studies annual conference, Atlanta, March 2007. I am grateful to Dr Rosenberg for a copy of his paper.

[34] Anon., *The barbarous & inhumane proceedings against the professors of the reformed religion* (London, 1655), emphasis supplied.

were taken up by Roman Catholics when Henry of Navarre, a Huguenot, succeeded to the French throne in 1589; and later its arguments were adopted by Protestant political radicals – it is no coincidence that the first full English translation was published in 1648, the year of the establishment of the British republic; or that it was republished in 1689, the year after the Glorious Revolution. In sum, the language of *VCT*, other monarchomach treatises and many martyrological works, which is more inclusive than the concepts underlying it, was so powerful that it shaped subsequent debate in ways the original authors had frequently not intended.

★

This can, finally, be seen in subsequent, seventeenth-century works on the Law of Nations. Although Hugo Grotius, the most significant legal theorist of the century, had to flee his native Dutch Republic after his religious moderation alienated the Calvinist authorities, he did not reject the arguments of the Calvinist author of *VCT* that there was a princely obligation to intervene against the worst tyrants. An underlying concern of Grotius's work was to bring order to the chaotic state of Christendom, but an underlying principle was that 'every human society' ought to be founded upon, yet also 'limited by', the 'principle of humanity'. This led him to significant conclusions about the legitimacy of intervention against tyranny; despite his concern for order, he rejected 'the conclusion that states had a duty not to intervene in each other's affairs'.[35]

Especially important are the views set out in 1625, in the influential *De jure belli ac pacis* (On the Law of War and Peace). Among the points addressed in this very long treatise is the question of 'whether a war for the subjects of another be just, [if] for the purpose of defending them from injuries by their ruler'.[36] Part of Grotius's purpose was to establish a universal law among states or rulers of states;[37] and as modern studies emphasise, in it he generally takes a high view of sovereignty, asserting that 'the treatment of subjects was a matter submitted only to the judgement of the sovereign', and that

---

[35] Abiew, *Evolution*, 34–5. Simon Chesterman, *Just War or Just Peace? Humanitarian Intervention and International Law* (Oxford: Oxford University Press, 2001), 9–10; R. J. Vincent, *Nonintervention and International Order* (Princeton: Princeton University Press, 1974), 23–4, at 23.

[36] William Whewell (ed. and trans.), *Grotius on the Rights of War and Peace, an Abridged Translation* (Cambridge: Cambridge University Press, 1853), 288, quoted in Abiew, *Evolution*, 35.

[37] Vincent, *Nonintervention and International Order*, 23.

generally a sovereign's subjects did not have a 'right to take up arms', 'even in extreme situations'.[38]

However, Grotius also declares that though sovereign rulers have legitimate claims over their own subjects, they do not therefore enjoy complete freedom; certain types of abusive action are illegitimate – so much so, that they actually are grounds for military action by neighbouring sovereigns. While subjects had no right to take up arms against their sovereign, Grotius (like Vitoria and *VCT*) accepts that another sovereign could take up arms on their behalf, in 'defence of innocents'.[39] And although only sovereigns could adjudicate on the treatment of subjects, he includes among the prerogatives of sovereignty a degree of responsibility for the actions of other princes or sovereign bodies and a right to hold them to account. He stresses 'that kings and those who possess rights equal to kings, have the right of demanding punishments ... on account of injuries', including even those 'which do not affect them' or their subjects, but which do 'excessively violate the law of nature or nations in regard to any persons whatsoever'. For, according to Grotius, 'Kings in addition to the particular care of their own state, are also burdened with a general responsibility for human society'.[40]

This responsibility included tyrannical actions and kings could do more than 'demand punishments' – they could impose them. In dealing with legitimate causes of war, Grotius cites four mythical and classical tyrants – men said to be guilty of killing children, human sacrifice, feeding men to horses, and cannibalism[41] – and then avows that if, like them, a prince 'should inflict upon his subjects such treatment as no one is warranted in inflicting, the exercise of the right vested in human society is not precluded'.[42] The original, 'Jus humanæ societatis', could also be translated as the 'right vested in humanity'.[43] Thus, this right 'not precluded' derived from common humanity, which in extreme cases trumped sovereignty. Grotius

---

[38] Fernando R. Tesón, *Humanitarian Intervention: An Inquiry into Law and Morality*, 3rd edn (Ardsley, NY: Transnational Publishers, 2005), 58; Vincent, *Nonintervention and International Order*, 24; Chesterman, *Just War or Just Peace?*, 15 and n.63.

[39] Hugo Grotius, *De jure belli ac pacis libri tres* [1646], vol. I (facsimile), vol. II (English edn) trans. 'John Damen Maguire' [F. W. Kelsey and others], Classics of International Law 3, ed. James Brown Scott (Washington, DC: Carnegie Institution, 1913–25), 2.25.8, at I, 414 ('defensione innocentium').

[40] *Ibid.*, II, 504–5, 508, quoted in Abiew, *Evolution*, 35n.

[41] Grotius, *De jure belli ac pacis*, 2.25.8, at I, 414.

[42] *Ibid.*, II, 584, quoted in Tesón, *Humanitarian Intervention*, 58.

[43] Grotius, *De jure belli ac pacis*, 2.25.8, at I, 414; on the translation, see Tesón, *Humanitarian Intervention*, 58n.; cf. Abiew, *Evolution*, 35.

makes plain that this right included the use of military action, which could legitimately be undertaken 'on behalf of others' because of 'the mutual tie of kinship among men, which of itself affords sufficient ground for rendering assistance'.[44]

In sum, from Vitoria to Duplessis-Mornay and Languet to Grotius, the men who founded what was to become the Law of Nations – men who included diplomats and statesmen, as well as academic theorists – had an enduring concern for the problem of how to deal with events that appalled the conscience of mankind. However, it is not only the theoretical literature of the sixteenth and seventeenth centuries that is significant. The principles proposed in it were, as we shall see in the remainder of this chapter, the basis for the policies of some early modern governments.

*

Early modern princes felt the domestic affairs of other states to be their legitimate business, in certain circumstances. These included the perpetration of massacres or egregious abuse by a prince, or with his effective consent, as outlined in the treatises examined so far in this chapter; but they could also include when order was on the verge of collapse as a result of misgovernment. Tyranny, in the eyes of some early modern princes (though this is only implicit in the monarchomachs or Grotius), could include allowing chaos and misery to proliferate and thereby endangering the *bien publique* (common wealth or common good) not only of the ill-governed polity, but also of its neighbours.

Elizabeth I (r.1558–1603) intervened in France against its Valois monarchs and the Netherlands against its Spanish Habsburg rulers, on multiple occasions. The grounds for her interventions, found both in public statements explaining and justifying intervention, and in internal government discussions, were, in France, the persecution, imprisonment and mass murder of French Protestants (the Huguenots); and, in the Netherlands, general Spanish tyranny, atrocity and oppression.

Religious hostility was a large part of the reason for English diplomatic and military interventions on behalf of the Huguenots and the Dutch rebels against Spain. Many Englishmen believed that, as co-religionists of French and Dutch Protestants, they owed them a duty of aid; this was particularly the view of the Puritans who, like the Huguenots and the most influential Dutch rebels, were Calvinist.[45] In addition, there was a widespread fear in Elizabethan England, not limited to Puritans, that the

---

[44] Grotius, *De jure belli ac pacis*, II, 582, quoted in Abiew, *Evolution*, 35n.
[45] D. J. B. Trim, 'Calvinist Internationalism and the English Officer Corps, 1562–1642', *History Compass* 4:6 (2006), 1029–31, 1035.

destruction of Protestantism in France and the Netherlands would leave Elizabeth 'bereft of allies' and presage an attack on England.[46] Nor were these fears unwarranted. The French crown had a close relationship with the Roman Catholic Church: medieval and early modern French writers identified the country's monarchy as 'a sacral institution'; the king was called 'the eldest son of the pope' and 'the most Christian king'; and he was believed to be divinely called to wage war to preserve the true church against infidels and heretics.[47] Philip II, King of Spain and ruler of a global empire that included the Netherlands, bore the title of 'the Catholic king'; he was determined to crush heresy throughout his dominions; and he eventually regarded himself as having been divinely appointed a champion of the Church.[48] Furthermore, although the rhetoric of Elizabethan intervention in France and the Low Countries frequently invoked tyranny, the context must be understood. As we have already seen, Protestants tended to identify the 'Popish' ecclesiastical regime as innately tyrannical. When English Protestants used the discourse of 'tyranny' it very often was conceptualised in confessional terms, even when there are no overt religious references.

One must be cautious, then, in analysing the reasons for the repeated Elizabethan interventions in France and the Netherlands. All that said, however, even though there is no doubt that confessional hostility shaped English policy to France, there is likewise no doubt that it was also shaped by genuine concern that the Valois and Habsburg monarchies were going to extremes. These extremes necessitated intervention both to protect those suffering persecution and atrocity, and to prevent France and the Low Countries falling into chaos and disorder, in which persons of all faiths would suffer.

*

Despite the underlying hostility between Catholic and Protestant, English policy in France had limited aims. It did not seek to overthrow the Valois monarchy or even to achieve absolute equality of the different confessions. It sought to moderate royal policy, so that the limited rights conceded to the Huguenots by repeated royal edicts of toleration would be honoured and observed; only when the French crown attacked the

---

[46] For example, Wallace MacCaffrey, *The Shaping of the Elizabethan Regime* (Princeton: Princeton University Press, 1968), 286–8, at 287.

[47] Mark Greengrass, 'France', in *The Reformation in National Context*, ed. Bob Scribner, Roy Porter, and Mikulás Teich (Cambridge: Cambridge University Press, 1994), 49, 57; Jöel Cornette, *Le roi de guerre. Essai sur la souveraineté dans la France du Grand Siècle* (Paris: Payot and Rivages, 1993), 151–2.

[48] For example, Geoffrey Parker, 'The Place of Tudor England in the Messianic Vision of Philip II of Spain', *TRHS*, 6th series, 12 (2002), 167–221.

Huguenot liberties, in violation of the laws, did Elizabeth's regime intervene. However, as the Wars of Religion wore on, resulting in escalating disorder, it also intervened on the basis that England, as the virtual neighbour of France, had a legitimate interest in its good governance, lest it slide into chaos (becoming something like the modern concept of a 'failed state'), the wider effects of which could be the same as tyranny.

The first English military intervention, in the autumn and winter of 1562–3, took place after a massacre of Huguenots in defiance of terms of a royal edict, which had granted limited religious liberty; and after the hijacking, as French Protestants believed, of the regency of the young king, Charles IX by a faction of powerful Catholic nobles. Crucially, Catholic aggression gave Huguenot actions a degree of legitimacy. However, Elizabeth tried to leverage her military intervention to regain lost English territory in northern France and, in consequence, as Wallace MacCaffrey observes, 'English aims were cloudy'.[49] Indeed, if Duplessis-Mornay was the author of the *Vindiciae contra tyrannos*, it may well have been his experience of this episode that prompted the observation that a prince ought not invade another's country, 'or convey their harvest into his floors', 'under pretext' of helping the people, albeit several princes had done so 'under such cover'. Yet, Elizabeth and her counsellors were also concerned about the threat to the Huguenots, regarding the English army as the only 'impediment lefte in Fraunce' to their potential destruction.[50]

In the late 1560s, with hostilities breaking out again, Elizabeth had her ambassador in Paris urge Charles IX to appoint 'persons of estimation not passionated' throughout the country, to enforce the edicts that granted limited religious toleration to the Huguenots. She told Charles's ambassador that the problem in France was 'that the King and Queen Mother were abused by some capital counsellors whereby these intestine troubles are nourished'.[51] Indeed, the English believed that the cause of oppression and persecution in France was the dominance of one faction – and part of Aquinas's legacy was that tyranny was defined as governing for personal or factional advantage, not the common good.[52] Thus in English eyes, by allowing itself to be dominated by Catholic

---

[49] MacCaffrey, *Shaping of the Elizabethan Regime*, 134.

[50] *VCT* (1581), 261 ('aussi ne suis-je pas d'avis sous tel pretexte un Prince enjambe sur l'autre & s'empare de ses pays, pour tirer en son aire le blé qui ne luy apartient pas, ce que plusieurs ont fait avec telle couverture'); *VCT–Apologie* (1588), sig. B6*r*; Earl of Warwick to Elizabeth, 22 Dec. 1562, NA, SP 70/47, fo. 103*r*.

[51] Elizabeth, instructions to Sir Henry Norreys, ambassador in Paris, 27 Aug. 1568, and to Bishop of Rennes, 30 Sept. 1568, *CSPFE*, VIII, 533, 558, nos. 2468, 2563.

[52] For example, Aquinas, *Summa Theologica*, II, ii, 42.2; *De regimine principum*, I.1–2.

interests, the French crown was acting tyrannically. Yet it was not perceived as being in and of itself tyrannical, by virtue of its religion. If it would return to governing impartially, then oppression or disorder in France would end; or so Elizabeth and her chief secretary of state, William Cecil, believed. Not long afterwards, Cecil wrote that it would be necessary to aid the Huguenots

> if the French Kyng will refuse to have the Q[ueen's] Majesty to be a mediator of peace ... She hath sent to offer the same, wherof as yet no answer is had, but if it be refused, then is it made apparent by them selves that ther intention is to prosequte the subversion of the Commen cause of relligion [i.e., Protestant religion].[53]

In other words, if the Huguenots genuinely were disloyal, other than in religion, Charles IX and his advisers had nothing to lose from Elizabeth's mediation; if they refused, then that would show that their real policy towards the Huguenots was one of oppression based solely on religion, despite the Huguenot leaders' loyalty if they, in turn, were permitted liberty of conscience and worship. Charles refused English mediation, suspecting Elizabeth's own bias, but confirming her and her ministers' suspicions.

These persisted throughout the 1570s, especially after the single most terrible episode in the whole thirty-six-year period of the French Wars of Religion: the St Bartholomew's Massacre. In Paris in 1572, beginning early on St Bartholomew's Day (24 August), some 3,000 Huguenots were killed in three to four days; this was only the first in a series of a dozen emulatory massacres in provincial cities, in which the deaths probably totalled around another 7,000.[54] In the autumn of 1574, after the fifth war of religion broke out, Elizabeth despatched an embassy to Henry III, who had recently succeeded his elder brother, Charles, and was pursuing an extreme anti-Protestant policy that was opposed even by leading Catholic nobles. The ambassador was instructed to express Elizabeth's belief that 'great mischefes and enormities' were taking place in France, because 'the Edictes' of toleration were now, because

---

[53] BL, Lans. MSS, vol. 102, fo. 146r.
[54] Estimates differ, but consensus seems now to be approaching a total of 10,000 killed across the whole of France. See Menna Prestwich, 'Calvinism in France 1555–1629', in *International Calvinism 1541–1715*, ed. Prestwich (Oxford: Clarendon Press, 1985), 91–2; Arlette Jouanna, *La France du XVIe siècle 1483–1598*, 2nd edn (Paris: Presses Universitaires de France, 1997), 471–3; R. J. Knecht, *The Rise and Fall of Renaissance France 1483–1610*, 2nd edn (Oxford: Blackwell, 2001), 363–6 (giving a lower total death toll for the provincial massacres); Philip Benedict, 'The Wars of Religion, 1562–1598', in *Renaissance and Reformation France*, ed. Mack P. Holt (Oxford: Oxford University Press, 2002), 155–6.

of 'factions & parcialities ... not well observed ... nor the execution of Justice so equallie administred', resulting in 'sonderie murthers & enormities commited agenst' the Huguenots.[55]

In addition to believing that the French crown was refusing to enforce its own laws, the Elizabethan regime also feared that by their policies the Valois kings were letting the country fall into chaos. The English government felt it had a legitimate interest in the good governance (or otherwise) of France, for if it 'languisshed in civill troubles' it would be contrary to 'the common benefit of ... all christendome'.[56] Elizabeth's ambassador in Paris warned in the winter of 1569 that 'this commen welthe is in so sick a state, that ... they [will] destroy them sellfes by ther owne division'.[57] Elizabeth had grave concerns about 'the contynewance and increase of troubles, in [France], tending to the great ruine and destruction of the same' and she feared that the consequences of 'such civill & intestin discentions' would be 'the undoing' of France.[58]

These, then, were the English government's concerns and grounds for intervening in France, which it did repeatedly over thirty-six years. Yet nominally cordial relations were maintained for much of this period, and were always resumed after interruptions. From the perspective of the French crown, Elizabethan England, where French 'rebells are either ayded openlie or comforted secretlie', was an enemy.[59] Yet the realities of its situation were that it could not cut itself off from the possibility of English help to assert royal authority over zealous Catholics. For its part, the English government was continually willing to work with France's Catholic monarchs. It was only when they were particularly oppressive of Protestants, or sacrificed stability and equity to the goal of confessional unity, that Elizabeth intervened. At other times, she and her ministers refrained from intervention – or even actively supported or literally wooed Valois kings and princes.

This helps to explain why there was no formal English action in the aftermath of the St Bartholomew's Massacre. Elizabeth and her ministers, especially William Cecil (now ennobled as Lord Burghley), were appalled, but they believed that the crown was not fully in control in

[55] FSL, MS X.d.90, unpag. [fo. 2r] (copy summarised in *CSPFE*, X, 560–2, no. 1573). See James Westfall Thompson, *The Wars of Religion in France 1559–1576* (Chicago: University of Chicago Press, 1909), 488–94, 499–501; Wallace T. MacCaffrey, *Queen Elizabeth and the Making of Policy, 1572–1588* (Princeton: Princeton University Press, 1981), 183–4.

[56] FSL, MS X.d.90, fo. [1v].

[57] Norreys to Elizabeth, 1 Jan. 1569, NA, SP 70/105, fo. 2v.

[58] FSL, MS X.d.90, fo. [1v].

[59] Report from Amyas Paulet (ambassador in Paris), 6 Aug. 1577, of a conversation with Henry III: HH, CP 9, fo. 75v.

Paris, and that the massacre was the work of the ultra-Catholic faction led by the Duke of Guise. Burghley, for example, observed that the horror of the massacre 'cannot be expressed with tongue to declare the cruelties, whereof now it is said that the king taketh repentance and that he was abused to cause it to be committed by the duke of Guise and the faction of the papists'.[60] The English still hoped that the Valois king, who seemed amenable to negotiation, might yet prove a counterbalance to the zealously Catholic Philip II of Spain, not least in the Netherlands. Therefore, despite their horror at the massacres, they sent only supplies and ships, not an army, to the Huguenots, desiring not to weaken the monarchy, lest the ultra-Catholics take control.[61]

Two years later, Burghley foresaw the imminent death of the ailing Charles IX and was determined to ensure the survival of his youngest brother, the Duke of Alençon, then under house arrest and in danger of execution. Charles's heir was the middle brother, Henry (then in Poland and soon to become Henry III), who had commanded royal armies in the third and fourth wars of religion and was perceived as one of the chief authors of the St Bartholomew's Massacre. Burghley wrote of the necessity that Alençon 'be preserved to counterpoise the tyrant that shall come from Poland'.[62] Elizabeth and Burghley objected to Henry, not because he was Catholic, for Alençon was Catholic too, but because Henry was perceived as an agent of Catholic tyranny in the past and an incipient 'tyrant' in the future.

English desires to have a French monarch who safeguarded Protestants from the Duke of Guise and the Catholic faction can also be seen in Elizabeth's willingness to consider marrying a French prince. In the late 1570s, the possibility of marriage to Alençon (Henry III's heir presumptive and now entitled Duke of Anjou) was strongly endorsed by one of Elizabeth's chief counsellors, the Earl of Sussex, since, as he told the queen, thereby 'you shall by your self & your husband be habell to assist the protestantes of fraunce from perrell of massacre by the papists'.[63] Sussex recognised that the 'Papists' sometimes acted in spite of the French crown – that tyranny and oppression of the Huguenots

---

[60] Burghley to Earl of Shrewsbury, 7 Sept. 1572, in Conyers Read, *Lord Burghley and Queen Elizabeth* (London: Jonathan Cape, 1960), 87.
[61] For example, see Read, *Lord Burghley and Queen Elizabeth*, 86–93; Susan Doran, *England and Europe 1485–1603* (London and New York: Longman, 1986), 58–9, 74–5; N. M. Sutherland, *The Massacre of St. Bartholomew and the European Conflict 1559–1572* (London and Basingstoke: Macmillan, 1973).
[62] To Walsingham, [26 May 1574], *CSPFE*, X, 506, no. 1431.
[63] Sussex to Elizabeth, 28 Aug. 1578, HH, CP, MS 10, fo. 30*v*; cf. G. D. Ramsay, 'The Foreign Policy of Elizabeth I', in *The Reign of Elizabeth I*, ed. Christopher Haigh (Athens: University of Georgia Press, 1985), 158–9.

sometimes stemmed from illegal usurpation of authority, rather than from the wishes of the French monarchy; if it could be induced, not least by a marital alliance, to act impartially and responsibly (as the English saw it), the French crown would be the best defence of the religious liberty of France's Protestant minority.

Intervention, then, was generally intended not to effect 'regime change' – but rather to change the regime's policy. On occasions, support for the French crown, in order to protect the Huguenots and preserve stability in France, merged with England's confessional interests. This was the case when Henry of Navarre succeeded to the throne as Henry IV in 1589. He was resisted by many of his Catholic subjects, until his conversion in 1593 brought all save the ultra-Catholic zealots over to the rightful heir. By a mix of military force, English assistance, and adept political manoeuvring, Henry finally brought the French Wars of Religion to an end in 1598. However, for over half of those wars' nearly four decades' duration, Elizabeth's French policy was not the policy that purely confessional considerations would have dictated. Even though many Englishmen, including some royal ministers and counsellors, thought that Catholicism *was* the problem in France, Elizabeth's policy was not to wage a religious war. Instead, she repeatedly used diplomacy, financial and logistical aid, and limited military action, to preserve freedom of worship and conscience for the Huguenots *and* to buttress royal authority and the rule of law.

It is entirely possible, moreover, that without the military interventions carried out in the 1560s, 1570s and 1580s by the Queen of England and two German princes, the Duke of Zweibrücken and the Elector Palatine, France would have witnessed genocide, rather than the mass murder that took place in the late summer and autumn of 1572. This is to use anachronistic language; but it is the correct modern term for what was occurring in France, bearing in mind that, according to modern international law, genocide can be committed against a 'religious group', as well as against 'national, ethnical, [or] racial' groups.[64] Elizabethan interventions on behalf of the Protestant population of France did not stop the worst massacres but probably helped to prevent their recurrence and did preserve the Huguenots into the seventeenth century. The policy had been reasonably successful.

*

When we come to the Revolt of the Netherlands against Spain (1567–1609), again, confessional factors were crucial in the English decision to provide the Dutch rebels first with financial aid, then covert military aid,

---

[64] United Nations Convention on the Prevention and Punishment of the Crime of Genocide, art. 2 (text at www.hrweb.org/legal/genocide.html).

then and by open military intervention. However, even more than in France, Elizabethan military interventions in the Netherlands took into account the general tyranny and oppression of the Habsburg monarch, Philip II, which threatened to ruin a prosperous nation, with which England had traditional strong bonds of friendship and cultural interaction, and with whose merchants their English counterparts had traditionally enjoyed rich trade.

Philip II saw the Dutch Revolt as essentially a revolt of Protestants, but in fact the rebels always comprised a spectrum of religious opinion, encompassing Roman Catholics, Lutherans, Calvinists, Anabaptists, Jews, and small radical Christian sects. The origins of the revolt were in protests against a Habsburg programme to extend central authority and diminish traditional liberties and privileges – a programme many Netherlanders believed to be illegal and incipiently tyrannical. Calvinist violence during early protests led Philip to identify the rebels as radical Protestants, when in fact Calvinists were a minority. But Philip sent an army under the inflexible and zealously Catholic Duke of Alba, who crushed both active resistance and moderate protest by force, and established what became known as the 'Council of Blood'. It went to extremes. To be sure, modern research shows that its exactions and excesses were greatly exaggerated, both at the time and since, but there was substance beneath rebel propaganda. The council certainly was widely hated, not least because it executed and imprisoned many Roman Catholics, many of them essentially loyal, who had neither converted to Protestantism nor denied Philip II's authority, but were victims of obsessive Spanish fears that they sympathised with those who had. Even the Counts of Egmont and Hoorn, who only fifteen years earlier had led Habsburg armies to victory over their French enemies, were put to death. Thus, in a way Philip and Alba's view of the resistance as a Protestant revolt became self-fulfilling, since the leaders who survived were Protestant and in many cases Calvinist.

Nevertheless, in the Dutch public discourse explaining their (by sixteenth-century standards) shocking act of rebellion, it was Philip II's illegal suppression of Dutch freedoms, and the oppressive tyranny of the Spanish soldiers and governors sent to impose Habsburg authority, that were emphasised much more than the Catholic–Protestant conflict that actually did underlie the revolt. This discourse consisted of the public declarations issued by the remaining leader of the rebels, William, Prince of Orange; the printed propaganda produced on his behalf; and the appeals the Dutch made to the rest of Europe for help. Thanks to the flourishing Dutch printing industry and the existence of something like a nascent 'public sphere' in the Netherlands, such tracts were printed, reprinted, pirated, copied, and adapted, in multiple languages; the result was a prolific literature of tracts and pamphlets setting out arguments for the rights of the Netherlanders and the legitimacy of their resistance to Philip II and his governors (and eventually their renunciation of Habsburg rule).[65]

The emphasis of this literature is overwhelmingly on the abolition of ancient laws by Spanish tyranny. It was a theme harped on in treatises written by William of Orange or his close associates such as Filip Marnix van St Aldegonde (one of the monarchomachs) and Jacques Wesembeeke. It was the loss of William's country's (and his countrymen's) legitimate, longstanding 'liberties and privileges' that these authors constantly emphasise, both in William's famous *Apology*, which was translated into several languages and widely disseminated, and in other tracts.[66] That Spanish abuses amounted to tyranny was a claim repeatedly made by rebel pamphleteers. They unsurprisingly emphasised the government of Alba, who (it was claimed) 'surpassed the most bloody tyrants in very strong cruelty' and had executed between 18,000 and 19,000 people (a wildly exaggerated figure) and the way that subsequent governors incited civil war, dividing the seventeen provinces of the Low Countries.[67] Religion is mentioned only infrequently. It is unsurprising that, in appeals to Netherlandish Catholic nobles and urban leaders for solidarity, or petitions to Catholic German princes to intervene in the Revolt, there is no mention of Protestantism. But even pamphlets aimed at readers in Protestant states, or Protestant statesmen, stressed Spanish tyranny. To take just one example, an anonymous tract, published in Antwerp around 1575 and translated into

---

[65] See, for example, Judith Pollmann and Andrew Spicer (eds.), *Public Opinion and Changing Identities in the Early Modern Netherlands: Essays in Honour of Alistair Duke*, Studies in Medieval and Reformation Traditions 121 (Leiden: Brill, 2007); Van Gelderen, *Political Thought of the Dutch Revolt*. A number of important texts are available in modern editions: E. H. Kossmann and A. F. Mellink (eds.), *Texts Concerning the Revolt of the Netherlands* (Cambridge: Cambridge University Press, 1974); Alistair Duke (trans. and intro.), 'William of Orange's Apology (1580): A New Annotated English Translation', *Dutch Crossing* 22 (1998), 3–96; and the *De Bello Belgico* website (http://dutchrevolt.leidenuniv.nl/default.htm) which includes a number of contemporary texts and documents, in different sections according to original language.

[66] See Duke, 'William of Orange's Apology'; Kossman and Mellink, *Texts*, 84–6 and 139–40, nos. 11 and 27; [Filip Marnix van St Aldegonde], *Oraison des ambassadeurs du serenissime prince Matthias Archiduc d'Austriche, &c. Gouverneur des païs bas: & des Estates generaux desdits païs* (Antwerp, 1578); Van Gelderen, *Political Thought of the Dutch Revolt*, 84–5, 123–6, 139–40.

[67] Anon., *Request presentee a son alteze*, 1 ('surpassé les plus sanguinaires tyrans en toute forte de cruaulté'); [Marnix], *Oraison des ambassadeurs*, sigs. C4r, D2r.

English, avowed that if a king was a murderer, instead of the father of his country, or a tyrant, rather than a prince and protector of his subjects, then the latter were 'no more bound to him'.[68]

There were all sorts of reasons to understate the confessional dimension, even in public statements in Protestant countries, since the revolt in the Netherlands was sustained by a multi-confessional coalition that religious disagreements threatened to tear asunder. Nevertheless, it seems clear, as Blair Worden argues, that influential advisers of William of Orange, including Marnix van St Aldegonde, genuinely 'believed [that] the crown was seeking to conquer its subjects and strip them of their liberties'.[69] That such actions were tyrannical was to be argued in the *Vindiciae contra tyrannos*.

English attitudes to the Dutch Revolt were shaped by confessional sympathy, but also by wider concern for the national interest, for the great bulk of English trade was with the Netherlands, Dutch culture was one of the chief influences on English culture, and England had traditionally found allies in the Low Countries. Now, it was also true that Spain had been England's firm ally throughout most of the first six decades of the sixteenth century, whereas France was its almost perpetual enemy. Among the first advice a veteran royal official had given the queen and Cecil after Elizabeth's accession to the throne was 'the necessity of friendship' with Spain. A policy of almost constant hostility to Spain (along, as we have seen, with periodic alliance with France, including against Spain) truly was an epochal change, leading Burghley to reflect thirty years later that 'the state of the world is marvellously changed'.[70] That change was made was partly, of course, for confessional reasons, but in addition, Elizabeth and her counsellors reluctantly concluded that the Spanish government had become egregiously abusive and tyrannical. The 'Spanish fury' at Antwerp in November 1576, when untold numbers of citizens of one of the greatest cities of Europe were killed during a three-day rampage by the Spanish army, confirmed the perceptions formed by Alba's rule. One of Elizabeth's Secretaries of State wrote to a fellow privy councillor in 1577 that Philip II was 'violent, wilful ... and not contented that right showlde everywhere take place'. The following year, the Earl of Sussex, who was no Protestant zealot and generally urged a conciliatory

[68] J. M. B. C. Kervyn de Lettenhove (ed.), *Relations politiques des Pays-Bas et de l'Angleterre sous le regne de Philippe II*, 11 vols. (Brussels: Académie Royale, 1882–1900), VIII, 55, no. 3021.
[69] Blair Worden, *The Sound of Virtue: Philip Sidney's* Arcadia *and Elizabethan Politics* (New Haven, CT, and London: Yale University Press, 1996), 287.
[70] Lord Paget to Cecil, Feb. 1559, quoted in Ramsay, 'Foreign Policy', 147; Burghley to Shrewsbury, 27 May 1589, quoted in Read, *Lord Burghley and Queen Elizabeth*, 456.

policy to the Catholic monarchies of France and Spain, nevertheless urged the queen to oppose 'the suppressyen of the lowe contryes by the Spanish tyranny'.[71] A history of Elizabeth's reign by a protégé of Burghley and written largely from the latter's papers surely reflected his view in its assertion that Elizabeth had not wanted to separate the Netherlands from Philip II or the Habsburg dominions, but had felt she had to act after she 'perceived the great cruelty of the Spaniards which they exercised upon the Dutch her neighbours'.[72]

The English accused the Spanish of attributing the conflict to religion, when it was really due to the abuse of power of Philip II's viceroys in the Low Countries; and the Elizabethan regime protested Spanish treatment of the population of the Netherlands in general, not just of the various types of Protestants. When Elizabeth finally went openly to war with Spain in 1585, she drew attention to the fact that, 'howso ever in the beginning of these cruell persecutions, the pretence thereof was for maintenance of the Romish religion, yet they spared not to deprive very many Catholiques and Ecclesiasticall persons of their franchises and privileges'.[73] Spanish government had been abusive and therefore was illegitimate. Moreover, because of England's 'natural' position as neighbour of the Low Countries, and the long history of much 'commerce and intercourse' and 'speciall mutuall amities ... betwixt the people and inhabitants' of both England and the Netherlands, Elizabeth had a right to offer 'continuall frendly advices to the king of Spain for restraining of the tyrannie of his governors'. This having been ignored, she had a right to do something about Spanish oppression.[74]

The comprehensive and indiscriminate nature of Spanish repression in the Low Countries was shocking to contemporaries. In addition, in their pursuit of total victory over heresy, Philip II and his lieutenants inflicted destruction and dislocation on all Netherlanders, even loyal ones. While Elizabeth wanted to see Philip II and his Dutch subjects reconciled, she also wanted him to govern them differently. She and her ministers decided to intervene for confessional reasons, but also for reasons arising from concern about tyranny and its wider ill effects.[75]

[71] Thomas Wilson to Earl of Leicester, 18 May 1577, HMC, *Salisbury MSS*, II, 151, no. 458. Sussex to Elizabeth, 28 Aug. 1578, HH, CP, MS 10, fo. 33r.
[72] William Camden, *The historie of the most high, mighty, and ever-glorious tmpresse, Elizabeth ... The third booke* (London, 1625), 101.
[73] Proclamation, 1 Oct. 1585, printed as *A declaration of the causes moving the queene to give aide to the oppressed in the lowe Countries* (London, 1585), 6.
[74] *Ibid.*, 2–3, 8.
[75] See R. B. Wernham, 'Elizabethan War Aims and Strategy', in *Elizabethan Government and Society: Essays Presented to Sir John Neale* ed. S. T. Bindoff, J. Hurstfield, and C. H. Williams (London: Athlone Press, 1961), 341, 343, 368.

Furthermore, one of the striking points about the *Vindiciae contra tyrannos* was the author's specific argument that the rhetoric of preventing tyranny must *not* be a pretence for the acquisition of territory or power. When we consider the English interventions in the Netherlands, which must have been in the mind of the *VCT*'s author (whether it was Duplessis-Mornay or Languet), it is notable that Elizabeth lived up to this principle; in 1576 she was offered the sovereignty of the County of Holland and rejected it; and in 1585, when offered the sovereignty of the whole United Provinces, she 'refused to take upon her their rule'.[76] If one lesson of the intervention in France in 1562 was not to invade or seek territorial acquisition under 'pretence of aid', Elizabeth had learned it. Nor is such a connection with the *Vindiciae* improbable; it is striking that the first English edition appeared in 1588, shortly after Elizabeth finally declared war on Spain, but printed only Quaestio 4 – the one most relevant to Elizabeth's intervention in the Netherlands (and much less objectionable to a sovereign than Quaestios 1–3, which justified subjects, rather than other sovereigns, resisting and removing kings) – and it is likely that the translation and publication of *A short Apologie* was sponsored by the government.[77]

★

As for the Spanish, they in turn also intervened, militarily in Ireland and used diplomatic pressure regularly against late Tudor and early Stuart England, in both cases on behalf of persecuted Catholics – a minority in England and Wales, the majority in Ireland. The Spanish, too, viewed tyranny through a confessional lens, but they conceptualised it – like their Protestant counterparts – as being government in the interest of just one faction, and as entailing violations of existing laws and customs. For this reason, when Philip II and Philip III looked to the British Isles, they saw tyranny.

The public justifications of the Spanish Armada included 'the brutal and cruel yoke' of persecution imposed on Catholics, which violated England's 'ancient laws'.[78] There can be no doubt that Philip II did not despatch the Armada to England in 1588, nor Philip III a Spanish army to Kinsale, in Ireland, in 1601, just to relieve the sufferings of English and Irish Catholics. The English interventions in France and the Netherlands were a major threat to the cohesion of the multiplex

[76] Camden, *Historie*, 100; see Simon Adams, 'Elizabeth I and the Sovereignty of the Netherlands 1576–1585', *TRHS*, 6th series, 14 (2004), 309–19.
[77] Salmon, *French Religious Wars in English Political Thought*, 17.
[78] Quoted in A. J. Loomie, 'Philip II's Armada Proclamation of 1597', *Recusant History* 12 (1974), 216, 221.

Spanish Monarchy and so, for confessional and for geopolitical reasons, Spain struck at England. Nevertheless, there is also little doubt that 'the brutal and cruel yoke' of persecution truly was *one* factor in Philip II's attempts to invade England in the 1580s and 1590s, and his son's intervention in the Irish rebellion. Again, concern about suffering and abuse of a foreign civilian minority, and concern for religion were mixed. And what is worth noting is that, as with Elizabethan justifications of intervention in France and the Netherlands, Philip II cited the fact that Elizabeth's persecution of Catholics actually broke England's laws.

There was, in fact, a developing rhetoric that where law and good governance were absent, other princes could legitimately interfere, or intervene, to restore them. As suggested at the start of the chapter, then, we arguably see the emergence of a norm in the Law of Nations and in state practice. This view is reinforced by subsequent developments in the seventeenth century. For example, during the 1610s and 1620s the French government attempted to influence by diplomatic means policy in England and the Dutch Republic towards religious minorities, including Protestants whose doctrines diverged from those of the national church, as well as Catholics. In the same period, Protestant and Catholic states alike were concerned by, and protested, depredations in the 1630s by Habsburg troops in the Grisons (or Grey Leagues, today part of the Swiss confederation). Most notably, Oliver Cromwell applied powerful diplomatic pressure to France to secure greater toleration for the Huguenots in the mid-1650s, when he also mobilised commercial, diplomatic and naval power to bludgeon Savoy into halting persecution of the Vaudois.

*

The foreign policy of the British republic, during the Protectorate, in fact affords some of the most significant precedents for the application of humanitarian principles to a nation-state's foreign relations. In Ireland, in 1649, Cromwell was brutal; as a Catholic bishop later recalled, 'Cromwell came over, and like a lightning passed through the land'.[79] He calculatedly initiated one of the first large-scale forced migrations, attempting with some success to drive large portions of the Catholic population of Ireland from the best agricultural land in order to make way for Protestant settlers. Elsewhere in the British Isles, however, he was magnanimous and humane to religious minorities, including groups that even contemporary advocates of religious toleration typically

---

[79] Quoted in Ciaran Brady and Jane Ohlmeyer, 'Making Good: New Perspectives on the English in Early Modern Ireland', in *British Interventions in Early Modern Ireland*, ed. Brady and Ohlmeyer (Cambridge: Cambridge University Press, 2005), 1.

agreed ought to be persecuted, such as Quakers, anti-Trinitarians and Catholics; and he played an influential role in the process of allowing Jews to be readmitted to England.[80]

Cromwell's government also successfully applied pressure on Louis XIV's France to help the Huguenots. By the mid-1650s, Cardinal Mazarin (Louis's chief minister, who dominated the young king) desired an English alliance, both to ensure that a war between England and France, which the anti-Catholic Cromwell certainly considered, was avoided, and to obtain help in France's decades-old war with the empire of the Spanish Habsburgs.[81] Since the death of Henry IV in 1610, France's Reformed community had faced ongoing encroachment on the liberty of conscience and of worship granted them by the one-time Huguenot king at the conclusion of the Wars of Religion in 1598. Cromwell used Mazarin's foreign policy agenda to influence French domestic policy, so that Mazarin somewhat ameliorated the developing persecution of the Huguenots.[82]

Then in 1655 the British republic intervened in Savoy, on behalf of the persecuted Waldenses (the name by which they were and still are most frequently known in England) or Vaudois (the local usage). They were the descendants of a medieval heretical movement, most of whose members lived in remote Alpine mountain valleys in what today is south-eastern France and north-western Italy. In the sixteenth century, most lived in the lands ruled by the Duke of Savoy, whose small sovereign principality, spanning parts of modern-day Italy, France and Switzerland, included the region of Piedmont, by which name the duchy was sometimes called. The dukes were firmly Roman Catholic; but, as rulers of a small state that perched precariously between larger, warring neighbours, and maintained its

[80] For an overview, see D. J. B. Trim, 'Oliver Cromwell and the Intolerant Inheritance of America's Religious Extreme', *Liberty*, 101:6 (Nov.–Dec. 2006), 12–15, 22–3, and 102:1 (Jan.–Feb. 2007), 8–13, 26–7. Concern for Jews was sadly rare before the mid-nineteenth century when it became an important factor in French and British policy, as Abigail Green shows in Chapter 6, below.
[81] See Charles P. Korr, *Cromwell and the New Model Foreign Policy: England's Policy Toward France, 1649–1658* (Berkeley: University of California Press, 1975), ch. 7; Timothy Venning, *Cromwellian Foreign Policy* (New York: St Martin's Press, 1995), chs. 3–4. Despite its title, Steven C. A. Pincus, *Protestantism and Patriotism: Ideologies and the Making of English Foreign Policy, 1650–1668* (Cambridge: Cambridge University Press, 1996) is largely focused on Anglo–Dutch relations, and almost entirely ignores the Anglo–French negotiations (and indeed Cromwell's intervention on behalf of the Vaudois).
[82] Philip A. Knachel, *England and the Fronde: The Impact of the English Civil War and Revolution on France* (Ithaca: Cornell University Press, 1967), 253; cf., for example, Sir George Downing to Secretary of State Thurloe, 25 Aug. 1655, *SP Thurloe*, III, 734.

independence by aiding them in their wars, they were rarely able to mount internal campaigns against dissidents.

In the 1520s the Vaudois were discovered by the Protestant Reformers, whose admiration for them cannot be overstated; but the Vaudois gradually adopted the doctrines, and merged into the mainstream, of the Reformed (or Calvinist) branch of the Reformation, whose Swiss heartland was adjacent.[83] In the following century and a half, the Vaudois's Catholic rulers alternated between persecution and a grudging limited toleration. European Protestants regarded the medieval Waldenses as an alternative tradition to that of Rome, making the Vaudois iconic figures for all kinds of Protestants, albeit the Calvinist connection led to a particular affinity with the Swiss, Huguenot, Dutch, and Scottish Reformed Churches and the Puritan community in England.[84] This was to be an important factor in motivating foreign Protestant action on behalf of the Vaudois.

In 1649 and 1653 Charles Emmanuel II, the Duke of Savoy, confirmed the free exercise of religion to his Vaudois subjects, as foreign Protestant sympathisers were aware; what they did not realise was that toleration was specifically limited to those living 'within the limits ... fixed' by the Covenant of Podio of 1561, which had granted freedom of worship to Vaudois living in certain valleys.[85] However, in the intervening century, the pattern of population in Piedmont had changed. On 25 January 1655, all Protestants living outside the valleys prescribed in 1561 were ordered to move to those valleys, or convert, on pain of death and confiscation of their properties.[86] But only twenty days was given for this major population movement to take place and, despite claims to the contrary by contemporary Catholic apologists, this was never likely to be sufficient time.[87] In the space of a few days in mid-April 1655 at least 300 Vaudois were massacred in what became known as 'Bloody Easter', while thousands

---

[83] See Euan Cameron, *The Reformation of the Heretics: The Waldenses of the Alps, 1480–1580* (Oxford: Clarendon Press, 1984), part III *passim*, esp. 138–9, 142–3, 157–9, 213–15.

[84] For example, Perrin, trans. Lennard, *Luthers forerunners*, sigs. A2r–v, Br–v; George Abbott, *A Treatise of the Perpetuall Visibilitie, and Succession of the True Church* (London, 1624), 52; cf. Cameron, *Reformation of the Heretics*, 201.

[85] Anon., *A short and faithfull Account of the late Commotions in the Valleys of Piedmont* (London, 1655), sig. A2r; Giovanni Stoppa, *A collection of the several papers ... concerning The Bloody and Barbarous Massacres, Murthers, and other Cruelties, committed ... in the Vallies of Piedmont* (London, 1655), 12–13; Samuel Rawson Gardiner, *History of the Commonwealth and Protectorate 1659–1656*, vol. IV (repr., New York: AMS Press, 1965), 179.

[86] Edict printed in *A short and faithfull Account*, 2–3; cf. Stoppa, *Collection*, 14–15; Gardiner, *History*, 180.

[87] Cf. *A short and faithfull Account*, 3.

more were driven from their homes, many of which were then burned.[88] Probably around another 1,400 refugees died as they fled through the Alps in bitter weather.[89]

News quickly spread of the 'bloudy and barbarous Massacre' and its 'horrid and barbarous Cruelties'; the events were 'so publickly known and evident, that it could not possibly be concealed or denied'.[90] 'The House of Savoy, through its ambassadors ... tried to minimize ... what had undoubtedly taken place. But it was to no avail.' The plight of the Protestants of Piedmont became one of the great *causes célèbres* of the seventeenth century, thanks to 'a stream of newspaper articles, tracts, pamphlets and special reports', which were widely distributed and sold across Protestant Europe.[91] Propaganda played its part: the stories that circulated undoubtedly included many exaggerations, as well as tales of deeds that are common to atrocity stories throughout history,[92] and hence are likely to have been inventions. Sometimes, however, atrocity stories are true.[93]

A captain whose company took part in the attacks recorded that he had seen women raped, bodies mutilated, some victims burned alive, and even children slain. Some children, though, were saved and forcibly adopted into Catholic families.[94] Other participants in the 'Bloody Easter' boasted of how they had killed 'a multitude

---

[88] See Gardiner, *History*, 181–5. Gardiner is rigorously sceptical about atrocity stories and rumoured death tolls; page 185 cites an official Savoyard contemporary source giving a death toll of 274 in two communes, not accounting for deaths in a third that had been the first to be attacked. I am grateful to Philippe Rosenberg for sharing his thoughts and information on the scale of the massacre.

[89] Philippe Rosenberg, 'Protestant Interests, Diplomatic Realism, and the Renewal of the Anti-Catholic Ethos, 1628–1658', unpubl. paper read at the annual meeting of the North American Conference on British Studies, Cincinnati, 3–5 Oct. 2008. Cf. Stoppa, *Collection*, 5, 34; anon., *The barbarous & inhumane proceedings against the professors of the reformed religion* (London, 1655), 3, 5; Gardiner, *History*, 185; Prescot Stephens, *The Waldensian Story: A Study in Faith, Intolerance and Survival* (Lewes: Book Guild, 1998), 175.

[90] Samuel Morland, *The History of The Evangelical Churches Of the Valleys of Piemont* (London, 1658), sig. a1*v*, 386, 548.

[91] Giorgio Tourn, *The Waldensians: The First 800 Years*, trans. Camillo P. Merlino, ed. Charles W. Arbuthnot (Turin: Claudiana, 1980), 125. Enea Balmas and Grazia Zardini Lana (eds.), *La vera relazione di quanto e accaduto nelle persecuzioni e i massacri dell'anno 1655: Le 'Pasque Piemontesi' del 1655 nelle testimonianze dei protagonisti*, Storici Valdesi 3 (Turin: Claudiana, 1987), 122–68, esp. 133–56.

[92] For example, Morland, *Evangelical Churches*, book II, ch. vi, 326–84, a detailed narrative of atrocities, based on testimony from 'persons who were both Eye and Ear Witnesses', interviewed by Morland (on which Gardiner casts doubt: *History*, 182n. 183–4n.); Stoppa, *Collection*, sig. A3*r*–4*r*, 3–6, 24–36; and anon., *Barbarous & inhumane proceedings*, 2–5 (and, for more atrocity stories, *ibid. et passim*).

[93] Cf. Gardiner, *History*, 184n.

[94] Morland, *Evangelical Churches*, 333; Gardiner, *History*, 183.

of enemies of God', who often 'could find no better way of escape than to kill themselves'.[95] The killing of children; suicides by those facing mutilation and death; rumours that some Vaudois were 'tumbled downe' precipices by soldiers; and eyewitness stories of how some mothers who fled through the mountains were 'frozen to death ... [with] Infants hanging upon their dry breasts': these combined are perhaps the origin of unsubstantiated stories, immortalised by John Milton in a famous sonnet, that mothers were forced off cliff tops with their children in their arms.[96] Even pro-Savoyard pamphleteers acknowledged that the duke's army had 'commit[ted] some cruelties'.[97]

Claims that Piedmont had witnessed genocide are greatly exaggerated, given the death toll; but it had been the site of an early example of ethnic cleansing.[98] The Vaudois in Savoy probably only numbered just over 23,000; while the casualties were small in absolute terms, they were significant as a proportion.[99]

In any event, although not genocidal, the massacres and forced emigration seemed to foreshadow the final extermination of the Waldenses, a prospect which horrified European Protestants. However, horror and dismay did not immediately produce action. The Calvinist Swiss Cantons all immediately protested the massacres and sent a special envoy to Charles Emmanuel II. However, Swiss protests were disregarded in Turin.[100] Having failed in 'their Intercession', the Swiss were not prepared to undertake an intervention; as an English diplomat, Samuel Morland, put it in his history of the affair: 'And the plain truth is, this Affair had thus in all probability fallen asleep and come to nothing, had it not been awakened ... in a most lively and vigorous manner, by ... the Lord Protector of England'. Crucially, as Morland

---

[95] Quoted in Stephens, *Waldensian Story*, 175.
[96] Anon., *Barbarous & inhumane proceedings*, 3; John Milton, 'On the Late Massacre in Piemont [sic]' (1655).
[97] For example, anon., *A short and faithfull Account*, 4.
[98] Tourn, *Waldensians*, 124, uses the term 'genocide'; Roger Hainsworth, *The Swordsmen in Power: War and Politics under the English Republic 1649–1660* (Stroud: Sutton, 1997), 204, uses 'ethnic cleansing'. It should be borne in mind that one of the chief markers distinguishing Croatians, Bosnians, and Serbs, whose conflicts in the early 1990s prompted the first use of the latter term, was religion – they effectively speak the same language, but historically Croatians are Catholic, Serbs are Orthodox, and Bosniacs are Muslim.
[99] See Enea Balmas, 'Introduzione', in *La vera relazione*, ed. Balmas and Zardini Lana, table in 32n.; Stoppa, *Collection*, 37.
[100] Teofilo Gay, *Histoire des Vaudois* (Florence: Imprimerie Claudienne, 1912), 103–4. See Morland, *Evangelical Churches*, Book IV, chs. i and ii, pp. 540–51, for details of the Swiss negotiations.

also noted, 'Neither indeed were the effects of his charity and Christian compassion at all inferiour to ... his zealous, earnest, and pathetick expressions'.[101] Cromwell, in fact, moved beyond hand wringing, to action.[102]

\*

The British republic's Council of State discussed the matter on 17 May and, at the Lord Protector's prompting, proclaimed 30 May a day of 'national humiliation', prayer and fasting. Cromwell launched a public appeal for funds to aid the decimated Waldensian communities, to which he donated £2,000 from his own purse.[103] But he did not merely act to help the survivors of the massacres, for he was well aware that they, too, might be put to the sword in due course. He therefore also took political action.

On 23 May, within a week of the original Council of State meeting on the Savoy massacres, a 'commissioner-extraordinary', Sir Samuel Morland, had been dispatched to Turin, to present a formal letter of protest to the Duke of Savoy and personally 'to intreat him to recall' his 'merciless' edicts; later, in July, another embassy was sent under Sir George Downing to add to the pressure on the Savoyard court.[104] Both embassies were sent via Paris, and as well as the letter to Charles Emmanuel II, Morland also had a letter to present to Louis XIV of France and a personal message for the youthful king's influential chief minister, Cardinal Mazarin.[105]

The government of France exercised considerable influence over its much smaller neighbour, which was normally a faithful French ally. As Cromwell and his councillors knew, Charles Emmanuel had borrowed several regiments from a French general and used them to supplement the ducal army in its attack on the Vaudois.[106] Cromwell seems to have realised that French involvement was not the result of royal policy, but the letter Morland carried to Louis (and, through him, Mazarin) urged

---

[101] Morland, *Evangelical Churches*, 552.
[102] For a detailed study, see Randolph Vigne, '"Avenge, O Lord, thy Slaughtered Saints": Cromwell's Intervention on Behalf of the Vaudois', *Proceedings of the Huguenot Society of Great Britain and Ireland* 24 (1983–8), 10–25.
[103] 'A Breife State of the Accompt of ... money collected for the Releife of the poore Protestants in Peidmount', NA, AO 3/1276, in box 1; C. H. Firth, *Oliver Cromwell and the Rule of the Puritans in England* [1900], World's Classics 536 (London: Oxford University Press, 1953), 371.
[104] Morland, *Evangelical Churches*, 563; see C. H. Firth and S. C. Lomas, *Notes on the Diplomatic Relations of England and France 1603–1688* (Oxford: Blackwell, 1906), 14–15; Gardiner, *History*, 190.
[105] Morland, *Evangelical Churches*, 563.
[106] Venning, *Cromwellian Foreign Policy*, 97. For the balance of Savoyard and French forces involved, see the detailed study of Balmas, 'Introduzione', *passim*.

him to use his 'Interest and Authority with the Duke of Savoy', to oblige Charles Emmanuel to let the Vaudois return to their valleys in peace and practise their faith. Wrapped up in the diplomatic language was a clear warning that if France did not oblige, then its alliance with England would be suspended. Persuading Savoy to stop persecuting Protestants would 'engage your Confederates and Allies, which posess the same [i.e., Protestant] Religion, in a far greater respect and good affection to your Majesty. As to what concerns us, what favour so ever in this kinde shall be ... obtained for the Subjects of others, it shall be no less acceptable to us, yea truly it will be more acceptable, and valuable, than any other profit and advantage, among those many which we promise unto our self from the friendship of your Majesty.'[107] Meanwhile, John Thurloe, Secretary to the Council of State, advised the French ambassador in London that the Anglo-French alliance treaty 'would not be signed until the Duke of Savoy had come to a satisfactory arrangement with his subjects'.[108]

In his personal meetings with Mazarin, Morland seems to have made it plain that negotiations would not be concluded, nor a treaty with France signed, until the persecution of the Vaudois was halted. He probably also hinted that, if it were not, the British fleet, then in the Mediterranean, might act against French maritime trade.[109] Cromwell had certainly sent orders to the British republic's redoubtable 'General-at-Sea', Robert Blake to use his fleet to interdict Savoyard commerce if diplomacy was rebuffed and was prepared to have the fleet bombard Nice or Villa Franca (Villefranche-sur-mer) (both then part of Savoy, not France).[110] In internal discussions, French ministers also discussed the possibility that the Protectoral government might hire mercenaries in the Protestant cantons of Switzerland, for service in Savoy, or stir up the Huguenots to rebellion in France, though this might have been their own inference rather than Morland's threat.[111]

In any event, Cromwell's threat not to conclude the Anglo-French alliance may have been significant enough – and it was no bluff.

[107] Cromwell to Louis XIV, 25 May 1655 (complete Latin text and English translation), in Morland, *Evangelical Churches*, 564–5, at 565; full English translation of Louis's reply (n.d.), *ibid.*, 566–7.

[108] Venning, *Cromwellian Foreign Policy*, 97; Gardiner, *History*, 186.

[109] Firth, *Cromwell*, 371; Gardiner, *History*, 185, 187–8, and 191 (only in July were letters of marque for privateering against French subjects revoked); Maurice Ashley, *The Greatness of Oliver Cromwell* (New York: Macmillan, 1958), 320–1; Hainsworth, *Swordsmen in Power*, 204.

[110] Firth, *Cromwell*, 371; Venning, *Cromwellian Foreign Policy*, 95.

[111] Gardiner, *History*, 189–90, citing AMAE, Correspondance Politique Savoie, 49, fos. 410, 446, 471, 479.

The Dutch ambassador in London was later told by English officials that 'the treaty with the lord embassador of [the French] crown was advanced so far ... that the lord protector and the council had been inclined to finish the said treaty, but that the inhuman murther of the Vaudois happened in the mean while, and prevented the same'.[112] As late as July, the Dutch ambassador in Paris observed: 'The treaty between France and England is not yet signed. The lord protector doth defer it till he hears from Savoy, in what manner that court will treat for the re-establishing of the Vaudois in Piedmont.'[113] The French ambassador knew that he had been on the brink of signing a treaty and was deeply frustrated at the delay.[114]

Seeing his coalition against Spain in danger, Mazarin, as he later told Ambassador Downing, so much 'desired a right understanding with' Cromwell,[115] that English demands were given high priority. Louis XIV formally notified Cromwell in early June that France would urge the Duke of Savoy to agree to English demands; and so strongly did France press Charles Emmanuel that Mazarin later took credit for 'the accommodation ... in Piemont'.[116] In September he wrote to the French ambassador in London observing that 'if the signing of the treaty [with England] did depend upon the accommodation of the Vaudois, it will be now performed, for the accommodation is now executed'.[117]

When Morland arrived in Turin, he presented Cromwell's formal protest. It conveyed no overt threat, but Morland's personal communications were surely stronger and the Savoyard government was shaken.[118] The British navy under Blake had reached a peak of effectiveness not reached again for another half-century, if not more; Cromwell's protests had to be taken seriously. So, too, even more, did the urgings of the King of France – yet he would not have even thought of acting were it not for Cromwell's influence on Mazarin. The Savoyard Court recognised that

---

[112] Despatch, 17 Sept. 1655 n.s., *SP Thurloe*, IV, 18.
[113] Despatch, 16 July 1655 (i.e., 6 July in England), *ibid.*, III, 619.
[114] Korr, *Cromwell and the New Model Foreign Policy*, 148–9.
[115] Downing to Thurloe, 25 Aug. 1655, *SP Thurloe*, III, 734.
[116] Louis XIV to Cromwell, 12 June 1655 [i.e., 2 June in England], AMAE, Correspondance Politique Angleterre, 66, fos. 631–2; Downing to Thurloe, 25 Aug. 1655, *SP Thurloe*, III, 734; Bordeaux to Count de Brienne, 9 Sept. 1655, *ibid.*, III, 745. See Knachel, *England and the Fronde*, 253; Firth, *Cromwell*, 371; Ashley, *Greatness of Oliver Cromwell*, 321; Korr, *Cromwell and the New Model Foreign Policy*, 154.
[117] Mazarin to Bordeaux, 8 Sept. 1655, *SP Thurloe*, III, 743.
[118] Tourn, *Waldensians*, 125; Hainsworth, *Swordsmen in Power*, 204–5. Cromwell's letter is printed in William S. Gilly, *Narrative of an Excursion to the Mountains of Piedmont* (London: C. and J. Rivington, 1827), 218–20.

it would have to stop the existing policy. In the resulting negotiations, the Vaudois delegation was supported by English and Swiss diplomats.[119] The resulting Treaty of Pinerolo (August 1655) ended the massacres and conceded to the Vaudois the right to return to their valleys; the British republic and Swiss Federation were co-guarantors of the treaty and the limited rights granted. It was not a wholly satisfactory settlement, for a variety of reasons that need not concern us here. Cromwell recognised it was imperfect; but 'he was hailed as the saviour of the Vaudois' in England, across Europe, and indeed by the Vaudois themselves. It was not the last time that they were to be vigorously persecuted, but at no other time was there such danger that they might be entirely exterminated.[120] If Cromwell achieved only limited success, it was still success: the massacres of the 'Bloody Easter' had been ended; ethnic cleansing had been partially reversed; possibly genocide had been prevented.

Over the next eighteen months Morland distributed the money that had been raised by popular donation in parishes across England, in response to Cromwell's appeal; it came to well over £38,000. The Vaudois had been spared and provided with a basis for rebuilding their lives. Cromwell understood that it was not enough merely to stop massacres: safeguards needed to be imposed that would stop them recurring; the communities destroyed or disrupted by massacre had to be reconstructed, and damage 'caused by the War, [such] as [by] pillaging, burning, and the like', needed to be made good.[121] In his comprehensive approach to intervention, integrating diplomacy, military power, and financial and economic assistance, Cromwell foreshadowed the Great Power interventions in Syria in the 1860s, Crete in 1868 and Macedonia in 1903–7,[122] and the NATO intervention in Kosovo, beginning in 1999.

The British republic's intervention in Savoy was undertaken even though special foreign embassies were expensive to mount and fleets expensive to maintain in foreign waters. Although force was not ultimately deployed, Cromwell was willing to have Blake's fleet bombard Savoyard ports, and to license privateers against French shipping.

[119] Gardiner, *History*, 188–90; Tourn, *Waldensians*, 126.
[120] Firth, *Cromwell*, 371; see Tourn, *Waldensians*, 126; Trim, 'Oliver Cromwell', 14–15; Gardiner, *History*, 190–3; Tourn, *Waldensians*, 126–8.
[121] 'A Breife State of the Accompt of ... the money collected for the Releife of the poore Protestants in Peidmount', NA, AO 3/1276, box 1; Morland, 'An Extract, or Abbreviate of the Accompt', in *A distinct and faithful accompt of all the receipts ... For the relief of the distressed Protestants ... of Piemont* (London: for the Council of State, 1658), 97–111, including 'Instructions ... for the Distribution of the collected Moneys among the poor people of ... Piemont', 1 June 1656, 103–5, quotation at 105.
[122] See Davide Rodogno, Chapters 7 and 9, below.

He put his government's aims in distant Piedmont ahead of the apparently more important diplomatic negotiations with France. A French alliance was seen as crucial for the war against Spain he had been planning since at least 1654; negotiations with France had been conducted, off and on, since 1652.[123] His willingness in 1655 to prioritise the Protestants of Piedmont over an alliance with France says much about the place of what would later become termed 'national interest' in his policy; instead he emphasised the Protestant interest.

This meant Cromwell's action was not disinterested. Morland praised the Lord Protector, because his 'great end' since becoming head of the British state was to promote:

The general interest of God's people throughout the Christian world … You have formed all Your Counsels in Order thereunto, and laying aside all other Reasons of State, have adhered onely to this, that Your own Interest may appear one and the same with the Universal Interest of the Evangelical Churches in their respective Nations.[124]

And there is no question that a consistent foreign policy priority, both for Cromwell and for several of his counsellors, was what the Lord Protector himself termed 'the Protestant interest abroad'.[125] A chief objective of Cromwellian foreign policy, as summed up by one of his ambassadors to Savoy, Sir George Downing, was to create an alliance of Protestant states that would form 'a Comon Bulwarke … against the bloody Inquisitions' of the Catholic powers; as the Venetian ambassador put it, Cromwell's policy was 'the ruin of … the Catholic faith'.[126] Cromwell urged the second protectoral parliament that England must 'have a brotherly fellow-feeling of the interest of all the Protestant Christians in the world', for 'he that strikes at but one species … to make it nothing, strikes at all'.[127] Prioritising the Protestant interest was in the Protector's eyes a way of enhancing national security.

---

[123] See Knachel, *England and the Fronde*, 250–71; see also Toby Barnard, *The English Republic 1649–1660* (Harlow: Longman, 1982), 43, 57; Firth, *Cromwell*, 303–5, 367–9.

[124] Morland, *Evangelical Churches*, sig. A2v.

[125] Cromwell, speeches to the first and second Protectoral Parliaments, 4 Sept. 1654 and 25 Jan. 1658, printed in Maurice Ashley (ed.), *Cromwell* (Englewood Cliffs, NJ: Prentice-Hall, 1969), 46–8 at 48, 51–4 at 52–3. See Pincus, *Protestantism and Patriotism*, 22–6, 58, 61, 79, 131–2, 181, 186–9; and Venning, *Cromwellian Foreign Policy*, 25, 75, 100–1, 194–6, 214–15. The later history of the 'Protestant interest' is examined by Andrew Thompson in Chapter 3, below.

[126] Quotations: Jonathan Scott, *England's Troubles: Seventeenth-Century English Political Instability in European Context* (Cambridge: Cambridge University Press, 2000), 159; J. W. Thompson and S. K. Padover, *Secret Diplomacy: A Record of Espionage and Double-Dealing: 1500–1815* (London: Jarrolds, 1937), 83.

[127] Cromwell, speech 25 Jan. 1658, in Ashley (ed.), *Cromwell*, 52.

Nevertheless, while this was the general context, there were no geopolitical or strategic benefits to be gained from the particular intervention in Piedmont-Savoy. The protectoral government saw the Spanish empire as the chief threat to the republic, for confessional-ideological reasons. In consequence, its *policy* was to create a strong coalition to wage offensive war against the Spanish Monarchy and weaken its economic strength and strategic position by stripping it of key territorial assets; protectoral *strategy* (to apply to Cromwell's thinking a term he would not have used himself)[128] was to conduct military operations against Spain, both with allies in the Low Countries, and unilaterally in the West Indies against Spanish colonies. Intervening in Savoy furthered neither Cromwell's strategy nor his policy; instead, it had the potential to harm both. Sending Blake's fleet to operate against Savoy's coast was a distraction from Cromwell's strategy. The Vaudois, moreover, were too weak to be useful future allies in any renewed war of religion; whereas Savoy, as English and British statesmen throughout the seventeenth century were well aware, had often been hostile to the Spanish Habsburgs. From a purely policy perspective, it would have been better to shrug off the death and forced migration of a small number of Protestants than to run the risk of losing both the French alliance and another potential Catholic ally in what was, for France, a vital strategic area – for it was through Savoy that Spanish armies from the Habsburg possessions in northern Italy could invade France. Thus, while Cromwell in aiding the Vaudois was aiding co-religionists, his 'laying aside [of] all other Reasons of State' to aid them (to use Morland's words) is hardly an exemplar of 'realist' foreign policy.

Furthermore, concerns about human suffering were major factors in Cromwell's decision-making. Morland is not an unbiased witness, but he was not greatly exaggerating when he emphasised 'how exceeding precious ... the lives and liberties of those poor distressed' people had been to Cromwell, 'and how deeply their bleeding condition hath always affected [his] very heart'.[129] As 'soon as ever the News thereof was brought him, [he] was so deeply affected with the poor peoples calamities, that he was often heard to say, *That it lay as near or rather nearer his heart than if it had concerned his nearest and dearest Relations.*' Cromwell told the French ambassador that he felt for the Vaudois as if they were his near kin; and the Dutch ambassador found Cromwell wanted him to

[128] See Hew Strachan, 'The Lost Meaning of Strategy', *Survival* 43:3 (Oct. 2005), 34–5.
[129] Morland, *Evangelical Churches*, sig. A2r–v.

discuss help for 'the poor people of Piedmont'.[130] Even on his deathbed in 1658, Cromwell was anxious not only for the future of the British republic after his death, but also for the future of the Vaudois, crying out 'what will they do with the poor protestants of the Piedmont'.[131] He aided the Vaudois partly because they *were* co-religionists and his 'own Interest [was] one and the same with the Universal Interest of the Evangelical Churches', but partly because he was genuinely outraged by the actions of the Duke of Savoy's government, which had violated 'the honest Maximes of Humane Policy'. He was moved, as Morland memorably puts it, in his 'Christian bowels of compassion for the poor afflicted' Piedmontese Protestants.[132] In sum, Cromwell's actions in 1655 can accurately be described as a humanitarian intervention.

*

This survey of the practice of early modern states shows that intervention on humanitarian grounds – intervention against mass atrocity and tyranny – has a very long pedigree, stretching back to the very origins of the modern state system. In each case, from Elizabeth I to Philip II to Oliver Cromwell, confessional interests were hugely important in the decision to undertake interventions; in all the examples considered, the victims of tyranny, atrocity or abusive government were largely conceptualised as suffering co-religionists, rather than as suffering humans; and they were described in terms of their confessional identity, not of their humanity. The only exception is the British republic: Cromwell's officials used the language of humanity, expressing concern for 'the honest Maximes of *Human*e Policy' and Cromwell himself voiced outrage at 'the *inhuman* murther of the Vaudois'. We have seen that thirty years earlier Grotius had characterised intervention as 'right vested in *human* society'; and that Protestant polemicists by the mid-seventeenth century were describing martyrs in terms of common humanity. But Cromwellian Britain was the only state that officially used similar language. The tendency to think of tyranny as something done to fellow believers, rather than to members of rival confessions, helps to explain why all the governments in question, including Cromwell's, persecuted and oppressed minorities in their own states.

---

[130] *Ibid.*, 552; Firth, *Cromwell*, 371; Nieupoort to Ruysch, 28 Jan. 1656 [new style], *SP Thurloe*, IV, 433.

[131] Anon. to William Clarke, in Frances Henderson (ed.), *The Clarke Papers*, vol. V, Camden Society, 5th series, 27 (2005), 272 (I owe this reference to John Morrill); despite lacking definite provenance, the story was circulating soon after Cromwell's death.

[132] Morland, *Evangelical Churches*, sigs. A3r, a1v–a2r.

Yet the fact that opposition to tyranny or abusive government was not applied uniformly does not mean it was insincere; it is not unusual for those who avow principles to apply them unevenly or to make (to them, obvious) exceptions. Few, for example, would question the sincerity of the British and American governments' defence of democracy in World War II, even though they were also defending their colonial possessions and in practice regarded democracy as appropriate only for some countries or ethnic groups.

It is important to note that there *was* concern about what can reasonably be called inhumane actions. Early modern governments did not see their interventions solely as support for fellow believers; they also saw them, and described them, as actions to stop unnecessary suffering – to strike down cruelty and tyranny. The fact that this language was used both in treatises about intervention in the Law of Nations, and by princes, officials and diplomats to explain intervention to the rest of Christendom, was vitally important. Even though in practice only co-religionists were intended to benefit, the language was rarely couched in exclusive or selfish terms; thus, it did not close off the possibility of action on behalf of people who were not co-religionists. The use of such language (regardless of the sentiments behind it) in official documents and legal treatises gave it an imprimatur, which surely helped to stimulate a development that probably would have happened in any case, for, since noble sentiments are attractive, the language evolved to become even more inclusive and altruistic. And so, by the 1650s, humanity (and inhumanity) started to be emphasised; and this in turn opened up still further the possibility of acting on behalf of people because their suffering was wrong, rather than simply because they were fellow believers.

Furthermore, as we have seen, action went hand-in-hand with the pronouncements of lawyers and political commentators, who were often also government officials and diplomats, and who therefore frequently helped to draft the official justifications for intervention and went on diplomatic missions to urge restraint on princes perceived as ruling tyrannically. The developing discourse against tyranny – the rhetoric that, where egregious oppression was present, or law and good governance absent, other princes could legitimately interfere, or intervene, to end the one and restore the others – was matched, to some extent, by state practice, which emerged in interplay with theoretical views. This conjuncture of state behaviour and principles underpinning and moulding it indicates that a norm of intervention had emerged in early modern Europe.[133]

---

[133] Cf. Sarah Percy, *Mercenaries: The History of a Norm in International Relations* (Oxford: Oxford University Press, 2007), 14–15.

In 1648, the Treaties of Westphalia created the modern international system and, along with it, a norm of non-intervention – or so scholars have said for several generations. In fact, recent scholarship shows that Westphalia did not suddenly produce states with a modern concept of sovereignty. In his chapter in this volume, examining intervention in the eighteenth century, Brendan Simms critiques the Westphalian myth.[134] But there is one point about Westphalia with which this chapter will conclude. The model of sovereignty that, in the eighteenth century, came to be associated with Westphalia has, almost ever since, been seen in terms of historical inevitability; yet it was not the only possible solution to the problem of endemic warfare in Europe. An alternative concept of sovereignty and interstate relations had already emerged in the Law of Nations, political theory, and state practice. It provided for a prince's exclusive authority within his domains, and the sovereignty of the developing state; it generally reiterated medieval presumptions that the lower orders were not normally permitted to resist the authority of the state; but while sovereignty was important, it was not absolute. It could not allow a ruler to engage in flagrant and awful breaches of Christian behavioural norms.

This view of sovereignty did not universally obtain in early modern Christendom, but it was widely held. It was far from being unproblematic, as the interventions by England in France and the Netherlands and by Spain in Ireland demonstrate; but it did provide an answer to the problem of what could be done if a state violated the bounds 'of pietie and justice', and if a 'prince use[d] tyranie towards his people'.[135] Other princes not only had the right to intervene on behalf of the abused and ill-governed foreign population: they even had a Christian obligation to do so; and some in fact did so. If it was a concept more honoured in the breach than in the observance, it nonetheless set a notable precedent – one that later generations were eventually to reclaim.

---

[134] Chapter 4, below.    [135] *VCT–Apologie* (1588), sig. B6*v*.

# 3   The Protestant interest and the history of humanitarian intervention, *c.* 1685–*c.* 1756

*Andrew C. Thompson*

> Kings, besides the Care of their own Kingdom, have lying upon them the Care of human society: Hence it is, that the Powers of the Earth enter into Alliances and Leagues to guard Men against the Oppression of their own Governours and others. And this accounts for the Original of a Guarantee, whose Office is, not only to see Articles perform'd in Treaties between Princes and Princes, but between Princes and their Subjects.
>
> Charles Owen (1725)[1]

Historians enjoy speculating on the past. There is a certain satisfaction in showing that ideas and developments that are more generally deemed to be novel and radical have a longer history than is generally accepted. The longevity of ideas of humanitarian intervention is something that a number of chapters in this volume seek to demonstrate and the present contribution concentrates attention on the late seventeenth and early eighteenth centuries. It considers how concern for oppressed peoples was articulated in the diplomatic and public discourse and practice of the period. Some of the techniques adopted and the problems faced have a surprisingly modern ring about them. This is not necessarily that surprising. Yet it is still worth recalling this history during discussions about the legitimacy or otherwise of humanitarian interventionism today.

Despite some of the similarities between the worlds of the eighteenth century and now, some substantial differences are apparent. The figures with whom this chapter is primarily concerned were very rarely motivated by a concern for common humanity. There were clear limits to the sorts of people for whom intervention in the internal affairs of another state – an inherently dangerous enterprise in itself – was deemed to be an acceptable risk. The focus of attention in this chapter is on the attempts by Protestants to defend their co-religionists who found themselves living within unfriendly territories elsewhere in

---

[1] Charles Owen, *An Alarm to protestant princes and people, who are all struck at in the popish cruelties at Thorn, and other barbarous executions abroad* (London, 1725), 29.

Europe. Attempts to defend Protestants worked on several levels. There were efforts made through the channels of what now might be called traditional diplomacy (although it is important to remember that much of what we regard as the essential rights and privileges of diplomats was still developing in this period). There were also substantial efforts made at a more popular level, through the use of a burgeoning print culture. One of the interesting features of interventionism in this period is seeking to determine whether it was being driven by popular feeling or whether popular feeling was being shaped by elite concerns. This chapter discusses the emergence of ideas of the 'Protestant interest' as a way in which concern for co-religionists could be discussed and as a tool in the rhetorical armoury of justifying intervention. The term 'Protestant interest', drawing on earlier notions of a 'Protestant cause', had (as seen in the previous chapter) been used by Cromwell to describe his efforts to support the Waldensians in the 1650s. Yet it began to be used more widely in the late seventeenth century, not least because disputes over the correct application of Protestant ideas were part and parcel of domestic partisan struggle in the period. This chapter charts the subsequent deployment of notions of the 'Protestant interest' to the start of the Seven Years' War.[2]

Much of the material in the chapter derives from Anglophone sources and commentators. This partly reflects the ways in which notions of the Protestant interest and a wider mission within Europe had a particular currency and utility for British politicians, especially of a whiggish stripe, in the period. It is worth pondering how much the defence of co-religionists was related to the growth of Britain's soft power in this period and, more broadly, how the acquisition processes for both hard and soft power connected with and fed off each other.[3] In other words, there is a need to think about the relationship between Britain's military capabilities and consequent coercive power (hard power) and the broader leverage that Britain gained through its cultural achievements, values and standing (soft power). This was, after all, the period commonly identified by international historians as marking Britain's ascent to great power status. Yet, it is also worth remembering that this was an age in which British concerns were increasingly intimately connected to a broader European agenda.[4] While James II and Anne may have wanted

---

[2] For further discussion of the ideas of the Protestant interest, see Andrew C. Thompson, *Britain, Hanover and the Protestant Interest* (Woodbridge: Boydell and Brewer, 2006), ch. 1.

[3] For the importance of soft and hard power, see Joseph Nye, *Soft Power* (New York: Public Affairs, 2004).

[4] The importance of the European dimension to British politics in this period has recently been highlighted by Brendan Simms, *Three Victories and a Defeat* (London: Allen Lane,

to turn their backs on the Continent (although both found it difficult to do so in practice), William III, George I and George II had political and dynastic ties to the Continent, not least through their extra-British territories. Consequently, this is British history that is very much rooted in a European context, not least because the sorts of concerns about the defence of Protestantism inevitably involved a transnational outlook and perspective.

The chapter begins by discussing the fate of the Huguenot diaspora in the aftermath of the revocation of the Edict of Nantes and the ways in which the fate of the Huguenots impinged on practical political considerations in the ensuing years. It then discusses other incidents that focused European attention on the position of Protestants in the early eighteenth century. All these incidents took place within central Europe, at Heidelberg, Thorn and Salzburg. The second half of the chapter also considers the different difficulties that attempts at intervention within eastern and central Europe faced when compared with France. The nature of ideas about persecution is also considered against a changing background of enlightened thought on toleration in theory and practice. Finally, the chapter also discusses both the options available to contemporary politicians and how they sought to ensure that the Protestant interest was consistently defended.

The revocation of the Edict of Nantes (or the Edict of Fontainebleau as it is sometimes known) in October 1685[5] was to have significant implications for how Europeans thought about the legitimacy of interfering in the internal affairs of other European states. In one sense, the feeling that the revocation was the result of clerical pressure heightened Protestant distrust of popish prelates. Yet from another point of view, it was merely the latest in a line of setbacks that made 1685 seem like an *annus terribilis* for the Protestant cause in Europe. In February 1685, Charles II had died, shortly after having been received into the Catholic faith, leaving his British thrones to his openly Catholic brother, James, Duke of York. In May 1685, another Charles II, this time the Elector of the Palatinate, died childless meaning that the last Protestant elector of a territory that had traditionally been the bulwark of German Calvinism would be replaced by one of his Catholic Pfalz-Neuburg cousins. Fears about the parlous state of British Protestantism proved to be short-lived.

---

2007) and Tony Claydon, *Europe and the Making of England, 1660–1760* (Cambridge: Cambridge University Press, 2007).

[5] See Brian E. Strayer, 'The Edict of Fontainebleau (1685) and the Huguenots: Who's to Blame?', in *Persecution and Pluralism: Calvinists and Religious Minorities in Early Modern Europe 1550–1700*, ed. Richard Bonney and D. J. B. Trim (Oxford and Bern: Peter Lang, 2006), 273–94.

In 1688, the invasion of William of Orange, James's son-in-law and nephew, put Britain back on a recognisably Protestant course. The Bill of Rights (1689) and the Act of Settlement (1701) ensured that British monarchs would have to be Protestant for the foreseeable future. In an age when the confession of the monarch was still seen as being an important signal for the confession of the people, Protestant subjects began to breathe more easily again.[6]

Yet, as the rest of the chapter shows, it was precisely because the belief that the confession of the monarch need not necessarily be the same as that of the people was becoming more widespread that many of the problems relating to the rights of oppressed minorities began to emerge, not least in France and the Palatinate. Why, then, did the Huguenot exodus mark such an important turning point? On the one hand, it is important to acknowledge that the Huguenots were certainly neither the first nor the last group to be displaced in the long struggles that marked Europe's religious history in the post-Reformation era.[7] What their expulsion did do, however, was to give further weight to a creeping sense that had been developing within European Protestantism over the course of the seventeenth century that perhaps the true light of the gospel might not be winning through as quickly as might have been hoped. The sheer scale of the emigration must also have contributed to a growing feeling of alarm. Wherever Protestants looked around the map of Europe, their faith seemed to be under attack. William's accession to the British thrones in 1688 was a bright spot in a sky that was looking increasingly dark. The Huguenot exodus was, therefore, both an important contributory factor to, and a mechanism by which, a general crisis of European Protestantism could be articulated.

How was that so? For one thing, the very size of the Huguenot diaspora meant that news of the terrors of the *dragonnades* and the other mistreatments that Louis XIV inflicted upon his Protestant subjects could spread both quickly and widely, despite the reluctance of James II to allow the issue to be discussed in the English press.[8] Huguenots fleeing France found refuge all around France's northern and eastern borders – in Protestant cantons like Geneva and Vaud, in Protestant

[6] For an overview of these events, see Tim Harris, *Revolution* (London: Allen Lane, 2006).
[7] See Patrick Collinson, 'Europe in Britain: Protestant Strangers and the English Reformation', in *From Strangers to Citizens*, ed. Randolph Vigne and Charles Littleton (Brighton: Sussex Academic Press, 2001), 57–67, and D. J. B. Trim, 'Protestant Refugees in Elizabethan England and Confessional Conflict in France and the Netherlands, 1562– c. 1610', in *From Strangers to Citizens*, ed. Vigne and Littleton, 68–79.
[8] Robin Gwynn, *Huguenot Heritage*, 2nd edn (Brighton: Sussex Academic Press, 2001), ch. 8.

territories in south-west Germany (although the confessional switch of ruler in the Palatinate, a traditional refuge for Calvinists, was hardly helpful in this regard) and even further afield in places like Hanover and Brandenburg, in the United Provinces, in Britain itself and, eventually, in British colonial possessions in either Ireland or North America.[9] Once settled in their newly adopted countries, Huguenots quickly began to petition on behalf of friends and family left behind in France. The papers of any British secretary of state from the late seventeenth and early eighteenth centuries will reveal a fair number of requests for aid and succour on behalf of those sent to the notorious galleys. These requests tail off over time but the Duke of Newcastle, the great British political survivor of the first half of the eighteenth century, was still being petitioned, albeit occasionally, in the 1750s in his role as secretary of state.[10] The sufferings of Protestants might also feature in parliamentary debates. Foreign policy frequently provoked considerable discussion in the House of Commons in the eighteenth century and several of the cases discussed in this chapter were the subject both of direct epistolary contact with ministers and of parliamentary comment.

Yet appeals to authority were not the only tactic available to displaced French Protestants. What the Huguenots also did was to draw the attention of a broader public sphere to their sufferings.[11] They were able to achieve a considerable impact through their writings, often graphically illustrated with engravings depicting their sufferings, and spread their message far and wide. Huguenot campaigns of the late seventeenth and early eighteenth centuries displayed considerable similarities with later efforts on behalf of distressed Protestants. Some attention was devoted towards direct appeals to those in power but some effort, and this became greater over time, was devoted to persuading a growing public of the importance of the cause.

As the work of Graham Gibbs and others has shown,[12] Huguenot political writers enjoyed considerable success as journalists and propagandists. One example will have to suffice to illustrate the ways in which

---

[9] For estimates of the size of the emigration, see Gwynn, *Huguenot Heritage*, 30–2.

[10] Secker to Newcastle, Lambeth, 30 Aug. 1751, BL, Add. MSS 32725, fo. 103. For British concern about the situation in southern France, see also Robinson to Albemarle, Whitehall, 28 March 1754, BL, Add. MSS 32848, fo. 372. A petition from a Peter Loubié can be found in Robinson to Albemarle, Whitehall, 6 May 1754, BL, Add. MSS 32849, fo. 122.

[11] For a short introduction to the vitality of the public sphere in the British context, see Peter Lake and Steven C. A. Pincus, 'Rethinking the Public Sphere in Early Modern England', *Journal of British Studies* 45 (2006), 270–92.

[12] Graham C. Gibbs, 'Some Intellectual and Political Influences of the Huguenot Emigrés in the United Provinces, c. 1680–1730', *Bijdragen en mededelingen betreffende de geschiedenis der*

Huguenot figures took full advantage of the opportunities that came their way in exile. Abel Boyer was born in the upper Languedoc around 1667.[13] He left France in the aftermath of the revocation and was among the 50,000 or 60,000 refugees who fled to the United Provinces. Poverty may have led Boyer, like many of his contemporaries, into military service in the army of the Dutch republic but he did not remain a soldier for long.[14] He crossed the Channel in the wake of William's invasion in 1689, bearing a letter of introduction from Pierre Bayle to Bishop Burnet of Salisbury. Burnet was a passionate supporter of the Huguenot cause and, as Tony Claydon has shown,[15] one of the cheerleaders for William's Protestant credentials during the 1690s. Boyer had some literary success in the 1690s, writing a French textbook and translating plays by Racine. Yet his historical and political work has attracted the greatest attention. He published the first history of William III's reign in 1702–3 and then published an annual digest of events for each year of Anne's reign from 1703 onwards. Boyer was also involved in the publication of several newspapers, including the *Post Boy*, and hoped in 1710 to succeed Richard Steele as editor of the *Gazette*, the government's official organ, following the latter's resignation. This was not to be, but Boyer started his own periodical in 1711, *The political state of Great Britain*, which provided monthly summaries of important events both inside and outside Britain long after Boyer's death in 1729. Boyer's reports in the *Political state* remain an important source for the parliamentary history of the period.[16] Indeed, Boyer found himself in trouble on several occasions for publishing unauthorised accounts of parliamentary proceedings and had to content himself with publishing summaries at the end of each session.

While Boyer may have stopped publishing parliamentary material immediately in England, it is unlikely he was so careful with material he distributed to his contacts elsewhere in Europe. For, in addition to his

*Nederlanden* 90 (1975), 255–87, and Gibbs, 'Huguenot Contributions to the Intellectual Life of England, c. 1680–c. 1720, with some Asides on the Process of Assimilation', in *La Révocation de l'Édit de Nantes et les Provinces-Unies 1685*, ed. J. A. H. Bots and G. H. M. Posthumus Meyjes (Amsterdam and Maarssen: APA–Holland University Press, 1986), 181–200.

[13] Details of Boyer's life are drawn from Graham Gibbs's article in the *Oxford Dictionary of National Biography*.

[14] For a broader consideration of Huguenot military service, see Matthew Glozier and David Onnekink (eds.), *War, Religion and Service: Huguenot Soldiering, 1685–1713* (Aldershot: Ashgate, 2007).

[15] Tony Claydon, *William III and the Godly Revolution* (Cambridge: Cambridge University Press, 1996).

[16] Jeremy Black, *Parliament and Foreign Policy* (Cambridge: Cambridge University Press, 2004), 149–50.

increasing attachment to his adopted land, Boyer still viewed himself as both a Huguenot and a member of the European republic of letters. He was a regular writer of manuscript newsletters whose output was distributed widely within Europe.[17] One of the easy ways for Boyer to make use of his material was to send it to Huguenot contacts who were now conveniently scattered across European capitals and share his news through them. The speed with which information could travel meant that news would often reach Amsterdam more quickly from London than letters sent to either Exeter or Edinburgh. What this discussion of Boyer's output shows is the extent to which Huguenots in this period could make use of networks within the diaspora, which were often both economic and familial, to spread news and to ensure that their particular spin on European events received the attention that they felt it deserved. More generally, religious groups provided a readily accessible structure around which to organise campaigning and propagandistic efforts. The Protestant cause was simultaneously a national and a transnational concern and organisation of its defence could take place at both levels.

This is not the place to explore the importance of Huguenot involvement in the early spread of enlightened ideas.[18] However, it is worth noting the importance more generally of both Huguenots and enlightened thinkers in stressing the value of religious toleration.[19] One of the important intellectual shifts that made the justification of intervention on behalf of oppressed religious minorities possible was the growth in the notion of the unacceptability of persecution as part of the state's means of dealing with the religiously different. The change in modes of justification is, in itself, important. Whereas seventeenth-century protagonists might have viewed the religious struggle as one between the forces of light and darkness (with Protestantism and Catholicism being apportioned to particular sides according to conviction), Protestants began to develop an asymmetrical view of the clash of confessions in the early enlightened period. Protestants regarded themselves as having moved beyond the apocalyptic struggles of the earlier period but they still thought that their Catholic opponents viewed persecution as a legitimate means of achieving their political ends. Hence, the case in favour of toleration and against persecution had to be made loudly and clearly.

---

[17] Thompson, *Britain, Hanover*, 86, for evidence of Boyer's newsletters surviving in Hanoverian archives.

[18] See Margaret Jacob, *The Radical Enlightenment* (London: Allen and Unwin, 1981) and Jonathan I. Israel, *Radical Enlightenment* (Oxford: Oxford University Press, 2001).

[19] For a thorough discussion of all aspects of this question, see John Marshall, *John Locke, Toleration and Early Enlightenment Culture* (Cambridge: Cambridge University Press, 2006), especially chs. 4 and 14.

Boyer's work also provides a link to one of the more important episodes in the history of intervention in the period – the Camisard rebellion in France. The Cévennes area of France had traditionally been an area of considerable Huguenot strength and the uncompromising physical geography of the area meant that the French state had to make significant efforts to enforce its will in the region. When the war of the Spanish succession broke out, the Cévenol Huguenots rose in revolt, taking the name Camisards from their distinctive shirts.[20] The bulk of the fighting was concentrated in the early years of the war and the initial surge of revolt had largely been controlled by 1704 when an agreement was reached between Jean Cavalier, one of the Huguenot leaders who was to end his varied career as governor of Jersey, and Marshal Villars, although intermittent skirmishing did continue thereafter.

The precise details of the campaign are of secondary interest here, although the degree of British interest in supporting the rebels was probably greater than Laurence Huey Boles allows.[21] What is more interesting is the ways in which contemporary writers justified the need to help the Huguenot rebels. Boyer argued in a pamphlet published soon after the outbreak of the rebellion that the revolt was a truly providential opportunity, given the way in which Louis's oppression of his own subjects had provoked divine wrath.[22] Boyer was keen to assert that the Huguenots were not, in fact, rebels. Rather, they were acting out of the same principles that had secured the Glorious Revolution in Britain for, as Grotius put it, 'it is a receiv'd Maxim, that subjects are not bound to obey the Magistrate, when he decrees any thing contrary either to the Law of Nature or of GOD'.[23] Importantly, Boyer glossed Grotius's comments by adding that, although the right to take up arms against the magistrate was disputed, it was clear that, as Seneca put it, 'a prince may make War upon another Prince his Neighbour, who oppresses his

---

[20] For a discussion of the revolt that tries to contextualise the Camisard experience within a broader framework of early modern revolt, see Linda and Marsah Frey, *Societies in Upheaval: Insurrections in France, Hungary and Spain in the Early Eighteenth Century* (New York: Greenwood Press, 1987).

[21] See Laurence Huey Boles, Jr, *The Huguenots, the Protestant Interest and the War of the Spanish Succession, 1702–1714* (New York: Peter Lang, 1997), chs. 5–6. Boles is generally sceptical of the success of Huguenot campaigns in influencing allied policy during the war although the range of material he uses is somewhat slight. For the efforts that the Royal Navy was able to make in support of rebels, see Andrew Wellum-Kent, 'The Role of Frigates in Royal Naval Operations in the Early Eighteenth-century Mediterranean' (BA diss., University of Cambridge, 2008).

[22] [Abel Boyer], *The lawfulness, glory and advantage of giving immediate and effectual relief to the protestants in the Cevennes together with the ways and means to succeed in such an enterprise*, 2nd edn (London, 1703), 4–5.

[23] *Ibid.*, 6. The reference appears to be to Grotius, *De jure belli ac pacis*, 2:25.

own Subjects; because such a War is often attended with the Protection of the Innocent'.[24] Boyer thought that such good policy had been characteristic of England's attitudes under Elizabeth I, although he was less convinced by her Stuart successors.[25] Boyer believed that an insurrection would be of great utility in disrupting Louis's armed forces, through the distraction that it would provide, and that strong British support would probably cause neighbouring Protestants to rise up as well, further weakening the French crown.[26] In terms of how aid might most effectively be given, Boyer argued that the first step was to send a strong naval squadron to the area.[27] Sea power alone would not be enough and some land forces would also be needed. While Boyer was aware that troops were in short supply, he argued that some of the Huguenot officers on the Irish establishment might be glad of the action and that they would quickly be able to raise troops. Additionally, both the United Provinces and Prussia had regiments of French Protestant troops who would be ideal for such an intervention.[28]

Boyer's overall claim was that helping the Protestants in the Cévennes was both legitimate and necessary. Like Pierre Jurieu, the Huguenot pastor and controversialist, Boyer was prepared to argue that those who practised intolerance had lost the right of obedience from their subjects.[29] While much later interest in the Camisard revolt has focused on the mystical and millenarian aspects, exemplified by the prophets Élie Marion and Durand Fage, figures like Boyer show how more pragmatic arguments in favour of intervention could be articulated.[30] Something much larger than simply the fate of the Huguenots was at stake – the very survival of European Protantism was tied in to resistance to the power of Louis XIV.

In this respect Boyer was very much in line with a growing tide of European Protestant opinion that saw in Louis XIV the ultimate expression of 'popish' rule. The epithet had been common currency in British domestic politics in the seventeenth century when it had frequently been coupled with 'arbitrary government' to indicate that which any right-thinking Briton would want to avoid. However, by the late seventeenth century, the outlines of a consistent Protestant opposition to popery in foreign affairs had begun to coalesce as well. The precise timing is difficult to ascertain, not least because those who advocated an approach to foreign affairs based around the defence of the Protestant interest wanted to situate themselves at the end of a long tradition, rather than

[24] Ibid., 7.      [25] Ibid., 8–9.      [26] Ibid., 10–11.      [27] Ibid., 21.      [28] Ibid., 22–3.
[29] Boles, Huguenots, 117–18, and Frey and Frey, Societies in Upheaval, 13.
[30] Boles, Huguenots, 132–3.

suggesting that what they were doing marked a departure from previous practice.[31] Yet, as Tony Claydon argues, it seems clear that the outlines of a different approach to foreign affairs were emerging by the end of the Nine Years' War.[32] Claydon argues that a shift took place both in the way that the threat posed by Louis XIV was portrayed and in the best means to combat it at around this point. Louis had already achieved the status of a bogeyman within British Protestant argument.[33] He was condemned for his persecuting zeal, for his threat to the reformation throughout Europe, for his cruelty and for his infidelity – as doubly captured in claims that he was a 'Christian Turk'.[34] The stage was now set for a shift away from a language that focused on the evils of Louis's rule, particularly emphasising the threat posed by his universal monarchist pretensions, to one in which the key component was how best to challenge it.[35] One aspect of this shift, as I have argued elsewhere,[36] was the growth of views of British interests that centred on notions of the balance of power as an effective counterweight to the popish threat. Yet for the purposes of the history of interventionist thinking, balance of power thinking alone was unlikely to be sufficient to commend action. Rather, other arguments had to be brought into play that, combined with strategic considerations of the general desirability of an equilibrium of forces within Europe, might tip the balance from passive observation into active intervention.

The early modern period was one in which considerable emphasis was placed on the importance of oaths and agreements. Natural law thinkers contended that human societies had originated in an agreement between the ruler and ruled to come together, under certain conditions, to move from a state of nature into civil society. The breaking of oaths and agreements was often seen, in an era marked out by the depth and violence of civil wars, as being the solvent of human society and the consequences of either rulers or ruled transgressing against either the law of nature or the law of God could be both serious and long-lived. In a period in which notions of religious toleration were emerging only slowly, John Locke could famously refuse to extend the benefits of

---

[31] Thus writers such as Charles Davenant, who argued for the importance of defending Protestant claims in the face of the universal monarchist threat from France, sought to place his recommendations about the direction of British policy as the logical outcome of British designs since at least the sixteenth century. See Thompson, *Britain, Hanover*, 36–8.

[32] Claydon, *Europe and the Making of England*, 192–3.     [33] *Ibid.*, ch. 3.

[34] *The most Christian Turk: or, a view of the life and bloody reign of Lewis XIV* (London, 1690).

[35] Claydon, *Europe and the Making of England*, 194.

[36] Thompson, *Britain, Hanover*, 39–42.

toleration towards atheists because their disbelief in divine punishment meant they had no reason to keep their oaths and contracts. Perfidy was, then, a serious offence.

At an international level, Louis XIV was accused not just of breaking his word but also of breaking international agreements. It was the structure of international agreements and guarantees that was to prove particularly important in the other instances of potential intervention discussed in the remainder of the chapter. The Treaties of Westphalia (1648) had brought the Thirty Years' War to an end and had attempted to regulate confessional affairs within the Holy Roman Empire. The defence of Westphalian provisions was to become fundamental to Protestant interventionism. One important aspect of the treaties was that the confessional map of the Empire had supposedly been fixed as a result of the treaties. On an individual basis, there was not supposed to be any civic discrimination on religious grounds. Those who were of a different confession to the prince were to be allowed to emigrate freely without loss of property. If Protestants or Catholics could show that they had enjoyed a measure of public or private toleration by specific agreement or custom in 1624, then these rights were to be preserved. More generally, the post-Westphalian legal framework allowed subjects to remove tyrannical princes.[37] The treaties had decreed that, unlike other issues where decisions were to be taken on the basis of majority votes, when it came to religious disagreements direct negotiations between Protestants and Catholics must take place to achieve a resolution. Yet, despite the seemingly clear provisions, areas of dispute soon arose.

One of these related to the question of what happened when a ruler changed confession. Earlier agreements within the Empire, most notably the Religious Peace of Augsburg (1555), had stressed the importance of the faith of the people following the faith of the ruler ('cuius regio, eius religio'). Yet this seemed to conflict with the Westphalian agreements. The issue was of more than theoretical interest to the Protestant community. The conversion traffic in the seventeenth century was nearly all one way. The situation in the Palatinate was but one example of a broader trend. Throughout the Empire the combination of a Catholicism revitalised by the efforts of the Counter-Reformation and the prospect of imperial patronage, not least within the *Reichskirche*, was exercising a considerable pull on German Protestant rulers. The balance of power within the electoral college was swinging dramatically in favour of the Catholic powers. Bavaria had been elevated to electoral status after

---

[37] Werner Trossbach, 'Fürstenabsetzungen im 18. Jahrhundert', *Zeitschrift für historische Forschung* 13 (1986), 425–54.

1648, adding another Catholic power to Bohemia and the archbishops of Mainz, Trier and Cologne. By 1700, although Hanover had been added to the Protestant party, the Palatinate had fallen into Catholic hands and Augustus of Saxony had decided that Poland was worth a mass and converted as well. This meant that Brandenburg and Hanover found themselves arrayed against seven Catholic electors, thus making it even more important that religious matters would be settled directly and not by majority votes.[38]

The continuing importance of confessional strife within the Empire has been a theme that has gained increasing importance within the historiography in recent years.[39] Historians now acknowledge that the result of the Westphalian treaties was to transfer confessional conflict into a new context – predominantly a legal one – rather than abolish it entirely. The records of the *Reichstag* (the Empire's representative body) for this period are full of disputes about religious questions. In part, this was a reflection of relative Protestant weakness. In circumstances where the Catholics increasingly enjoyed a majority in the each of the three colleges of the Empire (electors, princes, and cities) it made good tactical sense to ensure that problems were treated as 'religious' and therefore subject to direct negotiation, rather than majority voting. Yet it must also be acknowledged that the smoke was not entirely appearing without fire and that there was a series of incidents that provoked a Protestant reaction.

One of the more important of these incidents was a dispute over the use of the *Heiliggeistkirche* in Heidelberg. The trouble arose because the Catholic elector, Karl Philipp, had become dissatisfied with the arrangement whereby the church was divided, with the Catholics having the choir and the Protestants the nave. The church was one of a number in the Palatinate which had become subject to a so-called 'simultaneum' whereby use was shared between Protestants and Catholics. This could either involve a physically divided building, as in Heidelberg, or an arrangement that stipulated that Protestant services would take place at one time and Catholic ones at another. The potential for conflict in

---

[38] Thompson, *Britain, Hanover*, 18–20.
[39] Gabriele Haug-Moritz, 'Kaisertum und Parität: Reichspolitik und Konfession nach dem Westfälischen Frieden', *Zeitschrift für historische Forschung* 19 (1992), 445–82, and Haug-Moritz, 'Corpus Evangelicorum und deutscher Dualismus', in *Alternativen zur Reichsverfassung in der Frühen Neuzeit?*, ed. Volker Press (Munich: Oldenbourg, 1995), 189–207; Jürgen Luh, *Unheiliges Römisches Reich: der konfessionelle Gegensatz 1648 bis 1806* (Potsdam: Verlag für Berlin-Brandenburg, 1995); Dieter Stievermann, 'Politik und Konfession im 18. Jahrhundert', *Zeitschrift für historische Forschung* 18 (1991), 177–99.

such circumstances was readily apparent and it was often difficult to manage arrangements in practice. The 'simultaneum' had been introduced into the Palatinate as a result of the Treaty of Ryswick (1697). Louis XIV had invaded the Palatinate in 1688–9 at the start of the Nine Years' War. Faced with the steep hill on which Heidelberg castle sits, Louis had simply positioned his artillery at the bottom of the rise and blown the walls away, and the impact of his armies had been similarly destructive across the entire electorate. One of the things that French soldiers had done was to evict Protestants from their churches and put Catholic congregations in their place. The fourth article of the Ryswick treaty had allowed Catholicism to continue to be practised in those places where it had been introduced – hence the sharing arrangements. The Protestants, unsurprisingly, had been less than impressed by this and had sought clarification of their legal rights on several occasions (in 1705, for example, the Elector of Brandenberg had tried to broker an agreement). Matters had come to a head in 1719 with the elector's decision to end the sharing agreement in Heidelberg. This followed a ban on the use and publication of the Heidelberg catechism, a foundational text of the Calvinist faith, that the elector had introduced earlier in the year.

The situation for the Protestants of the Palatinate, therefore, looked distinctly bleak by the autumn of 1719. Yet there were other Protestant powers who were willing to offer their help. Both Britain-Hanover and Brandenburg-Prussia were quick to dispatch envoys to Heidelberg to negotiate with the elector on behalf of the distressed Protestants. Heidelberg was not the only place where the matter was discussed. The *Corpus Evangelicorum*, the umbrella organisation for the Protestant powers at the Imperial Diet at Regensburg, quickly took up the cause of the Palatine Protestants. The Hanoverian envoy Rudolf Johann von Wrisberg was keen to press for a broader restoration of Protestant rights and thought that this opportunity was too good to miss. Wrisberg's aim was for a complete abolition of the 'simultaneum' system and a return to Westphalian rights.[40] Prussian representatives also seemed keen to use the incident to press home broader Protestant claims.[41] Beyond these two sets of negotiations, the matter was also taken up with Emperor Charles VI directly by British diplomats in Vienna, François Louis de Pesme de Saint Saphorin and William, Earl Cadogan. Although one aspect of their negotiations was the recognition by Charles VI of

[40] Wrisberg to George I, Regensburg, 16 Oct. 1719 and 23 Oct. 1719, H HStA, Calenberg Brief 11, 2976, fo. 53r and fos. 106–7.
[41] Thompson, *Britain, Hanover*, 71.

George I's rights to the duchies of Bremen and Verden, they were also concerned to ensure that the religious problems within the Empire were satisfactorily resolved as well.

The strategies that British, Prussian and Hanoverian diplomats adopted during the course of these negotiations all had to deal with the Elector Palatine's consistent position that the internal religious disputes inside his territories were nobody's business but his own.[42] The response to these complaints was to insist that international agreements of various sorts had been broken and therefore some sort of restitution was necessary. One course of action that the British explored at this point was to see whether it would be possible for Britain to become a guarantor power of the Westphalian agreement.[43]

The advantages of such an arrangement were manifold. The emperor had claimed that it was impossible for princes within the Holy Roman Empire to make any sort of agreement with a foreign prince on their own initiative, about religious disputes or anything else. The status of the guarantor powers was, however, different. One reading of the legal situation was that a guarantor power, precisely because of that role, had a right to intervene (or interfere, to take another view). While it was unlikely that France would want to defend beleaguered Protestants, especially as it was a treaty with France that had created the difficult conditions in the Palatinate in the first place, a strong Protestant power, like Britain, was much more likely to be willing to fight the Protestants' corner. Sweden, although a guarantor power, was too busy with fighting for survival against Russian advances in 1719 to do anything within the Empire. Talk of Britain becoming a guarantor continued intermittently throughout the Palatine crisis. Stanhope raised the prospect again in a letter to Saint Saphorin and Cadogan in May 1720.[44] What this indicates is the importance of some sort of sense of international community and an international legal framework of rights and obligations for legitimating intervention. As Charles Whitworth, the British minister plenipotentiary in Berlin, put it, 'whereever a religion is established by law, the professors of it are at liberty to express their opinions in such terms as are thought most proper and significative'.[45] In the case of the Palatinate, military action, although threatened, never came to pass. Instead, the *Corpus Evangelicorum* insisted that after a deal had been brokered, a representative was sent to the Palatinate to ensure that the

---

[42]  See Haldane to Craggs, Neckerhausen, 25 Oct. 1719, NA, SP 81/120.
[43]  Stanhope to Whitworth, Göhrde, 27 Oct. 1719, BL, Add. MSS 37376, fo. 164*v*.
[44]  Stanhope to St Saphorin and Cadogan, Whitehall, 20 May 1720, NA, SP 104/42.
[45]  Whitworth to Haldane, Berlin, 28 Nov. 1719, BL, Add. MSS 37377, fo. 100*v*.

conditions of the agreement were being properly observed. A Hanoverian official was duly dispatched, although he encountered difficulties because all the Palatine officials had been forbidden to speak to him.[46] Although Karl Philipp could insist on practical non-cooperation with the representative of the *Corpus*, neither he nor the emperor had been able to prevent the dispatching of an observer to monitor the situation on the ground.

The pressure that had been brought to bear on Karl Philipp was not simply diplomatic. The public sphere had also been used extensively to illuminate the plight of the Palatine Protestants. Publications like Abel Boyer's *Political state of Great Britain* carried extensive reports on the developing crisis.[47] It is perhaps not entirely coincidental that a publication run by one religious refugee should include such detailed reporting of the fate of his co-religionists in another part of Europe. Beyond printed material, traces of interest in the events in the Palatinate can be found in manuscript newsletters circulating around Europe, such as the Dutch newsletters received by the Hanoverian ministry.[48] The Archbishop of Canterbury and the Bishop of Gloucester both mentioned the issue during speeches in the House of Lords.[49] Once again, the dual-track approach adopted by earlier Huguenot polemicists is visible. Part of the campaign of persuasion was directed specifically at those in authority, while efforts were also made to cultivate public support more broadly. The oxygen of publicity was also important during the next religious crisis that merits attention – the so-called massacre at Torun or Thorn in Royal (Polish) Prussia in July 1724.

The spark for the incident was a common source of tension in multiconfessional towns – how to behave appropriately during the religious ceremonies or processions of the other confession. A Catholic procession on 16 July 1724 deteriorated into a riot. The Catholics claimed that a Lutheran student had failed to remove his hat when the procession went by and had mocked the host. The Lutherans claimed that the student had been forced to bow to the host by students at the Jesuit Gymnasium. In the ensuing scuffle prisoners were taken by both sides. Protestants stormed the Jesuit school to free the imprisoned Lutherans. Eventually the town's mayor called out the militia and order was restored. The town's Jesuits complained to the Polish estates that the mayor had been

---

[46] Thompson, *Britain, Hanover*, 90.

[47] See *Political State of Great Britain*, XVIII (1719), 196–201, 221–2, 301–8, 414–15, and XIX (1720), 600–30.

[48] Newsletters from Amsterdam, 1 Mar. 1720 and 20 Apr. 1720. H HStA, Calenberg Brief 24, 2308, fos. 52r, 104r.

[49] Newsletter from London, 3 June 1720, H HStA, Calenberg Brief 24, 1726, fo. 289.

negligent in delaying the dispatch of the militia to quell the violence and this had led to the unnecessary destruction of Jesuit property, including damage to religious relics and statues of the Virgin. As a result, heavy fines were imposed upon the town and the last remaining Protestant church was confiscated and handed over to the Catholics. In addition, several prominent citizens, including the mayor and his deputy, were sentenced to death. The reaction to the sentences in Protestant Europe was one of disbelief, but disbelief was replaced by anger when the sentences were carried out on 7 December 1724. Although the deputy mayor was pardoned, a number of other executions took place. The precise number is disputed but it was certainly less than fifteen. Hence, to describe the events as a 'massacre' was to stretch the limits of the accepted understanding of the term.

Nevertheless, confessional quarrels like this continued to be able to provoke fierce reactions on both sides. As in the earlier Palatine case, the initial British and Prussian response was largely diplomatic. Letters were sent from both George I and Frederick William I to Augustus of Saxony-Poland decrying what had happened. Initial epistolary contacts were followed up with more concrete diplomatic pressure through the dispatch of diplomats to Augustus's court. Edward Finch, the British minister plenipotentiary at the *Reichstag* in Regensburg, was ordered by Townshend to travel to Dresden in January 1725. His instructions told him to cooperate closely with the Prussian minister. He should petition Augustus for the restitution of Protestant rights.[50] The basis for this appeal was the guarantees supplied by the Treaty of Oliva (1660) which, amongst other things, was supposed to regulate relations between Protestants and Catholics in Royal Prussia. Both Sweden and Brandenburg had been among the original signatories and Britain had become a guarantor power during the course of the 1660s. It was again on the basis of guarantor status that Britain and Prussia were prepared to justify their interference in the internal workings of the Polish state. British diplomats hinted at various courts that military intervention was a distinct possibility. Reports of Prussian troop movements with encampments close to the Saxon border surfaced. In the end military intervention did not take place. Some of the concerns about the position of Protestants in Poland were taken up in the negotiations that led to the Treaty of Hanover between Britain, Prussia and France in 1725. The first separate article, for example, related to how best the protection of Protestants in Thorn and other parts of Royal Poland might be secured. British officials were keen that this

---

[50] Townshend to Finch, Whitehall, 15 Jan. 1725, NA, SP 88/29.

aspect of the treaty should be communicated to both the Dutch and the Swedes, no doubt because they hoped that it would increase the chances of those powers joining the alliance.[51]

Printed reactions to events in Thorn displayed considerable interest in questions of how action against Catholic powers might be justified. There were some signs of a co-ordinated propagandistic effort with the Prussian court preacher Daniel Ernst Jablonski producing a number of works condemning Catholic actions.[52] Within English publications the events in Thorn were assimilated into a broader set of concerns about what might happen to Protestantism elsewhere in Europe. One tract explicitly linked events in Thorn to moves by Catholic powers within the Empire to attack Protestant rights and undermine Westphalian provisions.[53] The importance of upholding the Treaty of Oliva featured as well, as did the appeal for a greater degree of Protestant unity with Calvinists and Lutherans alike being called upon to set aside their differences to defend themselves against a common enemy.[54]

Another tract by Charles Owen took a stronger line.[55] Owen claimed that to remonstrate on behalf of distressed Protestants to Jesuits was 'to address the Dumb and Deaf'.[56] Owen considered whether direct retaliation by Protestant powers against their own Catholic subjects would be appropriate although on balance he thought that this was a bad idea. Some sort of use of force would probably be necessary to restrain Catholic advances.[57] Owen's preferred 'reasonable' solution was to allow Catholics to depart from Protestant states with their wealth and possessions, which he claimed had worked as a deterrent in certain circumstances.[58] Owen also considered how Protestants might best react to the situation. As private citizens, Christians had to remain subject to higher powers and not act on their own initiative. Yet, the same rules did not

---

[51] H. Walpole to Townshend, Fontainebleau, 15 Sept. 1725, BL, Add. MSS 32744, fo. 198r.

[52] For Jablonski's career more generally, see Hermann Dalton, *Daniel Ernst Jablonski* (Berlin: Warneck, 1903) and Norman Sykes, *Daniel Ernst Jablonski and the Church of England* (London: SPCK, 1950). For his involvement in Thorn, see Thompson, *Britain, Hanover*, 102. Jablonski was the author of *Das Betrübte Thorn, Oder die Geschichte so sich zu Thorn Von Dem II. Jul. 1724. biß auf gegenwärtige Zeit zugetragen, Aus zuverläßigen Nachrichten Unverfänglich zusammen getragen, und der Recht- und Wahrheit-liebenden Welt zur Beurtheilung migetheilet* (Berlin, 1725) and contributed material for *Thornische Deckwürdigkeiten, Worinnen die im Jahr Christi 1724 und vorhergehenden Zeiten verunglückte Stadt Thorn Im Königl. Pohlnischen Hertzogthum Preußen Von einer unparteyischen Feder gründlich vorgestellet wird* (Berlin, 1726).

[53] [Jean Bion], *A faithful and exact Narrative of the horrid tragedy; lately acted at Thorn, in Polish Prussia* (London, 1725), 35.

[54] *Ibid.*, 35–6.    [55] Owen, *An Alarm to protestant princes and people*.    [56] *Ibid.*, 21.

[57] *Ibid.*, 22.    [58] *Ibid.*, 24–6.

apply to princes. What had happened was a declaration of war against Protestants. To use another metaphor, if a house caught fire in a town, then all the neighbours would run to help to suppress the flames, even if this meant blowing up houses to stop the spread of the flames.[59] Owen discussed cases, mainly from the classical world, of the just suppression of tyrants who had put themselves at war with society.[60] Kings were not just responsible for their own subjects but had 'lying upon them the Care of human society'. Additionally, Protestants should be seen as one 'Body or Society, united for mutual Defence, animated by one Soul viz the Reformation, whose Interest is to preserve entire all its Parts, and make reprisals upon all Aggressors and their Allies'.[61] Owen concluded that when the shepherd of the people should become a wolf then a remedy did exist because 'Governments are not set up for the advantage, pleasure and glory of Princes, but for the good of society'.[62] He illustrated this claim by citing Aristotle and Plato, as well as Grotius and the history of British intervention on behalf of distressed Protestants in continental Europe.[63] Owen was, admittedly, a somewhat controversial figure, as a vigorous defender of both the Protestant succession and the rights of his fellow Protestant dissenters (he was a Presbyterian minister in Warrington). That said, his arguments show the extent to which it was possible to advance a consistent intellectual case for intervention when persecution was viewed as a direct attack on a common group that had rights that ought to be defended by other members of that group.

The reactions to the expulsion of the Protestant population of the archbishopric of Salzburg in 1731 differ slightly from those to the crises in Heidelberg and Thorn. Within the public sphere the events provoked a huge reaction and the history of the expulsion has probably also been better served by modern historiography.[64] Within Britain, news of the expulsions led to a concerted campaign by the Society for the Promotion of Christian Knowledge both to inform the public about the fate of the Salzburgers and to raise money on their behalf.[65] Yet there seemed to be a greater reluctance on the part of Britain and Prussia to intervene militarily on this occasion, partly due to the practical difficulties of doing anything.

---

[59] *Ibid.*, 26–7.     [60] *Ibid.*, 28.     [61] *Ibid.*, 29.     [62] *Ibid.*, 30.     [63] *Ibid.*, 30–5.
[64] Artur Ehmer, *Das Schrifttum zur Salzburger Emigration 1731/33* (Hamburg: Sonderschriften des Vereins für Familienforschung in Ost- und Westpreußen, 1975) has an extensive bibliography of over sixty pages of contemporary works on the expulsion while Mack Walker, *The Salzburg Transaction* (Ithaca and London: Cornell University Press, 1992) provides an excellent study of the impact of the expulsion and its resonances within German culture.
[65] Thompson, *Britain, Hanover*, 159–64.

Relations between Protestants and Catholics had worsened after the election of Leopold Anton, Baron von Firmian as archbishop in 1727. Firmian was determined to root out Protestants in the upland areas of his diocese and was keen to seek Jesuit aid to achieve this aim. In October 1731 he issued his *Emigrationspatent* ('patent of emigration'). All adult Protestants were compelled to leave his territories; children under twelve had to remain behind. Protestant representatives in Regensburg complained that Firmian had contravened the provisions of the Westphalian treaties that stipulated both the length of time in which such expulsions could be carried out and how much of their property the refugees could take with them.

The problem was that by the time the complaints were made at the *Reichstag* the flow of refugees had already started and the Protestant powers had to deal with a practical refugee problem rather than argue about the legal niceties of the events that had led to its creation. Thus much of the work on the expulsions has focused on the ways in which a number of Protestant powers stepped in to provide succour for the refugees in their hour of need.[66] The willingness of both Hanover and Prussia to intervene may also have been related to the negotiations over the Pragmatic Sanction, the attempt by Charles VI to ensure that on his death his territories could pass to his eldest daughter, Maria Theresa.[67] Austrian foreign policy had become almost entirely focused on getting acceptance of the Sanction both within the Empire and by the other powers in Europe. The ratification of the agreement was slowly proceeding through the *Reichstag* at the point at which the dispute in Salzburg erupted. Charles VI needed the support of Salzburg in the princely college to steer the Sanction through so was unlikely to come out strongly against Firmian's actions. Both Hanover and Prussia hoped to extract concessions in other areas and had some success in this regard – Frederick William's offer to extend the right of immigration to the Salzburg exiles provided him with a welcome increase in population in an age when population and national strength were seen as synonymous and Charles VI agreed to limit the activities of the Ostend company thus appeasing British and Dutch worries about a potential rival for colonial trade. In contrast to the 1720s, when relations between Austria and the

---

[66] See Walker, *Salzburg Transaction*, for the role of Prussia. For the role that Britain-Hanover played, see Thompson, *Britain, Hanover*, 152–64, which includes discussion of how a small group of refugees ended up in the newly founded colony of Georgia.

[67] For a brief overview of the Pragmatic Sanction, see Charles W. Ingrao, *The Habsburg Monarchy, 1618–1815*, 2nd edn (Cambridge: Cambridge University Press, 2000), 128–30 and 142–9.

leading north German Protestant powers had tended to be antagonistic, there seemed to be less of a willingness to push the defence of the Protestant interest to the limit during the period of the Salzburg expulsion.

Concern for the defence of the Protestant interest had not, however, disappeared entirely. Attempts to abolish the Ryswick clause and defend the terms of the Westphalian agreements continued during the 1730s.[68] The final example that this chapter considers is also related to the upholding of legal arrangements but in a context other than the abolition of the Ryswick clause. Royal marriages were an important means of cementing alliances and projecting power and identity. Lesser families sought to enhance status by marriage into the royal great and the good. Confession could also be an important factor. George II's wife, Caroline of Ansbach-Bayreuth, had refused the advances of the Archduke Charles because it would have necessitated conversion to Catholicism. The propagandistic value of her refusal was subsequently exploited in Britain and elsewhere.[69] Matrimonial politics was much more of an issue for George II, with his seven surviving children, than it had been for his father, with only two. In 1740, Mary, his penultimate daughter, was married to Frederick, the son of the landgrave of Hessen-Kassel. The match had come about for several reasons. The landgrave's elder brother was King of Sweden, Hessen-Kassel had been a fruitful source of troops for George II in times of need and the family was also Protestant. Like many royal marriages, dynastic expediency did not necessarily translate straightforwardly into marital bliss. Mary's new husband was brutal and violent and took several mistresses. Such behaviour was far from unusual. What was more extraordinary was Frederick's decision in 1749 to convert to Catholicism ostensibly to increase the likelihood of being reunited with his Catholic mistress in the afterlife. News of Frederick's decision did not become public until 1754.

Mary's father was not best pleased by the news that his son-in-law had turned papist.[70] George dispatched a trusted confidant, Count von der Schulenburg, to Kassel. George was clearly concerned about the broader implications that Frederick's conversion might have for the religious situation within the *Reich* and Europe.[71] Ultimately an

---

[68] Thompson, *Britain, Hanover*, 182–4.
[69] R. L. Arkell, *Caroline of Ansbach* (London: Oxford University Press, 1939), 13, and Hannah Smith, *Georgian Monarchy* (Cambridge: Cambridge University Press, 2006), 32–5.
[70] Much of the Hanoverian material on the conversion can be found in H HStA, Hann. 92, 1991.
[71] Draft George II to William of Hessen-Kassel, Kensington, [October 1754], *ibid.*, fo. 27.

agreement was reached by which Frederick promised to allow his wife to bring up his sons within the Protestant faith, a formal separation would take place and Mary would be given the revenues from the county of Hanau as a means to sustain herself and her sons. This agreement had been worked out between the landgrave and his son. George and his Hanoverian ministers were concerned that guarantees for the safety of Protestantism within Hessen-Kassel needed to be guaranteed by the *Corpus Evangelicorum* as well. The agreement was even scrutinised by the Lord Chancellor, the Earl of Hardwicke, who pronounced himself satisfied with its provisions.[72] Hardwicke had been asked about whether it was a good idea for George II to offer to guarantee the agreement in either his royal or electoral capacity. Hardwicke opined that such a guarantee would be 'an Act highly becoming His Majesty's greatness of mind; his care of His Royal Family, & of the Protestant Religion'.[73] Once more the pursuit of guarantees and assurances was seen as being an integral part of defending Protestant interests within central Europe.

This brief discussion of how early eighteenth-century Protestants set about defending the rights of their co-religionists is suggestive in several respects. The importance of legal agreements, particularly the Westphalian treaties, has emerged clearly. Ensuring that the rights of conscience, as established by law, were defended was an important component of Protestant argument. Attempts to justify intervention to aid Protestants were much easier in situations where the legal rationale was clear. One consequence of this was that it was, perhaps, the case that it was more difficult to apply pressure over attacks on Protestants inside France and in Habsburg lands outside the borders of the *Reich* because of the absence of the necessary legal framework within which to make such claims. Austrian territory had expanded rapidly eastwards and southwards during the late seventeenth and early eighteenth centuries and successive Habsburg rulers sought to colonise their newly won possessions. Promises of land were attractive to both Protestants and Catholics alike but Protestants found it difficult to claim that persecution, perceived or real, was illegal in the brave new legal world of the military border.

Moreover, intervention by Protestant powers in the face of Habsburg persecution was always likely to be a more difficult proposition than in France. For better or worse, for much of the late seventeenth and early eighteenth centuries, France was perceived to be the greatest threat to European stability and the Habsburgs an important component of the

---

[72] Hardwicke to Holdernesse, Powis House, 13 Dec. 1754, *ibid.*, fo. 237r.
[73] *Ibid.*, fo. 238r.

coalition to prevent French hegemony. Nevertheless, it was still possible to make arguments to justify intervention, even in the absence of overt treaty obligations. As some of the authors quoted in the chapter demonstrate, natural law theorists, like Grotius, could be combined with older work about the dangers posed by tyrannical regimes to show that intervention was not only right but also necessary. The notion that persecution was a declaration of war by rulers on their subjects was a potentially powerful argument as well, precisely because it was then possible to utilise a pre-existing set of arguments about just wars. This type of argument, designed primarily for the public sphere, had significant implications. Arguments that claimed that Protestants, regardless of their geographical location, were a group that enjoyed a particular set of rights and privileges could potentially be universalised and extended to cover the whole of humanity. The extent to which explicit arguments were made about the rights that all rulers had to defend human society as a whole is also noteworthy. Concerns about common humanity had, however, yet to separate themselves entirely from partisan confessional antipathy. From the point of view of the late seventeenth and early eighteenth centuries the degree of cooperation between different varieties of Protestant is remarkable in itself but the long-term implications of these changes are considerable.

# 4 'A false principle in the Law of Nations': Burke, state sovereignty, [German] liberty, and intervention in the Age of Westphalia

*Brendan Simms*

You hope, Sir, that I think the French deserving of Liberty? I certainly do. I certainly think that all men who desire it, deserve it. It is not the reward of our Merit or the acquisition of our industry. It is our Inheritance. It is the birthright of our species ... A positively Vicious and abusive Government ought to be changed and, if necessary, by Violence, if it cannot be (as is sometimes it is the case), Reformed.

Edmund Burke to Charles-Jean-François Depont, November 1789[1]

A more mischievous idea cannot exist than that any degree of wickedness, violence and oppression may prevail in a country, that the most abominable, murderous and exterminatory rebellions may rage in it, or the most atrocious and bloody tyranny may domineer, and that no neighbouring power can take cognizance of either or afford succour to the miserable sufferers.

Edmund Burke to Lord Grenville, Beaconsfield, 18 August 1792[2]

To many International Relations theorists and historians of international law, the Treaties of Westphalia which brought the Thirty Years' War to an end in 1648 represent a watershed in thinking about state sovereignty. Before then, the orthodoxy runs, European diplomacy was characterised by the post-Reformation antagonism between Catholicism, especially Counter-Reformation Catholicism, and various forms of Protestantism. Thereafter, so the argument continues, states

*The author would like to thank the following for their most helpful comments on various drafts of the text: Hamish Scott, Richard Bourke, Duncan Bell, Jo Whaley, Andrew Thompson, Stephen Wertheim, Chris Brown, Daniel Moyn, Patrick Milton, Jennifer Pitts, and David Trim. I am also most grateful for observations made on the original paper by Tim Blanning, Derek Beales, and Peter Mandler. Mark Austin and Charlotte Lee very kindly helped with preparing bibliographic materials.*

[1] Edmund Burke to Charles-Jean-François Depont, Nov. 1789, in Alfred Cobban and Robert A. Smith (eds.), *The Correspondence of Edmund Burke*, vol. VI: *July 1789–December 1791* (Cambridge: Cambridge University Press, and Chicago: University of Chicago Press, 1967), 41, 48.

[2] Edmund Burke to Lord Grenville, Beaconsfield, 18 Aug. 1792, in P. J. Marshall and John A. Woods (eds.), *The Correspondence of Edmund Burke*, vol. VII: *January 1792–August 1794* (Cambridge: Cambridge University Press, and Chicago: University of Chicago Press, 1968), 176–7.

accepted that religion was the preserve of the ruler; the principle of *cuius regio, eius religio*, which the Treaty of Augsburg had established in 1555, and which stipulated that populations should adopt the religion of their rulers, was put on a permanent footing. This, it is said, paved the way for the recognition of state sovereignty at the close of the Thirty Years' War nearly a century later.[3] Thus Thomas G. Weiss argues, 'the current foundations of international law with regards to sovereignty were shaped by . . . the Treaties of Westphalia in 1648'.[4] Central to this conception of sovereignty was the notion that in the state system – or the society of states, if you prefer – interference in the internal affairs of another state should be impermissible.[5] The United Nations clearly thought so too, as expressed in the General Assembly's December 1965 'Declaration on the Inadmissibility of Intervention in the Domestic Affairs of States and the Protection of their Independence and Sovereignty'.[6] It is on the basis of this understanding, for example, that many today speak of 'humanitarian intervention' in the 1990s as a break with the 'Westphalian System' only made possible by the end of the Cold War.[7]

It is not surprising that they should think this, because so many contemporaries spoke in similar terms, either out of genuine belief or because it suited them. Thus the early eighteenth-century German philosopher and political thinker Christian Wolff argued that 'To interfere in the government of another, in whatever way indeed that

---

[3] For a subtle restatement of this orthodoxy, see Daniel Philpott, 'The Religious Roots of Modern International Relations', *World Politics* 52 (January 2000), 206–45, esp. 211 and 213. See also Philpott, *Revolutions in Sovereignty* (Princeton: Princeton University Press, 2001).

[4] Thomas G. Weiss, *Humanitarian Intervention: Ideas in Action* (Cambridge: Polity Press, 2007), 14.

[5] For example, in K. J. Holsti's widely read *International Politics: A Framework for Analysis*, 4th edn (Englewood Cliffs, NJ: Prentice Hall, 1983), 4, 83–4. For a critical summary of this view and further literature, see Benno Teschke, *The Myth of 1648: Class, Geopolitics and the Making of Modern International Relations* (London: Verso, 2003), 216. A good discussion of the centrality of sovereignty and intervention to current understandings of the international order can be found in James Mayall (ed.), *The New Interventionism, 1991–1994: United Nations Experience in Cambodia, Former Yugoslavia and Somalia* (Cambridge: Cambridge University Press, 1996), esp. 3–7. (See now as a revised edition, Mats Berdal and Spyros Economides (eds.), *United Nations Interventionism, 1991–2004* (Cambridge: Cambridge University Press, 2007).) For the most effective critique of this idea of sovereigny, see Stephen D. Krasner's *Sovereignty: Organized Hypocrisy* (Princeton: Princeton University Press, 1999).

[6] See Hans J. Morgenthau, 'To Intervene or Not to Intervene', *Foreign Affairs* 45 (April 1967), 425–6.

[7] See Barry Buzan and Richard Little, 'Beyond Westphalia? Capitalism after the "Fall"', in *The Interregnum: Controversies in World Politics, 1989–1999*, ed. Michael Cox, Ken Booth, and Tim Dunne (Cambridge: Cambridge University Press, 1999), 89–104; Michael Ignatieff, *Empire Lite: Nation-building in Bosnia, Kosovo and Afghanistan* (London: Vintage, 2003), 57–9; Ignatieff, *Virtual War: Kosovo and Beyond* (New York: Macmillan, 2000), 163.

may be done is opposed to the natural liberty of nations, by virtue of which one is altogether independent of the will of other nations in its action'.[8] Another great theorist of eighteenth-century international law, Emmerich Vattel, also laid down very strict conditions under which it could be set aside – practically never, and then only if the state in question had already collapsed into factions. 'A nation', he wrote, 'is therefore mistress of her actions ... so that she is bound only by an internal obligation. If she abuses her liberty, she sins, but others must put up with it, having no right to tell her what to do'.[9] In fact, as Stephen Krasner, one of the few IR theorists to take recent research on seventeenth- and eighteenth-century Europe into account, suggests, the concept of inviolable state sovereignty was not so much elaborated by Wolff and Vattel as simply invented by them.[10]

The historical reality is that states had always intervened in each other's domestic affairs, either to secure strategic advantage, or to protect the rights of co-religionists, or the political liberties of the population, or for all three reasons combined. Indeed, there was an understanding among European powers that their freedom within the state system depended on the preservation of 'liberty' within certain states. At one level, of course, the 'liberty' that these sixteenth-, seventeenth- and eighteenth-century protagonists had in mind was very different from our twenty-first-century understanding of the term. They were referring to the legal or socio-economic 'privileges' which aristocrats or townspeople enjoyed either by contract or custom, on which the unequal and stratified European society of orders rested. In other respects, however, their conception of 'liberty' and 'freedoms' was more modern: an insistence on the limits of monarchical power, the defence of property, taxation by consent only, and the right to the free exercise of religion. One way or the other, there was a direct connection between the dynamics of the struggle for mastery between European states, and the battle for 'liberty' within them.

Thus, as David Trim has shown in Chapter 2, Elizabeth I – albeit with considerable reluctance – took on the cause of both Catholic and Protestant Dutch nobles because she wanted to deny Spain absolute control of the Low Countries and thus the base for a descent on England. Cardinal Richelieu intervened in the Thirty Years' War to defend French interests by protecting 'German liberties' (*Deutsche Freiheit*), the rights

---

[8] Cited in Stephen Krasner, 'Rethinking the Sovereign State Model', in *Empires, Systems and States: Great Transformations in International Politics*, ed. Michael Cox, Tim Dunne, and Ken Booth (Cambridge: Cambridge University Press, 2001), 20.
[9] Cited in Iain Hampsher-Monk, 'Edmund Burke's Changing Justification for Intervention', *Historical Journal* 48 (2005), 67.
[10] Krasner, 'Rethinking the Sovereign State Model', 17.

of the princes and representative assemblies, against the absolutist tendencies of the German emperor. Likewise, his ally, the Swedish chancellor Axel Oxenstierna, explained that his war aim was 'to restore German liberties ... and in this manner to conserve the equilibrium of all Europe'.[11] To be sure, all these interventions were carried out primarily for reasons of state rather than ideological sympathy, but they would not have been possible without a deep-rooted understanding of what these 'freedoms' were or should be. In short, the link many early modern protagonists made between domestic liberty – at least in other states, if not their own – the balance of power and the right to intervene is clear.

Against this background, the Westphalian treaties of 1648 were nothing less than a charter for intervention: by fixing the internal confessional balance between German principalities and within the empire, they provided a lever for interference throughout the late seventeenth and eighteenth centuries.[12] They laid down the toleration of the three major confessions, Roman Catholic, Lutheran and Reformed (Calvinist).[13] The political structure of the new Holy Roman Empire, though hierarchic with an emperor at the head, was a sophisticated form of early modern consociationalism, in which confessional matters – which was almost everything of substance – had to be settled by compromise rather than majority vote. Within territories, rulers were bound to respect certain rights, including the right to convert. Those religious minorities who had enjoyed toleration in 1624 were not only guaranteed it for the future, but could not be excluded from certain civic offices.[14] These arrangements, and the imperial constitution as a whole, were guaranteed by two outside powers, France and Sweden.

---

[11]  See Derek Croxton, 'The Peace of Westphalia of 1648 and the Origins of Sovereignty', *International History Review* 21 (1999), 583, with quotations on 589–90.

[12]  See Andreas Osiander, 'Sovereignty, International Relations, and the Westphalian Myth', *International Organization* 55 (2001), 251–87; Croxton, 'The Peace of Westphalia of 1648 and the Origins of Sovereignty', 569–91; Stephane Beaulac, 'The Westphalian Legal Orthodoxy – Myth or Reality', *Journal of the History of International Law* 2 (2000), 148–77. See also Krasner, 'Rethinking the Sovereign State Model', 35–8, and his *Sovereignty: Organized Hypocrisy* (Princeton: Princeton University Press, 1999), 3–4, 8 and esp. 20.

[13]  On this, see Joachim Whaley, 'A Tolerant Society? Religious Toleration in the Holy Roman Empire, 1648–1806', in *Toleration in Enlightenment Europe*, ed. Ole Grell and Roy Porter (Cambridge: Cambridge University Press, 2000), 175–95, esp. 176–7, 179.

[14]  See Beaulac, 'The Westphalian Legal Orthodoxy', 164–5, 168. More generally, see Joachim Whaley, 'Religioese Toleranz als allgemeines Menschenrecht in der fruehen Neuzeit?', in *Kollektive Freiheitsvorstellungen im fruheneuzeitlichen Europa (1400–1850)*, ed. Georg Schmidt, Martin van Gelderen, and Christoph Snigula (Bern and Frankfurt am Main: Peter Lang, 2006), 397–416.

More broadly, the politico-legal framework of the Holy Roman Empire hinged on the notion that a legitimate ruler could be brought into compliance with certain norms of good governance and even deposed if he continued to offend. In theory, rulers should only be deposed by a vote of all the German estates at a 'free' *Reichstag*, but in practice, most German rulers acquiesced in the emergence of an increasingly activist Imperial Aulic Council, dominated by the emperor. This took the initiative, usually by mandating the local 'circles' – which convened the regional authorities – to act with imperial authority. Dozens of German princes were in fact deposed, or at least suspended from power, for bankruptcy, imbecility, disturbing the peace, treasonable correspondence with outside powers – and abuse of power. Thus Ferdinand Karl Franz von Hohenems-Vaduz was deposed in 1683 for excessively cruel persecution of witches. The indictment specifically mentioned his use of torture, and the intervention rescued sixty-eight condemned men from execution, a huge number in a tiny principality. His cousin, William Hyacinth, the Catholic ruler of Nassau-Siegen, was sanctioned in 1708 for mistreating his Protestant subjects. The historian Bernd Marquardt has counted some fifty such interventions.[15] In none of these cases can an obvious pecuniary or strategic motive to intervene be discerned, and the rights being vindicated went well beyond that of religious toleration.

With the larger principalities, it was different. Here, intervention was both more hazardous and more contentious, but it still took place. In the Palatinate, for example, the Catholic prince attempted in 1719 to reverse the confessional power-sharing compromise agreed at Westphalia and subsequent settlements. According to this 'simultaneum', some Palatine churches were shared between Catholics and Protestants, either physically or by dividing up the timetable. This was not simply an internal matter between the prince and his subjects. If the 'simultaneum' were to be rendered null and void in one territory, the whole fabric of inter-confessional co-existence in the German Empire would unravel. For several years in the late 1710s and the early 1720s, the Palatinate therefore became the focus of a fierce struggle between the Catholic principalities, led by the Holy Roman Emperor Charles VI and their

---

[15] See Werner Trossbach, 'Fuersten Absetzungen im 18. Jahrhundert', *Zeitschrift für historische Forschung* 13 (1986), 425–54, esp. 437–30 on Nassau-Siegen, and Bernd Marquardt, 'Zur Reichsgerichtlichen Aberkennung der Herrschergewalt wegen Missbrauchs. Tyrannenprozesse vor dem Reichshofrat am Beispiel des suedoestlichen Schwaebischen Reichskreises', in *Prozessprazis im alten Reich. Annaeherungen-Fallstudien-Statistiken*, ed. Anette Baumann, Peter Oestmann, Stephan Wendehorst, and Siegrid Westphal (Cologne, Weimar, and Berlin: Boehlau Verlag, 2005), 53–89, esp. 62–8 (on Hohenems-Vaduz), and 85–9 (full list of interventions).

Protestant counterparts, led by Brandenburg-Prussia, Hanover and
Saxony. The Palatine case also reverberated far beyond Germany.
Andrew Thompson's chapter in this volume has shown that religion
mattered not only to the kings George I and II, who were also electors
of the mainly Protestant German principality of Hanover, but also to
their ministers in London and the wider political nation in parliament
and the pamphleteering public sphere.[16] George I championed the cause
of the Palatine Protestants on the grounds that 'we cannot abandon our
religious relatives in the face of such hard persecution and oppression'.[17]

There was also a strong element of *Realpolitik* involved. The defence of
German Protestantism had long been seen as part of the defence of the
European 'Protestant Cause' against popish 'Universal Monarchy'.
English and later British Whigs believed that it was better to tackle the
Catholic and absolutist threat well before it reached their own neigh-
bourhood. On this reading, Protestants everywhere should be sup-
ported, but those in the strategically vital Low Countries, and the
German lands adjoining them, should take priority. It was there that
the vital 'counterscarp' of England, and its buttresses to the east on the
Rhine, were to be found. In short, the defence of the European Protestantism and European liberties on which British freedoms depended,
required the defence of these rights in the Holy Roman Empire; *Deutsche
Freiheit* or 'German freedoms', the independence of the princes from
domination by the French, the Spanish or the emperor, were thus
critical to English constitutional freedoms.[18] Confessional sentiment
and strategic self-interest were almost synonymous here.

As with the smaller states, territorial sovereignty could be set aside on
grounds which had nothing to do with the confessional balance. In 1719,
for example, there was a Hanoverian-led intervention at the request of
the Holy Roman Empire against the tyrannical Duke Karl Leopold of
Mecklenburg, who was eventually deposed in 1728.[19] Religion played

---

[16] See Andrew Thompson's chapter above and Andrew C. Thompson, *Britain, Hanover and the Protestant Interest, 1688–1756* (Woodbridge: Boydell and Brewer, 2006).
[17] Quoted in Thompson, *Britain, Hanover*, 72.
[18] See Brendan Simms, *Three Victories and a Defeat: The Rise and Fall of the First British Empire, 1714–1783* (London: Penguin Press, 2007), *passim* and esp. 9–70; Tony Clayton, *Europe and the Making of England, 1660–1760* (Cambridge: Cambridge University Press, 2007), *passim*, esp. 125–219.
[19] See Karl Otmar von Aretin, *Das alte Reich. 1648–1806*, vol. II: *Kaisertradition und österreichische Grossmachtspolitik (1684–1745)* (Stuttgart: Klett-Cotta, 1997), 255–61, and Sigrid Jahns, '"Mecklenburgisches Wesen" oder absolutistisches Regiment? Mecklenburgischer Staendekonflikt und neue kaiserliche Reichspolitik (1658–1755)', in *Reich, Regionen und Europa in Mittelalter und Neuzeit. Festschrift für Peter Moraw*, ed. Paul-Joachim Heinig, Sigrid Jahns, Hans-Joachim Schmidt, Rainer Christoph Schwinges, and Sabine Wefers (Berlin: Duncker und Humblot, 2000), 340–2.

no role here: both the prince and his estates were Lutheran; the two intervening powers were Lutheran Hanover and Prussia, where a Calvinist monarch ruled over a largely Lutheran population. Instead, the justification for the *Reichsexekution* (Imperial Ordinance) against Karl Leopold was couched in terms of the duke's alleged tyrannical tendencies. The emperor's proclamation speaks of the duke's attempts to deprive the estates 'of their age-old privileges, freedoms and rights' through harsh measures, in order to 'force them into arbitrary subjection'.[20] Twelve years later, the imperial machinery swung into action once more. Again, Karl Leopold was accused of tyrannical behaviour. He was charged with undermining the local courts, establishing a *Blutgericht* (bloody assize). The decree then drew up a long list of physical abuses inflicted on the duke's subjects, including a graphic description of the torture of a refractory magistrate. Once again Karl Leopold was accused of 'arbitrary rule'.[21] The point here is that far from assuming that the duke could do what he liked within his territory, 'arbitrary' rule was specifically listed as a reason for intervening against him.

Admittedly, Karl Leopold was not sovereign in the strictly legal sense: he ruled over an 'estate' of the Holy Roman Empire, not a sovereign state in the modern meaning of the word. It is also true that the intervening powers were far from disinterested. Both Hanover and Prussia wished to maximise their power-political positions in northern Germany. Yet bringing Karl Leopold to heel, and deposing him as a last resort, reflected more than just a sense of obligation towards the estates of Mecklenburg; nor was it just a pretext. There was a broader fear that the duke's oppressive behaviour would cause a disturbance in the empire. The imperial decree warned that it 'might involve the Roman Empire as a whole or its parts in dangerous disturbances'.[22] In other words it was not just the inherent injustice of Karl Leopold's behaviour which gave rise to concern, but its disruptive impact on the stability of northern Germany. Here the ideological motivation was not simply a

---

[20] Kaiserliches Commissions-Decret, 17 Nov. 1717, Ratisbon, in Johann Joseph Pachner von Eggerstorff (ed.), *Vollstaendige Sammlung aller von Anfang an des noch fuerwaehrenden Teutschen Reichstags de Anno 1663 biss anhero abgefassten Reichs-Schluesse. Teil III 1701 bis 1718*, ed. Karl Otmar von Aretin and Johannes Burckhardt, rpt. (Hildesheim, Zurich, and New York: Historia Scientiarum, Editionsprogram der Fritz-Thyssen Stiftung, 1996), 740. See also Michael Hughes, *Law and Politics in Eighteenth-Century Germany: The Imperial Aulic Council in the Reign of Charles VI* (Woodbridge: Boydell and Brewer, 1988), which is principally about the Mecklenburg case (see, on sovereignty, 94–5).

[21] Kaiserliches Commissions-Decret, 13 June 1729, in Eggenstorff (ed.), *Vollstaendige Sammlung*, IV, 292–5.

[22] Kaiserliches Commissions-Decret, 17 Nov. 1717, *ibid.*, 741.

blind for some deeper strategic purpose, but inseparable from it. Only well-governed neighbours would be good neighbours.

Of course, the German Empire was a special case, and its practices are not necessarily generalisable across the rest of Europe. Other states, especially Great Britain and France, certainly aspired to a more strongly unitary conception of sovereignty. In practice, though, many powers found that the neat division between internal and external affairs quickly dissolved under the pressure of strategic imperatives, and almost invariably when the German Empire was concerned, as it usually was throughout the European struggles of the sixteenth, seventeenth and eighteenth centuries. This was as true for France, which ruled Alsace and other imperial territories, as it was for Britain, which was linked in personal union to the Electorate of Hanover.

*

Edmund Burke took from the Glorious Revolution of 1688 a Whiggish love of liberty and limited government, which found expression in his support for the American colonists.[23] He took from the Enlightenment a 'peculiar universalism', which was reflected in his concern for the rights of Indians in Bengal, and his opposition to the slave trade.[24] During the trial of Warren Hastings, Burke famously condemned 'the geographical morality by which the duties of men in public and private situations are not to be governed by their relations to the Great Governor of the universe, or by their relations to men, but by climates ... parallels not of life but of latitudes'.[25] Yet he was also as F. P. Lock says, 'by temperament and conviction ... a conservative', in that he was sceptical of any grand schemes to make society anew in disregard of history and tradition: this put him immediately at odds with the French Revolution.[26] More important still in explaining his passionate engagement in European affairs was his rootedness within the Whig interventionist tradition, which hinged on the assumption that Britain should not only actively defend European 'liberties', but that British liberties in turn had once

[23] J. C. D. Clark describes him as a 'Whig in politics' in J. C. D. Clark (ed.), *Edmund Burke: Reflections on the Revolution* (Stanford: Stanford University Press, 2001), 23.

[24] See Jennifer Pitts, *A Turn to Empire: The Rise of Imperial Liberalism in Britain and France* (Princeton: Princeton University Press, 2005), ch. 3: 'Edmund Burke's Peculiar Universalism', 59–95. For a critique of Pitts, see Karuna Mantena, 'Review Essay: Fragile Universals and the Politics of Empire', *Polity* 38:4 (2006), 543–55, and Duncan S. A. Bell, 'Historiographical Review: Empire and International Relations in Victorian Political Thought', *Historical Journal* 49 (2006), esp. 285–9. See also Nicholas B. Dirks, *The Scandal of Empire: India and the Creation of Imperial Britain* (Cambridge, MA: Harvard University Press, 2006), esp. 106–7.

[25] Quoted in Pitts, *A Turn to Empire*, 78.

[26] F. P. Lock, *Burke's Reflections on the Revolution in France* (London: Routledge, 1985), 31.

been saved by outside intervention in 1688. 'An abstract principle of public law', he later wrote, 'forbidding such interference, is not supported . . . by the practice of this kingdom, nor by that of any civilized nation in the world. This nation owes its laws and liberties, his Majesty owes the throne on which he sits, to the contrary principle.'[27]

Of course, Burke's idea of 'liberty' differed in many respects from modern conceptions of the term. It was explicitly opposed to 'democracy', at least in the Jacobin sense of the word; though far from intolerant, his fervent defence of 'religion' placed him at odds with the 'atheistical' French revolutionaries. Moreover, Burke's 'liberty', like that of other Europeans, was based on an unequal society of orders. That said, his opposition to 'tyranny', his support for limited government, his passionate defence of property rights, his insistence on consensual taxation and other constitutional freedoms, is recognisably modern. His concern for the rights of 'millions' of Indians, whom he wished to save from 'oppression and tyranny',[28] went well beyond a narrowly conservative defence of the caste system. More importantly for our purposes, Burke's conception of liberty and liberties profoundly shaped his approach to international affairs and the doctrine of intervention for which he became so famous.

It has often been remarked that Edmund Burke was many things: Irishman, Briton, a critical supporter of overseas empire; but above all these things, Burke was a *European*. 'He looked back', as R. J. Vincent has written, 'to the solidarity of medieval Christendom rather than forward to the plurality of sovereign states co-existing in a secular system'.[29] Indeed, as Jennifer Welsh demonstrates, by the end of the century, Burke's principal preoccupation was the 'Commonwealth of Europe'.[30] It became the increasingly dominant theme in his 'Great Melody',[31] which began when Burke came of age as a political polemicist in the context of three successive perceived blows to European

---

[27] Burke to Lord Grenville, 18 Aug. 1792, in Marshall and Woods (eds.), *The Correspondence of Edmund Burke*, VII, 176n.

[28] Introductory note to the speech on Fox's India Bill, in David Fidler and Jennifer Welsh (eds.), *Empire and Community: Edmund Burke's Writings and Speeches on International Relations* (Boulder, CO, and Oxford: Westview Press, 1999), 199.

[29] R. J. Vincent, 'Edmund Burke and the Theory of International Relations', *Review of International Studies* 10 (1984), 206.

[30] Jennifer M. Welsh, 'Edmund Burke and the Commonwealth of Europe: The Cultural Bases of International Order', in *Classical Theories of International Relations*, ed. Ian Clark and Iver Neumann (Basingstoke: Macmillan, 1996), 173–92. Jennifer M. Welsh, *Edmund Burke and International Relations* (Basingstoke: Macmillan, 1995), *passim* and esp. 70–88.

[31] Conor Cruise O'Brien, *The Great Melody: A Thematic Biography of Edmund Burke* (London: Sinclair Stevenson, 1992).

liberty and the balance of power. First, there was the French occupation of Corsica. France completed the purchase of the island from Genoa in May 1768, rapidly crushed the resistance of Corsican patriots under Pascale Paoli, and by mid-1769, was in full effective control of the island.[32] British public opinion was outraged, and James Boswell not only edited *British Essays in Favour of the Brave Corsicans* later that same year, but also raised enough in subscriptions to buy thirty artillery pieces for Paoli.[33] Burke's initial response stressed the strategic implications for Britain.[34] Later, however, in his coruscating attack on the administration, in the 'Thoughts on the Present Discontents' (1770), Burke condemned 'the conquest of Corsica, by the professed enemies of the freedom of mankind, in defiance of those who were formerly its professed defenders'.[35] Then in August 1772, King Gustavus of Sweden launched a coup against his parliament, with French support. Burke saw this as a threat to European and British freedoms more generally, which could be linked, more or less opportunistically, back to his own struggle against the allegedly despotic tendencies of George III. The following month he told one correspondent that he feared that 'the Court may assume as uncontrolled a power in this country as the King of Sweden has done in his'.[36]

At around the same time, Russia, Austria and Prussia announced that the old Polish Commonwealth would be partitioned between them. Interestingly, the partition was justified by the eastern powers at least in part as an intervention to curb Polish mistreatment of religious minorities such as Protestants and Orthodox. To Burke, however, the

---

[32] See Geoffrey W. Rice, 'Deceit and Distraction: Britain, France and the Corsican Crisis of 1768', *International History Review* 28 (2006), 287–315, and Thadd E. Hall, *France and the Eighteenth-century Corsican Question* (New York: New York University Press, 1971), 155–214.

[33] See Frederick A. Pottle, *James Boswell: The Earlier Years, 1740–1769* (London: Yale University Press, 1966), 390–5. Just before this chapter went to press, Jennifer Pitts very kindly let me have sight of her rich and suggestive unpublished paper 'The Stronger Ties of Humanity: Humanitarian Intervention in the Eighteenth Century', presented to the American Political Science Association annual meeting, Philadelphia, 28–31 August 2003, which focuses on Corsica. It is very much to be hoped that this pioneering paper, which complements this chapter and extends the analysis of humanitarian intervention in the eighteenth century well beyond what has been attempted here, will soon be available in published form.

[34] 'Speech on Address, 8 November 1768', in Paul Langford (ed.), *The Writings and Speeches of Edmund Burke*, vol. II: *Party, Parliament and the American Crisis, 1766–1774* (Oxford: Oxford University Press, 1981), 98–9.

[35] 'Thoughts on the Present Discontents', in Langford (ed.), *Writings and Speeches of Edmund Burke*, II, 283.

[36] Quoted in F. P. Lock, *Edmund Burke*, vol. I: *1730–1784* (Oxford: Oxford University Press, 1998), 341.

Polish partition was an affront to European freedoms. He spoke of 'the utter subversion of almost all the remaining monuments of public liberty', which did 'violence to humanity and justice'. Burke also regarded the partition as 'the first very great breach in the modern political system of Europe'. The unprovoked dismemberment of a large European state by a coalition of predators seemed to create an ominous precedent for 'Europe as a vast commonwealth', an early use of this term by him. Here Burke was enunciating not simply a principle of abstract international law, but rather a direct geopolitical threat to British security. He doubted that 'the insular situation of Great Britain weaken[ed] the application' of the principles of the balance of power as much as some claimed. Burke pointed out that no 'single state, in the present political and physical state of Europe could expect independence and safety, unconnected with all the others'.[37] In other words, the violence offered to 'liberty' and 'mankind' in Poland would eventually beat a path to England's door.

This was because the resulting territorial shifts had weakened the Holy Roman Empire and its barrier function, the neuralgic spot of traditional Whig strategic thinking. Hitherto, Burke argued, 'Poland was the natural barrier of Germany, as well as of the northern crowns, against the overwhelming power and ambition of Russia'. The partition now threatened 'totally to unhinge the ancient system of Germany and the north'. Poland might now be 'the road by which the Russians will enter Germany'.[38] Moreover, Burke feared that the partitions would set off a chain reaction of other partitions or 'exchanges', for example between the Duke of Mecklenburg-Schwerin (Mecklenburg again!) and Prussia. This might 'prepare the way for a total change of system in Germany'. Besides, Burke continued, the failure of noble liberty in Poland cast a harsh light on the viability of princely freedoms in a Germany surrounded by an unforgiving international environment. 'That empire', he wrote, 'seems to be in as precarious a situation as it has been at any time since its foundation. The equilibrium has been entirely overthrown ... The fate of the venal and arbitrary nobility presents a mirror to the German princes which they could not too long

---

[37] *The Annual Register for the Year 1772*, Preface p. 1 and 1–3, 6. See also G. L. Vincitorio, 'Edmund Burke and the First Partition of Poland', in *Crisis in the Great Republic: Essays Presented to Ross J. S. Hoffman*, ed. Vincitorio (New York: Fordham University Press, 1969), 14–46, esp. 33, 37, and 42 for quotations. Oddly, neither the first volume of F. P. Lock's magisterial biography, nor Paul Langford's classic edition of the writings and speeches, covers Burke on Poland.

[38] *The Annual Register for the Year 1772*, 3–5; *Annual Register for the Year 1773*, 3–4.

nor too attentively study'.[39] All this mattered, because the integrity of the German Empire was the foundation upon which the security of the Low Countries, Britain's strategic Achilles' heel, rested.

In short, the partition of Poland and the revolution in Sweden were not only devastating blows to European liberty *and* to the European balance; they were a threat to the balance *because* they were a threat to liberty and vice versa. 'No equal portion of time', Burke wrote, 'has been so fatal to public liberty, and the rights of mankind, as that which comprehends the overthrow of the constitution' in Sweden and Poland.[40] Military action to reverse these coups, to restore the rights of mankind, he implied, would be fully justified. 'Wars may be deferred', he wrote, 'but they cannot be wholly avoided; and to purchase present quiet, at the price of future security, is undoubtedly a cowardice of the most degrading and basest nature'.[41] In other words, the defence of liberty in Europe and the defence of the European balance were inextricably interconnected in Burke's mind well before 1789.

*

It was against this background that Burke formulated his response to the French Revolution. A great deal, of course, has been written about the subject and its implications for Burke's view of international affairs more generally, by R. J. Vincent, David Boucher,[42] extensively by Jennifer Welsh and, most recently and carefully, by Iain Hampsher-Monk. This chapter concurs with these authors on most points, but thinks the question worth revisiting for three reasons. First, all these authors are to some degree – Hampsher-Monk most especially[43] – in thrall to the Westphalian myth, and thus tend to exaggerate the novelty of Burke's interventionism. Second, they fail to see the connection between Burke's response to the Polish partitions, when he first enunciated the concept of a European 'Commonwealth', and his policies after 1789. Third, so far no Burke scholar has grasped the centrality of the (German) Empire in Burke's thinking about European liberties and the balance of power.

In the very early stages, Burke was ambivalent about the revolution, 'not knowing [in August 1789] whether to blame or applaud'.[44] Though

[39] *Annual Register for the Year 1773*, 8–9.
[40] *The Annual Register for the Year 1772*, Preface, p. 1.
[41] *The Annual Register for the Year 1772*, 3.
[42] David Boucher, 'The Character of the History of the Philosophy of International Relations and the Case of Edmund Burke', *Review of International Studies* 17 (1991), 127–48, esp. 142–4.
[43] See Hampsher-Monk, 'Edmund Burke's Changing Justification for Intervention', 65–100, esp. 72, 93 on the development of Burke's thinking on intervention and 65–6 on Westphalia.
[44] Quoted in Welsh, *Edmund Burke and International Relations*, 100.

he never shared the *Schadenfreude* with which many celebrated the apparent decline of French power in 1789, Burke did not completely reject the widespread belief that events in France were inspired by England's own 'Glorious Revolution' of 1688.[45] Within a year, however, Burke had tilted decisively and famously against the Revolution in his *Reflections on the Revolution in France* (1790), which Conor Cruise O'Brien has described as 'The manifesto of a counter-revolution'.[46] These were not merely a literary and political landmark but also a publishing sensation, selling between 17,000 and 19,000 copies (with a much greater readership) and provoking about another 100 pamphlets in turn. Many hated the *Reflections*, and most admired its 'eloquence' rather than its content, but almost everybody read it.[47] Not since Israel Mauduit's *Considerations on the Present German War* in 1760, and before that Jonathan's Swift's *The conduct of the allies* in 1711 had the British public been engaged in such lively debate about a single work.[48]

Burke condemned the Revolution as an attack on tradition, religion, property and 'chivalry', 'a revolution in sentiments, manners and moral opinions'.[49] The insults offered to the French royal family and especially Marie Antoinette, he argued, were really assaults on the institution of monarchy more generally. 'It appears to me as if I were in a great crisis',

---

[45] On the ambivalence of Burke's initial response, see Welsh, *Edmund Burke and International Relations*, 100.

[46] Conor Cruise O'Brien, 'Introduction' to *Edmund Burke: Reflections on the Revolution in France and on the Proceedings in Certain Societies in London Relative to that Event* (London: Penguin, 1968), 9.

[47] See L. G. Mitchell's 'Introduction' to Edmund Burke, *Reflections on the Revolution in France* (Oxford: Oxford University Press, 1993), ix–xi; J. C. D. Clark's 'Introduction' to his edition of *Edmund Burke: Reflections on the Revolution in France* (Stanford: Stanford University Press, 2001), esp. 97–108, and F. P. Lock, *Reflections*, ch. 5: 'Contemporary Reception', 132–65, esp. 133. Lock says some 17,500 in all were sold.

[48] Jonathan Swift, *The conduct of the allies and of the late ministry, in beginning and carrying on the war* (London, 1711), in Thomas Roscoe (ed.), *The works of Jonathan Swift containing interesting and valuable papers not hitherto published, in two volumes, with memoir of the author*, vol. I (London, 1841), 410–28; Israel Mauduit, *Considerations on the present German war* (London, 1760). See also Heinz-Joachim Muellenbrock, *The Culture of Contention: A Rhetorical Analysis of the Public Controversy about the Ending of the War of the Spanish Succession, 1710–1713* (Munich: Fink Verlag, 1997), and K. W. Schweizer, 'Pamphleteering and Foreign Policy in the Age of the Elder Pitt', in *Hanoverian Britain and Empire: Essays in Memory of Philip Lawson*, ed. Stephen Taylor, Richard Connors, and Clyve Jones (Woodbridge: Boydell and Brewer, 1998), 94–108.

[49] 'Reflections on the Revolution in France', in Paul Langford (ed.), *The Writings and Speeches of Edmund Burke*, vol. VIII: *The French Revolution, 1790–1794* (Oxford: Oxford University Press, 1989), 131. Religion also played a key role in European resistance to France: see T. C. W. Blanning, 'The Role of Religion in European Counter-Revolution, 1789–1815', in *History, Society and the Churches: Essays in Honour of Owen Chadwick*, ed. Derek Beales and Geoffrey Best (Cambridge: Cambridge University Press, 1985), 195–214.

Burke writes towards the beginning of the *Reflections*, 'not of the affairs of France alone but of all Europe, perhaps of more than Europe. All circumstances taken together, the French Revolution is the most astonishing that has hitherto happened in the world.'[50] 'The age of chivalry is gone', Burke later warned, 'That of sophisters, economists, and calculators has succeeded ... ancient chivalry ... which has given its character to modern Europe'.[51] What is striking about these passages is not just their prescience – all this was written well before the execution of the king, and the outbreak of the Terror – but the way in which Burke defined the problem from the beginning not in narrowly French, or even British, but very much in European, terms.

The explicitly ideological nature of Burke's hostility to revolutionary France did not place him outside the traditional British balance of power discourse, however. It is true, of course, that his doctrines ran directly contrary to the prevailing view of William Pitt's administration.[52] It is also true that London was uneasy about the French émigrés whom Burke championed, partly because it entertained grave doubts as to their military value, but primarily because any commitments to them might get in the way of a compromise peace with revolutionary France. Containing French power, in particular by restoring the integrity of the Low Countries, not reversing the revolution was Britain's war aim. All the same, Burke's response to the Revolution should be understood not as a simple repudiation of balance of power thinking – and thus of what we would today call 'realism' – but as a variation on it.

Burke believed that the Revolution posed a mortal threat to British liberty and security for three interconnected reasons. First, Burke famously feared the subversive example of the Revolution. In the *Reflections*, Burke pointed to the danger of revolutionary ideas. 'France has always more or less influenced manners in England', he wrote, 'and when your fountain is choked up and polluted, the stream will not run long, or will not run clear with us, or perhaps with any nation. This gives all Europe, in my opinion, but too close and connected a concern in what is done in France.'[53] Burke therefore spoke of the 'rights of men' as a 'grand magazine of offensive weapons'.[54] 'Formerly your affairs were your own concern only', he wrote, 'We felt for them as men; but we kept

---

[50] 'Reflections on the Revolution in France', 60.    [51] *Ibid.*, 127.
[52] On Pitt and Burke, see Jennifer Mori, *William Pitt and the French Revolution 1785–1795* (Edinburgh: Keele University Press, 1997), 81–2; and Jeremy Black, *British Foreign Policy in an Age of Revolutions, 1783–1793* (Cambridge: Cambridge University Press, 1994).
[53] 'Reflections on the Revolution in France', 131.    [54] *Ibid.*, 165.

aloof from them, because we were not citizens of France. But when we see the model held up to ourselves, we must feel as Englishmen, and feeling, we must provide as Englishmen.'[55] The answer, he said, was to 'keep at a distance' the revolutionary 'plague', against which 'the precautions of the most severe quarantine ought to be established'.[56] At this point, Burke was not yet making a plea for military intervention, but rather for placing the Revolution in an ideological quarantine.

Soon after, however, Burke became convinced that containment was not enough. In the course of the following year his 'Letter to a Member of the National Assembly' (1791), argued that only power 'from *without* [his italics]' would be sufficient to dislodge the Revolution. This, he continued, 'may be given ... in pity; for surely no nation ever called so pathetically on the compassion of all its neighbours'.[57] In speaking of 'compassion', Burke was surely expressing a humanitarian obligation towards France. For although his objections to the Revolution ranged across 'religion', 'property' and 'chivalry', they could all be subsumed under the single heading of 'tyranny'. The Revolution, Burke argued, 'oppressed' 'the small reliques of the persecuted landed interest', the 'burghers' and the 'farmers ... Two persons cannot meet and confer without hazard to their liberty ... numbers scarcely credible have been executed, and their property confiscated.'[58]

Burke was clearly demonstrating a secular and universal concern for liberty. The Revolution's war on the domestic freedoms of Frenchmen grieved Burke as much as the (alleged) threats to British freedoms had in the 1770s, or the rights of Indians had in the 1780s. He thought that 'all men who desire [Liberty] deserve it'. Far from seeing it as a geographically, historically or culturally contingent phenomenon, therefore, Burke regarded liberty as 'our inheritance, it is the birthright of our species'.[59] In early December 1794, Burke wrote that re-establishment of order in France was not merely in the 'interest of this kingdom [Britain]' but also of 'mankind in general' (*du genre humain en general*).[60] In the following year he referred to the Revolution as 'the most infernal Tyranny and

---

[55] *Ibid.*, 140; see also 203 and 205.     [56] *Ibid.*, 140.

[57] 'Letter to a Member of the National Assembly', in Langford (ed.), *Writings and Speeches*, VIII, 305–6. 'Compassion' is mentioned again on p. 308.

[58] 'Remarks on the Policy of the Allies', in Mitchell (ed.), *The Writings and Speeches*, VIII, 463.

[59] Edmund Burke to Charles-Jean-François Depont, Nov. 1789, in Cobban and Smith (eds.), *Correspondence of Edmund Burke*, VI, 41.

[60] Burke to Comtesse d'Osmond, 8 Dec. 1794, Beaconsfield, in R. B. McDowell (ed.), *The Correspondence of Edmund Burke*, vol. VIII: *September 1794–April 1796* (Chicago: University of Chicago Press, and Cambridge: Cambridge University Press, 1970), 93.

oppression that ever vexed or menaced the race of man'.[61] And the year after that Burke wrote that 'We cannot arrange with our enemy in the present conjuncture, without abandoning the interest of mankind'.[62] And here the context clearly shows that the words 'humanity' and 'mankind' are surely no mere appeal to sentimental moral principle, but refer to values and rights which are the birthright of all (or most) men of property.[63]

In such situations, Burke claimed, intervention was not only justifiable but imperative, because there was no other way of helping the victims. Right at the beginning of 1791, Burke wrote that he had 'no opinion at all of internal remedies ... I cannot persuade myself that any thing whatsoever can be effected without great force from abroad.'[64] In his 'Thoughts on French Affairs', published later that year, he noted simply that 'no counter-revolution is to be expected in France from internal causes solely'.[65] He was therefore sympathetic to arguments of French émigrés such as Pierre Gaeton Dupont, who told Burke in May 1791 'that in cases where the oppression is so great that the oppressed cannot even ask for help, it is enough that there is public and unequivocal notoriety of this to require the intervention of a foreign power'.[66]

What Burke was proposing was not mere benevolence, of course. 'Help', he wrote, 'may be given by those neighbours on motives of safety to themselves. Never shall I think any country in Europe to be secure, whilst there is established, in the very centre of it, a state (if so it may be called) founded on principles of anarchy, and which is in reality, a college of armed fanatics, for the propagation of the principles of assassination, robbery, rebellion, fraud, faction, oppression and impiety.'[67] 'How could we possibly avoid war', Burke asked parliament in 1792, 'when France had denounced [sic] destruction against all the Kings of Europe. We were forced, on principle of self-defence, into a confederacy with all the sovereigns of Europe.'[68] Later, in 1796, Burke described the

---

[61] Burke to Mrs John Crewe, c. 11 Aug. 1795 (summarising the views of the Duke of Portland), in McDowell (ed.), *Correspondence of Edmund Burke*, VIII, 300.

[62] 'First Letter on a Regicide Peace', in R. B. McDowell (ed.), *The Writings and Speeches of Edmund Burke*, vol. IX: *I. The Revolutionary War, 1794–1797. II. Ireland* (Oxford: Oxford University Press, 1991), 195.

[63] I am grateful to the Burke expert Richard Bourke for very illuminating correspondence on this matter, even if I have been unable to persuade him.

[64] Cited in Hampsher-Monk, 'Burke and Intervention', 70.

[65] 'Thoughts on French Affairs', in Langford (ed), *Writings and Speeches of Edmund Burke*, III, 368.

[66] Quoted in Hampsher-Monk, 'Burke and Intervention', 71.

[67] 'Letter to a Member of the National Assembly', 305–6.

[68] 15 Dec. 1792, William Cobbett (ed.), *The parliamentary history from the earliest period to the year 1803. Vol. XXX. Comprising the period from the thirteenth of December 1792, to the tenth of March 1794* (London, 1817), col. 115.

Revolution as 'an armed doctrine', a 'system, which, by its essence, is inimical to all other governments, and which makes peace or war, as peace or war may best contribute to their subversion'.[69] It therefore had to be confronted at both levels: that of 'compassion' as well as 'safety'.

The chief reason for this was that France was 'so powerful and so close'.[70] The very proximity – or 'vicinity'[71] as he put it – not merely of French power but French ideas, in 'a country but twenty-four miles from the shore of this island',[72] entitled Britain to move decisively against the source of the 'contagion'. Otherwise, he wrote 'They who are to live in the vicinity of this new fabrick, are to prepare to live in perpetual conspiracies and seditions; and to end at last in being conquered, if not to her dominions, to her resemblance'.[73] Indeed, Burke warned of France creating 'an universal empire, by producing a universal revolution'; Britain faced 'a sect aiming at universal empire, and beginning with the conquest of France'.[74] At one level, 'vicinity' referred to the fact that France lay only a short distance away across the Channel. But Burke was also referring to a more general European 'neighbourhood', or the 'grand vicinage of Europe'.[75] He claimed that in Europe as a whole, no 'new erection' or 'nuisance' was permitted which 'may redound, even secondarily, to the prejudice of a neighbour'. For the Revolution 'violates the rights upon which not only the community of France, but those on which all communities are founded'.[76] And when Burke's critics argued that 'our insular situation . . . is proof against every innovation', he responded that 'They talk as if England were not in Europe'.[77]

[69] 'First Letter on a Regicide Peace', 199.
[70] Burke to William Lushington, 26 Oct. 1796, in R. B. McDowell and John A. Woods (eds.), *The Correspondence of Edmund Burke*, vol. IX: *I. May 1796–July 1797. II. Additional and Undated Letters* (Chicago: Notre Dame University Press, 1970), 99.
[71] On 'vicinity', see 'Thoughts on French Affairs' (published after Burke's death in 1797), 307.
[72] 'Reflections on the Revolution in France', 185.
[73] Quoted in Welsh, *Edmund Burke and International Relations*, 113. For other examples of 'vicinity', see, for example, Burke to Lushington, 26 Oct. 1796, in McDowell (ed.), *The Correspondence of Edmund Burke*, IX, 99. See also the Letters on a Regicide Peace, *passim.*
[74] Cited in Welsh, *Edmund Burke and International Relations*, 113; 'Second Letter on a Regicide Peace', in McDowell (ed.), *The Writings and Speeches of Edmund Burke*, IX, 267.
[75] 'First Letter on a Regicide Peace', 250–1.    [76] *Ibid.*, 252.
[77] 15 Dec.1792, Cobbett (ed.), *The parliamentary history from the earliest period to the year 1803*, XXX, col. 112. In the same vein on the 'Commonwealth of Europe' and Britain's central role in it, see 'Fourth Letter on a Regicide Peace', in McDowell (ed.), *The Writings and Speeches of Edmund Burke*, IX, 56, 248; 'First Letter on a Regicide Peace', 195; 'Third Letter on a Regicide Peace', in McDowell (ed.), *The Writings and Speeches of Edmund Burke*, IX; 'Heads for Consideration on the Present State of Affairs', in L. G. Mitchell (ed.), *The Writings and Speeches of Edmund Burke*, vol. VIII: *The French Revolution* (Oxford: Oxford University Press, 1989), 399, 404.

For all these reasons, Burke claimed that French sovereignty needed to be set aside for the greater good. 'A positively vicious and abusive government', Burke had written even before the excesses of the Revolution had become clear, 'ought to be changed and, if necessary, by violence, if it cannot be (as it is sometimes the case) Reformed'.[78] After all, as we have seen, William of Orange had rescued English liberties in 1688. Burke therefore dismissed as 'mischevious' the idea 'that no neighbouring power can ... afford succour to' a population subjected to 'the most abominable, murderous and exterminatory rebellions' and 'the most atrocious and bloody tyranny'.[79] Indeed, Burke argued that the revolutionary regime had to be not merely contained, if necessary by intervention, but toppled. Iain Hampsher-Monk even refers to a 'specific policy of regime change'.[80] The right to intervene in the internal affairs of an independent state was conferred by neighbourhood: 'the vicinage itself is the natural judge. It is ... the assertor of its own rights' (251). Moreover, Burke argued, the 'Law of Neighbourhood' permitted Britain and its allies to undertake pre-emptive action to 'anticipate ... a damage justly apprehended but not actually done'. For this reason, he continued, 'the vicinage of Europe had not a right, but an indispensable duty, and an exigent interest, to denunciate this new work before it had produced the danger we have so sorely felt, and which we shall long feel'.[81]

This broader European 'vicinity' was crucial to Burke's interventionism, because it enabled him to resolve the tension between universal principles and practical limitations.[82] 'Men', he said, 'are rarely without some sympathy in the sufferings of others'. However, Burke continued, 'in the immense and diversified mass of human misery, which may be pitied, but cannot be relieved, in the gross, the mind must make a choice'. This being so, he continued, 'our sympathy is always more forcibly attracted towards the misfortunes of certain persons, and in certain descriptions: and this sympathetic attraction discovers, beyond a possibility of mistake, our mental affinities, and elective affections'.[83] This choice would be made on two grounds: practicality and necessity.

[78] Edmund Burke to Charles-Jean-François Depont, Nov. 1789, Cobban and Smith (eds.), *Correspondence of Edmund Burke*, VI, 48.
[79] Burke to Lord Grenville, Beaconsfield, 18 Aug. 1792, in Marshall and Woods (eds.), *Correspondence of Edmund Burke*, VII, 176–7.
[80] Hampsher-Monk, 'Burke's Changing Justification for Intervention', 77.
[81] 'First Letter on a Regicide Peace', 252.
[82] On this tension more generally, see Jennifer M. Welsh, 'Taking Consequences Seriously: Objections to Humanitarian Intervention', in *Humanitarian Intervention and International Relations*, ed. Welsh (Oxford: Oxford University Press, 2004), 52–68.
[83] 'Third Letter on a Regicide Peace', 307.

Thus when challenged as to why he did not urge intervention against the second partition of Poland in 1793, Burke responded that 'let our opinions on that partition be what they will, England, by itself, is not in a situation to afford to Poland any assistance whatsoever'.[84] He swatted back objections that the terrible crimes of the Barbary corsairs were going unpunished with the following statement: 'Algiers is not near; Algiers is not powerful; Algiers is not our neighbour; Algiers is not infectious. When I find Algiers transferred to Calais, I will tell you what I think of that point.'[85] Confronting tyranny in France was thus no precedent for a crusade without end. The principles of liberty were universal, but Britain's ability to vindicate them was limited. Burke therefore thought that while Britain should speak up for freedoms wherever they were endangered, it should pay particular attention to threats close to home. Intervention was essential to extirpate democracy and restore both religion and the social difference on which liberty rested. In practice this meant that Britain should halt the abuses of the East India Company because it could, and those of the French Revolution because it had to.

Secondly, Burke saw the Revolution as a specific geopolitical threat to British interests in the Holy Roman Empire. As we have already seen, Burke could boast an expert knowledge of the imperial constitution, which he paraded throughout the 1790s.[86] Whereas the *ancien régime* had been the 'author and natural support of the treaty of Westphalia', 'the natural guardian of the independence and balance of Germany', the new ideas were 'utterly irreconcilable with' the German imperial constitution. 'The treaty of Westphalia', he wrote, 'is, with France, an antiquated fable'. Not, as one might imagine because it had broken with traditional notions of state sovereignty, but because 'The rights and liberties [France] was bound to maintain [in the Holy Roman Empire] are now a system of wrong and tyranny which she is bound to destroy'.[87] Right at

---

[84] 'Observations on the Conduct of the Minority', in Mitchell (ed.), *Writings and Speeches*, VIII, 423. In the same vein, see Edmund Burke to Richard Burke jnr, 29 July 1792, in Marshall and Woods (eds.), *Corrrespondence of Edmund Burke*, VII, 158–9.

[85] 'First Letter on a Regicide Peace', 259.

[86] Burke used the term 'empire' for both the Holy Roman Empire and the British overseas empire. For example, Burke to Fitzwilliam, 14 Apr. 1795, in McDowell (ed.), *Correspondence of Edmund Burke*, VIII, 230 (Germany); Burke to Rev. Thomas Hussey, 18 May 1795, *ibid.*, 246 (British Empire). For Burke on the empire, see 'Burke to William Elliot', 26 May 1795, in *Writings and Speeches*, IX, 36–7, and 'Second Letter on a Regicide Peace', *ibid.*, 291. Surprisingly, the empire did not seem to feature much in his relations with the Hanoverian writer Ernst Brandes: Carl Haase, *Ernst Brandes, 1758–1810*, vol. I (Hildesheim: Verlag August Lax, 1973), 17, 115, 144–53, 338–51, 390–2.

[87] 'Thoughts on French Affairs', 352.

the top of the demonology of the revolutionaries were the petty German princes, who sheltered the hated émigrés in their residences just beyond the Rhine (particularly Koblenz), and the despised imperial constitution, which stood between the revolutionaries and the realisation of their ideological and strategic goals.[88] The 'liberté' of 1789 clashed with German liberties. Burke therefore predicted that 'A great revolution is preparing in Germany; and a revolution, in my opinion, likely to be more decisive upon the general fate of nations than that of France itself'.[89]

Burke believed this mattered because 'all the politics of Europe for more than two centuries' had shown 'the independence and the equilibrium of the empire to be ... the very essence of the system of balanced power in Europe, and the scheme of public law, or mass of laws, upon which that independence and equilibrium are founded'.[90] Echoing the ambivalence of an earlier generation of Whigs, Burke thought that the equilibrium was jeopardised by events in France in a double sense. French weakness would lead to a partition of Germany between Austria and Prussia: 'it is through her alone that the common liberty of Germany can be secured against the single or the combined ambition of any other power'.[91] At the same time, French subversion threatened 'to throw the empire into confusion'. Worse still, the French were known to 'hold out from time to time the idea of uniting all the other provinces of which Gaul was anciently composed, including Savoy on the other side, and on this side bounding themselves by the Rhine'.[92] For all these reasons, Burke foresaw that 'it is on the side of the ecclesiastical electorates that the dykes, raised to support the German liberty first will give way'.[93]

If that happened, the barrier system in the Low Countries would be in jeopardy. The so-called 'barrier fortresses' along the French border, in the territory of the Austrian Netherlands but occupied and garrisoned by the Dutch republic, Burke knew, were the rampart of British liberties, 'those outworks, which ever till now we so strenuously maintained, as the strong frontier of our own dignity and safety, no less than the liberties

---

[88] On this, see T. C. W. Blanning, *The Origins of the French Revolutionary Wars* (London and New York: Longman, 1986), esp. 99–104. On the clash between the 'new diplomacy' of the revolutionaries and the ancient regime, see Felix Gilbert, 'The "New Diplomacy" of the Eighteenth Century', *World Politics* 4 (1951/2), 15–17.

[89] 'Thoughts on French Affairs', 349.

[90] *Ibid.*, 350.    [91] *Ibid.*, 352.    [92] *Ibid.*, 353.

[93] *Ibid.*, 352. For further examples of Burke's preoccupation with the Holy Roman Empire and British security, see 'Heads for Consideration on the Present State of Affairs', 398; Marshall and Woods (eds.), *The Correspondence of Edmund Burke*, VII, 271ff., 277, 307, 316–17, 383, 387, 393, 430; and 'First Letter on a Regicide Peace', 195–6.

of Europe'.[94] Their loss would 'cut off all political communication between England and the continent'.[95] 'Holland', he told the House of Commons in 1791, 'might justly be considered as necessary part of this country as Kent'.[96] Later he wrote that the German emperor – to whom the defence of the Austrian Netherlands fell – was 'an integrant [*sic*] part of the strength of Great Britain, and in manner part of Great Britain itself'.[97] So France was in Burke's sights as a threat to the barrier as early as December 1791, long before French revolutionary armies had entered the Low Countries in 1793.[98] All this, of course, was classic Whig geopolitics stretching back to the Glorious Revolution, and further: the crucial role of the Low Countries; the consequent centrality of the (Holy Roman) 'Empire' and 'the common liberty of Germany'; the interplay of 'safety' and solidarity or 'compassion'; the language of 'dykes', 'balanced power' and 'equilibrium'.[99] The ideological and the strategic here cannot be usefully separated.

*

Burke's interventionist doctrine was thus no new departure, but an elaboration of traditional Whig thinking about British liberty, German freedoms, the liberties of Europe, and the reciprocal right of intervention in the internal affairs of another state within the European 'neighbourhood'. That said, Burke carried the concept of intervention a whole stage further, and put it on a firm intellectual footing. European notions of what or who deserved protection had already evolved from a narrow confessional solidarity to embrace (some of) those suffering arbitrary rule; now Burke had brought the much broader category of 'humanity' into play. The elimination of the Revolution was vital to the preservation of the German balance, and thus of the whole European equilibrium, was not just essential to safeguard British security, but necessary for the

---

[94] 'Third Letter on a Regicide Peace', 358.
[95] Observations on the Conduct of the Minority', in Mitchell (ed.), *Writings and Speeches*, VIII, 426. See, in same vein, 'Third Letter on a Regicide Peace', 305.
[96] 29 March 1791, Cobbett (ed.), *The parliamentary history from the earliest period to the year 1803*, XXX, col. 77.
[97] Burke to William Windham, 30 March 1797, in McDowell and Woods (eds.), *The Correspondence of Edmund Burke*, IX, 301. In 'Letter to a Noble Lord', in McDowell (ed.), *Writings and Speeches*, IX, 186, he refers to the barrier as 'the most precious part of England'.
[98] For Burke's subsequent concern with the French presence in the Low Countries, see, for example, 15 Dec. 1792, Cobbett (ed.), *The parliamentary history from the earliest period to the year 1803*, XXX, col. 114 Burke to William Windham, c. 2 Feb. 1795, McDowell (ed.), *The Correspondence of Edmund Burke*, VIII, 134; Burke to John Wilmot, 12 Dec. 1795, *ibid.*, 148–9. For his anxieties about 'the new system of giving to modern France the limits of ancient Gaul', see Burke to French Laurence, 1 March 1797, in McDowell and Woods (eds.), *The Correspondence of Edmund Burke*, IX, 265.
[99] See Simms, *Three Victories and a Defeat*.

protection of the universal rights of all 'humanity', without which the survival of individual members of the European Commonwealth would be meaningless.

Burke brought together all these themes in his broadside 'Heads for Consideration on the Present State of Affairs' (1792). He rebuked the courts of Austria and Prussia for suggesting 'that they had nothing to do with the interior arrangements of France', and he did so in terms which suggested that Burke fully understood the latitude which the true spirit of Westphalia gave to the counter-revolutionary powers. 'In this particular', Burke lamented, 'the two German courts seem to have as little consulted the publicists of Germany, as their own true interests, and those of all the Sovereigns of Germany and Europe'. Small wonder then that in the same document Burke dismissed the doctrine of non-intervention in the internal affairs of a sovereign state as 'a false principle in the Law of Nations'.[100]

---

[100] 'Heads for Consideration on the Present State of Affairs', 392–3.

*Part II*

# The Great Powers and the Ottoman Empire

RUSSIA

Vienna

Buda Pest

HUNGARY

Drava R.

Danube R.

TRANSYLVANIA

MOLDAVIA

Odessa

CROATIA

Sava R.

Braşov

WALLACHIA

BOSNIA

Belgrade

Bucharest

SERBIA

Danube R.

Split

Sarajevo

Vidin

Black
Sea

BOSNIA

Novi
Pazar

Niš

MONTENEGRO
Dubrovnik

Sofia

BULGARIA

Adriatic
Sea

Skopje

Plovdiv

Durrës

ALBANIA

Ohrid

Adrianople
(Edirne)

Constantinople

MACEDONIA

Thessaloniki

Sea of
Marmara

Janina

GREECE

Aegean
Sea

IONIAN ISLANDS
(British 1809–1863)

Athens

Mediterranean

Ottoman empire
Greece – independent from 1832
Territory ceded to Russia in 1812

CRETE

Sea

0   100   200   300   400 km
0   50   100   150   200   250 miles

Map 2  The Ottoman Empire in Europe, *c*. 1820s–1860s.

MEDITERRANEAN

SEA

Tripoli

Barid R.

Abu Ali R.

KURA

BSHARREH

Bsharreh

Jawz R.

Batrun

BATRUN

Duma

JBAIL

Jbail

Ibrahim R.

MNAITRA

KISRAWAN

Baalbek

Ghazir

Reifun

Bkerke

Ajallun

Zuk Mikayel

Baskinta

Bikfaiya

Beit Shebab

Brummana

Beirut R.

METN

Beit Meri

Salima

Zahleh

Beirut

Qabb Elias

SAHEL

Hazmiyeh

Baabda

Hadeth

Hammana

Bar Elias

SHUF BAYADI

Shwayfat

JURD

Ain Dara

to
Damascus

GHARB

Btater

ARQUB

Ammiq

Deir al-Qamar

R.

Baruk

Litani R.

Damur

Beit al-Din

Baaqline

Mukhtara

SHUF

Awwali R.

Jezzine

WADI TAYM

Sidon

Rashaiya

Jbaa

............ Province boundaries

Hasbaiya

Zahrani R.

| 0 | 5 | 10 | 15 | 20 | 25 km |

| 0 | 5 | 10 | 15 miles |

Marjayun

Map 3  Lebanon and Syria in the 1860s.

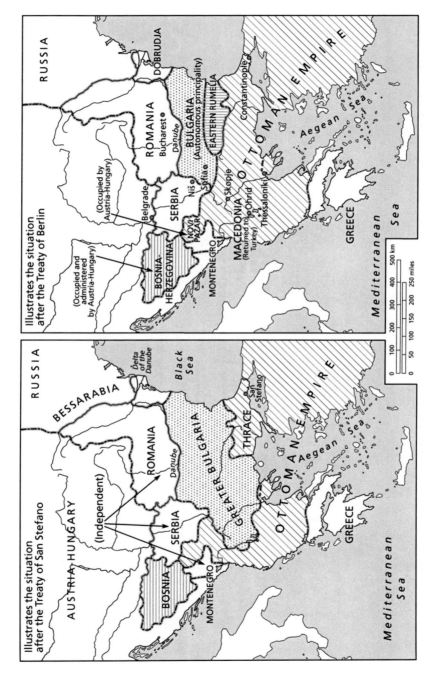

Map 4 The Ottoman Empire after the peace treaties of 1878.

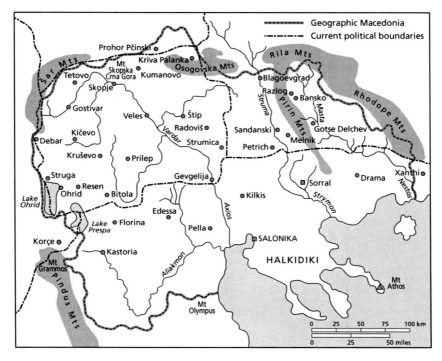

Map 5  Macedonia, *c.* 1900.

5    'From an umpire to a competitor':
     Castlereagh, Canning and the issue of
     international intervention in the wake
     of the Napoleonic Wars

*John Bew*

> There seems to be no little need that the whole doctrine of non-
> interference with foreign nations should be reconsidered ... with
> a view to establish some rule or criterion whereby the justifiableness
> of intervening in the affairs of other countries, and (what is sometimes
> fully as questionable) the justifiableness of refraining from intervention,
> may be brought to a definite and rational test.
>
> John Stuart Mill, 1859[1]

In seeking to outline the historical genesis of a modern political concept,
there is always the danger of anachronism and teleology. It is with that
in mind that this chapter focuses on a period in British history when
the *contra*-principle to humanitarian intervention – that is, the principle
of non-intervention – was in the ascendant. The aim is to provide an
insight into the twisted, accidental, but sequential origins of what was
later understood as humanitarian intervention. The focus is on British
foreign policy from the Battle of Waterloo in 1815 to the Battle of
Navarino in 1827. Although this volume contains a number of chapters
which pre-date the period of the Napoleonic Wars and it is misleading
to assume that these debates started in 1815 – or even 1793 – the reality
is that many theorists of intervention have traditionally taken, and still
do take, this period as the starting point for their analysis. That was as
true for John Stuart Mill, writing in the 1850s, as it is for Gary J. Bass
in his 2008 work, *Freedom's Battle: The Origins of Humanitarian
Intervention*.[2]

Some twentieth-century theorists, such as the German thinker Carl
Schmitt – a critic of intervention – have viewed humanitarian intervention as a modern incarnation of the 'just war' tradition, which could be

---

[1] J. S. Mill, 'A Few Words on Non-intervention', *Fraser's Magazine for Town and Country*,
60:360 (Dec. 1859), 766–76.
[2] G. J. Bass, *Freedom's Battle: The Origins of Humanitarian Intervention* (New York: Alfred
A. Knopf, 2008), 37–151.

traced back to St Thomas Aquinas.[3] A more recent view is that
humanitarian intervention derives from the theoretical application of
abstract moral principles at the expense of traditional notions of state
sovereignty and international law.[4] By contrast, this chapter argues that
the genesis of the concept of humanitarian intervention was more complex than a revival of the 'just war' tradition or the application of moral
universalism. It posits that there was a *realist* rationale at the core of
nineteenth-century interventionism from the outset and that intervention on the European continent – in the form that it took in the 1820s
and which has so clearly influenced later generations of theorists – came
about, above all, because of *strategic* necessities rather than *humanitarian*
imperatives. In this period, British foreign policy-makers, often reluctantly, moved outside what might be called the Westphalian paradigm.
In doing so, they set new precedents in the conduct of foreign policy,
entailing that their successors were less beholden to the strictures of the
principle of non-intervention (or, at least, an absolute application of
this principle), thus increasing the likelihood of humanitarian intervention in the future.

While the 'justifiableness' – in Mill's phrase – of intervention was to
become increasingly important, it was, initially at least, a secondary
consideration. That is not to say that a 'humanitarian imperative' was
not a prominent feature of contemporary debates. British foreign policy
was set against the background of the Philhellene movement of the
1820s.[5] More broadly, Peter Mandler has described the emergence of
a 'liberal universalist' mentality in early and mid-Victorian British
thought, based partly on a civic tradition of constitutionalism.[6] The
increasing use of the label 'liberal' was itself a product of heightened
interest in the affairs of other European states in this period, taken
from the Spanish *liberales*.[7] Much has also been said about the growing
influence of evangelical religion in this period, embodied in figures such as

[3] C. Brown, 'From Humanized War to Humanitarian Intervention: Carl Schmitt's
Critique of the Just War Tradition', in *The International Political Thought of Carl
Schmitt: Terror, Liberal War and the Crisis of the Global Order*, ed. L. Odysseos and
F. Petito (Abingdon and New York: Routledge, 2007), 56–70.
[4] R. Howard, *What's Wrong with Liberal Interventionism: The Dangers and Delusions of the
Interventionist Doctrine* (London: Social Affairs Unit, 2006).
[5] D. Beales, *From Castlereagh to Gladstone, 1815–1885* (London: W. W. Norton and Co.,
1969), 88.
[6] See P. Mandler, '"Race" and "Nation" in Mid-Victorian Thought', in *History, Religion,
and Culture: British Intellectual History, 1750–1950*, ed. S. Collini, R. Whatmore, and
B. Young (Cambridge: Cambridge University Press, 2000), 223–44.
[7] F. Rosen, *Bentham, Byron and Greece: Constitutionalism, Nationalism and Early Liberal
Political Thought* (Oxford: Oxford University Press, 1992).

Wilberforce and instrumental in the anti-slavery campaign.[8] Nonetheless, while these concerns were all part of the debate, they were not the foremost factor corroding Britain's commitment to non-interference in the internal affairs of other continental states. Rather than being *pushed* into intervention by a swell of domestic humanitarian sentiment – something which no government of the 1820s would have countenanced – Britain was actually *sucked* into intervention by the dictates of other foreign policy imperatives. The most important of these was a commitment to preserving 'the balance of power' in Europe. When foreign intervention did occur in a tangible military form, in the Battle of Navarino in 1827 – an episode which precipitated Greek independence and has often been interpreted as the first example of humanitarian intervention[9] – it was in fact 'accidental', to quote *The Times* editorial which appeared shortly after the episode.[10] Ultimately, Britain's increasing engagement with the Eastern Question – which culminated with Navarino – says more about the difficulties of avoiding such interventions – due to the necessities of *Realpolitik* – rather than the ideological, theoretical or moral considerations which fed into them.

If the origin of humanitarian intervention can be traced, it is arguably more discernible in the fusion of different strands of thinking, rather than in the search for a self-contained foreign policy tradition with a long historical lineage. In keeping with this, the first part of the chapter demonstrates how two otherwise separate concepts – interventionism and humanitarianism – were fused together in the unique context of the 1820s. Ultimately, however, the chapter also makes a bolder claim: that once Britain became drawn into active military intervention on the Continent, she was always likely to be drawn to the 'liberal' or 'humanitarian' side. In other words, the linkage between interventionism and humanitarianism was sequential; once it became clear that it was against the national interest to uphold a strict principle of non-intervention in every case, it was equally difficult for successive British governments to proceed without the consideration of humanitarian principles.

---

[8] For a broader discussion of the influence of evangelicalism, see B. Hilton, *The Age of Atonement: The Influence of Evangelicalism on Social and Economic Thought, 1785–1865* (Oxford: Oxford University Press, 1988).

[9] See, for example, L. Oppenheim in *International Law: A Treatise*, vol. I: *Peace*, ed. H. Lauterpacht, 8th edn (London: Longman Green, 1995), cited in N. Onuf, 'Humanitarian Intervention: The Early Years' (paper presented at the Centre of Global Peace and Conflict Studies Symposium on the Norms and Ethics of Humanitarian Intervention, University of California, Irvine), 5 May 2000, available at www.cgpacs.uci. edu/research/working_papers/nicholas_onuf_humanitarian_intervention.pdf.

[10] *The Times*, 21 Nov. 1827.

## The issue of intervention after the Treaty of Vienna

It would be a mistake to assume that, after 1815, the geopolitical landscape represented some sort of antediluvian world in the eyes of European statesmen. Nonetheless, the success of the Napoleonic army and the sheer reach of French conquests did have significant implications for traditional notions of state sovereignty and the restoration of the existing international order.[11] To a certain extent, the Treaty of Vienna of 1815 successfully papered over some of these cracks, at least momentarily.[12] After the defeat of Napoleon, the victorious allies – Britain, Austria, Prussia and Russia – proclaimed a desire to restore equilibrium in Europe and, with the exception of Britain, also expressed a specific preference for legitimist forms of government (stopping short of demanding the complete restoration of the pre-war status quo).[13] However, the corollary of this was that, in the eyes of the 'Holy Alliance' (Austria, Russia and Prussia), national sovereignty took second place to legitimacy. After 1815, Britain faced a European continent in which the main powers were more committed to intervening in the affairs of other states in a systematic way. Henry Kissinger has argued that the 'operational significance' of the Holy Alliance was that it introduced 'an element of moral restraint in to the relationship of the Great Powers'.[14] Equally, it might be said that its long-term consequences were more destabilising, actually jeopardising the 'balance of power' – which Kissinger also saw as the essence of the Vienna compromise – and forcing Britain to rethink its attitude to the Continent.

Commentators reflecting on British foreign policy in this period – such as Kissinger, or the Marquess of Salisbury, writing in the late

[11] For a compelling case for the exceptional nature of the Napoleonic Wars, see C. Esdaile, *Napoleon's Wars: An International History, 1803–1815* (London: Allen Lane, 2007). See also M. John, 'The Napoleonic Legacy and Problems of Restoration in Central Europe: The German Confederation', and B. Simms, 'Napoleon and Germany: A Legacy in Foreign Policy', in *Napoleon's Legacy: Problems in Restoration Europe*, ed. D. Laven and L. Riall (Oxford: Berg, 2000), 83–96 and 97–114.

[12] A. Zamoyski, *Rites of Peace: The Fall of Napoleon and the Congress of Vienna* (London: HarperCollins, 2007); H. Nicolson, *The Congress of Vienna: A Study in Allied Unity: 1812–1822* (London: Constable & Co., 1946); C. K. Webster, *The Foreign Policy of Castlereagh, 1812–1815: Britain and the Reconstruction of Europe*, vol. I (London: G. Bell & Sons, 1931) and Webster, *British Diplomacy, 1813–1815: Select Documents Dealing with Reconstruction of Europe* (London: G. Bell & Sons, 1921).

[13] P. M. Pilbeam, 'The "Restoration" of Western Europe, 1814–15', and B. Simms, 'The Eastern Empires from the Challenge of Napoleon to the Restoration, c.1806–30', in *Themes in Modern European History, 1780–1830*, ed. Pilbeam (London and New York: Routledge, 1995), 107–24 and 85–106.

[14] H. Kissinger, *Diplomacy* (New York: Simon and Schuster, 1994), 79–84.

nineteenth century – have placed great emphasis on the principle of 'non-intervention', which often appeared in diplomatic dispatches and parliamentary debates from the 1820s.[15] On the fundamental point that Lord Castlereagh (Foreign Secretary from 1812 until his death in 1822) adhered to a doctrine of non-intervention, there is no room for dispute. Where we must be careful, however, is in the concomitant assumption that, in pursuing such a policy, Castlereagh was resisting a significant bloc of pro-interventionist opinion, either from the Whig opposition or from his successor, George Canning. In reality, while there were deeply held divisions over the conduct of foreign policy, these were not fundamentally between interventionists and non-interventionists. The Whigs had a long history of willingness to intervene in Europe during the eighteenth century, largely through their commitment to Hanover. Likewise, William Pitt's government had also shown itself willing to intervene in the internal affairs of other states in the 1790s, because of the exceptional nature of the war effort. Nonetheless, in the period under consideration, both Whigs and Tories were generally anti-interventionist; despite marked differences on what this meant in practice, it might be said that they represented different species of the same creed.[16]

Significantly, insofar as there were active interventionists on the European stage, they were not humanitarian or liberal. Linked to the Holy Alliance, and conducted in defence of hereditary monarchs, the very notion of intervention had negative connotations in British politics in this period, and was seen as the greatest impediment to the emergence of liberal constitutionalist movements.[17] When Castlereagh was attacked by radicals and Whigs it was because of his complicity in a great power system which intervened in the affairs of other states. 'With a single stoke of his pen [at Vienna in 1815]', declared a radical pamphleteer in 1818, he 'laid the foundations of UNIVERSAL DESPOTISM'.[18] Or, as Lord John Russell claimed in his 1819 Letter to the Right Honourable Lord Holland on Foreign Politics, England had bound itself 'to interfere in the internal concerns of every state of Europe'.[19]

[15] R. Cecil (Lord Salisbury) on Castlereagh, Essays by the Marquess of Salisbury, vol. I: Biographical (London: John Murray, 1905), 3–70; Henry Kissinger, A World Restored: Metternich, Castlereagh and the Problems of Peace, 1812–1822 (London: Weidenfeld & Nicolson, 1957).

[16] R. J. Vincent, Nonintervention and International Order (Princeton: Princeton University Press, 1974), 70–2.

[17] Bass, Freedom's Battle, 47–87.

[18] Anon., Political Epitaphs, No. 1 Mr Canning ... No. 2 Lord Castlereagh (London, n.d. [1818?]).

[19] See also Lord John Russell, A Letter to the Right Honourable Lord Holland on Foreign Politics [1819], 4th edn (London, 1831).

In fact, Castlereagh's cooperation with these powers was more limited than is often assumed. He held aloof from the Holy Alliance, famously calling it 'a piece of sublime mysticism and nonsense'.[20] It is true that he did acquiesce in (rather than actively support) Austria's suppression of the Neapolitan revolt of 1821, which he had been appraised of by Count Metternich and which he refused to condemn in parliament. Nonetheless, Castlereagh became increasingly alarmed by the 'abstractions and sweeping generalities' associated with the Holy Alliance.[21] In contrast to the Holy Alliance, Britain was bound to protect the territorial settlement agreed to at Vienna for twenty years, but she had never agreed to collectively interfere in, or act as the guarantor of, any system of government within an independent state. Even in the case of France, Castlereagh was insistent that the allies 'could not justly claim any right of interference' unless they considered 'their own safety compromised'. 'The only safe Principles is that of the Law of Nations', he ventured, 'nothing would be more immoral or prejudicial to the Character of Government generally, than the Idea that their force was collectively to be prostituted to the support of established Power without any Consideration of the extent to which it was abused'.[22]

The most definitive expression of the principle of non-intervention was Castlereagh's State Paper of 5 May 1820, a response to another Russian dispatch which mooted allied intervention to put down a liberal rising in Spain. Castlereagh emphasised that his insistence on non-intervention was 'not absolute'; Britain would be found in her place 'when actual danger menaces the System of Europe'. However, he was also clear that 'this Country cannot, and will not, act upon the abstract and speculative principles of Precaution'. It was apparent that many European states were 'now employed in the difficult task of casting anew their Gov[ernmen]ts upon the Representative Principle' and 'the notion of revising, limiting or regulating the course of such Experiments, either by foreign Council or by foreign foe, would be as dangerous to avow as it w[ould] be impossible to execute'. The Congress system was never 'intended as an Union for the Government of the World, or for the Superintendence of the Internal Affairs of other States'. There were other practical problems with such a policy too; collective intervention had an 'air of dictation and menace', entailing that the 'grounds of the

---

[20] W. Hinde, *Castlereagh* (London: Collins, 1981), 233.
[21] A. Hassal, *Viscount Castlereagh* (London: Sir I. Pitman and Sons, 1908), 212.
[22] 'Memorandum on the Treaties of 1814 and 1815, Aix-la-Chapelle, October 1818', in H. Temperley and L. M. Penson, *Foundations of British Foreign Policy from Pitt (1792) to Salisbury (1902)* [1938] (London: Frank Cass, 1966), 39–46.

intervention thus become unpopular, the intention of the parties is misunderstood, the publick Mind is agitated and perverted, and the General Political Situation of the Government is thereby essentially embarrassed'.[23]

## The anti-intervention consensus

Castlereagh's position was based on a definition of national freedom as independence from other nations: 'the sense in which the word [freedom] is mostly used by the ancients' and which had been most famously articulated in Emmerich de Vattel's 1758 treatise on *The Law of Nations*.[24] Yet, this was not a particularly controversial mantra in the context of British political debate. Despite their differences of opinion, both the Whig opposition and George Canning – Castlereagh's successor as Foreign Secretary from 1822 to 1827 – did not deviate substantially from this premise. In his study of the Whigs in opposition in this period, Austin Mitchell argued that their basic foreign policy stance was as the 'advocates of change'. 'Palmerstonian before Palmerston', they 'urged the twin principles of national independence and self-determination'. But if this was a party that advocated change on the European continent, they also limited the scope for such change through their explicit commitment to a policy of non-intervention. Notably, Mitchell insisted that 'all other whig principles were subordinate to this encouragement of liberal regimes' and that non-intervention 'was never advanced in absolute terms'.[25] But it is hard to see how this caveat distinguished them in any concrete way from the position held by Castlereagh.

At various points during the eighteenth century, Whigs had been more willing than Tories to interfere in continental affairs, both for strategic reasons and in order to protect the Protestants against oppression.[26] However, one consequence – perhaps unintended – of Whig opposition to Pitt's entry into war against France in 1793 was a shift to an anti-interventionist stance – a position which hardened in opposition to Castlereagh from 1815. In 1831, one Tory writer characterised the

---

[23] Temperley and Penson, *Foundations of British Foreign Policy*, 48–63.

[24] T. P. Courtenay (a junior member of the government under Castlereagh), 'Foreign Policy of England: Lord Castlereagh', *The Foreign Quarterly Review* 8 (July 1831), 33–60.

[25] A. Mitchell, *The Whigs in Opposition, 1815–1830* (Oxford: Clarendon Press, 1967), 17–18.

[26] See B. Simms, *Three Victories and a Defeat: The Rise and Fall of the First British Empire, 1714–1783* (London: Allen Lane, 2007).

Whig position of the previous forty years as follows: 'Mr Pitt was for despotism and the Bourbons; Mr Fox for freedom and the people. Mr Pitt would interfere in the form of foreign government; Mr Fox would leave each nation to choose its own government . . . Interference, the principle of the Tories; non-interference, the watch-word of the Whigs.' If anything, as this writer observed, this was an inaccurate portrayal of Pitt's position – the latter had justified the intervention on the grounds of France's threat to the navigation laws of Scheldt and her breaking of existing European treaties. Instead, it was the former Whig Edmund Burke who had been the foremost exponent of the restoration of the Bourbons as a war aim, something which Pitt regarded as 'at variance with his political creed'. What is more, despite their support for Pitt, 'the disciples of Burke and Windham impute to . . . [Pitt] as a fault the disregard of that advice'.[27] Thus, the mainstream Whig position from 1815 represented a disjuncture with past traditions. Significantly, as early as 1817, Lord Grey wrote to Lord Holland to express concern about the self-imposed limits of this commitment to non-intervention.[28] As noted below, some Whigs began to shift back to a more flexible position in making a case for intervention in Portugal in 1826, in order to protect the constitutional government there against foreign interference. In practice, however, although the Whigs showed occasional glimpses of awareness about the potential contradictions in their position, they never satisfactorily resolved this internal tension and, for most of the 1820s, their foreign policy still pivoted around anti-interventionism.

The classic statement of the anti-interventionist Whig position was made by the jurist Sir James Mackintosh in response to Austria's intervention to suppress the Naples revolt of 1821. His key objection to such instances of intervention was that, once they began, they would be limitless. Moreover, even when humanitarian concerns were at stake, he was unprepared to countenance an exception. Referring to Austrian allegations of cruelty by the Neapolitan rebels (which he rejected), Mackintosh speculated about how dangerously open-ended such a justification could be:

Suppose the emperor of Russia had committed acts of flagrant injustice and cruelty towards some of his subjects in Asia; were we called on to express our opinions and to remonstrate on behalf of the Calmucs and Tongulsses? If such interference were justified, there would be no end to them. Suppose some foreign government had complained of our conduct towards the Catholics in Ireland,

[27] Courtenay, 'Foreign Policy of England'.    [28] Mitchell, *Whigs in Opposition*, 17–18.

and remonstrated on the ground that we had provoked a rebellion, and then suppressed it, in order to effect a union with Great Britain, should we have endured such meddling with our conduct towards any of our intermediaries.

Pursued to its full logic, the Holy Alliance position was, 'in effect a proposition for encamping a whole horde of Cossacks or croats in Hyde-park'.[29]

In responding to Mackintosh, Castlereagh identified a contradiction between the lofty moral tones assumed by the Whigs in foreign policy debates and their apparent squeamishness about intervention on the Continent. Following an attack on his policy of refusing to censure Austria for its suppression of the rebellion, he complained that, 'when reduction of every kind, and especially of our army, had been called for again and again, it was too much ... to be told that the British government ought to dictate moral lessons to Europe'. If we did speak, he stated, 'we ought to speak with effect':

He should deem it most pusillanimous conduct on our part, if, after interfering on a question of this nature, we limited our interference to the mere delivery of a scroll of paper, and did not follow it up with some more effectual measures. Were we to turn itinerant preachers of morality to the other nations of Europe, and to follow up the doctrines which we preached by nothing else but what was contained in our state papers?

When Napoleon had put down rebellions in Venice and Genoa, 'not a voice was raised in behalf of these republics by the gentlemen opposite [the Whigs]', who were more interested in negotiating a settlement with Napoleon, 'the grand subverter of the independence of states'.[30]

It would also be a mistake to see George Canning's appointment as Foreign Secretary in 1822 as the signature moment in the departure of a new, more 'interventionist' policy.[31] In fact, it is possible to argue that Canning was even more of a staunch anti-interventionist than Castlereagh. Over the issue of Austria's intervention in Naples in 1821, he had essentially backed his predecessor's position, reiterating the need for neutrality in 'deed' as well as 'word'. It was Canning who stated that intervention to uphold constitutionalist movements in other states was out of keeping with the aims of a country which mediated between 'Jacobinism' and 'Ultraism'.[32] The most obvious distinction was that Canning made a clearer break from the Concert of Europe.

[29]  21 Feb. 1821, *Hansard*, 3rd series, vol. IV, 838–58.
[30]  21 Feb. 1821, *ibid.*, 864–79.
[31]  H. W. V Temperley, *The Foreign Policy of Canning, 1822–1827*, 2nd edn (London: Frank Cass, 1966).
[32]  Vincent, *Nonintervention and International Order*, 84–5.

In emphasising Britain's opposition to French royalist intervention against the Spanish *liberales*, Canning effectively broke up the congress of Verona which had convened in October 1823. He also refused to attend a congress called by the tsar in December 1824, on the issue of the war between the Ottoman Empire and the Greeks. If anything, it was his staunch anti-interventionism that allowed him to sidestep Whig critiques more effectively. As Temperley has explained, Canning's 'English' foreign policy was often contrasted to Castlereagh's 'Europeanism'.[33] Furthermore, in demonstrating more disdain for the notion of 'legitimacy' adhered to by the Holy Alliance, he won some supporters in the liberal press, without making a substantial new departure in policy.[34]

In reality, Castlereagh had already been extricating himself from the Concert of Europe by the time of his suicide in 1822.[35] Speaking to parliament in 1823, Canning insisted that he had no intention of 'separating himself in any degree from those who had preceded him in it'. As the foundation-stone of his own position, he referred to Castlereagh's State Paper of 1820, 'laying down the principle of non-interference, with all the qualifications properly belonging to it'. Canning also made the ingenious point that the respective positions of Castlereagh and the Whigs were, in effect, two sides of the same coin. After acknowledging his debt to Castlereagh, he informed the Commons that he claimed to see no contradiction in also adhering to the guiding principles laid down by Mackintosh in 1821: 'respect for the faith of treaties – respect for the independence of nations – respect for that established line of policy known by the name of "the balance of power" in Europe – and last and not least, respect for the honour and interests of this country'.[36]

Canning was highlighting the fact that there was, in this period, a non-interventionist consensus, bound closely to the notion of the balance of power. However, just as he was articulating his own policy, doubts about the long-term sustainability of the non-intervention principle began to emerge. Before the Verona conference of October 1822, Canning (following Castlereagh's brief) had insisted that England would not tolerate a breach of the sovereignty of Spain by France, in defence of the royalist cause; once again, a policy of 'strict neutrality' was to form the crux of British policy. In the Commons, he tackled the argument that 'the invasion of Spain by a French force ought to be considered by

---

[33] Temperley, *The Foreign Policy of Canning*.
[34] See A. Briggs, *The Age of Improvement, 1783–1867* (London: Longmans, 1959), 218–19.
[35] *Ibid.*
[36] 14 Apr. 1823, *Hansard*, 3rd series, vol. VIII, 872–904. See also Temperley and Penson, *Foundations of British Foreign Policy*, 47–9.

England as an act of war against herself'. He was prepared to admit that a French invasion would be 'absolutely unjust' and he sympathised with those who 'seeing a strong and powerful nation eager to crush and overwhelm [with] its vengeance a less numerous but not less gallant people, were anxious to join the weaker against the stronger party'. Equally, however, in opposing such an action, he emphasised that, for military action to take place, 'the cause of it should not merely be sufficient, but urgent'. Moreover – here was the realist core – war had to be 'absolutely consistent with the interest and welfare of the country which first declared it'.[37]

When France did march on Spain, with the professed aim of restoring the legitimist government, Canning maintained British neutrality, despite requests for assistance from both the French government and the Spanish rebels. It was clear that vague warnings that Britain was opposed to the interference in principle had not been enough to prevent French action. But the French invasion created a number of other concerns, relating more directly to British interests in the New World, as well as Europe. Consequently, Canning now issued a stern warning to France against the permanent occupation of Spain, the appropriation of Spain's colonial possessions in the New World or the violation of territorial integrity of Portugal, Britain's traditional ally (with whom she had a defensive treaty). In doing so, he successfully acquired from Polignac, the French ambassador in London, a guarantee that France would not invade Cuba on behalf of legitimist Spain.[38] This 'hands off' warning to the European powers who might have designs on the New World was underpinned by an implicit threat that 'the junction of any foreign Power in an enterprise of Spain against the Colonies, would be viewed by them as constituting an entirely new question: and one upon which they must take such decision as the *interest* of Great Britain might require [my italics]'.[39]

Britain was effectively evoking the spectre of intervention in defence of the principle of non-intervention.[40] Although the logic was somewhat lopsided, the implications were increasingly difficult to ignore. A similar dilemma was soon caused by the progress of the Portuguese constitutionalists. Initially, Canning rejected appeals to intervene in Portugal on their behalf and rebuked Sir Edward Thornton, the British minister at

---

[37] Hansard, ibid.    [38] Vincent, *Nonintervention and International Order*, 86–9.
[39] 'The Polignac Memorandum, October 1823', in Temperley and Penson, *Foundations of British Foreign Policy*, 70–6.
[40] W. A. Phillips, 'Great Britain and the Continental Alliance, 1816–1822', in *The Cambridge History of British Foreign Policy, 1783–1919*, vol. II: *1815–1886*, ed. A. W. Ward and G. P. Gooch (Cambridge: Cambridge University Press, 1923), 67.

Lisbon, who had publicly advocated the liberal cause.[41] Ultimately, however, he was prepared to send British forces into Portugal in 1826, when absolutists – supporting the king's anti-constitutionalist younger brother Miguel – attacked Portugal with Spanish arms and equipment. Canning carefully justified this more substantive intervention on the traditional grounds that Britain was preserving the independence of an ally, with whom she had a defensive treaty. In these instances, it appeared that the principle of non-intervention was morphing into threats of counter-attack and *de facto* interventionism by Britain. Crucially, however, the humanitarian imperative was not explicitly evoked as a justification for action, despite widespread sympathy for the constitutionalist movements in the Iberian Peninsula. The tensions over Spain and Portugal during the mid- to late 1820s have often been viewed as 'an outgrowth of the fundamental clash and division in Europe between the constitutional West and the autocratic East'. In reality, as Paul Schroeder has pointed out, 'the two liberal-constitutional powers actively involved in the peninsula, Britain and France, were both playing a normal, non-ideological game almost entirely with and against each other'. Moreover, despite the supposed conflict of principles, the reality is that the Holy Alliance powers, who believed in the principle of intervention, did not intervene, and the Western powers, in particular Britain, intervened under the principle of non-intervention.[42] The balance of power remained central to all these actions; it was telling that British troops did not leave Portugal until French troops left Spain.[43]

### The Russian threat and the realist case for intervention

At this stage, it might be said that I seem to have been arguing against the existence of humanitarian interventionism as a serious foreign policy consideration in this period. Certainly, it was not a principle which was operationally recognisable or had any staunch advocates among those likely to exert a formative influence on the shaping of policy; there may well have been proto-interventionists – as Gary Bass has described, in the case of the London Greek Committee – but they did not exert a formative influence on the making of policy.[44] In fact, the dominant mantras of this period prompted Henry Kissinger to compare British

---

[41] Temperley, *The Foreign Policy of Canning*, 202–3.

[42] P. W. Schroeder, *The Transformation of European Politics, 1763–1848* (Oxford: Oxford University Press, 1994), 720.

[43] Vincent, *Nonintervention and International Order*, 86–9.

[44] Bass, *Freedom's Battle*, 51–151.

foreign policy with later American isolationism, as 'Britain felt impervious to all but cataclysmic upheavals'.[45] There was also a clear selfish,
strategic rationale behind the policy of non-intervention. Britain increasingly trained its sights on extending its empire overseas and had no
territorial designs on the European continent. It is worth repeating
Canning's definitive mantra: 'When people ask me . . . for what is called
a policy, the only answer is that we mean to do what may seem to be best,
upon each occasion as it arises, making the Interests of Our Country
one's guiding principle.' This was also the 'guiding principle' of Lord
Palmerston who declared that 'changes in the internal Constitution and
form of Government, are to be looked upon as matters with which
England has no business to interfere by force of arms'.[46] 'There is a
country in Europe, equal to the greatest in extent of dominion, far
exceeding any other in wealth, and in the power that wealth bestows,
the declared principle of whose foreign policy is, to let other nations
alone', wrote Mill.[47] The 'seductive policy of total abstention in continental affairs, an isolationism which would interpret the non-intervention
principle absolutely', was always under the surface of debate.[48]

But that still leaves us with an important question unanswered:
how did the idea of humanitarian intervention subsequently become
ingrained onto the diplomatic agenda, to the extent that John Stuart
Mill could seek to define it as a coherent principle in 1859, citing the
experiences of the 1820s? The short answer is that there was a growing
realisation that the successful operation of the non-intervention principle
did not always coalesce with British interests. From the time of
Castlereagh's tenure at the Foreign Office, a shared commitment with
other powers to maintain the peace of Europe entailed that the spectre
of intervention would raise its head at intervals. In accepting a role of
mediation on the Continent after Vienna, the prospect of becoming
embroiled in such interference had increased. To this it might be said
that both Canning and the Whigs advocated the extrication of Britain
from these alliances. Yet, although they could step away from the Holy
Alliance, they could not wish away its existence. Second, and most
importantly, non-intervention was not a purely abstract position, independent of any other considerations; it was nearly always invoked in the
same breath as another cornerstone of British foreign policy: the balance
of power. Castlereagh's strategic objection to great power intervention
was that it might jeopardise the equilibrium established at Vienna, which

---

[45] Kissinger, *Diplomacy*, 96.    [46] *Ibid.*
[47] Mill, 'A Few Words on Non-intervention'.
[48] Vincent, *Nonintervention and International Order*, 70–2.

ensured that no one power was dominant on the Continent.[49] Under Castlereagh, Britain had acted as a moderating check on the interventionist ambitions of other powers, such as Russia; consequently, once she had broken with the Congress system under Canning, the likelihood of intervention by the other European powers actually increased rather than diminished.

This problem – the growing spectre of great power intervention by other European states – had become increasingly obvious in the cases of Spain and Portugal. Canning's actions in both instances might be seen as a reluctant recognition of that reality. As Vincent has pointed out, Britain's generally *laissez-faire* attitude to forms of government in other states 'did not mean that she would refrain from intervention if pressing imperatives like the maintenance of the balance of power required it; what it did mean was that she could admit intervention only as an exception to the general of international conduct'.[50] In other words, Britain was being sucked back into European intervention, primarily on the basis of the old Pittite imperative: the balance of power. As Derek Beales has written, Castlereagh's objections derived from the fear 'that a Power which moved to suppress a revolution or a constitution in other states might have expansionist intentions'.[51] Thus, he was able to countenance Metternich's autocratic interference in the Italian and German states, chiefly because he did not regard Austria as a country which aspired to European hegemony.

By contrast, the prospect of Russian expansionism was the one variable which neither Castlereagh – as a key participant in the Congress system – nor much less Canning – as its critic – could control. In practical terms, the fear of Russian troops swamping Europe – rather than French resurgence – was the fundamental threat to British foreign policy interests.[52] One reason why England was slow to tackle the problem of Barbary pirates – and aimed to keep it off the table at the Congress of 1818 – was the risk of allowing the Russian fleet a free rein in the Mediterranean.[53] Concerted interventionism, wrote Castlereagh, would give Russian troops 'an almost irresistible claim to march through the territories of all the Confederate States to the most distant points of Europe to fulfil her guarantee [to maintain legitimist governments]'.[54]

---

[49] 'State Paper of 5 May 1820', in Temperley and Penson, *Foundations of British Foreign Policy*, 48–63.
[50] Vincent, *Nonintervention and International Order*, 71.
[51] Beales, *From Castlereagh to Gladstone*, 91.
[52] Kissinger, *Diplomacy*, 95.      [53] Hassal, *Viscount Castlereagh*, 212.
[54] Castlereagh to Lord Liverpool, 19 Oct. 1818, cited in Phillips, 'Great Britain and the Continental Alliance', 9.

The rationale in acting in congress was, to use Castlereagh's own phrase, to keep the tsar 'grouped' and less likely to behave in a renegade manner.[55]

The difficulty in reining in the tsar's ambitions first became apparent over the issue of the Greek revolt against the crumbling Ottoman Empire. From the Foreign Office perspective, the righteousness (or otherwise) of the cause took second place to fears about Russian ambitions in the region, as the self-styled advocates of the Christian Greeks. For this reason, Castlereagh was unprepared 'to embark on a scheme for new modelling the position of the Greek population at the hazard of all the destructive confusion and disunion which such an attempt would lead to'.[56] As one Irish advocate of the Greeks explained, 'the insurgents had perceived their ultimate dependency on the Courts of Europe' and had 'sought to conciliate their goodwill' at the Congress of Verona.[57] But Castlereagh's fear was that collective intervention would allow Russia to assume a predominant role in a region vital for British commercial and shipping interests. Shortly before his death, he successfully convinced the tsar not to act, suggesting that encouraging a revolt was a betrayal of the founding principles of the Holy Alliance (which was certainly Metternich's position). After Castlereagh's death, Britain lost something of its restraining influence on Russia. Moreover, by 1824, the Greeks had come close to achieving a *de facto* position of autonomy in the region, allowing Canning to grant them the status of belligerents in international law. It seemed that the conflict might be heading towards a conclusion without outside interference, until the Ottoman Sultan enlisted extra-European support in the form of Ali, the Pacha of Egypt. The latter's armies arrived in February 1825, adding a new intensity to the war and accentuating the impression that this was a struggle between Christians and Muslims. From this point, the issue was thrust back onto the diplomatic agenda; British public opinion was roused as the news began to emerge of Ottoman–Egyptian attempts to 'depopulate' some areas of its Greek population.[58]

In a protocol agreed in April 1826, both Britain and Russia had agreed a self-denying ordinance not to seek territorial advantage in the region. For his own part, Canning was still eager to avoid a joint commitment to upholding Greek independence, which would see Britain sucked into military intervention. Nonetheless, however undesirable this scenario was, it was the second worst option facing him. Much more dangerous was the

---

[55] Phillips, 'Great Britain and the Continental Alliance', 43.     [56] *Ibid.*, 43–4.
[57] James Emerson, *The History of Greece* (London, 1830), vol. I, cxvii–cxxiii.
[58] Bass, *Freedom's Battle*, 123–8.

prospect of Russia taking the matter into her own hands. Thus, Britain took the strategic decision to enter into more substantive negotiations with Russia (and France), leading to the Treaty of London on 6 July 1827. During the course of negotiations, as the Russians pushed for a secret clause which recommended the use of force, as Temperley has described, it was 'pretty clear now that unless he [Canning] consented to use force, Russia would go forward alone'. The conclusion reached was that 'if force was to be used, England must act with, and restrain, Russia'.[59] The basis of the treaty – accepted by the Greeks and rejected by the Turks – was to make Greece a tributary province, under sovereignty of the sultan, with permission to choose its own governors. It was accompanied by an offer to mediate in the dispute if an armistice was declared. Russian, French and English forces in the Mediterranean were immediately strengthened.

From this point, it was soon to become clear, Britain's Greek policy was devolved to its naval commanders. When supplies for Ibrahim Pacha's army arrived in the Greek port of Navarino, British forces prevented their movement to other ports in order to enforce the treaty.[60] However, the Turkish–Egyptian fleet broke the terms of an armistice signed on 25 September 1825 and reports soon reached the French and British navies that the Turks had resorted to what some called 'inhuman butchery' in the Morea. On 18 October 1827, the commanders of the three allied fleets, following instructions to enforce the treaty, entered the harbour of Navarino to remonstrate with the Turks and Egyptians.[61] The allied brief was to ensure the treaty and act as an arbiter, rather than to engage any of the combatants in warfare. The Commander-in-Chief of the British fleet, Edward Codrington, described how the allies sailed into Navarino on 20 October 'in order to induce Ibrahim Pacha to discontinue the brutal war of extermination which has been carrying on'. On the one hand, Codrington might be seen as an early exponent of humanitarian intervention; on hearing evidence of Ottoman atrocities in the region, he had commented that war might be 'a more humane way of settling affairs here than any other'. But much more important was the lack of precision in his brief. 'Neither I nor the French Admiral can make out', he had written, 'how we are by force to prevent the Turks, if obstinate, from pursuing any line of conduct which we are instructed to oppose, without committing hostility'.[62] When Turkish and Egyptian

---

[59] Temperley, *The Foreign Policy of Canning*, 390–409.    [60] *Ibid.*

[61] Emerson, *History of Greece*, vol. I, cxvii–cxxiii.

[62] Temperley, *The Foreign Policy of Canning*, 404–6. See also *Memoir of the Life of Admiral Sir Edward Codrington* (London, 1873), by his daughter Lady Jane Bourchier.

forces took fright at the sight of the approaching allies and opened fire, Codrington responded with his own fire, leading to a massive battle in which the Turkish and Egyptian fleets in the bay were almost entirely routed.[63]

There was clearly a humanitarian component to this act. Nonetheless, for all the horror at Ottoman atrocities, the only scenario in which the allied commanders were allowed to use force was in the event that they were attacked directly. Commenting on this surprise engagement – which had actually taken place after Canning's death on 8 August 1827 – *The Times* described the existence of 'humane and Christian feeling' as a contributory factor but also emphasised that the allied onslaught was, first and foremost, an act of 'self-defence'. Ibrahim Pacha had behaved 'grossly towards the Allies, and cruelly towards the Greeks', breaking the conditions of his armistice. Not only had the object of the treaty of 6 July been finally obtained, it also noted, 'the policy of Russia [had been] developed, explained, defined, and limited'.[64] However, within just a few days, *The Times* – which had been sympathetic to the intervention – also acknowledged the growing controversy about 'the rectitude of those principles on which the battle was fought by the Allies'. The battle itself was 'accidental', claimed the newspaper, and the British presence in the region was justified by the 'Law of Nations' and the Treaty of London. Notably, however, the humanitarian rationale loomed increasingly large in retrospective justifications of the action: 'Could ... the Turkish Government, *after* the conclusion and communication of ... [the] treaty, *expect* that it would be any longer permitted to direct the massacre of the Greeks?'[65] Moreover, the suggestion that 'public opinion has declared itself *against* the battle of Navarino as an act of violence and aggression' was quickly rejected: on the contrary 'it is universally regarded as an event as unavoidable as it was professionally glorious'.[66]

At the level of officialdom, bitter disputes were reported between the members of the government 'as to the causes, the conduct, or the consequences of that battle', and of the propriety of honouring Codrington, who was accused of gunboat diplomacy.[67] Writing three-quarters of a century later, Lord Salisbury bemoaned the Battle of Navarino as an unfortunate consequence of 'the practice of foreign intervention in domestic squabbles', and another example from the history of the last seventy years, 'strewn with the wrecks of national prosperity which these well-meant interventions have caused'. In the King's Speech of

---

[63] *The Times*, 12 Nov. 1827.    [64] *Ibid.*
[65] *The Times*, 14 Nov. 1827.    [66] *The Times*, 21 Nov. 1827.    [67] *Ibid.*

29 January 1828, it was dismissed as an 'untoward event'.[68] The legacy of the event is discussed further below. Ultimately, however, there is no escaping the fact that Britain's willingness to countenance intervention in Greece 'reflected the primacy of interest over doctrine'.[69] It was emphatically not the case, as one scholar has put it, that 'Humanitarian and religious concerns combined to inflame the liberal world and override the resistance to intervention so typical of the British government.'[70] Indeed, as one radical critic of Greek policy correctly identified in 1836, it was not 'the practice of intervention' but the 'balance of power' with had led to British involvement in the region in the first place. 'Not a war has broken out, but, either, in its origin or progress, it has had reference to this maxim', it was claimed. This, the radical complained, was what was always behind the sight of 'English statesmen of all parties and ages… rushing eagerly to participate in the dangers, and share the burdens, of commotions a thousand miles removed from its shores'.[71]

## The humanitarian context of intervention

Thus far, this chapter has illustrated the realist rationale which undermined the principle of non-intervention. With that having been established, it makes one further claim. When Britain was sucked into intervention, the 'humanitarian imperative' – the moral dimension to British political debate – increasingly came into play as an irreducible consideration. Even when it was accidental, military intervention of this kind, as the editorial commentary of *The Times* on the Battle of Navarino described above demonstrated, was much easier to defend when it had a moral justification.

Even Castlereagh had clearly recognised that British foreign policy could not proceed without a sufficient degree of public support. In his 1820 State Paper, he had stated that 'if embarked in a War, which the Voice of the Country does not support, the Efforts of the strongest Administration which ever served the Crown would be unequal to the prosecution of the Conquest'.[72] As he told his half-brother Lord Stewart in the same year, it was impossible to act militarily without 'the

---

[68] Cecil, *Essays by the Marquess of Salisbury*, vol. I, 24–5.

[69] Vincent, *Nonintervention and International Order*, 90.

[70] Onuf, 'Humanitarian Intervention'.

[71] C. I. Johnstone, 'England, Turkey, Russia: The Balance of Power, and the Non-Intervention Principle', *Tait's Edinburgh Magazine*, 3:28 (Apr. 1836), 240–6.

[72] 'State Paper of 5 May 1820', in Temperley and Penson, *Foundations of British Foreign Policy*, 48–63.

national sentiment' being behind the government: 'This is our compass, and by this we must steer; and our Allies on the Continent may be assured that they will deceive themselves if they suppose that we could for six months act with them unless the mind of the nation was in the cause'.[73]

By March 1823, Canning – who liked to shape public opinion rather than being driven by it[74] – had forewarned that there was a growing ideological dichotomy in continental politics; it was impossible 'to contemplate the struggles now going on in different parts of the world without anticipating struggles between the contending principles'. While insisting that it was not necessarily England's duty to be a party to these struggles, he was aware of the difficulties of remaining aloof. The 'perfect equilibrium' (balance of power and non-intervention) which Britain desired was not easy to maintain: 'the course we had to pursue was on a path which lay across a roaring stream; attempts might be made to bear us down on the one side or the other'. For Canning, the best approach was 'to preserve in an undeviating path, to preserve our resources entire until the period should arrive, if ever, when we might exercise our only legitimate right to interfere, from being called upon to quell the raging floods that threaten to distract the balance of Europe'.[75] Later the same year, in a famous speech in Plymouth, he pointed towards the warships in the town and compared them to England herself: 'apparently passive and motionless, she silently concentrates the power to be put forth on an adequate occasion'.[76]

By 1826 – as the European Concert had fractured over Spain, Portugal and then Greece – Canning had opened himself to the possibility that this 'adequate occasion' might be on the not-too-distant horizon, stating that he did not 'dread war in a good cause (and in no other may it be to the lot of this country ever to engage!)'. Reiterating that the next war in Europe would be a 'war not so much of armies, as of opinions', he prophesied that – if, for whatever reason, Britain was sucked into conflict – 'she will see under her banners, arrayed for the contest all the discontented and restless spirits of the age, all those – who whether justly or unjustly – are dissatisfied with the present state of their countries'. A year before the intervention in Greece, Canning was also prepared to admit: 'The consciousness of such a situation excites all my fears, for it

[73] Castlereagh to Lord Stewart, 24 Feb. 1820, quoted in Phillips, 'Great Britain and the Continental Alliance', 48.
[74] S. J. Lee, *George Canning and Liberal Toryism, 1801–1827* (Woodbridge: Boydell, 2008).
[75] Canning speaking on 5 March 1820, quoted in Phillips, 'Great Britain and the Continental Alliance', 53–4.
[76] Quoted in Phillips, 'Great Britain and the Continental Alliance', 64.

shows that there exists a power to be wielded by Great Britain, more tremendous than was perhaps ever yet brought into action in the history of making'. The best prospect, he believed, was 'to content ourselves with letting the professors of violent and exaggerated doctrines on both sides feel that it is not their interest to convert an umpire into their competitor'.[77] The stage was set. Britain was non-interventionist and she wished to remain so. But if some other consideration – such as a threat to her interests, or the balance of power – brought her into conflict, it was almost inevitable that she would intervene on the side of those who wished to overthrow autocracy.

I have argued that Britain was sucked into the Eastern Question as an 'umpire', not primarily because of its sympathy to the Greek cause but because the ambitions of Russia made her effectively – as Canning put it – a 'competitor' in the region. However, this should not detract from the long-term significance of the episode. With a slightly different emphasis, Gary Bass has suggested the 'litany of slaughter' committed by the Ottomans 'forced Britain out of its ostensible neutrality, and then to the brink of a humanitarian war'. This argument is perhaps clearly overstated; the pace and timing of Britain's engagement was dictated by Russian actions rather than news of Ottoman atrocities, but the fruition of the humanitarian agenda was an outcome of British policy. Indeed, Bass himself acknowledges that 'Russia, which had imperialistic as well as humanitarian motives, also pushed Britain closer to intervention'. What he does convincingly demonstrate, however, is how accounts of Ottoman atrocities kept the Greek issue on the political agenda in Britain.[78] Indeed, while unlikely, Canning had hinted that public outrage at Ottoman atrocities in the Morea might ultimately push him towards military action in Greece.[79] And even Castlereagh admitted that it was 'impossible not to feel the appeal' of the Greek cause.[80]

The fact remains that humanitarian ends were served – perhaps more effectively than strategic ones – and they became irrevocably tied to how British actions in Greece were understood: humanitarianism *de facto*, if not by design. This was the fusion of humanitarianism and intervention which was described at the outset of this chapter. 'It is too late in the day', John Stuart Mill later commented, 'after these precedents, to tell us that nations may not forcibly interfere with one another for the sole

[77] Canning, 'Extract from Speech of 12 December 1826', in Temperley and Penson, *Foundations of British Foreign Policy*, 66–7.
[78] Bass, *Freedom's Battle*, 49.
[79] Temperley, *The Foreign Policy of Canning*, 391–2.    [80] Bass, *Freedom's Battle*, 63.

purpose of stopping mischief and benefitting humanity'.[81] Writing in 1859, he argued that intervention was therefore justified in cases of 'protracted civil war, in which the contending parties are so equally balanced that there is no probability of a speedy issue; or, if the victorious side cannot hope to keep down the vanquished but by severities repugnant to humanity and injurious to the permanent welfare of the country'. He believed it was now 'an admitted doctrine' that the interference of a powerful neighbour, 'with the acquiescence of the rest', was permitted in such instances. 'Intervention of this description has been repeatedly practised during the present generation', he wrote, 'with such general approval that its legitimacy may be considered to have passed into a maxim of what is called international law'.[82]

This was not a case of Mill rewriting history to justify an abstract or philosophical position; he was completely aware that the selfish interests of Britain were always likely to be the primary concern in considering the 'justifiableness' of intervention. Even in the case of Britain's pro-active role in forcing the abolition of slavery on other states, he noted that 'The fox who had lost his tail had an intelligible interest in persuading his neighbours to rid themselves of theirs.'[83] But his most important insight – the same which dawned upon the makers of British foreign policy in the 1820s – was one which had strategic as well as moral implications. 'The doctrine of non-intervention, to be a legitimate principle of morality, must be accepted by all governments.' In other words, the 'despots must consent to be bound by it as well as the free States ... Unless they do, the profession of it by free countries comes but to this miserable issue, that the wrong side may help the wrong, but the right must not help the right.' Thus, for Mill, intervention 'to enforce non-intervention is always rightful, always moral, if not always prudent'.[84] There were indeed many people who believed British intervention in Portugal and Greece in the 1820s was both rightful and moral; nonetheless, it remains the case that intervention in both these cases had occurred because it was also deemed to be strategically prudent.

Critics of humanitarian intervention have often bemoaned the erosion of traditional Westphalian concepts of international order over the course of the nineteenth and twentieth centuries, due to the corrosive

---

[81] J. S. Mill in his 1849 essay 'Vindication of the French Revolution of February 1848, in Reply to Lord Brougham and Others', cited in Onuf, 'Humanitarian Intervention'.
[82] Mill, 'A Few Words on Non-intervention'. For a recent discussion of this article, see M. Walzer, 'Mill's "A Few Words on Non-Intervention": A Commentary', in *J. S. Mill's Political Thought: A Bicentennial Reassessment*, ed. N. Urbinati and A. Zakras (Cambridge: Cambridge University Press, 2007), 347–56.
[83] Mill, 'A Few Words on Non-intervention'.    [84] *Ibid.*

effect of philosophical abstractions. This chapter has argued that the post-War commitment to non-intervention was not simply undermined by humanitarian moralism, but because it was not always the most effective way of protecting the national interest. The realisation which occurred in the course of the 1820s – and which the experience of the Napoleonic Wars had already hinted at – was that the ideal of the Westphalian world in which all participants subscribed faithfully to the 'Law of Nations', however desirable, was itself an abstraction.

# 6    Intervening in the Jewish question, 1840–1878

*Abigail Green*

I cannot subscribe to the doctrine that the humanitarian treatment of
the Jews in the Principalities is not a subject for foreign interference.
The peculiar position of the Jews places them under the protection
of the civilised world.

> J. Green, British Consul-General in Bucharest to Stefan
> Golescu, Romanian Foreign Minister, 2 August 1867[1]

The Jews were a test case for humanitarian intervention in the nineteenth century, but the story of Great Power intervention in the Jewish
Question has received little attention from historians. With a few notable
exceptions, those working in Jewish studies have neglected international
politics in favour of social and cultural history.[2] Those working outside
Jewish studies have not grasped the relevance of this story to broader
humanitarian initiatives. Yet the Jewish story matters because this is an
early example of intervention on behalf of a group who (unlike Greeks or
Syrian Christians) were not 'people like us'. Great Power intervention in
the Jewish Question may have been diplomatic rather than military,
but it shaped the legal and political context in which Jews lived in the
Middle East, North Africa and the Balkans. As a result the balance
between interest and ideology is different. By lobbying for diplomatic
intervention in the name of 'humanity' and 'civilisation', Jewish activists
helped create a context in which the treatment of religious and ethnic
minorities became a precondition of acceptance into an international

---

[1] *Principalities. No.1 (1877) Correspondence Respecting the Condition and Treatment of the Jews
in Servia and Roumania 1867–1876* (London: Harrison and Sons, 1877), 47.

[2] Even studies of the *Alliance Israélite Universelle* have tended to see its origins in a narrowly
French perspective. See Michael Graetz, *The Jews in Nineteenth-Century France: From the
French Revolution to the Alliance Israélite Universelle*, trans. Jane Marie Todd (Stanford:
Stanford University Press, 1996), and Lisa Moses Leff, *Sacred Bonds of Solidarity: The
Rise of Jewish Internationalism in Nineteenth-Century France* (Stanford: Stanford University
Press, 2006). Noteworthy but honourable exceptions to this rule include Carole Fink,
*Defending the Rights of Others: The Great Powers, the Jews, and International Minority
Protection, 1878–1938* (Cambridge: Cambridge University Press, 2004), and Jonathan
Frankel, *The Damascus Affair: 'Ritual Murder', Politics, and the Jews in 1840* (Cambridge:
Cambridge University Press, 1997).

state system that was increasingly governed by Western norms. So what did Consul-General Green mean by 'the civilised world', and how did the condition of the Jews come to play such a critical part in defining it?

Barely a decade after Anglo-Jewish emancipation, the association between Jewish rights and European 'civilisation' could hardly be taken for granted. In 1867, Russia was already notorious for the oppression of its Jewish subjects, and even the Jews of Germany and Austria-Hungary lacked full political rights. Western Jewish activists and their non-Jewish compatriots preferred to ignore this gap between humanitarian rhetoric and reality. Instead, the former sought to identify their cause with a discourse of 'humanity' and 'civilisation' that was increasingly deployed by the Great Powers of Europe – particularly Britain and France – to legitimise their imperial ambitions. This discourse can be traced back to the 1760s, when the word 'civilisation' first entered the French language.[3] Its appropriation in the cause of international Jewish relief began with the Damascus Affair of 1840, when allegations of ritual murder in the East created a new context for European debates about Jewish emancipation.

Such debates had always engaged a transnational public. Proponents of Jewish rights were necessarily aware of the condition of Jews elsewhere and the arguments put forward on their behalf. Thus Abbé Grégoire drew on the work of John Toland, Jacques Basnage, Pierre-Louis Lacretelle, Christian Wilhelm von Dohm and Johann David Michaelis in his famous 1788 essay on the regeneration of the Jews.[4] Conversely, Jews exploited their transnational networks in times of crisis. This was exemplified in 1745, when the expulsion of the Jews from Prague sparked a Europe-wide campaign to overturn the initiative. The language used by Jewish communal leaders and the influential financiers known as 'Court Jews' did reflect an awareness of humanitarian considerations. More interestingly, perhaps, the letters of the British Foreign Secretary, the Earl of Harrington, referred unequivocally to 'the prejudice that the world might conceive against the Queen's proceedings', and to the fact that this 'severe and merciless resolution could not but be esteemed by all mankind as an indelible stain both in point of justice and clemency upon her hitherto moderate and equitable Government'.[5] Yet Jewish notables made no effort to appeal to a wider public sphere: discretion

---

[3] Stuart Woolf, 'French Civilization and Ethnicity in the Napoleonic Empire', *Past & Present* 124 (Aug. 1989), 96.

[4] Alyssa Goldstein Sepinwall, *The Abbé Grégoire and the French Revolution: The Making of Modern Universalism* (Berkeley: University of California Press, 2005), 62.

[5] See François Guesnet, 'Textures of Intercession – Rescue Efforts for the Jews of Prague, 1744/1748', *Simon Dubnow Institute Yearbook* 4 (2005), 373, and more generally.

was, in fact, their principal concern. Jewish success in persuading European governments to approach Maria Theresa appears to have been rooted in pragmatic concerns about the economic effects of expulsion on European commerce.[6] Arguably, moreover, the Jewish relief effort had more impact on Jewish political culture than it did on Maria Theresa herself.

Responses to the Damascus Affair inevitably drew on these antecedents. Yet these events marked a change of scale and tempo as the ability of Western European and North American Jews to exert influence on their governments combined with the birth of an international Jewish lobby to create a new synergy between imperialism, humanitarian ideology and the Jewish question.

For those unfamiliar with this seminal episode, a short introduction is in order. Early in 1840, news began to reach Europe that the leading Jews of Damascus had been convicted by the Egyptian government of ritual murder on evidence produced by the French consul, and that similar barbarities had been perpetrated in Rhodes.[7] The initial publicity surrounding these events reflected improved communications, the spread of missionary networks and the growth of European political influence in the Middle East. But the long-term impact of the Damascus Affair lay in demonstrating the interconnectedness of the Jewish world in an age of incipient globalisation – and interesting the Jews of the West in the plight of their brethren in the East.

Early that April, the *Sémaphore de Marseille* carried a gruesome description of the alleged murder in Damascus, presenting this as part of a wider Jewish cult of human sacrifice. The article was reprinted in newspapers all over Europe – not one of which mentioned the use of torture in extracting confessions from the Jews. Four days later, the *Journal des débats* published a devastating critique of the Damascus allegations. Its author, Adolphe Crémieux, was Vice-President of the *Consistoire central*, the governing body of French Jewry.[8] A leading liberal lawyer who had done much to remove the last vestiges of Jewish inequality, Crémieux contrasted the readiness with which even progressive French newspapers had accepted and disseminated 'this miserable

---

[6] Baruch Mevorach, 'Die Interventionsbestrebungen in Europa Zur Verhinderung der Vertreibung der Juden Aus Böhmen und Mähren, 1744–1745', *Jahrbuch des Instituts für Deutsche Geschichte* 9 (1980), 15–81. On the Court Jew paradigm, see Selma Stern, *The Court Jew: A Contribution to the History of the Period of Absolutism in Central Europe* (Philadelphia: Jewish Publication Society of America, 1950).

[7] See the seminal Frankel, *Damascus Affair*.

[8] On Crémieux, see S. Posener, *Adolphe Crémieux, a Biography*, trans. Eugene Golob (Philadelphia: Jewish Publication Society of America, 1940).

calumny born of the infamous prejudices of medieval Christianity'
with 'the ideas of progress and liberalism' they professed to support.[9]
Referring to France's role as a pioneer of Jewish emancipation during
the Revolution, Crémieux appealed to his Christian fellow-citizens to
'[s]erve as our shield having served as our support! May the press above
all embrace ... the sacred cause of civilisation and of truth!'

Crémieux's article provoked an unprecedented wave of agitation on
behalf of the Jewish prisoners in Damascus, as newspapers all over the
'civilised' world debated the allegations. The blood libel was centuries old
but involvement of the French Consul had lent the charge credibility.
With Jewish emancipation a live issue throughout Europe, Western
Jews could not afford to be guilty by association. But the impact
of this agitation reflected domestic political contexts in ways that
bore surprisingly little relationship to the degree (or otherwise) of
Jewish emancipation. And so, as the British emancipationist Van Oven
lamented, diplomatic calculation took precedence over humanitarian
considerations in 'modern, enlightened France'.[10]

Loss of French face was only part of the problem. The Damascus
Affair coincided with diplomatic crisis as Mehmed Ali, ruler of Egypt
and Syria, attempted to secede from his Ottoman overlord. France had
long supported Egypt as a vehicle for its own resurgence in the area. The
left-liberal Prime Minister Adolphe Thiers now began fomenting nationalist agitation at home in a vain attempt to stabilise both the regime and
his own precarious ministry. Given his celebrated role as historian of the
Revolution, Thiers's willingness to evoke the spectre of international
Jewish power in a jingoistic defence of his country's representative highlights the ambivalent place of Jews within the tradition of 1789 and,
more broadly, the national body politic. For despite the universal rhetoric of the Rights of Man, Jews only obtained emancipation belatedly in
1791. As Stuart Woolf has argued, the Napoleonic regime too viewed
them as an alien element that could only be raised to the level of French
civilisation with difficulty.[11]

The contrast with Britain is instructive. If the French consul took the lead
in the Damascus ritual murder accusations, then the British consul was the
ringleader in Rhodes. Neither Thiers nor Foreign Secretary Palmerston
were disposed to believe these allegations, but only Palmerston called his

---

[9] 'Horrible accusation contre les Juifs de Damas', *Archives Israelites* 1 (March
1840), 171, reprint of Adolphe Crémieux's article, which appeared in the *Journal des
Débats* on 8 Apr. 1840.
[10] *Morning Herald*, 25 June 1840, pasted in Board of Deputies Minutes, BDMB, LMA,
Acc/3121/A/005/A (fos. 180–4).
[11] Woolf, 'Civilization and Ethnicity', 117–18.

representative to account. His sympathetic response reflected the pivotal role of a religiously inflected humanitarianism in British political culture. The 1830s were a transformative moment in British politics. This was the era of slave emancipation and the Great Reform Act: Catholics and Protestant dissenters had just achieved political equality and Jews hoped to be next in line. It was a critical decade, when the Evangelical and dissenting middle classes first emerged as a force to be reckoned with – adopting the slogan 'Civil and Religious Liberty' as their battle cry.[12] These years have been seen as the high-water mark of humanitarian politics. Yet historians have ignored the place of international Jewish relief within the spectrum of humanitarian politics and the connections forged between the Jewish cause, anti-slavery and aboriginal rights in the trans-denominational world of the City. For personal, ideological and business contacts linked leading Jews like Moses Montefiore, Nathan Rothschild and Isaac Lyon Goldsmid with Quaker and Evangelical campaigners like Sir Thomas Buxton, Sam Gurney, Matthias Attwood, Thomas Hodgkin and Elizabeth Fry. It was no coincidence that Montefiore and Rothschild provided the finance for the massive government loan that purchased the freedom of British slaves in the West Indies. And it was no coincidence that the City of London proved a critical source of support for the Jews, repeatedly forcing the pace of the ongoing campaign for Jewish emancipation by electing Jews like Montefiore and Salomons to public office.

These associations between Jewish rights and the humanitarian politics of the 1830s only became explicit during the Damascus Affair, when Montefiore agreed to join with Crémieux on a mission of mercy to Damascus.[13] Announcing his departure at a public meeting in London's Great Synagogue, Montefiore stressed the universal implications of an expedition intended not just to free the prisoners and clear the Jews' name, but 'to infuse into the Governments of the East more enlightened principles of legislation and judicial procedure, and in particular to prevail on those Governments to abolish the use of torture, and to establish the supremacy of law over undefined and arbitrary power'.[14] As Lynn Hunt reminds us, torture had been widely accepted in Europe

---

[12] David Turley, *The Culture of English Antislavery, 1780–1860* (London: Routledge, 1991), 108–51.

[13] On Montefiore, see Abigail Green, *Moses Montefiore: Jewish Liberator, Imperial Hero* (Cambridge, MA, and London: Harvard University Press, 2010). The essays collected in Sonia and Vivian Lipman (eds.), *The Century of Moses Montefiore* (Oxford: Littman Library of Jewish Civilisation and Oxford University Press, 1985) and Israel Bartal (ed.), *The Age of Moses Montefiore* (Jerusalem: Kav Uketav, Institute for Research on Sephardi and Oriental Jewish Heritage, 1987) are also of interest.

[14] *Morning Herald*, 25 June 1840.

until the late eighteenth century, when it became a flagship issue in the development of a new, humanitarian sensibility.[15] Montefiore's emphasis on torture and his talk of 'the claims of humanity, outraged in the persons of our persecuted and suffering brethren' was calculated to resonate with this wider humanitarian milieu.

Ten days later, these themes took centre stage at a Grand Public Meeting in the Mansion House, where Evangelicals, Quakers, Radicals and anti-slavery activists declared their support for the Jewish cause.[16] The triumph of anti-slavery lent British imperialism a strong moral flavour and no one in the Mansion House felt any reservations about identifying Montefiore's expedition to Damascus with this wider sense of mission.[17] All England, according to G. Larpent, would support 'that champion and apostle Sir Moses Montefiore' in his efforts 'to stay the arm of the oppressor and the bigot, and to establish the character of Asian nations for toleration; and to place England with Europe at the head of those communities in this world which enforced religious toleration and civil liberty'. British identification with the biblical Israelites and the sympathetic climate created by Evangelical philo-Semitism facilitated the use of such patriotic rhetoric – although not all those who supported Jewish relief abroad necessarily endorsed emancipation at home.[18]

Studies of Victorian imperialism have emphasised the role of ideology as a motor for British expansion, while historians of the metropole have drawn attention to the importance of Christianity and humanitarianism in crystallising a sense of Britishness, and the role of liberal foreign policy in forging a national political consensus.[19] Linda Colley in particular has

---

[15] Lynn Hunt, *Inventing Human Rights: A History* (New York: W. W. Norton and Co., 2007), ch. 2.

[16] *Morning Herald*, 4 July 1840 pasted into BDMB, LMA, Acc/3121/A/005/A (fos. 249–55).

[17] For background, see Andrew Porter, 'Trusteeship, Anti-Slavery, and Humanitarianism', in *The Oxford History of the British Empire*, vol. III: *The Nineteenth Century*, ed. Andrew Porter (Oxford: Oxford University Press, 1999), 206–7, and John Cell, 'The Imperial Conscience', in *The Conscience of the Victorian State*, ed. Peter Marsh (Syracuse, NY: Syracuse University Press, 1979), 199–202. More generally, Niall Ferguson, *Empire: How Britain Made the Modern World* (London: Allen Lane, 2003), ch. 3; and Alan Lester, 'Humanitarians and White Settlers in the Nineteenth Century', in *Missions and Empire*, ed. Norman Etherington (Oxford: Oxford University Press, 2005), 64–86.

[18] On Anglo-Saxon philosemitism, see William and Hilary Rubinstein, *Philosemitism: Admiration and Support in the English-Speaking World for Jews, 1840–1939* (Basingstoke: Macmillan, 1999).

[19] On ideology, see John Darwin, 'Imperialism and the Victorians: The Dynamics of Territorial Expansion', *EHR* 112 (June 1997), 627. On Christianity, empire, and Britishness, see Susan Thorne, *Congregational Missions and the Making of an Imperial Culture in Nineteenth-Century England* (Stanford: Stanford University Press, 1999). On the importance of foreign policy at home, see David Brown, *Palmerston and the Politics of Foreign Policy 1846–55* (Manchester and New York: Manchester University Press, 2002).

argued that support for anti-slavery symbolised the superior freedom and morality of British political institutions, functioning as a powerful legitimation for Britain's claim to be the arbiter of both the civilised and the uncivilised world.[20] Palmerston's support for the Jews in Damascus needs to be understood in this context.[21] He instructed the British consul in Alexandria to express his outrage at 'the Barbarous enormities perpetrated' in Damascus; requested the Ottoman government to institute an immediate enquiry into the situation in Rhodes, and castigated the British Consul there for his complicity in the blood libel allegations.[22] In the event, Montefiore's mission proved a spectacular triumph. With British troops propping up the Ottoman Sultan, it was easy for Britain to exert different kinds of diplomatic pressure on both Abdul Mecid and Mehmed Ali. Montefiore and Crémieux claimed equal credit for liberating the Jewish prisoners in Damascus, but it was thanks to Palmerston that Montefiore emerged with a *firman* from the Ottoman Sultan, refuting the blood libel accusation and promising protection and religious toleration to his Jewish subjects – something guaranteed them, in any case, under Islamic law.[23]

The Damascus Affair was the first instance of diplomatic intervention in the Jewish question, but it took time for the practice to acquire deeper roots. In April 1841, Palmerston issued a general circular to British agents in the Ottoman Empire urging that they should

upon any suitable occasion make known to the Local Authorities that the British Government feels an interest in the welfare of the Jews in general, and is anxious that they should be protected from oppression; and that the Porte has promised to afford them protection, and will certainly attend to any representations which Her Majesty's Ambassador at Constantinople may make to it on these matters.[24]

---

[20] Linda Colley, *Britons: Forging the Nation 1707–1837* (London: Vintage, 1996), 350–60.

[21] This argument is elaborated in Abigail Green, 'The British Empire and the Jews: An Imperialism of Human Rights?', *Past & Present* 199 (May 2008), 175–205.

[22] Palmerston to Hodges, 5 May 1840, NA, FO 78/403 No. 9, fo. 20.

[23] For the text of the firman, see Louis Loewe (ed.), *Diaries of Sir Moses and Lady Montefiore, Comprising Their Life and Work as Recorded in Their Diaries from 1812 to 1883*, vol. I (London: Griffith Farran Okeden and Welsh, 1890), 278–9. More generally, see Bernard Lewis, *The Jews of Islam* (Princeton: Princeton University Press, 1984). Specifically on Ottoman Jewry, see Esther Benbassa and Aron Rodrigue, *Sephardi Jewry: A History of the Judeo-Spanish Community, 14th–20th Centuries* (Berkeley: University of California Press, 2000) and Benjamin Braude and Bernard Lewis (eds.), *Christians and Jews in the Ottoman Empire: The Functioning of a Plural Society* (New York and London: Holmes and Meier, 1982).

[24] Palmerston to the British Consuls and Consular Agents in the Turkish Dominions, 21 Apr. 1841, in Albert M. Hyamson (ed.), *The British Consulate in Jerusalem in Relation to the Jews of Palestine, 1838–1914*, 2 vols. (London: Edward Goldston, 1939), I, 39–40.

What this meant in practice varied from consul to consul. With formal diplomatic intervention restricted to those Jews legally recognised as British protégés, Jewish leaders like Montefiore continued to lobby their governments on a case-by-case basis. By the Crimean War, the habit of intervention had become ingrained in Britain and was beginning to make headway in France. This owed less to Jewish influence than to Anglo-French rivalry in the Middle East, where the rhetoric of 'civilisation' was central to both imperial projects. It also pointed to the emergence of an international humanitarian public and its growing political force.

Before the revolutions of 1848, Britain faced little competition in her self-appointed role as champion of Ottoman Jewry. Austrian representatives in Egypt and Syria had taken the lead in concerting European consular support for the Jews of Damascus in 1840, but their stance owed much to the Rothschilds' political connections. The Austrian consul-general in Alexandria was alive to the universal implications of the episode, contrasting the torture of the Damascus prisoners with Mehmed Ali's pretensions of civilisation in a letter to his Prussian colleague.[25] Metternich, however, did not frame his response to the ritual murder allegations in such terms.[26]

For most governments, considerations of *Realpolitik* appear to have been decisive. Long-term significance can perhaps be attributed to the intervention of the United States. Prompted by a letter from the Lord Mayor of London, the Secretary of State instructed the American *chargé d'affaires* in Constantinople to emphasise that a country 'acknowledging no distinction between the Mohammedan, the Jews and the Christian' would naturally use its 'good offices in behalf of an oppressed and persecuted race among whose kindred are found some of the most worthy and patriotic of our citizens'.[27] This formulation resonated with the rhetoric used in Britain, although the failure to abolish slavery would inhibit American diplomatic initiatives in the cause of international Jewish relief for some time to come.

France, meanwhile, saw herself as the protector of Eastern Catholics. Anglo-French rivalry in Syria and Egypt during the July Monarchy intensified the politicisation of these religious ties, particularly in Lebanon where the alleged plight of Maronite Christians was a central

---

[25] Laurin to von Stürmer, 5 May 1840, bound volume of transcripts of Austrian Foreign Office documents relating to the Damascus Affair, fos. 121–3 (Arthur Sebag-Montefiore Archive, Oxford Centre for Hebrew and Jewish Studies).

[26] Metternich to Laurin, 10 Apr. 1840, *ibid.*, fos. 257–60.

[27] Frankel, *Damascus Affair*, 226.

focus for French public opinion and foreign policy.[28] This nexus between French consuls and local Christians had proved critical in Damascus. Throughout the 1840s French representatives in the area lent a sympathetic ear to blood libel allegations – not always with the approval of their government. One such episode took place in the Lebanese town of Dayr al-Qamar in 1847, another in Damascus itself where the events of 1840 had created permanent scars.

In this context, defending Jewish rights abroad became an important site for strengthening the existing alliances between acculturated Jewish leaders and French liberals in the 1840s. This coalition included reformist deputies on the left, former Saint-Simonians, university professors, lawyers and a wide array of journalists and politicians, many of whom would emerge as leaders of the Second Republic. As Lisa Leff has argued, members of this milieu were committed to limiting the role of the Catholic Church in setting state policy and wished to see France embrace secularism in its foreign and colonial policy too.[29] The resulting alliance had a certain amount in common with the coalition forged in Britain during the 1830s between Jews like Montefiore and members of the Quaker–Evangelical milieu. In Britain, the imperial ideology of commerce, Christianity and civilisation was underpinned by a broad consensus in favour of exporting 'civil and religious liberty'. In France, however, foreign policy became an important battleground in the struggle between ultramontane Catholics and anti-clericals. Thus in 1846 Crémieux (now himself a deputy) opposed the values of 'Christian civilisation' in foreign policy to those of the Revolution: 'civilisation tout court'.[30]

The opposition between these two visions of French civilisation came to a head during the Crimean War. Fought over Catholic access to the Christian Holy Places in Jerusalem, this war raised crucial issues about Napoleon III's foreign policy and the French polity.[31] Archbishop Silbour of Paris – a well-known defender of traditional Catholic education – led public prayers for the troops engaged in what he saw as a new holy war, blessing them in the name of civilisation and Catholicism. More conservative Catholic writers referred to the conflict simply as a 'holy crusade'. Liberal anti-clericals, meanwhile, sought to reframe the war as a struggle between barbarism and civilisation. Men like Emile de Girardin defined this in terms redolent with Saint-Simonianism: modern government, freedom of conscience, equality before the law,

---

[28] For context, see Caesar E. Farah, *The Politics of Interventionism in Ottoman Lebanon, 1830–1861* (London and New York: I. B. Tauris, 2000).
[29] Leff, *Sacred Bonds of Solidarity*, ch. 4.     [30] *Ibid.*, 137.     [31] See *ibid.*, 141–2.

the liberation of oppressed nations, scientific and economic progress. Despite the avowed secularism of the anti-clerical camp, such terms were broadly consistent with the rival British imperial vision.

French Jewish activists were quick to grasp the implications of this polemic for their status as French citizens.[32] In 1854, the *Consistoire central* wrote formally, urging the French government to champion the cause of Ottoman Jewry during the coming conflict.[33] Reiterating their appeal a year later, the *Consistoire* framed their request rather more explicitly in terms of the French revolutionary tradition.[34] Since they confidently expected the sultan to grant equal rights to all his non-Muslim subjects, this well-publicised intervention had more to do with the politics of Jewish life in France than it did with concern for the plight of Ottoman Jewry. The French Foreign Minister chose to ignore it.

Once again, the contrast with Britain is instructive. The Board of Deputies had no difficulty eliciting the support of their government in the name of Ottoman Jewry.[35] Indeed, both Frederick Rodkey and Allan Cunningham have emphasised the importance attached by the British government to the equal treatment of Ottoman religious minorities during the Tanzimat reforms.[36] When the influential German Jewish activist, Ludwig Philippson, petitioned the British government on the matter, Lord John Russell replied politely pledging his government's intention to procure for Jews as well as Christians 'the benefits of equal law and impartial administration'.[37] Napoleon III declined to offer Philippson any such assurances, replying to his petition with a mere acknowledgement of receipt.[38]

In January 1856, Britain, France and Austria began to consult with the Porte over the terms of the peace agreement, with a view to trying to implement some of the conditions imposed by the Allies before the

---

[32] See *ibid.*, 145.
[33] Consistoire Central des Israelites de France, 24 March 1854 to Napoleon III, BDMB, LMA, Acc/3121/A/007, fos. 253–4.
[34] 'Lettre Adressé par le Consistoire Central au Ministère des Affaires Étrangères', *Archives Israélites de France* 16 (Apr. 1855), 217–18.
[35] Montefiore to Clarendon, 10 May 1854, BDMB, LMA, Acc/3121/A/007, fos. 272–300.
[36] Frederick Stanley Rodkey, 'Lord Palmerston and the Rejuvenation of Turkey, 1830–41', *Journal of Modern History* 2 (June 1930), 193–225; Allan Cunningham, 'Stratford Canning and the *Tanzimat*', in *Beginnings of Modernization in the Middle East. The Nineteenth Century*, ed. William R. Polk and Richard L. Chambers (Chicago: University of Chicago Press, 1968), 245–64.
[37] 'Magdeburg, 27. Februar. Adresse an Lord John Russel', *AZ* (5 Mar. 1855), 115–16.
[38] Eliyahu Feldman, 'The Question of Jewish Emancipation in the Ottoman Empire and the Danubian Principalities After the Crimean War', *Jewish Social Studies* 41 (Winter 1979), 45, which provides a general overview of these negotiations.

forthcoming Congress. The Fourth Point had originally referred only to Ottoman Christians, but the formulation now put forward by Stratford de Redcliffe, the British Ambassador, was phrased more generally. A commitment to freedom of conscience for all Ottoman subjects and to equal rights for 'non-Muslims' would also apply to the Jews. Negotiations were already in full swing when a further appeal from the Board of Deputies caused Clarendon to telegraph hastily that '[i]t would not do to leave the Jews out'.[39] Stratford de Redcliffe was able to report truthfully: 'I think it right to state that the Jews were included from the very first in all arrangements made towards the Fourth Point and that the Turks never made any difficulty on that head'.[40] This was unsurprising since Islamic law did not distinguish between Christians and Jews. The problem lay rather in Europe, where neither Jewish activists nor Christian statesmen could readily imagine a situation in which parity between the two groups was taken as read.

The *Hatt-i Hümayun* of 1856 transformed the context for diplomatic intervention in the Jewish question. Emancipating Ottoman Jewry created a precedent in the Muslim world and raised the stakes in Christian Europe, where most Jews still lacked political rights. Even Britain, which had championed their cause in Constantinople, waited until 1858 before allowing the first Jewish MP to take his seat in the Commons.[41] The countries in which Jews had achieved full emancipation now formed a solid core in Western Europe. The situation in Austria and the German Confederation was more ambiguous, while the legacy of the Inquisition continued to shape official attitudes in Spain and most of Italy. It was here in Bologna, in June 1858, that the kidnapping of an eight-year-old Jewish boy by the papal authorities prompted another major international outcry in defence of Jewish rights.[42]

Forced baptism had been a feature of Italian Jewish life for centuries. In theory, the Catholic Church condemned those who baptised children against the wishes of their parents. In practice, these baptisms were regarded as valid and the Church claimed such children as its own.[43]

---

[39] Clarendon to Stratford, 24 Jan. 1856, NA, FO 78/1159 Telegraph.
[40] Stratford to Clarendon, 13 Feb. 1856, NA, FO 78/1173 No. 177.
[41] The best account of Anglo-Jewish emancipation is M. C. N. Salbstein, *The Emancipation of the Jews in Britain: The Question of the Admission of the Jews to Parliament 1828–1860* (London and Toronto: Associated University Presses, 1982).
[42] See David I. Kertzer, *The Kidnapping of Edgardo Mortara* (London: Picador, 1997).
[43] See Cecil Roth, 'Forced Baptisms in Italy: A Contribution to the History of Jewish Persecution', *The Jewish Quarterly Review*, new series, 27 (1936–7), 117–36. There were at least eight cases of forced baptism after 1815: 1817 (Ferrara), 1824 (Genoa), 1826 (Ancona), 1836 (Modena), 1838 (Ferrara), 1840 (Rome), 1844 (Reggio d'Emilia), and 1844 (Lugo).

Just such a baptism was behind the abduction of little Edgardo Mortara, who was taken to Rome to be brought up as a good Catholic under the auspices of the Inquisition. The condition of papal Jewry was probably the worst in Western Europe and the Mortara family found they had no right of appeal. Elsewhere in Italy, the political climate was changing and the recently emancipated Jews of Piedmont did not hesitate to launch an international appeal to further the Mortaras' cause.[44] As the President of Turin's Jewish community explained pointedly:

> the civil and political conditions of several European States permit us now at least to express our abhorrence of those deeds of cruelty which are still committed in some parts of the civilised world, in the name of religion, by ignorant and fanatical ministers ... we ... avail ourselves of the universal Press to appeal to all mankind against acts which violate the most sacred rights of paternity ... and that we should endeavour by all possible means not only to obtain redress for the outrage in question, but to prevent the re-enactment of such an event.

Talk of 'civilisation', 'humanity', 'barbarous practices' and 'fanatical ministers' echoed the rhetoric of 1840 and the opposition between West and East invoked during the Damascus Affair. But even in 1840 the ritual murder allegations had been promoted through European influence. Now, the 'deeds of cruelty' decried by the Jews of Piedmont were perpetrated in the heartlands of Western Europe – and Catholics, not Jews, were in the dock.

This appeal by the Piedmontese Jewish community testified to the growing political maturity of the international Jewish public.[45] The decades after 1840 saw the emergence of a genuinely transnational public sphere in the Jewish world, with a growing number of newspapers and periodicals targeting a specifically Jewish audience in Western Europe, the United States and, by the 1860s, Eastern Europe. With the emergence of publications catering to a Jewish reading public, it had become relatively easy to disseminate specifically Jewish disaster news and co-ordinate an organised international response.[46]

---

[44] Extract from *The Times*, 9 Sept. 1858, pasted into BDMB, LMA, Acc 3121/B1/1, fo. 405.

[45] On the emergence of an international Jewish lobby, see Abigail Green, 'Nationalism and the "Jewish International": Religious Internationalism in Europe and the Middle East c.1840–c.1880', *Comparative Studies in Society and History* 50 (Apr. 2008), 535–58, and Green, 'Sir Moses Montefiore and the Making of the "Jewish International"', *Journal of Modern Jewish Studies* 7 (Nov. 2008), 287–307. For a trans-denominational and comparative approach to the globalisation of religious activism, see Abigail Green and Vincent Viaene (eds.), *Religious Internationals in the Modern World* (Leuven: Katholieke Universiteit Leuven, 2010).

[46] On the Jewish press, see Derek Penslar, 'Introduction: The Press and the Jewish Public Sphere', *Jewish History* 14 (2000), 3–8, and the rest of this special issue.

From a Jewish perspective, the Mortara Affair was merely the latest humanitarian outrage to transfix the Jewish public. But the anachronistic, theocratic regime of the papal states was a favourite whipping boy for European liberals, who associated Catholicism with superstition, backwardness and tyranny.[47] They, too, operated in an increasingly global public sphere. To French anti-clericals and patriotic British Protestants, the abduction of Edgardo symbolised the brutal exercise of arbitrary power by an illegitimate government. It was, in the words of Walewski, the French Foreign Minister, 'an outrageous violation of the most fundamental guarantees, that are the basis for respect of the home and paternal authority'.[48] This opposition between the traditional rights of the Catholic Church and the more fundamental human claims of the Mortara family enabled Jewish activists to formulate their case in universal terms. 'You cannot fail to perceive', wrote Montefiore in a circular, 'that this is a matter affecting not the Jews alone, but also every other denomination of Faith, except the Roman Catholic, further that it cannot be regarded exclusively under a Religious aspect, but as placing in peril, personal liberty, social relations and the peace of families'.[49]

Superficially, the Mortara agitation achieved very little since Edgardo was never returned to his family. The French Ambassador repeatedly raised the matter with Pius IX and Cardinal Antonelli, but the presence of French troops in Rome failed to sway the pope on what he saw as a point of principle. Arguably, however, the Mortara Affair shaped the process of Italian unification, persuading Napoleon III to abandon his support of the papacy and throw in his lot with Cavour and the liberal nationalist idea.[50] For Napoleon and for France, this marked a decisive break with the Catholic tradition of foreign policy.

In Britain, by contrast, the Mortara Affair fed into the existing tradition of trans-denominational activism centred on the cause of 'civil and religious liberty'. The limited influence exerted in Rome by a Protestant country did not stop Protestant lobby groups issuing multiple petitions to the British government – just as they had on behalf of various

---

[47] For the European context, see Christopher Clark and Wolfram Kaiser (eds.), *Culture Wars: Secular–Catholic Conflict in Nineteenth-Century Europe* (Cambridge: Cambridge University Press, 2003). On Britain, see D. G. Paz, *Popular Anti-Catholicism in Mid-Victorian England* (Stanford: Stanford University Press, 1992); also E. R. Norman, *Anti-Catholicism in Victorian England* (London: George, Allen and Unwin, 1968).

[48] Walewski to Grammont, 22 Sept. 1858, Archives du Ministère des Affaires Etrangères (Paris), Correspondance Politique, Rome 1008 (443).

[49] Circular from Montefiore, 25 Oct. 1858, BDMB, LMA, Acc 3121/B1/1, fo. 409.

[50] See the discussion in Kertzer, *Kidnapping*, 173–4.

types of Italian Protestant.[51] Yet recent experience had shown Foreign Secretary Malmesbury that heavy handed diplomatic intervention was likely to prove counter-productive.[52] Faced with his refusal to act, the Evangelical Alliance began organising an international Protestant deputation to Paris.[53] For its President, Sir Culling Eardley, the proposed expedition represented a unique opportunity to make an international and trans-denominational stand in defence of religious freedom; for tactical reasons, Montefiore refused to participate and Eardley dropped the plan.

Four months later, with Italian unification firmly under way, Eardley headed a deputation to the Foreign Secretary, urging him to raise the question of papal Jews and Edgardo Mortara at a putative congress on Italian affairs.[54] As Lord John Russell explained, the restrictions on Jewish rights in Austria, Prussia and Russia rendered such a suggestion eminently impractical. But the *Jewish Chronicle* suggested Russell might square this circle by establishing a wholly new kind of international framework, in which such interference was justified in terms of generally accepted moral principles: 'the only means we see for preventing the recurrence of any such crime is to memorialise the foreign Secretary to press upon the attention of the approaching Congress the expediency of establishing liberty of conscience ... as an international law of the civilised world'.[55] The congress never materialised, but the moment remains significant. Here, for the first time, we see the faint stirrings of an awareness of the role of international action in dealing with the problems of religious or ethnic minorities, and imposing universal standards of human rights.

The collapse of papal power shifted the spotlight from the Vatican. In the longer term, public attention focused on Persia, Morocco and the fledgling Christian states of the formerly Ottoman Balkans. The *Hatt-i Hümayun* had set a precedent for other Muslim countries and Jewish activists did not hesitate to exploit it. Just as emancipation was spreading across Western

---

[51] Mr Lord, Protestant Association Office, to Malmesbury, 11 Nov. 1858, enclosing the Memorial of the Committee of the Protestant Association, Memorial from the Scottish Reformation Society to Malmesbury, 19 Nov. 1858, and Shaftesbury to Malmesbury, enclosing Memorial of the Committee of the Protestant Alliance, 2 Dec. 1858, NA, FO 881/811 (20–1, 23).

[52] See Anna Lohrli, 'The Madiai: A Forgotten Chapter of Church History', *Victorian Studies* 33 (Autumn 1989), 29–50.

[53] 'The Mortara Case: Correspondence Between Sir Culling Eardley and Sir Moses Montefiore', *The Times*, 28 Dec. 1858, 5.

[54] 'The Mortara Protest', *JC*, 11 Nov. 1859, 7.

[55] 'The Deputation to Lord John Russell', *JC*, 18 Nov. 1859, 2. See also 'The Approaching Congress [Lead Article]', *JC*, 9 Dec. 1859.

Europe, so Montefiore hoped to set a similar process in motion across the Muslim world. In 1864, he travelled to the court of the Sultan of Morocco in Marrakesh, where he obtained a *dahir* from the sultan commanding his subjects 'to treat all the Jews residing in our dominions in the manner God Almighty prescribes, equally with the same balanced scales of justice and perfect equality in the courts of law as all other subjects, so that none of them be a victim of the slightest imaginable portion of injustice nor of any kind of malicious nor humiliating measures'.[56] Montefiore obtained a similar letter from the Shah of Persia in 1865, ordering his prime minister to treat the Jews with justice and kindness.[57]

In both cases, Montefiore's success owed a great deal to British influence – and was greeted as a triumph for British humanitarian values.[58] Yet the text of these declarations was carefully formulated to reflect Islamic law and local political traditions, which already held that the protection of Jewish minorities was a particular responsibility of Muslim rulers. The result was a sometimes violent clash between raised Jewish expectations and the entrenched attitudes and practices of local Muslims. Arguably, it did not matter if, in the short term, these concessions tended to exacerbate ethnic and religious tensions. The point was rather that – in principle if not in practice – Muslim countries were increasingly expected to apply British standards of civil and religious liberty to the treatment of their religious minorities. This marked a fundamental break with tradition in Muslim lands even if, back on the Continent, many European countries continued to discriminate against their Jewish subjects.

Nowhere was this more apparent than in Romania. Had Romania remained part of the Ottoman Empire, its Jews would already have been enjoying full civil equality under Article 23 of the Treaty of Paris.[59]

---

[56] Translation provided by Assia and Mohammed Kenbib, based on Ahmed Naciri, *Al Istiqsa Li Akhbar Duwwal Al Maghrib Al Aqsa* (Casablanca: Dar Al Kitab, 1956), 113–14. On the Jews of Morocco, see Mohammed Kenbib, *Juifs et Musulmans au Maroc, 1859–1948. Contribution à l'histoire des relations inter-communautaires en terre d'Islam* (Casablanca: Najah el Jadida, 1994), especially ch. 3 on Montefiore's mission and its aftermath. Specifically on British intervention in the Moroccan Jewish question, see Tudor Parfitt, 'Dhimma versus Protection in Nineteenth Century Morocco', in Parfitt (ed.), *Israel and Ishmael: Studies in Muslim-Jewish Relations* (Richmond: Curzon, 2000), 142–66.

[57] Alison to Clarendon, 21 Dec. 1865, NA, FO 60/291 No. 134. On the Jews of Persia, see Daniel Tsadik, *Between Foreigners and Shi'is: Nineteenth-Century Iran and its Jewish Minority* (Stanford: Stanford University Press, 2007).

[58] 'Mr Alderman Phillips' Motion in the Court of Common Council', *JC*, 15 Apr. 1864, 3.

[59] The best history of Romanian Jewry remains Carol Iancu, *Les Juifs en Roumanie (1866–1919). De l'exclusion à l'émancipation* (Aix en Provence: Editions de l'Université de Provence, 1978).

Instead, Romanian autonomy was guaranteed by the Great Powers under the 1858 Convention of Paris. This was ambiguous about Jewish emancipation. Article 46 tacitly recognised the existence of Jewish Romanians by guaranteeing all Moldavians and Wallachians equality 'before the law, in taxation, and ... access to public office in each principality', but explicitly restricted political rights to the adherents of 'all Christian confessions'.[60] Defenders of Romanian Jewry like the British Foreign Secretary Lord Clarendon would later claim that Article 46 granted Jews in the principalities 'full equality as regards legal and fiscal rights ... personal freedom and security for property'.[61] Romanians increasingly maintained Jews were aliens and denied them civil and political rights.

This fledgling nation-state had seen massive Jewish immigration in recent decades. Romania was also an unstable political partnership between two relatively independent principalities: rural Moldavia and more urban Wallachia, home to the new capital of Bucharest. Moldavia had borne the brunt of Jewish immigration, and Moldavians formed a large part of the new Romanian parliament.[62] The new government turned to anti-Jewish politics as the best way of creating a stable parliamentary majority. And so it was that men who had supported Jewish emancipation during the revolutions of 1848 changed their minds once they found themselves in government. Rather than grant the Jews citizenship under the Romanian constitution of 1866, ministers like Ion Brătianu began to implement a policy of mass expulsions and officially condoned police brutality As news of the official persecution of Romanian Jewry transfixed the 'civilised world', Jewish activists urged the Great Powers to assert their authority as Guarantors by imposing minimum standards of human rights.

Hitherto Britain and France had made most of the running when it came to diplomatic intervention in the Jewish question. This reflected a fusion of liberal political discourse and imperial aspirations, as both countries developed ideologies to legitimise their Great Power ambitions that were based on the idea of a civilising mission, the terms of which

[60] Carol Iancu, *Jews in Romania 1866–1919: From Exclusion to Emancipation*, trans. Carvel de Bussy, East European Monographs (Boulder, CO and New York: Columbia University Press, 1996), 33. (This translation is slightly abbreviated.)
[61] Feldman, 'Jewish Emancipation', 59. For more detail, see Privy Councillor Dr Bluntschli, Professor at the University of Heidelberg, *Roumania and the Legal Status of the Jews in Roumania: An Exposition of Public Law* (London: Anglo-Jewish Association, 1879).
[62] Keith Hitchins, *The Romanians, 1774–1866* (Oxford: Clarendon Press, 1996) provides the best history of pre-unification Romania.

were defined by domestic political traditions. Jews and Jewish rights carried a particular symbolic charge in both British and French political culture, representing either the twin causes of humanitarianism and civil and religious liberty, or the revolutionary tradition of state secularism and the universalism of the Rights of Man. Although Jews were fully emancipated in France long before this was the case in Britain, they remained a contentious feature of the domestic body politic in both countries. Yet their position was clearly far stronger than that of Jews living in Prussia, Austria and Russia for most of this period. Not until the spread of emancipation through Italy, the German states and Austria-Hungary during the 1860s was it possible for other countries to begin to appropriate the liberal rhetoric of 'humanity' and 'civilisation' as a dominant discourse. Since none of these states had imperial ambitions in the Middle East or North Africa, they were unlikely to take much interest in the status of Jews in the Muslim world. Now ruled by a Hohenzollern prince and situated on the fringes of both Habsburg and Russian spheres of interest, Romania was a very different matter.

News of the atrocities in Romania triggered a well-established pattern of activity among Jewish activists in London and Paris. As the Board of Deputies and leading Jewish MPs lobbied the British government, the *Jewish Chronicle* expressed its confidence in the good intentions of the Conservative ministry, concluding that while 'Liberals and Conservatives may differ in matters of general policy; in matters of common justice and humanity they are both alike'.[63] Crémieux, meanwhile, was peculiarly well placed to promote French universalism as a former minister in the second republic. As president of the *Alliance Israélite Universelle*, he travelled to Bucharest to address the constituent assembly, where he compared Jewish emancipation to the abolition of slavery – and recalled his own role emancipating French slaves during the revolution of 1848.[64]

With the Second Empire entering its liberal swansong, the French Foreign Minister assured Crémieux after renewed violence in Bucharest that the French agent would convey 'the sense of painful astonishment with which we have learned of these manifestations, as well as the sentiments of intolerance, so contrary to the light of present civilisation, evinced by the population of Bucharest'.[65] Recognising the importance of international public opinion to a country struggling for recognition,

---

[63] 'Deplorable Excesses in the Danubian Principalities', *JC*, 27 July 1866, 4.
[64] Isidore Loeb, *La situation des Israélites en Turquie, en Serbie et en Roumanie* (Paris: Joseph Baer, 1877), 154.
[65] 'Riots at Bucharest', *JC*, 3 Aug. 1866.

the Prefect of Jassy district warned the population against further anti-Jewish outbursts '[t]oday, when the eyes of Europe are upon us, and we must demonstrate that we are a civilised nation'.[66]

This, indeed, was the nub of the matter. The role of the Great Powers as guarantors of Romanian autonomy promised real scope for intervention under the Convention of Paris. As one correspondent of the *Allgemeine Zeitung des Judentums* put it, the riots compromised not just the Romanians but their Ottoman suzerain and the Powers overseeing the regeneration of the Romanian state.[67] Napoleon III apparently promised Crémieux 'immediate intervention', but although he wrote to Prince Carol it rapidly became clear that the Great Powers preferred threats and public remonstrance to more effective action.[68]

This line of action was broadly in tune with humanitarian opinion. The *Manchester Daily Examiner* spoke as the voice of the British liberal public, when it declared that there were 'cases in which it becomes the duty of all who have any share in guiding or expressing public opinion to raise their voice against the perpetration of wrongs which are an outrage upon humanity and a disgrace to the civilisation of the age'.[69] Yet even the *Daily Examiner* advised against appealing 'to a diplomatic document in a case which can be much more effectually met by a general and earnest expression of public opinion'. And so it was that diplomatic intervention in the Romanian Jewish question never moved beyond case-by-case admonitions from local consuls, and Montefiore's unsuccessful mission to Bucharest in 1867, which had the backing of all five Great Powers.

This rare unanimity reflected *Realpolitik* rather than humanitarian principles. Where France and Austria were inclined to support the new regime in the principalities, Russia wanted to strengthen her position in Moldavia, Prussia to stabilise Carol's situation, and Britain to maintain Ottoman suzerainty. Yet all were concerned by the direction of Brătianu's radical nationalist government – and the threat posed by dreams of national independence for a Greater Romania. In Britain and France, humanitarian concerns undoubtedly weighed with the

---

[66] 'Jassy, 20. Zeitungsnachrichten/ Donaufürstenthümer', *AZ*, 17 July 1866, 463–4.

[67] 'Bonn, 20. Juli (Privatmitth)', *AZ*, 31 July 1866, 491.

[68] For Napoleon's discussion with Crémieux, see 'Persecution in the Danubian Principalities', *JC*, 7 June 1867, 2. For examples of threats and collective action, see Stanley to Consul-General Green, 24 May 1867: *Correspondence Respecting the Persecution of Jews in Moldavia, Presented to Both Houses of Parliament by Command of Her Majesty* (London: Harrison and Sons, 1867), 2. See also *Aus dem Leben König Karls von Rumänien. Aufzeichnungen Eines Augenzeugen*, 2 vols. (Stuttgart: J. G. Cotta, 1894), I, 201.

[69] 'The Minister Bratiano and the Jews', *JC*, 14 June 1867, 3.

liberal public, while the presence of so many Austrian Jews in Moldavia was a particular consideration in Vienna.[70] But for all the Great Powers, the Jewish question provided an opportune excuse for interfering in Romanian internal affairs.

Arguably, the only exception to this rule was the United States. Back in 1858, with slavery a contentious political issue, President Buchanan had explicitly resisted calls to interfere in the Mortara Affair out of concern for 'the principle of non-intervention on the part of the United States between foreign sovereigns and their own subjects'.[71] The abolition of slavery now made it possible for the United States to claim the moral high ground in foreign policy.[72] In 1870, Benjamin Peixotto, a Cleveland journalist and Jewish activist, successfully petitioned to be appointed American Consul to Bucharest, with a view to intervening on behalf of his Romanian co-religionists.[73] The position was honorary, funded by Jewish activists, and Peixotto's letters of credentials stated that he was appointed for 'Missionary work for the benefit of the people he represents'.[74] As an attempt to change Romanian policy towards the Jews, Peixotto's mission was a failure. In the longer term, however, it marked growing acceptance in the international arena for the principle of humanitarian intervention in the affairs of another state.

This principle achieved formal recognition in 1878, when attempts to link existing international treaties to the defence of Romanian Jewry finally reached fruition. The long-running drama of Romanian Jewry had provided a critical focus for the international Jewish lobby during the 1870s. All were agreed that the Great Power guarantee of Romanian autonomy provided a vehicle for linking existing international treaties with the defence of the Romanian Jewry. Once Romania had declared independence during the Russo-Turkish war of 1876, the Congress of Berlin presented a last-ditch opportunity for Jewish activists to persuade the Powers to enforce respect for Jewish rights.[75]

---

[70] This is one of the central arguments made by Beate Welter, *Die Judenpolitik der Rumänischen Regierung 1866–1888* (Frankfurt am Main: Peter Lang, 1989).

[71] Bertram Wallace Korn, *The American Reaction to the Mortara Case: 1858–1859* (Cincinnati: American Jewish Archives, 1957), 63.

[72] A variation of this argument is made at much greater length in Robert Kagan, *Dangerous Nation: America and the World 1600–1898* (London: Atlantic Books, 2006), see, for instance, pp. 279–300 on the aftermath of the Civil War.

[73] See Lloyd P. Gartner, 'Documents on Roumanian Jewry, Consul Peixotto, and Jewish Diplomacy, 1870–1875', in *Salo Wittmayer Baron Jubilee Volume*, vol. I, ed. Saul Liebermann and Arthur Hyman (Jerusalem: American Academy for Jewish Research, 1974), 467–90, and Gartner, 'Roumania, America, and World Jewry: Consul Peixotto in Bucharest, 1870–1876', *American Jewish Historical Quarterly* 58 (1968), 25–117.

[74] Iancu, *Jews in Romania*, 62.    [75] See Fink, *Defending*, Prologue.

From this perspective, it was a triumph. Formally guaranteeing the religious, civil and political rights of Jews and other minorities in the Balkans under international law, Article 44 of the Treaty of Berlin marked a caesura in the history of human rights. Echoing earlier clauses that pertained to Bulgaria, Serbia and Montenegro, it asserted

In Romania the difference of religious creeds and confessions shall not be used against any person as a ground for exclusion of incapacity in matters relating to the enjoyment of civil and political rights, admission to public employments, functions and honors, to the exercise of the various professions and industries in any locality whatsover.

The freedom and outward exercise of all forms of worship shall be assured to all persons belonging to the Romanian state, as well as to foreigners, and no hindrance shall be offered either to the hierarchical organisation of the different religious communities nor to their spiritual leaders.[76]

Ironically, perhaps, this landmark development owed more to the old-fashioned influence of Bismarck's banker, Gerson von Bleichröder, than it did to international Jewish activism or the wider humanitarian public.[77] In the long term the Treaty of Berlin was also to prove a pyrrhic victory. The challenge of enforcing its provisions in the teeth of Romanian resistance would open a new (and disappointing) chapter in the evolution of humanitarian intervention.

[76] *Ibid.*, 29.
[77] Fritz Stern, *Gold and Iron: Bismarck, Bleichröder and the Building of the German Empire* (Harmondsworth and New York: Penguin, 1977), ch. 14.

# 7     The 'principles of humanity' and the European powers' intervention in Ottoman Lebanon and Syria in 1860–1861

## Davide Rodogno

The time is fast approaching when the imperative claims of Christianity and humanity must and ought to absorb all others in the much vexed Eastern Question.

Charles Churchill, *The Druzes and the Maronites* (1862)[1]

Previous chapters have identified several areas where the concept, rhetoric and practice of humanitarian intervention developed from the sixteenth century onwards. Nineteenth-century instances of humanitarian intervention certainly built on earlier precedents, especially as far as the discourse justifying and demanding protection, the groups of people deserving protection, and concepts such as 'rights of mankind' and 'rights of humanity' are concerned. In this chapter and then in Chapter 9, I deal more specifically with two instances of intervention, both related to the Ottoman Empire. The first (and the subject of this chapter) took place in Lebanon and Syria in 1860–1, and the second occurred in the European territories of the Ottoman Empire, known as Macedonian provinces, from 1903 to 1908. My objective is to illustrate when interventions took place, for what reason, who undertook them and on behalf of whom they were undertaken.

My starting assumptions are as follows: the structure of the nineteenth-century international system hindered unilateral intervention (whether for humanitarian or other purposes) by a European power within the boundaries of another European state, unless the latter wished to risk a war with the target state or a general war. Nevertheless, beyond the borders of Europe, and specifically within the boundaries of the Ottoman Empire, European powers undertook a number of military interventions during which massacres of Christian populations occurred. In each case, the intervention was a direct consequence of massacre, and its objective was to succour a Christian foreign civilian population by putting an end to, or avoiding repetition of, massacre. As far as the shape

---

[1] C. H. Churchill, *The Druzes and the Maronites under Turkish Rule from 1840 to 1860* [1862] (Reading: Garnet Publishing, 1994), v.

of intervention was concerned, the intervening states acted collectively politically and/or militarily (or mandated one or more states to intervene) on behalf of Christians in the Ottoman Empire. The interventions entailed protracted and comprehensive interference in Ottoman internal affairs and sometimes encompassed long-term protection of the victims of massacre by the implementation of a series of reforms, imposed by the intervening states. The shape of intervention was adapted to geopolitical (local and general) and military circumstances, and took into account the interests of all the intervening states. Intervention was the result of a multilateral negotiation among the intervening powers. The Ottoman Empire (the target state) participated in the negotiation but with a subordinate role. The victims of massacre played an irrelevant, or very secondary, role with respect to the decisions concerning their fate.

The governments of the intervening states were concerned about the violation of the 'rights of humanity', including the right to life of the Ottomans' Christian subjects. The European powers were equally concerned about finding evidence of the Ottoman authorities' unwillingness or incapacity to avoid massacre taking place. Evidence of the latter justified intervention in the internal affairs of a state, which the Europeans viewed as 'barbarous' and 'half civilised'. This brings me to another preliminary consideration: the importance of placing humanitarian interventions within the broader context of nineteenth-century European relations with the Ottoman Empire. On the one hand, humanitarian interventions should be examined in relation to the older practice of capitulation treaties, which specifically concerned the protection of Christian communities living in the Ottoman Empire. On the other hand, one should not forget that, during the nineteenth and early twentieth centuries, European powers wanted the Ottoman government to introduce reforms, in accordance with their view of 'good government'. The alleged failure of the Ottoman government to implement such reforms gave European powers evidence of the Ottoman Empire's 'barbarous' state, and justified further intervention in the empire's internal affairs. In the view of the European states, intervention following massacre was an action dictated by a state of emergency. In this context military intervention was an extraordinary last-resort measure undertaken when deemed necessary by the seriousness of the situation.

Nineteenth-century international law established a discriminatory hierarchy among European and non-European states, based on the principle of the alleged superiority of European civilisation. European countries, along with the United States of America, represented the community of 'civilised states', which enjoyed full membership of the so-called 'Family of Nations' (although the Great Powers intervened in the Low Countries in 1830–1 to compel the Kingdom of the Netherlands to halt military operations against the Belgian rebels and recognise Belgium's independence). Non-European states, such as the Ottoman Empire, were not members of the club of 'civilised' nations; their sovereignty was not absolute. In nineteenth-century European legal doctrine, intervention meant a hybrid politico-military process, a coercive and unsolicited action by an outside state (or states), lying at the intersection between peace and war. Notorious examples of the practice of intervention were the political and military actions undertaken within Europe by the Holy Alliance in the late 1810s and early 1820s, although these were to support governments against movements pressing for political liberalisation, rather than to stop governments' oppressive actions. European governments distinguished intervention – political and military – from an act of war by declaring themselves disinterested in political domination of the target-state, its territorial acquisition or the like. The adjective 'humanitarian' referred to the idea of help, of 'saving strangers'[2] or protecting foreign civilian populations. Reference to the term 'humanitarian intervention' emerged in European and US international law textbooks published in the second half of the nineteenth century as well as in the early twentieth century, whereas the term 'reasons of humanity' appeared as early as the European powers intervention against the Ottoman Empire in Morea (1827).

The *maître mot* of the nineteenth century, at least as far as European affairs were concerned, was non-intervention in the internal affairs of another state. After the end of the Napoleonic Wars, there was a consensus among the European powers that, in their individual and collective interest, it was best, as far as possible, to maintain peace and the existing international order. Nineteenth-century European statesmen, diplomats, philosophers and political thinkers clearly saw the potential for disruption to the international system posed by intervention, especially military intervention; they feared that, at any moment, the latter might degenerate into war. For this reason, humanitarian intervention in the Ottoman Empire must also be examined in the broader context of the 'Eastern Question', of European powers' imperial rivalries, and of the role played by nationalist movements. Keeping in mind the broader international context should help explain why on the one hand not all massacres within the boundaries of the Ottoman Empire were followed by intervention (for example, the massacres of Bulgarians in 1876, or of

[2] I use 'saving strangers' from the title of Nicholas Wheeler's study: *Saving Strangers: Humanitarian Intervention in International Society* (Oxford: Oxford University Press, 2000).

Ottoman Armenians during the 1890s and early 1900s). On the other hand, the nature of the nineteenth-century international system explains why military intervention on behalf of Lebanese and Syrian Christians was possible, whereas no military intervention on behalf of Catholic Poles, victims of harsh repression by Russia, was ever undertaken by a European power.

By massacre, nineteenth-century European governments and cultivated elites meant the loss of innocent human lives on a vast scale, brought about by deliberate acts.[3] Massacre was a collective form of action resulting in the widespread killing of non-combatants: men, women, children or disarmed soldiers. Nineteenth-century Europeans distinguished massacre from natural disaster, in that the former was understood as an organised process of destruction of civilian lives and properties. The authorities of a state could directly perpetrate a massacre; the state and its agents could also be indirectly involved in the massacre through being unwilling to put an end to it or by being unable to prevent its repetition. In a multi-ethnic state – such as the Ottoman Empire – the perpetrators of a massacre could also be a minority acting against another minority or an ethnic or religious majority acting against a minority for political or religious reasons. The states that intervened to put an end to massacre claimed their actions were motivated by the perpetrators' aim to eliminate a community from a more or less extensive territory of the target-state.

During the nineteenth century, European political and cultivated elites used the term 'massacre' in combination with 'atrocity' and, sometimes, with 'horror'. By atrocity, Europeans meant deliberate acts of violence (generally against innocent civilian populations) such as rape, pillage, slaughter, burning villages and destroying religious buildings. Atrocity was the means by which a perpetrator made his intention of hastening the departure of the undesirable 'other' clear. The term 'extermination' deserves particular attention. Since 1945, to exterminate has been intrinsically related to the concept of genocide – a word coined by Raphael Lemkin during 1943–4 – which refers to the 'intent to destroy' and 'deliberately inflict on a human group a condition of life calculated to bring about its physical destruction in whole or in part'.[4] During the nineteenth century the word 'extermination'

---

[3] Jacques Sémelin, *Purify and Destroy: The Political Uses of Massacre and Genocide,* trans. Cynthia Schoch (New York: Columbia University Press, 2007), 323. David El Kenz (ed.), *Le Massacre, objet d'histoire* (Paris: Gallimard, 2005).

[4] 'Convention on the Prevention and Punishment of the Crime of Genocide', UN General Assembly res. 260 (III) A, 9 Dec. 1948, art. 2 (www.hrweb.org/legal/genocide.html).

had a polysemic meaning: on the one hand, it was a synonym of massacre; on the other hand, it was close to the Latin word 'exterminare', by which Europeans meant to extirpate, expel, remove or displace indigenous populations usually to allow for the settlement of European colonies. Occasionally the two meanings overlapped so that the sense of extermination approximated yet another term used today: 'ethnic cleansing'.[5]

Sometimes the word 'annihilation' was used, as of the Ottoman Armenians during the 1890s and early 1900s. Some (not all) European observers and diplomats applied the word 'annihilation' to mean precisely the 'intent to destroy' a whole community carried out by local populations and Ottoman authorities with (and without) the consent of the sultan. With this possible exception, there is no convincing evidence that nineteenth-century Europeans in general connoted extermination and a fortiori massacre with the 'intent to destroy'. I have found no cases where, in the words and actions of the perpetrators, the notion of 'purifying' a territory became secondary in relation to the aim of totally annihilating a group: when their objective became to destroy all the members of a group, including children, when an entire community was killed without even having the chance to flee, or when it was slaughtered once they had been deported.[6] Besides, it is worth emphasising that, during the nineteenth century, the mass displacement of civilian populations was encouraged, recommended, and sometimes enforced, rather than viewed as a crime. For instance, in the aftermath of several interventions in the Ottoman Empire, the intervening states were clearly in favour of the non-forcible removal of civilian populations (often Muslims) as a way to attain the objective of forestalling the recurrence of massacre.

*

In 1840, Mount Lebanon (also known as the Mountain) was an autonomous administrative Ottoman entity, distinct from the province of Syria, comprising approximately 200,000 inhabitants. The Christian Maronites, who inhabited the northern and central regions of Mount

---

[5] Norman Naimark, *Fires of Hatred: Ethnic Cleansing in Twentieth-Century Europe* (Cambridge, MA: Harvard University Press, 2001), 3. See also Benjamin Lieberman, *Terrible Fate: Ethnic Cleansing in the Making of Modern Europe* (Chicago: Ivan R. Dee, 2006); Michael Mann, *The Dark Side of Democracy: Explaining Ethnic Cleansing* (Cambridge: Cambridge University Press, 2005).

[6] Sémelin, *Purify and Destroy*, 339: 'Some colonial massacres were probably perpetrated with this in mind, like that of the Herero population of Namibia in 1904 by the German settlers'.

Lebanon, were numerically preponderant.[7] They were also numerous in the mainly Druze area of Jezzine, and formed an enclave in the town of Dair al-Qamar. The Druze were a splinter group of Shi'a Islam, sufficiently far removed from Muslim doctrine to be sometimes considered a different religion. The Greek Orthodox community, also known as Orthodox Melkite, was the second largest in Lebanon settled mainly in the Kura district, the coastal region south of Tripoli. The Greek Catholics (Uniates), also known as Catholic Melkites, were concentrated in Zahleh. The Shi'a, Metwalis Sunni Muslim and Bedouins were scattered in various locations both north and south. In Mount Lebanon, local Druze and Maronite notables served as intermediaries between the Ottoman authorities and the urban population which they represented and controlled. The autonomy of Mount Lebanon depended on a network of alliances between leading Druze and Maronite families and on a chain of clan loyalties that cut across sectarian lines and took precedence over loyalty to village, district or church.[8]

In 1831, Ibrahim Pasha conquered Syria in the name of his father, Mohammed Ali of Egypt, and occupied it for a decade. The consequences of the Egyptian interregnum were to be long lasting. The Egyptian occupiers practised classic divide-and-rule politics, using the Druze against the Maronites, and encouraged the influx of missionaries, travellers, and economic and industrial prospectors from Europe. In July 1840, a British-sponsored coalition made up of Russia, Austria and Prussia agreed to put an end to Egyptian occupation and restored Ottoman sovereignty. In December 1842, the Mountain was divided into two self-governing districts, each with its own district governor: the northern district under a Maronite, and the south under a Druze. The price the sultan had to pay for European help was a considerable increase in the presence and interference in the affairs of Lebanon by European agents. The traditionally privileged classes of the region, whether Druze in Mount Lebanon or Sunni on the Syrian coast and

[7] Gérald Arboit, *Aux sources de la politique arabe de la France: le Second Empire au Machrek* (Paris: L'Harmattan, 2000); Dominique Chevallier, *La Société du Mont Liban à l'époque de la révolution industrielle en Europe* (Paris: Geunther, 1971); Caesar E. Farah, *The Politics of Interventionism in Ottoman Lebanon, 1830–1861* (London: I. B. Tauris, 2000); Ussama Makdisi, *The Culture of Sectarianism: Community, History, and Violence in Nineteenth-Century Ottoman Lebanon* (Berkeley: University of California Press, 2000); Bruce Masters, *Christians and Jews in the Ottoman Arab World: The Roots of Sectarianism* (Cambridge: Cambridge University Press, 2001); John P. Spagnolo, *France and Ottoman Lebanon 1861–1914* (London: Ithaca Press for the Middle East Centre, 1977); Leila Tarazi Fawaz, *An Occasion for War: Civil Conflict in Lebanon and Damascus in 1860* (Berkeley: University of California Press, 1994).

[8] Tarazi Fawaz, *Occasion for War*, 19.

interior, increasingly perceived the Christians who benefited from trade and close contact with Europe as a threat to their own status.

After 1840, both the British and French governments began to look upon local minorities as their clients and protégés and to play a role that went beyond the protection of religious matters of the previous centuries. France had staked out an early claim to the loyalty of the Maronite Christians. French Capuchins, Jesuits, Lazarists, Carmelites and Franciscans had been active in Lebanon and Syria since the seventeenth century. From the eighteenth century onwards, the French government instructed its diplomats to intervene on behalf of the Maronites whenever they became involved in disputes or trouble. However, this form of support, encapsulated in bilateral treaties, did not include the possibility of a military intervention by the French government. Protection was a discreet diplomatic action, generally an intercession undertaken by French consuls with local Ottoman authorities. In contrast, Britain had no toehold in Syria before 1840.[9] In the early 1840s, Lord Palmerston, then Foreign Secretary, had toyed with the idea of a 'special relationship' with the Druze, a vision made more attractive by missionary dreams of converting the Druze to Protestantism.[10]

It is possible that to some extent the massacres of 1860 were a consequence of the increased European presence in the area. In 1858, the introduction of the Ottoman Land Code allowed Europeans and their protégés to buy up both urban real estate and agricultural land. These newcomers often bought property from impoverished Muslim notables, especially in Damascus. The new laws, under which Christians could testify against Muslims, created further discontentment among the Muslims of the region. By 1860, tension was high and the Muslim population would have happily ejected the European consuls dwelling in their midst, although instead they moved against local Christians who were an easier target.[11]

A third element was the particular view the Europeans had of Lebanon and its people. A set of images and perceptions of Syria and Lebanon had circulated in Europe since the end of the eighteenth century, thanks to the works of orientalists, painters and poets who had brought impressions of Lebanon and Syria into the homes of the European cultivated elite. In the writings of Alphonse de Lamartine or in the paintings of

[9] A. L. Tibawi, *American Interests in Syria 1800–1901: A Study of Educational, Literary and Religious Work* (Oxford: Clarendon Press, 1966), 152.
[10] Ann Pottinger Saab, *Reluctant Icon: Gladstone, Bulgaria, and the Working Classes, 1856–1878* (Cambridge, MA: Harvard University Press, 1991), 38.
[11] Farah, *Politics of Interventionism*, 527.

David Roberts and Edward Lear, these Ottoman provinces evoked an Eden on earth, a timeless biblical land, a mountain refuge that was stagnant due to Islamic Ottoman domination. In the nineteenth century, European writers became prophets of the cultural redemption and religious salvation of Mount Lebanon, exuding confidence in European cultural, political, technological and military hegemony. In the words of historian Ussama Makdisi, they were 'gentle crusaders'; while they believed Mount Lebanon's populations, the Druze and the Maronites, to be completely separate entities, they wanted to see them both (though especially the Maronites) 'regenerated' and reconnected with the evolutionary 'stream of Time', from which they had been separated by Ottoman despotism and Islam. In particular, they argued that government by the 'fanatical' and 'anti-modern' Turk disproportionately harmed Christians.[12]

It is not that different religious communities did not exist, or that travellers' accounts were fabricated, but rather that they were conceptualised in certain terms that did not correspond to the way the inhabitants of Mount Lebanon perceived themselves. When the massacres of 1860 occurred, many in Western Europe saw intervention on humanitarian and civilising grounds as an obvious and urgent remedy. Massacres, British and French authors declared, were the consequence of 'native tribalism' and the 'barbarism' of Turkish rule; and they proclaimed the superiority of the Maronites with respect to Muslims.[13] The English soldier and traveller, Charles Churchill, and François Lenormant, author of many articles in the Catholic newspaper *L'Ami de la Religion*, argued that European governments were not bound by the principle of non-intervention in their dealings with the Ottoman Empire.[14] The massacres in Lebanon were widely reported by French newspapers such as *Le Moniteur* (close to Napoleon III), *Le Constitutionnel* (considered representative of the views of Edouard-Antoine de Thouvenel, the Minister for Foreign Affairs) and *Le Siècle*, which gave detailed accounts of atrocities and wholeheartedly supported intervention in Lebanon and Syria. As during the intervention in the Morea in the 1820s,

---

[12] Makdisi, *Culture of Sectarianism*, 21, 23–5, 68–9.

[13] See the title of ch. 11 in Henry Guys, *Beyrouth et le Liban: Relation d'un séjour de plusieurs années dans ce pays* [1850] (Beirut: Lahd Khater, 1985): 'Mœurs des chrétiens: ils sont supérieurs aux musulmans'. In another of his works, *Esquisse de l'état politique et commercial de la Syrie* (Paris: Chez France Libraire, 1862), Guys reiterated these views using as evidence the 'barbarity' of the massacres. See also Churchill, *The Druzes and the Maronites*, 54–5.

[14] Churchill, *The Druzes and the Maronites*, 8–9, 128–31. Lenormant, *Les derniers événements de Syrie* (Paris: Ch. Duniol, 1860).

public meetings on both sides of the Channel advocated the idea of an intervention and humanitarian relief; furthermore, Catholic deputies presented to the French Parliament a number of petitions from the Maronites of Lebanon and Christians of Damascus demanding military intervention by French troops 'to protect them'.[15]

★

As historian Cesar Farah argues, a great deal of distortion, exaggeration and extravagant claims characterised the descriptions of events. Some reports by European diplomats or merchants are not corroborated by historical evidence.[16] In March 1860, a series of skirmishes occurred in the mixed districts of south Lebanon. In the last two weeks of May, dispatches from the British and French consuls increasingly mentioned sectarian murders among the civilian populations of Lebanon. The leaders of the warring religious communities fomented and even led the revolt. By June, consular reports recorded the looting and burning of villages, the sacking of monasteries, churches and mosques, a number of forced conversions, the slaughtering of children, women and the elderly, and the rape and abduction of women and young girls. French consular reports included morbid details, such as the burning of women after they had been bathed in the blood of their children. In the view of Europeans who were present, massacre and atrocity spread because of the inability of the two district governors to put an end to the disturbances and because there was no adequate police or Ottoman military presence to stop it. As we shall see, the intervening powers claimed that the Ottoman Empire (the target-state) was unable – or unwilling as the French government claimed – to put an end to massacre.

European consuls gave precise information about and numbers of Christians killed, but they were not as accurate as to the number of Druze killed. The latter were much better organised militarily and almost systematically defeated the Maronites. The survivors from the inland districts fled to the coastal cities, for instance to Sidon. There they were refused admittance and so hid in caves along the coast and in gardens around the town. According to European eyewitness accounts, local bandits (Muslim and Druze) killed 250 to 300 people. In a typical contemporary account, Charles Churchill described the events that took place at the gates of Sidon as 'pure butchery':

300 bodies soon strewed the sea-beach and the gardens round about. The shrieks of the women and children rent the air. Some were slain; numbers violated. The young girls were hurried off by a mingled horde of Mohammedans and Metualis, who mysteriously appeared and pounced upon them like vultures ... Several

---

[15] Farah, *Politics of Interventionism*, 659, 672.    [16] *Ibid.*, 527.

Catholic convents and nunneries ... were invaded, robbed and pillaged with similar treachery. The nuns were turned out nearly naked into the fields ... The monks who failed in secreting themselves or escaping were pitilessly slaughtered; some speared in derision at the foot of their altars.[17]

The violence was short lived in the coastal areas of Lebanon, such as Jaffa, Haifa, Acre, Sidon (after the earlier massacre at the city gates), Tyre, Tripoli and Beirut, for in late June 1860, British and French ships anchored off the coast. Marines landed a number of times to protect British or French nationals and members of their households, as well as a number of Christian refugees. On 13 June, a French squadron anchored in Beirut and the French ambassador, Charles Jean, marquis de Lavalette, informed baron de la Roncière, commander of the frigate *Zénobie*, that his duty was: 'avant tout une *tâche d'humanité*'.[18] On 25 June, a small number of French marines landed in Sidon, to protect only French nationals; after that, the French government ceased all military operations.[19] The landing of troops was certainly not a humanitarian intervention for it was intended to protect European subjects and commercial interests. The visible presence of European warships had an unintended humanitarian consequence, for it effectively established peace in coastal towns and villages; however, it also generated an unforeseen humanitarian crisis, for thousands of civilian refugees (Maronite, Greek Orthodox, Greek Catholic and even Muslim) now abandoned the villages of the interior with the intention of reaching these towns, hoping to be rescued by the Europeans.

They did not find adequate structures or resources to care for them or for subsequent waves of refugees that continued to arrive. These people became victims of thieves, brigands and of other refugees, who looted just to survive.

Throughout the month of June in the towns and villages of the interior, massacre, atrocity and, as Churchill put it, a 'war of extermination' continued. On 3 June, the Druze massacred a group of 975 (according to French sources) Christian civilians of Hasbaiya.[20] In the Battle of Rashaiya, 900 more Christians perished. By that stage the European consuls, especially the French, highlighted what they saw as the obvious complicity of the local Ottoman authorities with the Druze. In their

---

[17] Churchill, *The Druzes and the Maronites*, 157.
[18] Lavalette to Thouvenel, MAE, *dépêche* 13 June 1860, AMAE, CP Tr., vol. 345, no. 7, annexe.
[19] Spagnolo, *France and Ottoman Lebanon*, 30.
[20] Consul Bentivoglio to Thouvenel, 17 and 26 June 1860, AMAE, CPC, Turquie, Beirut, vol. 12, nos. 22, 27. Consul Lanusse to Thouvenel, 19 June 1860, CPC, Turquie, Damas, no. 86.

reports they stressed the 'barbarity' of the Druze while portraying the Maronites as innocent victims.[21] Massacres occurred in Zahleh on 14 June and at Deir al-Qamar on 20 and 21 June. Civil war in Lebanon extended to Damascus, in the province of Syria, when Christian refugees arrived at the city. According to the British consul James Brant, refugees in Damascus numbered no fewer than 3,000; most were Greek Orthodox, and included many widows and children. These people overcrowded the city, especially its Christian quarter; most remained without shelter, begging in the streets.[22] On 8 or 9 July, after a minor incident, a violent mob moved towards the Christian quarter. At least 20,000 Druze and Muslims, not necessarily Damascene, poured into town over a period of some days. Ottoman forces initially tried to stop the angry mob. Some soldiers then joined the rioters and the local authorities simply melted away. Foreign consulates and European missions were early targets of the enraged mob. The plunder and killing at Damascus continued for eight days and nights. Around 2,000 Christians died during the riots, plus a few foreigners and an unknown number of refugees.[23]

*

From late May 1860, Stanislas d'Aragon, count de Bentivoglio, the French consul at Beirut, sent numerous and detailed reports of massacres and atrocities to Lavalette, the French ambassador at Constantinople. As the latter reported to the foreign minister, Edouard-Antoine de Thouvenel, all of the European ambassadors in the Ottoman capital were in agreement:

What imported above all, was to prescribe to the consuls in Beirut to put any disagreements to one side *in the interest of humanity* and to busy themselves, either collectively, or individually, but *in concert and agreement, as much as possible,* with the local authorities to stop the effusion of blood and to restore peace.[24]

Lavalette was in favour of a military operation to put an end to the massacre in Lebanon; the intervention would be on behalf of the

---

[21] French consulate at Damascus to Thouvenel, 19 June 1860, AMAE, CPC, Turquie, Damas, vol. 6, D. no. 86.

[22] Tarazi Fawaz, *Occasion for War*, 81.

[23] *Ibid.*, 259, citing Linda Schilcher Schatowski, *Families in Politics: Damascene Factions and Estates in the Eighteenth and Nineteenth Centuries* (Stuttgart: Franz Steiner Verlag, 1985), 89–91.

[24] 'Ce qui importait avant tout, c'était de prescrire aux consuls à Beyrouth de mettre de côté tout dissentiment *dans l'intérêt de l'humanité* et de s'employer, soit collectivement, soit individuellement, mais *de concert et d'accord, autant que possible, avec l'autorité locale à arrêter l'effusion du sang et à rétablir la paix.*' Lavalette to Thouvenel, 13 June 1860, AMAE, CP Tr., vol. 345, no. 7 (emphasis supplied).

Maronites and against the Druze and the Ottoman local authorities, whom he viewed as the accomplices of the Druze. In his view, a political and administrative reorganisation of the province ought to follow military intervention.[25]

Foreign minister Thouvenel, newly appointed in January 1860 (and an experienced diplomat who knew the Ottoman Empire well, as he had been ambassador to the Porte between 1855 and 1860), expressed grave concern over the violation of the rights of the 'French-protected Maronites' and over the likelihood that massacres of Christians might spread if no action were taken. He initially sought juridical legitimacy for intervention in the capitulation treaties between France and the Ottomans. However, Thouvenel knew that they did not give France a right of unilateral military intervention in an Ottoman province. Thouvenel and his government were fully aware that, for France to intervene further in Lebanon, he needed to internationalise the issue and to involve all the European powers in the decision. For that reason, he had to go beyond the capitulations and place new emphasis on the unprecedented scale of the massacres, on the likelihood of recurrences, and on acting in the interest of humanity rather than only on behalf of French-protected Maronites.

Before the Europeans could reach a collective decision and act, the sultan promised to exert all his power to re-establish order and security in Lebanon and Syria. By the end of June, the Ottoman government had despatched 6,000 men to Syria, and replaced the governor of Damascus. On 8 July, Fuad Pasha was appointed as envoy-extraordinaire to Syria with full civil and military powers in the region. He left Constantinople on 12 July along with 15,000–16,000 men and supplies of wheat, and reached Beirut five days later.[26] His mission was both punitive and humanitarian; he was in Syria to punish those who had committed crimes, to provide relief for destitute families with compassion and equity, to help rebuild towns and villages, and to re-establish order and local trust in Ottoman rule. Fuad strenuously attempted to avoid any European diplomatic and/or military intervention in Lebanon and Syria; had the massacre of Christians in Damascus not occurred he probably could have fulfilled his objectives and, most importantly, avoided intervention by the European powers.

When, on 5 July, Thouvenel met with the British ambassador in Paris, Lord Cowley, the latter rejected the French proposal of a joint monitoring of the Syrian coast with warships and the appointment of a European

---

[25] *Ibid.*, annexe.    [26] Tarazi Fawaz, *Occasion for War*, 106–7.

commission to investigate events in Lebanon. On 9 July, the British government directed the Vice-Admiral commanding the British naval fleet in the Mediterranean to proceed forthwith to the coast of Lebanon and Syria and to act with the British consul in protecting the lives and property of Christians. This would have included landing marines from the ships under his command if such measures were necessary. The British intended to assist the Ottoman government in 'protecting British subjects and Christians residing on the coast from massacre'.[27] By this means, the British government hoped that Fuad Pasha might be able at once to send succour to Damascus, where the lives of all Christians (including the British consul and other European consuls) were in imminent danger. In the meantime, the British Foreign Secretary, Lord John Russell, also hoped the representative of the European powers at Constantinople would reach an agreement concerning a general and permanent pacification of Syria and Lebanon.[28] Prime Minister Palmerston, too, seemed to trust Fuad's military and political mission and did not see the necessity of undertaking further military intervention, which in his view might have serious consequences for Great Power relations.

On 17 July, Jean Gilbert Victor, comte de Persigny, French ambassador in London, communicated to Russell a message from Thouvenel arguing that the events in Lebanon were exceptional, and that all European cabinets recognised that it was their duty to respond. Thouvenel doubted that the despatch of Ottoman troops would suffice to stop the spilling of blood. In his view, to satisfy the principles of justice and order, and to establish an enduring peace, suppress the insurrection, and oblige the Druze to lay down their arms, the situation required intervention by the Great Powers. He was in favour of sending a collective (European and Ottoman) commission of enquiry to ascertain the circumstances which had brought about the conflict and the extent to which the local administration was culpable, as well as to work out the compensation due to the victims, and, lastly, to review the arrangements that were to be adopted to avert future misfortunes. After the massacre of Damascus, Thouvenel could easily argue that, despite the peace between the Maronites and Druze in Lebanon, intervention was necessary not merely because the French consulate and property had been sacked (which, in his view, was of itself sufficient justification for intervention) and because 'Muslim fanatics' had murdered Christians (ditto), including French

---

[27] Lord J. Russell to Erskine, Foreign Office, 12 July 1860, in A. & P., 1861, Correspondence relating to the affairs of Syria 1860–61, no. 5.
[28] Lord J. Russell to Sir H. Bulwer, 10 July 1860, *ibid.*, no. 4.

missionaries (ditto), but also because massacre might spread elsewhere in the Ottoman Empire. Moreover, after the events of Damascus, it was difficult for the British government to contest the reports of atrocities, and allegations that the Ottoman authorities and soldiers had connived in the massacres of Christians.[29]

The French government sought the support of all the other European powers, claiming that France's initiative followed its earlier collaboration with the Sublime Porte in 1842 to create Lebanon's administrative system and that the military operation did not threaten the independence of the Ottoman Empire.[30] In other words, France did not wish to go to war against the Ottoman Empire. Thouvenel told the British ambassador in Paris, Lord Cowley, that he and Emperor Napoleon III both felt that events in Syria 'required a more active intervention on the part of Europe'.[31] Public opinion, Thouvenel added, would not brook the continued supineness of Europe in the event of such disasters. His plan was to send foreign troops and disembark them at various points along the coast of the disturbed districts; it would not be difficult for England, Austria and France to send detachments for that purpose. When Cowley remarked that they should weigh the consequences of such action, Thouvenel repeated that the consent of the Great Powers should be sought before any occupation of Ottoman soil. In Thouvenel's view, the order given to the commanders of the squadrons already anchored off the shores of Lebanon – to place their crews at the disposal of the consuls – would not stop the insurrection at the heart of Lebanon or in the towns of the interior:

A body of troops held ready to act according to circumstances would alone be capable of fulfilling the task. From all points of view, it would exercise a beneficial influence, not only by reason of the contingent aid which it would lend to the Turkish troops, but by the moral authority which its presence alone, by reassuring the populations, would not fail to have upon the attitude and conduct of the Ottoman functionaries themselves.[32]

This combination could only be executed in concert with the Porte and with the full agreement of the five European powers.

The intervention would thus, in principle, be collective, and the European troops, sent with common objectives, would only carry out a

[29] Earl Cowley to Lord J. Russell, Paris, 19 July 1861, received 20 July, *ibid.*, no. 13.
[30] Lavalette to Thouvenel, 18 July 1860, AMAE, CP Tr., vol. 345, no. 25.
[31] Cowley to Russell, Paris, 17 July 1860 (received 18 July). A. & P., 1861, Correspondence relating to the affairs of Syria 1860–61, no. 9.
[32] Thouvenel to Count Persigny, Paris, 17 July 1860 (communicated to Lord J. Russell by Persigny, on 20 July), *ibid.*, no. 11.

commission entrusted to them by the European powers in consultation with the Ottoman government. If the British government accepted Thouvenel's plan, the latter thought it possible to negotiate, without delay, an understanding with the other governments of Europe and with the Porte, and to agree on the most prompt means 'of obtaining the satisfaction *due to humanity, and of assisting in the reestablishment of peace in Syria*'.[33] In Constantinople, in the meantime, Lavalette explained to Ali Pasha that the reasons for the intervention were related to the manifest impotence of the Ottoman authorities, which made foreign help required if the collapse of the Ottoman Empire were to be avoided. Furthermore, France had a duty to fulfil and had to respect public opinion which 'would demand account for the blood of the Christians, which we let be shed without acting'. Hence, after having done so much to protect the Ottoman Empire it would be impossible for France to be 'impassive spectators of so much murder and carnage'.[34] The French plan as conveyed to its European counterparts and to the Ottoman government contrasted with Napoleon III's and his ministers' speeches for internal consumption in France, in which they avowed that the intervention was undertaken in favour of the Maronites, and *against* the Ottoman Empire.

The massacre of Damascus was the turning point with respect to intervention, for thereafter a significant element of British public opinion was in favour of some action. Two further elements contributed to the British involvement in the Lebanese and Syrian situations. On the one hand, Foreign Secretary Russell deeply distrusted French motives, yet, on the other, he feared even more the consequences of a Russo-French alliance and the possibility of British isolation. It was now very difficult for Russell to prove that news of peace in Lebanon was accurate; even if it were, as Thouvenel put it: What was this peace? Would it render all further intervention unnecessary? This peace would be unjust for it would be nothing more than the 'submission of the Maronites to the Druses, to save themselves from further massacre. But what reparation would they have for all the losses inflicted upon them? ... Was nothing to be done to prevent a repetition of such horrors?'[35] It was only on 23 July that Russell spoke openly of the frightful character of the massacre, asserting that 5,500 had been killed and that 20,000, including the widows and children of the murdered, were homeless and in a

---

[33] *Ibid.* (emphasis supplied).
[34] 'Demanderait compte du sang des chrétiens, que nous laissions verser sans agir ... Spectateurs impassibles de tant de meurtres et de carnage.' Lavalette to Thouvenel, 24 July 1860, AMAE, CP Tr. vol. 345, no. 31.
[35] Cowley to Russell, Paris, 22 July 1860, received 23 July, A. & P., 1861, Correspondence relating to the affairs of Syria 1860–61, no. 18.

state of famine. Russell admitted that while these dreadful scenes were going on, the Ottoman authorities appeared to have been bystanders, where, indeed, they were not participating in the massacre. Hence

> Indignant at this want of humanity and of energy, Her Majesty's Government have received, and accepted, a proposal of the Emperor of the French to send European troops to Syria to prevent further excesses.[36]

Russell very reluctantly sanctioned the deployment of foreign forces in Syria for, in his view, it could provoke a 'fiercer fanaticism among the Mussulmans' and it might delay, rather than hasten, the pacification of Syria. Both he and Prime Minister Palmerston feared grave international consequences and made it clear that the intervention should end as soon as the necessity for it no longer existed. In late July, Thouvenel organised a conference aimed at obtaining the Porte's explicit assent to intervention by foreign troops; this was essential to ensure the intervention was not deemed an act of war against the Ottoman Empire.[37] The first protocol located the juridical legitimacy of the intervention in the Treaty of Paris of 30 March 1856. The main argument was that Article IX, which guaranteed the rights of Ottoman Christians, had been violated in Syria. Thouvenel identified the political legitimacy for intervention in the continued unrest which threatened the integrity of the Ottoman Empire, and therefore peace in Europe, and requested that the Ottoman government re-establish the conditions under which Christians had lived prior to the massacres.[38]

The second protocol, dated 3 August (and signed on 5 September), embodied the conditions for intervention in Syria, a 'protocole de désintéressement' and included the declaration by the sultan claiming he wished to stop the spilling of blood in Syria.[39] The seven articles of the second protocol stipulated that a European military force of up to 12,000 soldiers would be sent to Syria to help re-establish order; France would provide half of them. The European powers would provide sufficient naval forces to monitor Syrian coastal towns (by August there were no fewer than twenty-two warships from 'great' and 'small' European powers, including Greece and Sardinia). A French expeditionary corps was mandated by the other European powers to undertake the military operation. France was to act in the name of all the signatories and, in conjunction with the Ottoman authorities, was to defend the best

---

[36] Russell to Cowley, 23 July 1860, *ibid.*, no. 22.
[37] Russell to Cowley, 28 July 1860, *ibid.*, no. 37.
[38] Protocol of a Conference held at Paris, 3 Aug. 1860, A. & P., 1861, *ibid.*, no. 59, encl. 2.
[39] *Résumé des Affaires de Syrie*, AMAE, Mémoires et Documents, vol. 122, no. 17.

interests of the Ottoman government as well as those of Ottoman Christians. The Ottoman government would provide the army's subsistence and supplies insofar as it was able. The European expeditionary force would remain in Syria for no more than six months, which the powers believed to be sufficient time to pacify the region.

The mission of General Charles-Marie-Napoléon Brandouin, marquis de Beaufort d'Hautpoul, as commander-in-chief of the French expedition, was not to conquer or occupy any territory. It was 'remedial and temporary', a response to public outcry and to the profound pity inspired by the misery of the Christians of the East. Napoleon III specified that the small army corps was to retain mobility, so as to bring justice anywhere in the country, rather than remain in garrison. It would catch, bring to trial and punish the guilty, return to the Christians their confiscated goods, disarm the Druze and force on them reparations as indemnity to the victims of the insurrection. It was intended to be seen to be a clear act of justice.[40] The *Moniteur* claimed that the mission was one in a long line of France's responsibilities in the East that had begun with the Crusades. Beaufort was entirely convinced that his mission was to bring progress, development, industrialisation and the civilisation of 'idées chrétiennes' to the Islamic world.[41]

Once in Lebanon, Beaufort quickly realised that the military and political objectives of the intervention as portrayed in French government speeches and newspapers, and by himself, were incompatible with the restrictive European mandate the French expeditionary corps was bound to act by and clashed with the objectives of Fuad Pasha, with whom Beaufort was to collaborate. The expeditionary corps did not ever engage in major military action. The representatives of the European powers, especially the British *in situ*, closely monitored every move and decision by the French commander and his troops. An even fiercer obstacle to the implementation of the French agenda was Fuad, who defended the imperial interests of the Porte. Beaufort had little room to manoeuvre and had to stick to the letter of his mandate.

As had happened in the Morea in 1827, after the naval battle of Navarino, the French military carried out a number of humanitarian activities in Syria and Lebanon, such as the burial of corpses and the cleaning of streets.[42] Beaufort viewed these 'humanitarian' actions with

[40] Hamelin to Beaufort, Paris, 2 Aug. 1860, Service Historique de l'Armée de Terre, Vincennes, G4/1, cited in Tarazi Fawaz, *Occasion for War*, 114–15.

[41] Farah, *Politics of Interventionism*, 543.

[42] C. Rochemonteix (ed.), *Le Liban et l'expédition française en Syrie (1860–1861). Documents inédits du Général A. Ducrot* (Paris: Librairie Auguste Picard, 1921). Lavalette to Thouvenel, Dépêche télégraphique, 12 Oct. 1860, AMAE, CP Tr., vol. 347.

contempt, regarding them as much less important than French military and political objectives. It was probably because of this disappointment that Napoleon III wanted his troops to remain until the administrative reorganisation of Lebanon was complete, officially to achieve their 'œuvre d'humanité'.[43] Thouvenel requested an extension of six months to the French mandate. The British government vetoed it, on the grounds that the frightful massacres that had filled 'all Europe with terror' were over; to augment the European force and maintain it in Syria with a view to preventing future outrages would be to alter entirely the original agreement between the European powers and the sultan. Russell feared that a longer occupation would soon degenerate into an annexation of Syria and become a precedent for the partition of the Ottoman Empire. For this reason, the British government wished to see the government of Syria restored to Ottoman control as soon as possible. Russell admitted that 'no security, it is true, would be thus obtained against a recurrence of the conflicts of Dru[ze] and Christians; but as long as the two races exist in the country no permanent security can be obtained'.[44] The achievement of a temporary peace was enough. In March 1861, the Europeans agreed that French troops would leave on 5 June, and that Britain would maintain its warships on the Lebanese coast and its soldiers would protect British and Christian civilians as well as the Druze population.[45]

*

On 26 September 1860, Fuad Pasha had met members of the newly instituted European Commission in Beirut, comprising representatives of France, Great Britain, Russia and Austria. The commissioners' task was to solve the problems of housing, indemnity and relief; they also had to determine who was responsible for the civil war, although punishing the guilty remained the responsibility of the Ottomans. Additionally, the Commission was to decide, in collaboration with Fuad Pasha, how Mount Lebanon should be administered in the future to prevent a recurrence of the massacres. The decision-making process was slow, further hindered by the commissioners' respective governments, which did not all agree with the decisions taken in Beirut.

The first problem the European commissioners attempted to solve was that of the refugees, especially the thousands amassed in Beirut. The local authorities, the Sublime Porte and the Europeans all lacked

---

[43] Thouvenel to count de Flahault, 18 Jan. 1861 (communicated to Russell by Flahault, 22 Jan.), A. & P., 1861, Correspondence relating to the affairs of Syria 1860–61, no. 253.
[44] Russell to Cowley, 7 Nov. 1860, *ibid.*, no. 172.
[45] Russell to Cowley, 27 Feb. 1861, *ibid.*, no. 324.

experience in dealing with a relief effort and refugee-related issues and found it difficult to assign energies and resources. The Ottoman government sponsored a relief programme, though it lacked sufficient funds to carry it out. Refugees were reluctant to return to their destroyed villages for fear of a repetition of events and because they believed that they could rely on relief indefinitely where they were.[46] The Druze and Christians of mixed villages were particularly reluctant to return home. When the French expeditionary corps departed, many Christians who had previously returned to their villages, headed back to the coast.[47] The French troops tended not to cooperate with the Ottomans, sometimes proceeding unilaterally with the disinfecting and clearing of towns, and with rebuilding roads and houses – all part of their 'civilising' mission.[48]

The European commissioners in Beirut realised that distribution of humanitarian aid needed to be centralised in order for it to be more effective. Existing national relief agencies were subordinated to the commission, which established a central relief committee to co-ordinate the use and distribution of donations. This committee also estimated the costs of rebuilding houses and used these estimates to determine the distribution of relief, though it did not become involved in assessing damages. The commission monitored Fuad's relief efforts in Mount Lebanon, including the distribution of grain and other necessities, the restitution of stolen goods, and all other aspects of government-sponsored relief. It maintained pressure on local authorities by making continual enquiries about how many people were benefiting from relief, how many houses and villages had been rebuilt, whether relief was interrupted and, if so, where and why, and whether or not Christians were returning.[49] Unfortunately, by October 1860, relief supplies from Europe had dried up. The Central Relief Committee had assisted Christian refugees on the coast significantly, but not those who remained in the war-torn districts.[50] In early 1861, civilians inland still lacked food and basic supplies; on the coast, overcrowded housing and hospitals resulted in outbreaks of typhoid, Egyptian ophthalymia and other contagious diseases, and efforts to raise money locally, by taxing the local Muslim populations, failed.

---

[46] Major Fraser to Russell, 2 Dec. 1860 (received 15 Dec.), *ibid.*, no. 203; Lord Dufferin to Russell, 4 Dec. 1860 (received 29 Dec.) and encl. 1 with same, *ibid.*, nos. 218–19.

[47] Lavalette to Thouvenel, 1 Jan. 1861, AMAE, CP Tr., vol. 348, no. 1; Dufferin to Bulwer, 13 Jan. 1861 in Dufferin to Russell, 10 Jan. 1861, NA, FO 78/1627, nos. 100, 50.

[48] Tarazi Fawaz, *Occasion for War*, 173.

[49] 'Protocol of the Third Meeting of the Syrian Commission', Beirut, 1 Oct. 1860, A. & P., 1861, Correspondence relating to the affairs of Syria 1860–61, no. 168, encl. 1.

[50] 'Protocol of the Seventh Meeting of the Syrian Commission', Beirut, 30 Oct. 1860, *ibid.*, no. 182, encl. 10.

When it came to punishing those responsible, the European commissioners distinguished between those responsible for the massacres (these were easier to identify in Damascus than in Mount Lebanon), the leaders of gangs, and common criminals. In the commissioners' minds, this differentiated between those who caused the civil war and those who simply got swept up in its violence. Those in the first category were deemed to be the most guilty. In Damascus on 3 August, the Ottoman military began to arrest men whose names were on lists drawn up by the European consulates, and within a few days almost 1,000 people had been arrested. The accused were delivered to an extraordinary tribunal made up of Ottoman functionaries brought in from Constantinople: they were judged by an Ottoman tribunal, according to Ottoman law.[51] On 20 August, 167 men were publicly executed; by early 1861, hundreds had suffered a similar fate, and hundreds more sentenced to forced labour. By punishing the perpetrators of the massacre of Damascus, Fuad intended to illustrate that the Ottoman government was 'modern', 'reformed' and not responsible for the massacres, which were contrary to 'the principle of civilisation current in the world'.[52] However, Fuad only agreed to the death penalty for the Governor of Damascus, Ahmad (Ahmet) Pasha, and his officers after strong pressure from the European commissioners.

Restoring order in Mount Lebanon proved to be more difficult than in Damascus. The administrative chaos that followed the massacres, as well as a lack of funds, generated problems. The European and Ottoman plan of relief, restitution, reconstruction and assessing responsibility, foundered on the issue of punishment, on which Europeans disagreed. The commissioners eventually reached a consensus on a moderate level of punishment for the Druze who, naturally, considered the sentences harsh and unjustified. Extraordinary tribunals were established at Beirut and Muktara (Moktara) to try the Druze.

The European powers considered the political and administrative reform of Mount Lebanon intrinsic to the intervention, arguing that in a reformed province, massacres were unlikely to occur, and that the reforms imposed by the European powers would be beneficial for local populations, for the Ottoman government, and for peace and tranquillity in Europe. It proved difficult to reach an agreement, because each of the intervening powers had its own interests to protect. Only on 9 June 1861 did the ambassadorial conference at Constantinople produce a sixteen-article draft that was accepted by the Sublime Porte.

---

[51] Lavalette to Thouvenel, 26 Sept. 1860, annexe, AMAE, CP Tr., vol. 346, no. 72.
[52] *Ibid.*, annexe, 'Proclamation de Fuad Pacha'.

The *Règlement et protocole relatifs à la réorganisation du Mont Liban* was a constitutional document which made Lebanon a 'Mutasarrifiyya' – the term was deliberately vague; the governor (*mutassarif*) was to be a Christian (brought in from outside, not a local Maronite), responsible directly to Constantinople, and would serve a three-year term. He had extensive powers, except over the courts. An administrative council composed of elected Christian and Muslim members was to assist the governor, and had to be consulted if Ottoman troops were to be called to active duty. A volunteer police force was established and was under the governor's control. The rest of the Ottoman province's territory was not subject to the *Règlement*. Apart from minor modifications, the *Règlement* remained in force until World War I.[53] As the historian Ussama Makdisi observes, the *Règlement* was an attempt to 'juridically replace a non-sectarian elite culture with a sectarian one that emphasised the important role that disciplined, reformed, and co-opted elites could and indeed had to play in the process of restoring an Ottoman social order' – and, I would add, ensure European interests in the region.[54]

\*

The intervention in Ottoman Lebanon and Syria has to be considered in the context of the European powers' imperial rivalries in the Mediterranean and in the Middle East, and of the European powers' relations with the Ottoman Empire in the aftermath of the Crimean War. The European powers' collective intervention was 'disinterested', for they did not seek territorial acquisition, exclusive influence, or any commercial concession for their subjects that might not be granted to the subjects of all other nations. Yet 'disinterested' did not mean that the intervention of 1860–1 was purely humanitarian. Despite Napoleon's proclamation – 'What interest other than humanity would move me to send troops to this region?' – it is abundantly clear that French motives for intervention were not exclusively humanitarian. French prestige and influence in the Middle East; the completion of the Suez Canal; the defence of the Syrian silk trade; and even the diversion of the French public's attention from domestic affairs and the dismemberment of the papal states that had alienated the sympathies

---

[53] Lavalette to Thouvenel, 12 and 26 June 1861, AMAE, CP Tr., vol. 350, nos. 85. 90. *Règlement pour l'Administration du Liban*, A. & P., 1861, vol. XVIII, pt ii: *Correspondence Relating to the Affairs of Syria (In Continuation of Correspondence presented to Parliament in April 1861)*, doc. 67, encl. 2.

[54] Makdisi, *Culture of Sectarianism*, 162. The irony of course is that the Ottomans (and the Europeans) never intended for this sectarian order to become a nationalist blueprint.

of the Catholics in France – all were issues of concern at this time.[55] Napoleon III certainly dreamt of Lebanon as a second Algeria in the Mediterranean, but the international nature of intervention meant that French troops were obliged to respect their mandate; expanding French involvement in Lebanon was not worth risking a European war.[56]

French public opinion was genuinely in favour of an intervention on behalf of the Christians. Through its deputies and senators it exerted pressure on the government. For instance, when, in June 1861, the French expeditionary corps was withdrawn from Lebanon, Catholic deputies opposed the emperor's decision, claiming that 'the departure of the army from the Lebanon would be followed there by regrettable scenes'. A committee of nine – including two Catholic priests and three deputies who would later actively advocate intervention to defend the Christian Armenians of Anatolia – addressed a petition to the French Senate requesting the prolongation of the French occupation of Syria; the petition was unsuccessful.[57] In Britain, the press, public opinion and Parliament all contested the government's initial decision not to support France. However, it was not public pressure that persuaded the government to support the French initiative, but rather foreign-policy considerations.

The European states not only wished to preserve the right to life and property guaranteed to the Christians of the Ottoman Empire by the 1856 Treaty of Paris, they also believed that further massacres threatened the internal stability of the Ottoman Empire and hence peace in Europe. The massacres of summer 1860 proved to many European diplomats and statesmen, and to cultivated public opinion, that the Ottoman Empire was a 'barbarous', 'fanatic' empire where anarchy prevailed. Hence, Ottoman Christians needed Europe to intervene on their behalf. European observers of the massacres and those who read their reports in the press had their responses shaped by civilisational considerations. One British observer declared:

It is to be remembered that this is a country of vendettas; in the war carried on between the *barbarian tribes* which inhabit it, usages prevail as horrible as those which disgraced the Middle Ages of Europe . . . Beneath the full blaze of modern

---

[55] 'Quel intérêt autre que l'humanité m'engagerait à envoyer des troupes dans cette contrée?' Alyce Edythe Mange, *The Near Eastern Policy of Emperor Napoleon III* (Urbana: University of Illinois Press, 1979), 91–2.

[56] Rochemonteix, *Liban et l'expédition française en Syrie*, 292–4. 'Mémoire du Comte Edouard de Warren . . . adressé à Napoléon III', Nancy, 18 July 1860, MAE, Mémoires et Documents, vol. 122, no. 19.

[57] Farah, *Politics of Interventionism*, 660. Chevallier, *La Société du Mont Liban*, 283–4, 'le départ de l'armée serait suivi dans le Liban de scènes regrettables'.

civilisation we find in Syria habits of thought and practices prevailing for which the only historical parallel can be found in the books of Moses.[58]

As Thouvenel perfectly understood, the compatibility of humanitarian concerns and *Realpolitik* made humanitarian intervention possible in 1860.

The intervention highlighted a number of features of emerging international practice. First, the European powers dealt with the Ottoman government as a sovereign entity only as long as it served the purpose of establishing that the intervention was not an act of war. Ottoman sovereignty was meaningless when it came to imposing a solution to prevent a repetition of the massacres. Nevertheless, to the intervening states (and to the Sublime Porte) it was clear that the intervention was not a war by the European powers against the Ottoman Empire.

Second, the intervention was a collective effort by all the major powers. While France took the leading role, it certainly did not act unilaterally.

Third, the intervention was humanitarian, for its main motivation was to prevent further massacres of Ottoman Christians in Lebanon and Syria. The French government clearly identified the Maronites (and the Greek Orthodox in Damascus) as the victims of massacre, and held the local and central Ottoman authorities, as well as the Druze, responsible. The British government – which initially opposed military intervention, preferring a political solution negotiated in Constantinople – changed its policy only when incontrovertible evidence of massacre in Damascus came to light. However, while it agreed to collective intervention in order to prevent further killings, after the intervention it insisted on including the Druze as victims of massacre. The British defended the Druze not because their idea of humanity was broader or less biased than the French, but to counter-balance French action in favour of the Maronites.

Fourth, throughout the crisis the Ottoman Christians were the recipients of rights, though they were not involved in the process that would have modified their lives after the events of 1860. The European commissioners in Lebanon, the diplomats in Constantinople, the statesmen in the European capitals, and the Sublime Porte – all seemed to know both what was best for the Christians and the nature of the political and administrative reforms that needed to be enforced in the Ottoman provinces. The military and political intervention of 1860–1 occurred too late to put an end to civil war and massacre; but it was

---

[58] Lord Dufferin, comments to Fuad Pasha, from the 'Eighth Sitting of the Syrian Commission', 10 Nov. 1860, A. & P., 1861, Correspondence relating to the affairs of Syria 1860–61, no. 190, encl. 1.

successful and effective in preventing any repetition, and brought peace and stability to those Ottoman provinces. The military intervention encompassed short-term rescue and long-term protection, which culminated with the 1861 *Règlement organique*. The social, economic, juridical and administrative reforms that were enforced were an intrinsic part of the intervention and indispensable to bringing peace, progress and civilisation to the Lebanese 'tribes'. The military and political dimensions of the intervention were the result of a compromise between the European powers, agreed before an accurate analysis of the well-being of the local populations had been carried out. The political settlement proved to be long-lasting, even though it consolidated the sectarian divisions of Mount Lebanon. It should be noted that, as was to be the case in the 1990s, the intervening states had different concepts as to the most appropriate 'exit strategy'. These differences revolved around the ever-controversial questions: Should the intervening states assume extensive administrative duties and full responsibility when they intervene? Should they stay until there is no reasonable doubt that massacre will not occur again?

Fifth, the work of the expeditionary corps and the European commission was unco-ordinated, but the creation of a multilateral *ad hoc* commission was an important innovation. Its ambitious aims and objectives were a significant precedent in the emerging international practice of humanitarian intervention, one that foreshadows the debate following the interventions of the 1990s, insofar as the intervening states aimed to solve the problem of refugees, to restore peace and enforce it through the implementation of a comprehensive set of reforms. It should be noted that the expeditionary corps achieved notable successes in sanitation and reconstruction. French soldiers who left France with the ambition of protecting indigenous Christians and consolidating French interests in the region instead accomplished a 'campagne de charité'.[59] Yet charity, humanitarian relief and reconstruction, as well as protection, were all clearly biased in favour of the Christians.

Finally, it must be stressed that in early June 1860, the British and French squadrons along the Syrian coast could have undertaken an intervention to prevent further disturbances. From the end of May, French and British ships had been clearly visible from Beirut, and the powerful Russian man-of-war *Vladimir* had 600 troops ready to land. These European forces refrained from intervening because their

---

[59] Rochemonteix, *Liban et l'expédition française en Syrie*, 213.

respective governments had yet to reach an agreement. This reveals that the European powers shared the same concept of what a humanitarian intervention entailed, including the risks involved. There were probably enough marines present to stop the massacres, at least in coastal areas, though not in the inland areas of Lebanon. They could have dissuaded some of the Christian bands from provoking the Druze, and allowed the Ottoman government to send fresh forces to restore peace. Preventive unilateral humanitarian intervention, however, was not an option for nineteenth-century European powers.

Intervention in Lebanon and Syria to protect Christians significantly shaped subsequent interventions (and non-interventions) on grounds of humanity within the boundaries of the Ottoman Empire. In the late nineteenth century and at the beginning of the twentieth, European foreign ministries identified the 1860–1 intervention and subsequent reforms as a model for political solutions in other areas of unrest in the Ottoman Empire where Christians lived: on the island of Crete (the *Règlement Organique* introduced there in 1868 was based on that of 1861); Rumelia in 1876; and Macedonia in the early 1900s (see Chapter 9). The 'principes d'humanité' of the intervention in Lebanon and Syria were evoked in diplomatic and governmental correspondence relating to other 'humanitarian' crises, and in the press and pamphlets. During the 1870s, the massacres of 1860 were reinterpreted in light of the Bulgarian atrocities (see Chapter 8) and came to be viewed as yet more proof of 'Ottoman barbarity'. Malcolm MacColl (one of the main figures of the Bulgarian agitation in Britain) wrote in 1877 that the events of 1860 were 'in every circumstance of bestial lust and fiendish cruelty ... on a par with the Bulgarian atrocities', even 'though the public mind of England' had not been 'equally excited' by them.[60] By the beginning of the twentieth century, moreover, the intervention in Lebanon and Syria was systematically integrated into the jurisprudence of humanitarian intervention, as it is in modern international law textbooks. The importance of the European response to the massacres in Lebanon and Syria is hard to overstate.

---

[60] Malcolm MacColl, *The Eastern Question: Its Facts and Fallacies* (London: Longmans, Green, & Co., 1877), 51–7 and 280–1.

# 8    The guarantees of humanity: the Concert of Europe and the origins of the Russo–Ottoman War of 1877

## *Matthias Schulz*

> If the Powers want serious results they must agree that the independence and integrity of Turkey should be subordinated to the guarantees demanded by humanity, Christian Europe, and interests of peace.
>
> Prince Gorchakov in conversation with Lord Loftus, 20 Nov. 1876[1]

The Eastern crisis from 1875 to 1878 represented a turning point in the history of the Ottoman Empire and a major challenge to the Concert of Great Powers.[2] Beginning like one of the episodic rebellions against Ottoman rule, a peasant revolt in the Herzegovina in July 1875 spread to Bosnia in January 1876 before spilling over to Bulgaria in late April, and Serbia and Montenegro, which declared war against Sultan Murad V in June/July 1876. The events caught the attention of diplomats and became a major issue in the press mainly because of the brutality with which irregular forces, the Bashi-Bazouks, commanded by Ottoman officers, crushed the Bulgarian insurgency. According to contemporary investigators, the Turks killed between 12,000 and 15,000 Christians, yet Bulgarian historians claim that between 30,000 and 60,000 must have perished in the massacres.[3] Whereas the powers intervened diplomatically at an early stage, the failure collectively to persuade the Ottoman government to implement reforms in the provinces led to the Russo-Turkish war in April 1877 which liberated the majority of the Balkan Christians.

What role, if any, did humanitarian motives play in the outbreak of the Russo-Turkish War in April 1877? Could it be understood as

---

[1] Lord Loftus to Earl of Derby, St Petersburg, 20 Nov. 1876, telegraphic, *BDFA*, I, B, vol. 3, doc. 383, 160.

[2] See Barbara Jelavich, *Russia's Balkan Entanglements, 1806–1914* (Cambridge: Cambridge University Press, 1993), 143–78; Winfried Baumgart, *Europäisches Konzert und nationale Bewegung, 1830–1878* (Paderborn: Schöningh, 1999), 416–28; Benedict H. Sumner, *Russia and the Balkans 1870–1880* (Oxford: Clarendon Press, 1937).

[3] L. S. Stavrianos, *The Balkans since 1453* (New York: Holt, 1958), 380. *The Times*, 8 Aug. 1876. This and all future references from *The Times* have been taken from *The Times Online Archives*, http://archive.timesonline.co.uk/tol/archive/.

a humanitarian intervention? Most historians have interpreted the war's origins in the light of Russia's and Austria's expansionist designs. According to this view, the Great Powers have furthered the disintegration of Turkey through their meddling in its internal affairs with a view to an eventual partition.[4] Russia's role, in particular, had been tainted by the publication, in 1877, of false documents fabricated by the Turkish government to incriminate the role played by the Russian ambassador in Constantinople, Nikolaj Ignati'ev, with respect to the Balkan uprisings.[5] Others, on the contrary, have argued that while the Great Powers competed for influence over parts of the Ottoman Empire, their reciprocal control and the fact that their 'designs' cancelled each other out helped to prevent the collapse of the 'Sick Man' of Europe until the First World War.[6] Austria-Hungary and Britain, in particular, had for a long time been stalwarts of Ottoman territorial integrity. And Russia, which burnt its fingers in the Crimean War, had ever since wished to keep out of the Eastern imbroglio, because Tsar Alexander II and Chancellor Alexander Gorchakov considered domestic reforms and economic modernisation their priority. From this perspective, Russian conquests in the Caucasus (Kazakh steppe, Samarkand, Tashkent and Kokand) in the 1860s were not part of a design, but the result of activities by uncontrollable officers on the fringes of the empire.[7]

To grasp the dynamics triggered by humanitarian crises in late nineteenth-century international relations, one has to take into account the changing framework of foreign policy-making. On the one hand, the regulative framework of the Concert of Europe, which consisted of close consultations, reciprocal control and conference diplomacy,[8] had been disturbed by the ascendancy of *Realpolitik* from around 1849 to 1870, i.e., the willingness of some governments to instrumentalise national sentiments in order to realise dynastic ambitions by limited wars – provided that the risks involved seemed manageable. During this period some governments, including Russia in 1853, put national ambitions

---

[4] See Ernst Engelberg, *Bismarck: Das Reich in der Mitte Europas* (Berlin: Siedler, 1990), 227; see also Mustafa Aksakal, *The Ottoman Road to War: The Ottoman Empire and the First World War* (Cambridge: Cambridge University Press, 2008), 4–5.

[5] The falsifications were uncovered only in 1960, so that several generations of historians had worked on the crisis with falsified documents. Cf. Gisela Hünigen, *Nikolaj Pavlovic Ignati'ev und die russische Balkanpolitik 1875–1878* (Göttingen: Musterschmidt, 1968), 8.

[6] Winfried Baumgart, *The Crimean War* (London: Arnold, 1999), 211, and *Europäisches Konzert und nationale Bewegung*, 349–50.

[7] Barbara Jelavich, *A Century of Russian Foreign Policy* (Philadelphia: Lippincott, 1964), 172–3.

[8] Matthias Schulz, *Normen und Praxis: Das Europäische Konzert der Großmächte als Sicherheitsrat 1815–1860* (Munich: Oldenburg, 2009).

above their commitment to international rules.[9] Yet after Italian and German unification and the revision of the Black Sea clauses in Russia's favour, the desire to stabilise the new balance of power became prevalent again in most European capitals. Was this tendency accompanied by a reaffirmation of rule-abiding behaviour and the virtues of moderation? One could suppose so, especially since cold-blooded realism did not universally appeal to public opinion, which exercised a growing influence on governments. Seeking to remain popular, some European monarchies conspicuously supported humanitarian causes during the Syrian and Cretan crises, issued appeals during the bombardment of Belgrade by the Turks in 1862 and assumed a leading role in the Red Cross movement. The tsar, although the addressee of humanitarian appeals and protests during the Polish uprising of 1863, was not alien to those tendencies. He launched the St Petersburg conference against explosive bullets in 1867, and promoted the Brussels conference on the law of war in 1873.

European policies in the Orient had been influenced by humanitarian considerations since the Greek War of Independence. British governments began to plead for reforms in favour of Christian minorities in the Ottoman Empire to prevent its disintegration. This policy was cast into a legal framework at the end of the Crimean War, in which England, France and Sardinia-Piedmont had fought against Russia for the survival of the Ottoman Empire. At the Congress of Paris in 1856, the Great Powers and Sardinia collectively guaranteed the Ottoman Empire's sovereignty and integrity to enhance its security. Russia had to accept the de-militarisation of the Black Sea and was deprived of its role of protector of Orthodox Christians in the Danubian principalities and in the rest of the empire. Instead, the Great Powers established the principle of dealing jointly with the Ottoman government whenever a problem concerning its Christian populations should arise.[10] In parallel, the Ottoman Empire was formally accepted into the European states system, i.e., protected by the *ius publicum europaeum*, and to the Concert's conferences (when its interests were concerned). However, important conditions were attached to the granting of those rights in Article IX of the Treaty of Paris, in which the Sublime Porte promised to introduce complete religious freedom, and equal taxation for Muslims and non-Muslims, and to admit its Christian subjects to public service. The article makes explicit the link between the sultan's *Hatt-i Hümayun*, decreed in February 1856 in

---

[9] See, on violations of norms before and after 1848: *ibid.*, 622–8.    [10] *Ibid.*, 341–8.

anticipation of the Great Powers' demands, and the admission of the Ottoman Empire to the European states system; the treaty made reforms in favour of Christians in the Ottoman Empire legally binding under international law, and implicitly entitled the European powers to make collective representations in favour of Ottoman non-Muslim subjects. In the case of the Danubian principalities, this right was embodied in a sort of joint European–Ottoman protectorate exercised by the Paris conference, which elaborated the constitution of, and granted full religious liberty in, these territories.

Within this politico-legal framework, the Concert of Europe continued to operate in Oriental matters with some success during the era of *Realpolitik*. It neutralised the selfish aims of each power during the Syrian crisis, put the Danubian principalities on the road towards independence (against the will of the Austrian and Ottoman governments), and managed the Romanian succession crisis in 1866 without major conflict, just as the parties to the London protocols of 1830/1 resolved the Greek succession crisis in 1863.[11]

Yet from an Ottoman perspective, the implications of the *Hatt-i Hümayun* were theoretically far-reaching and painful. It destroyed the hierarchical structure of Ottoman society, within which non-Muslims were separated from Muslims and considered to be the 'conquered race',[12] and allowed Muslims to convert to Christianity, which was forbidden under the Koran. The symbolic submission by the Sublime Porte to European expectations, made in the hope of gaining protection against Russia by the other Great Powers, signified the eclipse of the Ottoman concept of Islamic superiority. The Ottoman Empire acquiesced to the European 'standard of civilisation'.[13]

Unfortunately, the Ottoman Empire did not live up to European expectations. Domestic reforms were blocked by the desire of the establishment to maintain traditional Ottoman society and values. The notorious corruption and understaffing of the Ottoman administration rendered their implementation difficult. Conversely, the promises made raised expectations among the Balkan Christians and, when disappointed, increased their resentment against Constantinople. The Balkan nationalities began to strive for independence rather than for minor improvements of their condition. By the mid-1870s complaints were brought to the embassies and consular agents of the Great Powers on an almost daily basis. At the same time, the ties to Serbs and Croats

---

[11] See *ibid.*, 296–496, 524–34.    [12] Baumgart, *The Crimean War*, 207.
[13] Gerrit W. Gong, *The 'Standard' of Civilization in International Society* (Oxford: Clarendon Press, 1984), 112.

living within the Habsburg monarchy, and the emigration of Bulgarians to Moscow and Odessa, fostered nascent Pan-Serbian and Pan-Slav networks.[14]

In reaction to Balkan nationalism and Pan-Slavism, Turkish elite nationalism began to develop, and with it resistance to the European 'standard'. As one crisis after another erupted until the entire Balkans was in flames in 1876, the Ottoman government verged towards bankruptcy and political collapse. In May, Sultan Abdülaziz was deposed by a palace revolution, which was secretly supported by the British ambassador in Constantinople with a view to increasing his personal influence.[15] The sultan was assassinated a month later, as were two ministers. Yet his successor, Murad V, could keep himself in power only from 30 May to 31 August 1876, when he himself was deposed and passed on the throne to Abdul Hamid II. Against this background, the Great Powers reconfigured their policies towards the Ottoman Empire.

The Habsburg Monarchy, in which Slavs represented almost half of the population, moved first. Vienna had become sensitive to developments in the Balkans after its expulsion by Italy and Germany, and was frightened of the consequences which Serbian nationalism could entail for its own existence. Hence, the Habsburg policy to preserve the integrity of the Ottoman Empire gave way to a new strategy: if Balkan unrest was impossible to prevent, the only way to prevent the emergence of a Greater Serbia was to annex the Ottoman territories Serbia coveted. Thus from the beginning to the end of the Eastern crisis, Austria-Hungary's objective was the annexation of Herzegovina and Bosnia. During a meeting of ministers and military leaders with the emperor in January 1875 Minister of Foreign Affairs Count Julius Andrassy deemed an insurgency as the ideal means to occupy and seize the provinces.[16] While he continued to support the integrity of the Ottoman Empire in diplomatic discourse, Habsburg agents secretly helped to prepare the Herzegovinian uprising. On the advice of his generals, Emperor Francis Joseph travelled to Dalmatia near the border in April, where he received Catholic clerics and other leaders from the provinces in a show of support, thereby inflaming the situation.[17]

---

[14]   Charles and Barbara Jelavich, *The Establishment of the Balkan National States, 1804–1920* (Seattle: University of Washington Press, 1977), 128–40; Jelavich, *Russia's Balkan Entanglements*, 147–69; Sumner, *Russia*, 133–6, 141.

[15]   Hünigen, *Ignati'ev*, 94–5, 97–8. including notes 95 and 97 there, and 101.

[16]   Mihailo Stojanovic, *The Great Powers and the Balkans, 1875–1878* (Cambridge: Cambridge University Press, 1939), 12–27.

[17]   Sumner, *Russia*, 138–9.

When civil war broke out in Herzegovina in July 1875, the Habsburg scheme was countered by the Russian government, which wanted to prevent Austria from extending its influence in the Balkans.[18] Although Pan-Slav members of the Russian government considered a major insurgency as a good starting point for the Balkan provinces to achieve full autonomy,[19] St Petersburg wanted to avoid conflict with Constantinople. It ordered Ambassador Ignatiev to press the Turkish government to promise moderate reforms thereby calming the insurgency, preventing its spread and allowing the empire to maintain its territorial integrity. Russian pressure resulted in two reform acts promulgated by the sultan in October and December 1875.[20]

Andrassy understood that a premature occupation of the rebellious province might involve the Habsburg Monarchy in a war with Russia, and thus opposed military action for the time being. Instead, he took the lead in increasing pressure on Constantinople by demanding complete religious liberty and equality of all religions within the empire, the abolition of the farming of taxes in Herzegovina and Bosnia (a promise not fulfilled since 1856); a guarantee that direct taxes raised in the provinces would also be used within them, rather than for central government; the permission for Christian farmers to buy waste land; and the supervision of provincial finances and of all reforms by the Great Powers collectively as well as by a provincial Elective Council composed of Christians and Muslims equally.[21] With Bismarck mediating, and the Russian government anxious to avoid isolation, the tsar agreed to support Austria's exactions embodied in Andrassy's circular of 30 December 1875. However, the Ottoman Empire was unable to implement these demands due to the state of its finances and its public administration. Indeed, since annexation remained Austria's objective, Andrassy hoped for a negative outcome: either demands should be such that Turkey was unable to fulfil them or that it had to reject them on the grounds that they were humiliating; or the reforms proposed should be insufficient to stabilise the region. In both cases Austria-Hungary would sooner or later get the opportunity to 'save' the Christians by annexing the coveted territories.

The circular put the fate of the Balkan Christians on the European agenda. It mobilised public and government opinion to such a degree

---

[18] Hünigen, *Ignati'ev*, 62.
[19] Sir Henry Elliot to Derby, 23 Oct. 1876, telegraphic, *BDFA*, I, B, vol. 3, 85.
[20] Sumner, *Russia*, 149.
[21] Andrassy Circular of 30 Dec. 1875, in René Albrecht-Carrié, *The Concert of Europe, 1815–1914* (London: Macmillan, 1968), 249–59.

that the absence of great power intervention in Herzegovina and Bosnia comes almost as a surprise. As a special correspondent for *The Times* reported from the Herzegovina, 'some foreign occupation is absolutely necessary as a precaution to a most probable massacre of Christians'.[22] It would be tolerated by the Muslim population, and be better for the Ottoman Empire than a 'repetition of the Syrian affair'.[23] Otherwise, the inability of the Turks to quell the insurrection would lead to the greatest calamity and the occupation by European powers of 'all the Provinces of European Turkey'. Another *Times* article predicted a spread of the insurgency to Serbia, Montenegro and Bulgaria. It recommended immediate intervention to calm the situation before it got out of control, and considered Britain to be in a position of 'peculiar responsibility' to back the Austrians and summon the Ottomans.[24]

The Tory government, headed by Benjamin Disraeli aka Lord Beaconsfield, suspected, correctly, that Austria had ulterior motives. Nonetheless, London approved Andrassy's circular – as had France and Italy – to keep the Eastern Powers from resolving the issue unilaterally, and on the condition that it would be interpreted only as a recommendation by the Powers, not as a binding decision to be applied under the Concert's supervision. Reassured, Turkey accepted the circular, promising further reforms. However, the rebels were not satisfied by Ottoman promises. Receiving aid from Montenegro and Serbia, they refused to put down arms, demanded expropriations in favour of Christians, the withdrawal of Turkish troops, and a European guarantee for the implementation of reforms.[25]

Faced with the failure of the mediation, Gorchakov pleaded that the insurgents' demands be taken into account, including full autonomy for the provinces, and proposed a temporary occupation by Austria. However, during a meeting of the three emperors in Berlin,[26] the Austrian foreign minister rejected the Russian proposals which would maintain Ottoman suzerainty, including any guarantee of enforcement or temporary occupation. Andrassy also dismissed the involvement by the other European powers, since he wanted to retain control of the situation and persuade Russia to accept Austrian annexations.[27] Thus in the Berlin memorandum of 13 May 1876, the three emperors agreed only that the consular agents of the six Great Powers should report on the implementation of the reforms promised by Constantinople, demanded a two-month armistice and that a peace plan be worked out by a European

[22] *The Times*, 28 Dec. 1875.     [23] *The Times*, 5 Jan. 1876.
[24] *The Times*, 17 Jan. 1876.     [25] Hünigen, *Ignati'ev*, 79–82.
[26] *Ibid.*, 89–94.     [27] Cf. *ibid.*, 90.

conference. This was insufficient to quell the insurgency.[28] However, the memorandum was stillborn, first, because Disraeli rejected it – out of idleness, because his government had been excluded from the deliberations, and because he feared, prematurely, an Austro-Russian-German plot – and second,[29] because the *coup d'état* in Constantinople on 29/30 May posed the temporary problem of the new government's recognition.[30] The Russian chancellor put the blame for the Concert's ineffectiveness at this crucial juncture squarely on the British government.[31]

With 150,000 refugees from the rebellious provinces pouring into Austria and the neighbouring principalities,[32] and Balkan tensions spreading to Bulgaria, where Russia had exercised a moderating influence on the church and the national movement during the previous decades, the crisis reached boiling point.[33] Ignatiev warned from Constantinople that the fighting carried the 'symptoms of a war of religion and threatens to degenerate ... into a struggle for extermination'.[34] When, on 23 June, Serbia and, on 1 July, Montenegro declared war against Turkey, the Russian government wondered if it could control the tide of Pan-Slav sentiment.[35] Private Pan-Slav committees sprang up in Moscow, St Petersburg and elsewhere, providing financial, sanitary and military support to Serbians and Montenegrins. The churches and the press joined in, criticising the apparent inaction by the Russian government. Eventually the tsar secretly provided financial aid to Serbia against Gorchakov's will and allowed army officers to take leave to support the Serbs.[36]

In order to avoid being dragged into a war with Turkey and prevent the formation of an anti-Russian coalition, Gorchakov simultaneously pressed for a five- or six-power European conference. As Aleksandr

---

[28] Jomini to Giers, 14/26 May 1876, in Charles and Barbara Jelavich (eds.), *Russia in the East, 1876–1880: The Russo-Turkish War and the Kuldja Crisis as Seen Through the Letters of A. G. Jomini to N. K. Giers* (Leiden: E. J. Brill, 1959), 10; Hünigen, *Ignati'ev*, 100.
[29] See Sumner, *Russia*, 161–7; Jelavich and Jelavich (eds.), *Russia*, 7 (introduction by the editors to first chapter); Baumgart, *Europäisches Konzert*, 420f.; Hünigen, *Ignati'ev*, 99.
[30] Hünigen, *Ignati'ev*, 102–3.
[31] Loftus to Derby, St Petersburg, 20 Nov. 1876, telegraphic, *BDFA*, I, B, vol. 3, doc. 383, 160.
[32] Baumgart, *Europäisches Konzert und nationale Bewegung*, 420.
[33] Sumner, *Russia*, 108–17.
[34] See Ignatiev to Alexander II, 29 Apr./11 May 1876, quoted in Hünigen, *Ignati'ev*, 96 (translation by Matthias Schulz).
[35] Jelavich, *Balkan Entanglements*, 170.
[36] Monson to Derby, Ragusa, 20 Sept. 1876, *BDFA*, I, B, vol. 3, doc. 90, 29. Cf. also Baumgart, *Europäisches Konzert und nationale Bewegung*, 421. On Ignatiev's involvement, see Hünigen, *Ignati'ev*, 113–14. About the illegal voyage of Cernajaev, Russian general-major who inspected Serbian troops, and the tsar's order to return, see *ibid.*, 106, on civil society and the tsar's financial help, 114–15.

Jomini, the Russian foreign ministry's senior counsellor who accompanied the tsar and Gorchakov to Bad Ems from May to August 1876,
observed, it had been a mistake to exclude Britain from the talks in
Berlin: 'Russia does not seek diplomatic laurels, but the improvement of
the condition of the Balkan Christians and pacification ... We have to ...
bring back [the English] into the European Concert.'[37] During discussions with Disraeli in London, Russia demanded autonomy for Bosnia
and Herzegovina, access to the sea for Montenegro and a minor territorial enlargement for Serbia; but the failure of the London talks drove
Russia anew into Austrian hands.[38] On 8 July, Gorchakov and Andrassy
agreed at the Reichstadt jointly to mediate between the belligerents and,
for the present, to pursue a policy of non-intervention. In the event of a
Turkish victory – for which Andrassy secretly hoped and worked,[39]
because he did not want Serbia to proceed to annexation – they would
insist on the restoration of the *status quo ante* and the execution of the
reforms proposed in the Andrassy circular. If, however, Turkey was
defeated by the rebels, they envisaged major territorial changes in the
Balkans, which would allow for an equal division of influence of Russia
and Austria-Hungary, respectively. The latter provision came to naught,
for the Turks prevailed.[40]

Russia continued to focus on the Western Balkans until the extent of
the atrocities in Bulgaria was revealed in the press; this in turn unleashed
a wave of Pan-Slav activism in Russia and, in September 1876, reorien-
tated British policy.[41] In July and August, information about crimes
committed by Turks against unarmed Christian farmers, women and
children became ever more horrifying. Several newspapers sent report-
ers to the scene, and the Great Powers dispatched consular agents
to Adrianople, Philippopoli and their surroundings on fact-finding
missions. On 8 August, *The Times* replaced the word 'atrocities' with the
term 'general massacre':

According to testimony to which there can be no reasonable doubt, the helpless
and unresisting inhabitants of the district about Tatar Bazardjik and

[37] Jomini to Giers, Bad Ems, 30 May/11 June 1876, in Jelavich and Jelavich (eds.), *Russia*,
13 (this and all the following translations of Jomini's letters are by Matthias Schulz).
[38] Cf. Hünigen, *Ignati'ev*, 103–5.
[39] Andrassy refused to close the port of Klek by which armaments were delivered to the
Turks. Cf. *ibid.*, 110.
[40] See *ibid.*, 110, Engelberg, *Bismarck*, 227.
[41] Jelavich, *Balkan Entanglements*, 166–9; Jelavich and Jelavich (eds.), *Russia*, 4 (editors'
introduction to the first chapter); Richard T. Shannon, *Gladstone and the Bulgarian
Agitation 1876* (London: Nelson, 1963). The Russian government tried to calm the
domestic press by threatening to withdraw subsidies. Jomini to Giers, 23 Aug. 1876, in
Jelavich and Jelavich (eds.), *Russia*, 22.

Philippopoli – men, women and children – have been slaughtered literally by the thousands, and their towns and villages utterly destroyed ... The testimony of eye-witnesses, the admissions of the member of the British Embassy charged with the investigation, give reason to believe that there has been nothing less than a general massacre of the population against which the Turkish government had let loose its bands ... commanded by duly appointed officers.

The *Daily News* correspondent, Januarius A. MacGahan, gave graphic descriptions of what he had seen near the town of Batak:[42] fields covered with bones; a giant heap of skulls; over a thousand bodies in the local church and churchyard. He claimed that, of 9,000 inhabitants, almost 7,000 must have been killed or fled. Survivors reported that men had been tortured before being killed, bellies of pregnant women sliced open, young women raped before being murdered, and that a schoolhouse filled with women and children had been burnt. Investigations conducted by the American Consul-General Schuyler confirmed the worst.[43]

The British press began to open fire on Disraeli's government for having supported the wrong cause. The 'truth is so horrible', reported *The Times*, 'that even the fertile ingenuity of the advocates of Turkey can suggest no presentable apology'.[44] It attacked the British ambassador in Constantinople, Sir Henry Elliot, for not having formed 'a sound and accurate judgement upon the evidence on these Bulgarian atrocities',[45] and complained that, 'for some mysterious reasons', the Foreign Office withheld the report by the British diplomat Walter Baring.[46] A 'tempest of indignation' swept across the country.[47] Committees were established in Manchester, London and elsewhere to organise protest rallies against the government and the Turks.

The agitation reached a climax when, in September 1876, the foremost British opposition politician, William Gladstone, published his pamphlet 'The Bulgarian Horrors', in which he attacked the Conservative government for its desertion of the Concert. He argued that the Ottoman Empire should be denied any European assistance, and that the united 'Councils of Europe' should put moral pressure on the sultan to enact the necessary reforms immediately.[48] Turkey should oblige the Concert by granting Bulgaria and the other rebellious

---

[42] Shannon, *Gladstone*, 41–2, 54–9, 67–8, 77–8.     [43] *Ibid.*, 77–8.
[44] *The Times*, 2 Sept. 1876.     [45] *The Times*, 30 Aug. 1876.
[46] *The Times*, 2 Sept. 1876.     [47] *Ibid.*
[48] William E. Gladstone, *Bulgarian Horrors and the Question of the East* (London: Murray, 1876), 20.

provinces autonomy; and, since Ottoman promises had been worthless in the past, the Concert would have to guarantee and supervise the implementation. If, however, the Turks quarrelled and rejected autonomy, as in the Greek case, '[o]ur government ... shall apply all its vigour to concur with other states of Europe in obtaining the extinction of the Turkish executive power in Bulgaria',[49] the other provinces being treated accordingly. The Concert should then press for the provinces' full independence and modify their frontiers in accordance with the principle of nationality.[50] During a 'National Conference' on the Bulgarian question organised by the opposition, Gladstone advised the Concert to help weak nations against tyrannical, repressive governments.[51] Thus the British liberal became a spokesman for the Russian programme on the Balkans: 'Our demands', wrote Jomini, 'are limited to what public opinion has recognised as necessary, even in England, i.e. autonomy under [Ottoman] suzerainty, including for Bulgaria'.[52] The agitation overwhelmed British jingoists and forced the Disraeli government to take into account the values prevailing in British society.[53]

Yet although public opinion made British military action in defence of the Ottoman Empire inconceivable, Russia did not exploit the situation. Gorchakov consciously opted for a moderate programme to be pressed upon Turkey in order to win British support without alienating Austria. Assured of German agreement,[54] he suggested that Britain take the initiative for a European conference to pacify the East,[55] and accepted, on 15 September, British suggestions for peace terms: *status quo ante* for Serbia and Montenegro, administrative reforms for Bosnia and Herzegovina which should entail some form of autonomy, and a similar status for Bulgaria.[56] He added only that minor territorial concessions to Montenegro would probably be necessary to stabilise the situation, and demanded that reforms not simply be proposed, but categorically exacted by the European powers.[57] Gorchakov hoped that united European pressure would make Turkey comply. He also wished to contain Andrassy's ulterior designs, which 'would neither find support

[49] *Ibid.*, 31.    [50] *Ibid.*, 25.
[51] Gladstone, Speech at St James' Hall, 8 Dec. 1876, in James Joll (ed.), *Britain and Europe: Pitt to Churchill 1793–1940* (London: Kaye, 1950), 171–5.
[52] Jomini to Giers, 25 Aug. 1876, in Jelavich and Jelavich (eds.), *Russia*, 22.
[53] Sumner, *Russia*, 166.
[54] Jomini to Giers, Warsaw, 23 Aug. 1876, in Jelavich and Jelavich (eds.), *Russia*, 21.
[55] Jomini to Giers, Livadia, 1 Sept. 1876, in *ibid.*, 24. On the tsar's letter to Francis Joseph, 23 Sept. 1876, and to all other monarchs, see Hünigen, *Ignati'ev*, 135.
[56] Cf. Hünigen, *Ignati'ev*, 130.    [57] *Ibid.*, 131.

in any collective action of the Powers, nor . . . be agreed to by a European conference', as the British ambassador in St Petersburg, Lord Loftus, observed.[58]

Foreign Secretary Lord Derby thereupon brought British policy more into line with public opinion. Circumnavigating Andrassy's objection to autonomy for Bosnia and the Herzegovina, he formally proposed, on 25 September, the interposition of Europe in the dispute between the Ottoman Empire and its rebel subjects, on the condition that the other Great Powers would not question the territorial integrity of the Ottoman Empire and would vow not to seek any exclusive advantage. This stipulation conformed to the Russian chancellor's point of view and was expressly laid out in a memorandum by Ignatiev in late September 1876.[59] Publically, Andrassy had no choice but to accept, but he played foul by secretly encouraging the Porte to object to the British terms, which it did.[60]

By October, a crushing defeat of Serbia and Montenegro by Turkey loomed. Under mounting domestic pressure, Alexander was on the brink of intervening unilaterally. Eventually Lord Derby summoned the courage to demand an immediate unconditional armistice and threatened Constantinople with the suspension of diplomatic relations. Under the added pressure of a Russian ultimatum, the sultan complied on 31 October 1876.[61] The humanitarian crisis, however, endured; tens of thousands of refugees were afraid to return home; there was the danger of a famine because farmers had been forced to quit their lands; and there were 'incidents' taking the lives of Christians. The conference had to mediate peace, provide for the return of refugees, and guarantee the security of Christians.

Facing direct Russian intervention or a European conference, Sultan Abdul Hamid's government opted for the lesser of the two evils, yet only under certain conditions.[62] It demanded admission to the conference.[63] On this point, the Powers gave in with the important precondition that they would first assemble amongst themselves with a view to coordinating their position.[64] Furthermore, in an attempt to reduce the conference to a mere advisory counsel, Constantinople demanded that it

[58] Loftus to Derby, 2 Sept. 1876 (received 18 Sept.), *BDFA*, I, B, vol. 3, doc. 45, 12–13, citation p. 13.
[59] Cf. Hünigen, *Ignati'ev*, 127.      [60] *Ibid.*, 131.
[61] Doria to Derby, St Petersburg, 23 Oct. 1876, telegraphic, *BDFA*, I, B, vol. 3, doc. 256, 85; Elliot to Derby, Therapia, 1 Nov. 1876, *BDFA*, I, B, vol. 3, doc. 296, 99.
[62] Safvet Pasha to Musurus Pasha, Constantinople, 8 Nov. 1876, telegraphic, *BDFA*, I, B, vol. 3, doc. 345, 113.
[63] Derby to Elliot, 23 Oct. 1876, telegraphic, *BDFA*, I, B, vol. 3, doc. 255, 84–5.
[64] Count Schouvaloff to Derby, London, 27 Oct. 1876, *BDFA*, I, B, vol. 3, doc. 286, 96; Derby to Loftus, 3 Nov. 1876, *BDFA*, I, B, vol. 3, doc. 304, 101.

would only recommend, not decide, measures, and not interfere with domestic administration.[65] The Powers declined formally to acquiesce to those demands. Gorchakov argued that, the Turks having 'violated [their] Treaty obligations of 1856' by not implementing the reforms promised in favour of their Christian subjects, 'Europe had the right and duty to dictate [the] sole conditions on which it will maintain the political status quo', and, if necessary, to 'substitute its own action for the Porte's incapacity'.[66] In a similar vein, Jomini claimed that a rule for humanitarian intervention could be derived from the Syrian precedent:

> The principle was posited of the right of Europe to intervene, in the event of violence, in the internal affairs of Turkey. This was said for Turkey. The prince [Gorchakov] has written a superb dispatch demanding that this principle be extended to all the provinces of Turkey. It was rejected on the grounds that there had been no [other] outbursts [of violence]. However, now these outbursts took place. Thus the principle is applicable.[67]

And even Elliot, the British ambassador, concurred that the 'Guaranteeing Powers' were entitled to interfere in Ottoman domestic affairs as long as Constantinople failed to implement the reforms promised in the Paris Treaty. However, he warned his government that there could be no doubt as to which Powers would be able to use this right to their own advantage,[68] and this suspicion kept the British government from adopting a firm position towards Turkey.

There was no agreement as to what to do if Constantinople shunned the European counsels. Regarding the perennial dispute concerning the primacy of sovereignty over humanity or vice versa in international law, Gorchakov told Lord Loftus that 'if the Powers want serious results they must agree that the independence and integrity of Turkey should be subordinated to the guarantees demanded by humanity, Christian Europe, and interests of peace'.[69] This was, in a nutshell, the Russian doctrine of humanitarian intervention. Gorchakov suggested sending an

---

[65] Elliot to Derby, Constantinople, 18 Nov. 1876, telegraphic, *BDFA*, I, B, vol. 3, doc. 371, 125.

[66] Loftus to Derby, St Petersburg, 20 Nov. 1876, telegraphic, *BDFA*, I, B, vol. 3, doc. 383, 160.

[67] 'Le principe a été posé du droit de l'Europe d'intervenir en cas de violences dans les affaires de Turquie. Cela a été dit pour la Turquie. Le P[rin]ce [Gorchakov] a écrit une belle dépêche pour réclamer que ce principe soit étendu à toutes les provinces de la Turquie. On [l']a rejeté en disant qu'il n'y avait pas eu d'explosions [de violence]. Or ces explosions ont eu lieu. Donc le principe est applicable.' Jomini to Giers, n.d. [probably end of Sept. or early Oct. 1876], in Jelavich and Jelavich (eds.), *Russia*, 30.

[68] Elliot to Derby, 20 Oct. 1876, *BDFA*, I, B, vol. 3, doc. 306, 102.

[69] Loftus to Derby, St Petersburg, 20 Nov. 1876, telegraphic, *BDFA*, I, B, vol. 3, doc. 383, 160.

envoy of naval vessels to the Bosporus, and the temporary occupation of Bulgaria by Russia and of Bosnia and Herzegovina by Austria-Hungary under a European mandate.[70] The British government disagreed: Bismarck attempted both to convince Constantinople that some kind of occupation was necessary, because the Porte did not have the administrative capabilities to 'guarantee that the improved status quo that the Powers demand will be lasting and peaceful',[71] and to persuade it to accept occupation by agreeing to British intervention in Egypt and Syria to assure its naval interests.[72] Despite Bismarck's efforts, however, Lord Derby committed Britain only to continue consultations if Turkey rejected the demands,[73] and agreed that the Ottoman government should undertake under a European protocol to enact the reforms the Powers considered necessary. The 'mere announcement of reforms by the Porte', Derby admitted, 'cannot be accepted as sufficient', especially following the precedent of Syria.[74] Without the threat of force, it was unlikely that the Turks would yield.

Even before the conference began, the sultan's government was defiant: it dismissed a British demand to appoint, as a 'provisional measure, and without prejudice to ... future arrangements ... made in concert with the Powers', Christian commissioners to head the administration in the rebellious provinces. The British demand to 'repair the injuries which the apathy and misconduct of the local officials have allowed to be inflicted on the Christian population', was also rejected.[75] British attitude sobered. When the ambassadors began negotiating in Constantinople on 11 December, they agreed quickly on reforms which were more far-reaching than those proposed by Andrassy and comprised the Russian demand for autonomy of the rebellious provinces.[76] Under the leadership of Salisbury, whose nomination to lead the British delegation signified a 'victory of the moderates in the Cabinet over Disraeli', and Count Ignatiev, and following the terms suggested in London on

---

[70] Loftus to Derby, Yalta, 6 Nov. 1876, telegraphic, *BDFA*, I, B, vol. 3, doc. 329, 109; Derby to Musurus Pasha, 11 Nov. 1876, *BDFA*, I, B, vol. 3, doc. 349, 115.

[71] Lord Odo Russell to Derby, 6 Dec. 1876, *BDFA*, I, B, vol. 3, doc. 396, 166.

[72] Derby to Russell, 4 Dec. 1876, *BDFA*, I, B, vol. 3, doc. 387, 162. Following the Egyptian financial crisis of 1871/2, Britain established a protectorate.

[73] Derby to Loftus, 4 Oct. and 7 Nov. 1876, *BDFA*, I, B, vol. 3, docs. 113, 336, 39, 111.

[74] Derby to the Marquis of Salisbury, 20 Nov. 1876, *BDFA*, I, B, vol. 3, doc. 373, 134. On Syria see Chapter 7 above, by Davide Rodogno.

[75] Instructions by Derby for the Marquis of Salisbury, 20 Nov. 1876, *BDFA*, I, B, vol. 3, doc. 373, 138. Cf. Derby to Elliot, 24 Oct. 1876, telegraphic, *BDFA*, I, B, vol. 3, doc. 262, 86.

[76] Loftus to Derby, 3 Nov. 1876, telegraphic, *BDFA*, I, B, vol. 3, doc. 305, 101; Elliot to Derby, 20 Oct. 1876, *BDFA*, I, B, vol. 3, doc. 306, 102.

25 September,[77] the conference demanded that the Porte sign a protocol granting autonomy for a united Bosnia-Herzegovina; sanction a separation of Bulgarian lands into two administrative units; and accord far-reaching administrative reforms for all rebellious provinces, the implementation of which was to be supervised by three European Commissions and, in the case of Bulgarian lands, a European police force.[78] This was as much as London was prepared to countenance. As to the future peace between Turkey and Serbia and Montenegro, the conference demanded minor modifications to the borders in favour of the two provinces, though Turkey acquiesced only in the *status quo ante*.

The Ottoman government's response relied on the Powers' failure to agree on the use of force. On joining the conference, the Ottoman representatives immediately sought to sow disunion by promulgating, on 23 December, a Western-style constitution for the Ottoman Empire. In theory, it guaranteed all the individual liberties which religious minorities in the empire could hope for and provided for parliamentary elections. But by proclaiming the indivisibility of the empire, the constitution precluded any autonomy or special rights being granted to individual provinces or religious groups. The reformist Grand Vizier Ahmet Midhat Pasha, who had devised the constitution, declared that the deliberations of the conference had become pointless under the circumstances, and that the European demands violated Ottoman sovereignty and the constitution.

The conference did not break up at this spectacular rejection,[79] because Count Ignatiev had already advised the British representative on 4 December that the promulgation 'would be an affront ... to the European Powers', and was created for the sole purpose of 'defeating the object of the conference'.[80] Instead, the conference resumed its deliberations, and Salisbury and Ignatiev tried pragmatically to negotiate some of the differences with the Ottoman government. In choosing to negotiate, the Russian government, which would have been ready for war only in spring, demonstrated anew that it did not seek to precipitate war. The Turkish government refused to grant autonomy to the

[77] Shannon, *Bulgarian Agitation*, 253. Cf. Instructions by Derby for Salisbury, 20 Nov. 1876, *BDFA*, I, B, vol. 3, doc. 373, 133.

[78] Compare Sir A. Buchanan to Derby, Buda-Pest, 12 Dec. 1876, *BDFA*, I. B. vol. 3, doc. 413, 174; Derby to Buchanan, 19 Dec. 1876, telegraphic, *BDFA*, I, B, vol. 3, doc. 416, 175; and a letter by Derby to Buchanan, of the same date, *BDFA*, I, B, vol. 3, doc. 416, 175.

[79] Cf. Baumgart, *Europäisches Konzert und nationale Bewegung*, 422.

[80] Elliot to Derby, Constantinople, 4 Dec. 1876, telegraphic, *BDFA*, I, B, vol. 3, doc. 389, 163.

provinces, rebuffed a binding protocol and was unwilling to give Euro-pean commissions supervisory rights. In response, the Powers sent modified suggestions to the Ottoman government, which took into account some, but not all, of its reserves. At the same time, in order to increase the pressure, Bismarck and the emperor William tried to persuade Britain to rethink its position with respect to coercive meas-ures, and, when London rejected this, to apply political pressure, which it accepted.[81] However, this left the Russian government exposed, and it had to consider resuming its own policy. Ignatiev abstained, while Salisbury and the ambassadors of the other Powers presented the new terms to the Ottoman government with the threat of leaving Constantinople if it rejected them.[82] The Ottoman government scorned the revised proposals. Thereupon, and this was too little too late, the British government signalled to the Sublime Porte that, by repelling the advice of Britain, it had no claim whatsoever to British support.

The main participants reacted in different ways. The British ambas-sador Elliot reported that Russia merely sought a European cover for waging war. Andrassy, on the contrary, found that 'Russia, by her conciliatory attitude in the conference, has gained the moral cooperation of the Powers, which Turkey is losing by her resistance to their advice'.[83] And the French government, clearly less interested than Vienna, perceived the 'absolute and peremptory rejection by the Porte of the proposals by the Powers' as an 'insult to Europe, which it would be impossible to pass over'.[84] Russian officials had anticipated war since August 1876, not because they planned or even wished for it, but rather because the Turks, 'fanaticised, frantic, proud of their military victories, bearing the prophet's standard in their hands, do not doubt, do not listen' to anybody, and 'push for war', in the belief that, as in 1854, Britain would not let them down.[85]

The countdown to war began when Tsar Alexander and Austria's Francis Josef concluded a convention on 15 January 1877 in Budapest, which provided for Austrian neutrality in the event of a Russo-Ottoman war. Russia finally agreed to an annexation of Bosnia and Herzegovina by Austria-Hungary, while claiming only the retrocession of Southern Bessarabia (lost in 1856) for itself. Vienna agreed on the condition that no great Slav state would be established in the Balkans after the war.

---

[81] Russell to Derby, Berlin, 27 Dec. 1876, *BDFA*, I, B, vol. 3, doc. 431, 180.
[82] Safvet Pasha to Musurus Pasha, Constantinople, 15 Jan. 1877, *BDFA*, I, B, vol. 3, doc. 479, 198.
[83] Russell to the Derby, 4 Jan. 1876, *BDFA*, I, B, vol. 3, doc. 452, 189.
[84] Derby to Loftus, 2 Jan. 1877, *BDFA*, I, B, vol. 3, doc. 440, 184.
[85] Jomini to Giers, 25 Aug. 1876, in Jelavich and Jelavich (eds.), *Russia*, 23.

In the weeks before the outbreak of war, in April, the question of war and peace became one of national honour for Russia. Yet without the Bulgarian atrocities, Russia would not have been in this position.

Simultaneously the sultan continued to isolate his government. In February he sacked the reformist leader and drafter of the constitution, Midhat Pasha, banning him from the empire,[86] thereby signalling to the Great Powers that the promulgation of a revised constitution had been but a bluff to make them believe that there would be change. Nor did Abdul Hamid II have any intention of granting liberties to his subjects or submitting himself to constitutional government – after the outbreak of war, he dissolved parliament and ruled without it until the revolution of 1908. Furthermore, the trials organised by the Ottoman government against those responsible for the Bulgarian massacres were perceived as a farce by European observers: Tossoun Bey, officer of the empire and one of the chief orchestrators of the massacres, was acquitted 'in spite of conclusive evidence on his guilt'.[87]

Despite these insults, Russia invited the Turkish government to send an ambassador to St Petersburg to save the peace, which Turkey rejected. At the same time, Gorchakov strove to strengthen the accord of the European Powers. As a suspicious Bismarck complained, the Russian Chancellor tried to make 'Europe move as a collective force, as a sort of federal state, which should ... represent Russian interests as if they were European ones, and not only believe in Russia's disinterestedness, but also give cover to Russian designs by a European Commission'.[88] From Gorchakov's perspective, however, the amelioration of the condition of the Christians in the Balkans, pursued by Russia, was in the interest of humanity which justified, if necessary, Russian intervention in the name of Europe.[89] Accordingly, he pleaded disinterestedness and asked for the Powers' support.[90]

Ignatiev's negotiations with the Great Powers eventually culminated in the London Protocol of 31 March 1877. This reaffirmed the common European interest in the improvement of the Balkan Christians' situation, and reiterated that the Porte was bound by the obligations it had contracted with respect to the *Hatt-i Hümayun* in the Treaty of Paris, by its acceptance of the Andrassy memorandum and by other

---

[86] Safvet Pasha to Musurus Pasha, Constantinople, 6 Feb. 1877, telegraphic, *BDFA*, I, B, vol. 3, doc. 527, 219.
[87] Jocelyn to Derby, 7 Feb. 1877, telegraphic, *BDFA*, I, B, vol. 3, doc. 523, 218.
[88] Quoted in Engelberg, *Bismarck*, 225.
[89] Serge Goriaïnov, *La question d'Orient à la veille du traité de Berlin (1870–1876), après les archives russes* (Paris: Institut d'études slaves, 1948), 226.
[90] Loftus to Derby, 4 Feb. 1877, telegraphic, *BDFA*, I, B, vol. 3, doc. 510, 215.

declarations of reform.[91] The Powers repeated their demands for peace with Montenegro, including border rectifications, and urged the carrying out of the necessary reforms in Serbia and Montenegro to forestall unrest. The protocol also included a major concession by Russia: taking up a proposal made earlier by Midhat Pasha, it replaced the supervision of reforms by European commissions with a mode less insulting to Ottoman sovereignty – it gave the Ottoman government a year to enact reforms, at the end of which the ambassador conference in Constantinople would review progress.[92] However:

If their hopes should once more be disappointed, and if the condition of the Christian subjects of the Sultan should not be improved in a manner to prevent the return of the complications which periodically disturb the peace ... [the Great Powers] think it right to declare that such a state of affairs would be incompatible with their interests and those of Europe ... In such case they ... reserve to themselves to consider in common as to the means ... to secure the well-being of the Christian populations, and ... the general peace.

The protocol represented the last chance to avoid war. If Constantinople approved, Russia would demobilise. If it did not, Europe had the right to act.

Constantinople dismissed the peace terms with Montenegro, renewed the war with, and established a blockade against, the province at the expiration of the armistice, and not only rebuffed the London Protocol,[93] but even demanded its nullification. The sultan's government complained that it had been excluded from the conference, attacked the Powers for not having taken into account its objections, blamed Russia and Austria for the insurgencies, and Russia for it having to increase expenditure for war preparations. The government protested vigorously against any outside interference in its domestic affairs, even objecting to the reconvening of an ambassador conference after a year, and claimed that the clause of non-intervention of the Treaty of Paris applied also to its relations with its subject minorities. Furthermore, it repudiated the treaty's Article IX, by which it was bound to fulfil its promises of reform, and declared that the Powers' interference, on the

[91] Russell to Derby, 24 Feb. 1877, *BDFA*, I, B, vol. 3, doc. 549, 228; Derby to Loftus, 13 Mar. 1877, *BDFA*, I, B, vol. 3, doc. 554, 230; draft protocol by Count Schouvaloff, with alterations by Lord Derby, 13 Mar. 1877, *BDFA*, I, B, vol. 3, doc. 555, 231–2, 3rd draft, *BDFA*, I, B, vol. 3, doc. 572, 236–7; memorandum communicated to Derby by Schouvaloff, 17 Mar. 1877, *BDFA*, I, B, vol. 3, doc. 576; final version: Annex to letter, Derby to Loftus, 31 Mar. 1877, printed in Albrecht-Carrié, *Concert*, 265f.
[92] Elliot to Derby, 30 Dec. 1876, *BDFA*, I, B, vol. 3, doc. 465, 194.
[93] Safret Pasha to Musurus Pasha, 9 Apr. 1877, telegraphic, *BDFA*, I, B, vol. 3, doc. 611, 249–53.

basis of that article, was incompatible with the dignity of the empire. Denouncing the protocol as being devoid of any equity and legal obligation, the Ottoman government implicitly claimed impunity for its crimes against humanity: 'The Imperial Government does not comprehend ... why it has forfeited justice and civilisation up to a point where it sees itself reduced to a humiliating position without example in the world'.[94] In both form and substance, this provided a *casus belli* for the signatory powers, especially Russia, which had gone to great lengths to make the demands palatable. Thus no Power supported Turkey when Russia declared war. Russia lacked a legal mandate, but it had the sympathies of the European chancelleries.[95]

★

If the Eastern crisis had been inflamed by the Habsburg Monarchy's manoeuvres to obtain Herzegovina and Bosnia – not to save the Balkan Christians – the war of 1877 was essentially the result of a Russian humanitarian impulse re-enforced by Pan-Slavism and solidarity with the Orthodox Christians in the Balkans. The Russian leadership embraced a doctrine of humanitarian intervention which was solidly grounded in European diplomats' collective memory of savage violence between Muslims and Christians in the Ottoman Empire, of 'promises ... which have notoriously not been fulfilled' by Constantinople,[96] and of the customary practice of intervention, which had developed during the humanitarian emergencies in Greece and Syria.[97] Demands for reforms in the insurgent provinces were accepted by the other Great Powers before the massacres; after the atrocities in Bulgaria, domestic agitation modified the British stance and challenged the tsar's monarchical dignity. Confronted with blatant Ottoman insults, Russia had so many legitimate grievances that its minor territorial wishes (Southern Bessarabia) played almost no role in the outbreak of war.

At the same time, the intervention in 1876/7 was the product of an imperial mentality and a national and religious bias – and concomitant hubris. Polish rebels had been mercilessly repressed and assassinated in the name of Russian tsars during the insurgencies of 1830, 1846 and 1863; and Jews continued to be the object of discrimination and even

---

[94] 'Le Gouvernement Impérial ne vit pas ... en quoi il aurait démérité de la justice et de la civilisation au point de se voir faire une position humiliante et sans exemple dans le monde.' *BDFA*, I, B, vol. 3, doc. 611, 252; as well as *BDFA*, I, B, vol. 3, docs. 612–14, 617.

[95] Cf. annex of letter, Derby to Loftus, 31 Mar. 1877, in Albrecht-Carrié, *Concert*, 265–6.

[96] Elliot to Derby, 20 Oct. 1876, *BDFA*, I, B, vol. 3, doc. 306, 102.

[97] As discussed in Chapter 7, by Davide Rodogno.

pogroms under the reign of Alexander II.[98] Even so, during the Oriental crisis, the bias inherent in Russian Pan-Slav humanitarianism was sanctioned by the other Powers as being within the European 'standard of civilisation',[99] to which the Ottoman Empire was subjected. It was sanctioned, first, because investigations by journalists and diplomats ensured that the European deliberations were based on established facts; second, on account of Russia's readiness to abide by the customary procedures to arrive at a common point of view with the other Powers, based on normative reasoning and power compromises; third, since Russia tried at length to resolve the conflict by peaceful means before declaring war. Thus although Russia had no stellar 'human rights' record, its policy in support of Christians was legitimised by the only international authority recognised at the time, the Concert of Europe, which, in the London protocol, all but mandated Russian intervention.

Although coming between Turkey and its rebellious principalities, the Russo-Ottoman war was no humanitarian intervention in the strict sense, because it did not prevent the atrocities in Bulgaria, and it was savage.[100] It was characterised by a humanitarian intent, namely to prevent the recurrence of future savagery by liberating Balkan Christians, but once the war had begun, Gorchakov's moderate policy was side-tracked by military leaders who were driven by nationalist sentiment, and whose influence on the emperor temporarily eclipsed his own.[101] Herein lies the dilemma of most so-called 'humanitarian' military interventions. After the peace preliminaries of San Stefano, which provided for substantial Russian annexations and for the creation of a Great Bulgaria incompatible with the Austro-Russian agreement of January 1877, it took British and Austrian threats to rein in Russia and give diplomacy a chance. The Congress of Berlin enlarged Montenegro, Romania, Serbia; rendered them fully independent; and prescribed religious liberty and equality for all religions in the Balkans.[102] However, the autonomous Bulgarian province it created comprised only half of the Bulgarian population, and the Congress did not shy away from

---

[98] On oppression of Jews and attitudes thereto, see Chapter 6 above, by Abigail Green.
[99] The term used by Gong, *'Standard' of Civilization*.
[100] Memorandum by Queen Victoria, 7 Sept. 1877, in Joll (ed.), *Britain and Europe*, 176–8.
[101] Cf. the letters by Jomini to Giers written during the campaign, especially from 28 May to 2 July 1877, in Jelavich and Jelavich (eds.), *Russia*, 37–49.
[102] Ralph Melville and Hans-Jürgen Schröder (eds.), *Der Berliner Kongreß von 1878: Die Politik der Großmächte und die Probleme der Modernisierung in Südosteuropa in der zweiten Hälfte des 19. Jahrhunderts* (Wiesbaden: Franz Steiner Verlag, 1982).

distributing the spoils of war among the interested powers: Russia obtained Batum, Kars, Ardahan and Southern Bessarabia; Britain occupied Cyprus; and Austria-Hungary took Bosnia, Herzegovina and Novi-Pazar. To make the deal palatable to France, Bismarck offered Paris the future possession of Tunisia. Thus, the Congress of Berlin failed to respect the earlier nineteenth-century Concert's standard to eschew the pursuit of exclusive advantages.

## 9 The European powers' intervention in Macedonia, 1903–1908: an instance of humanitarian intervention?

### Davide Rodogno

We looked on in these ten last years at an appalling moral bankruptcy: the bankruptcy of European diplomacy at the time of the Armenian massacres. These are not only political failures there; they are moral failures, and they are paid for sooner or later . . . If we allow the renewal of this scandal in Macedonia, we will pay a still more expensive price. We will not have even bought, at the cost of this attack against humanity, a precarious and miserable peace, we moreover will have revealed forever that civilisation at present is no more for governments and for the people than a hypocritical cover for the workings of power.

Francis de Pressensé, *Pour l'Arménie et la Macédoine* (1904)[1]

For more than a year the financial commission has existed, with the civil agents and the military officers in place for more than three years. What have they done?

René Pinon, *L'Europe et l'Empire Ottoman* (1908)[2]

After the Congress of Berlin in 1878, the Ottoman government in Constantinople directly governed only six provinces (*vilayets*) in Europe: Adrianople (roughly corresponding to today's Thrace), Scutari (in today's Albania), Janina (north-western Greece) and the three Macedonian provinces of Kosovo (Kossovo, with its chief town of Skopje or Uskub),

---

[1] *Pour l'Arménie et la Macédoine. Manifestations Franco-Anglo-Italiennes* (preface by Victor Bérard, introduction by Pierre Quillard and report by Francis de Pressensé) (Paris: Société Nouvelle de Librairie, 1904), 248–50: 'Nous avons assisté dans ces dix dernières années à une effroyable banqueroute morale: la banqueroute de la diplomatie européenne au moment des massacres arméniens. Ce ne sont pas là des défaillances seulement politiques; elles sont morales, et elles se paient tôt ou tard . . . Si nous laissons se renouveler ce scandale en Macédoine, nous le paierons plus cher encore. Nous n'aurons pas même acheté, au prix de cet attentat contre l'humanité une paix précaire et misérable, nous aurons de plus démontré à tout jamais que la civilisation à l'heure actuelle , elle n'est, pour les gouvernements et pour les peuples qu'un manteau hypocrite pour les jeux de la force.'

[2] René Pinon, *L'Europe et l'Empire Ottoman* (Paris: Perrin, 1908), 209: 'Depuis plus d'un an la commission financière est constituée, depuis plus de trois ans les agents civils et les officiers sont à leur poste. Qu'ont-ils fait?'

Monastir (Bitolja) and Salonica.[3] The population was of an extremely mixed background. The Muslims comprised Turks, Albanians (especially in the western areas) and Pomaks; the Christians mostly comprised Slavs (Serbs and Bulgarians) but also Greeks and Vlachs (Arumanian or Kutzo-Vlach, a minority closely akin to the Romanians). The area was also inhabited by Roma (Gypsies) and Jews; the largest and most important Jewish community lived in Salonica. The area where the intervention of the European powers would take place was larger with even greater ethnic and religious diversity than Syria and Lebanon. Moreover, after the 1878 Treaty of Berlin, a number of newly independent states had nationalist aims with respect to extended areas of Macedonia.

Nationalism was a new and relevant factor that would affect the actions of the intervening states as well as of the target state, whereas it had played no significant role when massacres of Christians had taken place in Syria and Lebanon in 1860–1. Bulgarian nationalists made Macedonia the focal point of their expansionist projects. Bulgarian nationalist views clashed with those of Greek nationalists and, towards the end of the century, Romanian national propaganda in favour of the Vlach minority came to play a further destabilising role.[4] The Serbs entered the struggle for influence in Macedonia, claiming that the Slav population of Macedonia was mainly Serbian, that the tradition and culture of Macedonian Slavs was Serbian, and that the language was closer to Serbian than to Bulgarian. Last but not least, in October 1893 a revolutionary committee was founded in Salonica which claimed to work 'for the autonomy' of Macedonia with the Bulgarians as the leading population element. This committee did not opt for the direct annexation of Macedonia to Bulgaria, because this would have met with resistance from the European powers, the neighbouring Balkan states and the Ottoman Empire.[5] The organisation was named the Macedonian

[3] Vemund Aarbakke, *Ethnic Rivalry and the Quest for Macedonia 1870–1913*, East European Monographs (Boulder, CO, and New York: Columbia University Press, 2003); Douglas Dakin, *The Greek Struggle in Macedonia 1897–1913* (Salonica: Institute for Balkan Studies, 1966): Nadine Lange-Akhund, *The Macedonian Question, 1893–1908 from Western Sources*, trans. Gabriel Topor, East European Monographs (Boulder, CO, and New York: Columbia University Press, 1998); Michel Leo, *La Bulgarie et son peuple sous la domination ottomane. Tels que les ont vus les voyageurs Anglo-Saxons. Découverte d'une nationalité* (Paris: Editions d'Etat 'Science et Art', 1949); Victor Roudometof (ed.), *The Macedonian Question: Culture, Historiography, Politics*, East European Monographs (Boulder, CO, and New York: Columbia University Press, 2000); Vladimir Ortakovski, *Minorities in the Balkans* (New York: Transnational Publishers, 2000); and Alexandre Toumarkine, *Les migrations des populations musulmanes balkaniques en Anatolie (1876–1913)* (Istanbul: Les Editions Isis, 1995).
[4] Aarbakke, *Ethnic Rivalry*, 82.    [5] *Ibid.*, 97.

Revolutionary Organisation (IMRO, hereafter referred to as IO).[6] Another revolutionary organisation acted from Bulgaria: the Supreme Macedonian Committee (SMC), founded in 1895. The SMC's initial goal was to achieve autonomy for Macedonia. From their inception these nationalist movements and groups – which had before them the failure of the Armenians, whether pro-Bulgarian, pro-Greek, pro-Romanian or pro-Serb – made it clear they wanted to entice the European powers to intervene on behalf of the Christian population and tried to adapt their political ambitions and programmes to achieve this end.

Two of the Great Powers had a direct interest in Macedonia: Russia and Austria-Hungary. The latter had administered the two Ottoman provinces of Bosnia and Herzegovina since 1878 and maintained a garrison in the *sandjak* of Novi-Bazar. Germany, which openly defended the integrity of the Ottoman Empire, supported all initiatives undertaken by Austria-Hungary in agreement with Russia in order to preserve the European status quo. As far as the Western European powers were concerned, the French government's policy towards Macedonia was founded on the same principles which guided its diplomatic action *vis-à-vis* the rest of the Ottoman Empire, namely to defend and expand its economic interests as well as to preserve its traditional cultural ties (there were a dozen scholastic establishments, founded primarily by religious communities), thereby allowing it to exercise an influence appropriate to its position as a 'great' power.[7] France wanted to preserve peace in the Balkans and to maintain the Ottoman presence in the three Macedonian provinces, rather than allowing a territorial partition, the only beneficiaries of which would have been Austria-Hungary and Germany. Great Britain did not really have a Macedonian policy *per se*, subordinating Macedonian affairs to its general policy whose main targets were in Africa, Egypt, the Red Sea area and, especially, India.

With respect to the European powers' relations with the Ottoman Empire, the 'Macedonian Question' was affected by events that had recently occurred elsewhere in the empire and concerned the Armenians and the Cretans. Ottoman Armenians had been the victims of massacre in many eastern provinces of the empire during the 1890s. The European powers' divisions had hindered intervention on grounds of humanity, despite the considerable pressure from public opinion. In Crete, the

---

[6] It was to change name several times; in 1905 it became VMRO where 'V' stands for *vîtreshna*, 'inner'.

[7] Simeon Damianov, 'La diplomatie française et les réformes en Turquie d'Europe (1895–1903)', *Etudes Balkaniques* 2–3 (1974), 130–53, and 'Aspects économiques de la politique française dans les Balkans au début du XXe siècle', *Etudes Balkaniques* 4 (1974), 8–26.

European powers intervened to restore peace and tranquillity, rather than specifically to protect local Christians communities, in the hope that the issue could be avoided for as long as possible. A similar policy of avoidance characterised the European powers' policy towards Macedonia at a time when divisions and disagreement between the powers were important. When internal troubles and terrorist attacks began in Macedonia, European intervention seemed the only way to maintain peace in Europe as a whole. Was this intervention humanitarian?

*

On 23 September 1902, the Djumaya uprising began when about 300 men crossed the Ottoman frontier from Bulgaria. From its inception, and contrary to the case of Lebanon, the crisis was international, with those involved not from local civilian populations, but from neighbouring countries. Ottoman forces easily suppressed the uprising by the middle of November. According to Ottoman sources, about fifteen villages were damaged, 200 people fled to Bulgaria and thirty-seven were killed. Bulgarian sources record twenty-eight villages being completely destroyed by Ottoman regular and irregular forces, over 100 women violated, an unknown number of dead, and an influx of 3,000 refugees to Bulgaria. Discrepancies concerning the nature of violence, massacre and atrocity characterised events in Macedonia. As we shall see, reports of the massacre and atrocity would play a significant role in this crisis from its inception.

In 1902, information rapidly reached Europe from local (Macedonian), regional (from Balkan countries) and Ottoman sources and from the special correspondents of European newspapers. European correspondents of *The Times*, *Le Temps* or *Le Matin* received information via the IO staff, or from Bulgarian, Greek or Serbian diplomats. These sources organised campaigns of information that suited their political purpose. For instance, the SMC sent Stoyan Mihaylovski (a local intellectual) on tour to the European capitals to report that regular Ottoman troops massacred women and children. Macedonian nationalists were aware that indiscriminate massacre and atrocity increased the likelihood of intervention by the European powers, and that by generating public interest in the Macedonian question could potentially inspire the European powers to intervene on their behalf. These nationalists also knew that evidence (genuine, or fabricated if necessary) of the Ottoman authorities' unwillingness or incapacity to put an end to massacre would further increase the likelihood of a humanitarian intervention.

Throughout the crisis, the so-called *pro-memoria lists* generated public interest in events in Macedonia, possibly more efficiently than terrorist attacks and organised upheavals. These documents reported – yet also exaggerated, distorted and sometimes fabricated – news of massacres, atrocities and extermination, in the hope that pressure exerted by the European public on their respective governments might in turn trigger an intervention in Macedonia.[8] The *pro-memoria* denounced 'the barbaric actions' of Ottoman soldiers, the tortures and the murders; they contained detailed lists of demolished villages, gave – for once, accurate and truthful – accounts of the inhumane conditions in jails, and of deportation of convicts to northern Africa or Asia Minor.[9] The Ottoman government's counter-move was a strategy of information designed to portray the Macedonian uprising as a marginal action by some Bulgarian terrorists; the Sublime Porte refused to grant European journalists the permits they needed in order to journey across the region – as had happened when the 1894 massacres of Ottoman Armenians in Sasun had occurred – and circulated reports that were difficult to verify; this eventually aroused journalists' suspicions.

On the one hand, European journalists relied almost entirely on IO sources, which were critical of the Ottoman strategy. On the other hand, European diplomats were aware of the tactics and propaganda of local and foreign nationalists. This explains why European governments were cautious with respect to the action to be taken in Macedonia. The newly appointed British consul-general in Salonica, Alfred Biliotti, informed the Foreign Office that the majority of peasants who had sought refuge in Bulgaria during the uprising of Djumaya had returned to their Ottoman villages in late January 1903. They willingly surrendered their arms and did not mention instances of rape or of looting

---

[8]  Nadine Bonnefoi, '*Le Temps* (1903–1913) et *Le Monde* (1990–1993): miroirs d'une crise balkanique et européenne', *Guerres Mondiales et Conflits Contemporains* 184 (1996), 15–28. Among contemporary publications referring to newspaper articles, see Draganof, *Macedonia and the Reforms*, preface Victor Bérard (London: Hazell, Watson and Viney, 1908), 105ff. which focuses on the crimes committed against Bulgarian minorities living in Macedonia; Focief O. [alias Schopoff, Bulgarian commercial agent in Salonica], *La justice turque et les réformes en Macédoine. Aperçu sur leur histoire et leur organisation, leur fonctionnement et leur abus* (Paris: Plon, 1907); Gérard de Noirval, *Question Macédonienne et l'influence française en Orient. Considérations sur le dernier 'Livre Jaune'* (Brussels: Société Belge de Librairie, 1903); *The Population of Macedonia: Evidence of the Christian Schools . . . Added to which is a list of the Greeks killed at the instance of the Bulgarian Committees in Macedonia, from 1897 to November 1904* (London: Ede, Allom, and Townsend, 1905); Jean Ruby, *La guerre d'Orient. Une race qu'on extermine. Témoignages et documents* (n.p., n.d.); *Tragedies of Macedonia: A Record of Greek Victims of Bulgarian Outrages in Macedonia between 1897 and February 1903* (London: Ede, Allom, and Townsend, 1903).

[9]  Pinon, *Pour Arménie et la Macédoine*, 202–3; report by Dr Thom (American Mission at Mardin), Istanbul, 5 Apr. 1904 (received 11 Apr.), A. & P., vol. CX, 1904, Turkey, N.4 (1904), no. 151, encl.

or beating by Ottoman troops.[10] According to Biliotti, the publication of accounts of massacre and atrocities alleged to have taken place in Macedonia in 1902 was purely a strategy designed to rouse Europe to intervene on behalf of the Bulgarians. The SMC and IO did not deny this, and since the more public opinion was stirred up, the more chance there was for the agitators to achieve their ends, comparatively trifling incidents and opportune rumours were exaggerated into sensational stories. The British consul concluded that whilst the excesses which the troops and Muslim peasants had committed, in spite of the earnest endeavours which their officers and the civil authorities undoubtedly made to restrain them, were more serious than those which would have occurred in European states, they were by no means as serious as they had been portrayed by the IO, the SMC and the Bulgarian authorities.[11]

Meanwhile Sultan Abdul Hamid had appointed an inspector-general for the European provinces of the Ottoman Empire to prevent interference by the European powers. Hussein Hilmi Pasha arrived in Salonica on 8 December 1902 and set up a programme of reforms.[12] Before it could be initiated, the French consul in Salonica, Louis Steeg, criticised the Ottoman reforms, claiming they multiplied expensive and mindless mechanisms of resistance rather than progress.[13] According to Paul Cambon, French ambassador to Great Britain, the reforms of 1902 in Macedonia were similar to those intended, but never implemented, for the Armenians. He was sceptical about the three main pillars of the reform programme, namely the Ottoman authorities' competence to run a sound financial administration, to reform the gendarmerie, and to employ Christian subjects in public administration.[14] For Cambon, in order for the reforms to be effective, the European powers had to enforce them. In his view, the three Macedonian provinces had to become a single autonomous entity, with a Christian governor appointed by the consent of the European powers, a gendarmerie commanded by European officers,

[10] Consul-general Sir A. Biliotti to Sir N. O'Conor, Salonica, 15 Jan. 1903, A. & P., 1903, Turkey, N.3, doc. no. 29, encls. 1–3; Biliotti to Whitehead, Salonica, 31 Jan. 1903 (received 23 Feb.), *ibid.*, doc. no. 54.

[11] Biliotti to Whitehead, Salonica, 14 Feb. 1903, *ibid.*, encl. in doc. no. 56.

[12] O'Conor to Marquess of Lansdowne, Istanbul, 3 Dec. 1902 (received 8 Dec.), A. & P., 1903, Turkey N.1, no. 333; Aarbakke, *Ethnic Rivalry*, 107; Dakin, *Greek Struggle*, 86–91.

[13] Biliotti to O'Conor, Salonica, 1 Dec. 1902, A. & P., 1903, Turkey N.1, no. 347, encl.; French ambassador in Constantinople to Direction Politique MAE, 30 Dec. 1902, AMAE, CPC, nouvelle série 1897–1914, vol. 29, no. 254.

[14] Cambon to Direction Politique MAE, 23 Jan. 1903, AMAE, CPC, *ibid.*, vol. 30, no. 254.

and finances administered by European supervisors. Any other attempt at reform would only bring disappointment, disturbance and insurrection. It would have been, Cambon wrote, the Bulgarian atrocities all over again. The British Foreign Secretary, Henry Petty Fitz-Maurice, Marquess of Lansdowne, fully approved of this analysis.[15]

The Russian and Austria-Hungarian governments also realised that something had to be done to avoid further disturbances and massacre. Past experiences of intervention (as in Lebanon) or of non-intervention (as with the Bulgarians in 1876 and the Armenians in the 1890s) influenced European governments. On 21 February 1903, the Russian foreign minister, Count Wladimir Lamsdorff, and his Austrian-Hungarian counterpart, Count Agenor Goluchowski, presented the Ottoman authorities with a scheme of reform: the Ottoman inspector-general was to serve for a pre-ordained time-period in order to be able to carry out his task satisfactorily and was given the authority to dispense with troops without reference to the central government. The gendarmerie was to be reorganised by foreign officers (as in Crete) recruited from Muslims and Christians in a ratio reflecting that of the general population. The government had to take the necessary measures to suppress the crimes and offences committed during the revolt and to grant amnesty to all political prisoners. Fiscal reforms were also required. This amounted to a substantial interference in Ottoman domestic affairs by the European powers. In their view, however, these reforms would have introduced 'good government', brought peace and prosperity, and increased the well-being of all local populations; Europe would, in turn, benefit from tranquillity and stability in the region. The Ottoman government accepted the reforms with only minor amendments and nominally began implementation from 23 February 1903.[16]

The European powers' intervention did not mention autonomy for Macedonia and did not favour any of the nationalist movements. Intervention was certainly not intended to undermine what remained of Ottoman authority. The action taken by the European governments did not stop the agitation in favour of the Macedonians. For the agitators, the Macedonian issue was primarily a matter of humanity. Various groups had different views on the best solution to solve the problem, but they all agreed that intervention on behalf of the Macedonians had to go further. Some were in favour of independence for the entire region, others, more realistically, favoured a new status guaranteeing political and administrative autonomy under the supervision of the European powers.

[15] *Ibid.*    [16] Aarbakke, *Ethnic Rivalry*, 108.

French liberal, socialist and radical politicians, as well as journalists and intellectuals, became interested in the 'Macedonian Question' from 1901. As with the 'Armenian Question' and the 'Cretan Question', French international law reviews showed a great deal of interest too. The *Revue Générale de Droit International Public* published its first article on the subject in 1903 and others followed.[17] Interest was not only academic, however, for, starting in 1902, several French newspapers took strongly pro-Macedonian stances: *Le Temps*, *L'Aurore*, the *Correspondant*, the *Revue de Paris* (whose editor, Victor Bérard, was a particularly strident supporter of the Macedonians) and the *Revue Politique et Parlementaire*.[18] As had happened during the Armenian massacres of the previous decade, *ad hoc* reviews such as *La Macédoine (organe des revendications légales pour tous les Macédoniens)* were created.[19] Many of the pro-Macedonia agitators had previously supported the Armenians and the Cretans; now they followed the cause of the Christian populations of Macedonia, advancing the same political and humanitarian motives.[20] By 1903, as journalist Gaston Routier put it, the Macedonian issue had become more than political: it was a matter of justice and humanity (*une question de justice et d'humanité*). French pro-Macedonians frequently accused the Ottoman authorities of 'exterminating' Christian populations and, by awakening the conscience of French public opinion, as the London Committee aimed to do, they wished to help those Christians who belonged to the 'civilised races'.[21]

Pro-Macedonia agitation in France reached one of its peaks in early 1903, before the Macedonian terrorists' attack on Salonica. On 15 February, a meeting took place at the Paris theatre of Chateau-d'Eau. The convenor of the meeting was Paul Henry Benjamin d'Estournelles, baron de Constant de Rébeque, a French diplomat and an anti-colonialist who had won the Nobel prize for peace in 1909 and was later to become

---

[17] 'La situation en Macédoine – Le décret de réformes ottoman du 8 décembre 1902 – Les réformes nécessaires', *Revue Générale de Droit International Public* 10 (1903), 112–60. E. Engelhardt, 'La Question Macédonienne', *Revue Générale de Droit International Public* 12 (1905), 544–51, 636–44, and 13 (1906), 29–40, 164–74.

[18] Pinon, *Pour Arménie et la Macédoine*, 107. Bérard's involvement in the 'Macedonian Question' began very early indeed. In 1893 he published *La Turquie et l'Hellénisme Contemporain* (Paris: Ancienne Librairie Germer Baillière et Cie). It was followed by *Pro Macedonia* (Paris: Librairie Armand Colin, 1904).

[19] Lange-Akhund, *Macedonian Question*, 111. A number of these article are quoted by Gaston Routier, *La question Macédonienne* (Paris: Librairie H. Le Soudier, 1903).

[20] André Chéradame, *Douze ans de propagande en faveur des peuples balkaniques* (Paris: Plon, 1913), 60.

[21] Routier, *Question Macédonienne*, i–ii: 'des races [d']une intelligence des plus vives, un esprit très ouvert, très désireux d'apprendre, un sentiment extraordinaire de leurs droits à la liberté, à la sécurité, à la civilisation'.

president of the European Centre of the Carnegie Endowment for International Peace. A vigorous pro-Macedonia campaigner, he stressed that the aim of the meeting was 'humane' and, like other participants, claimed to be speaking on behalf of all the oppressed peoples of the Orient, not just the Macedonians. Among the other politicians, academics, intellectuals and journalists attending were the vice-presidents of the Chamber of Deputies MM. Etienne, Lockroy and Guillain; the administrator of the Collège de France, Gaston Paris; Anatole France; M. Vandal of the Académie Française who, four years later, would be among the organisers of the pro-Macedonia conference at the *École Libre des Sciences Politiques*; the dean of the Facultés de Lettres of the University of Paris, M. Croiset; Bérard, editor of the *Revue de Paris*; Etienne Lamy, editor of the *Revue des Deux Mondes*; Gaston Deschamps, editor of *Le Temps*; Pierre Quillard, editor-in-chief of *Pro Armenia*; and M. Herold, editor of *L'Européen*. There were no fewer than thirty-seven deputies and senators present, among them Clemenceau, Poincaré and Aristide Briand. When the convenors claimed to speak in the name of all the political parties of France, it was not mere rhetoric.[22] Many speakers used the example of the lack of intervention in favour of the Armenians in order to stress the urgent need to intervene in Macedonia. Like their British counterparts, they proclaimed themselves in favour of intervention and of autonomy for Macedonia and referred back to the precedent set in Lebanon. By early March, the pro-Macedonian deputies were exerting clear and very public political pressure on the French foreign minister, Théophile Delcassé.[23]

The British public was equally interested in the 'Macedonian Question', and many authors who had participated in the debate on the 'Armenian Question' now engaged with this related political issue.[24] The centre of philo-Macedonian agitation in Britain was the London Balkan Committee, a direct descendant of the Eastern Question Association founded in 1878 in the wake of the 'Bulgarian atrocities'. The Balkan Committee aimed to promote discussions and form opinion 'in a way which left no room for the more emotional and crude appeals to

---

[22] Pinon, *Pour l'Arménie et la Macédoine*, 6. See *Le question actuelles de Politique Etrangère en Europe*, Conférences organisés à la Société des Anciens Élèves de l'Ecole Libre des Sciences Politiques (Paris: Alcan, 1907), 161–211.

[23] Pinon, *Pour l'Arménie et la Macédoine*, 40.

[24] See, for instance, H. F. B. Lynch, author of *Armenia*, published in 1901, and of many articles published on the *Contemporary Review*, who published a series of articles in the *Morning Post* later reprinted under the title *Europe in Macedonia Being Five Articles Reprinted from the 'Morning Post'* (London: Edward Stanford, 1908).

which some of Gladstone's followers were wont to resort'.[25] James Bryce, president of the Balkan Committee, declared that the 'Macedonian Question' was primarily one of justice and humanity.[26] The Committee's members represented a direct continuity with past associations in terms of personnel, methods of action and ideas. Many members of the Balkan Committee had been previously involved in the Bulgarian agitation of 1876 and had later supported Armenians and Cretans. The vice-presidents of the Balkan Committee counted a number of bishops, Lord Herbert Gladstone and the Earl of Aberdeen among its incumbents; the executive committee included H. N. Brailsford, a newspaper correspondent and author of a study on Macedonia,[27] the archaeologist Arthur Evans, and the historian G. P. Its second president was K. C. Westlake, professor of International Law at Cambridge University.

The *modus operandi* of the Committee was similar to its predecessors: the Committee and its local branches organised meetings in large towns, generally attended by mayors, bishops, non-conformist churchmen, MPs and professional members.[28] The Committee presented large numbers of petitions to the Foreign Office from established and non-conformist church congregations. Many of these petitions were printed forms, with a space provided in which the name of the church would be entered. Non-conformist congregations sent by far the greatest number of petitions; others came from public meetings, trade associations, women's liberal associations, entire towns, working-men's brotherhoods and so forth. A vast number was submitted between 29 September and 16 November 1903 when the Balkan Committee organised over 150 meetings throughout Great Britain. As had happened during the Armenian crisis of the 1890s, British and French agitators and humanitarians met several times; for instance, the 1904 National Conference on the 'Macedonian Question', held at Caxton Hall in London, had a number of French guests, including Bérard (of the *Revue de Paris*) and Quillard (of *Pro Armenia*).[29]

[25] Dakin, *Greek Struggle*, 150. Noel Buxton, *Europe and the Turks* (London: John Murray, 1907), 134–5, provides the organisation chart of the Committee. Among the first publications of the Balkan Committee was *The Macedonian Crisis* (London: The Balkan Committee, 1903), which contained newspaper cuttings from *The Times*, *The Spectator*, *Pilot*, *The Speaker*, *The Guardian*, *The Daily News*, *The Westminster Gazette*, and *The Daily Chronicle*.
[26] 'Agent Diplomatique de France en Bulgarie', to M. Rouvier and the MAE, Sophia, 24 Sept. 1905, AMAE, CPC, nouvelle série 1897–1914, vol. 46, no. 234.
[27] Henry Noel Brailsford, *Macedonia: Its Races and their Future* (London: Methuen, 1906).
[28] *Report of the Proceedings at the National Conference on the Macedonian Question held at Caxton Hall, Westminster, S. W., on Tuesday, March 29th, 1904*, chaired by the Bishop of Rochester (London: The Balkan Committee, 1904).
[29] *Ibid.*

Despite this expertise, the Balkan Committee began with many preconceived ideas and was not well informed.[30] Noel Buxton's 1907 book, *Europe and the Turks*, epitomises the *Weltanshauung* and contradictory beliefs of many humanitarians and Balkan Committee members. Buxton was a Liberal, ideologically close to Gladstone and an active philo-Armenian; he stated that abominations such as those of the Congo were deplorable because they were carried out by Europeans, but that those of the Ottoman Empire were the 'greatest atrocity on the surface of the world, because the sufferers themselves are civilized beings'. His book was supposed to enlighten the British public about Macedonia: 'the field of the great battle between East and West – between barbarism and civilization'.[31] He emphasised 'the great mistakes' of previous British governments with respect to the Ottoman Empire (but completely misrepresented some previous policies). Although he did not quote his sources, he mentioned a number of massacres and thousands of victims among Macedonian, Christian and civilian populations. He admitted that the rise of nationalism had created problems, but roundly asserted that the 'cause of trouble' was the 'Turk', whose corrupt, inefficient and cruel government was based 'on barbarous ideas'.[32] The historic monster of British slavery itself, he wrote, had directly affected 700,000 souls; those whom 'Turkish rule degrades in body and in mind are many millions'.[33] Buxton concluded his book by suggesting that the importance of public opinion lay in its being the vector of the moral feeling of a nation:

Government is the reflection of public opinion and obeys the public will; ... every man or woman can do some tangible thing to make possible a life of decency and goodwill in a hundred thousand homes. We neglect the claim of those who have fallen among thieves at our peril. Nations equally with persons, must pay dearly for breaking moral law. And by what law are we bound? By the call of common human nature, to aid the victim of cruelty.[34]

Pro-Macedonia agitation rapidly became transnational, probably because of the previous experience with regard to the Armenians and, to a lesser extent, the Cretans. Meetings were organised in Milan and Rome (where Anatole France took part in the demonstration on 7 May 1903), as well as in smaller Italian towns, and in Brussels and Geneva. On 25 October 1903, sixty delegates from Great Britain, Belgium, the United States, Italy and France gathered in Paris. Buxton was among those attending, along with two other members of the London Balkan Committee, Evans and MacColl; François de Pressensé (author of the

---

[30] Dakin, *Greek Struggle*, 151.    [31] Buxton, *Europe and the Turks*, 130, 19.
[32] *Ibid.*, ch. iv, 'The Cause of Trouble', 60–74.    [33] *Ibid.*, 120.    [34] *Ibid.*, 131.

report *Pour l'Arménie et la Macédoine* which would be published early in
1904) and Bérard; and Atkin (the secretary of the Anglo-Armenian
Association). Evans declared that the issue of Macedonia was not merely
political but also a 'question humanitaire' – the aim was to save the lives
of the Bulgarians of Macedonia, and to give them good government for
the future. De Pressensé referred to hundreds of villages being destroyed; women, the elderly and even children being slaughtered, tortured or raped; and refugees tracked down and persecuted. He reminded
the audience and the European governments that the aim of the pro-
Macedonians was 'singulièrement modeste': to convince the three liberal
great Western powers to appoint a governor and humane system of
control and supervision in Macedonia. And, defending military intervention, he urged that this would be preferable to 'a precarious and
miserable peace' which was contrary to 'the conscience of humanity'.[35]

★

Terrorist attacks on the Ottoman bank of Salonica by young IO anarchists
on 28 April 1903 renewed pressure on European governments. European
consuls called on their governments to send naval vessels. The choice of
this particular action reflected the cautiousness of the European diplomats and governments: the military impact would be limited in terms of
saving the lives of Christians, but it would send a significant political
message. The European powers did not want to show any support for
the terrorists and also wanted to warn the Ottoman government. Historian
Mark Mazower writes that the consuls recalled the massacres of Bulgarians
of 1876 and feared an indiscriminate massacre of Salonica's Christians
by enraged Ottoman soldiers. As we saw in Chapter 7, in 1860 the
European powers sent warships to the coast of Lebanon for the same
reason. Even though the terrorist attacks failed, they succeeded at least
in making the Ottoman authorities look powerless, as they had during
the civil strife in Lebanon and Syria. And, as Fuad Pasha had done in
early July 1860, Ottoman soldiers, fearing a general uprising, scoured
the Bulgarian quarters of Salonica hunting down and killing many
suspects. The Ottoman authorities promised to protect Muslims living
in and around the town but, at the same time, warned them not to take
the law into their own hands. In fact, in contrast to what happened
in Damascus in July 1860, there was no reaction from the Muslim
population and no massacre followed.[36]

---

[35] Pinon, *Pour l'Arménie et la Macédoine*, 248–50: 'trois grandes puissances libérales de
l'Occident'; 'une paix précaire et misérable'; 'contra la conscience humaine'.
[36] Mark Mazower, *Salonica: City of Ghosts. Christians, Muslims and Jews 1430–1950*,
paperback edn (London: Harper Collins, 2005), 267.

Having failed to provoke a massacre in Salonica, Macedonian revolutionaries persisted in their subversive policy in the province of Monastir. The Ilinden uprising, which started on 2 August 1903 (St Elias's day), attempted to exploit the absence of the Ottoman troops in Monastir. The latter were stationed in the *vilayet* of Kosovo where the local Muslim population opposed the reform programme. The insurgents and the mob who participated in the insurrection destroyed the properties and goods of the Muslims of Monastir, who later retaliated by destroying neighbouring villages inhabited by a Christian majority. The escalation of violence was part of the strategy intended to induce foreign intervention, though the uprising did not have the result hoped for by its instigators, because members of the European public and those present were more shocked by the brutal deaths of innocent people at the hands of the insurgents than by the atrocities committed by Ottoman soldiers and local Muslims.[37]

Despite the organised and well-intentioned agitation in European countries in the summer of 1903, the massacres in the Macedonian provinces aroused less sympathy among the European public than the massacres of Armenians. First, whereas the Armenians were seen as defenceless victims of the sultan, Ottoman soldiers or the Kurds, European newspapers portrayed the Macedonian people as brave insurgents. Local Christian populations, or 'Macedonians' as they were sometimes called, were supposed to be able to defend themselves. Second, the Macedonian problem was much more complex to present to the public and could not be simplistically portrayed as 'oppressor versus oppressed'. Finally, due to the difficulties in obtaining reliable information, the Macedonian struggle was presented to the public as a succession of facts which were rarely related, and news reports were published only when they appeared sufficiently 'exciting' (or morbid) to awaken the readers' interest.[38]

\*

The European powers drew their own conclusions from the Ilinden uprising and the subsequent unrest in the entire region. Lord Lansdowne, the British Foreign Secretary, suggested in a note of 29 September 1903 that the Macedonian provinces should (1) have a Christian governor, or at least Christian assessors to help the governor if he were a Muslim; (2) that its gendarmerie should have Christian officers; and (3) that all irregular forces should be withdrawn. When,

---

[37] Lange-Akhund, *Macedonian Question*, 122. See also the French ambassador in Constantinople to 'Direction Politique MAE', Therapia, 22 Aug. 1903, AMAE, CPC, nouvelle série 1897–1914, vol. 36, no. 138.
[38] Lange-Akhund, *Macedonian Question*, 132–3.

three days later, the Russian tsar and Austrian emperor Nicholas II and Francis Joseph, with their foreign ministers, met at Mürzsteg, a few miles from Vienna, they drew up a programme along the lines of the British suggestions. Austria-Hungary and Russia primarily attempted to pacify the region. According to the French international legal scholar, Antoine Rougier, the two powers' action benefited from the general consensus in Europe.[39] This tacitly collective action was, in Rougier's view, a non-forcible intervention (or *intervention diplomatique*). The tone used by the two powers threatened recourse to sanctions, not to armed force, if the Porte refused to comply and compelled the Ottoman government to implement the reforms.

The Mürzsteg programme aimed to control the implementation of the reforms and the degree of interference in Ottoman internal affairs was significant. General inspector Hilmi Pasha was to be accompanied everywhere by two special civil agents from Russia and Austria who were to draw his attention to abuses and necessary remedies, to convey to him recommendations of the ambassadors in Constantinople, and to keep their own governments fully informed of affairs in Macedonia. The task of reorganising the gendarmerie in the three *vilayets* was to be entrusted to a general of foreign nationality. He was to be given European military officers and, if necessary, non-commissioned officers, to assist him. These officers were to supervise, train and reorganise the Ottoman gendarmerie, and to monitor the conduct of Ottoman troops. As soon as pacification of the country had been confirmed by the two civil agents, the powers would demand from the Ottoman government a modification of the territorial boundaries of the administrative units to reflect the grouping of the different nationalities. The powers also demanded that the Ottoman government allocate funds to cover the cost of repatriation of Christian families who had fled as refugees to Bulgaria or elsewhere; to aid the Christians who had lost their homes and property; and to pay for the repair of houses, churches and schools destroyed by Ottoman soldiers during the insurrection. In villages burnt down by Ottoman soldiers and irregulars, Christians were to be exempt from all taxes for twelve months. For count Agenor Maria Adam Goluchowski, the minister of Austro-Hungarian Foreign Affairs, the programme included two goals:

1. Implementation of the programme accepted by the sultan in February 1903, realisation of which would thereafter be subordinated

[39] Antoine Rougier, 'L'intervention de l'Europe dans la Question de Macédoine', *Revue Générale de Droit International Public* 13 (1906), 178–200, at 181.

to the control of the two civil agents representing Vienna and St Petersburg.

2. Humanitarian action in support of the Christian populations, which suffered greatly from the war and devastations, and were brutalised by the revolutionary committees as well as by the sultan's soldiers.

The process initiated by Austria-Hungary and Russia was avowedly aimed primarily at improving the security and fortunes of Christian populations in Macedonia.[40]

On 1 February 1904, an Italian general, Emilio De Giorgis, arrived in Constantinople and undertook the task of reforming the gendarmerie of the three provinces; intending to serve, like the civil agents, for two years, he in fact remained in office until 1908.[41] As historian Douglas Dakin emphasises, De Giorgis achieved exactly what he set out to do: the formation of a Macedonian gendarmerie elite. De Giorgis, unlike the ambassadors in Constantinople, was acutely aware that the gendarmerie was not a suitable force for suppressing bands of insurgents, a task which he considered to belong to the army.[42]

By 1905, the implementation of the reform programme, with the exception of the reorganisation of the gendarmerie, which was becoming a respectable though not particularly important force, had made little progress. The humanitarian measures listed above largely remained a dead letter, as Western journalists pointed out.[43]

In an attempt to accelerate implementation of the Mürzsteg programme, on 17 January 1905 the governments of Austria-Hungary and Russia proposed significant fiscal reforms in the three Macedonian provinces.[44] The Sublime Porte rejected these, as well as a proposal by Lansdowne to appoint four European financial experts in addition to the two civil agents. The European powers insisted, however, and on 6 October 1905 they collectively announced to the Porte that the four financial delegates would proceed forthwith to join Hilmi Pasha and the civil agents.[45] A second collective decree followed on 14 November

---

[40] Lange-Akhund, *Macedonian Question*, 147.
[41] A. & P., 1904, Further Correspondence respecting the Affairs of South-Eastern Europe, Turkey, no. 4.
[42] Dakin, *Greek Struggle*, 160–1.
[43] For example, Draganof, *Macedonia and the Reforms*, 86.
[44] Dakin, *Greek Struggle*, 245.
[45] 'Collective note communicated by the Ambassadors of the Great Powers to the Ottoman Government', 6 Oct. 1905; 'Instructions communicated by the Ambassadors of the Great Powers to the Financial Agents'; and 'Telegram to be communicated by the Ambassadors of the Great Powers to their respective Governments', A. & P., 1906, Further Correspondence respecting the Affairs of South-Eastern Europe, Turkey no. 1, encls. 1 to 3.

1905, demanding the Ottoman government's immediate approval, of a two-year extension of the reform programme, the reorganisation of the gendarmerie, the recognition of the four financial delegates, and the acceptance of the *règlement* governing the action of the International Financial Commission for the three *vilayets* of Macedonia.[46] On 5 October, the ambassadors at Constantinople advised their governments to take coercive action if the Porte did not comply.[47] The Ottoman ambassador in London complained that the demands of the European powers impinged on the integrity of the Ottoman Empire and were incompatible with the treaties guaranteeing it. The Sublime Porte offered a further compromise, but the European powers deemed it unacceptable.

As a consequence, the European powers undertook coercive action in the form of a naval exercise and the military occupation of Mytilene and Lemnos. The initial proposal for coercive action came from Austria-Hungary, with Russia's approval; it quickly gained the support of France, Great Britain and Italy. Germany only endorsed the naval exercise. On 22 November, under the command of Austrian vice-admiral Ripper, 617 European marines proceeded to occupy the island of Mytilene. On 26 November, they occupied the post and telegraph offices and the customs house. The squadron then advanced and invaded the island of Lemnos at the entrance to the Dardanelles strait. On 5 December, the Ottoman government conceded.[48]

The European powers' collective and coercive intervention was not an instance of humanitarian intervention unless one considers it an indirect and delayed response to the massacres. Nevertheless, it set an important precedent. The influential French jurist Antoine Rougier wrote that the armed intervention aimed at imposing a financial commission for Macedonia was a sign that modern international law no longer allowed for the idea of absolute sovereignty for states, because this would render them not responsible for their actions. The Ottoman government's protests, claiming that its sovereignty had been violated, were not important because this government was beyond the realm of international law.[49] 'La raison d'humanité' could have been invoked by the European powers to justify the military action aimed at preventing

---

[46] O'Conor to Lansdowne, Istanbul, 14 Nov. 1905 (received 20 Nov.), A. & P., 1906, Turkey no. 1, doc. no. 122.

[47] '"Règlement" for the Financial Service of the three Vilayets of Roumelia', A. & P., 1906, Turkey no. 2, encl.

[48] Dakin, *Greek Struggle*, 248–9. Sir Edward Grey became Secretary of State for Foreign Affairs on 11 December 1905.

[49] Rougier, 'L'intervention de l'Europe', 191–200.

disorder in the Balkans, but they did not make recourse to such an explanation. If the European powers did not cite humanitarian reasons it was because only a very indirect link existed between the symbolic occupation of these two islands and any action for 'saving strangers'.

In January 1908, Sir Edward Grey, the Liberal foreign secretary who had replaced Lansdowne in 1905, circulated a secret memorandum among members of the British cabinet on the state of the Ottoman Empire.[50] Grey emphasised that while there was 'nothing that we can do' for the Armenians except enable the population to emigrate, Britain could do something in Macedonia. He wished to ask the other powers whether they would consent to giving European officers executive control over the gendarmerie, and mentioned the possibility of using a mobile force of gendarmerie against insurgent bands. He was sceptical about a second European naval exercise to secure these measures and claimed not to be prepared to resort to coercive measures for any proposal that would achieve judicial reforms alone, which would not pacify the country; if coercion was to be used, it should be for something that would be effective. In the end, Grey did not suggest a new or more detailed scheme of reforms or a military operation on grounds of humanity. Either the powers worked together along the British lines or, if they refused, he could then report to parliament that there was nothing more to be done unless the European powers were of this mind.[51]

During the summer, while Great Britain and Russia negotiated various issues, the whole matter became purely academic, for the Young Turk revolution had broken out and a Turkish constitution had been proclaimed in Constantinople.[52] Reports from Macedonia showed that there had been a sudden and complete transformation. The insurgent bands disappeared as if by magic and, on 27 July 1908, both Grey and Isvolsky agreed to drop their proposals. Needless to say, the other powers concurred that the moment was inopportune for pressing any demands on Constantinople. Whether those demands would ever have been made and whether the powers would have been prepared to use coercion to impose them, is impossible to say. The triumph of the revolutionaries in 1909 did not and could not solve the problems of the Ottoman Empire. In some respects, it made them worse. In Macedonia, national hatreds still raged, and the revolution led to the withdrawal of

---

[50] Secret memorandum [6742 – 26 Feb. 1908], Jan. 1908, NA, FO 371/581.
[51] Ibid.; Dakin, Greek Struggle, 344. In a debate in the House of Commons in February, Grey repeated what he had said in the secret memorandum: see The Times, 26 Feb. 1908.
[52] Dakin, Greek Struggle, 359.

the foreign officers, the winding up of the financial commission and the recalling of civil agents. No guarantee of respect of basic rights of humanity existed in Macedonia and massacre and atrocity were likely to occur again.

★

The European powers knew that massacre and atrocity had occurred; they identified the victims of massacre and the perpetrators although, rather than openly targeting the Ottoman Empire as being solely responsible, they held the revolutionary committees equally culpable. The governments of Vienna and St Petersburg informed (threatened) the Sublime Porte (the target-state) that by not accepting the programme of reforms it might induce the signatory powers of the Treaty of Berlin to request more invasive measures. Although the Ottoman government initially agreed to implement reforms under the European powers' supervision, it was fully aware that the programme of reforms was a forcible imposition on its sovereignty. The intervention, with the exception of the naval exercise and the occupation of the islands of Mytilene and Lemnos, was a non-forcible coercive action; it was collective, although two particular powers played a more prominent role than the others, and it was 'disinterested': the powers gained no commercial or strategic advantage from their actions.

The Great Power intervention did not end the atrocities or massacres of civilian populations by military force, although it aimed to secure local Christians' right to life, property and religious liberty through a comprehensive peace-enforcement programme of social, governmental and economic reforms. Securing these basic rights had nothing to do with supporting any of the many nationalist groups and movements of the region, and none of the European powers showed particular sympathy towards any one of these groups. The intervention was against the way the Ottomans ruled these provinces but not in favour of a major political change in the region.

The programme of reforms and its enforcement were shaped by (and limited by) the primary objective of maintaining peace and security in Europe. Yet at the same time, as Grey put it in 1908, a sense of moral responsibility drove a policy that was intended to alleviate the sufferings of the population, to avert any threat to European peace, and to restore order and security of life and property.[53] There was also a degree of realism about the situation in the Macedonian provinces. The European powers could have initiated the intervention by claiming that the Ottoman

---

[53] Grey to F. Bertie, F. Lascelles, E. Egerton, A. Nicolson, E. Goschen, and O'Conor, 3 Mar. 1908, NA, FO 371/581, no. 1.

authorities were unable to restore peace and order but, in the early stages of the crisis, Ottoman soldiers had proved this not to be the case. Moreover, unlike the situation in Crete, the fact that Muslim civilian populations were equally the victims of massacre and atrocity could not be easily concealed.

Assessing the outcome of the intervention is complex. One could argue that the intervention succeeded in preventing massacres on the scale of those of the Ottomans' Armenian subjects in the 1890s. It is also true that the intervention kept Europe at peace by maintaining the unity of the Ottoman Empire. Alternatively, one could agree with the Balkan Committee's view that in 1908 the situation in the three provinces had assumed 'proportions of horror' and that, despite the Austro-Russian intervention, 'bloodshed, anarchy, and outrage of every description' still obtained.[54] Taking this argument to the extreme reveals that the reform programme, however well intentioned it may have been, or however beneficial it might have been had it been put fully into effect, in the end still spawned widespread massacre.

In 1908, the Balkan Committee's 'humanitarians' emphasised that since 1903, in a country of about 1,500,000 inhabitants, over 10,000 people had been murdered, and the monthly lists of victims were not getting any shorter. By 1908, the main victims were women and children, outrages of every kind were more numerous, and the destruction of houses, property and livestock had been extensive. Nationalist forces from outside Macedonia terrorised villages in order to bring about political conversions, while the Ottoman troops raided indiscriminately in the pursuit of maintaining 'order', though in general they avoided contact with armed insurgent bands and instead attacked defenceless villages. Some 30,000 people had emigrated to the United States, with the result that many villages in the central areas of Macedonia were depopulated.[55] In this respect alone, the humanitarian aim of the intervention was a total failure, not to mention the issues of reparation and reconstruction. Furthermore, when massacres did occur, the European officers could do little except photograph the corpses and report to their governments.[56] The partial enforcement of a weak scheme of reforms arguably enabled the ongoing war between rival bands. Christian populations wrongly interpreted the reforms as a guarantee of help from the

---

[54] *The Action of the Great Powers in Macedonia up to the End of 1907*, report of the Balkan Committee, signed by Westlake, Moore, and Buxton, 10 Jan. 1908, NA, FO 371/581.
[55] *Macedonia in the Winter of 1907–1908*, report of the Balkan Committee, in NA, FO 371/581.
[56] *Action of the Great Powers . . .*, report of the Balkan Committee, 10 Jan. 1908, in NA, FO 371/581.

European powers, behind which they would 'shelter' and organise their respective movements for independence.[57]

In defence of the intervening states, one could wonder what would have happened had no intervention whatsoever occurred. In his contemporary account of the 'Macedonian Question', René Pinon asserted that it was unfair to view the reforms as sterile or useless. They were insufficient to solve the problems of Macedonia: they could only moderately improve the living conditions of local populations, and were too weak to ensure security of life and property. But, in the end, the programme of reforms was 'a compromise between the adventurous politics of intervention and the concrete politics of the interests'.[58] Did other solutions exist? It is possible to argue that if European officers had assumed command of the troops, and the European commissioners had been given extensive executive powers to enable them to suppress rebel bands, they would have been more successful in restoring security of life and property. However, such a proposal was unrealistic, given that Austria-Hungary, Russia and Germany opposed any substantial military intervention, the Sublime Porte was resolutely prepared to resist any further interference in Ottoman sovereignty, and Great Britain was certainly not prepared to act unilaterally.

Finally, the ethnic solution to the 'Macedonian Question' was suggested in a memorandum of November 1903 by Lord Henry Percy, British parliamentary Under-Secretary for Foreign Affairs. It proposed a solution to the 'Macedonian Question' along the lines of the 'Lebanon Scheme' and praised the European occupation of Crete, which had prevented a 'war of extermination'. Percy concluded his report by pointing out that Cretan autonomy resulted in the voluntary exile of a large proportion of the Muslim population. If such a solution had been adopted in Macedonia, the numbers involved would have been 'infinitely larger'.[59] The expulsion or mass displacement of Muslim populations was often considered as a humanitarian solution to various Eastern 'problems'. Another solution – suggested by the Balkan Committee and based on the policy in Lebanon – was to effect the ethnic homogenisation of Macedonia by modifying 'territorial boundaries of the administrative units, with a view to the more regular grouping of the different nationalities'.[60] Such a plan would have entailed many displacements

---

[57] Lange-Akhund, *Macedonian Question*, 146.
[58] *Ibid.*, 146; Pinon, *L'Europe et l'Empire Ottoman*, 237–42, 164.
[59] Confidential Print: Memoranda by Lord Percy on Special Arrangements made for the Government of the Lebanon and Crete, Nov. 1903, NA, FO 881/8119.
[60] *Action of the Great Powers . . .*, report of the Balkan Committee, 10 Jan. 1908, in NA, FO 371/581.

and exchanges of civilian populations, who would have become Bulgarians, Greeks, Serbs or Arumanians according to decisions taken in one of the European capitals. This radical 'solution' which (as in Lebanon) might have achieved a significant increase in human security in Macedonia, at least in the short term, would thus have resulted in a 'humanitarian' tragedy not only for Muslim populations but also for the vast majority of Christians.

*Part III*

Intervening in Africa

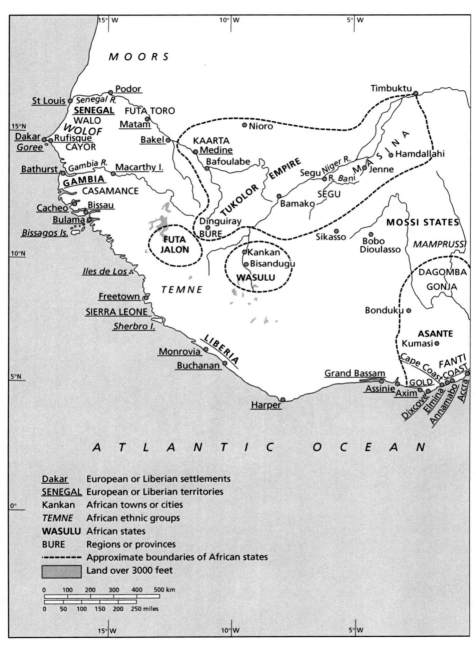

Map 6 West Africa in the first half of the nineteenth century.

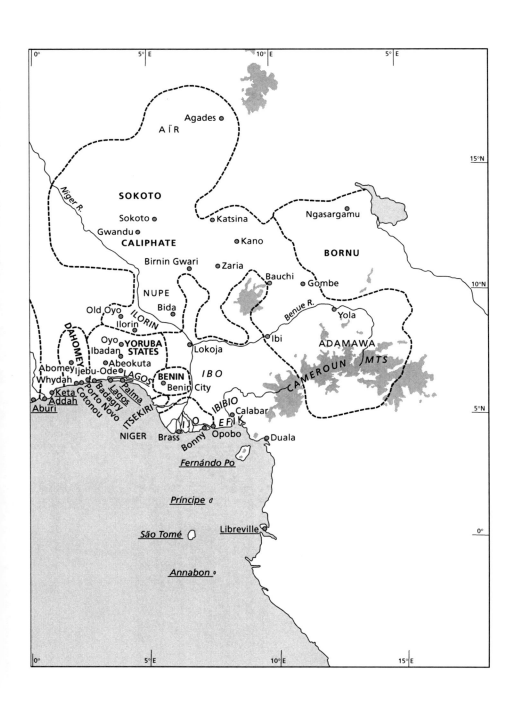

0°      5° E      10° E      5° E

Agades

A Ï R

15°N

SOKOTO

Niger R.

Sokoto

Gwandu

Katsina

Ngasargamu

CALIPHATE

Kano

BORNU

Birnin Gwari

Zaria

Bauchi

Gombe

10°N

NUPE

Bida

Old Oyo

ILORIN

Benue R.

Yola

Ilorin

Ibi

DAHOMEY

Oyo

YORUBA

Ibadan

STATES

Lokoja

ADAMAWA

Abeokuta

CAMEROUN MTS

Abomey

Ijebu-Ode

LAGOS

BENIN

I B O

Whydah

Lagos

Benin City

Keta

Badagry

Palma

Addah

Porto Novo

IBIBIO

Calabar

Aburi

Cotonou

ITSEKIRI

EFIK

NIGER

I J O

Opobo

Duala

Brass

Bonny

5°N

Fernándo Po

Príncipe d

São Tomé

Libreville

0°

Annabon o

0°      5° E      10° E      15° E

# 10 The price of legitimacy in humanitarian intervention: Britain, the right of search, and the abolition of the West African slave trade, 1807–1867

*Maeve Ryan*

> It rarely if ever happens that a foreign gov[ernmen]t gives up its selfish interests, its passions or its prejudices to the force of argument or persuasion; and the more such a gov[ernmen]t is in the wrong, the more pig headed it generally is, because its being very much in the wrong is a proof that it is deaf and blind to reason and right. Persuasion seldom succeeds unless there is compulsion of some sort, nearer or further off behind it.
>
> Lord Palmerston, September 1850[1]

By the turn of the nineteenth century, the idea that the slave trade constituted a humanitarian outrage was not really in doubt. Few if any educated minds believed the fate of the African trafficked as a slave to be an attractive or even benign one; certainly no strong argument was being made that it was so. Aside from the obvious upheaval of forcible transportation from freedom on one continent to slavery on another, the cruelty and inhumanity of the slave dealers engaged in the Atlantic slave trade was infamous. Newspaper reports in Britain and on the Continent portrayed the so-called 'Middle Passage' as an unqualified horror. Even aside from specific instances of violence such as rape and punishment beating, the day-to-day logistics of the trade were harrowing enough: hundreds of people shackled together and crammed into impossibly confined spaces without adequate nutrition, drinking water, ventilation, drainage or even space to stand upright. Many, many thousands died on these voyages, often children. Many more thousands fell victim to the rampant disease and other complications of the unnaturally close confinement of these slave ships and, having been judged dead weight not worth carrying to the Americas, were simply thrown overboard to drown.[2]

---

[1] Palmerston to Baring, 3 Sept. 1850, Broadlands MSS, GC/BA/310.
[2] W. E. F. Ward, *The Royal Navy and the Slavers: The Suppression of the Atlantic Slave Trade* (London: Allen and Unwin, 1969), 59–60.

It took an enormous popular campaign of unprecedented scope to persuade the houses of the British Parliament to pass in 1807 a bill outlawing the slave trade: the final step in turning Britain from its role as the foremost slave trading power to the leading figure in the cause of abolition.[3] This law had only domestic application, however, and while it prohibited slave trading in British territorial waters and precluded British-flagged ships from trading in slaves anywhere, it had no international jurisdiction, nor was it an expression of any kind of international consensus or *opinio juris* in support of a natural or customary law prohibition. British abolitionists recognised that the next step would be to bring the other powers to agree to pass domestic abolition laws and to institute an international enforcement mechanism. They saw in the Vienna conference the ideal opportunity to secure just such an agreement.

The other powers did not share Britain's newfound 'benevolent crotchet', however.[4] For many maritime states, slave trading was still a profitable commerce, and although the harsh reality of the traders' inhumanity was no secret in nineteenth-century Europe, the slave trade was not without its strong supporters. Proponents of the trade rarely condoned outwardly the humanitarian catastrophe that this commerce visited upon its victims, nor the demographic impact the slave marches had upon thousands of African villages every year. Instead they focused their defence of the trade on economics: on its significance to colonial empire and all the questions of commercial interest and national prestige this encompassed.

As with almost every example in modern history of proposed humanitarian intervention, it was not so much the British abolitionists' stated aim of ending a system of inhumanity that caused objection among the governments and populations of Europe; it was the process by which this was to be achieved. The fact that a naval enforcement strategy was central to Britain's abolition campaign was highly significant to the difficulties and disappointments that campaign would suffer over the six decades from the passage of the 1807 Abolition Act to the termination of the Cuban slave trade in 1867.

---

[3] Roger Anstey, *The Atlantic Slave Trade and British Abolition 1760–1810* (London: Macmillan, 1975); Davis Eltis and James Walvin (eds.), *The Abolition of the Atlantic Slave Trade: Origins and Effects in Europe, Africa and the Americas* (Madison and London: University of Wisconsin Press, 1981); Roger Anstey, 'A Reinterpretation of the Abolition of the British Slave Trade, 1806–7', *EHR* 87:343 (1972), 304–32; Chaim D. Kaufmann and Robert E. Pape, 'Explaining Costly International Moral Action: Britain's Sixty-Year Campaign Against the Slave Trade', *International Organisation* 53 (1999), 631–68.

[4] John Bright, House of Commons debate, 24 Apr. 1849, in T. C. Hansard (ed.), *The Parliamentary Debates*, 361 vols. (London: Hansard, 1829–91), CIV, col. 787.

Continental resistance to slave trade abolition was heavily influenced by broad hostility to the Royal Navy blockades during the Napoleonic Wars. In peacetime, this resentment coalesced to become a powerful force of opposition to a proposed abolition campaign waged at sea by the Royal Navy against merchants of all flags. The entire question of universal, internationally enforced slave trade abolition in the early nineteenth century hinged upon the question of the maritime 'right of search', and the sixty-year-long frustration of achieving this goal originated in suspicion and fear of Britain using a newly innovated power of naval interdiction as a smokescreen for hegemonic ambition. The principles of territorial sovereignty, individual property rights and the freedom of the high seas were too fundamental to international relations to be relinquished even in a small way, and even under agreed narrow restrictions.

Yet within three decades, the other powers were prepared to acquiesce while Britain successfully conducted unilateral naval interventions against the slave trading powers, Portugal and Brazil, in 1839, in 1845 and again in 1849–50. How did international thinking evolve in this short space of time from a strict, non-negotiable defence of territorial sovereignty, individual property rights and the freedom of the seas to legitimising unilateral, unmandated illegal intervention? Why did the other powers never protest?

*

Once the 1807 statute outlawing the slave trade had passed the British Houses of Parliament, the next question was how to enforce this law in practice. There were three options: tackle the trade at the level of source, demand or conveyance. To cut off the trade at its source would have involved the persuasion or coercion of the African kings and chiefs coordinating the hundreds of coastal slave-supply centres. It would also have required incursion into the African heartland to demolish the lines of slave transport infrastructure supplying the coastal stations. This was an enormous project of vast geographical and logistical scope that was not seriously considered until the 1840s. Nor was the idea entertained of tackling the slave trade at the level of demand. Slaves in British territories were not emancipated until 1838,[5] and neither before nor after this date was it a viable option to launch any kind of offensive against the slave holdings and plantations of other powers, even one of diplomatic pressure. Approaching the slave trade at the conveyance stage was the obvious choice: use naval warships to stop, search and seize slave ships in transit, then free the slaves, confiscate the ships and prosecute the crews.

---

[5] Although the law promising future emancipation was passed in 1835.

In practice, it would not prove to be so straightforward as simply sending the Royal Navy to the West African coast with orders to stop and search merchant ships suspected of being slavers. Only British-flagged ships and foreign ships found within the narrow confines of British territorial waters were legally subject to the 1807 statute. To this day, under the law of the sea, the flag flown by a ship on the high seas – provided it is genuine and backed up with supporting documentation – confers upon that vessel an extension of the home state's territorial sovereignty. Any act of force in peacetime, even the stopping and searching of a ship without harming its crew or interfering in any way with its cargo, constitutes a violation of sovereignty and can be interpreted, should the home state so choose, as an act of war. The rules are different in wartime, however, and thus from 1807 to the Peace of Paris in 1814, Britain was free to pursue a broad naval-based slave trade abolition campaign on the West African coast by indirect means: through the long-established wartime 'belligerent right of search' or, as Britain termed it in the early nineteenth century, 'Maritime Rights'. Under this right, a belligerent during wartime was entitled to stop and search ships suspected of being either enemy ships in disguise or neutrals carrying contraband, passengers or war *matériel* intended for the enemy. Britain was at war with virtually every slave trading power on the West African coast up to 1814, and although the use of the belligerent right of search to condemn slave traders was an innovation not specifically mandated in international law, it was nonetheless a simple matter of extending the definition of contraband to include slaves.[6] A special naval squadron, known as the West African Squadron, was commissioned for this purpose and based in Sierra Leone. From there the Royal Navy began to police the West African coast with a mandate to send all captured ships to Freetown for adjudication in a specially created Vice-Admiralty court under a prize jurisdiction.[7] The Vice-Admiralty court at Sierra Leone was, in theory, the impartial regulator of the activities of the West Africa Squadron, providing a forum for accused persons to defend themselves and their property against confiscation and conviction. In practice, the court was anything but impartial, with the judge himself playing a keen

---

[6] Tara Helfman, 'The Court of Vice Admiralty at Sierra Leone and the Abolition of the West African Slave Trade', *Yale Law Journal* 115:5 (2006), 1132–4; L. M. Bethell, 'The Mixed Commissions for the Suppression of the Transatlantic Slave Trade in the Nineteenth Century', *Journal of African History* 7:1 (1966), 79–93.

[7] Lynne Margaret Townley, 'Sir William Scott', unpublished LLM thesis, Admiralty Archives Portsmouth (1994), 159–85; H. Fischer, 'The Suppression of the Slave Trade in International Law', *International Law Quarterly* 3 (1950), 34; Bethell, 'Mixed Commissions', 79–93.

prosecutorial role.[8] The result was that the West Africa Squadron became a powerful focus for resentment and irritation among politically influential European commercial shipping interests.

*

While war continued, and with the whole orientation of British foreign policy dictated by the necessities of holding together an anti-French alliance and weakening the French military challenge, Britain responded to all international protests against the exercise of the belligerent right of search simply by maintaining it as a right and refusing to engage further with the question. For then, such protests were largely confined to representations of commercial interests and were not seriously pursued in diplomatic channels. With peace came accountability, however, and with attention suddenly focused on the need to formulate radically different military and civilian peacetime dispensations after decades of conflict, continental merchant opinion hostile to the Royal Navy coalesced into a powerful lobby. Arriving at the Congress of Vienna, although uniquely advantaged by her conduct and direct contribution to the war, Britain found the question of practical international slave trade abolition measures now hopelessly entangled with decades of latent resentment for actual and perceived abuse of her indisputable maritime supremacy. The right of search for the purposes of slave trade abolition could not be divorced from the related question of Maritime Rights, a powder keg to which no one – least of all the Foreign Secretary, Lord Castlereagh – wished to draw attention.[9] But by 1815, the idea of returning from Vienna with a settlement that achieved nothing for the cause of abolition was morally unthinkable to a British population overwhelmed by abolitionist fervour, and therefore politically unthinkable to a government that wished to stay in office.[10] The Vienna delegates were in a bind.

The question of a naval-based abolition campaign was a loaded one to bring to Vienna, since the closely associated belligerent right of search was not a right that Britain was prepared to review fundamentally, or even really discuss. 'Maritime Rights' were the basis of the effectiveness of the Royal Navy's capacity for blockade and as such would never be signed away, but even a debate on the question might have had

---

[8] Helfman, 'The Court of Vice Admiralty', 1133–5.
[9] Castlereagh to Cathcart, 14 July 1813, quoted in Harold Nicolson, *The Congress of Vienna: A Study in Allied Unity, 1812–1822* (London: Constable, 1946), 57.
[10] Jerome Reich, 'The Slave Trade at the Congress of Vienna: A Study in English Public Opinion', *Journal of Negro History* 53:2 (1968), 129–43; Boyd Hilton, *The Age of Atonement: The Influence of Evangelicalism on Social and Economic Thought, 1795–1865* (Oxford: Clarendon Press, 1988), 13–16.

disastrous consequences. Broad, weighty questions of geopolitical re-structuring of the European continent were at stake in Vienna, and if Britain was to be a key agent in the construction of the new balance, it was vital that a storm of united protest not be whipped up. It was for this reason that Castlereagh signed the Langres Protocol in January 1814, an agreement which guaranteed to keep the question of Maritime Rights off the table in Vienna.[11] By definition, this also precluded any real discussion of practical, cooperative slave trade abolition policies through the established strategy of naval interdiction. This was abso-lutely Castlereagh's intention from the outset, as outlined in a letter to Liverpool in November 1814.[12] 'I foresee', he confided, 'that ... we may be disappointed in obtaining such an arrangement [of co-ordinated measures towards universal abolition] during the Congress as Parliament would deem satisfactory as a final measure'. Therefore he was of the opinion that the convening of a separate body of negotiation, independent of the peace deliberations and therefore not an influential variable on the eventual outcome, 'may be made in itself a most power-ful instrument to enforce with good faith the engagements of the several Powers'. This would serve to resolve the dilemma by 'satisfy[ing public] feelings much' while also 'contribut[ing] to the success of our views'.[13] That is, this solution would appear to make progress towards a universal abolition consensus while preventing the Maritime Rights issue from interfering with the British government's more pressing geopolitical needs. The Congress of Vienna duly adjourned the slave trade question to a 'watching committee' to be convened at a later date. In the mean-time, the powers satisfied themselves with a vaguely worded declaration of the eight powers against the principle of slave trading.[14] The bind was thus escaped, successfully silencing the Maritime Rights issue while yet satisfying domestic abolitionist pressure that 'all [had been] done that could be done'.[15]

[11] Nicolson, *Congress of Vienna*, 65–71.
[12] Castlereagh to Liverpool, 21 Nov. 1814, in C. K. Webster (ed.), *British Diplomacy 1813–1815: Select Documents Dealing with the Reconstruction of Europe* (London: Bell and Sons, 1921), 233–5.
[13] *Ibid.*     [14] 'Déclaration des 8 cours ... 1815' in *BFSP, 1815–1816*, 972.
[15] This somewhat inaccurate assessment (William Wilberforce's, quoted in Nicolson, *Congress of Vienna*, 212) has prevailed. For example, 'Castlereagh was indefatigable in his endeavours to secure the abolition of the trade' in Vienna (W. E. Burghardt DuBois, *The Suppression of the African Slave Trade to the United States of America, 1638–1870* (New York: Russel and Russel, 1896), 134). See also Bernard H. Nelson, 'The Slave Trade as a Factor in British Foreign Policy 1815–1862', *Journal of Negro History* 27:2 (1942), 198. For an alternative interpretation, see Maeve Ryan, 'Britain, the Slave Trade and the Right of Search in Early Nineteenth Century European Diplomacy', unpublished MPhil. thesis, Cambridge (2007), 24–8.

The promised 'watching committee' was duly invited in 1817 to send its ambassadors to a conference in London with the specific aim of settling the future of the West African slave trade.[16] This meeting was no more successful in securing definite policies however. Although a politically safer environment to raise the question of the right of search, the ambassadors were not empowered to accede to British pressure and the conference achieved only a restatement of the Vienna declaration, that is, one couched in very general terms, condemning the slave trade as 'a scourge which had so long desolated Africa, degraded Europe and afflicted Humanity' to which they wished to put an end, though not 'without due regard to the interests, the habits, and even the prejudices of their subjects' and not 'prejudic[ing] the period that each particular Power may consider as most advisable for the definitive Abolition of the slave trade'.[17] Nor did subsequent conferences at Aix-la-Chapelle in 1818 and Verona in 1822 achieve anything more substantial than similar declarations, although the idea of excluding the colonial produce of slave trading powers from European markets was considered at Aix-la-Chapelle in the first historical international debate on economic sanctions,[18] and although the Verona conference did change the wording of the declaration slightly, going beyond the caution of the Vienna Declaration with the statement that the powers were 'ready to contribute to everything which could assure and accelerate the complete and definite abolition of this commerce'.[19] Still, neither this nor any prior declaration provided a solid, legally binding enforcement mandate to the task of slave trade suppression ongoing throughout the Congress years. For the moment, the declarations had no practical use. Their full significance would only come to be realised decades later.

By 1822, and no closer to an opposable legal instrument, it was clearly time for Britain to pursue the right of search through different means: bilateral treaties with every maritime power. A highly significant British High Court judgement, that of the *Le Louis* of 1817 which related to a French ship interfered with on the high seas by British naval patrols outside of any treaty mandate to do so, was taken as an authoritative statement of international law on the subject of naval interdiction on the high seas and was very influential in moving British policy towards a policy of bilateral treaties: 'without a general and sincere concurrence of

[16] Protocols 1–15, Foreign Office Papers, NA, FO 84/1, 84/2.
[17] 'Déclaration des 8 cours ... 1815', *BFSP, 1815–1816*, 972.
[18] C. K. Webster, *The Foreign Policy of Castlereagh, 1815–1822: Britain and the European Alliance* (London: Bell, 1834), 464. See also Ryan, 'Right of Search', 31–4.
[19] 'Résolution ... 1822', FO, *BFSP, 1822–1823*, 109–10.

all the maritime states', judged Sir William Scott, both 'in the principle and in the proper modes of pursuing it, comparatively but little of positive good could be acquired, so far ... as the interests of the victims of this commerce were concerned in it'.[20] Scott's words anticipated the difficulties with which British policy would be faced over the next three decades, as it shifted from seeking a general legal instrument to the strategy of creating a bilateral treaty web so tight that it would have the same practical effect. Drawing the maritime states of the world into a general concurrence on the need for reciprocal right of search treaties would prove challenge enough to the diplomatic skills of successive British administrations. Obtaining their sincerity was quite another thing.

★

In 1822, there existed only three reciprocal right of search treaties: those with Portugal, Spain and the Netherlands. None of these treaties was particularly effective in the practical pursuit of the aim to crush the slave trade, however. Ideally, Britain needed to secure treaties with 'all the maritime powers, whose flags could be abused or prostituted'[21] such as would allow the naval patrols of both parties to stop and search suspect ships sailing under the flag of the other party, and authorise the seizure of offenders, the liberation of slaves and the conviction of the crews under charges of piracy. In such an 'ideal' treaty, there would be no geographical limitation to the exercise of the right of search on the high seas. Furthermore, and most crucially to the humanitarian objective of ending slave trafficking, the 'ideal' treaty would specify that a ship's being equipped for trading in slaves constituted *prima facie* evidence of being a slaver and was enough to convict: the so-called 'Equipment Clause'.[22] In the absence of such a clause, slave ships could only be legally seized if a searching party discovered actual slaves on board. As the West Africa Squadron found to their horror, it was a simple matter for slavers simply to rid themselves of the damning evidence by 'disembarking' their slave cargoes upon sight of a naval patrol. If no convenient shore happened to be within reach, this could mean the mass murder of hundreds of people by throwing them overboard in shackles

---

[20] *Le Louis* case (1817), John Dodson, *Reports of Cases argued and determined in the High Court of Admiralty*, 2 vols. (London: A. Strahan, 1815–28), 265.

[21] Viscount Palmerston, House of Commons debate, 5 Aug. 1839, Hansard, *Parliamentary Debates*, XXXV, col. 939.

[22] Such equipment included: open gratings on hatches, spare bulkheads and planks for the creation of a slave-deck, shackles, bolts or handcuffs, extra mess tubs, boilers or an unreasonable amounts of water and food for the needs of the crew. See Foreign Office, *BFSP*, X, 559–60; Ward, *Royal Navy and the Slavers*, 119–37, and Jean Allain, 'Nineteenth Century Law of the Sea and the British Abolition of the Slave Trade', *British Yearbook of International Law* 78 (2008), 342–88.

and chains. Naval officers of the West Africa Squadron across decades of the abolition movement recorded their anger, frustration and disillusionment at being forced to watch helplessly as innocent victims drowned out of reach of assistance while the slave ship then sailed on immune to arrest.[23]

In practice, it was impossible to secure the 'ideal' treaty with every state; indeed it was enough of a challenge to get the maritime states to sign anything at all. By 1839, a quarter-century after the Vienna Congress's declaration against the slave trade, not one of the other Great Powers was bound by a fully comprehensive, effective and functioning treaty with Great Britain. In fact, there was only one 'ideal' treaty in place: that between Britain and the Netherlands.[24] All other states signatory to a bilateral treaty with Britain had negotiated such limitations to the practice of interdiction, arrest and conviction that their flags still remained almost wholly usable to a wily slaver dealer, and the volume of Africans being trafficked as slaves across the Atlantic was still increasing annually.[25] As the abolitionist parliamentarian Thomas Buxton would point out in an 1837 critique of the entire bilateral treaty network concept, there was little point in ensuring 'that ninety-nine doors are closed, if one remains open. To that outlet the whole slave trade of Africa will rush'.[26] By 1839, only two such 'doors' were effectively shut to the slave trade: the Dutch and British flags. Little wonder that the whole slave trade of Africa sauntered carefree through all others.

★

The year 1839 signalled a significant sea-change both in the British executive temper toward slave trade abolition and in the lengths to which it was prepared to take its practical policy on the question. By that year, two things had become very clear: France would never divorce the mechanisms of a cooperative slave trade abolition policy with Britain from the day-to-day rise and fall of rapprochement between the two countries, and Portugal would never, ever enforce its own treaty obligations in any way that it could avoid. Britain had recognised as early as

---

[23] Ward, *Royal Navy and the Slavers*, especially ch. 3. For direct testimonies of naval captains and Admiralty officers, see for example *Parliamentary Papers*, Slave Trade, vols. IV–VI.

[24] See Ryan, 'Right of Search', Appendix I.

[25] David Eltis, *Economic Growth and the Ending of the Transatlantic Slave Trade* (Oxford: Oxford University Press, 1987), 249; L. M. Bethell, *The Abolition of the Brazilian Slave Trade: Britain, Brazil and the Slave Trade Question, 1807–1869* (Cambridge: Cambridge University Press, 1970), 254–66.

[26] Thomas Buxton, quoted in Paul Michael Kielstra, *The Politics of Slave Trade Suppression in Britain and France, 1814–1848: Diplomacy, Morality and Economics* (Basingstoke: Macmillan, 2000), 193.

1815 that France and the Iberian states would prove by far the greatest challenge to the international legal norm it was striving to consecrate. By 1839, a dual-track policy had clearly emerged: on the one hand the rather gentle handling of France and, on the other, the very different treatment of Portugal.

\*

France was seen throughout the first half of the nineteenth century as potentially a very important jewel in the crown of abolition, and from the close of hostilities in 1814, British abolitionists had put great pressure on the government to make the land settlements at Vienna, specifically the return of colonies seized by Britain during the war years, conditional upon France implementing domestic abolition laws.[27] Castlereagh dismissed this approach as politically naive, however. The French had a strong commerce in slave trading and the trade would be dealt a significant blow by the removal of the French flag, it was true, but for broader political reasons, France simply had to be treated with more delicacy than outright coercion if the restored monarchy had any hope of survival past 1815. To dictate abolition to France in the language of a victorious conqueror was impossible. As Napoleon's plenipotentiary remarked at the Congress of Châtillon in 1814, such a tone might be appropriate 'with Denmark, but not with us. If you wish to abolish the slave trade, we will meet you half-way, and arrange it between ourselves'.[28] But a 'compulsory article' could 'never be tolerated by a great people who are not yet in a situation to be insulted with perfect impunity'.[29] Pressure from Britain to concede abolition could (and did) merely serve to mobilise the moderate and apathetic to a sudden attachment to France's right to trade in slaves and vocalised a great degree of cynicism as to Britain's insistence upon exporting this 'ethical foreign policy'.[30]

It was only in 1831, with the politically isolated July Monarchy seeking friends in a hostile Europe, that a reciprocal right of search agreement could be extracted from the French government. This was refined in 1833 to include the 'Equipment Clause', but the spirit of cooperation was short lived. Although there remained little French attachment to the slave trade, with the cooling of relations in the lead-up to the Eastern Crisis of 1840, the 1838 resurrection by Britain of the concept of a

---

[27] Nelson, 'The Slave Trade as a Factor', 192–209, esp. 194; See also Betty Fladeland, 'Abolitionist Pressures on the Concert of Europe, 1814–1822', *Journal of Modern History* 38:4 (1966), 355–73.

[28] Quoted in Martha Putney, 'The Slave Trade in French Diplomacy from 1814 to 1815', *Journal of Negro History* 60:3 (1975), 411.

[29] *Ibid.*        [30] Fladeland, 'Abolitionist Pressures', 355–61.

'Great Power Pact', intended finally to put teeth into the declarations of the Great Powers during the Congress years, met with fierce resistance in France, setting off a chain reaction of popular hostility that would ultimately culminate in the 1845 abrogation of the 1833 treaty. It was a major backtrack and a blow to the abolitionist movement to have a bilateral treaty with a fellow great power broken, never to be repaired. Significantly, however, the public Anglophobic hostility that forced the abrogation was not matched by the French government, nor was an end to British naval policing of the slave trade actually desired by the French executive. As relations between the two countries deteriorated in the aftermath of the Eastern Crisis with the tense atmosphere surrounding the Spanish Marriages question, the Moroccan and Tahitian crises of the early 1840s, the mounting popular Anglophobia resistant to any manifestation of Anglo-French cooperation irritated the French government as much as the British. The French government blamed the Great Power Pact project as the spark that set the whole edifice alight and criticised the British for pushing such an unnecessary idea, since a treaty binding such powers as Prussia and Austria could have little practical impact on a slave trade by then so much dominated by Spain, Portugal and Brazil. An incensed Guizot also blamed 'the bitterness' that 'Palmerston sowed' in popular 'memor[y] of 15 July, and of Tiverton' for undoing all the positive work of the past decade, since the right of search question between Britain and France had been all but forgotten until the British had raised it once again.[31]

Recriminations aside, it suited the British government as much as the French to prevent any further damage to cooperative policies. It was well understood in London that the French popular mood had to be accommodated and calmed if the government was to remain stable and if the Anglo-French reciprocal right of search had to be sacrificed for significant national political necessity, as far as the Foreign Secretary at this time, Lord Aberdeen, was concerned, so be it. Naturally, the outright acceptance of this reality had to be disguised from ardent British abolitionists, since it constituted in effect British acquiescence for broader European political purposes to a major backtrack on the part of the French government. Both executives therefore conspired in the 'extremely delicate combination of public theatre and secret negotiation' that was the Broglie-Lushington commission's 1845 investigation of the best means by which to henceforth pursue abolition.[32] By commissioning a prominent abolitionist from each country to consider this question, the

[31] Guizot to Saint-Aulaire, 1 Feb. 1842, BL, Add. MS 43132, fos. 38, 42.
[32] Kielstra, The Politics of Slave Trade Suppression, 208.

appearance of a steadfast commitment to the best interests of the cause could be maintained, though in reality the conclusions had been agreed in advance of the testimony of the first witness. A new arrangement, known as a 'joint cruising arrangement', was duly agreed in 1845.

★

By contrast with the treatment of France, Portugal's contemporaneous attempt to wriggle out of a reciprocal right of search treaty engagement was met with the full force of British opposition and, ultimately, the full force of British naval strength. Portugal was famously intransigent on the slave trade question. Although a heavily dependent (and hence rather loyal) junior ally of Britain, and one of the first states from whom an abolition treaty could be extracted,[33] Portugal consistently avoided committing to practical implementation of this agreement. It was extended to include a reciprocal right of search agreement in 1817 and an Equipment Clause in 1823, yet the terms of these agreements were limited to the high seas north of the equator. Therefore any slave ship intercepted south of the line, or whose journey originated south of the line, was exempt. From 1817 to 1839, subsequent Portuguese governments procrastinated, side-stepped and dodged all British efforts to sign a more effective treaty, using domestic political unrest as an excuse and claiming every reason of state from economics to national pride to continue facilitating the slave trade.[34] The volume of the Portuguese trade (and the trade of foreign slavers to whom Portuguese customs officers sold the shelter of its flag) increased with almost every passing year.

The reality was that few if any Portuguese governmental or colonial officials were actually committed to abolition. It had been an imposition of British will in 1810, and was resented as such even by those who were not directly interested in any way. With an entire African colonial economy based on the slave trade, Portuguese public opinion demonstrated no domestic political or humanitarian impetus to abolish. They could not see on what other basis the economic life of their empire could be arranged.[35] Exasperated, the British minister in Lisbon remarked in 1837 that 'notwithstanding [his] remonstrances ... slave vessels were

---

[33] The Anglo-Portuguese Treaty of Friendship and Cooperation of 1810, where British protection and support was made conditional upon the pursuit of abolition. See Nelson, 'The Slave Trade as a Factor', 196–8.

[34] L. M. Bethell, 'Britain, Portugal and the Suppression of the Brazilian Slave Trade: The Origins of Lord Palmerston's Act of 1839', *EHR* 80:317 (1965), 761–78; Jasper Ridley, *Lord Palmerston* (London: Constable, 1970), 182–95.

[35] Bethell, 'Origins of Lord Palmerston's Act', 762.

[being] equipped in the Tagus ... The law of Portugal under the very eyes of the Government, being allowed to be evaded, what was to be expected from the Governor of a colony?'[36] By 1839, patience in London had run out.

Unlike with the question of the rehabilitation of France in 1814 and 1815, the British government cared relatively little for Portuguese public opinion and had made it clear from 1807 that the future good relations of the two countries – that is, Britain's ongoing protection of Portugal – would depend upon Portugal's cooperation with Britain's abolitionist agenda. As the 1810 Anglo-Portuguese treaty demonstrated, this kind of coercive pressure made it possible to extract the desired concessions on paper. Yet in subsequent years, Britain was to discover the fundamental problem with which a government attempting to champion a humanitarian issue in international diplomacy was then and is still faced: where the promotion of a moral principle conflicts with an existing, significant domestic financial interest, no barter, bribe nor any application of political pressure successfully imposed upon a government can produce the same capitulation in its civilian population nor eliminate the commercial lobby from its domestic politics. Even the largest and most powerful navy in the world could not root out and destroy a slave trading interest where that interest had the passive inaction or the active corruption of government administrative agents working in its favour.

As early as 1817, British Consul-General in Rio de Janeiro Henry Chamberlain had predicted that the Portuguese slave trading interests would resist Britain to the end, flourishing 'until some great pressure either of interest or inconvenience forces the ministry to put a stop to it'.[37] By spring 1838, Palmerston had lost all vestiges of patience with the question.[38] He instructed Lord Howard de Walden in March 1838 to communicate to the Portuguese government that if the most recent treaty draft presented by Britain was not signed 'word for word as it stands' and with no further delay, Britain would not hesitate 'unceremoniously' to take 'what the Americans call high handed measures'.[39] Furthermore, 'not a crusado will we ever pay [in compensation] ... and if Portugal chuses to make war with us on that account we shall settle the question most effectively by taking possession of all her African

[36] Howard De Walden to Sabrosa, 1 June 1839, 'Memorandum on slave trade negotiations between Portugal and Great Britain', Foreign Office, BFSP, 1839–1840, 610.
[37] Chamberlain to Castlereagh, 24 Dec. 1817, NA, FO 63/204.
[38] Bethell, 'Origins of Lord Palmerston's Act', 761–75.
[39] Palmerston to Howard de Walden, 24 Mar. 1838, NA, FO 84/248; Palmerston to Howard de Walden, 24 Mar. and 7 Apr. 1838, Broadlands MSS, GC/HO/812–826.

settlements and colonies'. 'If', he added, 'like the wife in Molière they like and chuse to be beat, so let it be'.[40] By the end of the year he wrote: 'We are dealing with nothing but a stubborn, base and sordid desire to grasp till it is wrenched forcibly from their hold, the privilege of continuing to perpetrate a profitable crime'.[41]

By December 1838, with still no treaty forthcoming, Palmerston resolved to 'cut the knot' and unilaterally to assume the right Portugal still would not concede: the right of search against Portuguese-flagged ships both north and south of the equator.[42] He requested that the Treasury prepare a bill which would indemnify naval officers and commissioners acting under orders against private litigation actions in British courts arising from the captures, seizures and condemnation of Portuguese-flagged slave ships. The legal basis of the resulting bill was deliberately left somewhat vague and intentionally confusing. This was not commented upon when introduced to the House of Commons on 10 July 1839. It passed without difficulty and was handed up to the Lords, where the Duke of Wellington objected that the bill appeared intended to facilitate a vague war-like policy.[43] 'War was all very well', and Portugal deserved to be handled with severity but Wellington wanted to see things directed by the prerogative of the Crown and not the will of the legislature.[44] The lords were sufficiently confused about the intent of the bill and whether it purported to alter international law, and it was thrown out upon a narrow majority. In the second presentation Palmerston dropped the long preamble and stated the bill for what it was. It passed both houses with ease. Had it not, Palmerston had resolved in advance to 'go on with [the naval] measures; with a bill if possible; without one if none can be got'.[45] Even before this bill became law, Palmerston instructed the Admiralty immediately to authorise officers to assume full powers of search and seizure against the Portuguese flag.[46]

The dismissive executive approach to the passage of this act is instructive of the entire mentality behind Palmerston's Portuguese policy in the late 1830s. He was resolved upon the expansion of

---

[40] Palmerston to Howard de Walden, 10 Mar. and 28 Apr. 1838, Broadlands MSS, GC/HO/819; 825.
[41] Palmerston to Howard de Walden, 24 Dec. 1838, Broadlands MSS, GC/HO/829.
[42] Palmerston to Howard de Walden, *ibid.*
[43] Wellington, House of Lords debate, 19 Aug. 1839, Hansard, *Parliamentary Debates*, XLIX, cols. 1063–7.
[44] *Ibid.*
[45] Palmerston to Russell, 3 Aug. 1839 quoted in Bethell, 'Origins of Lord Palmerston's Act', 780.
[46] The bill became law on 24 Aug. 1839, but Palmerston sent the instructions to the Admiralty on 15 Aug., NA, FO 84/302.

naval operations and the crushing of Portuguese resistance, whether
supported by some kind of legislation or not. He was not greatly
troubled by the question of legality or the politics of alliance, considering
Portugal to be 'morally at war with us' and no longer privileged by 'terms
of friendly alliance'.[47] Nor was he troubled by the prospect of this policy
leading to Portugal's 'be[ing] physically at war with us also'.[48] The
second draft of the 1839 bill rested the justification for the expansion
of naval powers on the simple argument that Portugal had consistently
failed to fulfil the letter and spirit of obligation contacted to under all
previous engagements, and that Britain was entitled as a treaty partner
to seek the fulfilment of these promises.[49] This was a tenuous legal
argument at best. That it was accepted by parliament implies approval
of an express decision to exceed the widest interpretable bounds of treaty
rights, to breach international law. It was a victory for such proponents
as Palmerston of the argument of moral justification over strict legality.
It demonstrated the strong political will and lack of hesitation to take
decisive action against Portugal, to demonstrate by force that Britain was
sincere and firm in the policy of abolition.

By nature a far more conciliatory Foreign Secretary than his predecessor, Lord Aberdeen later commented that the 1839 act was

an act very little consonant with the friendly relations that subsisted between
England and Portugal; indeed it was rather an act of hostility and one which
might have led to interminable war had it been directed against any power of
greater weight and better able to cope with us.[50]

Yet when he was forced in 1845 – the same year, it is worth noting, as the
appeasing Anglo-French Broglie-Lushington commission – to tackle
ongoing Brazilian resistance to a renewed and more effective Anglo-
Brazilian right of search treaty, the solution he arrived at was of an
almost identical nature to Palmerston's 'high-handed measures' against
Portugal: the unilateral extension of naval enforcement powers on the
high seas. Aberdeen's decision was defended on the basis that Article 1
of the most recent Anglo-Brazilian treaty, that of 1826, had deemed
British and Brazilian slave traders on the high seas as pirates.[51] Though
Britain had never enforced this article, it claimed to have reserved the
right to do so for two decades. A bill was duly prepared and passed,

---

[47] Palmerston to Howard de Walden, 24 Jan. 1839, Broadlands MSS, GC/HO/830.
[48] *Ibid.*
[49] 14–19 Aug. 1839, Hansard, *Parliamentary Debates*, L, cols. 300–39; 366–7; 382–7.
[50] Aberdeen, 2 Aug. 1842, Hansard, *Parliamentary Debates*, LXV, col. 936.
[51] William Devereux Jones, 'The Origins and Passage of Lord Aberdeen's Act', *Hispanic
American Historical Review* 42:4 (1962), 502–20.

indemnifying the officers charged with the enforcement of this expanded right of search, much as the Palmerston precedent had done. Though Aberdeen considered it 'a great stretch of power, and open to many objections in principle' to ask parliament to legislate management mechanisms for such unilateralism, 'having been once sanctioned', it offered a useful and simple solution.[52]

When Palmerston returned to the Foreign Office in 1846, he found that Aberdeen's 1845 measure was still not proving a full success. The Brazilian flag still sheltered a trade of up to 60,000 Africans every year.[53] He resolved to expand its application as soon as he had the naval resources on hand to act. Thus in 1849, ignoring the legal limitation of the Aberdeen Act to action upon the high seas, Palmerston ordered naval ships in the area to enter Brazilian territorial waters, inland waterways and ports and destroy whatever slave trading vessels, equipment and slave depots they could find. Though of very uncertain legality, this move marked the beginning of the end of the Brazilian slave trade.

It is no coincidence that the most legally dubious impositions of the British navy happened while Palmerston was Foreign Secretary, and it is no accident that the term 'gunboat diplomacy' is often preceded by the description 'Palmerstonian'. Yet the contrast between the delicate handling of French sensibilities and the blunt imposition on Portugal and Brazil had more to do with international political hierarchy than personality. It is interesting to reflect that the 1839 decision against Portugal was predicated on the basis that Portugal had consistently ignored the spirit of the Vienna and Verona declarations, and had failed to demonstrate a sincere desire to fulfil the treaty obligations undertaken in 1810, 1815 and 1817. France had also failed successfully and permanently to fulfil the spirit of the 1831 and 1833 engagements, undermined the 1841 Quintuple Treaty and even abrogated the 1833 obligations in 1845, replacing them with new provisions through a treaty which excluded the mutual right of search. Far from protesting this about-turn or attempting unilaterally to assume rights France had once conceded and then retracted, Britain actively sought to minimise the embarrassment the entire incident caused the French government, even in the context of the very poor Anglo-French relations of the late 1830s.

The recognised willingness of successive French governments to cooperate on this question undoubtedly played a part. By comparison, two decades of correspondence with Portugal was characterised by

---

[52] Aberdeen to Peel, quoted in *ibid.*, 510.
[53] Bethell, *The Abolition of the Brazilian Slave Trade*, Appendix I.

mounting irritation on one side and evasion on the other.[54] But it was more than a simple question of executive goodwill, as Aberdeen's above-mentioned remarks to the House of Lords indicate. Even had France been uncooperative, such 'act[s] of hostility' as the Palmerston Act would never have been considered. *The Times* reflected on this demonstration of political hierarchy among supposedly sovereign equals, calling Palmerston's 1839 orders to the navy

a very tyrannical measure – the insolent assumption of supremacy of a great power over a small one ... a cowardly system of bullying. Would Lord Palmerston venture to treat France as he does Portugal![55]

The British government never even considered passing a law to authorise the forcible seizure of French shipping. The mere suggestion might have triggered war. By contrast Palmerston was not overly concerned with the idea of triggering war with Portugal:

'If Portugal should chuse to declare war against us', for the violation of sovereignty, 'so much the better; there are several of her colonies which would suit us remarkably well, and having taken them in war, we should retain them at the Peace which she would soon beg on her knees to obtain from us'.[56]

Portugal could never have hoped to rival Britain in a naval contest in 1839, it is true. Nor could Brazil have done so in 1845 or 1849. Yet the decision to act with force against Portugal, and later Brazil, was more than a simple calculation of strength and probable military capacity for retaliation: there was the calculation of the international response it was likely to elicit.

*

In the aftermath of the Napoleonic Wars, the very suggestion that Britain might be granted broad policing powers of the high seas in peacetime was met with outraged condemnation. Yet when precisely the species of 'tyranny' so feared in the early years was actually exercised against Portugal and Brazil in recognised excess of the enforcement powers conferred by bilateral treaties with these states, the European

---

[54] Palmerston to Howard de Walden, 28 Apr. and 10 Feb. 1838, Broadlands MSS, GC/HO/825, 816.

[55] *The Times*, 2 Aug. 1839. See also *Diario do Governo*, 28 July 1839, NA, FO 84/282.

[56] Palmerston to Howard de Walden, 24 Dec. 1838, Broadlands MSS, GC/HO/829/1–3. Palmerston's remarks should not be misinterpreted in the light of his contemporaneous interest in acquiring Goa from Portugal or ongoing friction in relation to unpaid Portuguese debts to British subjects. Abolition was a consistent policy pursued by successive administrations (not always willingly) in response to public demand. Its significance to broader foreign policy issues was always secondary. See Ridley, *Lord Palmerston* 182–95, for contemporary Anglo-Portuguese relations.

powers acquiesced silently. This represents a fundamental shift in international perceptions of the legitimacy of Britain's pursuit of abolition. Indeed it represents a shift in the international acceptability of when, where and with whom Britain could legitimately push and ultimately exceed the limits of legality. International suspicion, at least at government level, had evidently lessened in the years since Vienna. Since 1817, Britain had professed to adhere to the legal advice of the *Le Louis* judgement, to 'obtain the concurrence of other nations' through a web of bilateral treaties.[57] But now, two decades later, did not this new, aggressive policy against Portugal and Brazil at least partly resemble 'forc[ing] the way to the liberation of Africa by trampling on the independence of other States'?[58] Could it not be claimed that the unilateral assumption of the right to capture and adjudicate upon the property of another sovereign state, even for humanitarian reasons, was an example of Britain's 'press[ing] forward with a great principle by breaking through every other great principle that stands in the way of its establishment'?[59]

To the few domestic British opponents of the policy, the 1845 enforcement action against Brazil looked very much like 'the pacification of Africa by making war against the rest of the world'.[60] Significantly, this particular criticism was borne not of concern for the policy's broad political or legal implications, but of anxiety about the detrimental impact a war-like state of relations with Brazil might have on British trade with that country. In fact, no serious concern was ever voiced in parliament that the European allies might abreact to an aggressive and internationally illegal policy towards Brazil, and indeed they did not. Although approached by the Brazilian government in July 1850, the French ambassador to Rio de Janeiro made it absolutely clear that on this issue Brazil stood entirely alone.[61]

It is unlikely that Brazil had genuinely expected any assistance from Europe, since Portugal had been faced with the same international stony silence to its protests in 1839. The Portuguese government responded to the so-called Palmerston Act of that year with fury, deluging the Foreign Office with referred complaints and demands for reparations.[62] When no such reparations were forthcoming, Portugal broadened the appeal to the courts of Europe ('whose opinion', it claimed, was

---

[57] *Le Louis* case discussed in depth in Allain, 'Law of the Sea'.    [58] *Ibid.*    [59] *Ibid.*
[60] Debate on Brazil policy, 24 Apr. 1849, Hansard, *Parliamentary Debates*, CIV, 757–807.
[61] St George, 23 July 1850, quoted in Bethell, *Abolition of the Brazilian Slave Trade*, 333, n.2.
[62] For example, Moirao to Ouseley (plus encls.) 22 Jan. 1840, *PP*, Slave Trade, XIX, 97–105.

'the supreme Jury in the contests of Nations')[63] through a circular note to 'the sovereigns of the signatory Powers of the Congress of Vienna, as the steadfast supporters of the European balance', asking them to reject Britain's 'venturing to obtain' the end of the slave trade 'by coercion'.[64] The note concluded with a warning regarding 'the consequences which may ensue for Portugal and the whole of Europe from this extraordinary and new example of the greatest abuse of force towards an independent Sovereign and nation'.[65] The implication of this note was clear: that the unmandated imposition of the Royal Navy on Portuguese slavers in 1839 was effectively a realisation of what France in particular had fought from the outset to prevent: the unilateral and unregulated use of British naval power to impose a moral objective not shared by the recipient of the forceful acts. Portugal presented the events of 1839 as the unmasking of British hegemonic ambition from its humanitarian guise, and in addressing its protest to all powers signatory to the Vienna declaration, looked primarily to a French spirit of Anglophobic suspicion.

Although Palmerston considered the Portuguese circular 'feeble',[66] he decided to answer it directly. In doing so, he evidently had an eye to France, with whom relations were then particularly frosty. In a short missive, Palmerston appealed to the spirit of consensus on the moral invalidity of supporting the slave trade. He first referred the reader to five pieces of enclosed correspondence exchanged between the Portuguese and British governments and stated that this evidence was all that was necessary to 'exhibit an example of long enduring forbearance on the part of Great Britain, and of deliberate bad faith and persevering breach of engagement, on the part of Portugal, rarely to be paralleled in the history of modern times'.[67] Britain had warned Portugal repeatedly over the previous year that it would extract unilaterally 'the fulfilment of the Portuguese government of the obligations of existing treaties' if no new treaty was signed.[68] (Or as Palmerston stated more bluntly in his private correspondence, 'we ... shall simply take the leave they will not give'.[69]) He was careful to emphasise in his circular that this latest expansion of the activities of the Royal Navy was neither a permanent measure nor was it applicable to any state but Portugal. He reaffirmed this in his instructions to the British minister in Paris to

[63] *Diario do Governo*, 28 July 1839, NA, FO 84/282.
[64] *PP*, Slave Trade, XVIII, 100–1.     [65] *Ibid.*
[66] Palmerston to Howard de Walden, 17 Aug. 1839, Broadlands MSS, GC/HO/843.
[67] *BFSP, 1839–1840*, 566.     [68] Howard de Walden to Baron de Sabrosa, *ibid.*, 604.
[69] Palmerston to Howard de Walden, 24 Dec. 1838, Broadlands MSS, GC/HO/829.

communicate the reassurance that Britain was not harbouring any intent to abuse existing treaties with other states:

With respect to vessels sailing under the flag of a state with which Great Britain has a treaty granting a mutual right of search, that Act of Parliament is not intended to authorize ... visit and search [of] such vessels, in any other way than that which is prescribed by such treaties.[70]

The French response to Palmerston's circular is instructive. First Minister Soult confined himself to a brief note remarking on the 'care' that the British government was taking in its ongoing struggle against the 'crime' of slave trading to ensure that naval commanders confine the policy of coercion to dealing with Portugal alone, and maintain the 'conventional' limits of operation with other powers.[71] There is no mistaking the veiled warning implicit in Soult's compliment, yet it is remarkable that this was the limit of French reaction to the entire incident. The argument was strong that Britain was actively transgressing the bounds of international law, yet it was equally clear that Britain held the moral high ground over those collaborating with the slave trade. Although of course this did not confer unqualified legitimacy on any British act of force against Portugal, the pursuit of the recognised moral objective at play between Portugal and Britain on this unprecedented clash of powers rendered the boundaries of justifiable action rather intangible and unquantifiable in specific terms. The French administration therefore took the view that it would wait and see what transpired. Should there be an excess of zeal in the enforcement against Portugal, or should France find the handling of her own merchant shipping by the Royal Navy to change in any way, then would be the time for protest. For their part, Prussia, Russia and Austria declined to comment on the Portuguese circular, stating that they did not feel themselves called up to comment in any way.[72] The Portuguese government was dismayed to find this 'supreme Jury in the contests of Nations'[73] so indifferent to its appeal.

The position taken by the Great Powers on this question cannot be simply explained by political expediency or dismissed because Portugal held a junior status in the European system and was not a vital security

---

[70] Palmerston to Granville, *BFSP, 1839–1840*, 795–6.

[71] Soult to Granville, 29 Nov. 1839, *BFSP, 1839–1840*, 696–7: 'J'ai remarqué le soin qu'a pris le Gouvernement de sa Majesté britannique de prévenir les Commandans [*sic*] de ses croiseurs contre l'extension de ses mesures à des bâtimens [*sic*] appartenant aux puissances qui ont réglé conventionnellement avec la grande bretagne, le mode poursuite et de répression du crime de traite.'

[72] Correspondence of the Great Powers on the Slave Trade, Sept.–Dec. 1839, NA, FO 84/291.

[73] *Diario do Governo*, 28 July 1839, NA, FO 84/282.

or trading interest of any of the major powers. The European powers were more than capable of using minor incidents as principles upon which to base conflict; one need look no further than Anglo-French relations in the previous few decades to see this. The silence with which the Great Powers – particularly France, at whom it was most pointedly directed – accepted Portugal's circular note held a more deeply seated implication: that Lisbon's confidence was misplaced and outdated. The Vienna declaration against the slave trade represented the first of several declarations of intent. Almost twenty-five years later, though no state had pursued this end with the zeal and commitment of Britain, most states had manifested at least a sincere wish to see the trade abolished. Most significantly, all recognised that Portugal had not. In the two decades since Vienna, continental public opinion had progressed a good deal towards viewing slave trading as morally reprehensible, and although British motives were still regarded with suspicion in France, the defence of another power's right to engage in slave trading on purely anti-British grounds had lost popularity. Furthermore, although popular opinion lagged far behind, it was clearly understood at a government level in Paris that in its abolition policy, Britain was not cloaking an aggressive imperialist agenda with philanthropy. If that were the case, it would have manifested itself by that point in either financial or territorial gain or in the relative gain of destroying the colonial assets of her rivals. Instead, the abolition movement was a constant and increasing drain on the British exchequer and the manpower of the Royal Navy.[74] Furthermore, Britain had conspicuously refrained from attempts to make any territorial gains or encroachments at the expense of the slave trading powers. The sincerity of British abolition policy was not in question by 1839. The Russian Foreign Minister Count Nesselrode acknowledged in 1839 that 'the complete extinction' of the slave trade, which was 'stipulated by solemn transactions, is an object of the most generous solicitude and the most constant efforts by the Cabinet of Her Britannic Majesty'.[75] Even more significantly, the British pursuit of abolition was patently not a threat to the European balance of power. Although Britain's unilateralism lacked unquestionable legality, the context in which it occurred – following decades of diplomatic delicacy and in parallel with an evolving humanitarian public awareness – lent it a certain

---

[74] Ryan, 'Right of Search', 3 n.4. For lives lost, see William Law Mathieson, *Great Britain and the Slave Trade* (New York and London: Longmans, Green, and Co., 1929), 52–6, and Ward, *Royal Navy and the Slavers*, 99–118.

[75] 'Dont l'extinction entière stipulée par des transactions solenelles, est pour le Cabinet de la Majesté Britannique, un objet de la plus généreux sollicitude et des plus constans efforts.' Nesselrode to Clanricarde, 23 July 1839, NA, FO 84/291.

legitimacy. In this respect, Palmerston's use of the words 'flagrant violation of the law of nations' in the abovementioned circular is highly significant.[76] Unilateral use of force against Portuguese slavers was technically a breach of international law but was being employed by British naval cruisers in the pursuit of an agreed objective of the Great Powers to combat a trade now not simply considered 'repugnant' but accepted as a 'crime'. It presented a limited threat, one solely and explicitly restricted to a state which had not only persistently failed to implement treaty promises, but also demonstrated an ongoing contempt for international cooperation against the slave trade and a complicity in its continuation tantamount to collaboration. Portugal's invocation of the Vienna status quo reflected that state's failure to realise that the Great Power perception of justifiable action against slave trading was evolving towards the British point of view. It is significant in this respect that in his response to Palmerston's circular, Soult also referred to the 'répression du *crime*', a word that had not even featured in the Verona declaration.[77]

It is worth noting that the only state to maintain a vocal and consistent six-decade-long protest to both the principle and the practice of British policing of the slave trade was the United States. Although this state had passed legislation to abolish the slave trade under its flag in 1807, it had gone to war against Britain in 1812 in part because the Royal Navy had impressed sailors who were American citizens under the pretext of a belligerent right to visit neutral ships during the Napoleonic Wars to check for contraband. The idea of 'admitting the right of search by foreign officers of our vessels upon the sea in time of peace' was universally denounced as being equivalent to 'making slaves of ourselves',[78] and twenty-three years later, the line had not changed. Instructions issued in 1843 to a United States naval commander on the West African coast read thus:

1. You are charged with the protection of legitimate commerce.
2. While the United States wishes to suppress the slave trade, she will not admit a Right of Search by foreign vessels.
3. You are to arrest slavers.
4. You are to allow in no case an exercise of the Right of Search or any great interruption of legitimate commerce.[79]

---

[76] Palmerston circular, *BFSP, 1839–1840*, 566.
[77] Soult to Granville, 29 Nov. 1839, *BFSP, 1839–1840*, 696–7. Emphasis mine.
[78] John Quincy Adams to Stratford Canning, 1820, quoted in Hugh Soulsby, *The Right of Search and the Slave Trade in Anglo-American Relations 1814–1862*, Johns Hopkins University Studies in Historical and Political Science, 51:2 (Baltimore: Johns Hopkins University Press, 1993), 18. See also Allain, 'Law of the Sea', 33.
[79] To Commodore Perry, 30 Mar. 1843, quoted in DuBois, *Suppression of the African Slave Trade*, 160 n.2.

In the light of the history of Anglo-American tension on the question of the right of search, the Brazilian Foreign Minister also considered appealing to the United States in 1849 on the grounds that Britain was exercising an unmandated and illegal extension of the right of search. Furthermore the British land incursions and naval intervention in Brazilian territorial waters and inland waterways constituted a blatant violation of the Monroe Doctrine. Yet the United States did not even respond to feelers on the matter, and Sousa rapidly dropped the idea.[80]

*

Palmerton considered the outcome of the Brazilian policy a vindication of 'strong measures' and he remarked with evident satisfaction that 'the naval operations of our squadron have accomplished in a few weeks what diplomatic notes and negotiations have failed for years to accomplish'.[81] He went on to reflect upon the near impossibility of converting other powers to the policy of abolition by persuasion alone, as demonstrated by the previous three and a half decades of effort:

> It rarely if ever happens that a foreign gov[ernmen]t gives up its selfish interests, its passions or its prejudices to the force of argument or persuasion, and the more such a gov[ernmen]t is in the wrong, it is a proof that it is deaf and blind to reason and right. Persuasion seldom succeeds unless there is compulsion of some sort, nearer or further off behind it.[82]

'I have always been perfectly aware', he continued, 'that whenever we chose to strike the Brazilians *must* give in'.[83] Palmerston was famously consistent in his belief that 'power is valuable only for its employment', and applied this maxim wherever he felt British foreign-policy priorities necessitated it.[84] A coercive policy to Brazilian slave traders was always going to work, in his view, because 'Right and Might' were 'both on our side', and had he had the naval resources to act earlier, he would have.[85]

It is clear that measures of coercion taken under Palmerston broke from the overarching legal framework put in place by the *Le Louis* case, which had held that 'to procure an eminent good by means that are unlawful is as little consonant to private morality as to publick justice'. That the European states could acquiesce and ignore Portugal's complaints in 1839 indicated that ideas of this 'publick justice' had changed over time. The Vienna declaration of 1815 held the slave trade to be wrong, but reserved the manner and time of remedy to individual state

[80] Bethell, *Abolition*, 333 n.2.
[81] Palmerston to Baring, 3 Sept. 1850, Broadlands MSS, GC/BA/310.    [82] *Ibid.*
[83] *Ibid.* Emphasis in original.
[84] Palmerston speech draft, undated, Broadlands MSS, SLT/26.
[85] Palmerston to Russell, 15 Mar. 1851, NA, PRO 30/22/9B.

discretion. The Verona declaration of 1822 expanded upon this to commit all states in abstract terms to the continued, unbroken search for a collective solution. By 1839, the implicit mandate existed for Britain to act with legitimacy such that even in the context of poor Anglo-French relations, the French minister Soult approved of Britain's assumed mandate to police against the 'crime'. This shift in states' perception of the legitimate bounds of British action was a result of decades of delicate diplomacy. This was necessary to prove to a suspicious international community that slave trade suppression by naval interdiction was being pursued genuinely and constituted no security threat. The *Le Louis* case had stated that 'a Nation' is not legally entitled to 'make regulations [it] cannot enforce without trespassing on the rights of others' in matters in which its own 'safety is in no degree concerned'.[86] By mid-century, Britain was tacitly empowered to enforce abolition regulations regardless of the conflicting rights of Portuguese and Brazilian sovereignty, provided she was careful to see that the enforcement was restricted to its stated aims and that no other state's 'safety' was at issue. It was a significant reformulation.

The cost of slave trade abolition as an international moral action undertaken by Britain was restricted to financial expense and lives lost in naval service.[87] Through the careful choice of when and how to push the limits of legality, Britain never challenged a power outside the bounds of defensible legitimacy and so no real threat to British national security ever resulted. Although in command of the most powerful navy in the world at the close of the Napoleonic Wars, for almost twenty-five years British governments sacrificed the option of putting a swift and forcible end to the humanitarian outrage of the slave trade, believing overwhelming, forcible, unmandated interdiction of slave ships to be an inappropriate and dangerous violation of state sovereignty. Instead (until 1839) they opted for the politically safer option of constructing a diplomatic consensus. Although this diplomatic track was pursued genuinely by Britain for decades, its limited effectiveness was evident as the slave trade continued to grow in volume every year, with annual importations to Brazil alone ranging between 15,000 and 20,000 slaves, progressively swelling to over 60,000 in later years.[88]

It is difficult to know how much sooner the international community might have endorsed forcible action, and whether legitimacy might have

---

[86]  *Le Louis* case (1817). See Allain, 'Law of the Sea'.
[87]  Kaufmann and Pape, 'Costly International Moral Action', 631–68.
[88]  Bethell, *Abolition*, Appendix I; Philip Curtin, *The Atlantic Slave Trade: A Census* (Madison and London: University of Wisconsin Press, 1969).

been retrospectively granted to a more immediate intervention. As the post-World War examples of Cambodia, Rwanda, Darfur, Somalia and, most recently, Burma, have illustrated, the primacy of state sovereignty still prevails over the immediate urgency of halting a nascent humanitarian catastrophe. The 1999 NATO intervention in Kosovo was conferred with legitimacy only in retrospect; at the time, critics of the US-led initiative upheld the same principles of sovereign independence and non-interference as had been espoused in early nineteenth-century arguments against British naval forcible slave trade suppression. As a comparative model for the present-day study of international relations, the unprecedented example of the British slave trade suppression campaign is perhaps most useful as an illustration of how very high the price of legitimacy in humanitarian action can be set. Contemporaries did not measure this price in human lives lost to the slave ships, but in diplomatic notes and treaty negotiations, in demonstrably restricted endeavour and enforced passivity, until opinion in Europe and America had evolved to allow the limits of legality to be acceptably exceeded in certain restricted ways. Yet the real price was paid by upwards of two million Africans trafficked as slaves during this period.

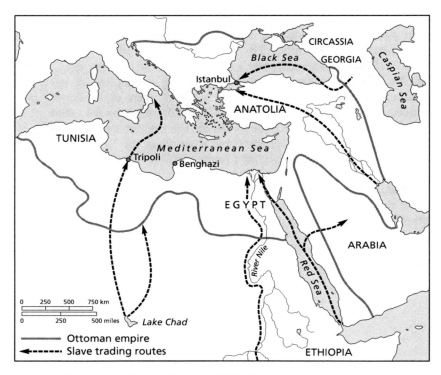

Map 7 The East African and Middle Eastern slave trade, late nineteenth century.

# 11 British anti-slave trade and anti-slavery policy in East Africa, Arabia, and Turkey in the late nineteenth century

*William Mulligan*

> There is no feeling so strong in England as the Anti-Slave Trade feeling.
> Lord Northbrook to Baring, 7 March 1884

> Philanthropy decidedly costs money.
> Goschen to Gladstone, 19 September 1871

The abolition of the slave trade in East Africa, Arabia, and Turkey was a lengthy process, the most intense and climactic period occurring in the final third of the nineteenth century. This coincided with the conquest of Africa by European states. Just as the link between capitalism and abolitionism in the late eighteenth century has been the subject of controversy, so too has the link between imperialism and the ending of the slave trade in Africa. Whereas slavery was abolished at a stroke in British colonies in 1833, anti-slavery policies had a more gradual effect in Africa, starting with anti-slave trade agreements in the early nineteenth century and concluding with abolition in the late nineteenth century. Thereafter, coercive labour systems and slavery persisted.[1] This lengthy process necessarily involved ambiguities, compromises, and missed opportunities, but it was a process in which British humanitarian public opinion was the driving force.

Changing historical perspectives have mirrored broader attitudes to empire. In the first part of the twentieth century, the suppression of the slave trade was considered a humanitarian triumph, untainted by political and economic interest. The tone was set by memoirs of key figures. 'Cynical commentators', wrote Lady Gwendolen Cecil in her life-and-times panegyric to Salisbury, 'have doubted the genuineness and extent of the revolt of conscience which was roused by this revelation of preventable human agony on a vast scale ... More than once in these later years, a consent to compromise on this issue with the Arab and other dominant slave-making races would have smoothed the way

---

[1] M. W. Daly, *Empire on the Nile: The Anglo-Egyptian Sudan, 1898–1934* (Cambridge: Cambridge University Press, 1986), 142, 231–9.

257

for national ambition or individual profit and saved expenditure in
money and the lives of men. But consent was always refused.'[2] Publishing Gerald Portal's account of his mission to Uganda posthumously,
Rennell Rodd, later ambassador to Rome, portrayed anti-slavery policy
as part of Britain's noble imperial mission.[3]

Even those contemporaries concerned that the abolition of slavery
would jeopardise social stability and damage British interests, purveyed
a similar line. Rodd criticised humanitarian opinion in Britain for ignoring 'the hard fact ... that at this time we were holding on to East Africa
by a very slender thread and preserving it from a worse fate by the faith
and exertions of a mere handful of men'.[4] Yet, arguably their works
accentuated the nobility of Britain's civilising mission. Their doubts
about suppressing slavery and their criticisms of the humanitarian lobby
suggested that Britain had neither political nor economic interests in
ending African slavery.

The most notable early historian of the suppression of the East African
slave trade, Coupland, embedded the humanitarian narrative in several
of his books. He pointed out that Britain's anti-slave trade stance risked
losing influence to France. But potential political sacrifice did not make
one jot of difference to 'Britain's inflexible determination to destroy the
slave trade'.[5] He suggested that the principle of anti-slavery was so firmly
rooted in British policy that, unlike the 1830s, there was no need for
popular campaigns and monster petitions. Ministers were so committed
to the anti-slavery agenda that the House of Commons did not require a
repetition of the great debates of nineteenth-century parliamentary
lore.[6] This version enjoys little support, although it surfaces occasionally
in some works.[7]

Since the early 1970s, historians have been more sceptical of British
humanitarian claims and anti-slavery strategy. A variety of arguments,
none of which are necessarily incompatible, stress different issues.
Suzanne Miers, in the most detailed study of Britain's anti-slavery
diplomacy, argued that anti-slavery and slave trade policy was largely
determined by political interest. It was used as a means to justify

---

[2] Lady Gwendolen Cecil, *Life of Robert, Marquis of Salisbury*, IV (London: Hodder and Stoughton 1932), 223–4.

[3] Rennell Rodd (ed.), *The British Mission to Uganda in 1893* (London: Arnold, 1894), 349–51.

[4] James Rennell Rodd, *Social and Diplomatic Memories*, I (London: Arnold 1922), 338, 347.

[5] R. Coupland, *The Exploitation of East Africa, 1856–1890* (London: Faber and Faber, 1939), 13, 101.

[6] *Ibid.*, 136, 148–51.

[7] Raymond Howell, *The Royal Navy and the Slave Trade* (London: Croom Helm, 1987); R. W. Beachey, *The Slave Trade of Eastern Africa* (London: Collings, 1976).

imperial expansion to an electorate which, until the 1880s at least, was sceptical about the acquisition of colonies: 'those whose job it was to defend British interests abroad did not let humanitarianism dictate their policy. They were happy however to present that policy to the world in an anti-slavery guise.' The extension of British influence, in Miers's view, 'depended upon the suppression of the slave trade'.[8] Her research marginalised the role of humanitarian public opinion. Foreign Office officials saw humanitarian associations as 'well-meaning busybodies', but Miers doubted whether there was much popular support for humanitarian aims.[9] R. J. Gavin's study of the 1873 treaty with Zanzibar argued that Bartle Frere, the special envoy for the mission, pursued a forward policy in East Africa, designed to secure Indian interests. In a classic account of the man-on-the-spot version of imperial history, Gavin shows how Bartle Frere roused public opinion in Britain in order to bring pressure to bear on Gladstone's reluctant government. Bartle Frere offered a grand fusion of humanitarian, commercial, and strategic reasons to the British public.[10]

Others have laid more stress on the argument that as capitalism spread, slavery would die out. In these writings, free labour is seen as a central characteristic of the capitalist system. British hegemony in East Africa was geared towards the promotion of trade and economic opportunities for British and Indian merchants. Paul Lovejoy suggests that European policies had little impact, with the impetus for the ending of slavery emerging from African societies, which were in the process of adjusting to the global economy. The 'modern industrial economy' and 'a slave-based social formation' were incompatible: 'In Marxist terms, the clash was based on the contradictions between different modes of production. The demise of slavery was inevitable in the context of absorption into a capitalist world-economy.'[11] Pressure from the metropolis was commercial, rather than humanitarian.

Finally, historians have questioned whether British anti-slavery policies had much impact on the ending of slavery. Cooper and Lovejoy have stressed the self-mobilisation of slaves, who ran away from their masters or negotiated an improved relationship. On this reading, the

---

[8] Suzanne Miers, *Britain and the Ending of the Slave Trade* (London: Longman, 1975), 35–8.

[9] *Ibid.*, 31–3.

[10] R. J. Gavin, 'The Bartle Frere Mission to Zanzibar, 1873', *Historical Journal* 5:2 (1962), 122–48.

[11] Paul Lovejoy, *Transformations in Slavery: A History of Slavery in Africa* (Cambridge: Cambridge University Press 1983), 246–7; Jacques Depelchin, 'The Transition from Slavery, 1873–1914', in *Zanzibar under Colonial Rule*, ed. Abdul Sheriff and Ed Ferguson (London: J. Currey, 1991), 21–2.

slave–master relationship was always precarious. Slaves seized the initiative, argued Lovejoy, and 'were largely responsible for changing the social and economic structures of Africa'. Indeed, he contended that colonial regimes became 'defenders of slavery' and 'the greatest single impediment to full emancipation'.[12] Baer has suggested that the ending of the slave trade and slavery in Egypt was largely the result of the end of the guild system and opening up of a free labour market.[13]

A number of questions must be asked of these revisionist accounts. First, there is nothing inherently anti-capitalist about slavery. As far as slave traders were concerned, slaves were just another commodity to be traded. Contemporaries distinguished between legitimate commerce and the slave trade, not between capitalism and a slave-based economy. Slaves were important in several capitalist enterprises, such as the Zanzibar clove fields.[14] Moreover, work on other slave systems has undermined the view that capitalism and slave labour are antithetical. Indeed the economic problems in the West Indies after abolition were a potent lesson to those forming anti-slavery and slave trade policies in late nineteenth-century Britain.[15] Although British and Indian subjects could not employ slaves, this was a self-denying ordinance, rather than an attempt to gain a competitive advantage. They could easily have operated in an economic system, based on slavery – as the loans of Indian bankers to Arabs in Zanzibar indicated. Therefore the relationship of capitalism and the suppression of the slave trade in East Africa needs to be reassessed.

Second, Britain's political interests were far more likely to be jeopardised than advanced by the suppression of the slave trade. Imperial policy, particularly before the Scramble for Africa in the 1880s, sought cooperation with local rulers. This often involved turning a blind eye to practices regarded as barbaric in Britain. Advocating anti-slave trade policies risked destabilising local political systems and pushing East African

[12] Lovejoy, *Transformations*, 247–8.
[13] Gabriel Baer, *Studies in the History of Modern Egypt* (Chicago: University of Chicago Press, 1969), 182–8.
[14] Ralph Austen, 'The Trans-Saharan Slave Trade: A Tentative Census', in *The Uncommon Market: Essays in the Economic History of the Atlantic Slave Trade*, ed. Henry A. Gemery and Jon S. Hogendorn (New York: Academic Press, 1979), 50; Abdul Sheriff, 'The Peasantry Under Imperialism, 1873–1963', in *Zanzibar under Colonial Rule*, ed. Sheriff and Ferguson, 109–12.
[15] Seymour Drescher, *The Mighty Experiment: Free Labor Versus Slavery in British Emancipation* (Oxford: Oxford University Press, 2002), 6, 166–75, 218–28; Drescher's arguments have been challenged in a recent article: David Beck Ryden, 'Does Decline Make Sense? The West Indian Economy and the Abolition of the Slave Trade', *Journal of Interdisciplinary History* 31:3 (2001), 347–74.

potentates into the arms of rival powers. Indeed to a certain extent, rulers sought to exploit Britain for their own interests by concluding anti-slave trade agreements. Rulers hoped for British support against internal opposition or external threats following the signature of an anti-slave trade agreement. Anti-slave trade policies complicated the pursuit of British interests in East Africa, introducing an ideological dimension to relationships in the region.

Of course, anti-slavery policies may have been guided by domestic political considerations. The only study of the Aborigines' Protection Society (APS) argued that its main achievements were a 'few cases of individual hardship relieved and petty wrongs righted'.[16] The links between humanitarian public opinion and government anti-slavery policy require further consideration. It should be borne in mind that many other groups, aside from the APS and ASS (Anti-Slavery Society), were active in humanitarian politics, including missionaries and local political activists. Kevin Grant has uncovered the networks of humanitarians, including missionaries, chambers of commerce, and political figures, which made an impact on imperial policies in the early twentieth century.[17]

Finally, the claim that British policy had little bearing on the ending of the slave trade and slavery in Africa requires scrutiny. As Patrick Manning points out, the enslavement of Africans ended 'as a result of European conquests'.[18] Austen's research, showing a major decline in the slave trade from the 1870s, led him to conclude that the European presence was of major significance.[19] Studies by Toledano and Erdem show that there was little impulse from within the Ottoman Empire to suppress the slave trade. It was notable that any steps in that direction were taken after foreign pressure, the firman of 1857 after the Crimean War being an excellent example.[20] Slavery found many defenders

---

[16] Charles Swaisland, 'The Aborigines Protection Society, 1837–1909', *Slavery & Abolition* 21:2 (2000), 271–8.

[17] Kevin Grant, *A Civilized Savagery: Britain and the New Slaveries in Africa, 1884–1926* (London: Routledge, 2005).

[18] Patrick Manning, *Slavery and African Life: Occidental, Oriental, and African Slave Trades* (Cambridge: Cambridge University Press, 1990), 160.

[19] Austen, 'Census', 66; Austen, 'From the Atlantic to the Indian Ocean: European Abolition, the African Slave Trade, and Asian Economic Structures', in *The Abolition of the Atlantic Slave Trade: Origins and Effects in Europe, Africa, and the Americas*, ed. David Eltis and James Walvin (Madison: University of Wisconsin Press, 1981), 117–32.

[20] Ehud R. Toledano, *The Ottoman Slave Trade and its Suppression, 1840–1890* (Princeton: Princeton University Press, 1982); Y. Hakan Erdem, *Slavery in the Ottoman Empire and its Demise, 1800–1909* (Basingstoke: Palgrave, 1996); for a contrary view, see William Gervase Clarence-Smith, *Islam and the Abolition of Slavery* (London: Hurst and Co., 2006).

amongst Islamic scholars, as well as Europeans familiar with Islamic and African cultures.[21] In any case, the coincidence of the ending of the slave trade and the European conquest and occupation of Africa suggests a close relationship.

For whatever reason, current scholarship has played down the humanitarian bent of British policy. But the alternative explanations do not offer a wholly convincing account. Dismissing humanitarianism as a motive on the basis that other interests – economic or political – had a role sets the bar for humanitarian politics at an impossibly high level. Debates amongst policy-makers show that they were concerned that the implementation of an anti-slave trade policy could damage British interests, could upset the balance of local economies, and could open the space for other powers to gain influence. No doubt there was a good deal of cant and arrogance amongst British officials. The process of ending the slave trade was slow, often purposefully. The outcomes were sometimes disastrous and often destabilising. The motives were occasionally shady and cut to fit commercial and political interests. Yet, as we shall see, in the final analysis, humanitarian concerns remained a powerful force in British policy.

## British interests and motivations in ending the slave trade

The driving force behind British anti-slave trade and anti-slavery policy in the late nineteenth century came from humanitarian public opinion, not from the political interests of leading politicians or the commercial interests of merchants and financiers. Popular humanitarianism had existed in Britain since the late eighteenth century. The mobilisation of humanitarian opinion in the late Victorian era varied, according to the issues at stake. There was a high degree of self-mobilisation on slavery issues amongst non-Conformists, radical working-class groups, and Liberals. Party politics also played an important role, as did the impact of a single, energetic figure, like Frere. But in comparison to the first half of the century, the influence of renowned humanitarian associations, the APS and ASS, was limited. Before turning to explore the role of popular humanitarianism in greater depth, it is important to examine the constraints on policy at the highest levels of government.

Amongst the leading members of the Liberal and Conservative governments, there was little sustained interest in anti-slavery politics.

---

[21] Eve M. Troutt Powell, *A Different Shade of Colonialism. Egypt, Great Britain, and the Mastery of the Sudan* (Berkeley: University of California Press, 2003), 139–46.

Despite Salisbury's repugnance towards Ottoman rule and Gladstone's championing of (some of) the oppressed, the fate of slaves rarely figured in their private letters and public pronouncements. Kirk condemned Lord Derby as a fair-weather supporter of anti-slave trade policies. He hoped that Lord Salisbury, who replaced Derby as Foreign Secretary in April 1878, would 'be more firm than Derby, who was a man I felt I could never rely upon for support unless all went smooth and proved a success. Luckily they did and I was supported.'[22] Salisbury showed some energy in negotiating an anti-slave trade convention with Turkey in 1880, but in his private letters to the ambassador in Constantinople, Austen Layard, he only occasionally referred to anti-slavery policy, generally tacking on a single sentence at the end.[23] He was cautious about abolishing slavery in Zanzibar, fearing it would provoke a Muslim revolt against Britain in Africa and India.[24] Neither were Gladstone's governments more committed. Charles Gordon complained to Charles Allen, secretary of the ASS, that the slave trade would continue and 'our govt will not do anything, except shift the subject'.[25] The lack of interest among the political elite meant that the impulse for British policy would have to come from outside the political elite, in the form either of public pressure or external interests.

Indeed many politicians saw anti-slave trade policies as damaging to British interests. For a start, suppressing the slave trade cost money in an era when economy was a prized political asset. Gladstone sought to reduce military and naval expenditure in the early 1870s. Goschen, the First Lord of the Admiralty, identified the East African anti-slave trade squadron as a possible target for cuts. 'The fact is', he told Gladstone, 'half of our expenditure is not for war service in the strict sense but for keeping the police of the seas, of protecting commerce during times of peace, and for carrying out our views as to protecting those barbarous and backwards races against kidnapping and various forms of outrage. Philanthropy decidedly costs money.'[26] Ministers also reasoned that the suppression of the slave trade was beyond Britain's means, as the naval squadron could not police effectively the East African coast. 'Ministers', wrote Vivian, 'look at the great expense,

[22] Kirk to Wylde, 7 July 1878, NLS, Acc 9942/7.
[23] Salisbury to Layard, 24 July 1879, 27 Nov. 1879, 29 Jan. 1880, HH, 3MA/33, fos. 64, 102, 127.
[24] G. N. Uzoigwe, *Britain and the Conquest of Africa: The Era of Salisbury* (Ann Arbor: University of Michigan Press, 1974), 156–7.
[25] Gordon to Allen, 9 Mar. 1881, BL, Add. MS 47609, fos. 118–19; more generally, see Roland Quinault, 'Gladstone and Slavery', *Historical Journal* 52:2 (2009), 363–83.
[26] Goschen to Gladstone, 19 Sept. 1871, BL, Gladstone Papers, Add MS 44161, fos. 177–82.

which has already been incurred in our futile attempts to suppress the traffic (which they estimate at about £50,000 a year) and they point with considerable show of justice to the wretched results of our efforts, and ask whether any increased expenditure upon ships and Consuls can be justified and whether, judging from past experience, it would not be likely only to raise the price of slaves by the increased risk of capture, and to increase the inducements to continue the Traffic.'[27]

The Treasury continually blocked anti-slave trade measures, such as an agreement between the British and Indian governments to share the costs of the Consul and Political Agent at Zanzibar, who had the dual role of protecting Indian trading interests and supervising anti-slave trade measures.[28] The Treasury refused 'to pay a farthing' towards the maintenance of the Zanzibar, claiming it could not be justified in terms of the national interest.[29] Shortly after coming to office, Lord Derby reduced expenditure on anti-slave trade measures in East Africa, building on plans developed in the last months of the Gladstone government.[30]

Future commercial opportunity, the development of thriving free labour economies, and increased revenues from trade were put forward by humanitarians to advance their cause. Like their early nineteenth-century counterparts, they recognised the importance of appealing to the motives of material gain and political advantage. Fowell Buxton, a philanthropist and brewer, asked Kirk for information on Zanzibar 'showing the interest we have ... in suppressing the ST in consequence of our own commercial connection with the place'.[31] Africa's potential wealth was regularly cited as a reason for stamping out the slave trade. 'How is England interested in the East Coast of Africa – namely in every way – Commerce – Humanity to improve the well-being of the inhabitants of the Country and the suppression of the slave trade. Commerce is the foundation of England I have always been taught.'[32] In a series of articles on the slave trade, the *English Independent* noted that commercial benefits would follow from the suppression of the slave trade.[33] Yet the

[27] Vivian to Kirk, 12 Dec. 1871, NLS Acc 9942/6.
[28] *Parliamentary Papers, 1871. Reports from Committees, Slave Trade (East Coast of Africa)*, v–vii.
[29] *Ibid.*, 13–21.
[30] *The Diaries of Edward Henry Stanley, 15th Earl of Derby, 1869–1878*, ed. John Vincent (London: Royal Historical Society, 1994), 27 Feb. 1874, 167; *The Gladstone Diaries*, ed. H. C. G. Matthew (Oxford: Oxford University Press, 1999), 15 Nov. 1873, VIII, 411.
[31] T. Fowell Buxton to Kirk, 4 Feb. 1869, NLS, MS 20311, fos. 237–8.
[32] Wylde to Gordon, 2 Oct. 1880, BL, Add MS 47609, fos. 57–8.
[33] 'East African Slave Trade', *English Independent*, 20 Aug. 1874.

voices of merchants were largely absent from the humanitarian chorus. Kirk had grave doubts about the humanitarian claims of William Mackinnon and the East African Company. He pointed out that the whole of the Zambesi basin, 'the very hot-bed of the East African Slave Trade', was excluded. Kirk concluded: 'if the suppression of the Slave Trade is the object in view, surely these great slave-holding fields that furnish Egypt with the raw material must be included'.[34] Entrepreneurs showed little interest in opening up Africa's interior and ending the slave trade.[35]

If the suppression of the slave trade promised few commercial benefits, then one might look to strategic interests as a motivating factor. The area between the eastern Mediterranean and Zanzibar lay on the route between Britain and India. The maintenance of naval power and political influence was a, if not the, central preoccupation of British policy-makers. Officials and politicians tried to keep anti-slave trade issues separate from broad political concerns. The ASS tried to push its concerns onto the agenda of the 1874 Brussels Conference on the rules of war and the 1876 conference at Constantinople on Ottoman reforms, supervised by the Great Powers. On both occasions, the Foreign Office politely declined.[36] Anti-slavery policy complicated the pursuit of strategic interests and often ran against pragmatic political arguments. During the row in 1875 and 1876 over the Fugitive Slave Circular, issued to the Royal Navy, Sir Stafford Northcote, the Chancellor, suggested an international treaty with other Great Powers, aiming at the ending of slavery. Lord Tenterden, the under-secretary of state at the Foreign Office, warned that any such treaty would give Great Powers the right to interfere in the domestic politics of weaker states, enabling Russian intervention in Turkey, French in Egypt, and American in Brazil and Cuba: 'I therefore deprecated any sort of appeal to Foreign Countries of this kind. It would do no good in regard to the Fugitive Slave Circular and would do a great deal of harm in other respects.'[37]

Diplomats recognised that the pursuit of anti-slave trade policies could alienate local potentates along the crucial strategic route from

[34] Kirk to Derby, 7 Mar. 1877, NA, FO 881/3183, 1–2.
[35] John S. Galbraith, *Mackinnon and East Africa, 1878–1895: A Study in the 'New Imperialism'* (Cambridge: Cambridge University Press, 1972), 10–14; Miers, *Ending the Slave Trade*, 147–53; A. C. Unomah and J. B. Webster, 'East Africa: The Expansion of Commerce', in *The Cambridge History of Africa, 1790–1870*, ed. John R. Flint (Cambridge: Cambridge University Press, 1976), 277–83.
[36] Bourke to ASS, 24 June 1874, Bodl., Rhodes House, MSS Brit Emp S18, C 162, fo. 7; Minutes of Anti-Slavery Society, 3 Nov. and 1 Dec. 1876, MSS Brit Emp S20, E 2/10.
[37] Tenterden to Derby, 28 Feb. 1876, Liverpool Record Office 920 DER (15), 16/2/10.

the Mediterranean to India. Anti-slave trade policies could interfere with political priorities. Beyond those officials, specifically charged with an anti-slave trade brief, diplomats showed little enthusiasm for pursuing humanitarian policies. When a British consul showed too much zeal in applying anti-slave trade agreements in Salonica, the British ambassador to the Porte, Henry Elliot, noted that the Turkish government had no intention of implementing the decrees, issued after the Crimean War. The Turks 'have often wished to throw dust in the eyes of European Govts by a pretence of putting an end to slavery', but Elliot was willing to ignore the traffic, as Turkey was an important barrier against Russian expansion.[38] In early 1876, when the possibility of an anti-slave trade agreement between Britain, Egypt, and Turkey was discussed, Elliot warned that any such agreement would be seen in Turkey as further foreign interference.[39] Negotiations with Turkey did not begin until 1878.

Following the 1877 convention with Egypt, Vivian warned consuls in Egypt about the enforcement of the agreement:

I should also strongly recommend to you to combine a firm insistence upon the loyal and faithful execution of the Convention in all cases of Slave Trading with prudence and tact in any proceedings you may have to take to enforce its stipulation so as not needlessly or unreasonably to irritate or arouse Musulman susceptibilities which would do far more harm than good to the cause that England has at heart.[40]

Anti-slave trade policies had to fit the grain of Britain's broader imperial and foreign policy.

Before the scramble for territory in the 1880s, Britain sought to maintain and expand influence. Friendly relations with local rulers could be jeopardised by a heavy-handed humanitarian policy. Respect for the sovereignty (over their own subjects, not Europeans) of these states was an important assumption of British policy-makers. This helps to explain the gradual approach to ending slavery and the slave trade. Suppressing the slave trade, they hoped, would end slavery owing to low birth rates. As Rothery, the Treasury official in charge of anti-slavery policy, told the Parliamentary Select Committee in 1871, the aim was the 'suppression of the slave trade, not slavery'.[41] When discussing the possibility of an anti-slave trade convention with Egypt in 1873, Granville noted that

---

[38] Elliot to Hammond, 18 Aug. 1870, NLS, Elliot Papers, MS 13069, fo. 60.
[39] Elliot to Derby, 12 Feb. 1876, NA, FO 881/3423, 25–6.
[40] Vivian to Consuls at Alexandria, Port Said, Suez, Cairo, Khartoum, 22 Aug. 1877, NA, FO 84/1473, fos. 119–20.
[41] Rothery, 24 July 1871, *PP*, 61.

'however desirable it would be to suppress domestic slavery it would not be expedient to press the point as an indispensable condition of the agreement'.[42] Criticising Britain for its gradual approach to ending the slave trade raises the bar for humanitarian policy too high – and also overestimates greatly the extent of British power. A successful policy required the matching of means and ends. Humanitarianism was not exempt from the dictum that politics is the art of the possible.

Nor was anti-slavery policy a central part of the reforms that Britain proposed to Turkey and Egypt in the 1870s and 1880s. Salisbury doubted whether all societies were on the same historical trajectory as liberal Britain.[43] He doubted the capacity of 'the Mahometan races' to adapt to British or European political and social institutions. 'I should deprecate the attempt to establish complicated occidental forms of Government – India furnishes a far safer model than Europe'.[44] India had abolished the legal status of slavery in 1843, but when a proposal was made to apply a similar model to Egypt, Evelyn Baring, the influential British consul in Egypt, counselled: 'it would be most unwise to attempt at present the introduction of so radical a reform ... I fully sympathise with the view generally entertained by Englishmen on this subject, but it is also necessary to consider the question from the point of view of local circumstance and of local opinion. It cannot be denied that there is at present great discontent amongst all classes in Egypt. The people, moreover, have not remained altogether indifferent to the successes of the Mahdi. Any measures likely to lead to a recrudescence of Mahomedan fanaticism is much to be deprecated.'[45] Order and stability served British interests more effectively than humanitarian liberalism.[46]

It is significant that the anti-slave trade agreements with Zanzibar, Egypt, and Turkey came when those countries were going through major internal and external crises. Bright and Geyer have argued that while globalisation was largely driven by European and American states and societies, weaker powers could try to turn the process to their advantage.[47] In these states there was neither a significant anti-slavery movement nor the intellectual traditions to promote abolition. Indeed,

---

[42] Granville to Elliot, 11 July 1873, NA, FO 881/3423, 1.
[43] Michael Bentley, *Lord Salisbury's World: Conservative Environments in Late Victorian Britain* (Cambridge: Cambridge University Press, 2001), 220–5.
[44] Salisbury to Layard, 25 June 1878, HH, 3MA/32, fo. 37.
[45] 'Despatch from Sir E. Baring respecting slavery in Egypt', *PP*, 1884, LXXV, 3.
[46] Roger Owen, *Lord Cromer: Victorian Imperialist, Edwardian Proconsul* (Oxford: Oxford University Press, 2004), 298–9.
[47] Charles Bright and Michael Geyer, 'World History in a Global Age', *AHR* 100 (1995), 1034–60.

intellectuals defended Muslim slavery, pointing out that it was a more gentle institution than the plantation slavery, which Europeans had established in the Americas.[48] Egypt, Turkey, and, to a lesser extent, Zanzibar, signed these treaties to improve their image in Britain. Of course, the rulers of these states had other reasons to end the slave trade. The Khedive Ismail aimed to expand his empire and to bring slavers and their military forces under control.[49] Sultan Abdul Hamid eventually acceded in 1880 to British demands to end the slave trade as a gesture of diplomatic goodwill.[50] Kirk noted the Sultan of Zanzibar had come to appreciate that the anti-slave trade policy was 'if not what he thinks right at least a political necessity and he adapts the situation'.[51] Anti-slave trade policies, therefore, were not simply an imposition on these powers, as rulers considered potential political benefits.

The negotiations for an anti-slave trade convention with Egypt began in July 1873, after the Sultan issued a firman allowing the Khedive to conclude non-political agreements with foreign powers. Since the early part of the nineteenth century, the Khedives of Egypt had sought to assert their autonomy and even independence from the Ottoman Empire. The firman of 1873 represented an important addition to his powers. Elliot reported that the Khedive was 'anxious to let it be seen that he has enlightened and progressive views, which will enable him to turn to good account any additional privilege or liberty of action which he may obtain'.[52] Negotiations failed to produce an agreement, but were taken up again in early 1876. By then, Britain's influence in Egypt had increased further, following the purchase of the Suez Canal Company shares. An anti-slave trade treaty would bolster the Khedive's image, tarnished by alleged financial mismanagement. Britain was also concerned at the expansion of the Egyptian empire after its war against Ethiopia, as Derby feared that extension of Egyptian rule would lead to an increase in slave hunting.[53] British approval appeared dependent on an anti-slave trade commitment from Egypt. As Vivian told Wylde in June 1877, 'the Khedive is only too anxious to do all and everything that England wants'.[54]

---

[48] Troutt Powell, *Different Shade of Colonialism*, 140–6; Clarence-Smith, *Islam and the Abolition of Slavery.*
[49] M. F. Shukry (ed.), *Equatoria under Egyptian Rule: The Unpublished Correspondence of Col. C. G. Gordon with Ismail, Khedive of Egypt and the Sudan, 1874–1876* (Cairo: Cairo University Press, 1952), 19–26.
[50] Erdem, *Slavery and the Ottoman Empire*, 128–36.
[51] Kirk to Wylde, 1 June 1876, NLS Acc 9942/7.
[52] Elliot to Granville, NA, FO 881/3423, 3.
[53] Derby to Vivian, 2 Feb. 1877, NA, FO 84/1472, fos. 11–12.
[54] Vivian to Wylde, 9 June 1877, NA, FO 84/1472, fo. 324.

Negotiations with Turkey for an anti-slave trade convention began as Russian troops moved towards Constantinople in February 1878. Austen Layard, the ambassador to the Porte, pointed 'to the good effect it would have in this Country, if the Porte should cooperate with us in the suppression of the Slave Traffic'.[55] The 1877 agreement with Egypt was difficult to implement as Britain only had the right to search Egyptian vessels whose flag was identical to the Turkish one. The larger context was Turkey's need for British support against Russia. While anti-Russian sentiment had flourished in late 1877 and early 1878, this did not mean that attitudes to Turkey had become any more favourable since the Bulgarian atrocities campaign. The Turkish Foreign Ministry began negotiations, but they fizzled out by the time of the Berlin Congress. Talks recommenced a year later, with the British once again stressing Ottoman isolation. By the end of January 1880 a Convention had been agreed. Layard urged a rapid conclusion to the negotiations as the Porte 'is, at the moment, anxious to show its desire to please and satisfy Her Majesty's government'.[56] On this occasion, the thorny issue of implementing the treaty of Berlin preoccupied the sultan.

Therefore the Khedive and Porte expected benefits from pursuing an anti-slavery policy. These benefits never materialised. Derby noted that the Sultan of Zanzibar 'has alienated most of his subjects and half-ruined himself, in putting down the slave trade at our request, and as yet we have given him nothing but good words in return'.[57] Gladstone, who became Prime Minister in 1880, had little sympathy for the Ottoman Empire and Britain occupied Egypt in 1882. Nonetheless, Egypt and Turkey had mainly pragmatic reasons for concluding an anti-slave trade agreement with Britain and sought to delay full implementation. Anti-slavery measures were an instrument to advance political interests, not an end in themselves. Commenting on the ineffectiveness of the Anglo-Egyptian Convention, the Khedive Tewfik told Frank Lascelles that 'he was not surprised that the Convention had not hitherto worked in a satisfactory manner, as his father had in reality no intention of its being seriously put into execution'.[58] Britain took advantage of these moments of crisis to pursue its anti-slave trade policy, looking for, as Layard put it, 'a small end of the wedge which can be driven home afterwards if it should be found necessary to do so'.[59]

---

[55] Wylde, minute on Layard's telegram, 2 Mar. 1878, NA, FO 84/1658, fo. 3.
[56] Layard to Salisbury, 24 Jan. 1880, NA, FO 84/1570, fos. 81–5.
[57] *Derby Diaries*, 23 Oct. 1877, 447.
[58] Lascelles to Salisbury, 12 Sept. 1879, NA, FO 881/4066, 1–2.
[59] Layard to Salisbury, 13 Jan. 1880, NA, FO 84/1658, fos. 59–60.

While Britain coerced Zanzibar into signing the 1873 slave trade treaty, ministers and diplomats sought to deal with the slave trade within the boundaries of international law. The conception of international law amongst diplomats and politicians differed from that of the humanitarian public. The former sought to uphold and develop existing treaty stipulations, dating from the first half of the nineteenth century. In 1889, before the Brussels Conference, Edward Hertslet listed the anti-slave trade declarations and agreements, dating back to Vienna in 1815, as a justification for an international treaty.[60] In matters regarding the slave trade, they respected the sovereign control of these governments over their own citizens. They did not accept that humanitarian concerns overrode international law, as set down in treaties. The 'wedge', as Layard put it, was the conclusion of a treaty or convention, which Britain could then use to put pressure on the signatories, if their anti-slavery enthusiasm waned. Treaty law, therefore, restrained the anti-slave trade measures, but it also served British interests in maintaining regional stability. Humanitarian opinion was less clear about exactly which moral code the institution of slavery violated – it could be natural law, Christian morality, or human rights. In any case, humanitarian opinion did not consider treaties acknowledging slavery as binding.

These different perceptions of international law came to the fore during the Fugitive Slave Circular agitation in 1875 and 1876.[61] The Foreign Office, the Law Officers, and the Indian government were adamant that fugitive slaves, who took refuge on board British vessels in territorial waters, were to be returned to their masters. 'The immunity from the law of the country and the privileges conceded to public ships when under territorial waters', the Law Officers argued, 'cannot be extended to cases in which the practical result would be, in the first instance to encourage and assist in a breach of the laws of the country, and next to protect the person breaking that law'.[62] In their view, the local laws could override the concerns of humanity; international law did not allow Britain to impose its values on other societies. On the other hand, the ASS felt 'alarmed for the cause of humanity' when it learned that fugitive slaves were to be returned to their masters, while the Sheffield Council declared the circular 'at variance with the principles

---

[60] E. Hertslet, 'Memorandum on the bearing of International Law on the Slave Trade', 9 Nov. 1889, NA, FO 881/5853.

[61] William Mulligan, 'The Fugitive Slave Circulars, 1875–76', *Journal of Imperial and Commonwealth History* 37:2 (2009), 183–206.

[62] Confidential Print, Précis of Correspondence relative to Reception of Fugitive Slaves on board Her Majesty's Ships, 17 Feb. 1876, Liverpool Record Office, 920 DER (15), 30/3/4, 'Report of the Law Officers', 18 Apr. 1874, 5.

of the Constitution of this country and the obligations of humanity'.[63] With some amendments, namely that slaves were returned on the promise of good treatment, the government's view of international law trumped the radical demands of the humanitarian public.

The Fugitive Slave Circular was just one illustration of the continued interest of the public in humanitarian politics. Humanitarian public opinion was the predominant factor in the formation of British anti-slavery and anti-slave trade policy. Indeed, each of the anti-slave trade conventions signed between 1873 and 1880 can be related to public pressure, as well as to the crises of the other signatory state. Frere's mission to Zanzibar was sanctioned after he had roused anti-slavery sentiment into a significant political force.[64] Britain decided to reopen negotiations for an anti-slave trade convention with Egypt in December 1875, when the Disraeli government was coming under sustained attack for its 'unEnglish' policy on fugitive slaves.[65] Finally the convention with Turkey was concluded just before an election, as Disraeli's government faced further attacks for its failed policy in Afghanistan and South Africa. In other words, domestic political circumstances in Britain and crises in East Africa and the Ottoman Empire coincided to give an impetus to anti-slavery policies.

Historians have generally ignored the popular humanitarian politics in the 1870s and 1880s. For the most part, they have assumed that the abolitionist zeal of the first half of the nineteenth century had largely died out by the end of the American Civil War.[66] Yet there is a good deal of evidence to the contrary, suggesting that humanitarian concerns continued to appeal to the British public. The outrage over the murder of Bishop Patteson led to the Pacific Islanders' Protection Act, Frere's campaign led to the anti-slave trade treaty with Zanzibar, the cult of Livingstone drew attention to slave hunting in the interior of Africa, the first criticisms of the Conservative government as 'unEnglish' arose during the Fugitive Slave Circular affair, and Gladstone's career revived on the back of the Bulgarian atrocities campaign. British imperial expansion and policy in Egypt and Sudan in the 1880s and in East Africa in the 1890s drew on humanitarian arguments to bolster public support. Humanitarianism enabled many otherwise sceptical Britons to accept

---

[63] Memorial of the Anti-Slavery Society to the Admiralty; Sheffield Council to Lord Derby, 13 Oct. 1875, NA, FO 84/1430, fos. 127–30, 243.

[64] Gavin, 'Frere'.

[65] Memorandum by Mr Wylde, 19 Dec. 1875, NA, FO 881/3423, 19–21.

[66] Catherine Hall, *Civilising Subjects: Metropole and Colony in the English Imagination, 1830–1867* (Cambridge: Polity, 2002), 337–9, 347, 390; Howard Temperley, *British Anti-slavery, 1833–70* (London: Longman, 1972), 256–8.

and even demand the expansion of empire.[67] While conventional humanitarian associations were weak, humanitarian politics continued to thrive, because the issues – Britain's role in the world, the constitution, international law – were relevant to other causes.

The composition and mobilisation of the humanitarian coalition varied from case to case. The old coalition of non-Conformists, missionary societies, radical Liberals, working men's associations, and secular humanitarians coalesced at moments when anti-slavery concerns arouse in the 1870s and 1880s. In 1872, Frere's energetic campaign mobilised opinion in favour of an anti-slave trade treaty with Zanzibar. During the controversy over the Fugitive Slave Circular in 1875 and 1876, there was a high degree of self-mobilisation, with little direction from the established humanitarian associations. Meetings were held in large towns and cities, churches organised petitions, working men's clubs invited MPs to speak on the issue, and members of the Liberal party exploited the issue to embarrass Disraeli's government. An editorial in the *Liverpool Daily Post* noted 'there are matters on which they [the English people] are capable of being raised to a white heat of anger that burns up sooner or later the object of their hate. And Slavery is one of them.'[68] In the 1880 election campaign, Liberal speakers raised the affair on several occasions, offering it as proof of Disraeli's disregard for British liberties.[69] Conservatives were able to turn the tables during the 1880s, when the Liberal government encountered problems in Egypt and the Sudan.

The most obvious manifestations of public opinion were the great political meetings, often held at Exeter Hall, at which a leading figure spoke.[70] These set-piece occasions were reported in the press, drew attention in the House of Commons, and put pressure on the government to take some form of action, if only to fob off public pressure.[71] Smaller meetings were also important and often resulted in a petition to the Foreign Office. Moreover, these meetings put direct pressure on local MPs. The humanitarian message was transmitted in books and pamphlet literature. The latter were often extracts from a speech or an article in one of the major reviews. The ASS had its own journal, the *Anti-Slavery Reporter*, but it was more useful at keeping members of the

---

[67] C. C. Eldridge, *England's Mission: The Imperial Idea in the Age of Gladstone and Disraeli* (London: Macmillan, 1973).

[68] *Liverpool Daily Post*, 1 Jan. 1876; 3 Jan. 1876, 5.

[69] Holms' address to his constituents, 27 Mar. 1880, NLS Acc 8449/2, fos. 2–3; *The Times*, 18 Oct. 1878, 'Parliament out of session'; 5 Jan. 1879, 'Mr Forster at Bradford'.

[70] 'The Slave Trade', *The Times*, 26 July 1872; *The Post*, 26 July 1872, carry accounts of Frere's speech at the Mansion House.

[71] *Daily Telegraph*, 5 Nov. 1872, on the Mansion House speech by Frere.

society informed than in spreading the humanitarian message. Finally, events such as the death of Livingstone in 1874 provided occasions during which humanitarian idealism was married to national identity. British history was cast as a story of fighting for liberty, not just at home, but around the globe.

Politicians reacted to public opinion on anti-slavery issues. During the agitation concerning the Fugitive Slave Circulars in 1875 and 1876, Derby made frequent references to the 'noise' and the 'popular cry'.[72] Two occasions serve as examples – the Frere mission to Zanzibar and the decision to oppose Gordon's request, in early 1884, to put Zobeir, a prominent (and infamous) slave dealer, in charge of the Sudan. Frere's mission was linked in the public mind to the relief expedition to find Livingstone. H. W. Bates, President of the Royal Geographical Society, reported to Kirk that 'the public is wild and it is impossible to keep pace with all that is said and done, the latest phase is the suppression of the E African slavery movement, which is supported by all parties with greater or lesser enthusiasm'.[73] Concerns about the East African slave trade had been growing since Livingstone's reports in the mid-1860s, but they were given a decisive fillip and direction by Frere's 1872 campaign. The Treasury made a series of concessions on funding the anti-slave trade campaign in Zanzibar, following pressure from public opinion.[74]

By late 1883, the Liberal government's policy on Egypt was coming under increasing attack. Having ostensibly occupied Egypt to stave off the military despotism of Arabi, the Egyptian nationalist leader, the government needed to burnish its liberal credentials. Lord Northbrook, the First Lord of the Admiralty, suggested that the 'suppression of the slave trade might do real good, and besides get the advantage of some popularity for our policy, which seems to be getting unpopular here'.[75] The appointment of Gordon to organise the withdrawal of Egyptian forces from the Sudan was bound up with his humanitarian credentials, but it developed in an unexpected way, when Gordon asked Zobeir, a notorious slave trader with whom he had fallen out in the 1870s, during a previous stint in Egypt, to take charge. Gordon's decision to approach Zobeir, supported by Baring, was based on his assessment that the Sudan required a powerful figure to hold the Mahdi in check, while Egyptian forces were withdrawn. But in Britain, his suggestion was met with disbelief and turned down. 'I am sure this country won't stand his appointment by us', Northbrook wrote to Baring. 'They have winced a

[72] *Derby Diaries*, 7 Oct. 1875, 25 Feb. 1876, 245, 280.
[73] H. W. Bates to Kirk, 8 Nov. 1872, NLS, Acc 9942/6.     [74] Gavin, 'Frere', 137–41.
[75] Northbrook to Baring, 26 Dec. 1883, NA, FO 633/4, 14–15.

little at Gordon's Slave Proclamation ... There is no feeling so strong in England as the Anti-Slave Trade feeling and, once roused, it will not be easy to allay it.'[76] Gladstone saw some merit in Gordon's proposal, but recognised any revival in the slave trade in the Sudan was 'likely to cause great excitement in this country'.[77] After Gordon's death, Gladstone claimed that the decision not to approve Zobeir – who might have prevented Gordon's death – 'was the judgment of the cabinet, it was no less the judgment of parliament and the people'.[78] Ministers believed that they would have lost a vote in the House of Commons, precipitating a dissolution or a Conservative government, had they approved Gordon's request. Public opinion, moved by anti-slavery sentiment, shaped policy at this crucial juncture in Anglo-Egyptian relations.

However, public enthusiasm could not be maintained at a high level for long periods of time. Once the initial goal was achieved, humanitarian sentiment waned and so did the vigour of government measures. 'Since the news of the signature of the Treaty [of 1873]', commented the orientalist, George Badger, 'all interest in the question has subsided and not even the publication of the blue books has revived it'.[79] George Clerk warned Frere that 'you must not expect that this Government cares, or that the next will care "tuppence" for slavery out there – except for party purposes'.[80] Yet 'party purposes' had its own value, particularly in keeping governments aware of anti-slavery issues, as the debate over Zobeir demonstrated. Governments, of whatever hue, did not want to face accusations that they had besmirched the British tradition of helping the oppressed and spreading liberty. Questions in parliament, public meetings, and the well-placed editorial or letter ensured that the government could not ignore humanitarian concerns, even in the absence of the periodical and intense public campaigns.

### Strategy and impact

Before the conquest of large parts of Africa, British strategy to suppress the slave trade was based on naval power, diplomatic pressure, and

---

[76] Northbrook to Baring, 7 Mar. 1884, NA, FO 633/4, 32.
[77] Gladstone to Granville, 22 Feb. 1884, in Agatha Ramm (ed.), *The Political Correspondence of Mr Gladstone and Lord Granville, 1876–1886*, II (Oxford: Oxford University Press, 1962), 160.
[78] Cited in John Morley, *The Life of William Ewart Gladstone*, vol. III: *1880–1898* (London: Macmillan, 1903), 160.
[79] Badger to Kirk, 24 Sept. 1873, NLS, Acc 9942/8.
[80] Clerk to Frere, 26 June 1873, in John Martineau, *The Life and Correspondence of Sir Bartle Frere*, II (London: John Murray, 1895), 113.

Table 1 *The slave trade of East Africa in the nineteenth century*[81]

| Sector | Volume in thousands | Percentage |
|---|---|---|
| Arabia, Persia, India | 347 | 23.3 |
| South-east Africa | 276 | 18.6 |
| Mascarenes | 95 | 6.4 |
| East African Coast | 769 | 51.7 |

Table 2 *Imports of slaves, in thousands, into Egypt, 1800–1880*[82]

| Decade | P/A average | Total | Decade | P/A average | Total |
|---|---|---|---|---|---|
| 1810–20 | 3 | 30 | 1850–60 | 3 | 30 |
| 1820–40 | 8 | 160 | 1860–70 | 20 | 200 |
| 1840–50 | 5 | 50 | 1870–80 | 2 | 20 |

cooperation with local officials. Strategy reflected the strengths and weaknesses of British power around the globe – dominance of the seas, economic hegemony, the support, albeit inconstant, of public opinion, the unwillingness to commit land forces, and cooperation with local elites. Britain dented the slave trade and harassed slavers, but it would require the presence of land forces and the occupation of territory to bring an end to the slave trade (especially on the East African Coast – see Table 1) and to slavery itself. The limits of British strategy and power explain, in part, the gradual suppression of the slave trade. Even after occupation and conquest, British policy progressed cautiously, making use of institutions set up in the 1870s. Moreover, assessments of British policy are complicated by incomplete data.

It is important to bear in mind that reductions in the slave trade (evident in Table 2) were linked to changing economic circumstances, war, and famine, as well as British policy.[83] In 1887, Baring reported that 2,628 slaves had been manumitted in 1886 and 2,075 the previous year. 'I certainly regard slavery in Egypt as a moribund institution', he told Salisbury.[84] Given that about 2,000 slaves per annum were imported into Egypt in the 1870s, the rate of manumission was

[81] Lovejoy, *Transformations*, 150.
[82] Austen, 'Trans-Saharan Slave Trade', 35.
[83] Lt Col. Miles to Granville, 1 Mar. 1883, *PP*, 1884, XXV, 80–2.
[84] Baring to Salisbury, 12 Feb. 1887, *PP*, 1887, XLII, 7–8.

impressive. The manumission bureaux and the anti-slavery institutions, in general, became more effective under British occupation. The basis for these institutions had been laid by agreements concluded in the 1870s. The numbers of slaves captured in Zanzibar and liberated by the Vice-Admiralty court were very low. It would require the occupation of Egypt and the establishment of a protectorate over Zanzibar, leading to the abolition of slavery in 1897, to prosecute the anti-slave trade and anti-slavery policy with a much greater degree of success.

The navy was the obvious instrument of British power in the Red Sea and further south as far as Zanzibar. The threat of bombardment forced the Sultan of Zanzibar to accept the terms of the 1873 treaty. Kirk claimed that the threat of bombardment was essential in securing the agreement of the sultan, as he was able to show his Arab subjects the dangers of rejecting British entreaties.[85] The presence of gun-boats could make clear to local administrative elites that Britain expected the implementation of anti-slave trade agreements.

The naval squadron in East Africa was also expected to intercept dhows, which carried the slaves from East Africa to Arabia. Rear Admiral Corbett, in his 1879 report on the slave trade in East Africa, argued that naval patrols had reduced the trade to a 'mere smuggling business' between the mainland and the island of Pemba.[86] However, there were a number of problems with this reliance on the naval squadron. First and foremost, the coastline was vast and the number of ships was small. 'Slaves continue to pass from Zeila, our cruisers are useless to prevent their passing', Gordon told Allen.[87] The chances of capturing dhows were low, though the navy tried various schemes of deployment to maximise their coverage of the maritime slave trade routes. For instance, journeys only took place at certain times of the year, when there were favourable winds. It was possible to concentrate ships at particular ports. Officers were also frustrated by their inability to stop the slave trade in the Red Sea, where slavers enjoyed the protection of the Turkish flag, at least until the convention of 1880.[88] The anti-slave trade convention with Turkey ensured that the major powers along the East African and Red Sea coast now formed a treaty network with Britain aimed at suppressing the slave trade. Until then, there were significant holes in the network.

[85] Martineau, *Frere*, 111.
[86] Rear Admiral Corbett to the Admiralty, 8 Aug. 1879, *PP*, 1880, LXIX, 315–18.
[87] Gordon to Allen, 29 Sept. 1880, BL, Add MS 47609, fo. 51.
[88] Rear Admiral Corbett to the Admiralty, 8 Aug. 1879, *PP*, 1880, LXIX, 315–18; Rear Admiral Jones to Admiralty, 24 Sept. 1880, *PP*, 1881, LXIX, 419–22.

Even naval officers accepted, later, that a land-based strategy would have produced more effective and immediate results.[89] Naval power only affected the immediate coastline, as a blockade was meaningless in the context of African economic and social structures – with the exception of the island of Zanzibar. Kirk, assessing the 1873 treaty with Zanzibar, argued that the real breakthrough came with the decision of the sultan to attack the slave trade on the East African mainland. The number of 'raw slaves' captured by British cruisers had fallen from 458 in 1876 to 102 in 1878 to 15 in 1879 – yet he estimated that around 10,000–12,000 slaves were transported to Pemba each year.[90] By the time of the 1890 Brussels Conference, Kirk claimed that the 'extension of Port[uguese] and German influence on the mainland will do more than our cruisers to stop it'. The memorandum concluded: 'Very exaggerated views have been held about the value of cruisers. The Slave Trade at sea has been reduced on the East Coast by work on shore, not afloat … At present our cruisers are the most expensive and least valuable of all the means we employ.'[91] Gordon pointed out that the naval measures had the paradoxical effect of actually increasing the suffering of the captured slaves, who now were marched on longer and more gruelling routes to points along the coast, where the Royal Navy was absent.[92]

However, a naval squadron could complement other measures against the slave trade. Britain relied on cooperation with local elites. Vivian described the division of labour: 'We must look to the Egyptian authorities to do their duty in putting a stop to the Slave Traffic on land, and as far as we are concerned do our utmost to put a term to it by sea'.[93] Yet Britain did not completely ignore anti-slave trade measures in the interior. Often cooperation was underpinned by the appointment of a British subject to implement the anti-slave trade measures on behalf of the local ruler. These appointments bolstered British prestige and influence.[94] The best-known example is Charles Gordon, who headed the Khedive's administration in the Sudan and took control of anti-slave trade measures in the Sudan and on the East African coast, after forcing the resignation of another British officer, Captain Malcolm, from the Khedive's service.[95] Despite his messianic temperament, Gordon was

---

[89] 'Memoirs', NMM, FIE 43, fos. 103–4, 137–8.
[90] Kirk to Salisbury, 23 Feb. 1880, PP, 1881, LXIX, 296–7.
[91] Kirk, 'The Brussels Conference', NLS Acc 9942/14.
[92] Gordon to Cooper, 18 May 1874, BL, Add MS 47609, fos. 1–4.
[93] Vivian to Salisbury, 15 May 1879, NA, FO 84/1545, fo. 99.
[94] FO to Vivian, 22 Nov. 1877, NA, FO 84/1473, fo. 58.
[95] Alice Moore-Harell, Gordon and the Sudan: Prologue to the Mahdiyya, 1877–1880 (London: Frank Cass, 2001).

realistic about the abolition of slavery and the slave trade in Africa. On occasion, he argued that as long as there was a demand for slaves, the slave trade would continue to exist.[96] This did not mean that Britain should not try to suppress the slave trade, but it signalled his understanding that anti-slave trade measures would take considerable time to have an effect.

Gordon was the land-arm of British anti-slave trade policy. Although he was appointed and paid by the Khedive, he was in regular contact with British officials. Vivian held Gordon in high regard, though Gordon called the diplomat a 'stuck-up donkey'.[97] The Khedive approached the British government on several occasions for advice about appointments to anti-slave trade posts and the credibility of the British officers in the Egyptian service derived from their nationality.[98] When Captain Malcolm resigned, following a row with Gordon, Foreign Office officials expressed their concerns and looked for reassurances that this did not signal an easing of Egyptian anti-slave trade policy.

The internal weakness of states, such as Egypt and Zanzibar, thwarted the implementation of British anti-slave trade strategy. Gordon, familiar with the frailties of the Khedive's authority, argued that the Khedive was too weak to take effective action against powerful slave traders.[99] In the late 1870s, Foreign Office officials expressed their annoyance at Gordon's refusal to push the anti-slave trade agenda. Wylde conceded that Gordon had a 'difficult position', but refused to shut his eyes to the fact that Gordon 'supports authorities who have been taken red-handed in Slave Traffic in defiance of the Khedive's orders'.[100] The Foreign Office preferred to turn a blind eye to these incidents, regarding them as internal Egyptian affairs. Vivian summed up the new policy: 'On the whole I am well satisfied with the way in which the Slave Trade is being attacked in its strongholds; the measures taken may not satisfy the zealous champions of the abolition of slavery, but I believe that if Colonel Gordon be allowed to continue his work as hitherto, strongly supported by the central government, the cure he will effect will be radical and complete'.[101] Vivian's accommodation with Gordon over anti-slave trade policy was based on hope and reflected the absence of any alternatives.

[96] Gordon to Cooper, 18 May 1874, BL, Add MS 47609, fo. 1; Gordon to Tenterden, 23 Aug. 1878, NA, FO 363/1, fos. 464–5.
[97] Gordon to his sister, 12 Feb. 1877, BL, Add MS 51294, fo. 8.
[98] FO to Vivian, 20 Mar. 1878, NA, FO 84/1511, fos. 25–30.
[99] Vivian to Derby, 22 Mar. 1878, NA, FO 84/1511, fo. 135.
[100] Wylde, minute, 18 June 1878, NA, FO 84/1511, fos. 205–6.
[101] Vivian to Salisbury, 31 Aug. 1878, NA, FO 84/1511, fos. 248–9.

If Britain had pursued its anti-slave trade policy more vigorously, it could have been counter-productive. Britain was already relying on weakened states – Turkey, Zanzibar, and Egypt – whose authority in their outlying regions was dependent on local elites. These elites had commercial and cultural interests in the maintenance of slavery and the slave trade. Even when anti-slave trade measures were implemented with caution, as was the case in Zanzibar and Egypt, anti-slave trade policies generated significant local opposition and weakened the states further. There were outbreaks of violence in Arabia, especially Jeddah, revolts on the East African coast, the growing discontent of Arab subjects in Zanzibar, conflicts in Lower Egypt, and the rise of the Mahdi in the Sudan.[102] Anti-slave trade policies were only one of the external pressures on these states; wars and the global, capitalist economy were others. For instance, the drop in slave imports in Egypt in the 1870s can be attributed to the re-emergence of American cotton production after the civil war and the collapse of Egyptian cotton production. The modernisation process, often financed by loans from European creditors and governments, undermined social structures in East Africa and the Ottoman Empire.

The weakness of local administrative structures and the resistance of societies to the imposition of humanitarian values threatened British strategy against the slave trade. The collapse of these states – Egypt in the early 1880s and Zanzibar in the 1870s and 1890s – led to British occupation and firmer implementation of anti-slavery measures. It is important to distinguish, however, between motive, cause, and effect. Britain did not pursue an anti-slave trade strategy in order to prompt the collapse of states and enable them to occupy territory. This was the outcome of a wider process, driven by the cumulative effect of numerous decisions in an era of globalisation – in the world economy and also in human rights. The capitalist economy was one feature of this process of globalisation, but it ran parallel, rather than being specifically related, to anti-slave trade policies.

The suppression of the slave trade and the abolition of slavery were the outcome of a gradual process. Neither the British government nor the rulers in East Africa had a sustained interest in the issue. The humanitarian context was crucial to the formation and implementation

---

[102] P. M. Holt, *The Mahdist State in the Sudan, 1881–1898: A Study of its Origins and Overthrow* (Oxford: Oxford University Press, 1958), 29–30; Alexander Schölch suggests that Arabi would have abolished slavery, had his movement not been overthrown by Britain's occupation, *Egypt for the Egyptians: The Socio-Political Crisis in Egypt, 1878–1882* (London: Middle East Centre, St Antony's College, 1981), 221.

of policy. The impetus came from the British popular humanitarianism, the persistence of a small number of officials, and the desire (at times) of Egyptian, Turkish, and Zanzibar rulers to present their rule in a light that appealed to Britain. These impulses were often short lived. Nonetheless, the achievements were significant, especially in the 1870s, when a number of treaties and conventions were agreed, which set up the institutions that would enable a more vigorous implementation of British policy after the occupation of Egypt in 1882 and the establishment of a protectorate in Zanzibar in 1890. Given that policy was framed by treaty law and the desire to maintain stability, the process of suppressing the trade and abolition was gradual, but the trend was unmistakable, as slavery became a moribund institution in large parts of Africa in the late nineteenth and early twentieth centuries.

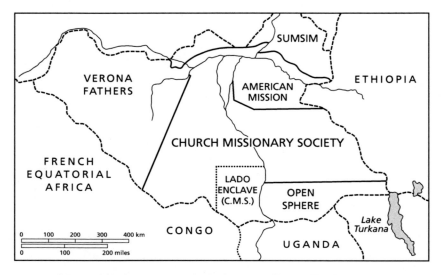

Map 8 Missionary zones in Sudan since World War II.

# 12   The origins of humanitarian intervention in Sudan: Anglo-American missionaries after 1899

*Gideon Mailer*

> We have no other way to conceive of anything which other persons act or suffer, but by recalling and exciting the ideas of what we ourselves are conscious we have found in our own minds; and by ... substituting ourselves in their place.
>
> Jonathan Edwards, *The Nature of True Virtue* (1758)[1]

During the nineteenth century, the origins of the Anglo-American Protestant missionary spirit were often attributed to the writings of Jonathan Edwards.[2] Composed between 1730 and 1758, his main works discussed the nature of subjective moral discernment. They depicted humans as imprisoned by their sensory perceptions, each objectively disconnected from the other. Without acknowledging this isolating predicament, individuals were prevented from achieving the salvation of grace, and its communal connection.[3] In *The Nature of True Virtue*

---

[1] Jonathan Edwards, *The Nature of True Virtue* (1765), ed. William K. Frankena (Ann Arbor: University of Michigan Press, 1960), 64.

[2] See Oliver W. Elsbree, *The Rise of the Missionary Spirit in America, 1790–1815* (Williamsport, PA: Williamsport Printing, 1928); Wolfgang Eberhard Lowe, 'The First American Foreign Missionaries: "The Students", 1810–1820', PhD diss., Brown University (1962), chs. 2–3; R. Pierce Beaver, 'Missionary Motivation through Three Centuries', in *Reinterpretation in American Church History*, ed. Jerald Brauer (Chicago: University of Chicago Press, 1968), 121–6; Clifton J. Phillips, *Protestant America and the Pagan World: The First Half Century of the American Board of Commissioners for Foreign Missions, 1810–1860* (Cambridge, MA: East Asian Research Center, Harvard University, 1969), ch. 1; Charles L. Chaney, *The Birth of Missions in America* (South Pasadena, CA: William Carey Library, 1976), 74–84, 188–9, 192–5, 269–74; Joseph Conforti, *Samuel Hopkins and the New Divinity Movement: Calvinism, the Congregational Ministry, and Reform between the Great Awakenings* (Grand Rapids, MI: Christian University Press, 1981), 157–8; Genevieve McCoy, 'Reason for a Hope': Evangelical Women Making Sense of Late Edwardsian Calvinism', in *Jonathan Edwards' Writings: Text, Context, Interpretation*, ed. Stephen J. Stein (Bloomington: Indiana University Press, 1996), 175–92; Dana L. Robert, *American Women in Mission: A Social History of Their Thought and Practise* (Macon, GA: Mercer University Press, 1996), 3–10.

[3] See Jonathan Edwards, 'The Beauty of the World', in *The Sermons of Jonathan Edwards: A Reader*, ed. Wilson H. Kimnach, Kenneth P. Minkema, and Douglas A. Sweeney (New Haven: Yale University Press, 1999), 14; Edwards, *Nature of True Virtue*, 64; *The Works of Jonathan Edwards: Scientific and Philosophical Writings*, ed. Wallace E. Anderson (New

(written 1755–8, though not published until 1765), Edwards described conversion as a harmony 'between individual being and Being in general'. Humans perceived the suffering of others only by 'recalling and exciting the ideas of what we ourselves are conscious'. The lack of sympathy between unregenerate beings inevitably resulted in warfare and violence.[4] What could be done to prevent common affliction resulting in communal disorder in areas untouched by New Testament theology? If depravity was universal, how could individuals and nations justify intervention in the lives of others, to reduce their miserable lot?

By the nineteenth century, Anglo-American missionaries responded to these questions.[5] They outlined the common need for 'regeneration': oppressor was to achieve 'true' sympathy with the oppressed, persecuted with persecutor. In an 1816 sermon before the American Board of Commissioners for Foreign Missions, Henry Davis, the 'New Divinity' head of Middlebury College, noted that all peoples in the world were 'members of the same family; as candidates for the same immortality; and to be saved, if saved at all, with the same everlasting salvation'.[6] Privileged Americans and Britons were no better off eternally than the 'millions grovelling in ignorance, in sottishness and pollution'.[7] As Andrew Walls has more recently argued, the transatlantic revivalism that connected Britain and America during the eighteenth century also clarified the unity between the sinful homeland and the sinful heathen further abroad:

That spiritual parity of the unregenerate of Christendom and the heathen abroad had important missionary consequences ... A consistent view of human solidarity in depravity shielded the first missionary generation from some of the worst excesses of racism.[8]

Haven: Yale University Press, 1980), 344. For the biblical precedent they used, see Gal. 5.17–21; Eph. 2.4–10; Rom. 5.6–8; Col. 2:13–15.

[4] Susan Manning, *The Puritan-Provincial Vision* (Cambridge: Cambridge University Press, 1990), 35.

[5] See David W. Kling, 'The New Divinity and the Origins of the American Board of Commissioners for Foreign Missions', in *North American Foreign Missions, 1810–1914*, ed. Wilbert R. Shenk (Grand Rapids, MI: Eerdmans, 2004), 12; Joseph Conforti, 'David Brainerd and the Nineteenth Century Missionary Movement', *Journal of the Early Republic* 5 (Fall 1985), 309–29; Conforti, *Jonathan Edwards, Religious Tradition, and American Culture* (Chapel Hill: University of North Carolina Press, 1995), ch. 3.

[6] Henry Davis, *A Sermon, delivered before the American Board of Commissioners for Foreign Missions* (Boston: Samuel T. Armstrong, 1816), 24.

[7] *Ibid.*

[8] Andrew Finlay Walls, 'The Evangelical Revival, the Missionary Movement and Africa', in *Evangelicalism: Comparative Studies of Popular Protestantism in North America, the British Isles and beyond, 1700–1990*, ed. Marc Noll (Oxford: Oxford University Press, 1994), 310.

If individuals acknowledged that they were as morally estranged from those within their community as those without, they could be reconciled with their warring enemies.

Evangelicalism provided a framework for cooperation between nations, whose missionaries sought to intervene in the affairs of a third party. It inspired joint operations between British and American missionaries towards the end of the nineteenth century, particularly in Southern Sudan.[9] They provide the focus for this chapter.

The provinces of Bahr el Ghazal, Equatoria and Upper Nile had been ravaged by slavery and killing during their occupation by Ottoman and Mahdist forces. Their various ethnic groups were suspended in suspicion and animosity against Northern Sudanese communities. Missionaries gained permission from the British government to enter the south in 1899. Much of their theology was covenantal. This was particularly the case among American Presbyterians. Reflecting the 'Puritan' origins of Anglo-American revivalism, missionaries claimed that covenants were always to be tested.[10] Support for southerners was framed as a divine gift, which followed their own 'test' of suffering. Despite the universality of human affliction, its specific manifestation in their lives (slavery and war) provided the means to receive salvation. The common connection provided by grace was perceived as an empowering response to the violent onslaughts they continued to endure.[11] Many missionaries harnessed their role as non-state actors to gain greater legitimacy among those with whom they worked. They appeared to some in the south as a buttress against both

---

[9] So famous was Edwards in Britain that historians have even linked his 1746 work on *The Life of Brainerd*, with its call for a 'United Concert of Prayer', to Britain's growing support for foreign missions and foreign interventions in the lives of troubled communities. Missionaries carried copies of the *Life of Brainerd* into the field with them, especially in the context of warfare. Gideon Hawley wrote from his position amongst the Oneida: 'I read my Bible & Mr. Brainerds life the only Books I bro't with me, and from them have a little support.' Diary entry, June 3, 1753, American Congregational Library, Boston, MA, The Papers of Gideon Hawley. For the continuation of this Edwardsean sentiment in the nineteenth century, see Conforti, *Jonathan Edwards*, 62–86; Conforti, *Samuel Hopkins and the New Divinity Movement*.

[10] See, for example, Sacvan Bercovitch, *The Puritan Origins of the American Self* (New Haven: Yale University Press, 1977).

[11] On the ability for evangelical revival to break down boundaries between southern communities through its equalising tendency, see, for example, Charles R. Watson, *The Sorrow and Hope of the Egyptian Sudan: A Survey of Missionary Conditions and Methods of Work in the Egyptian Sudan* (Philadelphia: United Presbyterian Church of North America, 1913).

British and northern 'Arab' forces. The developing southern perception of missionaries caused much anxiety in London during the colonial period. After Sudan's independence, suspicion was transferred to Khartoum, and emanated from its 'Arab' political elites. In 1964, missionaries were officially expelled by the northern-dominated Sudanese government. Tragically, we will see, no further intervention from any outside actor took place in these later years, which witnessed the death of an entire generation of young southerners.

### Missionary opposition to slavery in Sudan: a cover for secular rule?

In what was formally an Anglo-Egyptian condominium, with Khartoum's governor appointed by 'Khedival Decree', Britain assumed most institutional power in Sudan after 1899.[12] British public opinion supported this consolidation of power against the Mahdi army partly because of the memory of Charles George Gordon's massacre alongside 50,000 other people during the fall of Khartoum in 1885.[13] Gordon had been fighting alongside Egyptian authorities to prevent Sudan's more 'indigenous' Islamic revival from gaining a hold on the region, and threatening Anglo-Egyptian control of the Suez Canal.[14] Anti-slavery societies in London, however, understood Gordon's defeat in moral terms: his devout faith, and his professed wish to intervene against slavery and injustice in Sudan, resulted in an intercession that brought about his own martyrdom. During Sudan's Condominium period (1899–1955), Anglo-American missionaries made known their opposition to the system of slavery that had developed during the Turco-Egyptian and Mahdist regimes (1821–97). They linked their opposition to the legacy of Gordon.[15]

The entry of the American Presbyterian Church mission (APM) and the British Anglican Church Missionary Society (CMS) followed a more

---

[12] See Robert Collins, *The Southern Sudan in Historical Perspective* (New Brunswick: Transaction, 2006), 32–67.
[13] See John Wolffe, *God and Greater Britain: Religion and National Life in Britain and Ireland, 1843–1945* (London: Routledge, 1994), 226–7.
[14] See Stephen J. Lee, *Gladstone and Disraeli* (London: Routledge, 2005), 105.
[15] See Roland Werner et al., *Day of Devastation, Day of Contentment: The History of the Sudanese Church Across 2000 Years* (Nairobi: Pauline Publications, 2000), 194–5.

informal and largely European Catholic missionary presence in the region since the early nineteenth century. Catholics had been met with suspicion in southern Sudan. White missionaries were often associated with the 'Turks' who came before them. A missionary report of 1850 stated:

We sailed along deserted banks, because the poor savages living near the river are in constant fear of the Turks, from whom they often receive cruel treatment, especially from the annual expedition.[16]

Historians have reserved similar suspicion for Anglo-American missionaries. While stopping short of associating them with Ottoman slavers, they are often connected to Britain's secular colonial hegemony, which used the fear of slavery to divide South against North, 'African' against 'Arab'. There remains a degree of scepticism regarding the moral claims of missionaries who professed their wish to protect southern Sudanese communities from warfare and slavery directed from the North. For Beshir Said, these claims 'left no stone unturned to intensify the feelings of Southerners against the North'.[17] Daly argues that the sense of southern separateness in the provinces of Bahr al-Ghazal, Upper Nile and Equatoria continued as an open sore because of the 'constant reminders of the nineteenth century slave trade'.[18]

Indeed, Charles George Gordon's subsequent reputation among missionaries was not entirely accurate. As he tried to form a coalition within Sudan against the Mahdi Army, he made significant compromises with those who supported the trafficking of slaves from southern 'African' regions to those in the 'Arab' north.[19] While he continued to oppose slavery publicly, he felt that its eventual eradication might necessitate compromises with slave traders in the short term.[20] Instances of slavery even increased during the final decades of the nineteenth century.[21] These facts suggest to some that the legend of Gordon was a convenient cover for

[16] Cited in E. Toniolo, 'The First Centenary of the Roman Catholic Mission to Central Africa, 1846–1946', *Sudan Notes and Records* 27 (1946), 102.

[17] Mohamed Beshir Said, *The Southern Sudan, Background to Conflict* (New York: Frederick A. Praeger, 1968), 22–7.

[18] Martin Daly, 'Islam, Secularism, and Ethnic Identity in the Sudan', in *Religion and Political Power*, ed. Gustavo Benavides and Martin Daly (New York: State University of New York Press, 1989), 84–5.

[19] See Alice Moore-Harell, 'Slave Trade in the Sudan in the Nineteenth Century and its Suppression in the Years 1877–80', *Middle Eastern Studies* 34:2 (1998), 113–28; Robert O. Collins, *Civil Wars and Revolution in the Sudan* (Hollywood: Tsehai Publishers, 2005), 332.

[20] See M. A. Gordon, *Letters of General C. G. Gordon to his Sister* (London, 1897), l, 13; G. B. Hill, *Colonel Gordon in Central Africa 1874–1879*, 4th edn (New York: Kraus Reprint Co., 1969), 225–6; Moore-Harell, 'Slave Trade in the Sudan', 118.

[21] See Moore-Harell, 'Slave Trade in the Sudan', 122–4.

missionaries. Their humanitarian impetus was less related to abolitionism than it was to the manufacture of divisions between North and South, and the spread of 'Western' religion within this conflicted context. American and British missionaries are charged with the partial creation and fermentation of Sudan's subsequent problem of national unity, the so-called 'Southern Problem'.[22] Their humanitarian rhetoric has been deemed a Western chimera, designed to keep two subaltern peoples in conflict.[23]

### Missionaries as non-state actors and the growth of southern political identity

Despite this critique, it is a stretch to suggest that communities in southern and Nuban regions would somehow have forgotten their experiences of slavery, only to be reminded of the issue by those with a vested interest in fomenting animosity. The destruction of the Nuba people through enslavement and violence occurred between 1850 and 1900. They, along with their neighbours in Southern Darfur and Western Bahr el Ghazal, were devastated by a slave route that followed the ivory trade directly through their region. Zubeir Pasha, a northern slave lord, established a monopoly in these areas. Those who survived his campaigns mostly took refuge in the Nuban Mountains. There they remained after Kitchener's victory in Khartoum, subject to repeated slave raids well into the twentieth century. Their mountainous asylum was not a missionary invention. K. D. D. Henderson, who had surveyed the surrounding region over previous decades, wrote in 1965:

Up till the middle 'twenties the Baggara were still lifting slaves south of the river and disposing of them to inaccessible markets far to the north. When not slave raiding they were poaching elephants or hunting giraffe or lifting cattle.[24]

---

[22] See, for example, Beshir, *The Southern Sudan*, 22–7; Martin Daly, 'Islam, Secularism, and Ethnic Identity in the Sudan', in *Religion and Political Power*, ed. Gustavo Benavides and Martin Daly (New York: State University of New York Press, 1989), 84–5.

[23] On supposed American and Anglo-American missionary 'imperialism', see especially Arthur Schlesinger, Jr., 'The Missionary Enterprise and Theories of Imperialism', in *The Missionary Enterprise in China and America*, ed. John K. Fairbank (Cambridge, MA: Harvard University Press, 1974), 336–73; William R. Hutchinson, 'A Moral Equivalent for Imperialism: Americans and the Promotion of Christian Civilisation, 1880–1910', in *Missionary Ideologies in the Imperialist Era: 1880–1920*, ed. Hutchinson and Torben Christensen (Aarhus: Christensens Bogtrykkeri, 1982), 167–78.

[24] K. D. D. Henderson, *Sudan Republic* (London: Frederick A. Praeger, 1966), 162.

Given the sustained threat to southern communities after 1899, we ought to view the humanitarian zeal of missionaries during the Condominium period with less cynicism. The invocation of the slave legacy was explicitly discouraged by colonial administrators, who feared that any increased consciousness of the issue in the south would cause unrest, and make governance more difficult. North and South were administered as separate colonies, even if joint jurisdiction had been implemented in principle by early colonial legislation.[25] Just as Gordon was forced to placate pro-slavery forces during the 1880s, British leaders feared upsetting northern Arab elites by focusing on the issue of slavery after 1899.[26] Since 1905, specifically 'moral' and religious teaching, including references to the immorality of servitude, had been banned in the context of 'official' education. It was feared that a heightened perception of collective persecution would lead to an enhanced 'southern' identity.[27] Instead, missionaries were implored to teach secular subjects such as literacy and numeracy.[28] That they continued to invoke their moral cause against slavery, despite British opposition, further separated their role in the region from colonial authorities.[29]

In 1930, Rev. Wilson Cash, Secretary of the Church Missionary Society, recalled the development of a 'neutral' British policy over the previous decades, which failed to prevent continued slaver incursions. In a typically jaundiced view of the time, he associated the alternative to the missionary presence in the region with the 'capture' and servitude of Southerners, which British authorities would do little to prevent. After referring to continued forced labour and violence against southern communities, he wrote:

[25] See Martin Daly, *Empire on the Nile: The Anglo-Egyptian Sudan, 1898–1934* (Cambridge: Cambridge University Press, 2004), 71–82.

[26] See Harold MacMichael, *The Sudan* (London: Frederick A. Praeger, 1955), 91–118, 137–40; Lillian M. Sanderson and Neville G. Sanderson, *Education, Religion and Politics in Southern Sudan, 1899–1964* (London: Ithaca Press, 1981), 51–71, 147–63.

[27] See Charles R. Watson, *The Sorrow and Hope of the Egyptian Sudan: A Survey of Missionary Conditions and Methods of Work in the Egyptian Sudan* (Philadelphia: United Presbyterian Church of North America 1913).

[28] See Oliver Albino, *The Sudan: A Southern Viewpoint* (London: Institute of Race Relations and Oxford University Press, 1970), 16–19; Sanderson and Sanderson, *Education, Religion, and Politics*, 78–103; Abdel Rahim, 'The Development of British Policy in the Southern Sudan, 1899–1947', *Middle Eastern Journal* 2:3 (April 1966), 238.

[29] See Robert O. Collins, 'The Establishment of Christian Missions and their Rivalry in the Southern Sudan', *Tarikh* 3 (Jan.–Mar. 1969), 96, 39; Collins, *Land Beyond the Rivers: The Southern Sudan, 1898–1918* (New Haven and London: Yale University Press, 1971), 284, 286.

The Government is scrupulously fair to Moslems ... and in religious matters adopts a strictly neutral attitude. The task of evangelization is no part of the Government's work and it falls to the mission alone to decide whether these Southern pagan tribes shall be left to be captured ...[30]

As a result of such sentiment, CMS activity in the region was distinctly politicised: it was linked to the support of southern Sudanese against 'capture' after 'neutral' British authorities had failed to offer the necessary protection. Within this uneasy framework, missionaries even connected their 'secular' teaching to the fight against slavery: if 'African' Sudanese were equipped with basic administrative skills, they would at least be less likely to journey to those rural areas where slave raiders still threatened. Despite the restrictions under which they worked, this was part of the justification that CMS representatives used in order to pioneer more formal schooling for girls, many of whom were also slave descendants. This was especially the case in the schools founded in and around Omdurman in 1900. American Presbyterian Missionaries opened schools in Khartoum, populated mainly by Sudanese ex-slave boys. The CMS followed suit with a similar school in 1902, for girls. They used their experiences in Omdurman to educate slave descendants in a more formal setting.[31]

Colonial administrators had divided the various Anglo-American and European missionary denominations into separate 'spheres' that matched the separate ethnic regions they delineated in the South.[32] Authorities also placed missionary centres away from administrative headquarters, fearing that colonial legitimacy would be threatened by any alternative source of support for indigenous communities in close proximity.[33] Yet in the eyes of some southern Sudanese, this policy emphasised the humanitarian cause of missionaries. The geographical separation of missionary and colonial centres allowed religious groups to present themselves as a 'third party' acting on behalf of those who were caught between two other interests (Northern and British).

[30] Wilson Cash, *The Changing Sudan* (London: Christian Mission Society, 1930), 54.
[31] Heather Sharkey, 'Christians among Muslims: The Church Missionary Society in the Northern Sudan', *Journal of African History* 43:11 (2002), 63–4.
[32] See Wal Duany, 'Neither Palaces nor Prisons: The Constitution of Order among the Nuer', PhD diss., Indiana University (1992), 298; Richard L. Hill, 'Government and Christian Missions in the Anglo-Egyptian Sudan, 1899–1914', *Middle Eastern Studies* 1:2 (1965), 123–4; Philip Legge Pitya, 'A History of Western Christian Evangelism in Sudan, 1898–1964', PhD diss., Boston University Graduate School (1996); Collins, *Land Beyond*, 291–3.
[33] See Pitya, 'History of Western Christian Evangelism', 207–20; Arnaldo Violine, 'The History of Our Mission, Lul', *The Messenger*, Wau (Feb./Mar. 1937), 13.

Local southern leaders were more likely to de-couple missionaries from colonial governance, which provoked more ambivalent, or even negative, reactions. According to Lamin Sanneh:

By their root conviction that the gospel is transmissible in the mother tongue, I suggest, missionaries opened the way for the local idiom to gain the ascendancy over assertions of [colonial] foreign policy.[34]

In southern Sudan in the first half of the twentieth century, the colonial 'assertion of foreign policy' did not explicitly oppose existing injustice, even if its authority prevented a resurgence of slavery on nineteenth-century levels. If missionary actions were distanced from colonial power, they were likely to be seen by indigenous Southerners as more 'humanitarian', offering greater 'vernacular' appeal.[35]

Francis Deng was born the son of tribal leader Deng Majok in southern Sudan in 1938. He has suggested that 'Christianization' took place partly because missionaries were associated with a specifically external intervention against slavery and persecution, separate from the more ambiguously perceived colonial political order:

Christianity also benefited from the sense that Europeans had come to rescue the Southerners from enslavement by Arabs. This understanding was, of course, a bit innocent, for some nineteenth-century Europeans were in fact engaged in the slave trade, but their involvement was hidden by their reliance on Egyptian or Northern Sudanese middlemen whom Southern Sudanese saw as the sole culprits.[36]

Having carried out extensive interviews with those who lived in the South during this period, as well as their offspring, Deng goes as far as to use the term 'intervention' in his description of missionary efforts, and their attempt to alter the course of British colonial policy:

Some elders even present the British intervention [in conjunction with Christian missionaries] in the Sudan as motivated by the desire to save the black man from Arab slavers. In view of the pressures by European missionaries on the British

[34] Lamin Sanneh, *Encountering the West: Christianity and the Global Cultural Process: The African Dimension* (London: HarperCollins; Maryknoll and New York: Orbis Books, 1993), 19.

[35] G. Whitehead, 'Social Changes among the Bari', *Sudan Notes and Records* 5:1 (1929), 91–7; Lilian Sanderson, 'Education in the Southern Sudan: The Impact of Government–Missionary–Southern Sudanese Relationships upon the Development of Education during the Condominium Period, 1898–1956', *African Affairs* 79:315 (1980), 166; Sharkey, 'Christians among Muslims', 68.

[36] Francis Mading Deng, 'Sudan – Civil War and Genocide', *Middle East Quarterly* 8:1 (Winter 2001), 8.

government before condominium rule ... this view is not an entirely naïve version of history. Chief Makuei Bilkuei presents the English [who were in fact allied with American Presbyterians] as having been 'brought' by the chiefs to rescue their people: 'It is our fathers – people like Bilkuei, people like Kwol Arob – who brought the English ... [because of] the indignity of the Ansaw were inflicting upon us ... If no one had been taken away to be sold, the English would not have come.'[37]

According to Deng, 'virtually every chief and elder interviewed made the same point' about these 'interventions' in their history.[38] Indeed: 'What is particularly significant about these accounts – however naive they may sound to someone with a sophisticated understanding of history – is that they reflect a perspective of alienation from the North and a degree of moral affinity with the more distant European'.[39]

John Spencer Trimingham, the secretary of the Church Missionary Society in 1945, opposed the 'laissez-faire policy' of the British government towards the maltreatment of the South. He claimed that missionary educational efforts necessarily undermined British attempts to ignore slavery. They had catalysed a 'southern' political 'awakening':

> During the war years the south has been awakening. Many new points of contacts have been set up between southerners [and Anglo-American missionaries]. Those who have received education in mission schools are becoming increasingly conscious of the economic and intellectual disabilities under which they live.[40]

Trimingham associated the role of missionaries as non-state actors with their ability to enhance the political demands of the marginalised South. With the potential for independence from colonial rule becoming more apparent in the late 1940s, he highlighted the moral pressure exerted by missionaries on colonial administrators in the last years of their rule: 'This awakening has brought home to the Government its moral obligation to foster their moral and material welfare so that they can play their part in modern Africa, to which end plans for very considerable future development are now (1945) being prepared'.[41]

As Abel Alier has shown, and as contemporary documents attested, the majority of new southern leaders who called for political equality in the 1940s were missionary-educated, many of them being devout

---

[37] Francis Mading Deng, *War of Visions: Conflict of Identities in the Sudan* (Washington, DC: Brookings Institution Press, 1995), 82.
[38] *Ibid.*    [39] *Ibid.*, 63.
[40] John Spencer Trimingham, *The Christian Approach to Islam in the Sudan* (Oxford: Oxford University Press, 1948), 73.
[41] *Ibid.*

Christians.[42] Those who attended the Juba conference in June 1947, however, were to be bitterly disappointed. Missionaries had 'awoken' the British government's 'moral obligation' towards the South too late in the day. North and South were formally united in Juba, with the interests and representation of the former dominating the resulting agreement.[43] The missionaries who remained in Sudan as it moved towards independence during the following decade were to experience this domination first hand.

## The continued need for intervention in the south after 1953

On the surface, the need for outside support in the South was not apparent in the early days of Sudan's independence. The Arabic-speaking Northerners who came to dominate Sudan's new government initially spoke of religious pluralism within the nation, and the protection of southern Christian communities. At a conference in Juba on 19–22 October 1953, missionary educational and medical support was praised by Awad Satti, the first Sudanese Director of Education. While clearly pointing towards the imminent departure of British secular rulers, he also sought to reassure Southerners that the 'Sudan would continue to rely on the help and cooperation of the missions and would continue to need the fruitful work carried out by them'.[44] Sayed Kosmas Rababa, a Southern Member of Parliament, stated on 26 April 1954:

For fifty years the Southerners have got all their education from the Missions; and the Sudan Government should be grateful ... had it not been for the Missionaries, there would be no Southerners in parliament now.[45]

---

[42] See Abel Alier, *Southern Sudan: Too Many Agreements Dishonoured* (Exeter: Ithaca Press, 1990), 5, 7, 24–35, 73–4, 83–9; Abel Alier, 'The Southern Sudan Question', in *The Southern Sudan: The Problem of National Integration*, ed. Dunstan M. Wai (London: Frank Cass, 1973), 15–18; Victor Ramadan, 'Uses of Education', *The Messenger*, Wau (Sept. 1948), 63; Joseph H. Oduho, 'Senior Education', *The Messenger*, Wau (Sept. 1948), 63; William G. Gbendi and Tarcizio Ahmed, 'School Fees', *The Messenger*, Wau (Sept. 1948), 63.

[43] Oliver Albino, *The Sudan: A Southern Viewpoint* (Oxford: Oxford University Press, 1970), 20–35.

[44] Verona Fathers Mission, *The Black Book of the Sudan on the Expulsion of the Christian Missionaries from Southern Sudan: An Answer* (Milan: Istituto Artigianelli, 1964), 75.

[45] Cited in Scopas Sekwat Poggo, 'War and Conflict in the Southern Sudan, 1955–1972', PhD diss., University of California, Santa Barbara (1999), 159.

Sayed Edward Odhok, another southern politician, added that 'the Missionaries have educated ... the Southern clerks[,] Sub-Mamurs and Ministers. The Missionaries should be thanked for this work.'[46]

This rhetoric of religious pluralism, however, vanished in less than a decade. The racialised language used to justify a potential ban on missionary activity demonstrated just why some saw the continued need for their presence in the South. During the 1950s and 1960s, it became clear that missionaries were resented by new ruling elites not because of the religious differences they helped to create, but because of the ethnic identity of those amongst whom they worked. A dominant form of nationalism corresponded to 'Arab' identity, which was threatened by any intervening force that cemented the southern 'African' cause. This included the indigenisation of missionary activity.[47] The language used by strident northern Sudanese officials differed from their initial statements regarding religious missions. In 1955, the new Department of Religious Affairs sought to spread 'Islam and Arab culture in the non-Arab and non-Islamic parts of the Sudan'.[48] The coupling of the words 'Islam' and 'Arab culture' was particularly telling: religion and race were becoming even more intertwined in this post-colonial setting.[49] Ali Abdel Rahman, Minister of the Interior in the Peoples' Democratic Party (PDP)–Umma Party coalition government of Abdalla Khalil stated in 1958 that 'the Sudan is an integral part of the Arab world ... Anybody dissenting from this view must quit the country.'[50] Northern Sudanese elites saw Islam and Arabism as a mutually inclusive bulwark against any other elements in the country.[51]

---

[46] *Ibid.*
[47] *The Black Book of the Sudan*, 16–17; 'Relations between the Government and the Missionary Organisations during the Era of Foreign Rule', in *Memorandum on Reasons that led to the Expulsion of Foreign Missionaries and Priests from the Southern Provinces of the Sudan* (Khartoum, 1964), 3–4.
[48] 'The Memorandum Presented by the Sudan African National Union to the Commission of the Organization of African Unity for Refugees' (Kampala, Uganda, November 1964), 57.
[49] Such an interpretation is in accordance with the latest historiography of Sudan, which seeks to move our understanding away from any easy dichotomy between northern Muslim and southern Christian, in favour of a north–south conflict based on ethno-racial, rather than religious, difference. See, for example, Gerard Prunier, *Darfur: The Ambiguous Genocide* (Ithaca: Cornell University Press, 2005).
[50] Albino, *The Sudan: A Southern Viewpoint*, 6, citing 'Parliamentary Proceedings: Second Sitting of the First Session of Parliament' (1958), 3.
[51] See 'Relations between the Government and the Missionary Organisations during the Era of Foreign Rule', 3.

Dr Kamal Baghir, the Northern Sudanese head of the Department of Religious Affairs, outlined a missionary policy that demonstrated profoundly racial concerns, and an anxiety regarding the role of missionaries as outside actors. In the Arabic newspaper *Rai El Amm*, he wrote the following on 30 September 1959:

The nationalization of the Mission schools was an important step in the direction which recognizes cultural unification ... and we, of the Department of religious affairs, are ready to do our duty. We have begun with the opening of Islamic centers in the Southern Provinces and we will not cease to work (and are still) in the direction until we have realized the *cultural Islamic unity* which we seek.[52]

The phrase 'Cultural Islamic Unity' represented an ethno-cultural rather than a specifically religious concern. 'Islam' was conflated with a 'culture' that was, by its northern nature, 'Arabic'. Southern students admitted into government schools in the 1960s were 'threatened with loss of education if they go [went] to church on Sunday'.[53] An official of the Ministry of Education in Khartoum testified that children of Christian parents were usually told that no room existed for them. Abboud's publicly stated aim of 'One religion (Islam), one culture, one language (Arabic), one nation (Sudan)' was increasingly apparent.[54] The nationalisation of mission schools in 1957 led the *Voice of Southern Sudan* to link increasing threats against missionaries to Sudan's new national language policy, which restricted the use of English in schools, offices and government departments. Editorial comments related both to the reduction of the South to 'political slavery'.[55]

After the various southern student riots of 1962/3, the Sudan Government accused 'outside' Christian missionary forces of stoking the troubles. Southern spokespeople, as well as Anglo-American religious leaders, warned the world that missionaries were the last line of defence against the imminent racial persecution of Southerners. In a letter to *The Times*, John V. Taylor, the General Secretary of the Church Missionary Society of England (CMS), urged the international media not 'to mask the far more serious issue of the political clash between the Arab-North and the African-South' with the easy diagnosis of religious tension.[56] According to an American *Time Magazine* report filed in February 1963:

[52] Dr Kamal Baghir, *Rai El Amm*, 30 Sept. 1959 (italics supplied).
[53] 'Editorial Comment', *Voice of Southern Sudan* 1:2 (Sudan African National Union, Negritude and Progress, 1963), 12.
[54] *Ibid.*, 2.   [55] *Ibid.*, 9.
[56] 'Letter to *The Times*', London, 13 Mar. 1964, cited in *Voice of Southern Sudan* 2:1 (Apr. 1964), 7–8.

Sudanese officials have cracked down on missionaries on the flimsiest of excuses. Priests and brothers have been fined or jailed for 'illegally' administering medicine to the sick, or admitting orphans to mission compounds.[57]

*The Voice of Southern Sudan* warned that accusations against Western missionaries were meant 'solely to divert and mislead public opinion'. Missionaries were the 'victims of Arab religious chauvinism ... Arab propaganda and double talk'. Religion was used by the Sudan government as a basis for 'national unity' – a phrase that masked northern 'racial chauvinism' over the black South.[58] The word 'Islam' was never mentioned by the southern Sudanese authors of this lament. Rather, they cast themselves, and missionaries, as victims of 'Arab religious' prejudice. To southern representatives, missionaries were their last connection to the outside world, which needed to be made aware of their perilous position.[59] Unfortunately, in 1964 Prime Minister Abdalla expelled missionaries from Sudan.[60] The beginning of heightened racial persecution coincided with their departure. There was a 'growing realization during the 1960s of a servile future that appeared to be confirmed in 1964 by the expulsion of Christian missionaries few of whom had not quoted the Victorian administrators and the Bible about the iniquities of slavery and the slave trade in the Southern Sudan'.[61]

The period 1955–72, especially after the expulsion of missionaries in 1964, amounted to what most historians have termed a civil war.[62] Thousands of southern Sudanese died, and many southern leaders were murdered.[63] Southern communities recognised that their deteriorating relationship with the ruling centre in Khartoum reflected their racial marginalisation, whose roots were to be found in the nineteenth century. Their perception did not need to be stoked by missionary rhetoric. The latter had acted as a buttress against the British colonial and Arab interests that had perpetuated slavery in the nineteenth century, even if British authorities had opposed slavery officially after 1870. During the 1950s and 1960s, when punitive patrols were launched into the countryside against southern Sudanese insurgents, 'they appeared reminiscent of the nineteenth century *razzia* for slaves, the stories of which every child in the South has learned around the cooking fires of the tukul

[57] 'Sudan v. Christians', *Time Magazine*, 1 Feb. 1963.
[58] 'Editorial Comment', *Voice of Southern Sudan* 1:4 (1964), 16.     [59] *Ibid.*
[60] See Ann Mosely Lesch, *The Sudan: Contested National Identities* (Oxford: James Currey, 1998), 39.
[61] Collins, *Civil Wars and Revolution*, 336.
[62] Deng, *War of Visions*, 96.     [63] *Ibid.*, 145

and the cattle camp'.[64] The attempt to crush popular dissent in the South was 'matched by political manipulation in the North to create a unity in the Sudan by Arabisation and Islamisation. This policy only reinforced the perception by the southern Sudanese that they would be the hewers of wood and the drawers of water, the slaves, in any future Sudan.'[65] During the Condominium period missionaries justified their evangelical presence in the South by highlighting their opposition to servitude and collective punishment. Their justification seemed more legitimate in the light of events that followed their expulsion.

### The Edwardsean south: retroactive humanitarianism after 1964

The 1970s and early 1980s heralded a 'second civil war' in which over one million southern Sudanese were killed.[66] The region saw a resurgence in slavery.[67] Some southerners even sought refuge in enslavement, seeing it as an institutional alternative to death.[68]

The Christian religion adhered to by many in the South offered some solace in the face of this new wave of destruction: the suffering of Christ was understood in light of their own persecution, and his death in light of the thousands who lost their own lives. The work of Anglo-American missionaries in Sudan after 1899 was partly responsible for the growth of southern Christianity. By the 1970s, their interventions were reconceived in more universal religious and humanitarian terms: not 'Western', but 'Christian'. This reconception followed the statements of official missionary organisations after their expulsion in 1964. Representatives of the United Presbyterian and Reformed missions had issued a joint declaration to Abboud's government:

We hope that the fact that Christianity is not a Western religion will enable the Sudanese government to reconsider its action on the basis of the fact that in their service to the people of the Sudan the missionaries represent the worldwide Christian community.[69]

Khartoum's subsequent rejection of these statements emphasised the afflicted humanity of missionaries, and allowed their previous actions to be framed as 'humanitarian' in the evangelical sense. Southern converts came to believe even more deeply that 'Christianity and their

---

[64] Collins, *Civil Wars and Revolution*, 336.    [65] *Ibid.*    [66] *Ibid.*, 307–10.
[67] *Ibid.*, 337–8.    [68] *Ibid.*
[69] 'Sudan Expels Missionaries', *Christian Century*, 2 Jan. 1963, 19.

traditional religious and ancestral beliefs derived from the same source'.[70] Northern rhetoric portrayed missionaries as an outside force whose interference in Sudan had therefore lacked legitimacy. Many ethnic groups in the South inverted this reasoning. Their perception of external Christian intervention fused with indigenous conceptions of the spiritual 'Jok', which had long been conceived as a 'protector' that would enter their region from without.[71] After the 1950s, Bari communities identified Jesus and Mary with their local and legendary ancestral heroes and heroines, 'Konyi' and 'Kiden'. With growing assaults on their communities from northern armed militias during the 1970s, Jesus was also identified with 'Mor', an ancient 'unifier' king, who might have come from without.[72] A similar understanding developed among the Nuer communities.[73] American missionaries had translated Christian scriptures into the Nuer vernacular, creating a literate pool of Nuer who began to 'gain access to a literary tradition somewhat more congenial with their own (Nuer) covenantal theology.'[74] Covenants were always to be tested. This notion was maintained – even strengthened – after the official expulsion of missionaries in the later post-colonial period. They were seen by some southern communities as afflicted beings, whose humanitarian efforts had not been an outside imposition.

By uncoupling missionary humanitarianism from colonial realism, this chapter has demonstrated why some religious groups were eventually accepted by Southerners. Their continued presence after Sudan's independence from British rule in 1956 offered a buttress against further northern incursions. For northern elites, missionaries prevented their own proxies from assuming power in the South after the imminent

---

[70] Pitya, 'History of Christian Evangelism', 555.
[71] See Marc Nikkel, 'Dinka Christianity: The Origins and Development of Christianity among the Dinka of Sudan, with Special Reference to the Songs of Dinka Christians', PhD diss., University of Edinburgh (1993); Francis Mading Deng, *The Dinka and their Songs* (Oxford: Clarendon Press, 1973), 49–54. See also John Burton, 'Nilotic Cosmology and the Divination of Atuot Philosophy', in *African Divination Systems: Ways of Knowing*, ed. Philip M. Peek (Bloomington: Indiana University Press, 1991), 41–2; Isidore Okpewho, *African Oral Literature: Backgrounds, Character, and Continuity* (Bloomington: Indiana University Press, 1992), 107.
[72] Pitya, 'History of Christian Evangelism', 586.
[73] *Ibid.*, 650–5. Lowrey has demonstrated that, among the Nuer, some Christians 'saw a relationship between former Nuer prophets, especially Ngundeng, Nuer covenantal theology and the new Christian message [in the later twentieth century]'. William Olsen Lowrey, 'Passing the Peace ... People to People: The Role of Religion in an Indigenous Peace Process Among the Nuer People of Sudan', PhD diss., Union Institute and University (1996), 130.
[74] Cited in Duany 'Neither Palaces nor Prisons', 299.

departure of secular colonial administrators. British and American evangelism had been slowly indigenised. Southern Christianity influenced communal resistance to northern coercion during the post-colonial era. Yet greater southern cohesion was met with greater force, and a need for further international support. During the 1970s and 1980s, no intervention ever took place. Over one million Southern Sudanese died.[75]

---

[75] Collins, *Civil Wars and Revolution*, 337–9.

*Part IV*

# Non-European states

# 13 Humanitarian intervention, democracy, and imperialism: the American war with Spain, 1898, and after

*Mike Sewell*

[T]he American people never shirk a responsibility and never unload a burden that carries forward civilization. We accepted war for humanity. We can accept no terms of peace which shall not be in the interest of humanity. [Great applause]

William McKinley, October 1898[1]

Ambassador (later Secretary of State) John Hay's remark that the American war with Spain in 1898 was a 'splendid little war' is well known. His next phrase, 'begun with the highest motives' is not.[2] President William McKinley repeatedly defined the war as humanitarian. It was 'a triumph of our humanity' begun 'for freedom and to relieve our neighbors of oppression'.[3] One recent commentator sees in human rights 'one of the primary reasons why the United States went to war with Spain', although this ignored 'the contradiction inherent in the joint pursuit of democracy, a dynamic concept, and stability, a static one'.[4] In September 1949, Secretary of State Dean Acheson commented on commitments in Latin America: 'to protect security, defend democracy, and refrain from intervention in the internal affairs of other American nations, a prescription, it might seem, for inaction ... or sacrifice of one of our purposes or principles in pursuing others'.[5] The McKinley administration went to war to free Cuba. It then limited freedom in former Spanish colonies. I shall argue that a core of humanitarian principles informed both decisions, but also stimulated opposition to the second.

---

[1] Speech at Cedar Rapids, Iowa, 11 Oct. 1898, *Speeches and Addresses of William McKinley From March 1, 1897, to May 30, 1900* (New York: McClure's, 1900), 87. The phrase 'accepted war' echoes Abraham Lincoln.

[2] Hay to Theodore Roosevelt, quoted in W. R. Thayer, *The Life and Letters of John Hay* (London: Constable, 1915), II, 337.

[3] Speeches at Belle Plaine, Iowa, and Kokomo, Indiana, 11 and 21 Oct. 1898, in *Speeches and Addresses*, 89, 140.

[4] W. Zimmermann, *First Great Triumph: How Five Americans made their Country a World Power* (New York: FSG, 2002), 494–9, quotations at 497 and 499.

[5] D. Acheson, *Present at the Creation: My Years in the State Department* (London: Norton, 1969), 330.

Intervention presented as purely self-interested or purely humanitarian did not command enough support to force war. Building an overwhelming interventionist consensus took Spanish and Cuban intransigence and circumstances that created a coalition demanding intervention for often contradictory reasons. Previous efforts to buy, seize or encourage Cuba's 'gravitation' to the United States failed due to Spanish control, reluctance to take territory without the consent of the governed, slavery politics and naval weakness. The *Virginius* affair brought the prospect of Spanish–American war. Cuban-Americans claimed the protection of the American flag when a filibustering expedition ended in capture and trials. Despite a potentially strong legal case, the Grant administration saw off Congressional demands for war. Spain made reparation for the execution of American citizens, press coverage was balanced, Secretary of State Hamilton Fish opposed an 'unnecessary' war, and Reconstruction politics intruded divisive race questions. Naval weakness made victory uncertain. A multilateral solution emerged.[6] Much had changed by 1895, when rebellion again broke out in Cuba, leading to intervention in April 1898.

The attitude of Spain was key. Madrid refused expedient concessions in 1895–6 then gave too little, too late, too slowly. Spanish informants depicted to American diplomats a fragile government preferring hopeless war to the peaceful loss of Cuba. Nor must Cuba become independent lest it witness a repeat of events a century before in Saint Domingue.[7] Neither Spain nor the rebels would cease fire on the other's terms or make concessions to initiate negotiations. Intervention came when it became apparent that no short-term scheme of pacification could meet the two sides' conditions and satisfy American insistence upon an end to the horrors. The calls of honour and humanity were not new but the American response was a function of greater power. Significant recent investments increased direct American interests. The 'new Navy' made success in war more likely, easing willingness to risk conflict.[8] Citing Grant's precedent, the Democrat Cleveland administration resisted pressure for intervention. It

---

[6] R. H. Bradford, *The Virginius Affair* (Boulder, CO: Colorado University Press, 1980), 97–136; J. Sexton, 'The United States, the Cuban Rebellion, and the Multilateral Initiative of 1875', *Diplomatic History* 30 (2006), 335–66; I. Musicant, *Empire by Default: The Spanish–American War and the Dawn of the American Century* (New York: Henry Holt, 1998), 13.

[7] Woodford to Sherman, 9 Mar. 1898, *FRUS 1898*, 682–4; J. L. Offner, *An Unwanted War: The Diplomacy of the United States and Spain over Cuba, 1895–1898* (Chapel Hill: University of North Carolina Press, 1992), 114–17.

[8] R. Kagan, *Dangerous Nation: America and the World, 1600–1898* (London: Atlantic, 2006), 305, 309–13, 354–6, 409–10; Zimmermann, *Great Triumph*, 38, 265.

encouraged reforms, especially Cuban autonomy, to end fighting. More pro-Spanish than pro-Cuban, it was criticised for following Wall Street's preferences over humanitarian priorities.[9] Strategic concerns underlay Cleveland's approach. Influenced by American planters with Cuban interests to whom the rebels were a 'nigger rabble' prone to arson and other crimes, he and Secretary of State Richard Olney worried that independent Cuba might become a second, nearer, bigger Haiti.[10] They resisted the 'Junta' of Cuban exiles' propaganda that helped create 'one-sided'[11] American reporting of sufferings which actually resulted from both rebel efforts to wreck the colonial economy and the Spanish response. General Valeriano Weyler's 'reconcentration' of the population undermined the insurgency but was counter-productive. Historian J. L. Tone suggests that it 'backfired by creating an outcry in the United States against Spanish barbarism'. A mix of fact, exaggeration and fiction marginalised more balanced accounts. American journalists and consular officials produced rebel-inspired accounts of suffering blaming Spain alone.[12] Junta propaganda stressed civilised qualities, to American eyes, of the insurgency and damned the Spanish as monsters.[13] The affinities of the rebels to American civilisation were emphasised and aspects of the rebellion, notably the racial background of the rebel forces, were obfuscated.

From his inaugural address in March 1897, McKinley's Republican administration added sympathy for the Cubans to insistence on Americans' rights and welfare.[14] It increased pressure on Spain to make concessions. A change of Spanish government brought the replacement of Weyler and, apparently, his policies. By the New Year hopes began to fade. Neither the rebels nor the Spanish would compromise over sovereignty.[15] Resistance to reforms took the form of riots which, reported Consul General Richard Henry Lee from Havana, had a strong anti-American aspect. Spanish dilatoriness over reforms and more riots brought the despatch of ships to Cuban ports, including the USS *Maine* to Havana.

---

[9] L. L. Gould, *The Spanish–American War and President McKinley* (Lawrence: University Press of Kansas, 1982), 25; Kagan, *Dangerous Nation*, 377–94.
[10] Musicant, *Empire by Default*, 83–7.
[11] R. F. Hamilton, *President McKinley, War and Empire*, 2 vols. (New Brunswick: Transaction, 2006), I, 105.
[12] J. L. Tone, *War and Genocide in Cuba, 1895–1898* (Chapel Hill: University of North Carolina Press, 2006), 218–24, quotation at 224.
[13] Hamilton, *McKinley*, I, 232–40; Tone, *War and Genocide*, 139–88.
[14] Kagan, *Dangerous Nation*, 387–93.    [15] Gould, *Spanish–American War*, 17–23.

From Washington the Spanish Minister reported that the American mood had shifted; 'any sensational occurrence' might disturb relations.[16] The revelation on 9 February of a private letter in which he criticised McKinley and advocated a duplicitous course in negotiations to buy time caused uproar. On 16 February, news of the sinking of the *Maine* triggered war fever. McKinley insisted on awaiting the results of an enquiry, but the press and politicians leapt to the conclusion that the Spanish were either responsible for the explosion that sank it or incapable of fulfilling their duty to protect the ship. Suggestions that there may have been an internal explosion were swamped by denunciations of Spain. The enquiry reported, probably wrongly, on 24 March that external agency had sunk the *Maine*. The administration faced overwhelming pressure to intervene and concluded that Spain must quickly concede Cuban independence and a cease-fire. American diplomacy stressed that Weyler's conduct had been such as to raise the possibility of breaking off relations had he not been dismissed. War would have been preferable to a continuation of his methods. Yet the suffering continued. If fighting was not over by mid-April, the rainy season would bring further famine and epidemics of yellow fever that might spread to the US, which was thus obliged to intervene if Spain was impotent.[17] Spanish concessions were insufficient to avert an American ultimatum. On 11 April McKinley invited Congress to consider the issues. War came. American victories followed. An armistice was signed on 12 August, the Treaty of Paris on 10 December. Cuba was under military rule until 1902 when independence was qualified by the 1901 Platt Amendment. Intervention to secure order followed as early as 1906. The United States retained Guantanamo Bay and Puerto Rico, vital relative to any isthmian canal. Guam's cession was uncontroversial. Colonialism in the Philippines was not.

*

McKinley's claims that intervention served the cause of humanity have been debated ever since. American interests included commercial, strategic and sanitary considerations. Public statements gave priority to self-determination, freedom and the relief of suffering. Congress imposed limits on American ambitions through the self-denying Teller amendment guaranteeing Cuban self-determination and disavowing permanent annexation.[18] Wartime proclamations stressed benevolence:

---

[16] Musicant, *Empire*, 126.
[17] Woodford to Sherman, 2 Mar. 1898, *FRUS 1898*, 674–5.
[18] Gould, *Spanish–American War*, 47–50.

'[W]e come not to make war upon the inhabitants of Cuba ... but to protect them in their homes, in their employments, and in their personal and religious rights'.[19]

Historians' interpretations have mirrored the preoccupations of their times. Post-war American accounts regarded it positively as regards Cuba, ambivalently over the Philippines. A 1910s biographer thought McKinley 'the first of our Presidents to respond to the call of a broad philanthropy towards other less fortunate people'.[20] Between the world wars intervention was criticised. Strategic concerns were rehabilitated in mid-century. Post-Vietnam revisionism argued economic determinism and dismissed humanitarian professions. This scepticism remains prominent in textbooks. At its best, it poses important challenges to those who would define the intervention as humanitarian.[21] It sometimes ignores evidence that business opinion was reluctant to go to war and that Cleveland and McKinley resisted jingo pressures. Political scientist Richard Hamilton criticises over-determined interpretations, stressing instead contingency and elite leadership of a public sentiment responsive to humanitarian rhetoric.[22]

Such scholarship takes the rhetoric of humanitarianism seriously, probing such influences as partisanship and Christian duty.[23] Gerald Linderman's 1974 analysis remains influential. He found 'two formulations widely accepted by Americans in 1898: the popular dedication to the Spanish–American War as a humanitarian and anti-materialist crusade, and the popular denunciation of the American businessman-financier as an internal enemy... [trying to] block a war for humanity'.[24] Values shaped policy-makers' priorities. Ninkovich quotes one contemporary: 'We want not to acquire the Philippines for ourselves, but to give the Philippines free schools, a free church, open courts, no caste, equal rights for all'. He argues that 'more than any other

[19] McKinley to Secretary of War Russell Alger, 18 July 1898, *Correspondence Relating to the War with Spain, April 15, 1898 to July 30, 1902*, 2 vols. (Washington, DC: Center of Military History reprint, 1993), I, 159–60.

[20] E. K. Smith, 'William McKinley's Enduring Legacy: The Historiographical Debate over the Taking of the Philippine Islands', in *Crucible of Empire: The Spanish–American War and its Aftermath*, ed. J. C. Bradford (Annapolis, MD: US Naval Institute Press, 1993), quotation at 211.

[21] P. A. Kramer, *The Blood of Government: Race, Empire, the United States and the Philippines* (Chapel Hill: University of North Carolina Press, 2006); L. A. Perez, *The War of 1898: The United States and Cuba in History and Historiography* (Chapel Hill: University of North Carolina Press, 1998).

[22] Hamilton, *McKinley*, I, 115, 195–7, 29.    [23] Offner, *Unwanted War*, 187–8.

[24] G. F. Linderman, *The Mirror of War: American Society and the Spanish–American War* (Ann Arbor: University of Michigan Press, 1974), 6–7.

argument, it was the call of duty and civilization, the internationalist rhetoric of empire, that appears to have had the greatest impact'.[25]

Linderman emphasises deep-rooted stereotypes of Catholic Spain as barbaric, unchangingly cruel, incapable of good government and uncivilised. American leaders who took the country to war were schooled on 'Black Legend' histories of Counter-Reformation Spanish cruelty. Weyler was a new Duke of Alba, who featured in that tradition as the brutal enemy of the Dutch Revolt. When faced with contentious evidence from Cuba, many Americans reverted to such assumptions.[26] Offner thus sees reconcentration, not the *Maine*, as the key issue, preparing the ground for McKinley's emphasis on humanitarian themes.[27] Minister to Spain Woodford reckoned the *Maine* sinking could be resolved, 'but there remain general conditions in Cuba which can not longer be endured and which will demand action on our part unless Spain restores honourable peace, which will stop starvation of people and give them opportunity to take care of themselves and restore commerce'. He suggested 'the time has come when the United States must, in the interest of humanity and because of the great and pressing commercial, financial and sanitary needs of our country, ask that some satisfactory agreement be reached within a very few days'. Assistant Secretary of State William R. Day replied that McKinley 'cannot look upon the starvation in Cuba save with horror. The concentration of men, women and children in fortified towns and permitting them to starve is intolerable to a Christian nation geographically so close as ours to Cuba. All this has shocked and inflamed the American mind, as it has the civilized world.'[28] Europeans stressed that for the protection of its own citizens 'and for the sake of humanity and civilization, the United States must accept the duty which our position in the western hemisphere imposes upon us'.[29] The proximity of the suffering, and the prospect that epidemic disease might spread, played a role in easing the creation of an interventionist consensus but was only part of the explanation. Tone comments:

When a state – especially a populist republic – embarks on foreign military adventures, it is essential to prepare the ground by clothing war in the

---

[25] F. Ninkovich, *The United States and Imperialism* (Oxford: Blackwell, 2001), 40, 47, 150–2; also K. Phillips, *William McKinley* (New York: Henry Holt, 2003), 93–5, 156; Musicant, *Empire*, 590–600.

[26] Linderman, *Mirror*, 115–28.

[27] Offner, *Unwanted War*, 48, 80, 84–7, 112–13, 136–41, 183–4.

[28] Woodford to the President, 21 and 25 Mar. 1898; Day to Woodford, 26 Mar. 1898; *FRUS 1898*, 695, 699, 704.

[29] Woodford to Sherman, 13 Sept. 1897, *ibid.*, 562–5. Consular reports, *ibid.*, 596–7, describing 'alarming rates of starvation' and powerless colonial authorities, were held back by McKinley from Congress whilst he sought a settlement.

language of human rights and a civilizing mission. Reconcentration gave the American jingoes just the tool they needed to do this. As a result the American public went to war in Cuba confident that their cause was righteous.[30]

McKinley dwelt upon reconcentration: 'it was not civilized warfare, it was extermination. The only peace it could beget was that of the wilderness and the grave.' Pacification must immediately end such misery.[31] To his Peace Commissioners, he stressed: 'We took up arms only in obedience to the dictates of humanity and in the fulfilment of high public and moral obligations. We had no design of aggrandizement and no ambition of conquest.' He had gone to war to right wrongs.[32] Kagan sees American policy as aimed to expand civilisation by spreading democracy: McKinley reluctantly took the nation to war because of overwhelming political pressures generated by a widely reported humanitarian crisis. Honour, human rights and humanity demanded intervention against savagery and tyranny.[33]

Historian Kristin Hoganson stresses gendered values. To proponents, the war was chivalrous: '[n]o man ever went to the assistance of a weak and defenseless fellow-being who was being tortured by a brutal master and did not feel that he had done a good act, and did not receive the encouragement and plaudits of manly men'. The *Maine* incident engaged American honour, tipping the views of some hesitant leaders 'because it has become necessary to fight if we would uphold our manhood'.[34] Trask quotes a McKinley confidant on considerations of humanity and justice in motivating 'a selfless war for Cuba' and 'public enthusiasm for Cuban independence'. The humanitarian objective of Cuban independence achieved, expansionist appetites were stimulated.[35]

Perez portrays a historiographical myth of a 'relief mission' derived from American views during the war, but concedes that many Americans *believed* their cause to be humanitarian.[36] McKinley, a cautious imperialist, fits Perez's characterisation of the American self-image. Several future critics of intervention in the Philippines shared the President's

---

[30] Tone, *War and Genocide*, 224, 249; and 218–22 on Junta manipulation of the black legend.

[31] Message to Congress, 11 April 1898, in J. D. Richardson (ed.), *A Compilation of the Messages and Papers of the Presidents, William McKinley* (n.p.: Biblio-Bazaar reprint, 2006), 31–5.

[32] McKinley instructions, *FRUS 1898*, 16 Sept. 1898, 906–7.

[33] Kagan, *Dangerous Nation*, 296, 386–90, 406–7, 411–12.

[34] K. L. Hoganson, *Fighting for American Manhood: How Gender Politics Provoked the Spanish–American and Philippine–American Wars* (New Haven: Yale University Press, 1998), 43–5, 67–73, 85, quotation at 70–1.

[35] D. F. Trask, *The War with Spain in 1898* (Lincoln, NB: University of Nebraska Press, 1981), 36, 474–83.

[36] Perez, *War of 1898*, 20–41.

views. Senator George Frisbie Hoar (R-Mass) favoured intervention in Cuba after events eroded hopes of Cuban freedom through peaceful means. Andrew Carnegie reluctantly accepted war for Cuban independence. Mark Twain supported fighting to free Cuba from foreign rule as noble, just as he later opposed American rule in the Philippines.[37]

Economic considerations featured in justifications, but rarely dominated.[38] Vehement denunciations of timid capitalists by advocates of a large policy were prominent. Targets included John D. Rockefeller and J. P. Morgan. Investors in Cuban sugar urged caution rather than risk a conflict. Senator Henry Cabot Lodge and Assistant Secretary of the Navy Theodore Roosevelt lambasted business timidity, indicting commercial society for undermining manly virtues.[39] The values of Main Street prevailed over Wall Street. A broad coalition demanded action against disorder and for democracy over business hesitation.[40] Business resistance was reduced by the events of February and, notably, by a Senate speech following a visit to Cuba by conservative millionaire businessman Redfield Proctor (R-Vt) on 17 March. Alluding to the Inquisition and St Bartholomew's Night massacre, he described a misgoverned people striving for deliverance. Although prepared for horrors, the reality was worse than he had imagined. Proctor's account of 'desolation and distress, misery and starvation' raised the prospect of war 'founded on an undiluted humanitarianism'. He brought from Hoar the comment that intervention would be 'the most honourable single war in all history'.[41]

Proctor reinforced the view that Spain lacked the capacity to govern Cuba humanely and effectively. The *Maine* disaster provided evidence that this posed a threat to Americans.[42] Such key figures as Republican Senators William E. Chandler (R-NH) and Joseph B. Foraker (R-OH) switched just as Democrats seized on the *Maine* to garner support for action.[43] Lawyer, Republican loyalist and future Secretary of War Elihu Root, motivated by Proctor's speech and the *Maine* report, switched

[37] E. T. L. Love, *Race over Empire: Racism and U.S. Imperialism, 1865–1900* (Chapel Hill: University of North Carolina, 2004), 151–8; Hamilton, *McKinley*, I, 228–9; 123, the archetypally pro-corporate Mark Hanna (R-OH), thought war 'a damn nuisance'. J. Zwick, *Confronting Imperialism: Essays on Mark Twain and the Anti-Imperialist League* (New Haven: Infinity, 2007), 125–8, 158–9; Zimmermann, *Great Triumph*, 330–8.
[38] Hamilton, *McKinley*, I, 195–9.    [39] Hoganson, *Fighting*, 36–9.
[40] L. D. Langley, *The Banana Wars: United States Intervention in the Caribbean, 1898–1934* (Wilmington: Scholarly Resources, 2002), xvii–xx; Hamilton, *McKinley*, I, 105–9, 120–6, 246; II, 85–94.
[41] Linderman, *Mirror*, 7, 40–5, 58.    [42] Perez, *War of 1898*, 62.
[43] Hamilton, *McKinley*, I, 218–31; Tone, *War and Genocide*, 249.

from pro-business reluctance to regretful interventionism to uphold American principles and human rights.[44] Phillips describes a president close to the business community, opposed to war, facing hawkish criticism. Only after Proctor's speech made the business community less apprehensive and more favourable to humanitarian arguments did the president bow to pressure.[45]

The yellow journalism of Hearst and Pulitzer was Democrat and followed opinion. Their shrill attacks on McKinley reflected the partisan dimension to debates. Having chafed under Republican attacks on Cleveland, Silver Democrats castigated McKinley for subservience to banking interests.[46] Business leaders thought war might endanger economic recovery. Party fears of electoral losses pushed the reluctant president to accept war despite his lingering hopes for a peaceful solution.[47] McKinley bowed to the popular consensus despite his desire to avoid war. Ernest May describes him as 'jumping aboard a vehicle he could not brake'.[48] He stayed silent until April then capitulated. A leading pro-business Republican doubted that the president could resist popular clamour after the report on the *Maine*: 'if he cannot end it by negotiations, the people will insist that he shall do so by force'. Nothing, thought Senator Thomas C. Platt (R-NY), would restrain Congress from declaring for intervention and war. The November elections would be a disaster if the administration resisted.[49] Pushed by his party, McKinley manifested his preference to stay close to public opinion. His decision was eased by humanitarian considerations that had gained popular currency in an 'emotional response to what many Americans considered the intolerable conditions of the Cuban people'.[50]

American victories followed. By August, American forces held the bay and city of Manila, parts of eastern Cuba, and much of Puerto Rico. Humanitarian war to liberate suffering Cubans expanded with far-reaching consequences. Americans faced new responsibilities. Tensions between order and democracy surfaced in debates about how to translate the humanitarian values that helped take the country to war into a settlement. The Junta promoted a vision of the Cuban insurgents

[44] Zimmermann, *Great Triumph*, 256–9.    [45] Phillips, *McKinley*, 91–5.
[46] Hamilton, *McKinley*, I, 149ff., 190–2, 232.
[47] Offner, *Unwanted War*, 15–18, 153; Linderman, *Mirror*, 33–4; Musicant, *Empire*, 172–5.
[48] E. R. May, *Imperial Democracy: The Emergence of the United States as a Great Power* (New York: Harcourt, Brace, 1961), 243. May argues that partisan politics played a crucial role.
[49] Phillips, *McKinley*, 94–5; Musicant, *Empire*, 168–73; Linderman, *Mirror*, 21–37.
[50] Linderman, *Mirror*, 27–30; Bradford (ed.), *Crucible*, xiii–xiv; J. Dobson, *Reticent Expansionism: The Foreign Policy of William McKinley* (Pittsburgh: Duquesne University Press, 1988), 5–14; Zimmermann, *Great Triumph*, 253–8.

as disciplined, orderly, conventional warriors, not the guerrilla reality. The Spanish were presented as cowardly, inhumane butchers. A re-evaluation occurred when Spanish troops fought bravely, treated American prisoners properly, and surrendered rather than inflicting needless casualties. Where interventionist propaganda had depicted rebels' affinities with American values, Spanish commanders now stressed theirs. Rebel forces were viewed differently. Junta-fuelled expectations were disappointed. Ragged Afro-Cuban irregulars assisted American landings in ways not obvious to the arriving soldiers. Ill-suited to conventional warfare, they could not prevent Spanish reinforcements reaching Santiago. They looked to the Americans like bandits, scavenging for food and equipment, gaining a reputation for importuning their friends, avoiding work details and not engaging the enemy. Their treatment of prisoners seemed arbitrary and brutal. American perceptions shifted. A war critic commented: 'The noble army of Cuban martyrs has become an armed rabble as unchivalrous as it was unsanitary'. This re-evaluation of Cubans was mirrored in the Philippines.[51]

★

The war for Cuba united Americans. That for the Philippines divided them. Naval plans for a war over Cuba were predicated on a strategy to bring Spain to favourable terms. There was no joint planning for combined Pacific operations as there was for the Caribbean. McKinley's aim in sending a fleet to the Philippines and invading Puerto Rico was to discomfort Spain, protect commerce and force negotiations on American terms without major operations near Havana. Annexation was 'an unintended by-product of the war ... accident rather than calculated design'.[52] After victory McKinley faced the question of retention.[53] Outgoing Secretary of State Day commented as he took on the role of Peace Commissioner: 'Because we had done good in one place, we were not therefore compelled to rush over the whole civilized world, six thousand miles away from home, to undertake tasks of that sort among people of whom we knew nothing'.[54] Until Dewey's victory brought a 'radical change of mission', no thought was given to sending an army to

[51] Tone, *War and Genocide*, 280–5; Hoganson, *Fighting*, 107–9; Linderman, *Mirror*, 134–47, quotation at 144.
[52] Trask, *War with Spain*, 73–8, 367–8.
[53] E. K. Smith, '"A Question From Which We Could Not Escape": William McKinley and the Decision to Acquire the Philippine Islands', *Diplomatic History* 9 (1985), 363–75; Hamilton, *McKinley*, II, 18–21.
[54] Offner, *Unwanted War*, xi; diary entry for 16 Sept. 1898, H. Wayne Morgan (ed.), *Making Peace with Spain: The Diary of Whitelaw Reid* (Austin: University of Texas Press, 1965), 28.

the Philippines.[55] Numbers rose incrementally from 5,000 to 20,000 as commanders sought clarification of their orders.[56] Neither quite by accident nor by design, imperial ventures developed. Dewey drew a parallel between the Filipinos and freed slaves during the Civil War – they augmented the forces facing a common enemy. He and American Consuls initially encouraged Filipino rebels to join the war effort and form a government.[57] For months McKinley hesitated, causing Henry Cabot Lodge to worry about political repercussions of restored Spanish rule: 'Democrats will unite in attacking us for doing so as false to freedom & humanity & we shall have no answer'.[58]

Dissent became more prominent after the peace treaty was signed. Annexation of the Philippines turned Twain and others anti-imperialist. But the treaty was ratified. Simultaneously, fighting, the counter-insurgency phase of which lasted until 1902, broke out between Filipinos and Americans. Anti-imperialists held that American traditions were being violated and worried about Filipino economic competition. Imperialists countered with strategic and prestige concerns, economic potential, and the duty of the United States to follow through on humanitarian war aims. Anyway, the alternatives were worse.

Policy-makers placed their faith in God to show them what destiny intended but also relied upon local expertise. Filipino and Cuban elites sought American protection. The colonial state was built 'in dialogue with Hispanicized Filipino elites'.[59] General Otis reported that Manila residents preferred American protection.[60] Sceptics about American humanitarian professions suggest that 'wealthy Filipinos clamored for US rule because they distrusted democracy', reinforcing American racial and class biases.[61] There was considerable variation, by island, ethnic group, province and village in American–Filipino relations. Linn

---

[55] D. F. Trask, 'American Intelligence During the War', in *Crucible*, ed. Bradford, 25–8; Musicant, *Empire*, 237–61; Love, *Race over Empire*, 159, notes that not even expansionists initially advocated annexation.

[56] Trask, *War with Spain*, 167, 422, 479–80.

[57] B. M. Linn, *The Philippine War, 1899–1902* (Lawrence: University of Kansas Press, 2000), 5–7; Trask, *War with Spain*, 398–407; Musicant, *Empire*, 550; Gould, *Spanish–American War*, 61–2.

[58] Lodge quoted in L. L. Gould, 'William McKinley: "The Man at the Helm"', in *Commanders in Chief: Presidential Leadership in Modern Wars*, ed. J. G. Dawson (Lawrence: University of Kansas Press, 1993), 60; Love, *Race over Empire*, 171–2.

[59] Kramer, *Blood of Government*, 84–5, 112–13, 215, quotation at 226; D. J. Silbey, *A War of Frontier and Empire: The Philippine-American, 1899–1902* (New York: Hill and Wang, 2007), 128, 135.

[60] Otis to Adjutant General, 3 Sept. 1898, *Correspondence*, II, 786.

[61] T. Schoonover, *Uncle Sam's War of 1898 and the Origins of Globalization* (Lexington: University Press of Kentucky, 2003), 98.

depicts 'a series of regional struggles bewildering in their complexity' and stresses intra-Filipino divisions.[62] Spanish troops also affected American attitudes. Preferring surrender to the Americans to defeat by their subjects, Spanish commanders agreed to fight enough to satisfy honour. At Manila as at Santiago de Cuba, they surrendered only to the *Americans*. Filipino forces were excluded. The exclusions caused recriminations. This smacked to the American forces of ingratitude. Although the sufferings of white populations did not play a particular role in stimulating intervention, Europeans were able to influence how humanitarian principles were interpreted as intervention turned into pacification.

Edging to his decision, McKinley sought expert advice. He then moulded public consensus by effective communication of his priorities.[63] In June, McKinley's ambitions only encompassed a coaling station and secure harbour. By September he desired Luzon as the best way to secure them. Men with experience of the Philippines suggested that the Filipinos lacked capacity for effective self-government without American tutelage. 'Nearly all expert testimony' to the Peace Commissioners considered it 'a naval, political, and commercial mistake to divide the archipelago'.[64] Islands a cannon-shot away from American possessions might fall into the hands of rival powers if left independent, and there was a moral obligation not to return any to Spain's 'oppressive power'.[65] Military reports derived from Manila elites suggested Filipino opinion was favourable to American rule and that Emilio Aguinaldo's republic was unrepresentative, even unpopular. General Francis V. Greene's visit to Washington after his tour in the Philippines was important. He met McKinley over several days in late September and early October, playing a key role in convincing the president to choose American control of the whole archipelago: Filipinos wanted an outcome similar to Cuba with growth into self-rule under American protection.[66] Consuls also denigrated the republic, echoing the local urban elite.[67] Their reports added weight to Greene's view that to relinquish control would bring anarchy and civil strife to the islands. Split control

---

[62] Linn, *Philippine War*, ix–xi, 75–82, 59–61, 185–99, quotation at 185.
[63] Phillips, *McKinley*, xvii, 100.
[64] Commissioners to Secretary of State Hay, telegram, 25 Oct. 1898, *FRUS 1898*, 932.
[65] Trask, *War with Spain*, 450–1; Dobson, *Reticent Expansionism*, 105–6, 138–40; Gould, *Spanish–American War*, 82–3, 101.
[66] Gould, *Spanish–American War*, 100–3.
[67] For example, Consul Williams, 12 May, forwarded by Day to the War Department, *Correspondence*, II, 718–19; Trask, 'American Intelligence', 40–3; Musicant, *Empire*, 546.

was risky with other powers, notably Germany or Japan, hovering.[68] Reports of McKinley's conversations in November mirror Greene's arguments: the war's origins made return to Spain impossible; control by other powers would be only marginally less ignominious; turning control over 'to the Tagal insurgents' would endanger stability and progress; splitting islands so close together was fraught with dangers. That left American control.[69] The Peace Commissioners received similar advice from military men. Whitelaw Reid recorded its particular effect on Day, who was initially reluctant to take more than a coaling station, citing Commander Bradford's memorandum of 14 October, forwarded by the president, on the strategic impossibility of splitting the archipelago. Further military testimony diminished Day's and Democrat Senator George Gray's (D-Del) resistance to annexation. One report included accounts likening Spanish torture of suspected freemasons to the Inquisition or the worst acts of North American Indians. It thought Aguinaldo manageable 'with tact'.[70]

Negative images of the Spanish and a perception of the Filipinos as unready for self-rule encouraged annexation. In July, with Aguinaldo still praising the Americans as humanitarian 'liberators' and 'redeemers', Lodge opined that, the war having been fought for ethical reasons, it would be 'infamy' to hand 'people whom we have set free' back to Spain.[71] Concern about other powers was genuine. Dewey enjoyed tense relations with a German squadron that appeared in Manila Bay. American voices worried about Japanese ambitions in Hawaii as in the Philippines. Whitelaw Reid's diary of the treaty negotiation described conversations with German diplomats about their country's Pacific interests. British diplomats stressed possible rivals.[72] The concern sharpened misgivings about Filipino capacity for stable and orderly self-government. A mere Protectorate might bring complications.

★

By 13 November, when the Commissioners were instructed to demand the whole archipelago, McKinley had ensured that they received plenty

---

[68] General Otis to the Adjutant General, 13 Nov. 1898, *Correspondence*, II, 836; E. K. Smith, 'McKinley's Enduring Legacy', in *Crucible*, ed. Bradford, 234–5; Musicant, *Empire*, 600–2; Trask, *War with Spain*, 452–3.

[69] Smith, 'A Question', 372, echoing another military man's mid-October memorandum.

[70] Morgan, *Making Peace*, 54–6, 73–4, 178, 214–15. S. C. Miller, *Benevolent Assimilation: The American Conquest of the Philippines, 1899–1903* (New Haven: Yale University Press, 1982), 20.

[71] Kramer, *Blood of Government*, 84–5; Trask, *War with Spain*, 439.

[72] Morgan, *Making Peace*, 186, 3 December, for example.

of material to shape their discussions.[73] With the decision crystallising, he undertook a speaking tour in the Midwest from 11 to 21 October. This was an effective exercise in leading public opinion. His emphasis on the interests of humanity, not shirking responsibility, promoting liberty, and fulfilling duty and destiny in a Godly cause rallied support for annexation.[74] Destiny imposed a duty on the United States to exercise a civilising role by ending suffering and injustice.[75] High-minded American tutelage for self-rule and 'benevolent assimilation' would promote Filipino welfare.[76]

In contrast to his public silence in early 1898, McKinley was the main promoter of annexation of the Philippines, emphasising humanitarian themes. He had not wanted the islands, having no imperial designs, but to be true to national principles, the blessings of freedom must be brought to the islands: 'We cannot escape the obligations of victory ... We are bound in conscience to keep and perform the covenants which the war has sacredly sealed with mankind. Accepting war for humanity's sake, we must accept all obligations which the war in duty and honor imposed upon us.'[77] Privately he reported agonising over the fate of the Philippines. Dewey's destruction of the Spanish fleet had been undertaken for short-term aims but it became imperative to strip Spain of her colonies. Return was impossible 'for the very reasons which justified the war'. Handing them to European powers would bring war 'in fifteen minutes'. It 'would be to escape responsibility for our own acts and that we could not do; our duty and destiny demanded that we undertake our own responsibilities'. In the interests of humanity the United States must accept its destiny.[78] Some accounts intrude a more overt religious note, portraying McKinley adverting to prayer. Rather than dismiss this self-portrayal, we should, as Preston has urged, connect the sacred and the secular.[79] Lincoln 'won the war with metaphors' by leading public opinion to accept novel policies. McKinley strove to do likewise.[80] McKinley's presentation of the country as God's instrument

---

[73] Hay to Commissioners, 13 Nov. 1898, *FRUS 1898*, 949; by 25 October, a majority favoured annexation, 932–4.

[74] Gould, *Spanish–American War*, 104.     [75] Musicant, *Empire*, 614–15.

[76] Zimmermann, *Great Triumph*, 386–92; Love, *Race over Empire*, 192–3.

[77] Gould, *Spanish–American War*, 117–19; McKinley, speech at the Citizens' Banquet in the Auditorium, Chicago, 19 Oct. 1898, in *Speeches and Addresses*, 133–4.

[78] Smith, 'A Question', 369–70.

[79] A. Preston, 'Bridging the Gap Between the Sacred and the Secular in the History of American Foreign Relations', *Diplomatic History* 30 (2006), 783–812.

[80] J. McPherson, 'How Lincoln Won the War with Metaphors', in his *Abraham Lincoln and the Second American Revolution* (New York: Oxford University Press, 1991), 93–112; D. L. Wilson, *Lincoln's Sword: The Presidency and the Power of Words* (New York: Knopf, 2007), 145, 231, 233–5, 244.

connected their wars. They shared the same humane ends: liberation and emancipation. Such allusions defined the war, even the Philippine counter-insurgency, as morally just. As Lincoln taught that God's providence, through events, expanded his war beyond original aims,[81] so McKinley's outgrew freeing Cuba.

McKinley's September instructions to the Peace Commissioners stressed the war's unselfish purpose:

[W]e took up arms only in obedience to the dictates of humanity and in the fulfilment of high public and moral obligationsm ... Without any original thought of complete or even partial acquisition, the presence and success of our arms at Manila imposes upon us obligations that we cannot disregard. The march of events rules and overrules human action.[82]

The president told Philippine Commissioner Jacob G. Schurman that 'events had governed him'. Secretary of the Navy John D. Long agreed. A responsibility was acquired once Manila fell, 'I cannot shut my eyes to the march of events – a march which seems beyond human control'.[83] To the Boston Home Market Club in February 1899, McKinley stressed:

The evolution of events, which no man could control, has brought these problems upon us ... The Philippines, like Cuba and Porto Rico [sic], were intrusted to our hands by the war, and to that great trust, under the providence of God and in the name of human progress and civilization we are committed {Great applause}.

A 'higher Power' than presidents' or generals' plans determined the outcome of wars. McKinley then stressed Greene's themes. Return to Spain or for the islands shamefully to be 'tossed into the arena of the strife of nations' would be 'a weak evasion of duty'. Self-government was unacceptable:

Could we, after freeing the Filipinos from the domination of Spain, have left them without government and without power to protect life or property or to perform the international obligations essential to an independent state? Could we have left them in a state of anarchy and justified ourselves in our own consciences and before the tribunal of mankind? Could we have done that in the sight of God or man? ... We were obeying a higher moral obligation, which rested on us and did not require anyone's consent. {Great applause and cheering} We were doing our duty by them, as God gave us the light to see our duty.

---

[81] R. C. White, *Lincoln's Greatest Speech: The Second Inaugural* (New York: Simon and Schuster, 2002), 97, 123.
[82] Instructions to the Peace Commissioners, 16 Sept. 1898, *FRUS 1898*, 906–7.
[83] Trask, *War with Spain*, 454–5.

Grave responsibilities fell unsought on 'American emancipators'. Filipinos would enjoy 'the blessings of freedom, of civil and religious liberty, of education, and of homes ... [their] children and children's children shall for ages hence bless the American republic because it emancipated and redeemed their fatherland'.[84]

Civil War echoes abound. Lincoln's Second Inaugural evoked 'firmness in the right, as God gives us to see the right'. The passive voice recalls Lincoln's advocacy of controversial wartime policies. The insistence on events, and their providential nature, sanctified McKinley's war as humanitarian. Republicans of McKinley's generation would recall Lincoln's 'I do not claim to have controlled events, but confess plainly that events have controlled me'.[85] John Hay had been one of Lincoln's private secretaries and co-authored the definitive biography in which he revealed how Lincoln invoked Divine Will, making human agents 'the instrumentalities of another will'.[86] The theme recurred in his Second Inaugural: 'The Almighty has His own purposes'. Lincoln supposed God had given both north and south their terrible war 'as the woe to those by whom the offence came'.

His countrymen should seek God's will in the conflict.[87] Carwardine has stressed how, 'tapping into the Union's deep well of religio-patriotic sentiment', Lincoln proclaimed a direct providential role for an interventionist God and thus rallied support from important religious constituencies. McKinley, a religious man who 'personified American Protestantism',[88] rallied support by following Lincoln's themes. He too fused patriotism with 'the forces of mainstream Protestant orthodoxy, the most potent agent of American nationalism'. Patriotic attachment to the nation as the chosen instrument of God's will, a quest for liberty and justice for all, and military necessity justified unanticipated policies.[89] The Republican constituency that responded to these themes represented a body of opinion amenable to calls to intervene on humanitarian grounds. Grand Old Party rank and file remembered the Civil War as a

---

[84] Speech to the Boston Home Market Club, 16 Feb. 1899, in *Speeches and Addresses*, 185–93.

[85] The phrase occurs in the 'Hodges letter' of April 1864, White, *Greatest Speech*, 96–9; A. C. Guelzo, *Lincoln's Emancipation Proclamation* (New York: Simon and Schuster, 2004), 7.

[86] D. E. Fehrenbacher, 'The Weight of Responsibility', in his *Lincoln in Text and Context: Collected Essays* (Stanford: Stanford University Press, 1987), 162.

[87] J. Takach, *Lincoln's Moral Vision: The Second Inaugural Address* (Jackson, MS: University Press of Mississippi, 2002), 94–7, 125–42; Guelzo, *Emancipation Proclamation*, 167–8.

[88] R. Carwardine, *Lincoln: A Life of Purpose and Power* (New York: Knopf, 2006), 266, 227, 245–8; Phillips, *McKinley*, 15–16, 83.

[89] Carwardine, *Lincoln*, 313; Guelzo, *Emancipation Proclamation*, 203.

conflict justified by God's Providence and seem, from the evidence of McKinley's speaking tours, to have responded enthusiastically to his efforts to associate his aims with Lincoln's. Without amounting to a humanitarian constituency akin to abolitionists, the party faithful formed a reservoir of support for humanitarian military action.

The providential theme and McKinley's religiosity make sense only when linked to the Civil War heritage.[90] McKinley, having seen war, wished never to 'get into a war until I am sure that God and Man approve'.[91] Kagan has suggested that the Civil War's outcome made future foreign interventions easier. This seems too simple. Race politics continued to affect debates over intervention, usually making it less likely. Southern segregationists opposed bringing more people of colour under American rule. There was a constituency that responded to humanitarian impulses to export American values, including self-rule. But it overlapped with an anti-imperialist impulse that derived from similar roots. The attitudes of the two senators from Massachusetts at this time, Henry Cabot Lodge and George F. Hoar, exemplify this diversity of post-abolitionist sentiment.

Kagan's view of the Union's Civil War as encompassing themes typical of nineteenth-century foreign policy – nation-building through force to change enemy values and society, hard war for libertarian ends – is closer to the mark. 'The moral logic of Lincoln' animated those wielding American power in 1898.[92] McKinley had fought insurgent 'rebels' in the Shenandoah Valley. Lincoln twice used the term 'insurgent' in his Second Inaugural to describe Confederates conspiring against established government. In the Philippines General Orders governing military treatment of the local population derived directly from the Union army's and frontier warfare.[93] GO 100, issued by Lincoln in 1863, prescribed humane treatment of civilians as long as they did not resist. If they did, harsh treatment would follow. Those who wilfully resisted a constitutional order had no justification for seeking its protection. Combatants out of uniform would be treated like highwaymen or pirates, not soldiers. Ribbons worn at the 1865 inaugural celebrations proclaimed 'No compromise with armed rebels'.[94] Once Filipino resistance was defined as

---

[90] Linderman, *Mirror*, 10; Ninkovich, *The United States and Imperialism*, 39–40.

[91] Phillips, *McKinley*, 92.

[92] Kagan, *Dangerous Nation*, 264–84. J. R. Holmes, *Theodore Roosevelt and World Order: Police Power in International Relations* (Washington, DC: Potomac, 2006), links Roosevelt's vision of trusteeship to his view of providential lessons of history, and especially the Civil War use of police power: 75, 84, 144–58.

[93] Kramer, *Blood of Government*, 335, 88, 136–7; Linn, *Philippine War*, 7–9, 198–201, 212.

[94] Guelzo, *Emancipation Proclamation*, 220; White, *Greatest Speech*, 83.

rebellion, the Filipinos' turn to guerrilla tactics determined the American response. Theodore Roosevelt compared them to Apaches for their 'savage' behaviour.[95] Governor William Howard Taft saw guerrilla resistance as criminal conspiracy, murder and assassination. Criminals deserved appropriate treatment.[96]

The tension between non-intervention, democracy promotion, and security concerns that Acheson later sketched from his experience also faced McKinley, as a similar one had faced Lincoln three decades previously. Intervention originated in concerns about instability and human suffering in nearby areas of vital interest. Americans went to war for Cuba feeling righteous over human rights, democracy and mission. Missionary opportunities to uplift the benighted, advance civilisation and self-government were more important than permanent acquisition of territory.[97] Elections were, in Lincoln's words, crucial: 'We can not have free government without elections'.[98] Elections depend on stability and order. Promoting the latter contradicted interventionist principles when tactics mirrored reconcentration, or troops used torture.[99] American counter-insurgency in the Philippines caused an outcry reminiscent of that against Spain's in Cuba. Failure to live up to humanitarian intent broke the pro-war consensus. Lincoln's redefinition of freedom added to republican self-rule a commitment to freedom as state-facilitated self-realisation.[100] Tensions between these definitions were apparent in debates over imperialism. After a war for Cuban freedom, Americans debated how to secure self-rule *and* self-realisation. Instability and lawlessness created a humanitarian crisis. Intervention followed to protect the weak. But what if, unlike the Puerto Ricans, the population resisted? An analyst of Roosevelt's thought on the international police power roots comments that a 'rhetoric of militant decency' linked moral, education and health reforms for all to justice, and justice to obedience to laws. Force was needed to uphold the laws that were the key to civilisation.[101]

The issue of capacity for self-rule was a key American concern. Secretary of War Root characterised American rule as democracy 'on

[95] Miller, *Benevolent Assimilation*, 152, 171; Kramer, *Blood of Government*, 87–90, 101.
[96] Ninkovich, *The United States and Imperialism*, 52–9; also Kramer, *Blood of Government*, 103–4, 121–8, 134–43, 146–9, 215–26.
[97] Hamilton, *McKinley*, II, 159–83; Offner, *Unwanted War*, 227–34.
[98] Quoted in J. L. Weber, *Copperheads: The Rise and Fall of Lincoln's Opponents in the North* (Oxford: Oxford University Press, 2006), 198.
[99] Tone, *War and Genocide*, 224.
[100] G. Wills, *Lincoln at Gettysburg: Words that Remade America* (New York: Simon and Schuster, 1992), 121–47.
[101] Holmes, *Roosevelt*, 25–35, 160–4.

training wheels'. Freedom, stipulated Roosevelt, depended upon self-restraint.[102] Criticism of Spanish governance in Cuba was validated by events. Proctor's account clinched the argument that Spain lacked the capacity to govern humanely or effectively.[103] The failure of the colonial state in Cuba to provide effective governance was a key element in the creation of an interventionist consensus. Failed states (or colonies) made bad neighbours. Woodford pressed for intervention against a 'horrible and unchristian' regime to stop 'this cruel, useless, and horrid warfare'.[104] Wanting to end 'the present hell of famine and anarchy', he opposed Cuban independence because 'I do not believe that the population is fit for self-government'. In a 'mad-house', only American control would restore peace.[105] McKinley refused to recognise the Cuban republic: 'until there is within the island a government capable of performing the duties and discharging the functions of a separate nation'.[106]

A paternalistic attitude to people considered lacking capacity for self-rule brought humanitarian interveners to champion American control. The Teller Amendment reflected idealistic pre-war desire to liberate Cuba. Post-intervention, however, the creation of institutions that lived up to the unselfish ideals was not straightforward. Cuban elections took place on a limited franchise in 1900. In 1902, an independence constitution was adopted, but American concerns that internal disorder might provoke European intervention brought the Platt amendment, 'virtually a substitute for formal annexation', forced on reluctant Cubans as a condition of independence.[107] Limitations on self-government cast doubt on the sincerity of humanitarian motives. Critics viewed and view the stress on mission, providence and God as cover for more worldly motivations.[108] They point to the Platt amendment and to the Philippine counter-insurgency's sometimes brutal treatment of the local population. Behaviour that contradicted McKinley's proclamations of altruism upset former allies.[109] Excesses fuelled a backlash at home.

Policy emerged piecemeal and came into conflict with the ideals underpinning it. Intervention for humane and patriotic motives was so popular it overwhelmed McKinley's resistance to war. Wartime events

---

[102] Ninkovich, *The United States and Imperialism*, 57–70, 87–8, 92–3.
[103] Perez, *War of 1898*, 62.
[104] Woodford to Sherman, 13 Sept. 1897, *FRUS 1898*, 563–5.
[105] Woodford to McKinley, 17 Mar. 1898, *FRUS 1898*, 685–8.
[106] Message to Congress, 11 Apr. 1898, in Richardson, *Messages and Papers*, 39, 40.
[107] J. Smith, *The United States and Latin America: A History of American Diplomacy, 1776–2000* (London: Routledge, 2005), 64.
[108] Miller, *Benevolent Assimilation*, 15, 242.    [109] *Ibid.*, 42–3.

produced a presence in the Philippines that turned, *faute de mieux*, into colonial control. Debates raged over how much discipline and military control were appropriate. Critics denounced as un-American the imposition of the values of the Declaration of Independence 'at cannon's mouth'.[110] Atrocity stories provoked Congressional investigations. Lodge then reminded colleagues of the nation's divinely ordained mission to promote freedom. The vehemence of such debates derived from principles both sides drew upon. The issue lay in how best to be true to them. Critics often considered intervention tactically misguided or insufficiently true to humanitarian principles rather than plain wrong.

Mark Twain supported war with Spain but turned anti-imperialist when the repercussions highlighted the contradictions inherent in using force to promote democracy. Filipino home rule did gradually grow, and the Platt Amendment was repealed in 1933. Contradictions remained between democracy, order and stability. Interventions followed to enforce good government and order. One commitment was sacrificed in pursuit of the others.

[110] Silbey, *Frontier and Empire*, 89–97; Zimmermann, *Great Triumph*, 409.

# 14    The innovation of the Jackson–Vanik Amendment

*Thomas J. W. Probert*

> Mankind's sole salvation lies in everyone making everything his business, in the people in the East being vitally concerned with what is thought in the West, the people of the West being vitally concerned with what goes on in the East ... there are no internal affairs left on our crowded Earth.
>
> Henry M. Jackson quoting Alexandre Solzhenitsyn, US Senate[1]

This chapter contends that in the early 1970s there emerged a major ideological challenge to the very rationale of the American foreign-policy paradigm. A newly universalised discourse of human rights questioned the underpinning of a conservative international system, by disputing the notion that states should not interfere in the internal business of other states: instead, for human rights to have any meaning whatsoever, other states must be able to intervene in order to protect them.

The challenge took the form of an amendment, proposed in the Senate by Henry Jackson (D-WA) and in the House of Representatives by Charles Vanik (D-OH), and hence known as the Jackson–Vanik Amendment. It directly linked the granting of Most-Favoured-Nation status (MFN) to the Soviet Union with the number of citizens they allowed to emigrate. Though the planners carefully avoided any hint of it in the actual wording of the Amendment, it was clear that the motivation was the Soviet restriction on Jewish emigration. The contention here is that the debates surrounding this Amendment were debates within the American polity about the role it could play in international affairs. They were debates about the international legitimacy of a diplomatic (non-military) humanitarian intervention.

The Nixon Administration's Trade Reform legislation was part of the broader programme of détente. This programme was constructed on two interacting pillars of policy: resistance to Soviet territorial expansionism

*I would like to thank John Bew and Brendan Simms, who guided me through the dissertation on which this chapter is based, along with so many other things.*
[1] *Congressional Record*, 27 Sept. 1972, 32428–9.

coupled with a willingness to negotiate on concrete issues and a readiness to explore the principles of coexistence.[2] Détente was couched in doctrines of non-interference, making no reference to the way in which the Soviets treated their own citizens.[3] Jackson–Vanik challenged this, making a clear, legislative link between the external relations of the USA with another state and the internal behaviour of that state.

The idea of the Amendment emerged in a meeting of congressional staffers in August 1972. Prominent among them were Richard Perle, Peter Lakeland and Morris Amitay who have been collectively accredited with coming up with the idea.[4] Perle wrote the Amendment, a fundamental shift in American policy, certain that Jackson would agree with it. Historians have not, however, paused to explain the cause of Perle's certainty: the intellectual context of Jackson's career is crucial to understanding how and why Jackson–Vanik came to pass, but has been left, hitherto, unexamined. Instead, simplistic caricatures, either endorsing Jackson as a leader of the Jewish movement or condemning him as a 'Cold War ideologue', have sufficed to shape historians' understanding of the period.[5]

A small number of historical works have partially grasped the implications of the Amendment: one is Paula Stern's *Water's Edge*. Stern's argument, that 'domestic politics neither stops at the water's edge nor does it necessarily begin at the water's edge of this nation', ironically highlighted the fundamental principle of Jackson–Vanik – that the internal and external policies of a regime (the Soviet Union) are linked – but applied it to the United States, positing that Jackson's foreign-policy objectives were intimately connected with his domestic agenda.[6] Jackson doubtlessly did consider the impact the Amendment would have on his 1976 campaign, particularly on the Jewish constituency, but, when one examines his intellectual background it becomes clear that this was far from his primary motivation. Stern's most significant disadvantage, however, is a lack of hindsight: writing in 1979, she could not possibly

---

[2] Henry A. Kissinger, *Years of Upheaval* (London: Weidenfeld and Nicolson, 1982), 982.

[3] For the extent to which Kissinger subscribed to non-interference, see Henry A. Kissinger, *American Foreign Policy*, 3rd edn (New York: W. W. Norton and Co., 1977), 11–12. Also see Henry A. Kissinger, *Diplomacy* (New York: Simon and Schuster, 1994), 17–18.

[4] Petrus Buwulda, *They Did Not Dwell Alone: Jewish Emigration from the Soviet Union, 1967– 1990* (Washington, DC: Woodrow Wilson Centre Press, 1997), 95.

[5] An example of the former is Henry L. Feingold, *'Silent No More': Saving the Jews of Russia, the American Jewish Effort, 1967–1989* (Syracuse: Syracuse University Press, 2007), ch. 4; for the phrase 'cold war ideologue', see Peter J. Ognibene, *Scoop: The Life and Politics of Henry M. Jackson* (New York: Stein and Day, 1975), 153.

[6] Paula Stern, *Water's Edge* (Westport, CT: Greenwood Press, 1979), ix.

foresee the longer-term impact on the American foreign-policy landscape, or the role that human rights, so significantly advanced by the Amendment, would play in the post-Cold War era. It is with a mind to this perspective that Jackson–Vanik must be re-examined.

Another substantive account of the Amendment is in an unpublished doctoral thesis by Robert Dow based on the Jackson Papers at the University of Washington.[7] While this lifts Jackson–Vanik from its Jewish-centred legacy and places it within the context of a comprehensive biographical analysis of Jackson's opposition to détente, Dow does not examine previous Congressional attempts to address this humanitarian issue (nor indeed Congressional records at all).[8] He consequently fails to acknowledge the way in which Jackson–Vanik was a response not only to particular circumstances but also to far-reaching and potent international issues.

This chapter is a contextual study: it examines how these issues fermented during the 1960s, through public opinion, the press, the legislature and finally to the highest diplomatic circles. It presents the records of Congressional subcommittee hearings, which offer unexamined background to the Amendment. This Amendment made a substantive contribution to the foreign-policy debate in the shadow of which today's geopolitical discourse is framed: its thematic basis – the linking of internal and external considerations in foreign-policy planning – became a central dimension of neoconservative thought.[9]

## I

American activism on the issue of Soviet anti-Semitism began in earnest when the horrors of the 'Doctors' Plot' emerged in 1953: 3,500 people attended a rally in Manhattan calling for the Soviets to allow Jews to emigrate,[10] and two separate petitions were sent to President Eisenhower.[11] This call to action 'fizzled out' after the doctors were

---

[7] Robert M. Dow, 'Senator Henry M. Jackson and the US–Soviet Détente', PhD diss., University of Oxford (1995).
[8] Though for more understandable reasons, the same could be said of Robert Kaufman's biography of Jackson, *A Life in Politics* (Seattle: University of Washington Press, 2000).
[9] For example, Natan Sharansky, *The Case for Democracy* (New York: Public Affair, 2004).
[10] *New York Times*, 17 Feb. 1953, 11. For more on the resolution produced, see Lucy Dawidowicz, 'American Reaction to Soviet Anti-Semitism', *American Jewish Yearbook* 55 (1954), 149.
[11] Albert Chernin, 'Making Soviet Jews an Issue', in *The Second Exodus: The American Movement to Free Soviet Jews*, ed. Murray Friedman and Chernin (Hanover, NH: Brandeis University Press, 1999), 22.

exonerated,[12] but was soon reignited by the 'Economic Trials'. Prominent public intellectuals began to lend their weight to the movement: Bertrand Russell (an erstwhile and self-professed Soviet sympathiser) and Jean-Paul Sartre both wrote open letters to Khrushchev.[13] The number of American activists and organised protests steadily increased: the 'Soviet Mission' rally in 1964, Jacob Birnbaum's 'Student Struggle for Soviet Jewry', and then, in June 1965, the 'American Jewish Conference on Soviet Jewry' (AJCSJ) convened the largest ever rally on the issue, gathering nearly 20,000 people at Madison Square Garden.[14] President Johnson, addressing this rally, expressed his hope, 'in the spirit of peace and reason ... that the Soviet leadership ameliorate the situation of its Jewish minority. Doing so would go a long way toward removing a moral and emotional barrier between us and contribute to a relaxation of tensions.'[15] This aspiration would charac-terise the Administration over the whole of the next decade: a public rhetoric of peaceful cooperation designed to induce the Soviet Union to change its policy.

Eisenhower's private Camp David meeting of September 1959 was the only time before Jackson–Vanik that a US president directly addressed his Soviet counterpart regarding the issue. He was informed that Jews in the Soviet Union were treated in the same way as all other citizens; Secretary of State Christian Herter's similar enquiry had been met with the more standard Kremlin response, that Jews were 'an internal matter'.[16] The Administration soon realised that any attempt at diplo-matic intervention would stumble over this simple fact: that treatment of Soviet Jews was a matter of Soviet domestic jurisdiction. In reaction to the Economic Trials, President Kennedy raised the issue with Gromyko, but he did so sceptically.[17] Whenever the executive took up the issue it was always in private and never with any confidence that it would make a difference. But this passive policy had to be reconciled with a dynamic public opinion. In November 1963, Associate Justice of the Supreme Court, Arthur J. Goldberg, expressed to the Conference of Presidents of

[12] *Ibid.*, 23.
[13] Bertrand Russell and Aron Vergels, 'Soviet Anti-Semitism: An Exchange', *Commentary* (Jan. 1965); also Chernin, 'Issue', 29.
[14] In several accounts, but most fully in Yaacov Ro'i, *Struggle for Soviet Jewish Emigration* (Cambridge: Cambridge University Press, 1991), 198–9. Interestingly, Philip Baum, then director of the International Commission of the American Jewish Congress, played a key role in organising this rally – he was subsequently very critical of Jackson's efforts, see Philip Baum, 'Rethinking Jackson–Vanik: New Approaches to Soviet Emigration?', *Congress Monthly* 43 (June 1976), 7–9.
[15] Quoted in Chernin, 'Issue', 41.
[16] Gunther Lawrence, *Three Million More?* (New York: Doubleday and Co., 1970), 8.
[17] *Ibid.*, 170–1. Also see Chernin, 'Issue', 30.

Major American Jewish Organisations his reservations about the diplomatic route and his preference for responsible public protest. However,
he cautioned that protest must never be linked with any direct relationship between the USA and the Soviet Union – 'The question of the Jews
in the USSR should always be *kept on the humanitarian plane, above
political consideration*'.[18] There could be no better statement of the
divided policy-paradigm against which Jackson–Vanik reacted.

The same position was taken in a secret White House memorandum
precipitated by the Eternal Light Vigil of September 1965.[19] The memorandum, sent to McGeorge Bundy, the President's Special Assistant for
National Security Affairs, summarised secret intelligence reports
describing the relaxation of some minor restrictions. Though warning
that these concessions did not change 'the Communist purpose of
forcing Jews to forget their heritage and assimilate', it argued that 'the
fact that they've been made at all suggests the climate may improve, at
least for a time'. It speculated that world opinion may have helped to
'prod' Soviet leadership into concessions but, crucially, concluded:
'State has clearly decided it shouldn't lead on this one but will lend a
hand to private efforts. Given our limited ability to achieve anything
officially and our other priorities, the balance seems about right.'
A handwritten note on the original suggests Bundy agreed.[20]

This memorandum is a crucial foundation of the Administration's
policy in this period, yet, along with the Goldberg meeting, it has been
ignored by previous studies. It is impossible completely to understand
the debates around this issue in the 1970s, and the substantive change
made by Jackson–Vanik, without having acknowledged this prior position. This context makes clear, contrary to the impression conveyed, for
example in Noam Kochavi's recent study, that Kissinger was by no
means the first State Department official to suggest humanitarian issues
should be subordinated to 'other priorities'.[21] Jackson's Amendment
challenged not Kissinger, but the system of which Kissinger was a part.

[18] Quoted in Lawrence, *Three Million More?* 174 (emphasis added).
[19] For more on the Vigil itself see the *Washington Post*, 20 Sept. 1965, A4; also Ro'i,
*Struggle*, 199.
[20] 'Memorandum from Harold Saunders of the National Security Council Staff to the
President's Special Assistant for National Security Affairs', 5 Oct. 1965, Johnson
Library, National Security File (State Department Archive at http://www.state.gov/r/
pa/ho/frus/johnsonlb/xiv/1378.htm {Doc.130}).
[21] Noam Kochavi, 'Insights Abandoned, Flexibility Lost: Kissinger, Soviet Jewish
Emigration and the Demise of Détente', *Diplomatic History* 29 (June 2005), 503–30.
This criticism should not, however, detract from Kochavi's distinction in acknowledging
the impact of the Amendment on détente, see esp. 503–5.

The Administration's stance was firm; but it became clear that Congress was not willing to be constrained by White House aspirations for détente. There was a broad sympathy for the idea that this was an issue much larger than just Soviet Jewry, and that Americans should continue to protest vocally.[22] In May 1965, the House Committee on Foreign Affairs convened to discuss 'Anti-Religious Activities in the Soviet Union and in Eastern Europe'.[23] The testimonies given were illustrative of the mood in Congress at the time: aware of both 'the *opportunity* and the *responsibility* to take the lead'.[24] A young Donald Rumsfeld clarified this responsibility, couched in 'considerations of humanity and justice', arguing that it was 'incumbent upon those who believe that the protection of human rights and fundamental freedoms is basic to the cause of peace to weigh these reports carefully and to give serious consideration to appropriate action'.[25]

In late 1970, the dramatic trials of the Leningrad Nine 'catapulted' the issue back into the international limelight.[26] The trial was an opportunity to resurrect other concerns about the treatment of Soviet Jews. Issues such as internal passports, access to religious and cultural life, literature and education, and the right to emigrate had been discussed in American-Jewish journalism throughout the 1960s.[27] However, whereas Congressional hearings in 1965 had only discussed a vague 'regression' of freedom of conscience,[28] by May 1971, with more information available and a more overt transgression evident, Arthur Schneier was able to confidently assert that, while 'building bridges' was desirable, a clear

[22] See Arthur Schneier's recollection of the foundation of the Appeal of Conscience Foundation in early 1965 at *Denial of Human Rights to Jews in the Soviet Union: Hearings before the Subcommittee on Europe of the House of Representatives Committee on Foreign Affairs*, May 1971, CIS (Microfiche) Vol. 2/H381–14, 23; also see Senator Hubert H. Humphrey's letter of support (15 Jan. 1965), appended to the record at p. 41. Senators Kennedy and Javits subsequently made a speech on the Senate Floor based on essentially the same themes: see *Congressional Record* (10 Feb. 1965).
[23] *Antireligious Activities in the Soviet Union and in Eastern Europe: Hearings before the Subcommittee on Europe of the House of Representatives Committee on Foreign Affairs*, May 1965, Senate Library (Microfiche) Ref.(89)H2129–2.
[24] *Ibid.*, 55 (emphasis added).
[25] *Ibid.*, 52. His 'appropriate action', however, was little more than strongly worded condemnation.
[26] Kochavi, 'Insights Abandoned', 510.
[27] For example in *Commentary*: Mark Neuweld, 'The Latest Soviet Census and the Jews' (May 1960); Mark Richards, 'The Answer to Soviet Anti-Semitism' (Sept. 1960); Chanan Ayalti, 'Moscow's Jews' (Dec. 1962); Elie Weisel, 'Will Soviet Jewry Survive' (Feb. 1967); and Maurice Friedberg, 'Soviet Jewry Today' (Aug. 1969).
[28] Congressional Hearing: 'Antireligious Activities', 1.

'understanding' had to be established, 'that there can't really be an improvement of climate when there is such a flagrant violation of human rights'.[29]

The humanitarian issue of Soviet Jewish emigration could evoke reaction from large segments of American society, and these reactions could be conveyed from bottom to top of the political system. But while sympathy pervaded, action was avoided within the political community – sovereignty was respected, and 'lending a hand' was as far as the Administration was willing to go. This previously unacknowledged context casts the controversies around Jackson–Vanik in a new light.


## II

By prohibiting the so-called 'refuseniks' from emigrating, the Soviets were directly contravening Article 13 of the Universal Declaration of Human Rights. The Six-Day War had coalesced Jewish opinion in the Soviet Union: emigration provided a tangible cause that could be measured both by themselves and, more importantly, by international opinion. This internationalisation of the issue was one of the crucial tenets underlying the May 1971 Hearings, and was made more explicit by November.[30] Appreciation of the power of world opinion changed understandings of the substantive difference between supporting private efforts and Congress making a firm statement of its position regarding Soviet behaviour. In 1970, Morris Abram highlighted Soviet sensitivity to world opinion by relating to a Congressional subcommittee how, in 1968, they had contrived to have Ambassador Goldberg's testimony to the UN Human Rights Commission on the plight of Soviet intellectuals expunged.[31] The conviction that global political opinion could stimulate reform within the Soviet Union, whether justified or not, constituted an important mid-way point between the 1960s policy and the mindset of Jackson–Vanik; it also correlates with one of the key themes of this collection: that of controlling *norms*.[32] By making public statements,

---

[29] Congressional Hearing: 'Denial of Human Rights', 25.

[30] Congressional Hearing: 'Denial of Human Rights' (May 1971) and *Soviet Jewry: Hearings before the Subcommittee on Europe of the House of Representatives Committee on Foreign Affairs*, Nov. 1971, CIS (Microfiche) Vol. 3/H381–19.

[31] *25th Anniversary of the United Nations: Hearing before the Subcommittee on International Organisations and Movements of the House of Representatives Committee on Foreign Affairs*, Feb./Mar. 1970, CIS (Microfiche) Vol. 1/H381–11, 207.

[32] For more on the role of world opinion within a liberal internationalist paradigm, see Stanley Hoffman 'The Crisis of Liberal Internationalism', *Foreign Policy* 98 (1995), 159–77.

Congress could define acceptable international behaviour while avoiding the dilution (and consent) required for a formal treaty. In the development of international law this is a key phase. In 1971, the potential of condemnatory measures was understood to be making the issue so 'nettlesome'[33] to the Soviet government that it would become preferable simply to abandon it. Some columnists were suggesting that this was already happening.[34]

However, there remained dissenting voices: at the November Hearings, the Deputy Assistant Secretary of State, Richard T. Davies, provided one. He shrugged off the treatment of 'refuseniks' (such as the omnipresent KGB-tail) as being no different to the condition of any person in Soviet society expressing deviant opinion.[35] When asked whether the issue should be linked to Arms Control Negotiation, Davies made clear that he believed the problem should be handled as a discrete one – doing otherwise would be *ineffective*. This was the State Department's bottom line: that enforcement (in the sense of making vital interests contingent on humanitarian vectors) would have a negative impact.

Moderate opinion beyond government also counselled reserve. Predictably, the most measured statement came from Professor Hans Morgenthau, arch-realist, testifying in his capacity as Chairman of the Academic Committee of the AJCSJ, an allegiance that only gave greater credence to his advice. He claimed that the Soviets were sensitive to outside pressures in a dual sense: refusing to yield to pressure they considered insulting or dangerous to key interests, while yielding, generally surreptitiously, to other more subtle pressures, especially when doing so improved their position in the world community. It followed 'that the effectiveness of such pressures stands in inverse relation to their violence and ostentatiousness'.[36] Morgenthau's recommendation was pragmatism: that the President make clear to Brezhnev that this was an issue that agitated his population and that there was only so far he could go against public opinion. The chairman, Benjamin Rosenthal (D-NY), countered the more ideological alternative: for the President to add that 'freedom denied anywhere is freedom denied everywhere ... and our people are rightly concerned about denial of freedom anywhere in the world'. Morgenthau pointed out that, in response to the explanation 'we're a moralistic country', Brezhnev might well remark,

---

[33] F. Lee Bailey (a representative of the League for the Repatriation of Russian Jews) testifying at Congressional Hearing: 'Soviet Jewry', 5.
[34] Robert G. Kaiser in *Washington Post*, 6 Nov. 1971, A10.
[35] Congressional Hearing: 'Soviet Jewry', 39–54.    [36] *Ibid.*, 134.

'That's your problem.'[37] Morgenthau cautioned against 'sweeping and essentially Utopian' language inapplicable to the totalitarian nature of the Soviet regime. Rosenthal debated this too, stating that 'when this Congress writes a resolution, we have to consider the motivations of the American people. We have to begin with our traditional beliefs ... We can't scale down congressional action to meet the situation that we are trying to deal with.'[38] This episode is illustrative of what became an important strand of the debate around this issue: reconciling a policy maximising the number of Jews allowed to leave the Soviet Union, with one publicly critiquing the moral and humanitarian propriety of the Communist regime.

On the eve of Jackson–Vanik, the debate had progressed to one not of whether government should act, but of what form that action should take. Morganthau's pragmatic suggestion of discreet diplomacy to maximise emigration figures was challenged by arguments couched in American values, but also by arguments suggesting that such efforts served a wider purpose: Vanik noted that 'It is surprising how many other people, how many non-Jews have this feeling of confinement and suppression under the Soviet pressure and I think our efforts for Soviet Jewry gives all of them a symbol of freedom, a hope. I think that it is a service for the liberty of all mankind that this effort is being made.'[39] But there was no suggestion of any means of *enforcing* change: this was the innovation of Jackson's Amendment.

The immediate context of the Amendment is readily acknowledged to have been the Soviet 'Diploma Tax', news of which became public in the West in August 1972. This tax was levied against emigrants, supposedly to recover the cost of educating them: a thinly disguised deterrent for the generally well-educated Jewish population, but one which undoubtedly underestimated the vigour of the West's reaction. In September, public rallies and statements condemning 'quiet diplomacy' coincided with Jackson's speech to the Senate announcing his intention to introduce legislation.[40] The victory détente had achieved earlier in the year at the Moscow Summit began to look less clear-cut.

The genesis of the Amendment itself lay in an informal meeting of some Senate staffers, convened to discuss the appropriate response to the Diploma Tax, at which one, Richard Perle, then a thirty-year-old staffer for Jackson, recalled that 'there was a lot of hand-wringing'.[41] At this meeting, Peter Lakeland, a staffer for Jacob Javits, suggested that

[37] *Ibid.*, 136.    [38] *Ibid.*, 138–9.    [39] *Ibid.*, 92.
[40] *New York Times*, 28 Sept. 1972, 12; *Congressional Record*, 27 Sept. 1972, 32428–9.
[41] Quoted in Buwulda, *They Did Not Dwell Alone*, 95.

one way of dealing with the situation would be to deny the Soviets trade-credits. Perle added the idea of linking MFN-status with emigration flow figures.[42] The mood of the meeting quickly changed and Perle drew up the first draft of the Amendment, certain that Jackson, himself working on a response to the Moscow Summit, would agree. Jackson skilfully located the Amendment within the humanitarian critique that had been building up over the previous decades: 'the tyranny the Soviet Government continues to inflict on its minorities of all faiths and persuasions, on its dissidents, its scholars, its scientists, and men of letters is a crime in which all who choose to acquiesce are implicated'.[43] 'The unconscionable attempt ... to ransom human beings'[44] was only the most recent addition, 'one small part of an elaborate system of threats, obstacles, reprisals and intimidations designed to prevent Soviet citizens from exercising the right to free emigration'.[45]

The way in which Jackson–Vanik fits into the contemporary debate about the Soviet Union's humanitarian record is clear. But this is not the only context: we must now consider Jackson himself, since concern for the Jewish people was only one dimension of his political consciousness. He perceived an obligation to the international community to preserve and nurture human rights globally. But what is fundamental to understanding both Jackson and his Amendment is an appreciation of the fact that, for him, human rights had a *dual function*: they were obviously humanitarian, but there was a concurrent geopolitico-strategic element. As one of Jackson's chief aides later recalled: 'In his view, nations, especially powerful ones, that deny the basic freedoms deprive themselves of an effective public opinion to control their conduct – a situation that not only leaves their citizens unprotected from lawlessness and oppression, but is a menace to international peace'.[46] Even before introducing his Amendment, Jackson had campaigned that the US ought to be actively supporting the principle of the open society because 'our own freedom is intimately tied to the freedom of others ... our bitter experience in this century demonstrates that closed societies which deny freedom to their own citizens are made uneasy by the persistence of freedom in open societies – and this uneasiness and the fear and ambition it breeds threatens us all'.[47]

[42] Interview with Richard Perle (4 Dec. 2007) (hereafter cited as 'Perle Interview').
[43] *Congressional Record*, 4 Oct. 1972, 33658.     [44] *Ibid.*
[45] Press release of 15 Mar. 1973 (the same day as the reintroduction of Jackson–Vanik to the Senate), quoted in Buwulda, *They Did Not Dwell Alone*, 98.
[46] Dorothy Fosdick, 'Introduction', in *Staying the Course: Henry M. Jackson and National Security*, ed. Fosdick (Seattle: University of Washington Press, 1987), 5–6.
[47] Speaking in proposition of Concurrent Resolution 33 (which he co-authored), *Congressional Record*, 12 July 1971.

These conflating themes can be found in Jackson's autumn speeches. The reference to past mistakes was made clear: 'Once before within our memory, the world stood by while an innocent people was all but exterminated ... That Israel should exist is a modern miracle; that the Russian Jews should be denied the right to go there is a cruel and inhuman irony. It must be ended.'[48] The previous week, Jackson had drawn heavily on Alexandre Solzhenitsyn's Nobel Lecture, and his 'profound message that "mankind's sole salvation lies in everyone making everything his business, in the people in the East being vitally concerned with what is thought in the West, the people of the West being vitally concerned with what goes on in the East"'.[49] The challenge to conventional international norms of sovereignty and independence is clear. John J. Rhodes (R-AZ) declared that 'the borders of the Soviet Union should not be prison walls behind which human beings are stripped of fundamental human liberties'.[50] Jackson repudiated suggestions that Soviet emigration policies were Brezhnev's internal affairs by again quoting Solzhenitsyn: 'there are no internal affairs left on our crowded Earth'.[51]

Jackson made the innovation of his Amendment clear from the outset: 'It is a simple plea for simple justice. But unlike other such pleadings, it has some teeth.'[52] This demonstrates the critical transition that was being made: away from rhetoric and towards 'effective' policy.[53] Jackson–Vanik was, in Ribicoff's words, pioneering a 'vehicle which can be attached in the future to any appropriate legislation' to 'get the message across to the leaders of the Soviet Union'.[54] Senator Humphrey highlighted the connection central to Jackson–Vanik, the ambition 'to bring some sense of decency and humaneness into the relationship between countries and the practices of government with their own people'.[55]

Jackson was able to set his Amendment against contemporary policies quite easily: he explicitly criticised Kissinger for 'rejecting Dr. Andrei Sakharov's wise counsel against promoting a "détente" unaccompanied by increased openness and trust'. He insisted he was not opposing détente itself; the debate was not between proponents and detractors of peace, rather 'between those who wish a genuine era of international

[48] *Congressional Record*, 4 Oct. 1972, 33658.
[49] *Congressional Record*, 27 Sept. 1972, 32428.
[50] Congressional Hearing: 'Soviet Jewry', 197.
[51] *Congressional Record*, 27 Sept. 1972, 32429.     [52] *Ibid.*, 32428.
[53] Abraham Ribicoff used the word 'effective' to distinguish Jackson–Vanik from the other measure that had been considered but 'wisely rejected'. See *Congressional Record*, 4 Oct. 1972, 33661.
[54] *Ibid.*     [55] *Ibid.*

accommodation based on progress toward individual liberty and those who, in the final analysis, are indifferent to such progress'.[56] Jackson's personal view of human rights as a strategic tool in the restraint of tyranny was implicit.

The Amendment had no difficulty attracting support in the Congress – from the start it had the support of more than three-quarters of the Senate, including vociferous proponents of expanded trade and co-sponsors of the East–West Trade Bill itself.[57] The Administration was, however, confident that it could derail the Amendment from 'below' – exerting pressure on Republican Senators, or on the American Jewish community.[58] But it became evident that this tactic alone would be insufficient. Finally, in March 1974, Kissinger agreed to meet with Jackson for the first time, and there ensued a prolonged and carefully scrutinised negotiation.[59] The important aspect of this was the way in which Kissinger, by attempting to appease Jackson with emigration figures, either failed to acknowledge, or was trying to dilute, the Amendment's very powerful, yet dangerous, wider implications, which will now be examined.[60]

### III

This chapter attempts, among other things, to challenge the simplified account of Jackson–Vanik as utopianism inimical to American interests better served by gradualism, an analysis that ignores the nuances both of the context and of Jackson's view and consequently misinterprets the Amendment.[61] As illustrated above, Jackson believed that America's 'commitment' to safeguard and encourage human rights in the Soviet Union arose from both moral *and strategic* considerations. Totalitarian nations, especially geopolitically powerful ones, that systematically invoked expansionist, universalistic ideology to repress their own citizens

[56] Henry M. Jackson, 'Détente and Human Rights' (Address to the *Pacem in Terris* Conference, 11 Oct. 1973) in *Henry M. Jackson and World Affairs: Selected Speeches, 1953–1983*, ed. Dorothy Fosdick (Seattle: Washington University Press, 1990), 186–91. Kissinger had addressed this conference three days previously and endorsed détente as a system of moving from confrontation to negotiation: see Kissinger, *American Foreign Policy*, 115–30.

[57] *Congressional Record*, 4 Oct. 1972, 33660.

[58] On the 'heavy-handedness' of these methods, see Kochavi, 'Insights Abandoned', 517.

[59] Kissinger, *Upheaval*, 991; also Perle Interview.

[60] For details of the correspondence and the debate surrounding the 'letters' and the diplomacy of 1974, see Kissinger, *Upheaval*, 991–8; for the eventual collapse of the talks, and the causes, see Kochavi, 'Insights Abandoned', 521–4.

[61] Kissinger, *Diplomacy*, 751–4.

were likely, he argued, to commit or threaten aggression abroad.[62] Peace and stability could only be achieved by the international acceptance of certain common values – in short, international order was ephemeral without a *society* of states, not simply a *system* of states.[63]

Jackson took great effort to ensure that his thinking about the Soviet Union was very well informed. He used his chairmanship of the Sub-committee on National Security and International Operations (SNSIO) to invite all kinds of authorities to give testimony on the state of the Soviet Union: Robert Conquest, James Schlesinger and Bernard Lewis were all brought to Washington. Commonly known as 'The Bunker', this subcommittee's work was aimed, as Robert Conquest identified during hearings in December 1969, at correcting the 'unsatisfactory approach to international affairs' arising from the assumption that the Communist leadership was, if not quite the same type as America's, 'at any rate susceptible to more or less the same pressures and manoeuvres'.[64] Conquest recommended firmness in impelling the Communist states: 'to end their siege policy and siege economy, particularly on thought – without, in principle, their abandoning their particular social attitudes'.[65] The correlation with Jackson's views about the importance of standing firm and anticipating that the Soviets would eventually yield is clear.

The crucial lesson of these hearings was the rejection of the distinction drawn between negotiation and confrontation with the Soviets. As Robert Byrnes asserted, 'we have been confronting them and negotiating with them simultaneously since 1947'.[66] The point was not that the Soviets would not negotiate, but that they would not comprehend (and certainly not reciprocate) concession.[67] Many of the experts were pessimistic about

---

[62] For an example, see his speech to the Congress in July 1971 (quoted above); see also, Kaufman, *Life in Politics*, 252.

[63] For the system/societal distinction, see Hedley Bull, *The Anarchical Society: A Study of Order in World Politics* (London: Macmillan, 1977). The connection between Jackson's thinking and this canonical text of International Relations scholarship has been highlighted by Dow, 'Senator Henry M. Jackson and the US–Soviet Détente', 124–7.

[64] *International Negotiation: Hearing Before the SNSIO*, US Senate (Part I (with Robert Conquest)) Dec. 1969, CIS (Microfiche) Vol. 1/S401–5, 2. For more on The Bunker, see Jay Winik, *On the Brink: The Dramatic Behind-the-Scenes Saga of the Reagan Era and the Men and Women Who Won the Cold War* (New York: Simon and Schuster, 1996), esp. 55–6.

[65] Congressional Hearing: 'International Negotiation' (Part I), 19.

[66] *International Negotiation: Hearing before the SNSIO*, US Senate (Part V (with Robert F. Byrnes)) Apr. 1971 CIS (Microfiche) Vol. 2/S401–5, 131.

[67] Almost all experts appearing before the SNSIO comment on negotiation (as one might expect given the title of the set of hearings); William R. van Cleave is particularly lucid – see *International Negotiation: Hearing before the SNSIO*, US Senate (Part VII (with William R. van Cleave)) July 1972 CIS (Microfiche) Vol. 4/S401–1.

the future; Leonard Shapiro warned: 'I don't believe that the regime wants to liberalise in the slightest'.[68] While Shapiro would have agreed with Kissinger's analysis that the Soviets aimed at undermining the balance of power, his assertion that they would not liberalise over time was one counterpoised to most justifications of détente, most importantly the 'convergence theory', that, given time and space, the Soviet system would gradually 'converge' with that of the West. Jackson saw this theory as an effort to grasp at a happier prognosis than the realities of the Soviet leadership and system allowed. Conquest (in his second SNSIO testimony) was a little more sophisticated: he saw it as an economic-determinist interpretation of history, which ignored 'the preponderant weight of the whole civil and political tradition of the country'. As before under Peter the Great and Stalin, 'a merely technological "convergence" was accompanied by a social and political *divergence* into ever-greater difference from the Western methods'.[69] Walter Laqueur, in a separate hearing, gave an equally damning condemnation of the 'para-Marxist tendency' of connecting increased trade and improved relations.[70]

Jackson insisted that Soviet policy must be based on 'true reciprocity', and highlighted human rights as a sphere where the USA should take 'stronger initiatives', because without greater freedom 'there can be no genuine détente; there can be no real progress toward peace'.[71] Leopold Labedz (quoting Solzhenitsyn) made the parallel with Munich: 'The timid civilised world has found nothing with which to oppose the onslaught of a sudden revival of barefaced barbarity, other than concessions and smiles'.[72]

That historians of Jewish activism have omitted the context of these hearings from their cursory examination of Jackson–Vanik is understandable; that historians of détente have failed to examine the contributions of the many intellectuals who appeared before them prior to concluding that the Amendment was symptomatic of, at worst, sordid electioneering and, at best, obsolete cold-warriorism, is less so. The corollary of basing one's foreign policy on the internal regimes of other

---

[68] *Ibid.*, 37; compare this with Leszek Kolakowski, 'The Case for Reform in Communist Countries: Hopeless or Not?', *New Politics* 9 (Fall 1971), 38–54.

[69] Congressional Hearing: 'International Negotiation' (Part VI), 187–9.

[70] *Negotiation and Statecraft: Hearing before the Permanent Subcommittee on Investigations of the Committee on Government Operations*, US Senate (Part I (with Walter Laqueur)) April 1973 CIS (Microfiche) Vol. 4/S401–5, 15.

[71] *Negotiation and Statecraft: Hearing before the Permanent Subcommittee on Investigations of the Committee on Government Operations*, US Senate (Part II (with Leopold Labedz)) July 1973 CIS (Microfiche) Vol. 4/S401–5, 51.

[72] *Ibid.*, 62.

states is far more fundamental: a challenge to the distinction between accepting normative-internationalism when it concerns external behaviour, but staunchly rejecting it regarding internal policy. Jackson was trying to bring Soviet domestic behaviour, as it had been documented in his hearings, to account in the international sphere. It would, however, be reductionist to suggest that the debate over this amendment was driven by a straightforward disagreement concerning the nature of American foreign-policy goals, with Jackson on one side arguing that moral issues ought to be considered, and the Nixon–Kissinger nexus on the other, determined that they should not. It is of course worth considering the sophistication of the Administration's position.[73]

*

Henry Kissinger has written extensively about the design of American foreign policy: 'to build peace on reciprocal restraint; to suffuse our concept of order with our country's commitment to freedom; to strive for peace without abdication and for order without unnecessary confrontation'.[74] He understood American perceptions of international affairs as traditionally being Manichean – with international relationships being either peaceful or warlike and never anything in between. The Soviet Union fulfilled the traditional image of irreconcilable conflict between good and evil, but their hostility translated itself into 'ambiguous' attempts to 'nibble away' at the balance of power.[75]

These considerations engendered White House policy that strove 'to end America's traditional oscillation between over-commitment and isolationism, between crusading and escapism [and] to ground American policy in a realistic sense of national interest and the requirements of the balance of power'.[76] From this followed 'détente', the dual policy of resisting expansion while demonstrating willingness to negotiate on issues such as deterrence and to explore principles of coexistence, such as trade. The Administration had initially resisted pressure to expand East–West trade, on the grounds that the Soviets should first demonstrate 'a commitment to restrained international conduct' and to settling issues such as Vietnam and Berlin, a policy dubbed 'linkage'.[77] When, in 1972, the trade initiative was resuscitated, it was 'linkage' that was altered to justify Jackson–Vanik, often by men who had originally opposed it. Jackson viewed the unamended Trade Bill as an

---

[73] It is noted that governments speak with more than one voice, and that some in the White House were much closer to Congress on this issue than others. This study has used 'White House' and 'Administration' to signify Nixon, Kissinger and détente, but further study of the plurality of Administration views in this period could be profitable.

[74] Kissinger, *Upheaval*, 979.     [75] *Ibid.*, 980–1.     [76] *Ibid.*, 981.     [77] *Ibid.*, 985.

unacceptable concession: undermining this conciliatory policy was at all stages as important to Jackson as freeing Jews.[78]

Kissinger's interpretation of Jackson's position was informed, and at times sophisticated, but, in totality, demonstrative of the fundamental division being drawn. He saw the issue as one on which conservatives and liberals cynically converged: the conservatives uneasy about the number of agreements being made with the Soviets and the liberals converted by a 'blood-feud' with Nixon.[79] Kissinger suggests that this convergence led to an intellectual chaos that might well have remained 'inchoate sniping' had not Jackson emerged as a leader. However, as demonstrated (for the first time) above, the 'inchoate sniping' was *not* the product of Nixon's administration. The desire to take action concerning Soviet anti-Semitism had a long pedigree in both the legislature and executive branches of government, and an even longer one in public opinion and the press. Jackson did not emerge a leader of this movement but rather a political innovator challenging the *modus vivendi* of foreign-policy planning. Initially supportive of his efforts, the Administration was, in Kissinger's view, too slow realising that 'Jackson's whole crusade depended on proving that our sense of what was attainable was flawed'.[80] While demonstrating that Jackson's struggle against détente was not merely self-perception, Kissinger does not mention the crucial consistency between internal and external politics, and instead insists that the distinction was between a gradualist Administration and an absolutist Jackson caucus.[81]

To suggest that Jackson pursued the goal of stalling détente at the cost of increasing emigration figures is to suggest that there was an opportunity to make a choice.[82] But Jackson believed that he could achieve both goals concurrently and, importantly, that they were mutually reinforcing. For Jackson, the issue was always much broader than Russian Jews. This is a reality that has been tremendously distorted by studies of the activist movement. For those who worked on the Amendment, the issue was the much larger one of human rights, and its intrusion into the diplomatic arena.

Jackson–Vanik precipitated a transformation of liberal public opinion regarding trade. In September 1972, the *New York Times* printed a conventional liberal endorsement of expanded trade as something 'sufficiently

---

[78] Perle Interview.    [79] Kissinger, *Upheaval*, 983.    [80] *Ibid.*, 985.    [81] *Ibid.*, 984.
[82] Kissinger's analysis of Jackson–Vanik assumes that it was counter-productive, that 'quiet diplomacy' worked and that Soviet accommodations on emigration were contingent on the overall state of US–Soviet relations, tarnished by Jackson (*Upheaval*, 987). Kochavi refutes this as 'possibly disingenuous and certainly self-serving and inaccurate' ('Insights Abandoned', 509).

beneficial to both sides that it ought to be considered . . . on its own merits, independent of particular secondary disputes in other areas'. Two months later, there was a complete reversal, and a warning against becoming 'so eager to expand Soviet–American trade as to forget the continuing sensitivity of the American people – and of Congress – to Soviet political behavior both inside and outside the USSR's borders'.[83] By September 1973, as the Soviets intensified their campaign against the dissenters, the *New York Times*, while still broadly advocating expanded trade, suggested that the Soviets ought to recognise 'that American moral indignation over the fate of the Russian dissenters is a fact of political consequence. We would like to see this concern also expressed openly and at the highest levels of the United States Government.'[84]

The Administration, however, maintained that a presidential declaration would contravene accepted diplomatic conduct; that confrontation by the White House would only aggravate the Kremlin and escalate tensions that were otherwise being relaxed. After Jackson–Vanik was signed into law, these fears were realised: on 10 January 1975, the Soviets rejected the entire trade package.[85] Kissinger was vindicated: the Soviets had reacted badly to America 'contravening . . . the principle of non-interference in domestic affairs', making a non-military humanitarian intervention.[86] However, some studies of Brezhnev's politburo have suggested that they may have been using Jackson–Vanik to cover their retreat from a now-unfavourable trade negotiation.

★

For Jackson the issue had always been much larger: he insisted that the Soviet reaction was a deliberate effort to demonstrate the folly of human rights legislation, of which Jackson–Vanik was just one step.[87] The Amendment was the first American legislation to draw explicitly on the 1948 Declaration: Jackson interpreted this document as having brought internal behaviour into the sphere of the international, to be

---

[83] *New York Times*, 13 Sept. 1972, 46, and 25 Nov. 1972, 30. For Kissinger's view of this contrast, see *Years of Renewal* (New York: Simon and Schuster, 1999), 105.

[84] *New York Times*, 18 Sept. 1973, 42. Interestingly, however, this article was critical of ongoing Congressional attempts to resolve the problem: 'We do not believe that it is appropriate, in a foreign trade or in any other kind of bill, for Congress to legislate on the internal affairs of another country'.

[85] This had not been anticipated by the planners of the Amendment: they had considered it possible that the Soviets would refuse to accept and then renegotiate, but not accept and then renege (Perle Interview).

[86] At a press conference the following week; full text in the *New York Times*, 15 Jan. 1975, 4.

[87] 'Remarks to NCSJ Leadership Assembly' (5 May 1975), quoted in Dow, 'Senator Henry M. Jackson and the US–Soviet Détente', 254.

judged and arbitrated in the same way as external conduct.[88] Having submitted his Amendment, Jackson and those around him became increasingly aware of the supremacy of the right to emigrate among all the other rights. Perle has referred to it as 'the mother of all rights'.[89] Jackson came to the conclusion that this was a very powerful tool in the struggle against totalitarianism – if people were capable of voting with their feet then any government was forced to make life tolerable. This was a view shared by Anatoly Dobrynin in his memoirs: the Soviets feared 'an escape hatch from the happy land of socialism' which would destabilise their domestic situation.[90] It is interesting to note that emigration was immediately recognised by Eleanor Roosevelt in 1948 as an insuperable barrier for the Soviets regarding human rights.[91] The importance of emigration had been acknowledged by a 1963 UN study noting that, unlike many rights set forth in the UDHR, comparatively few countries constitutionally, legally or administratively recognised the right of nationals to leave: 'this lack of recognition not only opens the door to arbitrary action, but seriously reduces the possibility of an effective remedy when discrimination occurs'.[92] This was the radical departure made by Jackson–Vanik: dictating that unless this fundamental right was acknowledged and respected, the US would not grant trade concessions.

Jackson–Vanik is an interestingly early example of a unilateral, if non-military, US humanitarian intervention. The inaction of the UN and (more startling) of Israel is something deserving further study. Jackson's own understanding of America's place in the world was unapologetic: he saw a strong United States as crucial to the defence of Americo-Western concepts of government.[93] After the Soviets had rejected the trade agreement, Jackson did not relent: he insisted that the Amendment was just the first step in a long-term struggle to use American foreign policy as a means of

---

[88] William Korey, *The Promises We Keep: Human Rights, the Helsinki Process, and American Foreign Policy* (New York: St Martin's Press, 1993), 54.
[89] Perle Interview.
[90] Anatoly Dobrynin, *In Confidence: Moscow's Ambassador to America's Six Cold War Presidents (1962–1986)* (New York: Times Books, 1995), 268. Also Sharansky, *Case for Democracy*, 118–20.
[91] 'Making Human Rights Come Alive', in *What I Hope to Leave Behind: The Essential Essays of Eleanor Roosevelt*, ed. Allida M. Black (New York: Carlson, 1995), 565–6, 573.
[92] *A Study of Discrimination with Respect to the Right of Everyone to Leave Any Country, Including His Own, And to Return to his Own Country*, prepared by José D. Ingles (New York: UN, 1963), UN-Ref.E/CN.4/Sub.2/220/Rev.1, 60.
[93] Perle Interview.

increasing Soviet human rights compliance.[94] He criticised Kissinger as a 'poor student of the American people', for dismissing their historical commitment to human rights as a luxury that could not be afforded in the nuclear age.[95] The reality, he insisted, was that their tradition of promoting individual liberty and democratic government was one of America's most important *strategic* assets.[96]

## IV

Jackson–Vanik's influence on the American debate was quickly apparent: in October 1975, Andrei Amal'rik wrote in the *New York Times* that the 'old-fashioned European political mentality' was not likely to long dominate US foreign policy. With clear resonances of Jackson he asserted: 'When the USSR must pay for every bushel of grain and for every technological secret not so much with gold as with a step toward democratisation of its society, only then will its foreign policy cease to present a threat to the West'.[97]

It has been demonstrated that the Amendment passed several significant watersheds: it was a policy which linked the way in which America treated another state with the way in which that state treated its own citizens; and it was one which operated with an understanding not only of America's role in the world, but also of more intangible problems of universalism and human rights. This study has emphasised the earlier efforts to ease the plight of Soviet Jewry at all levels – public, intellectual, Congressional and Presidential – through the late 1960s, to illustrate the innovation of Jackson–Vanik's method, combining humanitarianism and soft power in accordance with Jackson's understanding of geopolitical strategy.

Jackson–Vanik highlighted the possibilities for human rights in geopolitics but, at the same time, demonstrated the dangers: while challenging Kissinger's reservations about involving human rights in international politics, it concurrently highlighted the risks to détente of trying to expand human rights.[98] However, this study has demonstrated

---

[94] 'Memorandum re. meeting with Soviet Jewry leadership on July 28' (25 July 1975); also see 'America Hasn't Lost its Nerve' (8 February 1976) both quoted in Dow, 'Senator Henry M. Jackson and the US–Soviet Détente', 255, 257.

[95] *Ibid.* On the relationship of America and human rights, see Arthur M. Schlesinger, 'Human Rights and the American Tradition', *Foreign Affairs* 57 (1978), 503–26.

[96] 'America and Human Rights' Address to the World Affairs Council of Philadelphia (19 April 1976), quoted in Dow, 'Senator Henry M. Jackson and the US–Soviet Détente', 258.

[97] Andrei Amal'rik, 'Andrei Amal'rik on Détente', *New York Times*, 22 Oct. 1975, 45.

[98] Harold Molineu, 'Negotiating Human Rights: The Helsinki Agreement', *World Affairs* 141 (Summer 1978), 27.

that the Amendment was more than an attempt to free Soviet Jews with unintended consequences: it was the culmination of ideas that had been fomenting for a decade at all levels of the American polity. The American ideals identified here were in escalating conflict with the official foreign-policy paradigm of non-interference. The Amendment, and the ideas it embodied, have both a provenance and a legacy that stretch well beyond the détente they were so critical in undermining.

## 15 Fraternal aid, self-defence, or self-interest? Vietnam's intervention in Cambodia, 1978–1989

*Sophie Quinn-Judge*

> The righteous actions of the Vietnamese people and the people of Kampuchea are in harmony with the principles of the Non-aligned Movement and the United Nations Charter.
>
> Truong Chinh, *Ve Van De Cam-pu-chia* (1979)[1]

Vietnam's march into its smaller, weaker neighbour in late 1978, with weapons supplied by the Soviet Union, looked to many observers like a classic annexation. The Vietnamese themselves did not attempt to defend their action as a 'humanitarian intervention', although they expected much of the world to approve their removal of the Pol Pot regime. This obsessively secretive Cambodian government had cut off its population from most contacts with the outside world since coming to power in April 1975. Over the nearly four years of Pol Pot's rule, news of the brutal agrarian regime he inflicted on Cambodia had seeped out via refugees who made their way to the Thai border. A Khmer-speaking US diplomat, Charles Twining, had spent months in these border camps interviewing refugees and cross-checking their stories of hunger and executions.[2] Another Khmer speaker, Father François Ponchaud, had published his findings on Khmer Rouge brutality in *Le Monde* in February 1976, when he estimated that as many as 800,000 killings had occurred.[3] The basic outlines of what was going on in Cambodia were thus becoming well known when Twining testified at hearings of the House International Relations Subcommittee in July 1977.

But the complexities of international politics, in particular the US obsession with spreading Soviet power in the Third World, made it difficult for the Democratic administration of President Jimmy Carter to condone Vietnam's unilateral toppling of the government known as

---

[1] Truong Chinh, *Ve Van De Cam-pu-chia* [*On the Kampuchean Question*] (Hanoi: NXB Su That, 1979), 29.

[2] Samantha Power, '*A Problem for Hell*': *America and the Age of Genocide* (New York: Basic Books, 2002), 115–17.

[3] *Ibid.*, 120.

the Khmer Rouge (KR). The policy which the American government would follow for roughly the next eleven years, however, was more than one of neutrality – it amounted to an unspoken tactical alliance with the Khmer Rouge and a denial of any positive or humanitarian aspects linked to Vietnam's removal of Pol Pot. Thus one of the few successful humanitarian interventions in the decades of the Cold War passed without recognition or serious examination by international bodies until the Cold War ended in 1992.

Looking back, one can affirm that this was a military invasion that made a marked improvement in the lives of the people of Cambodia. In spite of the political and ideological posturing that surrounded the overthrow of the Khmer Rouge, with thirty years' hindsight we can say that the Vietnamese action amounted to an undeclared but successful humanitarian intervention. As political scientist Thomas G. Weiss puts it, this was an intervention with a 'very substantial humanitarian payoff'.[4] A despotic, deluded leader who had turned his country into a prison camp was pushed to the Thai border, where the harm he could inflict on his people was limited. The new Vietnamese-controlled regime in Phnom Penh was a less-than-ideal replacement, but it ended the slavery of Cambodia's people, who under Pol Pot had become malnourished, unpaid workers in a nationwide, labour-intensive agricultural development project.

After President Clinton signed the Cambodian Genocide Justice Act in 1994, two US attorneys determined that the Khmer Rouge could be tried for genocide on the grounds of '*prima facie* culpability for acts against religious and ethnic groups, such as the Cham Muslims, Vietnamese and Chinese communities, and the Buddhist monkhood'. They also found *prima facie* culpability for war crimes and other crimes against humanity.[5]

In the paragraphs that follow, I will first address the genesis of Vietnam's decision to intervene in Cambodia, behind the screen of a Cambodian resistance movement. I will then look at the international reaction to the Vietnamese occupation, and the Khmer government they erected. Finally, I will discuss the ongoing process of study and documentation of the brief Khmer Rouge rule, which only in 2007 made it possible to open a UN-sponsored war crimes tribunal to try the leaders of this regime.

---

[4] Thomas G. Weiss, *Humanitarian Intervention: War and Conflict in the Modern World* (Cambridge: Polity Press, 2007), 37.
[5] Craig Etcheson, *After the Killing Fields: Lessons from the Cambodian Genocide* (Westport, CT, and London: Praeger, 2005), 55.

I will not attempt to produce here a systematic description of the Pol Pot system and how it came into being. For excellent scholarly studies of the Khmer Rouge see Ben Kiernan's *How Pol Pot Came to Power* and *The Pol Pot Regime*.[6]

★

Much of the confusion surrounding the Vietnamese conflict with the Khmer Rouge's Democratic Kampuchea (DK) stemmed from the closed nature of the two states. Few outside analysts were reading the KR's theoretical journal *Tung Padewat* (*Revolutionary Flag*) in the years when Pol Pot's soldiers were attacking settlements in Vietnam, so there was little awareness of the regime's irredentist objective to take back the Mekong Delta, the area which the Khmers referred to as Kampuchea Krom or Lower Cambodia. However, eyewitness accounts of events in 1977 collected by Ben Kiernan confirm that by May 1977 KR cadres were talking of conquering 'Kampuchea Krom'.[7] They were also *acting* on their beliefs by beginning a series of violent attacks across the border into Vietnam at that time. (They must have believed that China would come to their rescue in the event of a Vietnamese counter-attack.)

The Vietnamese were slow to condemn the new Communist government in Cambodia, which had come to power less than a month before South Vietnam fell to Hanoi's final offensive on 30 April 1975. The Khmer Rouge leadership had kept their political distance from the Vietnamese since roughly 1962, but after Prince Sihanouk was overthrown in 1970, the two parties collaborated closely enough to overwhelm the US-supported army of Lon Nol. Around 1973 the KR began to attack and assassinate members of their movement whom they suspected were too close to Vietnam, but whether the Vietnamese were aware of the elimination of those Khmers trained in Hanoi is not known. As they returned to Cambodia from Vietnam, these men were simply swallowed up within the ranks of the party. By 1973, however, US intelligence was hearing accounts of rival factions within the Cambodian Communist party, one of which, the *Khmer Krahom* or 'Red Khmer' was the more hard-line and objected to cooperation with North Vietnamese forces. In fact, as later interviews established, the Red Khmer were already killing off their rivals, the *Khmer Rumdos* ('Liberation Khmer') in 1973–4, in districts where their forces were dominant.[8]

[6] Ben Kiernan, *How Pol Pot Came to Power: Colonialism, Nationalism and Communism in Cambodia, 1930–1975*, 2nd edn (New Haven and London: Yale University Press, 2004) and Kiernan, *The Pol Pot Regime: Race, Power and Genocide under the Khmer Rouge, 1975–79*, 2nd edn (New Haven and London: Yale University Press, 2002).
[7] Kiernan, *The Pol Pot Regime*, 360–6.      [8] *Ibid.*, 65–76.

With their joint victory over American power in South-east Asia, the two Communist governments would have had ample reason to continue their cooperation. Both nations were emerging from devastating wars that had destroyed much of their infrastructure and delayed their participation in the rapid development that was occurring in other parts of South-east Asia. Although both of these countries were caught up in a wave of revolutionary optimism in 1975 (the Vietnamese were often described as 'drunk with victory'), it is hard to imagine that either leadership was ready for a new phase of war.

The border disputes that first brought the two into conflict in April 1975 could have been settled by negotiation over the months to come, and that is certainly what the Vietnamese expected. These border problems were the legacy of the French colonial mapping of Indochina, as well as the drawn-out Vietnamese war against the United States. In the latter case, the Vietnamese had made use of Cambodian territory for sanctuaries and supply routes, until 1970 with head-of-state Sihanouk's tacit acceptance. It has never been entirely clear how many Vietnamese troops remained inside Cambodian territory after mid-1975, but most observers agree that the Vietnamese complied with Cambodian requests that they leave.[9] There were two factors that transformed what started as border conflicts into an irreconcilable argument: one was the irredentism of Democratic Kampuchea's little-known Communist party leader, Saloth Sar, revealed to the world in 1976 under the name Pol Pot; the second was his fear of internal rivals, whom he suspected of being allied with Vietnam.

Pol Pot was an exemplar of the relatively privileged colonial subject who developed into an anti-colonial leftist during his studies in the metropole. He became a member of a tight-knit Marxist studies group in Paris, which in the 1960s provided most of the core members of the Communist Party of Kampuchea. A middling technical student who failed his exams in radio technology, Pol Pot would become a popular teacher of French in Phnom Penh as he rose in the ranks of the party during the 1950s.[10] Along with most other educated Khmer, Pol Pot was distrustful of Vietnamese intentions in Cambodia. After 1978, the Cambodian leadership and their allies held to the story that the

---

[9] *Ibid.*, 106–7. Kiernan cites a Chinese report by Geng Biao, secretary-general of the CCP military commission.
[10] Philip Short, *Pol Pot: History of a Nightmare* (London: John Murray, 2004), is the most recent and comprehensive biography of Pol Pot. While the book provides much interesting detail and unique interviews with KR leaders, it gives a one-sided view of Cambodian–Vietnamese relations and does not endorse the view that the KR leadership should be brought to trial.

Vietnamese coveted Cambodian territory and had a long-term plan to re-create the French colonial Indochinese Union of Laos, Cambodia and Vietnam.

Outside assumptions about Vietnam's territorial ambitions were based on two episodes in Vietnam's past, and almost certainly exaggerated the Vietnamese capacity for long-term planning in 1975. The history of Nguyen Emperor Minh-Mang's efforts to transform Cambodia into a sinicised vassal between 1835 and 1841 was the first example cited by Vietnam's critics. Alexander Woodside has explained these efforts as an outgrowth of Vietnam's adoption of the Chinese model of international relations.[11] In order to claim the status of emperor, the Nguyen rulers had to wield influence over vassal states or peoples. Even though their efforts failed and they had to be content after 1841 to share their influence over Cambodia with the kingdom of Siam, the Nguyen continued to view themselves as representatives of a higher form of civilisation, in contrast to the less organised, Indianised Khmers. The Vietnamese Communists no doubt continued to make assumptions about their cultural superiority to the Cambodian people in the 1970s, but they had learned from years of difficult inter-party relations that the Khmer Rouge would not play the little brothers. Just as the Vietnamese demanded autonomy from the Chinese in formulating their foreign policies, the Khmer Rouge refused to accept anything that resembled a tributary relationship with Vietnam.

The second episode began with the creation of an Indochina Communist Party in 1930, and continued until at least 1939, through the iterations of a left-wing, supra-national political programme for the territories of French Indochina, at that time approved by both the Soviet and Chinese parties.[12] With Ho Chi Minh's return to prominence in the Vietnamese party in 1941, this programme was replaced by an explicitly nationalist programme for the Vietnamese revolution. While Cambodia remained strategically vital to the Vietnamese, talk of an Indochina Federation ended. Still, based on these two pieces of evidence, foreign observers in the 1980s claimed to see something akin to a genetic or essentialist Vietnamese disposition to gobble up Cambodia.

The simultaneous unravelling of their relations with Cambodia and China was, however, not part of the Vietnamese long-term plan in

---

[11] Alexander Barton Woodside, *Vietnam and the Chinese Model* (Cambridge, MA: Harvard University Press, 1971), 246–55.
[12] Thomas Engelbert and Christopher E. Goscha, *Falling Out of Touch: A Study on Vietnamese Communist Policy Towards an Emerging Cambodian Communist Movement, 1930–1945* (Clayton, Victoria: Monash Asia Institute, Monash University, 1995), 7–14.

1975–6. As one Foreign Ministry expert explains, the unexpected turn of events in 1977–8, including vicious KR attacks on Vietnamese villages and the suspension of Chinese aid, left them scrambling to come up with a policy.[13] By the time they had established their presence throughout Cambodia in 1979, they settled on self-defence as their primary legal justification for the invasion. This explanation was laid out by ideologist Truong Chinh in a 1979 article. His argument was aimed at the UN, where the KR retained their seat until 1981; from then until 1990 the seat was held by the Coalition Government of DK, a fig-leaf for the KR in which Prince Sihanouk participated. Truong Chinh's plea of self-defence combined this 'legitimate right of an independent people' with a defence of the right of the Khmer people to 'overthrow the genocidal yoke of the lackeys of Beijing'. He also insisted that their Cambodian allies had a right to assist the people of Vietnam in defending themselves against an invasion from Cambodian soil. These rights were in line with the principles of non-alignment and the UN Charter, he pointed out.[14]

But in 1978, as they planned their move into Cambodia, the Vietnamese placed more emphasis on the crimes of the Pol Pot regime against their own people. They also maintained the rather thin fiction that the invasion was led by a Cambodian opposition force. An argument in support of a humanitarian intervention was not within their repertoire of international law. This is not surprising, as the newly independent Asian states had been born after World War II, when national self-determination and peaceful co-existence had become sacred notions, enshrined in the declaration of the 1955 Bandung Conference.

★

By the summer of 1975, the Vietnamese should have known quite a lot about the government in Phnom Penh. In the first month of Khmer Rouge rule, Pol Pot's forces had forced most of the 150,000 Vietnamese residents of Cambodia, including families that had lived in the country for several generations, back over the border into Vietnam. A Vietnamese Embassy was one of the few diplomatic representations in Phnom Penh until the KR severed relations at the end of 1977. Vietnamese delegations visited occasionally, both to promote friendship and to engage in border negotiations. But in the early years of peace, the Vietnamese chose to cover up any tensions that existed between their country and the new Democratic Kampuchea. They may have hoped that their allies within the Khmer party would gain the upper hand, or that with

[13] Personal interview with Luu Doan Huynh, Hanoi, Jan. 2009.
[14] Truong Chinh, *Về Vấn Đề Cam-pu-chia* (Hanoi: NXB Su That, 1979), 28–9.

the death of Mao and the ousting of the Gang of Four leftists from power in October 1976, the Chinese would take a greater interest in moderating KR behaviour.

In 1975, the Vietnamese also had ambitious development plans for their country. Although they did not force the evacuation of the urban areas, as the Khmers Rouges had done, the Vietnamese Communists placed strong pressure on urban populations to move to the countryside to help rebuild the country's agriculture. For the new Communist rulers, the urban sprawl of Saigon represented Western decadence and the American enemy's culture, just as Phnom Penh did for the KR. By mid-1978 this pressure was combined with a campaign to 'end capitalism' in the towns and cities, aimed at traders and producers of all economic strata. The government that was implementing these policies was neither as gradualist nor as committed to reconciliation among Vietnamese as their wartime programmes had promised. But in contrast to Cambodia in those years, the Vietnamese individual was still free to leave the rural 'New Economic Zones' and return to the towns, even though he may have lost his residence permit and right to enrol his children in school. Still, the pressures the Communist government placed on middle-class, urban Vietnamese increased the small trickle of people fleeing southern Vietnam by boat to a flood, what became known as the exodus of 'boat people'. As Vietnam's ethnic Chinese minority, the Hoa, was predominantly composed of urban traders, they came to form a high percentage of those leaving Vietnam by boat. (Ethnic Chinese in Cambodia suffered far more severely in the Pol Pot years, being forced to move to the countryside, where they laboured under the same conditions as other urban people, and were forbidden to speak their own language.)

At the same time, Vietnam was growing estranged from their neighbour to the north. The Vietnamese had become adept during the war years at balancing relations with the two giants of the Socialist Bloc. This had not been an easy process, since from the late 1950s, the Soviet Union and the People's Republic of China (PRC) had been competing aggressively for leadership of this bloc. The Vietnamese Worker's Party had been dominated by its pro-Chinese wing for much of the 1960s, but as their need for heavy weaponry increased after 1965, they grew more dependent on the USSR for its military technology. Relations with China had gone into decline in 1968, as the Cultural Revolution engulfed this once secure rear base in civil war. Political conflict increased when the Chinese refused initially to support the opening of Vietnam's peace negotiations with the United States in Paris. This deterioration in Sino-Vietnamese relations only accelerated when the Chinese and Americans began their rapprochement in 1971, culminating in President Nixon's visit to China in 1972. Still, North Vietnam, before its official reunification with the South in 1976, had been dependent on China for food aid and low-cost consumer goods and continued to rely on Chinese aid after the war ended.

After 1977, however, polite neutrality in the Sino–Soviet dispute was no longer an option. When the Chinese demanded that the Vietnamese stop receiving aid from the Soviet Union, the Vietnamese refused to make such a concession. China in 1976 was just emerging from the Cultural Revolution and could never have supplied the level of technological aid that the Vietnamese were counting on from their Soviet supporters. But this reality did not lessen the Chinese leadership's discomfort with the idea of a resurgent Soviet satellite on its southern border, in place of the loyal vassal that they counted on Vietnam to be. Still, there is ample evidence that the Vietnamese had hoped, until 1978, to avoid a dependent relationship with the Soviet Union.[15] They did not sign a Friendship Treaty with the USSR until November 1978, when their options had become extremely limited. They joined the COMECON pact a few months beforehand, as economic aid from other sources had not been plentiful.

In these years Vietnam was finding that its wartime popularity as a Third World underdog was ebbing away, while relations with both Cambodia and China deteriorated. Negotiations aimed at normalising relations with the United States did not go well, in part because the Vietnamese continued to demand that the United States supply aid for post-war reconstruction, as agreed by President Nixon in 1973. A Western European tour by Prime Minister Pham Van Dong in 1977 had resulted in a splendid reception at the Elysée Palace in Paris, but very little in the way of financial commitments to help Vietnam rebuild.[16] It was also unhelpful that DK Foreign Minister, Ieng Sary, made a tour of ASEAN (Association of South East Asian Nations) capitals in early 1977, during which he complained to his counterparts of Vietnamese territorial expansionism.[17] Although there was no known evidence to support this claim, his interlocutors tended to give credence to his complaints, given the wartime history of Vietnamese use of Cambodian territory. This was the period when the Cambodian party's Central Committee seems to have formulated what journalist Nayan

---

[15]  This view is convincingly developed by journalist Nayan Chanda in *Brother Enemy: The War After the War, A History of Indochina Since the Fall of Saigon* (New York: Collier Books, 1986), see, in particular, 181–7.

[16]  *Ibid.*, 158.

[17]  Personal communication with Singapore diplomat Kishore Mahbubani.

Chanda calls a 'final solution' to deal with the perceived threat from Vietnam. On 1 April the party Central Committee, then known as '870', issued a directive calling on local organisations to turn over to the party's security service all ethnic Vietnamese, as well as any Khmers who spoke Vietnamese or had Vietnamese friends. According to one villager from Oudong District, a Vietnamese woman was bludgeoned to death after being turned over.[18] Then the Khmer Rouge launched a surprise series of attacks on Vietnamese villages on 30 April 1977, leaving around 100 civilians dead in the Mekong Delta's An Giang province. The Cambodians ignored a Vietnamese offer of peace negotiations that June. A particularly vicious KR attack was launched on Vietnamese villages in Tay Ninh province on 24 September 1977, which left hundreds of Vietnamese civilians dead and mutilated. Still the Vietnamese tried to prevent news of these clashes from reaching the outside world. A Hungarian journalist who had been taken to the border to view the devastated villages was prevented from filing his stories or photos when he returned to Ho Chi Minh City and Hanoi.[19] On Christmas Day 1977, Vietnam launched its own retaliatory attack on Cambodia, a multi-pronged operation penetrating to the outskirts of two provincial towns, Svay Rieng and Kompong Cham. They followed this up with a proposal for a cease-fire and negotiations in February 1978, but without any response from the Cambodian side. Instead, on 31 December 1977 the Cambodians announced to the world that they were ending their diplomatic relations with Vietnam.

Once the KR had made this inter-Communist argument public, the gloves also came off on the Vietnamese side. In 1978, they began to publicise the background to the violence taking place on their border with Cambodia. They revealed to the world that some 300,000 Cambodians, Chinese and Vietnamese had fled from Cambodia into Vietnam since 1975; 60,000 Khmers came with the Vietnamese troops when they returned to Vietnam from their operation to punish the Pol Pot troops. These refugees would form an official resistance movement under Vietnamese tutelage and accompany the Vietnamese into Phnom Penh in the winter of 1978–9, to set up a new government.

In August of 1978, the Vietnamese Communist press would begin to develop their arguments for intervention against the Pol Pot regime. *The Communist Review* (*Tap Chi Cong San*) wrote that the overthrow of the US-supported Lon Nol regime on 17 April 1975 had led to its replacement by another oppressive regime, one that was much crueller and

---

[18] Chanda, *Brother Enemy*, 86.    [19] *Ibid.*, 192–6.

more savage. This was the 'oppressive, fascist system marked by medieval barbarism of the reactionary Pol Pot-Ieng Sary group. By their concrete acts of the past three years, the reactionary Cambodian rulers have clearly revealed that they are enemies who do not represent the people of Kampuchea.'[20] The people not only did not have any democratic rights – they were treated like animals. A former student of Phnom Penh University who had escaped to Vietnam was quoted as saying that the power holders in his country viewed their people as water buffalo and oxen, or as even less than these beasts. Sometimes the people were less important than animals – they killed people more quickly than they would kill a buffalo or cow. 'We are just slaves, poor serfs, who keep our mouths closed both day and night', the student said.

The Vietnamese indictment was loose with its numbers, but there is no doubt that they presented the basic outlines of the Khmer Rouge crimes against their people truthfully. Western experts such as Charles Twining and Father François Ponchaud had already laid out this case against the Khmer Rouge, after all. The article spoke of 'millions of people who had fallen under their cruel hand. Tens of thousands of Chinese and Vietnamese residents have met a similar fate. The Pol Pot-Ieng Sary gang kills with rifles, clubs, knives and hoes; they gouge out eyes, disembowel and pull out the livers of their victims . . . They kill for a variety of reasons: they kill the soldiers and officers of the Lon Nol army, as well as the civil servants of the former puppet government (for officers from the rank of major and up, they kill the entire family to "eliminate future problems"); they kill monks, who are also viewed as enemies; they kill workers who lack strength, because they are unable to follow orders; anyone who complains of hunger or hardship can be accused of opposing the system and killed'. This passage ends with the assertion that 'the crime of genocide is being committed in Kampuchea today'.[21] In addition to detailing the treatment of the Cham minority, this article describes the extreme social policies implemented by the KR: the separation of families, forced marriages, and the elimination of money, education and any form of communication that would have enabled family members to stay in touch.

As noted, the Vietnamese were far from the first to make these accusations. And yet the warnings of more respected international voices had not led to any action by the UN or other international bodies to stop

---

[20] Quyet-Tien, 'Cac nha cam quyen Trung-Quoc dang ung ho Bon Phat Xit Diet Chung o Cam-pu-chia' [Chinese Support for the Fascist, Genocidal Gang in Kampuchea], *Tap Chi Cong San* [*Communist Review*] (Aug. 1978), 17.
[21] *Ibid.*, 17–18.

the killing in Cambodia. Rather than let what they were coming to see as a joint Cambodian–Chinese operation to undermine them continue, the Vietnamese began to make plans for their own intervention. Starting in April 1978, they started to train anti-Pol Pot guerrillas chosen from the refugees living along the border. These forces were eventually introduced to the world as the Kampuchean National United Front for National Salvation (KNUFNS). (By October, Vietnamese troops, who would compose the bulk of the fighting force during the invasion, were also deploying along the border, from Dac Lac to An Giang.) The KNUFNS would be the leaders of the 'authentic Cambodian revolution', which would restore the rights of the people. This would be one of the Vietnamese defences of their occupation of Cambodia: that they were assisting the Kampuchean people to implement the correct policies of socialism. (Unfortunately, the precedents for such an intervention were not attractive ones – the 'Fraternal Aid' offered by the Brezhnev regime to Czechoslovakia in August 1968 was still fresh in many memories.)

On the international front, Hanoi continued efforts to normalise relations with the United States; but in spite of the fact that they dropped their demand that the United States provide the reconstruction aid once promised by Richard Nixon, these negotiations never bore fruit. This may have been linked to the growing influence of National Security Council head Zbigniew Brzezinski, who favoured closer US ties with China. His May 1978 trip to China established a new level of security and intelligence cooperation between the two sides. At the same time, Vietnamese relations with China continued to deteriorate, with skirmishes on the northern border reported in February 1978. The most damaging blow to Vietnam's international reputation came when the Chinese sent a freighter to the coast of Southern Vietnam, with the provocative offer to rescue 'victimised' Overseas Chinese. The ship left Vietnamese waters in July before it could collect any refugees, but in the meantime, many trusting Hoa had registered to depart. This led to a semi-official exodus organised by the Vietnamese security organs, which allowed Hoa to depart from Ho Chi Minh City on rusting Hong Kong freighters in exchange for a hefty fee in gold. By this stage, the Vietnamese had become convinced that the Chinese were egging on the KR in their violent forays into Vietnam.[22] But this did nothing to improve the sinking image of Vietnam, as a nation that was carrying

---

[22] Chanda, *Brother Enemy*, 215. Chanda was informed by Vietnamese Foreign Minister Nguyen Co Thach that after November 1977 talks in China, Vietnamese party leader Le Duan had come to believe that the Chinese 'will use Pol Pot against us'.

out ethnic discrimination by encouraging its Chinese residents to depart. Altogether approximately 450,000 Chinese left Vietnam between May 1975 and September 1979, with about 260,000 of these leaving over the northern border.[23]

In contrast, the Soviets were cooperative when the Vietnamese were ready to sign a twenty-five-year friendship treaty in November 1978. This treaty would outlive the Soviet Union. The Vietnamese rationale for entering Cambodia would be tailored to please the ideologues in the Soviet Politburo. In 1978, the aging Soviet leadership grouped around Leonid Brezhnev was experiencing a final burst of enthusiasm for Communist-led revolutions in the Third World, in part as a result of the success of their Communist clients in Vietnam. Events in Africa also appeared to be going their way in those years, after the collapse of the Portuguese empire and the coming to power of a movement aligned with the Soviet Union in Angola. It was also in 1978 that the Soviets threw in their support to the Ethiopian revolution in its Ogaden war with Somalia. Moreover, the Russians were still mired in confrontation with the Chinese and were eager to increase their reach into South-east Asia. By the early 1970s, in fact, they had concluded that 'Indochina will become the key for us to all of South-east Asia'.[24]

The idea that the Vietnamese were installing an 'authentically revolutionary', pro-Moscow Communist party in power, in a country previously allied to China, was enough to win Soviet backing for the incursion. As the Vietnamese phrased it, the 'revolutionary struggle of the Cambodian people ... although it would encounter difficulties and hardships, would surely win the final victory'.[25] Three 'popular revolutionary movements' would be employed to return Cambodia to the right path. These were the movement to fight the enemy and his propaganda, the movement to produce and build the people's livelihood, and the movement to build up the forces of the revolution. All three movements would have to be developed together, without neglecting or subordinating any one facet, according to the Vietnamese general in charge of the

[23] Odd Arne Westad and Sophie Quinn-Judge, *The Third Indochina War: Conflict between China, Vietnam and Cambodia, 1972–79* (London and New York: Routledge, 2006), 234–7.

[24] RGANI (Russian State Archive for Contemporary History), collection 8, record series 54, report 10, 1: Political Report from the USSR Embassy in the DRV, 21 May 1971, 'The Policy of the Lao Dong Party regarding a Solution of the Indochina Problem and our Tasks arising from the decisions of the Twenty-fourth Congress of the Communist Party of the Soviet Union'.

[25] Quyet-tien, 'Cac nha cam quyen Trung-Quoc dang ung ho Bon Phat Xit Diet Chung o Cam-pu-chia', 20.

Cambodia operation.[26] In other words, the Vietnamese regarded the reconstruction of a friendly Cambodian political party to be just as important as overcoming hunger.

Ironically, almost as soon as the Vietnamese had completed their sweep into Cambodia, their faith in the 'authentic revolutionary' doctrines which they were applying at home would begin to waver. The years from 1978 to 1986 would be ones of hardship for Communist Vietnam, because of their international isolation and the backward state of their economy. It would also be a time of disillusionment with Marxist–Leninist–Stalinist doctrines of development and deep disagreement and debate regarding the country's future path. This growing loss of faith would be compounded by post-Brezhnev debates in Moscow on the USSR's wasteful expenditures in the Third World. By the time the Vietnamese managed to extricate themselves from Cambodia in 1989, the internationalist socialism which they had been defending in Cambodia would be all but dead. By then, the humanitarian aspects of the Vietnamese intervention had been largely forgotten under the weight of the years of war and hardship suffered by those Cambodian people who had neither the credentials nor the luck to make it to the West.

*

The Vietnamese needed only ten days following their initial attacks on Cambodia in December 1978 to take Phnom Penh and push the KR towards the Thai border. Until the very last moment the propaganda machinery of Democratic Kampuchea was churning out news bulletins lauding their own victories over the advancing Vietnamese. They had consistently spread the idea that the Vietnamese were conniving to subvert DK and carry out a *coup d'état* against its leadership. For a very long time, they said, the Vietnamese had planned 'to annex and swallow Cambodia', as part of their goal to establish an 'Indochinese Federation'.[27] Once the Vietnamese carried out their lightning attack, this appeared to be a prophecy that had been fulfilled. Experts on South-east Asia spoke of the tensions between Cambodia and Vietnam as, in part, a proxy war between the Chinese and the USSR. But they were often

---

[26] Le Duc Anh, *Quan Doi Nhan Dan Viet Nam va Nhiem Vu Quoc Te Cao Ca Tren Dat Ban Campuchia* [*The People's Army of Vietnam and their Noble Mission on the Friendly Soil of Campuchia*] (Hanoi: NXB Quan Doi Nhan Dan, 1986), 57–61.

[27] Democratic Kampuchea, *Livre Noir: Faits et Preuves des actes d'aggression et d'annexion du Vietnam contre le Kampuchea* (Phnom Penh: Département de la Presse et de l'Information du Ministère des Affaires Etrangères du Kampuchea Démocratique, 1978), 2.

quick to add that the Khmers and Vietnamese were 'traditional enemies' or that 'ancient resentments' had determined the break-down in relations between the two neighbours. Stephen J. Morris, for example, saw no need to look beyond these factors in his explanation of events.[28]

American policy in 1978–9 was defined by a growing closeness with China and fear of Soviet expansionism. The foreign policy pioneered by Henry Kissinger and Richard Nixon in 1971, at the time of the Indian intervention to free East Pakistan, was a precedent for the US response to Vietnam's overthrow of Pol Pot. In 1971, Kissinger read the darkest intentions into India's intervention, convincing himself that the Indian army was set on destroying West Pakistan. He formulated policy, not based on humanitarian considerations, but out of concern for Chinese sensibilities.[29] The same might be said for Brzezinski's reading of the 1979 crisis in Indochina. He saw it as an extension of the 'arc of crisis' fomented by Soviet actions from the Horn of Africa to the Middle East and Afghanistan. Thus rolling back this Soviet gain in South-east Asia became the US government's overriding aim. It is instructive to contrast the US response to these events in South-east Asia to their reaction to Tanzania's 1978–9 involvement in regime change in Uganda. Tanzania's removal of Idi Amin, in circumstances very similar to those existing in Indochina, was met with relief in Western capitals. The key difference was that the Tanzanians were not Soviet clients.

Initial shock at the speed of the KR defeat was soon replaced by a clear political choice in Washington. US Secretary of State Cyrus Vance called almost immediately for the Vietnamese to remove their troops from Cambodia – the USA could not condone cross-border aggression or applaud this change in the balance of power in South-east Asia. Thus a course was set by the Democratic Carter Administration which would continue throughout the Republican Reagan years, with support from all major European allies, as well as the PRC and ASEAN (Association of South East Asian Nations). The Vietnamese would be portrayed as aggressors and proxies of the Soviet Union, while the needs of the people they had freed from Pol Pot would take second place to the goal of punishing Vietnam. The idea that the international community, led by the United Nations, could take steps to de-politicise this situation by offering aid and recognition to the new rulers in Phnom Penh, in exchange for a gradual Vietnamese withdrawal, never seems to have

---

[28] Stephen J. Morris, *Why Vietnam Invaded Cambodia: Political Culture and the Causes of War* (Stanford: Stanford University Press, 1999), 235.
[29] Raymond L. Garthoff, *Détente and Confrontation: American–Soviet Relations from Nixon to Reagan*, rev. edn (Washington, DC: The Brookings Institution, 1994), 299–303.

been entertained. Instead, when the bedraggled remnants of the KR started to appear on the Thai border in the spring of 1978, they were fed and eventually housed in camps where they could rebuild their strength and receive weapons shipped to them from China via the good offices of the Thai military.

Of course the emaciated state of the refugees who crossed the Thai border in March and April of 1979 called out for immediate intervention. This came at first via non-governmental agencies such as Catholic Relief Services and the UN's World Food Program. By October 1979, Thai Prime Minister Kriangsak Chomanand had agreed to construct holding centres for the refugees on Thai soil, with funds from the UNHCR, and the UN had issued a major appeal for aid to Cambodia. The US Embassy in Bangkok established its own coordinating group, the Kampuchea Emergency Group or KEG, to coordinate aid and refugee work. Inevitably humanitarian and political objectives became intertwined within their activities, as William Shawcross reported in his study of the Cambodia relief effort. He was told that KEG's three purposes were, 'to increase food deliveries and improve medical care along the border; to explore the ways in which Cambodian resistance to the Vietnamese could be helped; and to lobby for resettlement of Cambodian refugees in the United States'.[30]

In early 1979 a new coalition of forces to oppose Vietnam took shape in South-east Asia with impressive speed. On 13 January, KR Foreign Minister Ieng Sary was in Beijing for meetings with the *de facto* Chinese leader Deng Xiaoping and President Hua Guofeng, where he was assured of Chinese support. By 15 January Deng had flown to a secret airbase in Thailand to do a deal with Prime Minister Kriangsak, to permit a supply of Chinese weapons and medical supplies to reach the KR. The Thai requirement for cooperation was that the Chinese and KR renounce their support for the Thai Communist Party, a movement that had flourished in 1977–8. Contacts between the KR and the Thai leadership would have to go through the Chinese embassy in Bangkok, while the Chinese would maintain a mobile embassy to DK on the border.[31] Over the years this arrangement would benefit the Thai military in a number of ways. The Chinese paid the Thai army a transport fee for trucking the weapons from Thai ports to the Cambodian border; they also permitted the Thais to keep a portion of the weapons. Later

[30] William Shawcross, *The Quality of Mercy: Cambodia, Holocaust and Modern Conscience* (New York: Simon and Schuster, 1984), 183–4.
[31] Christopher Goscha, 'Vietnam and the Meltdown of Asian Internationalism', in *The Third Indochina War*, 177–9.

they provided the technology for the manufacture of anti-tank weapons in a Thai factory, with the agreement that a portion of the weapons would be given to the KR.[32]

The Americans and Chinese together worked to maintain an acceptable face for the KR, first of all by persuading Prince Sihanouk to avoid an official break with their government-in-exile, by defecting to the US or France. Sihanouk, who had passed most of the KR period under house arrest, was once again needed to attract international support for Pol Pot's organisation. The brief, destructive Chinese attack over the northern Vietnamese border in February 1979 would be a hiccup in the campaign to isolate Vietnam diplomatically. In the longer term, both the Chinese and US governments seemed to prefer the option of propaganda and diplomatic initiatives to paint Vietnam as 'an aggressive Cuba of the East'.[33] This policy did succeed in keeping Vietnam isolated and economically weak, but it also punished those Cambodians who had survived the KR nightmare and now had to rebuild their country.

Singapore and its Foreign Minister Sinnathamby Rajaratnam played a key role in this coalition to isolate Vietnam. He helped to shore up support for DK in the UN, where each autumn efforts by the Vietnamese and the Soviet bloc failed to dislodge the KR from their seat. ASEAN insisted on a full Vietnamese troop withdrawal from Cambodia before they would contemplate a change in their position. In June 1982, with strong pressure from Singapore, a Coalition Government of Democratic Kampuchea was cobbled together, in which two non-Communist factions joined the KR. Prince Sihanouk led one of these smaller factions, which included his son and other émigrés returned from France, while one of his former ministers, Son Sann, headed the other non-Communist group. Together they claimed to have 11,000 men fighting in-country, as compared to the 30,000 to 40,000 fighters claimed by the KR. In the meantime, the bulk of the Cambodian population living under control of the Vietnamese-sponsored government was denied development aid, in an almost unprecedented boycott by the UN agencies.

Former Oxfam representative in Phnom Penh, Eva Mysliwiec, has documented the use of UN aid to Cambodia as a political instrument. There was a sharp disparity in aid distributed to refugees and KR personnel who made their way to the Thai border, and the aid made available to the people who lived under the Vietnamese-controlled

[32] Chanda, *Brother Enemy*, 381.
[33] Chanda, in *Far Eastern Economic Review* (12 Jan. 1979), 14.

Heng Samrin government. As Mysliwiec explains, half of the US $663.9 million from Western donors channelled through UN agencies between 1979 and 1981 went to a joint UN/ICRC assistance programme to displaced people and refugees at the Thai–Cambodian border. This aid benefited a population that at one point rose to almost one million people, including the remnants of the KR. The other half of the aid was distributed via the government in Phnom Penh to its surviving 6.5 million people. After 1982, when the food emergency within Cambodia was deemed to be over, the UN was unwilling to shift from emergency aid to providing aid for reconstruction and development projects. Thus, as Mysliwiec wrote in 1988, 'the 7 million Kampucheans who remain in the country are still denied development aid while those living under the control of the opposition forces in Thailand benefit from generous relief programmes in the border camps'.[34] At that time, Kampuchea was the only Third World country to be denied UN development aid – not even Afghanistan under Soviet occupation was dealt with so severely.

★

The long, slow process of making the Khmer Rouge leadership accountable for their actions is a story of dogged persistence on the part of a handful of researchers and jurists. Had some force other than the Vietnamese been the liberators, clearly things would have been different. But the desire to weaken and punish the Vietnamese was so strong on the part of the United States and China, that the inconvenient issue of KR crimes was ignored by the US State Department until 1994. This change of heart followed the 1993 UN-supervised election of a coalition government in Cambodia, as stipulated in the Paris Agreement on Peace in Cambodia, signed in 1991. This negotiated resolution to the stand-off in Cambodia became possible in the late 1980s, once the Soviet Union moved to defuse the Cold War by withdrawing their troops from Afghanistan, negotiating serious arms control agreements with the United States and settling their simmering border conflicts with China. The Chinese had set three conditions for the normalisation of relations with the Soviet Union, including the resolution of the regional conflict in Cambodia. Under heavy pressure from their over-stretched Soviet allies, the Vietnamese withdrew all or most of their troops by September 1989, and President Mikhail Gorbachev was able to make his historic trip to China that June. This was by no means the end of the Khmer Rouge, but it greatly decreased their value to the coalition that had been opposing

---

[34] Eva Mysliwiec, *Punishing the Poor: The International Isolation of Kampuchea* (Oxford: Oxfam, 1988), 72–3.

the Vietnamese role in Cambodia.[35] By then, economic reform was in the air throughout the Communist bloc, and the Vietnamese were well into their process of reform or *Doi Moi*, which was making them more attractive to Western investors and governments.

Even before the Vietnamese troop withdrawal, a 1985 UN sub-commission's investigation of the KR's crimes had described them as 'the most serious that had occurred anywhere in the world since Nazism'.[36] By that time the documentation of the percentages of ethnic Chams, Vietnamese and Buddhist monks killed made it possible to accuse the KR of the crime of genocide. All the same, the USA did not even give up its support for the KR's control of the UN seat (via the Democratic Kampuchea coalition government) until 1990. In the 1980s and early 1990s, Australian Ben Kiernan was one of a handful of historians of Cambodia who continued his research to document what had happened under the Khmer Rouge, work he had begun in 1979. This involved hundreds of interviews inside Cambodia, on the Thai border and in France. In 1990, he wrote that the 1948 UN Convention on Genocide could be applied to the KR's persecution and slaughter of three categories of their Cambodian victims. These are: 'religious groups', such as Cambodia's Buddhist monks; 'ethnical or racial groups', such as the country's Cham or Vietnamese minorities, and at least one 'part' of the majority Khmer 'national' group – the eastern Khmer population from the provinces near Vietnam (and possibly the Khmer urban population too). All were targeted for destruction 'as such', and are therefore cases of attempted genocide by the Khmer Rouge.[37] In the case of the ethnic Chinese, for example, he claims that under Pol Pot they 'suffered the worst disaster ever to befall any ethnic Chinese community in Southeast Asia'. Of the 1975 population of 425,000, only 200,000 survived until 1979.[38] Of the majority Khmer population, Kiernan estimated that 15 per cent of the rural population perished, compared to 33 per cent of urban dwellers.[39]

Finally, once a peace settlement agreeable to the West had been achieved in Cambodia, serious research money was provided for the study of the Khmer Rouge crimes. In 1994, as a professor at Yale University,

---

[35] Ironically, it was the firmly anti-Communist Thai military which was the last hold-out in protecting Pol Pot. In 1997, they prevented a scheme to kidnap Pol Pot from his base inside Cambodia, to have been organised jointly by Sihanouk's forces and the USA. See Short, *Pol Pot*, 439–40.

[36] Power, *America and the Age of Genocide*, 154.

[37] Ben Kiernan, *Genocide and Resistance in Southeast Asia: Documentation, Denial and Justice in Cambodia and East Timor* (New Brunswick: Transaction Publishers, 2008), 217 (republished from *The Far Eastern Economic Review* (1 Mar. 1990)).

[38] Kiernan, *Genocide and Resistance in Southeast Asia*, 218.     [39] *Ibid.*, 219.

Kiernan established the Cambodian Genocide Program with a $500,000 grant from the US Department of State. In January 1995, they opened a branch in Phnom Penh, the Documentation Center of Cambodia (now an independent entity). Kiernan was repeatedly attacked by the *Wall Street Journal*'s editorial page as a Communist, Khmer Rouge sympathiser or stooge of Vietnam. However, with growing acceptance of his research findings within the legal and scholarly communities, at last a new phase of systematic research began, on the documentation generated by the Khmer Rouge security and political systems.

The manpower and resources available to the Documentation Center of Cambodia (DCC) have made it possible over the last decade to develop a fuller understanding of the systematic nature of the arrest and execution of class, political and ethnic enemies carried out under Pol Pot. As Craig Etcheson, Ben Kiernan's colleague, explains in his review of this research, data on the frequency, distribution and origin of mass graves, combined with data gleaned from newly discovered Khmer Rouge internal security documents, have given us new insight into the question of the economy of violence within Democratic Kampuchea. The data lead inexorably to the conclusion that most of the violence was carried out pursuant to orders from the highest political authorities of the Communist Party of Kampuchea.[40] This evidence goes a long way towards putting to rest the argument that the violence was local, the result of indiscipline in a peasant army. As Kiernan has explained, 'as early as March 1976, a Pol Pot regime memorandum divided up what it called "the authority to smash people inside and outside the ranks". Some political killings were held to be the prerogative of the "Centre", others were delegated to the regime's regions'.[41]

Documents generated by the staff at the Tuol Sleng prison, headquarters of the S-21 internal security apparatus, have confirmed the existence of a three-person 'national security committee' composed of Nuon Chea, Deputy Secretary General of the Party, Son Sen, Deputy Prime Minister in charge of National Security, and Yon Yat, Son Sen's wife, assistant to the Committee. These individuals, with Pol Pot at their head, received daily reports on the confessions obtained at Tuol Sleng and reports of executions. One log from Tuol Sleng, dated July 1977, reports the execution and biographies of eighteen prisoners. At the bottom of the page, a handwritten note adds that 160 children have also been killed that day, for a 'total of 178 enemies killed'.[42]

[40] Etcheson, *After the Killing Fields*, 78.
[41] Kiernan, *Genocide and Resistance in Southeast Asia*, 217.    [42] *Ibid.*, 83.

After years of debate and delay, while many responsible experts continued to argue about the wisdom of trying the KR leadership, the 'hybrid' UN–Cambodian tribunal finally opened at the end of 2007. Still, in early 2009, as the trial of Tuol Sleng director 'Duch' or Kaing Kek Iev moved forward, the tribunal faced obstacles that seem to arise from political doubts about this process, or the low priority attached to it by the relevant international actors. The tribunal's Supreme Court chief judge, Kom Srim, announced in 2008 that both sides of the hybrid tribunal face financial problems, although they should be able to complete the case against Duch. Meanwhile, of the inner core of the KR leadership, only a few remain alive, including former foreign minister Ieng Sary, Khieu Samphan and 'Brother Number Two' Nuon Chea. Pol Pot died in his sleep in 1998, while his former security chief Son Sen was murdered in factional fighting not long before that.

*Part V*

# Postscript

# 16    Humanitarian intervention since 1990 and 'liberal interventionism'

*Matthew Jamison*

> Where our values and our interests are at stake, and where we can make a difference, we must be prepared to do so.
>
> Bill Clinton, speech of 10 June 1999
>
> Global interdependence requires global values commonly or evenly applied. But sometimes force is necessary to get the space for those values to be applied.
>
> Tony Blair, speech of 7 April 2002

If, as this volume has tried to show, there were many interventions for humanitarian purposes before 1980, their number increased exponentially after the end of the Cold War. This chapter briefly summarises the interventions of the 1990s, and considers in more detail their political and conceptual underpinnings, paying particular attention to debates within Britain, whose Labour Prime Minister, Tony Blair, emerged as a torchbearer of 'liberal' and 'humanitarian' 'interventionism'.

Its starting point is the fact that with the end of the Cold War in 1989–90 hopes were widespread that power politics would increasingly be replaced in international relations by moral and ethical considerations, mediated by the newly non-polarised United Nations and imposed, where necessary, by its Security Council. In particular, with the breakdown of the bi-polar balance of power between the United States and the Soviet Union, many hoped that the number of humanitarian interventions, authorised and overseen by the United Nations, predicated upon the rule of law and principle of collective security, would increase.[1] At least in Western countries, there was enthusiasm among statesmen, scholars, media commentators and the public, for using diplomacy and military power to protect human rights. By the early 2000s an 'emerging norm' of intervention to protect human rights was widely

---

[1] J. Rosenau, *The United Nations in a Turbulent World* (London: Lynne Rienner Publishers, 1992), 44. See also Anthony Parson, *From Cold War to Hot Peace: UN Interventions, 1947–1994* (London: Penguin, 1995), 184–5.

recognised.[2] Yet it was a highly contested norm. Successful interventions had been undertaken throughout the 1990s; but there had been only a very delayed response to genocide in Bosnia, and no effective response to genocide in Rwanda and Southern Sudan, or to immense humanitarian crises, caused by failure of government, in the Congo and Zimbabwe. The fact that interventions have been conducted selectively, and sometimes seemingly in the strategic interests of the intervening powers, so that some human rights abuses and genocides have gone unchecked, has helped to discredit the concept of intervention; so too has the widespread perception that US-led military action in Afghanistan and Iraq is less interventionist than imperialist.

Yet if the concept of intervening in a nation-state's domestic affairs on moral, humanitarian grounds is controversial, it nevertheless retains advocates, simply because sometimes 'use of force [is] the only means of ending atrocities on a massive scale'.[3] In an interdependent global community, the concept of intervention on humanitarian grounds is not moribund; rather, it remains the subject of vigorous debate among military, policy and development practitioners, academics, and peace and human rights activists, with the media and the public keen followers. In this debate, history is vital. A clear interventionist consensus failed to emerge in the post-Cold War international community partly because of the failure to see recent interventions as part of a long-term historical continuum. This probably led to mistakes by intervening powers but it also certainly led to continuing perceptions of illegitimacy. Going over the familiar territory of both the practice of intervention in the 1990s and 2000s and the debates surrounding them is important, because it is the concluding stage (at least for now) of the journey begun in the middle years of the sixteenth century. The focus up to now on interventions before 1980 is to reinforce the point that the tendency to treat intervention only in late twentieth-century terms is flawed.[4] But in order to have a full perspective on the whole history of humanitarian intervention, it is essential to look at events since the end of the Cold War.

*

In the immediate aftermath of the fall of the Berlin Wall, humanitarian emergencies arose in Central America, northern Iraq, the former Yugoslavia, Kosovo, Somalia, Rwanda and the Great Lakes region of Africa.[5]

[2] Report of the UN 'High-Level Panel on Threats, Challenges and Change', in *A More Secure World: Our Shared Responsibility* (New York: United Nations Department of Public Information, 2004), 66 (I owe this reference to David Trim).
[3] Nicholas J. Wheeler, *Saving Strangers: Humanitarian Intervention in International Society* (Oxford: Oxford University Press, 2000), 295.
[4] See Trim and Simms, Chapter 1, above.
[5] T. Weiss and C. Collins, *Humanitarian Challenges and Intervention* (New York: Westview Press, 2000), 71.

Indeed, between 1991 and mid-1993 the international system witnessed an eight-fold increase in the number of UN peacekeeping troops deployed and a quadrupling of the UN's peacekeeping budget. This was paralleled by the proliferation in the type of operation undertaken to include crisis prevention, peace enforcement and the idea of humanitarian intervention in an on-going conflict.[6] This chapter will focus on four cases: Iraq, the Balkans, Somalia, and Sierra Leone, and reflect on them in historical perspective.

After the cessation of hostilities during the first Gulf War on 27 February 1991 and the expulsion of Iraqi forces from Kuwait, popular insurrections against Saddam Hussein's regime exploded in the north and in the south, and Iraq's Republican Guard responded with brutal force.[7] Some 1.5 million Iraqi Kurds fled to the Turkish border and into Iran.[8] Within one month's time, that number would reach nearly 2.5 million. The United Nations was faced with one of the first major humanitarian challenges since the balance of power had altered with the end of the Cold War. To cope with the resulting humanitarian catastrophe in April 1991, United Nations Security Council Resolution 688, which set up 'safe areas' to protect the Kurds of northern Iraq against Saddam Hussein, established a crucial precedent for legitimising UN involvement in the internal affairs of a country in order to alleviate suffering. The troop composition of the militarised humanitarian Operation Provide Comfort initially included elite units from the United States, the United Kingdom, France and the Netherlands, without the consent of the sovereign authority. Resolution 688 insisted 'that Iraq allow immediate access by international humanitarian organizations to all those in need of assistance in all parts of Iraq'. The resolution also established a no-fly zone and banned Iraqi military personnel from the protected area.[9] These international developments led the UN Secretary-General, Javier Perez de Cuellar, to claim that there had occurred a shift in public attitudes towards the belief that the defence of the oppressed in the name of morality 'should prevail over frontiers and legal documents'.[10]

---

[6] A. Dorman and T. Otte, *Military Intervention: From Gunboat Diplomacy to Humanitarian Intervention* (Dartmouth: Dartmouth Publishing Company, 1995), 162.

[7] Weiss and Collins, *Humanitarian Challenges and Intervention*, 78.

[8] M. Chelliah, C. Mackinlay, and T. Weiss, *United Nations Coordination of the International Humanitarian Response to the Gulf Crisis 1990–92*, Thomas J. Watson Jr. Institute for International Studies, Occasional Paper 13 (Providence, RI: Brown University Press, 1992), 1.

[9] See J. Welsh, *Humanitarian Intervention and International Law* (Oxford: Oxford University Press, 2006), 149; Weiss and Collins, *Humanitarian Challenges and Intervention*, 78–9; and see Wheeler, *Saving Strangers*, ch. 5.

[10] UN Press Release SG/SM/4560, 24 Apr. 1991.

Within three years, the Iraqi precedent was applied in Europe.[11] Between 1991 and 1995, first Croatia and then Bosnia was wracked by a campaign of ethnic cleansing sponsored by Slobodan Milošević in Belgrade. Somewhere in the region of 100,000 Bosnians were killed, and about two million were displaced or expelled in an attempt to carve an ethnically pure state out of the ruins of multi-national Yugoslavia.[12] Very slowly, the international community became involved, first in the distribution and protection of aid, before eventually intervening to end the bloodshed.[13] On 13 August 1992, the United Nations Security Council passed resolution 770 authorising the use of 'all necessary measures' to ensure the passage of humanitarian aid. In March of the following year, the UN Security Council endorsed NATO air forces to enforce flight bans over Bosnia-Herzegovina and Croatia.[14] In June 1993, Resolution 836 set up 'safe areas' to guard the Bosnian Muslim population and empowered regional organisations, such as NATO, to deploy the necessary force to 'deter attacks' on them. NATO also received UN approval to establish a naval blockade of Yugoslavia.[15] After the infamous Srebrenica massacre in July 1995, when Bosnian Serb forces killed 7,000 Muslim men and boys, an American-led air campaign was mounted in the autumn of that year. Together with Bosnian and Croatian army ground offensives, it inflicted a series of crushing defeats on the Bosnian Serbs and forced them to agree to a settlement at Dayton at the end of the year.

The UN had meanwhile confronted a grave humanitarian disaster in Somalia. Exacerbated by a complete breakdown in Somalian civil order, the United Nations established UNOSOM I mission in April 1992. However, the efficacy of UNOSOM I was undermined by the obdurate local warlords and their faction fighting. The mission never reached its mandated strength.[16] Circumstances in Somalia deteriorated during the closing months of 1992. By November, General Mohamed Farrah Aidid

---

[11] See Spyros Economides and Paul Taylor, 'Former Yugoslavia', in *United Nations Interventionism, 1991–2004*, ed. Mats Berdal and Spyros Economides 2nd edn (Cambridge: Cambridge University Press, 2007), 65–107.

[12] The best account of the systematic nature of ethnic cleansing is James Gow, *The Serbian Project and its Adversaries: A Strategy of War Crimes* (London: Hurst, 2003).

[13] For a list of Security Council Resolutions on the former Yugoslavia, see B. G. Ramcharan (ed.), *The International Conference on the Former Yugoslavia: Official Papers* (The Hague, London, and Boston: Kluwer Law International, 1997), 1161–74. For a critical view of the United Nations performance, see George Stamkoski (ed.), *With No Peace to Keep. United Nations Peacekeeping and the Wars in Former Yugoslavia* (1995), 2nd edn (London: Grainpress, 2002).

[14] UNSC, Res. 816, 31 Mar. 1993.       [15] UNSC, Res. 958, 19 Nov. 1994.

[16] UN Mission in Somalia, UN Dept of Peacekeeping: www.un.org/Depts/DPKO/Missions/unosomi.htm.

had grown confident enough to formally defy the Security Council and demand the withdrawal of peacekeepers, as well as declaring hostile intent against any further UN deployments.[17] Faced with intense and mounting public pressure, UN Secretary-General Boutros Boutros-Ghali formulated several options for the Security Council to consider. Diplomacy having been exhausted Boutros-Ghali argued that a serious display of force was required to bring the armed groups to heel. Chapter VII of the Charter of the United Nations allows for 'action by air, sea or land forces as may be necessary to maintain or restore international peace and security'. Boutros-Ghali believed the time had come for employing this clause and moving on beyond peacekeeping.[18] Significantly, this invocation of Chapter VII waived the need for consent on the part of the state of Somalia. However, Boutros-Ghali felt that such action would be difficult to apply under the mandate for UNOSOM. Moreover, Boutros-Ghali recognised that eradicating Somalia's problems would require a much more muscular deployment than the UN Secretariat was capable of implementing. Accordingly, he recommended that a large intervention force be constituted under the command of member states but authorised by the Security Council to carry out operations in Somalia. The goal of this deployment was 'to prepare the way for a return to peacekeeping and post-conflict peace-building'.[19]

Following up on this proposal on 3 December 1992, the Security Council unanimously adopted Resolution 794, authorising the use of 'all necessary means to establish as soon as possible a secure environment for humanitarian relief operations in Somalia'.[20] Resolution 794 was unanimously adopted by the United Nations Security Council on 3 December 1992, and the United States offer to help create a secure environment for humanitarian efforts in Somalia was welcomed.[21] President George H. W. Bush responded to this by initiating Operation Restore Hope on 4 December 1992, under which the United States would assume command in accordance with Resolution 794. This policy was continued by his successor, Bill Clinton.

By 1998, the question of Kosovo, where the Albanian majority was passively resisting the Milošević government and the 'Greater Serbia' project and demanding either the restoration of autonomy or full

---

[17] UN, 1992, Secretary-General to President of UNSC, 24 Nov. 1992.
[18] UN, 1992, Secretary-General to President of the Security Council, 29 Nov. 1992.
[19] UN Mission in Somalia, UN Dept of Peacekeeping: www.un.org/Depts/DPKO/Missions/unosomi.htm.
[20] UNSC, Res. 794 (1992), 24/4/92, para. 3.
[21] G. H. W. Bush, *Address to the Nation on the Situation in Somalia*, 4 Dec. 1992: http://bushlibrary.tamu.edu/.

independence, was exploding onto the international scene. The Kosovo Liberation Army (KLA) started a guerrilla campaign against Belgrade's security forces, provoking a brutal backlash. On 31 March, UNSC Resolution 1160 condemned both sides and expressed hope for a peaceful outcome. By 23 September, the continued violence of the Serb regime had led to Resolution 1199 which demanded an immediate ceasefire, and threatened Belgrade with the use of air power if it failed to comply. Instead, Milošević launched an all-out attack on the KLA and the Albanian population causing the flight of hundreds of thousands. No further UN resolution was passed, primarily because Russia and China objected to intervention in the internal affairs of a sovereign state. In March 1999, NATO attacked Serbia just the same in order to prevent a humanitarian crisis. After a seventy-day air campaign, Milošević backed down and allowed an international, primarily NATO force into the area. UNSC Resolution 1244 provided the retrospective legal backing for the intervention, even though it had taken place without express UN authorisation.[22]

Not long after, the African country of Sierra Leone was rocked by a severe humanitarian crisis. The civil war which raged throughout the 1990s saw nearly half the country's 4.5 million population displaced. At least 50,000 people died and tens of thousands more were victims of amputations and rape, mainly at the hands of the Revolutionary United Front (RUF), a gang of thugs which controlled much of the country.[23] The RUF however stepped up their offensive after successful British-funded elections in 1996. In early March 1998, Nigerian forces deployed under a United Nations umbrella restored Kabbah to power.[24] However, a subsequent peace agreement between Kabbah and the RUF disintegrated and the UN force charged with keeping order was poorly resourced and inexperienced in dealing with such a combat situation. As the fighting intensified, the international force became unable to cope. It retreated into its compound and then came under attack. In February 2000, the UN Security Council adopted a resolution expanding UN operations to 11,000. In spite of the increasing numbers, RUF forces managed in May to take 500 of the foreign soldiers hostage. In London 'that was a trigger for action'.[25] Acting on military intelligence that Freetown was about to be taken again, Britain's Defence Secretary Geoff Hoon, and Foreign Secretary, Robin Cook, took the decision to scramble a 'spearhead

---

[22] For the latest discussion of Kosovo, see Marc Weller, *Contested Statehood. Kosovo's Struggle for Independence* (Oxford: Oxford University Press, 2009), 115–16 *et passim*.
[23] *Ibid.*, 66–9.    [24] *Ibid.*, 67–8.
[25] R. Cook, *The Point of Departure: Diaries from The Front Bench* (London: Pocket Books, 2004), 35.

battalion' of about 700 troops, ostensibly to evacuate foreign nationals from Freetown.[26] Having been sent in to evacuate the foreign nationals and secure the airport, British forces morphed into the only stabilising force that existed in the country. The UK military had undertaken an operation grounded in humanitarian and liberal policies of restoring law and order and upholding the democratically elected power. Mr Blair himself later proudly claimed that Britain went into Sierra Leone 'on our own, where a country of six million people was saved from a murderous group of gangsters who had hijacked the democratically elected government'.[27] All of this was, in effect, a unilateral action by Britain without UN approval, based upon the premise that, as the Prime Minister put it, 'global interdependence requires global values commonly or evenly applied. But sometimes force is necessary to get the space for those values to be applied: in Sierra Leone or Kosovo for example.'[28]

Of course, the catalogue of cases where the international community did not intervene in a timely fashion, but debated doing so, is much longer. Top of the list is Rwanda in 1994, where intervention was delayed until it was too late to help the victims. The key lesson derived by Jan Nederveen Pieterse from the Rwandan Genocide is not the need for early warning, for there was adequate intelligence and notice in several quarters which, for various reasons, was not acted on; the key problem was the lack of early action.[29] These experiences hastened the emergence of the revised concept of 'humanitarian intervention', as elaborated in the report of the Canadian government-sponsored independent 'International Commission on Intervention and State Sovereignty', *The Responsibility to Protect*, which was released in December 2001. Under certain circumstances, this emerging consensus held, state sovereignty could be set aside for the good of 'humanity'.[30] It was fiercely resisted by non-Western powers such as the People's Republic of China and the Russian Federation, which nearly came to blows with NATO over Kosovo. Among the Western powers, however, the concept of 'humanitarian intervention' found more and more widespread acceptance.

★

[26] J. Kampfner, *Blair's Wars* (London: Free Press, 2003), 69.
[27] T. Blair, 'Speech to the George Bush Snr Presidential Library', 7 Apr. 2002, available at www.number10.gov.uk/output/Page11.
[28] *Ibid.*
[29] J. N. Pieterse, *World Orders in the Making* (London: Palgrave Macmillan, 1998), 12.
[30] ICISS, *The Responsibility to Protect: Report of the International Commission on Intervention and State Sovereignty* (Ottawa: International Development Research Centre, 2001).

As we have seen, the progressive centre-left administrations of 'New Democrat' Bill Clinton and 'New Labour' Tony Blair had been engaged in a series of military interventions abroad to uphold human rights, promote democracy and halt ethnic cleansing long before September 11 2001 and the Iraq War.[31] Clinton and Blair practised a post-Cold War 'Third Way' between state socialism and free-market capitalism with heavy emphasis upon the principles of 'community', applied in both the domestic and international spheres. In fact, throughout his two terms in office, Clinton's administration, under the guidance of humanitarian interventionists and liberal hawks such as Madeline Albright, Anthony Lake and Samuel Berger, was accused by isolationist Republicans of 'hyper-interventionism', with a foreign-policy record of 'deepening intervention in Somalia, invading Haiti, bombing Bosnia, and finally going to war over Kosovo'. Clinton's revolutionary *National Security Strategy* of 1994 prescribed a 'strategy of enlargement' for democracy, coupled with the growth of American power into a global hegemony, well before the advent of George W. Bush. Commenting on the National Security Strategy unveiled in 1994, then National Security Advisor Anthony Lake outlined that the successor to Cold War containment, 'must be a strategy of enlargement ... of the world's free community of market democracies'. The blueprint focused on four points: (1) to 'strengthen the community of market democracies'; (2) to 'foster and consolidate new democracies and market economies where possible'; (3) to 'counter the aggression and support the liberalization of states hostile to democracy'; and (4) to 'help democracy and market economies take root in regions of greatest humanitarian concern'.[32]

In a speech on 26 February 1999, President Clinton posed the question 'What are the consequences to our security of letting conflicts fester and spread ... where our values and our interests are at stake, and where we can make a difference, we must be prepared to do so'. Clinton added that 'we can say to the people of the world, whether you live in Africa, or Central Europe, or any other place, if somebody comes after innocent civilians and tries to kill them en masse because of their race, their ethnic background or their religion, and it's within our power to stop it, we will stop it'.[33]

[31] J. Callaghan and M. Phythian, *The Labour Party and Foreign Policy: A History* (London: Routledge, 2006), 45.
[32] *National Security Strategy of the United States 1994–1995: Engagement and Enlargement* (Washington, DC: Potomac Books, 1994), 5.
[33] W. J. Clinton, *Speech on Kosovo Agreement*, 10 June 1999: http://millercenter.org/scripps/archive/speeches.

Since then, the 'New Democrat' Progressive Policy Institute, under the aegis of Will Marshall, has published the robust and interventionist *Progressive Internationalism: A Democratic National Security Strategy* which endorsed the removal of the Taliban and Iraqi Baathist regimes.[34] It is therefore hardly surprising that the leading liberal interventionist author Paul Berman has argued that the 2001 invasion of Afghanistan and 2003 invasion of Iraq were justified by the doctrine of 'liberal interventionism' – intervention to safeguard and promote liberal demo-cratic freedoms.[35] It seemed that in the space of little more than a decade, a new and ever-broader concept of international interventionism had swept the board in the Western world. But was it really that new?

Common to both advocates and critics of what has come to be called 'humanitarian intervention' after 1989 were some extremely tenacious historical myths about the role of sovereignty in the international state system. Both enthusiasts and detractors assumed that the concept, at least as practised by governments, was a completely new departure. Advocates of humanitarian intervention pointed to the 'lessons' of appeasement, and the gruesome fate of the Armenians.[36] They argued that the international system had always had difficulties dealing with genocide, the 'problem from hell' to borrow the title of Samantha Power's bestselling book of the same name. This appeared in 2002, but was written very much under the impression of the author's experi-ences as a journalist reporting the Bosnian war of the 1990s.[37] Oppon-ents of humanitarian intervention likewise appealed to history, in order to argue that the concept was an unwarranted departure from a well-founded tradition of non-intervention in the internal affairs of another country.

Nowhere was this belief more prominent than in the Britain of John Major, who served as Prime Minister from 1990 to 1997. Thus Malcolm Rifkind, who served in the British Conservative government as Defence Secretary, and then Foreign Secretary throughout the Bosnian war, rejected any intervention on the grounds of Palmerston's famous dictum that 'the furtherance of British interests ought to be the sole object of a British foreign secretary'. His predecessor, Douglas Hurd, to whom the

---

[34] *Progressive Internationalism: A Democratic National Security Strategy*, available at www. ppionline.org/ppi_ci.cfm?contentid=252144&subsecid=900020&knlgAreaID=450004.

[35] P. Berman, *Terror and Liberalism* (New York: W. W. Norton and Co., 2004), 25.

[36] B. Simms, 'Bosnia: The Lessons of History', in *This Time We Knew: Western Responses to Genocide in Bosnia*, ed. T. Cushman and S. Mestrovic (New York: New York University Press, 1996), 65–78.

[37] S. Power, *A Problem From Hell: America and the Age of Genocide* (London: Harper Perennial, 2003), 57.

conduct of the crisis had principally devolved, trenchantly stated that 'there is no such thing as "the international community"'. And – he might have added, had the terms then been in vogue – there could therefore be no such thing as 'humanitarian intervention' or a 'responsibility to protect'.[38]

British foreign policy was spoken of and conducted purely through the prism of the narrow national interest, adopting a non-interventionist posture and emphasising the limitations of British and Western power. While Foreign Secretary, Hurd told the House of Commons: 'I do not believe and have never used rhetoric that would lead anyone to believe, that it was part of Britain's interests to pretend that we could sort out every man-made disaster in the world, of which there are many at the moment'.[39] At the United Nations in New York, he warned Western powers 'it is empty to pretend that we can impose peace with justice on every disorder or dispute outside our national borders'.[40] What this meant in practice, Hurd told the Royal Institute of International Affairs, was that 'we [Britain] shall probably have to say no more often than yes'.[41] He explicitly rejected what he called 'the concept of benevolent international interventionism'. That concept, he warned 'might be attractive, but we should not wander down the new road without serious thought'.[42]

The notion that Britain and the West should support the imposition of universal values for their own sake and pursue an expansive, interventionist foreign policy freed from the constraints of the Cold War, provoked a kind of 'conservative anti-imperialism'.[43] 'We have no right, power or appetite', Hurd told the European Parliament, 'to re-establish protectorates in Eastern Europe in the name of European order'.[44] Almost exactly a year later he elaborated on this theme to the Carlton Club Political Committee:

We must not promise more than we can deliver. We must not let rhetoric run ahead of reality in this new [post-Cold War] world. NATO is not a world policeman. It is certainly not an army of crusaders marching forward to

---

[38] B. Simms, *Unfinest Hour: Britain and the Destruction of Bosnia* (London: Penguin, 2001), 7.

[39] D. Hurd, in *Hansard*, 9 May 1994: www.publications.parliament.uk/pa/cm/cmhansrd.htm.

[40] 'Hurd Addresses UN', *The Independent*, 14 Sept. 1994, http://web.lexis-nexis.com/professional/.

[41] D. Hurd, 'Speech on "Britain's Role in Fighting the New World Disorder" Delivered at the Royal United Services Institute', *Journal of the Royal United Services Institute* 142:4 (1994), 15.

[42] D. Hurd, 'Speech to Young Conservatives Conference', 6 July 1992, Bodl., CCO 150/7/2.

[43] Simms, *Unfinest Hour*, 46.

[44] D. Hurd, 'Speech to the European Parliament', 9 July 1992, Bodl., CCO 150/7/2.

separate combatants by force or to plant the flag of conquest on foreign soil. NATO cannot be expected to solve all the problems on its borders and it must not be blamed for failing to do so.[45]

These sentiments were widely shared in the Conservative parliamentary party, which frequently harked back to Disraeli's steadfast refusal to intervene on behalf of the embattled Balkan Christians in the 1870s. 'What we lack', the Conservative MP Nicholas Budgen claimed, 'is a Disraeli. There is a case for inaction and, now, disengagement, but it has never been put.'[46] The reluctance to intervene in the Balkans surpassed party lines, however: the independent peer Lord Chalfont objected to 'interfering in the affairs of sovereign nations'.[47]

Hurd, Rifkind and their realist Conservative colleagues were swept from power by the Labour victory in the 1997 general election. Complementing the liberal interventionist foreign policy pursued by the Clinton adminis-tration, the rise of Tony Blair's New Labour to power in Britain injected into British foreign policy a 'liberal conscience' placing heavy emphasis on the problems created by the internal nature of sovereign states and their regimes, rather than viewing them as pillars for international order and stability.[48] Good government, democracy, and political rights within states were seen as the main factors determining international peace and stability and should be exported and spread abroad.[49] This was not mere rhetoric. New Labour's interventionist foreign policy was grounded in the Strategic Defence Review (SDR) of UK military posture, initiated by the Defence Secretary, George Robertson, on 28 May 1997. Its aim was to provide the basis for a coherent, long-term defence programme up to 2015, fit for the needs of the post-Cold War world.[50] The 'Grand Strategy' that emerged for Britain's power projection from the SDR was an overarching strategy that would define Britain's role abroad for the duration of Tony Blair's government. This 'Grand Strategy' revamped Britain's defence posture away from the main emphasis of fighting a conventional, high-intensity war in Europe and instead created a flexible, rapid, expeditionary posture in order to actively manage risks and undertake humanitarian interventions 'seeking to prevent conflicts rather than suppress them'.[51]

[45] D. Hurd, 'Speech to the Carlton Club Political Committee', 1993, Bodl., CCO 150/7/2.
[46] Simms, Unfinest Hour, 278.    [47] Ibid., 290.
[48] H. Larsen, Foreign Policy and Discourse Analysis: France, Britain and Europe (London: Routledge, 1997), 75.
[49] P. Williams, British Foreign Policy under New Labour (London: Palgrave Macmillan, 2005), 125.
[50] C. McInnes, Labour's Strategic Defence Review (London: Journal of British Historical Studies, 1998), 1.
[51] G. Robertson, Introduction: Strategic Defence Review, 3, www.mod.uk/NR/rdonlyres/65F3D7AC-4340–4119–93A2–20825848E50E/0/sdr1998_complete.pdf.

There were some early straws in the wind as to where this approach would lead. Defending the 1998 bombing of Saddam Hussein's suspected weapons programmes during 'Operation Desert Fox' in the South African Parliament in January 1999, Blair observed: 'People say – and I understand – you can't be self-appointed guardians of what is right and wrong. True – but when the international community agrees certain objectives and then fails to implement them, those that can act must.'[52] This was an embryonic form of the doctrine he would soon elaborate in greater detail in Chicago, and became the intellectual linchpin for successive interventions abroad under his New Labour Government, often in alliance with the United States. The self-styled 'ethical foreign policy' of the Blair government was soon put to a severe test. During the Kosovo Crisis of 1999, the Western powers – led in Europe by Great Britain – were forced to respond to the attempt by the Serbian leader Slobodan Milošević to expel almost the entire Kosovar Albanian population. Mr Blair's 'Doctrine of the International Community', formulated in a groundbreaking speech given to the Chicago Economic Club in April 1999, at the height of the conflict, explicitly rejected the traditional 'realism'. Instead, it promulgated a new paradigm, blending 'mutual self-interest with moral purpose'.[53] Blair asserted that 'the spread of our values makes us safer. As John Kennedy put it "Freedom is indivisible and when one man is enslaved who is free?"' The Kosovo war, on his reading, was thus 'based not on any territorial ambitions but on values'. He therefore called for a 'new framework' in addressing international security concerns, arguing that Western actions were now guided by a 'more subtle blend of mutual self interest and moral purpose in defending the values we cherish'. It was Blair's vision of establishing and spreading the values of liberty, the rule of law, human rights and an open society, which was within the 'national interest' as well. Mr Blair therefore qualified the principle of non-interference in the affairs of other states by stating that acts of genocide could never be a purely internal matter, rather oppression in foreign countries should be viewed properly as a threat to international peace and security.[54]

According to one leading scholar of international relations and politics, Blair's 'Doctrine of the International Community' speech 'was one

---

[52] T. Blair, 'Speech to the South African Parliament', 8 Jan. 1999, available at www.number-10.gov.uk/output/Page1172.asp.
[53] T. Blair, 'Speech to the Chicago Economic Club', Chicago, 24 Apr. 1999, available at www.number10.gov.uk/Page1297.
[54] *Ibid.*

of the most theoretical speeches ever made by a British Prime Minister on the fundamentals of foreign policy.'[55] It 'repays close attention for the self-conscious way in which it attempts to signal a new departure in British foreign policy', indeed, in international relations more generally.[56] Although its centre-piece was an attempt to rewrite the just-war doctrine for the new millennium, this was set in the midst of a discussion of globalisation, political as well as economic, which was fostering, the Prime Minister argued, 'the beginnings of a new doctrine of international community'.[57] Moving on to international politics Blair argued that 'the principles of international community apply also to international security' and identified the key foreign-policy problem of the modern state – at least, of those like Britain with the pretensions and perhaps power to have a global role: how 'to identify the circumstances in which we should get actively involved in other people's conflicts'. The classical rule of non-interference (enshrined somewhat ambiguously in the UN Charter) needed qualifying in three ways: to justify action against genocide; to deal with 'massive flows of refugees' which became 'threats to international peace and security'; and to deal with regimes based on minority rule.[58]

The most striking element of the Blair Doctrine and the accompanying war aims in Kosovo was the explicit call for a political framework in Kosovo, which would advance Western liberal values. The ensuing humanitarian intervention in Kosovo was accompanied by the creation of a liberal international administration in Kosovo with a European High Representative and provision of aid that keeps Bosnia and Kosovo running, and soldiers as an indispensable stabilising force.[59] It is not just soldiers that come from the international community; it is police, judges, prison officers, central bankers and others. Elections were organised and monitored by the Organization for Security and Cooperation in Europe (OSCE). Local police are financed and trained by the UN. As auxiliaries to this effort – in many areas indispensable to it – are over a hundred NGOs.[60] Intervention in Kosovo was acceptable to other member states of the UN in involving that organisation in the post-conflict situation, provided that it did not entail the unilateral alteration of sovereign borders.[61] However, the Kosovo intervention illustrated

[55] C. Hill, 'Putting the World to Rights', in *The Blair Effect 2001–05* (Cambridge: Cambridge University Press, 2005), 386.
[56] R. Little and M. Wickham-Jones, *New Labour's Foreign Policy: A New Moral Crusade?* (Manchester: Manchester University Press, 2000), 109.
[57] T. Blair, 'Speech on the Doctrine of the International Community', available at www.number10.gov.uk/Page1297.
[58] *Ibid.*    [59] Little and Wickham-Jones, *New Labour's Foreign Policy*, 8.
[60] *Ibid.*, 10.    [61] *Ibid.*, 170.

that once Western powers use military and diplomatic power to right human rights abuses, inevitably a course is set upon of altering sovereignty and even altering borders.[62] It also affirmed the principle in international relations that states can lose sovereignty over a portion of their territory if they oppress the majority population.

★

Mr Blair believed – and most observers tended to concur – that his approach represented a fundamentally new departure in international politics, rather than a development of a long-standing tradition. Jonathan Powell, chief of staff for Tony Blair during his ten years at Downing Street, maintains that 'the principle of non-interference in other nation's affairs was established by the Peace of Westphalia in 1648', and, musing on the rationale for the Iraq War, Powell reflects the Blair Government 'should have been clear we were removing Saddam [Hussein] because he was a ruthless dictator suppressing his people'.[63] Yet, as this volume has tried to demonstrate, states have throughout history repeatedly intervened to end human rights abuses and uphold good governance. They have always been prepared to set aside state sovereignty, usually in pursuit of their own strategic interests but also for purposes that we would today broadly classify as humanitarian; sometimes the two impulses cannot be usefully separated. Thus Elizabeth I intervened in the Netherlands, albeit reluctantly, with the explicit aim of upholding the rights of the Dutch nobility, Protestant and Catholic. Throughout the seventeenth and eighteenth centuries German and outside powers routinely intervened, usually diplomatically but sometimes militarily, to prevent German princes from abusing the rights of their subjects. During the Greek War of independence, Britain and France intervened, albeit rather confusedly, in order to stop the sultan from massacring his Christian subjects. European powers did the same in the Levant and the Balkans later in the century. At the end of the century, the United States put an end to Spanish atrocities in Cuba. Nor is this list exhaustive.

Looked at in this light, the interventions of the 1990s seem to be far less innovative. The huge debate over Bosnia resembles that over Greece in the 1820s, and that over Bulgaria in the 1870s, when – as Matthias Schulz has shown – the Russian intervention was justified very much in 'humanitarian' terms. A primary motivating factor, particularly in the early modern period, was often confessional or religious

---

[62] *Ibid.*, 171.
[63] J. Powell, 'Why the West should Not Fear to Intervene', *The Observer*, 18 Nov. 2007.

solidarity, but less and less so as time progressed. We see the same tensions between *Realpolitik* and humanitarian concerns. If at one level, George I's intervention on behalf of the oppressed Palatines was a gesture of confessional solidarity, it was also a blow against the perceived pretensions of Charles VI towards Catholic 'universal monarchy'. The same could be said, *mutatis mutandis*, of most of the other interventions described in this book. Likewise, the protection extended to the Kurds needs to be seen in the context of the Western desire to contain Saddam Hussein. The interventions in Bosnia and Kosovo were strongly influenced by the need to show the ability of NATO to provide security in the new Europe.

At the same time, the remote and the more recent past provide us with many examples of purely humanitarian interventions. For example, when Cromwell espoused the cause of the Vaudois he did so at the expense of relations with Savoy, a valued ally in the strategically vital area of northern Italy. Similarly, as Maeve Ryan has shown in this volume, Britain's campaign against the international slave trade was a huge deployment of national resources in pursuit of an aim which was far more moral than strategic. In the same way, the interventions in Sierra Leone and East Timor were hardly driven by the 'national interest' of Western powers; indeed, in the latter case, it cut across a long-standing desire to appease powerful Indonesia. Moreover, both past and present have shown that humanitarian and strategic concerns are not only hard to disentangle, but may in fact sometimes be indistinguishable. Since the sixteenth century, for example, confessional solidarity with fellow Protestants across Europe was a survival strategy in the face of Counter-Reformation assaults. To Burke, the French Revolution was a threat to the international order *because* of its contempt for the rights of Frenchmen. In early eighteenth-century Mecklenburg, late eighteenth-century Poland and late nineteenth-century Cuba, neighbouring powers feared that bad governance destabilised the area and thus constituted a threat to their own security. Similarly, in the mid-1970s, the Jackson–Vanik amendment proceeded from the principle that forcing the Soviet Union to respect human rights was part and parcel of US national interests. Likewise, Bosnia and Kosovo in the 1990s became geopolitical problems because they were humanitarian ones. It was no longer possible for the Great Powers to tolerate ethnic cleansing and instability in the heart of Europe. In short, 'humanitarian intervention' did not spring fully formed from the minds of post-Cold War Western statesmen, human rights activists and international theorists. It represented the fusion of several long-standing strands in Western international practice and discourse. The road which leads from the sixteenth century to the present day may be a crooked one, complicated by many distracting turns and forks, but for those who want to understand the origins of the most transformative idea of the twenty-first century, it is a path worth travelling in the opposite direction.

# 17 Conclusion: Humanitarian intervention in historical perspective

## D. J. B. Trim

One of the most important conclusions of this collaborative historical investigation concerns the Westphalian concept of sovereignty.[1] Our findings confirm those of Stephen Krasner and other scholars who argue that the alleged emergence of a new concept of state sovereignty after the treaties of Westphalia (1648) has been greatly exaggerated.[2]

Closer historical investigation of the 'recalcitrant' question of sovereignty has shown it to have been a very relative term indeed. In particular, Krasner shows that what most scholars – and confusingly he – call 'Westphalian Sovereignty', the absolute freedom from intervention by an outside power, has in fact nothing to do with the Peace of Westphalia. The arrangements made there, he points out, enshrined minority rights at the expense of central sovereignty. One way or another, sovereignty has 'always' been violated throughout history.[3]

Most recent criticisms of the supposedly Westphalian paradigm have been made from the explicit disciplinary perspectives of International Relations or Political Science, or on overtly political grounds. The historical studies in this volume confirm that the concept of Westphalia as originating a system of states whose sovereignty was absolute simply is not true, and that, in consequence, the idea that the modern

*I am grateful to Brendan Simms and Winifred Trim for their comments on earlier drafts.*

[1] It should be noted that the so-called Peace of Westphalia comprised three separate treaties: the treaty of Münster, between the Spanish Monarchy and the Dutch Republic (Jan. 1648); a second treaty of Münster, between France and the Holy Roman Empire (Oct. 1648); and the treaty of Osnabrück, between Sweden and the Empire (Oct. 1648). (Hence the Dutch term *vrede van Münster*, 'peace of Münster', instead of 'Peace of Westphalia'.)

[2] For example, Stephen Krasner, *Sovereignty: Organized Hypocrisy* (Princeton: Princeton University Press, 1999) and 'Rethinking the Sovereign State Model', *Review of International Studies* 27 (2001), 17–42; Benno Teschke, *The Myth of 1648: Class, Geopolitics, and the Making of Modern International Relations* (London and New York: Verso, 2003); Stéphane Beaulac, *The Power of Language in the Making of International Law*, Developments in International Law 46 (Leiden: Martinus Nijhoff, 2004), 70 *et passim*.

[3] Krasner, *Sovereignty*, 20 *et passim*.

international system derives solely from Westphalia is, at best, highly dubious. This means that the presumption of some vocal scholars, policy practitioners and human rights activists, that humanitarian intervention is illegitimate simply because it contravenes Westphalian principles, is not so much erroneous as baseless.

First, as Chapter 2 argues, intervention was compatible with seventeenth-century concepts of sovereignty; intervention arguably was widely, though not universally, normative in early modern Europe. Second, as Chapter 3 highlights, the peace treaties of Westphalia specifically included guarantees of freedom of conscience for some religious minorities within the empire – and made some states from outside the empire guarantors of the rights of religious minorities in other states. Sweden was, for example, the Westphalian guarantor of the rights of Protestants within the Holy Roman Empire. In such cases, not only was sovereignty not absolute, but interventions actually were legally mandated. Third, as Chapters 3 and 4 bring out, within the empire there were, even for sovereign princes, well-established mechanisms, endorsed at Westphalia, which existed to warn and, on occasions, to depose tyrannical princes, which were employed against both Catholic and Protestant. The Imperial Aulic Council (*Reichshofrat*) had been established in 1498 as an instrument of imperial power, but in 1648 at Westphalia it received its first Lutheran members.[4] The Westphalian settlement made it a far more consensual body, with the result that in the late seventeenth century and throughout the eighteenth century it was more active and assertive, intervening in the affairs of individual sovereign territories to defuse confessional tension and constrain tyrannical rulers.

The (actual, as opposed to mythical) Westphalian model was copied outside the empire. Provisions making states guarantors of the rights of religious minorities in other states were built into treaties throughout the second half of the seventeenth century and into the eighteenth. Britain and the Swiss Confederation guaranteed the provisions of the Treaty of Pinerolo (1655), by which the Duke of Savoy granted limited religious toleration to the Vaudois (see Chapter 2); Sweden and Brandenburg-Prussia guaranteed the rights of Protestants in Polish Prussia by the terms of the Treaty of Oliva (1660) and Britain was added as a third guarantor power a few years later (see Chapter 3). In 1704, Great Britain and the Dutch Republic made a treaty of alliance

---

[4] See Peter Wilson, *From Reich to Revolution: German History, 1558–1806* (Basingstoke: Palgrave, 2004), 179.

with Victor Amadeus of Savoy conditional on his conceding to the Vaudois the 'entire and inviolable observance' of their religion, and the two Maritime Powers guaranteed their religious liberty by the same treaty. Contracting powers took these obligations seriously – in 1719–20 Britain was willing to 'become a guarantor power of the Westphalian agreement', so as to have a basis for halting oppression of Protestants in Heidelberg; in 1724, Prussia, as guarantor power, mobilised troops to force the Polish government to protect Protestants in Thorn from Catholic violence.[5]

What today is typically identified as the 'Westphalian model' emerged, but only later in the eighteenth century. Even then it did not monopolise attitudes to sovereignty; the concept that how a government treated the governed ought to be a factor in sovereignty retained its influence. In 1774, the treaty of Kutchuk–Kainardji effectively established Russia as guarantor of the rights of Orthodox Christians in the Ottoman Empire, when the Sublime Porte conceded to Russia the right to protect its Orthodox subjects (rights the Russians later exercised).[6] In 1790, during the early and idealistic days of the French Revolution, Jérôme Pétion de Villeneuve, a lawyer and member of the National Assembly, denounced monarchy for its record of *'crimes de lèse-humanité'* – 'crimes against humanity'; he urged the 'extermination' of contemporary princes who perpetrated such crimes, including the rulers of the piratical Barbary States. The excesses of the French Revolution in the following two years led the Anglo-Irish statesman Edmund Burke to urge foreign military intervention in France on the grounds that the revolutionaries consti-tuted a 'positively Vicious and abusive Government', which was guilty of 'the most atrocious and bloody tyranny' – thus echoing the sixteenth- and seventeenth-century opponents of oppression.[7] For nearly eight decades after 1648, then, the supposed Westphalian system did not, in fact,

---

[5] Randolph Vigne, 'Richard Hill and the Saving of Liberty of Conscience for the Vaudois', in *The Development of Pluralism in Modern Britain and France*, ed. Richard Bonney and D. J. B. Trim (2007) (Oxford, Bern, Berlin, Brussels, Frankfurt am Main, New York, and Vienna: Peter Lang, 2010), 163. Andrew Thompson, Chapter 3, above, pp. 80–82 (at 80).

[6] I. Young, 'Russia', in *New Cambridge Modern History*, VIII, ed. A. Goodwin (Cambridge: Cambridge University Press, 1965), 325; R. J. Crampton, *A Concise History of Bulgaria* (Cambridge: Cambridge University Press, 1997), 52; J. A. S. Grenville, *Europe Reshaped 1848–1878*, 2nd edn (Oxford: Blackwell, 2000), 171. The treaty is mentioned by G. J. Bass, *Freedom's Battle: The Origins of Humanitarian Intervention* (New York: Alfred A. Knopf, 2008), but for criticism of his interpretation, see Adam Hochschild's review, in the *New York Times*, 29 Aug. 2008 (available at www.nytimes.com/2008/08/31/books/review/Hochschild-t.html?pagewanted=all).

[7] Pétion, quoted in David A. Bell, *The First Total War: Napoleon's Europe and the Birth of Modern Warfare* (London: Bloomsbury, 2008), 102. Burke, quoted by Brendan Simms, in Chapter 4, above, p. 89.

provide for absolute sovereignty; and earlier models of sovereignty continued to be influential even into the last decade of the eighteenth century.

Thus, the chapters in Part I confirm the findings of recent scholarship: even in its heyday, the Westphalian system in practice provided neither for truly absolute sovereignty, nor an unconditional principle of non-intervention. Some rulers' sovereignty was not absolute in some parts of their territories; other rulers had both a right and obligation to intervene in other princes' affairs.

By 1815, when the Congress of Vienna redrew the map of Europe after the Napoleonic Wars, intervention was not on the table and the West-phalian myth was given substantive form. European statesmen seem to have had a shared image of Westphalia that, at least in terms of a norm of non-intervention, was at odds with its realities, even if Burke's comments, quoted above, reveal that the early modern norm of intervention was remembered in some quarters. But perhaps as important to the statesmen at Vienna as the myth of Westphalia was the fact that the French revolutionaries were perceived as being interventionists.[8] In the early, pre-Napoleonic days of the revolutionary wars, French troops had helped parties of revolutionaries in the Dutch Republic, the Swiss Confederation, and some states in Germany and Italy, to overthrow their absolutist or authoritarian governments. Interventionism thus came to be associated with revolution.

To be sure, the Vienna settlement asserted the right of the Great Powers, acting collaboratively (as the so-called 'Concert of Europe') to intervene in domestic affairs on behalf of a government facing a rebel-lion, or in the case of the collapse of a government's authority. Indeed, as John Bew observes in Chapter 5, 'the main powers were more commit-ted to intervening in the affairs of other states in a systematic way'.[9] The principle of intervention endorsed at Vienna was not at all the same thing, however, as asserting a right to intervene *against* an oppressive government on behalf of the (oppressed) governed, over the govern-ment's objections. In fact, what was envisaged truly was allied action, more than intervention, its purpose being to maintain existing govern-ments, rather than checking their abuses. The Vienna settlement was intended to result in a kind of stasis in the international system. Yet instead of marking the death knell of the concept of intervention, the nineteenth century ironically was to be its apogee.

---

[8]  Michael Broers, 'The French Revolution and the Napoleonic Wars', unpubl. paper read at the conference 'The Changing Character of War', St Anthony's College Oxford, 19–21 Mar. 2009.

[9]  Above, p. 120.

The founders of the Concert of Europe were conservative, but they also identified it as a 'guardian of civilisation' and hoped it would foster moral policy-making.[10] As a result, and as a result, too, of the wider rise of 'liberal' values in Western Europe, especially in Britain and France, the Concert actually became an informal mechanism for taking collective action against regimes or actions regarded as uncivilised, illiberal and ultimately inhumane; it became the basis for intervention.

However, it must be stressed that the revival of intervention in the nineteenth century was not a radical departure: not in terms of international law, nor of state practice. For, as we have seen, the century after 1648 had seen a weakening of the earlier norm of intervention, yet even in the Age of Westphalia, both the Law of Nations and state practice allowed for the possibility of intervention.

A final point on sovereignty: it is increasingly likely that, in the future, NGOs, rather than states, will become humanitarian interveners. Gideon Mailer's examination (Chapter 12) of interventionist activity by missionary NGOs in the Sudan highlights the importance of NGOs in the twenty-first-century world. Many of them are Christian – either informally, in origin or sympathy, or overtly and organisationally – and they are especially significant in the developing world, where they wield considerable economic power and, increasingly, political influence. Relationships between missionaries and colonial authorities were often tense, not least because missionaries were key players in the emergence of 'the humanitarian public' (see below), and helped to pressure their own governments into actions they frequently did not want to take, against oppressive regimes. After the end of empire in Africa, Western missionaries, who often strongly identified with native converts, remained behind. Seeing indigenous Christians increasingly suffering oppression, but failing to interest foreign governments in taking action to help them, missionaries started to take unilateral action, though it usually was financial and logistical, not violent.

Similar points could be made about the activities of church-based Western NGOs in Burma; some have done no more than provide food and medical aid to persecuted Karen Christians, but others have undoubtedly paid for weapons, other military equipment, and training. There is some evidence of relationships between Western NGOs and militias in Rwanda and the Democratic Republic of the Congo. This is a

---

[10] For example, Matthias Schulz, 'Did Norms Matter in Nineteenth-Century International Relations?', in *An Improbable War: The Outbreak of World War I, and European Political Culture before 1914*, ed. Holger Afflerbach and David Stevenson (New York and Oxford: Berghahn, 2007), 43–60, esp. 45–7.

grey area, one that needs more research, but it highlights the important role of non-state actors, though scholarly literature is full of references to 'Westphalian sovereignty'. Just as this concept has to be deconstructed for the seventeenth and eighteenth centuries, it may be becoming increasingly irrelevant in the twenty-first century.

★

The second key conclusion is about the way that concepts of who or what should be protected have developed over time. Ethical concern for the sufferings of people of other nationalities or ethnicities started as a primarily confessional solidarity, and then expanded to encompass ever-broader groups. It is a Whiggish progression, but one that moved in fits and starts. The effect of the Enlightenment probably was to secularise solidarity and see the emergence of a 'humanitarian sensibility'. That said, Elizabeth I in the sixteenth century had already expressed concern for the 'privileges' of both Catholic and Protestant Dutch nobility, while religion clearly played an important part in Burke's sense of solidarity with the victims of the French Revolution. This is a subject on which more research is needed. Indeed, the present book does not claim to be an exhaustive history of all the precedents for humanitarian intervention; it *is* intended to demonstrate that a long-term history exists and needs to be fully recovered.

Furthermore, several important points have emerged. In taking the sixteenth and seventeenth centuries as its starting point for a history of humanitarian intervention, this volume is going further than many scholars will feel right or proper. Some historians will be alarmed at our identification of and emphasis on long-term trends, seeing it as teleological, or Whiggish (or other pejorative characterisations). Historians are rightly wary of an overly 'present-centred agenda', in which concern 'to chart the stepping-stones on the path towards "modern" democratic society' results in merely identifying and linking 'disparate pieces of evidence which draw the route-map between a pre-modern world and the modern system of representative politics'.[11] However, scholars must not be deterred from trying to understand the origins and development of the ideas, paradigms and practices that obtain in the present-day world. This is what we endeavour to do. Our pursuit of this end has not been teleological; the preceding chapters sought the causes of the various episodes they examined and viewed them as historically contingent, rather than only explaining them as forerunners of a later phenomenon.

---

[11] Lloyd Bowen, review of George Yerby, *People and Parliament: Representative Rights and the English Revolution* (Basingstoke: Palgrave Macmillan, 2008), in *Parliamentary History* 28 (2009), 301, 299–300.

Taken together, the chapters identify a series of 'slow-moving processes, sequences, and developmental paths'.[12] But they also reveal a relatively clear line of development: not, to be sure, one of simplistic or mechanistic 'progress', whose outcome in twentieth- and twenty-first-century concepts is natural or inevitable – indeed, attitudes to intervention on moral, ethical or humanitarian grounds have swung backwards and forwards over the last four-and-a-half centuries, undermining ideas of progress.

Over the more than four-and-a-half centuries we have covered, there were significant shifts: in the types of people who were thought to deserve interventionist protection; in the rationale for protecting them; and in the rhetoric used both at home and abroad to justify the use of force to protect foreign peoples. All of these changed. The concept of people deserving protection evolved: from confessional co-religionists, to all fellow Christians, to all human beings. The concept of what was illegitimate evolved: starting with 'tyranny' and religious persecution, it then encompassed slavery (once a staple of civilised commerce) and 'uncivilised' governance, and then focused on war crimes, before expanding to crimes 'against humanity'. The concept of what the international system ought to support and maintain evolved too: from Christendom; to liberty, liberalism and civilisation; to universal human rights.

However, the final, inclusive stage, which is relatively recent, was only arrived at via the initial stages. There is a clear and interconnected series of evolutions and developments, each emerging out of, and to some extent developing or expanding, earlier concepts and praxis, and forming, as it were, links in a chain. The recent and present concept of 'humanitarian intervention' was not bound to have emerged from earlier concerns about tyranny, persecution, atrocity, slavery and massacre, because at certain periods in the last 500 years these concerns were downplayed by international society as a whole, or were subordinated to other concepts and values. Yet nor was it created *de novo* by inspired humanitarians in the nineteenth or twentieth centuries. Without knowing and understanding the earlier links in the chain, we will not understand how the most recent link – the twin concepts of universal human rights and of using power to protect them – came to be forged. Without the earlier links in the chain, humanitarian intervention, in its current sense, simply would not exist.

*

Another important area of change was in the means by which governments were persuaded to act, and the associated rise in public awareness

---

[12] George Lawson, 'The Promise of Historical Sociology in International Relations', *International Studies Review* 8 (2006), 415.

and consciousness of tyranny, atrocities and crimes against humanity. What was consistent, across the period, is that there was widespread interest in humanitarian crises and especially in oppressive, tyrannical misgovernment. What changed was the sheer breadth of knowledge within (especially Western) societies and this created a dynamic of its own. What has eventually emerged is what we term a 'humanitarian public'.

In the sixteenth and seventeenth centuries, governments began to take their decisions not only based on what seemed right and good to sovereigns and their counsellors. Kings saw foreign policy as part of the *imperium arcana* and exempt from public discussion. As Chapter 2 shows, however, the Dutch insurgents against Spain used the printing press to excellent effect, to publicise Spanish atrocities and generate international support; and Oliver Cromwell, Lord Protector of the British republic, called for public donations to aid the Vaudois in 1655 along with a day of prayer and fasting – calls that were effective partly because the massacre of the Vaudois in Savoy had been widely reported across Europe in pamphlets, broadsides and books. Cromwell capitalised on the extraordinary reportage to mobilise public opinion in order to aid the Vaudois more effectively. By the end of the century, as Chapter 3 reveals, newspapers and pamphlets regularly disseminated news of the sufferings of Protestant minorities across Europe; presentation of the sufferings of Protestants was one of the means used to garner support for them. It helped to influence nascent 'public opinion' and thus government policy in Britain and the Dutch Republic.

Chapters 6, 7, 9, 11, and 13 show the emergence of more sophisticated pressure groups in the middle and later decades of the nineteenth century, both across Europe and in North America. These capitalised on the press, which had developed since the early eighteenth century into an almost omnipresent medium in Western society, with extraordinary influence.

The transnational pressure groups that emerged in the nineteenth century were susceptible to manipulation: by politicians who saw intervention as an easy way to expand an empire, or gain glory from defending persecuted fellow Christians; and by oppressed foreign people groups, who by the 1890s understood that if they could induce intervention by the Great Powers they could achieve otherwise unobtainable results. However, manipulation went two ways. Transnational humanitarian pressure groups were also able to push politicians, normally devoted to *raison d'état*, into humanitarian action that they would rather have avoided.

Lobbying for diplomatic [and military] intervention in the name of 'humanity' and 'civilisation' . . . activists helped [to] create a context in which the treatment of religious and ethnic minorities became a pre-condition of acceptance into an international state system that was increasingly governed by Western norms.[13]

This had both positive and negative consequences. It pushed states outside Europe to accept that they could not mistreat minorities; but it could also provide justification for European states to subjugate supposedly 'uncivilised' peoples.

The humanitarian groups mixed gullibility and sophistication towards atrocity stories, and they could be patronising to ethnic and religious minorities whom they hoped to 'save'. Their obsessive preoccupation could alienate Western politicians as well as persuade them to act. Furthermore, the rhetoric, and sometimes the objectives, of the humanitarian lobby could overlie, or blur into, those of imperialist and expansionist lobbies. Yet the humanitarian groups in Europe did help to ameliorate the lot of oppressed peoples in the Ottoman Empire and East Africa. Their attitudes lived on into the twentieth century, in some of the societies that supported missionary work in Africa, as shown in Chapter 12. There is increasing scholarship on the emergence of humanitarianism in the twentieth century; we suggest it needs explicitly to take into account the transnational humanitarian pressure groups of the nineteenth century.

From these roots eventually emerged today's humanitarian public: a large group within Western society of people who either feel committed to human rights and ethical conduct of foreign policy, or are fascinated by atrocity stories. Their support generates reporting of humanitarian crises (not necessarily limited to those caused by war and brutal government), but also consumes it; the audience is in a symbiotic relationship with the media. We have seen that this humanitarian public had forerunners in the seventeenth century, but it probably required the emergence of the communicative space of large-circulation newspapers before it could itself emerge. It certainly developed over the nineteenth century: as Chapters 6–7, 9–10, and 13 indicate, it became an important factor in government attitudes to intervention. Mobilising public opinion became a necessary step for governments undertaking interventions. As referred to earlier, the rhetoric of humanitarianism has not only been deployed top down, by governments seeking to manipulate public opinion; it also has been used from the bottom up, by activist groups seeking to push governments into action.

---

[13] Abigail Green, Chapter 6, above, pp. 139–40. Cf. Bass, *Freedom's Battle*, 7, 375.

Governments have preferred to choose the time and place of interventions, even when they are ethically and morally grounded; but popular opinion has frequently demanded greater consistency. However, while public pressure for intervention has usually reflected genuine emotion, it has rarely been wholly spontaneous, and is often orchestrated by skilful activists, such as the transnational pressure groups mentioned above. Alternatively, the émigré representatives of oppressed peoples have used the ostensible Western attachment to civilisation, liberal values and (more recently) human rights to influence Western governments, including by stirring up popular opinion. Sometimes, too, it has been governments or opposition parties that have manipulated the public with humanitarian rhetoric, to obtain popular sanction for geopolitically motivated policy.

Yet it is also the case that governments in their turn have been influenced or pressured by the humanitarian media and public. Interventions have sometimes been impelled against a government's wishes, or shaped in ways that were partly contrary to its designs, by popular response to reportage of atrocities and persecution. Examples include British action against the East African slave trade in the late nineteenth century, US diplomatic efforts against the Soviet Union in the late 1960s and early 1970s, and the Australian military intervention in East Timor in 1999.[14]

In sum, the interrelationships between governments, the media, the humanitarian public and the general public have been complex. Yet its history has rarely been a subject of explicit consideration.[15] The preceding chapters have opened up this terrain, but it needs to be explored further. This is another area in need of more research.

*

Once interventions have been decided on, whether through popular pressure or not, they can take different forms – as we argued above, interventions need not involve military operations. To be sure, overtly military interventions – such as those undertaken by England in France and the Netherlands in the late sixteenth century, by Britain against slave traders at various times in the nineteenth century, by Russia against the Ottoman Empire in 1877, by the United States against Spain in 1898, by

---

[14] Chapters 11 and 14; John Connor, 'Intervention and Domestic Politics', in *Australian Peacekeeping: Sixty Years in the Field*, ed. David Horner, Peter Londey, and Jen Bou (Cambridge: Cambridge University Press, 2009), 60.

[15] Bass has sustained consideration of the role of the press and public pressure groups: *Freedom's Battle*, 6–7, 24–36, 273–81, 290–1, 372–5. For a (rare) examination of the media's role in a very recent intervention, see C. de Landtsheer, J. Palmer, and D. Middleton, 'Een "framing" analyse over de Kosovo–oorlog in de Nederlandse pers (vergeleken met de Britse en Italiaanse pers)', *Tijdschrift voor sociologie* 23 (2002), 403–39.

Austria (briefly) against the Ottomans in 1905, by Vietnam in Cambodia in 1978, or demanded by Burke against the French revolutionary regime in the 1790s – have certainly been the most visible form of intervention. However, intervention has taken many forms; some did not involve the use of force. Diplomatic and financial, or commercial, influence has also been put to effective use.

For example, as noted earlier, the treaties of Westphalia not only guaranteed the rights of certain religious minorities, they also provided that other states were to act to ensure those rights were maintained. This system did not work perfectly, but it did achieve some protection of minority rights. The British government in 1655 used diplomacy (as well as the threat of force), in both France and Savoy, to oblige the Duke of Savoy to ease restrictions on the Vaudois, and it sent large sums of money to help them reconstruct their communities. In the first decade of the eighteenth century, Britain and the Netherlands used diplomatic pressure to persuade the duke to concede rights to the Vaudois, which were guaranteed by the British and Dutch governments.[16] In the first half of the nineteenth century, Britain painstakingly constructed a web of international treaties against the slave trade. The British government used diplomacy to foster the rights of Jews in the Ottoman Empire in the 1840s–70s, while British and French voluntary groups supported them financially; and, it is worth adding that at least three times in the first half of the nineteenth century the British government interceded in Italian affairs on behalf of persecuted religious minorities, not deploying coercive force, but using strong diplomatic measures against the King of Piedmont and the Grand Duke of Tuscany.[17] In addition to Austria's military action against the Ottomans in 1905, for several years Austria, Russia and Italy invested manpower and financial resources into efforts to reconstruct and reorganise Macedonia in the first decade of the twentieth century. In the 1970s, the Jackson–Vanik amendment tied the granting of 'most favoured nation' status to the Soviet Union to the right of emigration. And for much of the twentieth century, missionaries educated Sudanese people and funded social progress, though in a way that proved incompatible with the nationalist and Islamic agenda of the government in Khartoum.[18]

However, military force as often as not has been really the only way to achieve concrete results and even limited successes. Even when

---

[16] Chapters 2–3; Vigne, 'Richard Hill and Liberty of Conscience'.
[17] Chapters 10, 6; John Wolffe, 'British Protestants and Europe, 1820–1860: Some Perceptions and Influences', in *Development of Pluralism*, ed. Bonney and Trim, 207–26.
[18] Chapters 9, 14, 12.

diplomacy succeeded, it often did so *because* of the implicit or actual threat of force. Savoy accepted British demands in 1655 partly because of the threat of the British fleet. Without the 'compulsion' of British naval action off the West African coast, the Atlantic slave trade would not have ended, as Palmerston knew; British naval and military action in East Africa and the Indian Ocean helped to reduce the slave trade there. European naval ships and marines saved lives in Lebanon during the initial atrocities in 1860; and though French troops did not fight in Lebanon in 1861, their presence helped to ensure killing did not recur. There was no recurrence of atrocities against the Christian population of Bulgaria after the notorious massacres of 1876 partly because Russian military action in 1877–8 led to the creation of an autonomous Bulgarian polity. The Ottoman government only accepted the reform of Macedonia after Austrian military action in the Aegean. Foreign missionaries in Sudan were eventually frustrated by the Sudanese government's persecution of their fellow believers, and assisted them in a struggle for 'self-determination'.[19] Violence has almost always been implicit in interventions, even when not actually used.

This makes the reluctance of many present commentators and statesmen even to contemplate armed intervention a problem. For example, former Irish President Mary Robinson roundly declared in 2008 of the 'Responsibility to Protect' doctrine: 'We should be clear that it is not a justification of military intervention'.[20] Strictly speaking, this is incorrect: the original *Responsibility to Protect* report includes a section on when military intervention is justified and how it ought to be undertaken.[21] In addition, however, the implicit rejection of 'military intervention' is misguided. Of course, prevention is always preferable to remedial action (as the original *R2P* report stressed) and peaceful resolution of humanitarian crises (as in Kenya in 2008) is preferable to solutions imposed by force. But there have always been crises that are impervious to mediation – and historically speaking, these have been the majority.

*

Diplomatic interventions are usually less controversial than military ones, but regardless of the form intervention takes, when they are conducted, there tends to be controversy about their wider objectives. Once atrocities are stopped, what next? This can raise the contentious question of 'regime change', which in recent actual or suggested

---

[19] Chapters 2, 10 (see p. 253), 11, 7, 8, 9, 12.
[20] 'Remarks', at the Global Centre for Responsibility to Protect, 14 Feb. 2008 (available at http://globalr2p.org/pdf/RobinsonGCR2Plaunch.pdf), 2.
[21] *Responsibility to Protect*, I, 30–7, paras. 4.6–4.42.

interventions has been highly controversial. However, the issue of regime change is not new, although the terminology is and it probably has been the subject of greater debate recently than in the past. Associated with regime change are arguments about so-called 'failed states' – here, too, while the terminology is recent, the concept and the difficulties it creates have a long history, though it is often ignored in debates about failed states and nation-building.[22]

In one sense, all interventions are to bring about a change *in* a regime: if there was no imperative to change a regime's policy, there would be no need for intervention in the first place. The question has been: will change be made *by* the regime, or will there be a change *of* the regime?

Arguments against tyrannical rule can and do shade into arguments for regime change, which in turn can become arguments for expansionism or imperialism. This is rightly a concern among critics, and some proponents, of humanitarian intervention. However, it is important to note that sovereignty historically has rarely been necessarily permanent; the notion of the 'failed state', far from being new hegemonic parlance, has existed for hundreds of years. While the term 'failed state' is a recent neologism, the concept clearly dates back at least to the sixteenth century, when Elizabethan England intervened in France partly from fears that the French kingdom was on the point of collapse into anarchy.[23] When states ceased to function, sovereignty no longer was inherent in them.

Poland was the classic eighteenth-century 'failed state', whose instability perpetually threatened to suck in outside powers. As the British Secretary of State Henry Seymour Conway put it in August 1767, the main aim was to 'prevent the effect of those unhappy commotions from spreading wider, or endangering the public tranquility'. He argued that 'The continuance of the confusions in Poland is far from being an indifferent object & may be attended with events which cannot, at present be exactly foreseen'. Intermittent concern was expressed for 'the Toleration of the [religious] dissidents'.[24] On the other hand, in the aftermath of the partition of Poland in 1772, one newspaper correspondent welcomed the event as a well-deserved comeuppance for the bigoted Polish nobility. The sufferings of Poland, he wrote, 'have been greatly

---

[22] For example, Michael Ignatieff, 'State Failure and Nation-building', in *Humanitarian Intervention: Ethical, Legal and Political Dilemmas*, ed. J. L. Holzgrefe and Robert O. Keohane (Cambridge: Cambridge University Press, 2003), 299–321, an essay that is entirely focused on events after 1990, despite some references to 'Westphalian sovereignty'.

[23] Chapter 2.

[24] Quoted in Brendan Simms, *Three Victories and a Defeat: The Rise and Fall of the First British Empire* (London: Allen Lane, 2007), 547–8.

her own fault. Her intolerancy in religion, her tyrannical oligarchy, her senseless *liberum veto*, her systematic corruptness, could not well afford a prospect of a less deplorable catastrophe than what they are now undergoing'. Now that the eastern empires had finally decided to foreclose on this failed state, the argument ran, this could only be for the greater good.[25] Thus, the failure of the state was a major factor in the destruction of Poland as a nation, partitioned between Austria, Prussia and Russia.

The concept of regime change, while again a neologism, also has a long history in response to the problem of 'failed states'. The German philosopher, Immanuel Kant, sanctioned 'forced constitutional change against regimes that were persistent and serious violators of international law',[26] although admittedly this did not include violation of principles of good internal government based on divine law. Yet his view provides support for the approach, eventually taken in the war crimes trials at Nuremberg, that some violations of human rights are so egregious as to constitute in effect a breach of international law, justifying coercive action by other state actors. The notion that 'good governance' should be a requirement of states, whether for ethical or security reasons, thus has long-standing roots.[27] However, regime change has a mixed history, rather like humanitarian intervention itself. At times it has been favoured but at other times clearly not.

As Chapter 2 reveals, some influential early modern writers argued that princes who violated behavioural norms sufficient to prompt war by neighbouring princes had forfeited their right to sovereignty; however, other writers disagreed, as indeed did the princes who practised military intervention, such as Elizabeth I of England. In her eyes, while tyranny made a prince's rule illegitimate, this was temporary rather than permanent; intervention was intended to induce a prince to abandon transgressive behaviours, rather than to remove a prince whose right to rule had been permanently lost. This also seems to have been the attitude of late seventeenth- and early eighteenth-century governments, who used diplomatic intervention and sometimes the threat of force to induce changes in policy in other states.[28]

By the late eighteenth century, however, Edmund Burke argued for regime change in revolutionary France. The Congress of Vienna, which laid the groundwork for Europe in the aftermath of the French

---

[25] Quotations are *ibid.*, 566.
[26] John MacMillan, 'Liberal Interventionism', in *International Relations Theory for the Twenty-First Century: An Introduction*, ed. Martin Griffiths (London and New York: Routledge, 2007), 28.
[27] *Ibid.*     [28] Chapters 2, 3.

revolutionary and Napoleonic Wars, rejected the very concept of regime change, and military intervention against the Great Powers was to remain out of the question – but elsewhere was a different story. In the 1810s and 1820s, the Ottoman Turks responded to rebellion in Greece with atrocities that were widely publicised across Europe.[29] The answer, in effect, was a kind of regime change: although the Ottoman sultan was not removed, he was compelled by military intervention to agree to Greek independence – the regime in Greece *had* been changed. Thereafter, however, despite some limited annexation of Ottoman territory by the Great Powers, intervention in the Ottoman Empire, as in sixteenth- and seventeenth-century Europe, was often intended to produce a change in policy, rather than in the regime. Arrangements for local governance *were* subject to sometimes considerable 'reform', but Syria, Lebanon, Crete and Macedonia all remained under Turkish rule.[30]

Nineteenth-century Western European liberals were generally sympathetic to independence struggles in a range of countries, including Hungary, Poland and Italy, as well as Greece, and yet military intervention in Hungary and Poland seems never to have been even considered, certainly not seriously. This partly reflects the power of the Austrian and Russian empires and the Kingdom of Prussia, so that intervention targeted against them simply was unfeasible. This is not to say that nothing can be done to ameliorate oppression in powerful states – diplomacy has achieved some humanitarian goals.[31] But it is notable that intervention has typically been undertaken against weaker states.

The failure to intervene on behalf of oppressed peoples in nineteenth-century Central and Eastern European empires was due to more than geopolitical realities, however. To some extent it reflected a double standard among European liberals: civilised states and peoples might be guilty of excesses from time to time, but intervention ought not be practised against them, since all civilised polities were at a roughly equal stage of development. Uncivilised peoples and kingdoms, however, were not full members of the international system (invented and self-defined by European states!); they were thought to be at a more primitive stage of development, which meant they were inherently likely to commit acts of appalling barbarism, brutality and cruelty.[32] Intervention by civilised, enlightened polities against uncivilised peoples or rulers was perceived as almost natural. This perspective was not limited to imperialists: even some of the staunchest advocates of liberalism in nineteenth-century

[29] Chapters 4, 5.    [30] Chapters 6–9.    [31] Chapters 6, 14.    [32] Chapter 7.

Europe, including John Stuart Mill, 'went so far as to sanction despotism as a legitimate mode of government for "uncivilized" non-Europeans'.[33]

The Austrians, Prussians and Russians (although there were occasional doubts about the last named among Western Europeans) were seen as civilised. The Ottomans were regarded as being *almost* civilised. This, along with concerns about the balance of power, help to explain why intervention in the Ottoman Empire was invariably limited in its goals. Not only would the collapse of the empire create a vacuum that would upset the balance of the Great Powers; it was also thought that, with the right blend of encouragement, punishment and tutelage, the Ottomans could attain the civilisation of Christian Europe. Thus, military intervention was something that could legitimately be carried out in the Ottoman Empire. The youthfully self-confident United States could undertake it against the decrepit Spanish Empire, which in American eyes similarly verged on uncivilised.[34] In contrast, diplomatic intervention was the most that would be carried out in Eastern Europe, despite the fact that minorities there faced persecution as much as those living in lands ruled by the Turk.[35]

Military intervention was perceived as even more legitimate in Africa and Asia, where local peoples and rulers were, it was assumed, steeped in barbarism. Initially during the nineteenth century, African rulers, as well as European and American trading companies and individual merchants, were targeted for intervention to end the slave trade. In this early phase, there was little desire to overthrow local rulers.[36] Ironically, it was only after the slave trade had been successfully ended in West Africa that native princes, rather than their policies, became the target. By this time, the rhetoric was no longer that of abolishing the slave trade, but rather that of spreading 'liberty' and civilisation to peoples benighted, as it was thought, by barbarism and tyranny. This rhetoric of liberty and humanity resulted in the replacement of local rulers by protectorates, or outright colonial annexation. Regime change was very much the order of the day.

Where intervention was avowedly against tyranny, persecution, slave-trading and owning, or ethnic cleansing, it arguably was more likely to remain limited, because all of these are 'behaviours' that a target government or faction can choose to modify. When an intervention has allegedly been against general brutality or barbarism, or in the interests of liberty or humanity, it has arguably been more likely to drift into imperialism, or something similar, because it has then been concerned with national, ethnic or cultural qualities or characteristics. These are

---

[33] MacMillan, 'Liberal Interventionism', 29; cf. Chapter 5.    [34] Chapter 13.
[35] Cf. Chapter 6.    [36] Chapter 10.

rather more difficult to modify, even where there is willingness to attempt it; if change does not take place, or its pace is too slow for the interveners' liking, the temptation becomes to change the regime instead, whether by finding a replacement of the same nationality, or by bringing in a new government from outside the target state.

Ultimately, however, it is important to recognise that there have been times and places where, simply put, regime change has been necessary. It was, at the least, desirable for the Netherlands to achieve independence from Spanish rule in the 1570s–1580s; for Greece to become independent of the Ottoman Empire in the 1820s, and Cuba of the Spanish Empire in the 1890s; and for Southern Sudanese peoples to achieve independence today from a northern government that commits mass atrocities. Independence was absolutely essential in East Pakistan in 1971 and East Timor in 1999. And it was vital that the Khmer Rouge regime be overthrown in Cambodia in 1978 and Idi Amin removed from power in Uganda in 1979.

*

Regardless of the means used in an intervention and its objective, it must have a basis. Intervention has often been claimed as a right, though that claim has also often been denied. Sometimes, however, intervention has also been couched as a duty.

Strikingly, indeed, as I have shown in Chapter 2, the *Vindiciae contra tyrannos* – a text first published in the sixteenth century but translated and reprinted throughout the seventeenth century – sets out a theoretical basis for something almost foreshadowing what would, in 2001, be dubbed by the International Commission on Intervention and State Sovereignty 'the responsibility to protect'. The *Vindiciae* argues *inter alia* that princes had a duty to defend the subjects of other princes against egregiously abusive tyranny and oppression – what could be termed the 'obligation to aid' or the 'duty to defend'. Similar ideas were avowed by Edmund Burke in the late eighteenth century. As Brendan Simms shows in Chapter 4, Burke believed that it was not just desirable that a 'positively Vicious and abusive Government' should be changed; the principles of 'humanity and justice' dictated that it 'ought to be changed and, if necessary, by Violence'. By the 1860s and 1870s, as Abigail Green, Davide Rodogno and Matthias Schulz demonstrate, there was widespread agreement across Western Europe that (in the words of a British newspaper) in some 'cases ... it becomes the duty of all who have any share in guiding or expressing public opinion to raise their voice against the perpetration of wrongs which are an outrage upon humanity'.[37]

---

[37] Quoted above, p. 156.

Thus, when a junior minister of the Mitterand government, Bernard Kouchner, was appalled by events in Yugoslavia in 1991 and argued for the existence of a '*droit d'ingérence humanitaire*', he was not 'inventing' the concept of a right of humanitarian intervention, as some commentators claim.[38] Such a right had explicitly been asserted – and been the basis for state practice – much earlier. Even the concept of a 'Responsibility to Protect', significant though it is, is not entirely new, though the sixteenth-century antecedent had long been forgotten.

The idea that a state is obliged to intervene to protect foreign civilians against brutal tyranny, genocide, mass atrocities or crimes against humanity has been rejected as much as embraced in the twenty-first century. Although R2P has been officially endorsed by the UN General Assembly and Security Council, and the European Union, except for France (at the urging of Kouchner), individual states have been more sceptical, despite considerable efforts by today's transnational humanitarian pressure groups.[39] The altruism of an 'obligation to aid', or 'duty to defend' or indeed a 'responsibility to protect', may naturally seem to sit uncomfortably with the reality of power politics. How relevant, then, have such idealistic concepts been?

The foregoing chapters confirm the importance, and usually the primacy, of *Realpolitik* in international relations. Almost all the interventions discussed in this book were carried out for more than humanitarian reasons alone. Elizabeth helped the Dutch rebels partly because she wanted to deny Spain bases for a cross-channel invasion of England, and because members of her government suspected Philip II of harbouring desires for universal monarchy. The English government of the 1690s and 1700s suspected Louis XIV of a similar aspiration.[40] George I backed Protestant princes in order to frustrate the Holy Roman Emperor Charles VI's suspected plans to dominate Germany and thus the continent of Europe.[41] France hoped to obtain commercial and possibly

---

[38] Michael Ignatieff, *Empire Lite: Nation-building in Bosnia, Kosovo and Afghanistan* (London: Vintage, 2003), 57; Evans, *Responsibility to Protect*, 32–3.

[39] By several research centres, commissions and consultancies: for example, the Global Centre for the Responsibility to Protect (www.GlobalCentreR2P.org); the International Coalition for the Responsibility to Protect (www.responsibilitytoprotect.org); the International Crisis Group (www.crisisgroup.org); the World Federalist Movement–Institute for Global Policy (www.wfm-igp.org/site); and the Montreal Institute for Genocide and Human Rights Studies (see its important 2009 report, *Mobilising the Will to Intervene: Leadership and Action to Prevent Mass Atrocities*).

[40] Chapters 2–3; see also Steven C. A. Pincus, *Protestantism and Patriotism: Ideologies and the Making of English Foreign Policy, 1650–1668* (Cambridge: Cambridge University Press, 1996).

[41] Chapters 3–4.

territorial concessions in Lebanon in the 1860s, and Russia sought to gain territory at the expense of the Ottoman Empire in the 1870s. Many Americans wanted to create an empire in the 1890s; unsatisfied with the annexation of Hawai'i, and with Africa having been carved up by the European powers, Spain's Caribbean and Pacific possessions were great temptations. In 1972, while Senator Henry Jackson and Congressman Charles Vanik hoped to benefit would-be Soviet émigrés, whose plight had been the subject of sustained lobbying by well-organised pressure groups in the United States, Vanik and Jackson also wanted to embarrass the Soviet Union and gain an advantage in the Cold War competition for influence.[42]

Yet, in marked contrast, the British republic had no strategic or commercial interests at stake in Savoy. Cromwell's intervention on behalf of the Vaudois in 1655 was more likely to harm, than to benefit, British interests. Diplomatic efforts to help Jews in the nineteenth century were largely idealistic and altruistic. The Great Powers who agreed with France to intervene in the Ottoman province of Syria in 1860–1 had less to gain than the French, and across Europe, including in France, there was genuine outrage and concern at the mass atrocities in Lebanon and Damascus. The Russian government was genuinely concerned about the fate of Christian minorities in the Ottoman Empire, as well as wanting to profit at the Turks' expense.[43]

Furthermore, there has also been a long history of interest in good governance. Rulers and governments have long identified that chaos in a neighbour is a recipe for disaster. Without peace and stability, there can be no human rights. If a neighbouring state 'fails', it will immediately affect its own inhabitants, who will suffer by acts of omission as well as of commission; however, the effects are likely to spread. One abusive or failing state can, through the departure of waves of refugees or insurgents' disregard for borders, destabilise an entire region. As a result, humanitarian and geopolitical concerns can merge to some extent. It is both in a state's interest and for the good of the people in a state collapsing into anarchy and disorder for intervention to take place. As Tony Blair argued in his celebrated Chicago speech in 1999, in an interdependent world it is impossible to localise risk.[44] But this principle had been recognised long before, albeit on a regional rather than global scale.

England intervened in France and the Netherlands in the sixteenth century precisely because, as Chapter 2 argues, Elizabeth I and her ministers identified anarchy in England's neighbours as their legitimate

---

[42] Chapters 7–8, 13–14.     [43] Chapters 2, 6–9.
[44] 'Speech to the Chicago Economic Club', Chicago, 24 Apr. 1999, available at www.number10.gov.uk/Page1297.

concern. Interventions in eighteenth-century Poland and Mecklenburg-Schwerin (discussed in Chapters 3 and 4) were partly driven by a perceived need to protect rights of inhabitants, and partly because the collapse of law and order in those states was a standing invitation to outside interference. In 1860, the Ottoman Empire accepted European intervention in Syria, as Chapter 7 shows, because the central authorities acknowledged that they had lost control of events in the province. Vietnam invaded Cambodia late in 1978 partly because the truth about 'the killing fields' had begun to emerge but also, as Chapter 15 relates, because having a genocidal and anarchic neighbour was very dangerous.

Moreover, the two categories are not always easy to distinguish. Many statesmen and commentators in late eighteenth- and nineteenth-century Europe argued that the stability of the European states system depended on good governance within its constituent parts – that, in fact, *Realpolitik* and humanitarian concerns were inseparable. As Chapter 16 shows, similar concerns motivated intervention in the former Yugoslavia in the 1990s. There can be little doubt that there *is* a relationship between good governance and security; or that regional, multilateral initiatives to ensure democracy and human rights tend to be more likely to succeed than isolated ones.

Not only do national security and humanitarian concerns often go hand-in-hand, but also, even where a state benefits from an intervention but is still protecting oppressed people groups, the intervention can still reasonably be regarded as 'humanitarian'. In Chapter 5, John Bew concluded that 'humanitarian ends were served' in Greece in the 1820s, even though that was not the intention of the British government; central in any analysis of an intervention must be its effects on the activity or behaviour it was undertaken to halt. Now, to be sure, interventions undertaken for naked national or imperial self-interest are problematic, but Ignatieff is surely right: 'Humanitarian action is not unmasked if it is shown to be the instrument of imperial power. Motives are not discredited just because they are shown to be mixed.' Indeed, in Weiss's words: 'Motives behind humanitarian interventions are almost invariably mixed. Looking for parsimony in motives does not really advance the discussion, because not all political motivations are evil.' As Wheeler powerfully argues, 'the existence of non-humanitarian motives undermines the humanitarian credentials of [an] action only if these undermined a positive humanitarian outcome'.[45]

---

[45]  Bew, above, p. 136; Ignatieff, *Empire Lite*, 23; Thomas G. Weiss, *Humanitarian Intervention* (Cambridge and Malden, MA: Polity, 2007), 7; Nicholas J. Wheeler, *Saving Strangers: Humanitarian Intervention in International Society* (Oxford: Oxford University Press, 2000), 133.

In sum, the studies in this volume collectively indicate that the perceived dichotomy between *Realpolitik* and humanitarian concerns has frequently been a false one. Statesmen have rarely had to choose between acting ethically or morally, to promote human rights, and acting sensibly, in the national interest. Very often these are the same option – more, sometimes one is not possible without the other.

# Index

94, 138, 179–80; and NGOs 20, 23, 385
*see also* Sudan; opposition to 16, 23–4, 80,
133, 252–3, 356, 373–5; pre-emptive
106, 182–3; and public pressure 22, 67–8,
186, 243, 387–8; and *Realpolitik* 118, 379,
398, 400–1; and regime change 47, 106,
392–5, 396; and religious freedom 152;
and revolution 384; and sovereignty 2, 6,
10, 66, 90–1, 118, 133, 181, 220, 254–5,
329, 370, 371, 393, *see also*
*Responsibility to Protect*; and threat
of force 6, *see also* Heidelberg
dispute, Macedonia, slave trade,
Thorn 'Massacre', Vaudois; types of 6–7,
390–1
Hussein, Saddam (President of Iraq) 367,
376, 378, 379

Ignatieff, Michael (Canadian statesman)
8, 400
Ignatiev, Nikolaj (Russian diplomat) 185,
189, 191, 195, 197
imperialism 22, 32, 136, 144, 366; and
abolition of slave trade 257–8
India 17, 18, 207, 356;
*see also* Indo-Pakistani War
Indo-Pakistani War (1971) 7, 17, 24, 356
international community 1, 30, 80, 254,
368, 371, 376
international law 31, 47, 99, 152, 186, 187,
237, 244–5, 270, 330, 348, 394; origins
29 *see also* Aquinas, St Thomas; and slave
trade 234
Iraq 366; and Kurdish insurrection 367; *see
also* Iraq War (2003) 367
Iraq War (2003) 367, 372–3, 378
Ireland 53, 124; Spanish intervention in
*see* Anglo-Spanish War

Jackson, Henry (US statesman) 323, 325,
332–41, 399
Jackson–Vanik Amendment (1974) 323–5,
327, 329, 331–4, 379, 391
James II (King of England, 1685–8) 68–9, 70
Jews 48, 139–58, 206, 324, 399; in Britain
54; emancipation of 140, 142, 143,
157–8; in Europe 149, 155; in France
142, 147 in Italy *see* Mortara affair; in
Ottoman Empire 148–9, 391; *see also*
Damascus affair; in Romania 153–8; in
Russia 140, 202; in Soviet Union
323–40, 325, 331, 341–2, 399; *see also*
Jackson–Vanik Amendment
Jordan 5
just war 31, 88, 117, 377

Kampuchea *see* Cambodia
Karl Philip III (Elector of the Palatinate,
1716–42) 78–81
Kissinger, Henry (US statesman) 120, 128,
and Indo-Pakistani War of 1971 356; and
Jackson–Vanik Amendment 327, 333–4,
336, 337
Kosovo 205, 217, 366, 371, 377–8;
*see also* Kosovo War
Kosovo War (1998–9) 61, 255, 369–70,
372, 376–8, 379; and NATO
intervention (1999) 7

Law of Nations 6, 13, 21, 29, 122, 133,
*see also* Grotius, Hugo
Lebanese and Syrian crisis of 1860–1 7,
167–83, 186, 190, 202, 206, 208, 216;
and Britain, *see* Palmerston;
and European intervention 7, 10, 61,
169–83, 187, 196, 211, 213,
224–5, 392, 399; and France 175–6, 399
*see also* Thouvenel; its origins 164–5; and
Ottoman reaction 170, 176–8, 400; and
*Règlement Organique* 16, 178–9, 182
Lebanon 5, 163, 206, 395; its ethnical and
religious composition 163 French
interests in 146, 398–9; Western
perceptions of 165–6; *see also* Lebanese
and Syrian crisis of 1860–1
'liberal interventionism' 365–73, 375–80
Lincoln, Abraham 316, 318–20
Louis XIV (King of France, 1643–1715)
54, 77, 79, 398; and Huguenots 70, 74;
in Protestant political writings 75–6; and
Vaudois 58, 60
Low Countries, 63, 91, 94, 100, 108–9,
161; *see also* Belgium, Dutch War of
Independence, Netherlands

Macedonia 205, 395; and Austrian naval
demonstration (1905) 220, 391, 392; its
ethnical and religious composition 206;
intervention by Great Powers 7, 11, 61,
210–11, 221, 391; Ottoman involvement
in 210, 220; uprisings and nationalist
violence 208, 216–17, 223–4
Maria Theresa (Archduchess of Austria,
1740–80, and Holy Roman Empress) 85,
140–1
Mazarin, Cardinal Giulio (French Italian
statesman) 54, 58–60
McKinley, William (US President) 303,
318–20, 321; and Cuba 305–11; and
Philippines 312–17
Mecklenburg 94–5, 99, 379, 400

Lightning Source UK Ltd.
Milton Keynes UK
UKOW051328110412

190501UK00001B/125/P